# Positive Obligations under the European Convention on Human Rights

# Positive Obligations under the European Convention on Human Rights

*Within and Beyond Boundaries*

Vladislava Stoyanova
*Associate Professor in Public International Law and Wallenberg Academy Fellow, Faculty of Law, Lund University, Sweden*

Great Clarendon Street, Oxford, OX2 6DP,
United Kingdom

Oxford University Press is a department of the University of Oxford.
It furthers the University's objective of excellence in research, scholarship,
and education by publishing worldwide. Oxford is a registered trade mark of
Oxford University Press in the UK and in certain other countries

© Vladislava Stoyanova 2023
Cover art by Josefina Söderberg. © Ragnar Söderbergs stiftelse, 2016

The moral rights of the author have been asserted

First Edition published in 2023

Some rights reserved. No part of this publication may be reproduced, stored in
a retrieval system, or transmitted, in any form or by any means, for commercial purposes,
without the prior permission in writing of Oxford University Press, or as expressly
permitted by law, by licence or under terms agreed with the appropriate
reprographics rights organization.

This is an open access publication, available online and distributed under the terms of a
Creative Commons Attribution – Non Commercial – No Derivatives 4.0
International licence (CC BY-NC-ND 4.0), a copy of which is available at
http://creativecommons.org/licenses/by-nc-nd/4.0/.

Enquiries concerning reproduction outside the scope of this licence
should be sent to the Rights Department, Oxford University Press, at the address above

Published in the United States of America by Oxford University Press
198 Madison Avenue, New York, NY 10016, United States of America

British Library Cataloguing in Publication Data

Data available

Library of Congress Control Number is on file at the Library of Congress

ISBN 978-0-19-288804-4

DOI: 10.1093/oso/9780192888044.001.0001

Printed and bound by CPI Group (UK) Ltd, Croydon, CR0 4YY

Links to third party websites are provided by Oxford in good faith and
for information only. Oxford disclaims any responsibility for the materials
contained in any third party website referenced in this work.

# Preface

The idea behind this book started with my postdoctoral project funded by the Ragnar Söderberg Foundation and was possible to complete with the funding provided by the Knut and Alice Wallenberg Foundation and the Swedish Academy of Sciences.

Parts of the book have been published as articles including 'The Disjunctive Structure of Positive Rights under the European Convention on Human Rights' (2018) Nordic Journal of International Law; 'Causation between State Omission and Harm within the Framework of Positive Obligations under' (2018) Human Rights Law Review; 'Common Law Tort of Negligence as a Tool for Deconstructing Positive Obligations under the European Convention on Human Rights' (2020) The International Journal of Human Rights; 'Fault, Knowledge and Risk within the Framework of Positive Obligations under the European Convention on Human Rights' (2020) Leiden Journal of International Law; and 'Framing Positive Obligations under the European Convention on Human Rights: Mediating between the Abstract and the Concrete' (2023) Human Rights Law Review.

I would like to thank the Faculty of Law, Lund University, and, in particular, the former dean, Professor Mia Rönnmar, the former vice-dean, Professor Xavier Groussot, and Professor Ulf Maunsbach for their support. The idea at the core of the book was originally inspired by conversations with Professor Gregor Noll, to whom I would like to acknowledge an intellectual debt of gratitude. The book has benefited from discussions with many colleagues, among whom I should mention Professor Janneke Gerards, Dr Kristof Gombeer, Professor Ulf Linderfalk, Professor Rick Lawson, Dr Johan Vorland Wibye, Serde Atalay and Emiliya Bratanova. Any errors are attributable to me. I would like to also thank Dr Eleni Karageorgiou, without whom my working environment would never have been so enjoyable. Nicu Costea's unsettling and challenging observations have always pushed my limits and made me ultimately increase the academic rigour with which I pursue my work.

I wrote this book at a time when States imposed massive restrictions on our liberties in a manner hitherto unimaginable so that we are better protected from known, unknown, or unknowable risks. Faced with the COVID-19 pandemic and the benevolent objective of protecting lives, asking for a debate about the limits of state power and the proper role of human rights *law* appeared not only superfluous but also unscientific and uncompassionate. This disturbed me and helped me to understand the importance of my work.

I devote this book to my grandmother, Dochka Delcheva, who for years has been helping me to take care of my two children with so much love. Without her nothing would have been possible. My parents, Nedyalka Stoyanova and Petar Stoyanov, have always supported us and have been a source of emotional peacefulness and strength. My sister could always make me laught!

Посвещавам тази книга на баба ми Дочка Делчева, която с години ми е помагала да се грижа за двете ми деца с толкова много любов. Без нея нищо не би било възможно. Благодаря ти бабо! Родителите ми, Недялка Стоянова и Петар Стоянов, винаги са ни подкрепяли и са били източник на емоционално спокойствие и сила.

Vladislava Stoyanova<br>
January 2023<br>
Lund, Sweden

# Contents

*Table of Cases* xi

**Introduction** 1

**1. Deconstructing Positive Obligations** 7
Introduction 7
1.1 The State as an Institutional Mediator 8
1.2 Justifications for Positive Obligations 10
1.3 Plurality of Obligations Owed by the State 12
1.4 Priority of Rights as Organizational Principles 16
1.5 Trigger, Scope, Content, and Types of Positive Obligations 18
Conclusion 20

**2. State Knowledge** 21
Introduction 21
2.1 The Role of Fault in State Responsibility 21
2.2 Triggering and Breach of Positive Obligations under ECHR 24
2.3 Actual Knowledge versus Putative Knowledge 26
    2.3.1 Different Possible Ways of Assessing Putative Knowledge 26
    2.3.2 State Knowledge Necessarily Implies Normative Assessment 29
2.4 Assessment of Knowledge 29
2.5 No Benefit of Hindsight 31
2.6 Burden of Proof 32
2.7 The Nature and the Level of Risk 33
    2.7.1 The 'Real and Immediate Risk' Standard 33
    2.7.2 Man-made versus Natural Harms 38
2.8 Contributory Fault of the Victim 40
Conclusion 42

**3. Causation** 45
Introduction 45
3.1 The Role and the Standard of Causation 46
3.2 Control and Causation 49
    3.2.1 The Rules on Attribution 49
    3.2.2 The Role of Control and the Extension of the Logic of the Rules on Attribution 51
    3.2.3 Control and Prevention of State-inflicted Harm 53
    3.2.4 Assumption of Control in the Area of Public Services 55
    3.2.5 Source of the Harm and the Related Level of Control 58
    3.2.6 Assumption of Control over the Victim 60

## Contents

|  |  |
|---|---|
| 3.3 Techniques for Avoiding Causation | 63 |
|     3.3.1 Domestic Legality | 63 |
|     3.3.2 Procedural Protection | 66 |
| 3.4 Technique for Limiting Responsibility when Causation is Present | 67 |
| Conclusion | 70 |

## 4. Reasonableness     73

|  |  |
|---|---|
| Introduction | 73 |
| 4.1 Intertwinement with Knowledge and Causation | 75 |
|     4.1.1 Weak Causation Counterbalanced by the Reasonableness Standard | 76 |
|     4.1.2 Strong Causation Counterbalanced by the Reasonableness Standard | 78 |
|     4.1.3 Reasonableness and Immediacy of the Risk | 79 |
|     4.1.4 The Importance and the Justifiability of the Analytical Distinctions | 80 |
| 4.2 Consideration of Alternative Protective Measures | 81 |
|     4.2.1 Levels of Abstraction/Concreteness and the Burden of Proof | 83 |
|     4.2.2 Place and Formulation of the Alternative | 85 |
|     4.2.3 The Standard of Protectiveness | 88 |
| 4.3 Margin of Appreciation | 89 |
|     4.3.1 Delineation between Structural Deference and Appreciation of Alternatives | 89 |
|     4.3.2 Scrutiny in the Appreciation of Alternatives | 92 |
| Conclusion | 93 |

## 5. Competing Obligations     95

|  |  |
|---|---|
| Introduction | 95 |
| 5.1 Specification for Tensions to Become Cognizable | 97 |
| 5.2 The Distinction between General Interests and Interests that Form the Basis of Human Rights | 99 |
| 5.3 Addressing the Competition | 103 |
|     5.3.1 Equal Moral Status | 103 |
|     5.3.2 The Relative Importance of the Interests and the Obligations Triggered | 104 |
|     5.3.3 Action versus Omission | 107 |
|     5.3.4 Determinacy of the Harm and the Affected Individuals | 117 |
| 5.4 Accommodation of Obligations | 119 |
| Conclusion | 121 |

## 6. Procedural Positive Obligation to Investigate     123

|  |  |
|---|---|
| Introduction | 123 |
| 6.1 Conditions that Trigger the Obligation | 127 |
|     6.1.1 Harm Inflicted by State Actors | 129 |
|     6.1.2 Harm Inflicted by Non-state Actors | 131 |
|     6.1.3 Harm Linked with Arguable Omissions | 134 |
| 6.2 Content and Scope of the Obligation | 138 |
|     6.2.1 Type of Proceedings | 138 |
|     6.2.2 Initiation of the Proceedings | 148 |

|  |  |  |
|---|---|---|
| | 6.2.3 Effectiveness | 150 |
| | 6.2.4 Cooperation with Other States in Cross-border Contexts | 159 |
| Conclusion | | 167 |

## 7. Substantive Positive Obligations — 171

Introduction — 171
7.1 Obligation to Develop Effective Regulatory Frameworks — 171
    7.1.1 Diversity of Regulatory Spheres and the Role of Criminal Law — 174
    7.1.2 Types of Deficiencies in the Regulatory Framework — 176
    7.1.3 Concrete or Abstract Reasonableness Review of the Regulatory Framework — 181
7.2 Obligation to Develop Effective National Procedures — 197
    7.2.1 Not a Self-standing Positive Obligation — 198
    7.2.2 The Content of the Obligation — 200
7.3 Obligation to Take Protective Operational Measures — 203
    7.3.1 The Test as Originally Developed in *Osman v the United Kingdom* — 204
    7.3.2 Modifications of the Test Regarding the Actors of Harm, the Objects of Harm, and the Immediacy of the Risk — 205
    7.3.3 Adjustment of the Test by Adding Risk Assessment as an 'Integral Part' — 211
    7.3.4 Adjustment of the Test by Adding Harm-related, Temporal, and Geographical Specifications — 214
    7.3.5 Content and Scope of the Obligation—the Operational Measures — 215
Conclusion — 217

## 8. Extraterritorial Positive Obligations — 219

Introduction — 219
8.1 Positive Obligations' Normative Preconditions — 223
    8.1.1 The Role of the State in Society — 224
    8.1.2 Democratic Legitimacy and Territorial Boundedness — 225
    8.1.3 Not Contingent Exclusively on Actual Capacity — 228
8.2 Deconstructing Jurisdiction — 228
    8.2.1 The Territorial Paradigm — 229
    8.2.2 Effective Control over an Area — 231
    8.2.3 Physical Power and Control over a Person — 235
    8.2.4 Acts of Diplomatic and Consular Agents — 238
    8.2.5 Exercise of Public Powers — 244
    8.2.6 Extraterritorial Effects — 250
    8.2.7 Procedural Link — 257
    8.2.8 Conclusion — 263
8.3 Adapting Jurisdiction to the Obligations? — 265
    8.3.1 Dividing and Tailoring — 266
    8.3.2 Dividing the Tailoring Brought to a Breaking Point — 270
    8.3.3 Conclusion — 273

8.4  Deconstructing Extraterritorial Positive Obligations    273
       8.4.1  Legality and Legal Competence                      275
       8.4.2  Reasonableness and Balancing of Interests           293
       8.4.3  Causation                                           303
  Conclusion                                                     306

# Conclusion                                                     **311**

*Select Bibliography*                                            **315**
*Index*                                                          **329**

# Table of Cases

*A. v Croatia* no 55164/08, 14 October 20102010...................................87n.65
*A. and B. v Georgia* no 73975/16, 10 February 2022.....................179n.51, 212n.201
*A. and B. v Romania* no 48442/16 and 48831/16, 2 June 2020................40n.115, 82n.41
*A., B. and C. v Ireland* [GC] no 25579/05, 16 December 2010.......................82n.41
*Abdu v Bulgaria* no 26827/08, 11 March 2014...................................155n.195
*Abdul Wahab Khan v the United Kingdom* (dec.) no 11987/11, 28 January 2014 ......240n.112
*Abdülsamet Yaman v Turkey* no 32446/96, 2 November 2004......................157n.217
*Aftanache v Romania* no 999/19, 26 May 2020 .................................167n.269
*Ageyevy v Russia* no 7075/10, 18 April 2013 ............................131n.42, 140n.97
*Aksu v Turkey* [GC] no 4149/04 and 41029/07, 15 March 2012 .........19n.78, 116nn.102–3
*Albekov and Others v Russia* no 68216/01, 9 October 2008 ..........................51n.46
*Al-Jedda v the United Kingdom* [GC] no 27021/08, 7 July 2011..............219n.2, 298n.389
*Al Nashiri v Romania* no 33234/12, 31 May 2018 ...............................152n.170
*Al-Skeini and Others v the United Kingdom* [GC] no 55721/07,
    7 July 2011........................ 130n.38, 139n.90, 153n.183, 219n.2, 230–31, 232,
        235n.82, 236–37, 238, 243–47, 248–49, 257, 266, 268–69, 268n.249, 270, 298n.387
*Anna Todorova v Bulgaria* no 23302/03, 24 May 2011 .....................123n.5, 137n.81
*Andreou v Turkey* (dec.) no 45653/99, 3 June 2008.....................253n.183, 298n.388
*Animal Defenders International v the United Kingdom* [GC] no 48876/08,
    22 April 2013.........................................................198n.132
*Antonov v Ukraine* no 28096/04, 3 November 2011 ............................152n.168
*Armani Da Silva v United Kingdom* [GC] no 5878/08, 30 March 2016 ..........126nn.15–16,
        150n.158, 151n.162, 152n.167, 153n.179, 157n.212, 169n.280
*Arskaya v Ukraine* no 45076/05, 5 December 2013 .............................. 176–77
*Asiye Genc v Turkey* no 24109/07, 27 January 2015 .....................143n.117, 144n.123
*Assanidze v Georgia* no 71503/01, 8 April 2004.................................278n.285
*Assenov and Others v Bulgaria* no 24760/94, 28 October 1998 .....................130n.33
*Association Accept and Others v Romania* no 19237/16, 1 June 2021.....175–76nn.31–37, 203n.157
*Association Innocence en Danger and Association Enfance et Partage v France*
    no 15343/15 and 16806/15, 4 June 2020 ......................................31n.66
*Aydoğdu v Turkey* no 40448/06, 30 August 2016................................. 176–77
*Axel Springer AG v Germany* [GC] no 39954/08, 7 February 2012.... 96n.7, 189n.96, 200n.143
*Azer Ahmadov v Azerbaijan* no 3409/10, 22 July 2021 ............................131n.41

*Babylonova v Slovakia* no 69146/01, 20 June 2006 ................................19n.78
*Bagiyeva v Uktraine* no 41085/05, 28 April 2016................................140n.98
*Bakanova v Lithuania* no 11167/12, 31 May 2016.......128n.22, 134n.66, 138n.83, 143n.117, 150–51,
*Bălşan v Romania* no 49645/09, 23 May 2017....................................140n.99
*Banel v Lithuania* no 14326/11, 18 June 2013 ........ 1n.6, 35n.86, 80n.33, 134n.66, 147n.136
*Bankovic and Others v Belgium and Others* [GC] (dec.) no 52207/99,
    12 December 2001 ........................229n.38, 230n.44, 236, 245–46, 252, 253,
        256n.199, 258, 261n.224, 266, 266n.237, 267, 275n.271, 288n.330
*Basu v Germany* no 215/19, 18 October 2022 .......................................131
*Bărbulescu v Romania* [GC] no 61496/08, 5 September 2017.........18n.74, 82n.40, 140n.94,
    174n.19, 174n.23, 181n.63, 189n.96, 198n.135, 199, 200n.144, 200n.147, 202, 202n.154

## xii  Table of Cases

*Beganoviç v Croatia* no 46423/06, 25 June 2009 . . . . . . . . . . . . . . . . . . . .10n.24, 125n.8, 132n.52,
  138n.84, 152n.177, 168n.275
*Behar and Gutman v Bulgaria* no 29335/13, 16 February 2021 . . . . . . . . . . . . . . . . . . . . .201n.148
*Beizaraz and Levickas v Lithuania* no 41288/15, 14 January 2020 . . . . . . . . . . . . . . . . . . .19n.79
*Belenko v Russia* no 25435/06, 18 December 2014 . . . . . . . . . . . . . . . . . . . . . . . . . . . . . . .70n.145
*Berkman v Russia* no 46712/15 1 December 2020 . . . . . . . . . . . . . . . . . . . . . . . . . . . . . . . .118n.109
*Bevacqua and S. v Bulgaria* no 71127/01, 12 June 2008 . . . . . . . . . . . . 62n.112, 82n.39, 140n.100
*Big Brother Watch and Others v the United Kingdom* [GC] no 58170, 25 May 2021 . . . .264n.232
*Bilbija and Blazevic v Croatia* no 62870/13, 12 January 2016 . . . . . . . . . . . . . . . . . . . . . . .70n.145
*Binişan v Romania* no 39438/05, 20 May 2014 . . . . . . . . . . . . . . . . . . . . . . . . . . .193n.111, 195n.119
*Bljakaj and Others v Croatia* no 74448/12, 18 September 2014 . . . . . . .47n.11, 59–60, 79n.32, 207
*Boljević v Serbia* no 47443/14, 16 June 2020 . . . . . . . . . . . . . . . . . . . . . . . . . . . . . . . . . . . . 176–77
*Botoyan v Armenia* no 5766/17, 8 February 2022 . . . . . . . . . . . . . . . 123n.3, 147n.137, 154n.190,
  155n.200, 190, 191
*Bouyid v Belgium* [GC] no 23380/09, 28 September 2015 . . . . . . . . . . . . . . 125n.10, 130nn.38–39,
  148n.144, 153n.182
*Branko Tomašić and Others v Croatia*, no 46598/06, 15 January 2009 . . . . . . . . . .18n.73, 136n.76
*Brincat and Others v Malta* no 60908/11, 24 July 2014 . . . . . . 27n.39, 29–30nn.52–53, 42, 58–59
*Budayeva and Others v Russia* no 15339/02, 20 March 2008 . . . . . . . . . .25n.32, 26n.35, 38n.107,
  39, 48–49, 59, 66n.127, 73n.2, 75n.18, 82n.38, 84, 92n.81, 134n.63
*Budina v Russia* no 45603/05 (dec) 18 June 2009 . . . . . . . . . . . . . . . . . . . . . . . . . . . . . . . . . .60n.99
*Budinova and Chaprazov v Bulgaria* no 12567/13, 16 February 2021 . . . . . . . . 116–17nn.102–4
*Burlya and Others v Ukraine* no 3289/10, 6 November 2018 . . . . . . . . . . . . . . . . . . . . . . .133n.58
*Burzykowski v Poland* no 11562/05, 27 June 2006 . . . . . . . . . . . . . . . . . . . . . . . . . . . . . . . .70n.145
*Butolen v Slovenia* no 41356/08, 26 April 2012 . . . . . . . . . . . . . . . . . . . . . . . . . . . . . . . . . .152n.176
*Buturugă v Romania* no 56867/15, 11 February 2020 . . . . . . . . . . . . . . . . . . . . . . . . . . . . .140n.99

*C. v Romania* no 47358/20, 30 August 2022 . . . . . . . . . . . . . . . . . . . . . . . . . . . . . . . . . . . . .133n.59
*Calvelli and Ciglio v Italy* [GC] no 32967/96, 17 January 2002 . . . . . . . .56n.65, 126n.16, 137n.82,
  141n.106, 155n.199
*Carter v Russia* no 20914/07, 21 September 2021 . . . . . . . . . . . . . . . . . . . . . . . . . . . .229n.38, 237
*C.A.S. and C.S. v Romania* no 26692/05, 20 March 2012 . . . . . . . . . . . . . . . . . . . . . . . . . .132n.52
*Case "Relating to Certain Aspects of the Laws on the Use of Languages in Education in
  Belgium" v Belgium (Merits)* no 1474/62, 23 July 1968 . . . . . . . . . . . . . . . . . . . . . . . . .74n.13
*Catan and Others v the Republic of Moldova and Russia* [GC] no 43370/04,
  19 October 2012 . . . . . . . . . . . . . . . . . . . . . . . . 219n.2, 232n.55, 233–34, 270n.252, 298–99
*Cavit Tınarlıoğlu v Turkey* no 3648/04, 2 February 2016 . . . . . . . . . . . . . . . . . . . .30n.57, 39n.110
*C.E. and Others v France* no 29775/18 and 29693/19, 24 March 2022 . . . . . . . . . . . . . . . 174–75
*Centre for Legal Resources on Behalf of Velntin Câmpeanu v Romania* [GC]
  no 47848/08, 17 July 2014 . . . . . . . 21n.1, 62n.112, 73n.3, 84n.45, 92n.82, 206n.167, 207n.176
*Cevrioğlu v Turkey* no 69546/12, 4 October 2016 . . . . . . . . . . . . . . . . . . . .1n.6, 25n.31, 26n.35,
  29–30, 33n.75, 41, 57, 73n.1
*Chiragov and Others v Armenia* [GC] no 13216/05, 16 June 2015 . . . . . . . . . . . 232n.54, 298–99
*Choreftakis and Choreftaki v Greece* no 46846/08, 17 January 2012 . . . . . . . . . . 25n.27, 105n.48
*Christine Goodwin v United Kingdom* [GC] no 28957/95, 11 July 2002 . . . . . . . . . 11n.33, 19n.78
*Ciechońska v Poland* no 19776/04, 14 June 2011 . . . . . . . . . . . . . . . . . . . . . . . . . . .135n.68, 154n.187
*Corsacov v Moldova* no 18944/02, 4 April 2006 . . . . . . . . . . . . . . . . . . . . . . . . . . . . . . . . .153n.182
*Cordella and Others v Italy* no 54414/13 and 54264/15, 24 January 2019 . . . . . . . . . . . . . . .33n.74
*Costello-Roberts v United Kingdom* no 13134/87, 25 March 1993 . . . . . . . . . . . . . . . . . . . .55n.64
*Coţofan v Moldova and Russia* no 5659/07, 18 June 2019 . . . . . . . . . . . . . . . . . . . . . . . .279n.289
*Craxi v Italy (no. 2)* no 25337/94, 17 July 2003 . . . . . . . . . . . . . . . . . . . . . . . . . . . . . . . . . .133n.59
*Cuence Zarzoco v Spain* no 23383/12, 16 January 2018 . . . . . . . . . . . . . . . . . . . . . . . . . . .179n.54
*Cyprus v Turkey* [GC] no 25781/94, 10 May 2001 . . . . . . . . . . . . . . 50n.41, 64n.117, 231, 233n.66,
  245–46, 268–69, 280n.291

*Darboe and Camara v Italy* no 5797/17, 21 July 2022 .......................... 201–2n.153
*De Giorgi v Italy* no 23735/19, 16 June 2022 .................. 210n.189, 210n.192, 212n.201
*Demir and Baykara v Turkey* [GC] no 34503/94, 12 November 2008................ 116n.98,
*Denis Vasilyev v Russia* no 32704/04, 17 December 2009 ........ 61, 125n.8, 128n.22, 138n.84
*Derenik Mkrtchyan and Gayane Mkrtchyan v Armenia* no 69736/12,
　30 November 2021 .................................205–6n.164, 210n.191, 211n.198
*D.H. and Others v the Czech Republic* [GC] no 57325/00, 3 November 2007 ......... 62n.113,
*Dodov v Bulgaria* no 59548/00, 17 January 2008....................48n.16, 55n.64, 57n.73,
　　　　　　　　　　　　　　　　　　　　　　　　　　　70n.145, 73n.9, 206n.165
*Dordevic v Croatia* no 41526/10, 24 July 2012..............................83n.44, 87–88
*Drašković v Montenegro* no 40597/17, 9 June 2020..............................201n.152
*Draon v France* [GC] no 1513/03, 21 June 2006 ............................ 48n.17, 85n.51
*Drozd and Janousek v France and Spain* no 12747/87, 26 June 1992.............247, 249n.158
*Dubetska and Others v Ukraine* no 30499/03, 10 February 2011.....................48n.18
*Dubská and Krejzová v The Czech Republic* [GC] no 28859/11 and 28473/12,
　15 November 2016 .....................................................80n.34
*Dupate v Latvia* no 18068/11, 19 November 2020 ........................... 200nn.145–46
*Dvořáček v the Check Republic* no 12927/13, 6 November 2014 ....................145n.124

*E. and Others v the United Kingdom* no 33218/96, 26 November 2002................85n.53
*E.G. v the Republic of Moldova* no 37882/13, 13 April 2021.......................157n.216
*Elena Cojocaru v Romania* no 74114/12, 22 March 2016.............................64
*El-Masri v the former Yugoslav Republic of Macedonia* [GC] no 39630/09,
　13 December 2012 ....................................... 130n.33, 130n.38, 149n.145
*Enukidze and Girgvliani v Georgia* no 25091/07, 26 April 2011 .....................158n.221
*Eremia v the Republic of Moldova* no 3564/11, 28 May 2013 ............ 25n.27, 82n.39, 87n.65
*Ergi v Turkey* no 66/1997/850/1057, 28 July 1998........................132n.50, 296n.375
*Evans v United Kingdom* [GC] no 6339/05, 10 April 2007 .............. 14n.53, 93n.85, 96n.5

*Fabris et Parziale v Italy* no 41603/13, 19 March 2020 ...................... 82n.42, 98n.15
*Fadeyeva v Russia* no 55723/00, 9 June 2005 ..... 19n.78, 26n.35, 33, 48n.21, 65n.124, 82n.38, 172n.8
*Fernandes de Oliveira v Portugal* [GC] no 78103/14, 31 January 2019 .......... 28n.46, 35–36,
　　　　　　　　　　　　　37n.102, 38n.106, 48n.15, 171n.1, 175n.25, 178, 182n.67,
　　　　　　　　　　　　　192n.106, 193n.109, 194–97, 205–6n.164, 214–15
*Fedotova and Others v Russia* no 40792/10, 13 July 2021 ..............19n.78, 174n.18, 176–77
*Fergec v Croatia* no 68516/14, 9 May 2017.................................. 134nn.64–65
*Fernández Marínez v Spain* [GC] no 56030/07, 12 June 2014 ................. 1n.6, 100n.24
*Finogenov and Others v Russia* no 18299/03, 20 December 2011 ......38n.108, 53n.51, 54–55 ,
　　　　　　　　　　　　　　　　　　　　　　　　　　　　88n.67, 269n.251, 296n.377
*Florea v Romania* no 37186/03, 14 September 2010...............................60n.97
*F.O. v Croatia* no 29555/13, 22 April 2022 ....... 56n.68, 140n.95, 175n.27, 179n.51, 203n.157
*Firstov v Russia* no 42119/04, 20 February 2014 ...............................158n.229
*Frick v Switzerland* no 23405/16, 30 June 2020 ............................29n.51, 84n.46
*Furdík v Slovakia* (dec.) no 42994/05, 2 December 2008 ..........................40n.115

*Gäfgen v Germany* [GC] no 22978/05, 1 June 2010 ......................106n.55, 108n.61
*Gaskin v the United Kingdom* no 10454/83, 7 July 1989 ..........................199n.140
*Genderdoc-M and M.D. v Moldova* no 23914/15, 14 December 2021 ...............155n.194
*Georgel and Georgeta Stoicescu v Romania* no 9718/03,
　26 July 2011................................................33–34n.76, 37n.100, 158n.224
*Georgia v Russia (II)* [GC] no 38263/08, 21 January 2021 ........ 167n.267, 231, 232, 235n.82,
　　　　　　　　　　　　　　　　　　　　　246n.143, 252, 255n.190, 256n.200, 261n.224,
　　　　　　　　　　　　　　　　　　　　　263n.229, 270n.253, 281n.301, 282–83
*Giacomelli v Italy* no 59909/00, 2 November 2006 ...............................65n.121

*Giuliani and Gaggio v Italy* [GC] no 23458/02, 24 March 2011................ 48n.23, 53–54, 110n.72, 111n.75, 152n.170, 156n.206
*Gjikondi and Others v Greece* no 17249/10, 21 December 2017 .................... 155n.195
*Gökdemir v Turkey* (dec.) no 66309/09, 19 May 2015............................. 40n.115
*Gorgiev v The Former Yugoslav Republic of Macedonia* no 26984/05, 19 April 2004..... 38n.109, 136
*Gorovensky and Bugara v Ukraine* no 36146/05 and 42418/05,
    12 January 2012 .................................................... 207, 284n.315
*Gross v Switzerland* no 67810/10, 14 May 2013................................... 178n.47
*Gvozdeva v Russia* no 69997/11, 22 March 2022........................ 196n.122, 210n.191
*Guerra and Others v Italy* [GC] no 14967/89, 19 February 1998...................... 58n.79
*Gustafsson v Sweden* [GC] no 15573/89, 25 April 1996 ........................... 116n.99
*Güzelyurtlu and Others v Cyprus and Turkey* [GC] no 36925/07, 29 January 2019 .... 159, 161, 162, 163, 164n.253, 165n.262, 240n.111, 258, 259, 260–62

*Haas v Switzerland* no 31322/07, 20 January 2011 ............................... 98n.15
*Hájovsky v Slovakia* no 7796/16, 1 July 2021 .................................. 200n.145
*Halime Kilic v Turkey* no 63034/11, 28 June 2016 ................................ 31n.64
*Hanan v Germany* [GC] no 4871/16, 16 February 2021......... 151n.165, 156n.202, 167n.267, 261n.224, 262, 263n.229, 270, 273, 286, 287n.327, 299–300
*Hämäläinen v Finland* [GC] no 37359/09, 16 July 2014............................... 86
*Harroudj v France* no 43631/09, 4 October 2012 ................................. 19n.78
*Hassan v the United Kingdom* [GC] no 29750/09, 16 September 2014......... 235–36, 280–81, 283–84, 298n.389
*Hatton and Others v the United Kingdom* [GC] no 36022/97,
    8 July 2003................................. 12n.40, 66n.127, 67, 82n.40, 92–93, 198
*H.F. and Others v France* [GC] no 24384/19, 14 September 2022........ 219n.2, 229nn.38–39, 230n.44, 238n.99, 239n.106, 241–44, 247n.151, 255n.190, 258n.209, 259n.213, 260n.217, 267n.239, 268n.244, 270, 271, 272, 273, 275n.271, 278n.285, 284n.314, 285–86, 300–1
*Hiller v Austria* no 1967/14, 22 November 2016.............. 34n.83, 48–49, 80n.36, 228n.33
*Hirsi Jamaa and Others v Italy* [GC] no 27765/09, 23 February 2012................ 237n.93, 267n.239, 278n.285
*Hristozov and Others v Bulgaria* no 47039/11 and 358/12..... 14n.53, 74n.11, 93n.85, 174n.24
*Hudorovič and Others v Slovenia* no 24816/14 and 25140/14,
    10 March 2020............................ 19n.81, 40n.115, 85nn.54–55, 182n.67, 188

*I. v Finland* no 20511/03, 17 July 2008 ........................................ 64n.116,
*Ibrahimov and Mammadov v Azerbaijan* no 63571/16, 13 February 2020 ............ 126n.14
*I.E. v The Republic of Moldova* no 45422/13, 26 May 2020........................ 206n.166
*I.G. and Others v Slovakia* no 15966/04, 13 November 2012...................... 145n.127
*Ilaşcu and Others v Moldova and Russia* no 48787/99, 8 July 2004 ............... 51nn.42–43, 232n.55, 250n.163
*Ilbeyi Kemaloglu and Meriye Kemaloglu v Turkey* no 19986/06,
    10 April 2012............................................ 56–57, 57n.71, 92n.83
*Ilhan v Turkey* [GC] no 22277/93, 27 June 2000 ................................ 133n.56
*Ilia Petrov v Bulgaria* no 19202/03, 24 April 2012...................... 41–42, 57, 73n.8, 86,
*Ilse Hess v United Kingdom* no 6231/73, 28 May 1975 ......................... 305n.421
*Issa and Others v Turkey* no 31821/96, 16 November 2004 .......... 232, 252n.175, 277n.279
*Isaak and Others v Turkey* (dec.) no 44587/98, 28 September 2006 .................. 235–36
*Isayeva v Russia* no 57950/00, 24 February 2005.............. 53–55, 282nn.306–6, 283n.312, 284–85n.316, 296n.376, 297n.383,
*Isayeva, Yusupova and Bazayeva v Russia* no 57947/00, 24 February 2005 .......... 296n.376
*Ivantoc and Others v Moldova and Russia* no 23687/05, 15 November 2011.. 232n.55, 299n.393

Table of Cases    xv

*Jabłońska v Poland* no 24913/15, 14 May 2020 .................................153n.180
*Jaloud v the Netherlands* [GC] no 47708/08, 20 November 2014 ........231, 232, 233, 234–35,
                                                                       274n.269, 298n.387
*Jansons v Latvia* no 1434/14, 8 September 2022 .....................133n.62, 140n.100, 180
*Jashi v Georgia* no 10799/06, 8 January 2013......................................60n.97
*Jeronovičs v Latvia* [GC] no 44898/10, 5 July 2016 .............. 128n.22, 156n.206, 158n.226
*J.I. v Croatia* no 35898/16, 8 September 2022 ...........................127n.20, 155n.197
*Jivan v Romania* no 62250/19, 8 February 2022 ........................................179

*K. and T. v Finland* no 25702/94, 12 July 2001.......................... 119–20nn.113–14
*Kalender v Turkey* no 4314/02, 15 December 2009...............................65n.121
*Kalicki v Poland* no 46797/08, 8 December 2015 ........................... 137nn.79–80
*Kalucza v Hungary* no 57693/10, 24 April 2012 .................................93n.84
*Kapa and Others v Poland* no 75031/13, 14 October 2021...................73n.7, 172–73n.9
*Karpylenko v Ukraine* no 15509/12, 11 February 2016............................47n.11
*Keenan v United Kingdom* no 27229/95, 3 April 2001 ............... 60nn.94–96, 206n.166
*Keller v Russia* no 26824/04, 17 October 2013...........................62n.105, 284n.315
*Khadija Ismayilova v Azerbaijan (no 3)* no 35283/14, 7 May 2020 ..................200n.145
*Khudoroshko v Russia* no 3959/14, 18 January 2022.....................196n.122, 210n.191
*Khusnutdinov and X. v Russia* no 76598/12, 18 December 2018....................120n.115
*Kitanovska Stanojkovic and Others v Macedonia* no 2319/14, 13 October 2016 .......158n.222
*Koky and Others v Slovakia* no 13624/03, 12 June 2012......125n.8, 152n.177, 155n.196, 168n.272
*Kolyadenko and Others v Russia* no 17423/05, 28 February 2012......39n.113, 58, 75n.18, 82n.38, 87
*Konrova v Slovakia* no 7510/04, 31 May 2007 ...................................31n.62
*Kotilainen and Others v Finland* no 62439/12, 17 September 2020...... 25n.34, 34n.79, 38–39,
                               47n.11, 49n.27, 59n.89, 65n.123, 105, 106, 108n.65, 114n.91,
                                  120nn.118–19, 128n.22, 136n.76, 179n.50, 182n.67, 187,
                                          192n.108, 196n.121, 206nn.172–73, 208n.184, 216n.220
*Kovačič v Slovenia* [GC] no 44574/98, 3 October 2008 ..........................253n.184
*Kraulaidis v Lithuania* no 76805/11, 8 November 2016......................138n.85, 147
*K.U. v Finland* no 2872/02, 2 December 2008.............................28n.47, 133n.59
*Kudra v Croatia* no 13904/07, 18 December 2012 ...............................51n.45
*Kuppinger v Germany* no 62198/11, 15 April 2015.................................85n.51
*Kurt v Austria* [GC] no 62903/15, 15 June 2021 ........... 27n.44, 31n.65, 34–35n.84, 36–37,
                                              82n.43, 111, 114–15, 175n.28, 182n.67,
                                      183–84, 187, 205n.162, 209, 210--13, 214–15

*Labita v Italy* [GC] no 26772/95, 6 April 2000..................................131n.40
*Landi v Italy* no 10929/19, 7 April 2022 .....................210n.192, 213n.205, 216n.221
*Lambert and Others v France* [GC] no 46043/14, 5 June 2015.................56n.65, 82n.38
*L.C.B. v United Kingdom* no 14/1997/798/1001, 9 June 1998 .........46–47, 58n.79, 81n.37
*Leray and Others v France* (dec.) no 44617/98, 16 January 2001....................40n.115
*Loizidou v Turkey* (preliminary objections) no 15318/89, 23 March 1995 ....231n.51, 245–46,
*Loizidou v Turkey* (Merits) [GC] no 15318/89, 18 December 1996 ..........231n.52, 245–46,
                                                                            252, 298–99
*Lopes de Sousa Fernandes v Portugal* no 56080/13, 15 December 2015 ................48n.18
*Lopes de Sousa Fernandes v Portugal* [GC] no 56080/13, 19 December 2017 ......1n.9, 32n.69,
                                   36–37, 39, 48n.19, 68, 127n.18, 128n.22, 134, 134n.67,
                                       138n.86, 141n.107, 144n.123, 148n.142, 149n.150,
                                          152n.169, 154nn.190–91, 158n.225, 168nn.274–75,
                                      174n.22, 179n.50, 182n.67, 192, 193n.109, 194, 195n.119, 196
*López Ribalda and Others v Spain* [GC] no 1874/13 and 8567/13,
    17 October 2019 ..............................................73n.4, 198n.136

## xvi  Table of Cases

*Loste v France* no 59227/12, 3 November 2022 . . . . . . . . . . . . . .179n.51, 210n.191, 215–16n.217
*Lozovyye v Russia* no 4587/09, 24 April 2018 . . . . . . . . . . . . . . . . . . . . . . . . . . . . . . . .172–73n.9
*Lyubov Vasilyeva v Russia* no 62080/09, 18 January 2022 . . . . . . . . . . . . . . . . . . . . . . .210n.191

*M. v Denmark* (dec.) no 17392/90, 14 October 1992 . . . . . . . . . . . . . . . . . . . . . . . . . . . . . . . .239
*M. and Others v Bulgaria* no 41416/08, 26 July 2011 . . . . . . . . . . . . . . . . . . . . . . . . . . .278n.286
*M. and Others v Italy and Bulgaria* no 40020/03, 31 July 2012
*M.A. v Denmark* [GC] no 6697/18, 9 July 2021 . . . . . . . . . . . . . . . . . . . . . . . . 188n.91, 198n.132
*Maiorano and Others v Italy* no 28634/06, 15 December 2009 . . . . . . . . .25n.27, 59–60, 136n.76
*Makaratzis v Greece* [GC] no 50385/99, 20 December 2004 . . . . . . . . . . . 48–49, 53–54, 139n.92
*Makuchyan and Minasyan v Azerbaijan and Hungary* no 17247/13,
 26 May 2020 . . . . . . . . . . . . . . . . . . . . . . . . . . . . . . . . . . . . . . . . . . . . . . . . .157n.218, 158n.219
*Malagić v Croatia* no 29417/17, 17 November 2022 . . . . . . . . . . . . . . . . . . . . . .203n.157, 213n.206
*Marckc v Belgium* no 6833/74, 13 June 1979 . . . . . . . . . . . . . . . . . . . . . . . . . . . . . . . . . . .174n.20
*Mangîr and Others v Moldova and Russia* no 50157/06, 17 July 2018. . . . . . . . . . . . . . . .232n.55
*Marguš v Croatia* [GC] no 4455/10, 27 May 2014. . . . . . . . . . . . . . . . . . . . . . . . . . . . . .158n.220
*Markovic and Others v Italy* [GC] no 1398/03, 14 December 2006 . . . . . 258, 258nn.205–10, 259, 260
*Manitaras and Others v Turkey* (dec.) no 54591/00, 3 June 2008 . . . . . . . . . . . . 231n.53, 233n.67
*Maurice v France* [GC] no11810/03, 6 October 2005 §121 . . . . . . . . . . . . . . . . .74n.11, 198n.132
*Marius Alexandru and Marinela Ştefan v Romania* no 78643/11,
 24 March 2020 . . . . . . . . . . . . . . . . . . . . . . . . . . . . . . . . . . . . . . . . . 1n.3, 192n.107, 196n.124,
*Mastromatteo v Italy* [GC] no 37703/97, 24 October 2002 . . . . . 1n.7, 25n.27, 25n.34, 67, 69, 78,
 79n.29, 128n.22, 136n.76, 206–7
*Mazepa and Others v Russia* no 15086/07, 17 July 2018. . . . . . . . . . . . . . . . . . . . . . . . . .155n.192
*Mažukna v Lithuania* no 72092/12, 11 April 2017 . . . . . . . . . . . . . . . . . . . . . . . . . . .129n.27, 147
*M.C. v Bulgaria* no 39272/98, 4 December 2003. . . . . . . . 132n.46, 133n.58, 154n.185, 169n.279,
 169n.280, 175n.29, 176n.36
*M. and C. v Romania* no 29032/04, 27 September 2011 . . . . . . . . . . 168n.276, 169n.279, 169n.280
*McCann and Others v United Kingdom* [GC] no 18984/91,
 27 September 1995 . . . . . . . . . . . . . . . 53n.53, 128n.24, 129–30, 130n.36, 183n.71, 297n.383
*McKerr v the United Kingdom* no 28883/95, 4 May 2001 . . . . . . . . . . . . . . . . . . 140n.93, 153n.183
*Medova v Russia* no 25385/04, 15 January 2009 . . . . . . . . . . . . . . . . . . . . . . . . . . . 11n.32, 51n.46
*Medvedyev and Others v France* [GC] no 3394/03, 29 March 2010 . . . . 230n.41, 230n.44, 235–36,
 236n.88, 237, 278n.285, 279n.287, 280–81, 283–84, 288n.333, 289n.338
*Mehmet Şentürk and Bekir Şentürk v Turkey* no 13423/09, 9 April 2013 . . . . . . . . . . . . . 176–77
*Mikayil Mammadov v Azerbaijan* no 4762/05, 17 December 2009 . . . . . . . . . . 40n.115, 55n.62,
 136n.76, 150n.153, 154n.186
*Mikheyev v Russia* no 77617/01, 26 January 2006. . . . . . . . . . . . . . . . . . . . . . . . . . . . . . .168n.274
*Mikhno v Ukrain* no 32514/12, 1 September 2016 . . . . . . . . . . . . . . . . . . . . . . . . . . . . . . . .79n.32
*Milanović v Serbia* no 44614/07, 14 December 2010 . . . . . . . . . . . . . . . . . . . . .132n.52, 155n.196
*M.H. and Others v Croatia*, no 15670/18 and 43115/18, 18 November 2021. . . . . . . . . . . . . . 127
*M.N.and Others v Belgium* (dec) no 3599/18, 5 May 2020. . . . . . . . . . . 219n.2, 229n.37, 239–41,
 243–44, 246–47, 251n.166, 254, 259, 260, 264n.231, 285–86, 288n.330
*Mocanu and Others v Romania* [GC] no 10865/09, 17 September 2014 . . . . . . 123n.2, 130n.34,
 130n.38, 157nn.214–16, 167n.267
*Mohammed Ben Al Mahi and Others v Denmark* no 5853/06, 11 December 2006 . . . . .254n.186
*Moldovan and Others v. Romania (no. 2)* no 41138/98 and 64320/01, 12 July 2005 . . . . . 133n.58
*Molie v Romania* (dec.) no 13754/02, 1 September 2009 . . . . . . . . . . . . . . . . . . . . . . . . . . 40n.115
*Monteanu v Moldova* no 34168/11, 26 May 2020 . . . . . . . . . . . . . . . . . . . . . . . . . . . . . . . . . . .179
*Mosley v United Kingdom* no 48009/08, 10 May 2011. . . . . . . . . . . . . . . . . 48n.14, 73n.10, 86n.61
*Movsesyan v Armenia* no 27524/09, 16 November 2017 . . . . . . . . . . . . . . . . . .140n.93, 158n.227
*M.S. v Croatia* [GC] no 60561/14, 25 June 2020 . . . . . . . . . . . . . . . . . . . . . . . . . . . . . . . . . .125n.9
*M.S. v Italy* no 32715/19, 7 July 2022 . . . . . . 210n.189, 210n.192, 213n.205, 214n.210, 216n.221

Table of Cases    xvii

*M.S.S. v Belgium and Greece* [GC] no 30696/09, 21 January 2011 . . . . . . . . . . . . . . . . . . . .62n.109
*Mozer v the Republic of Moldova and Russia* [GC] no 11138/10, 23 February 2016 . . . . .232n.55
*Mukuchyan and Minasyan v Azerbaijan and Hungary* no 17247/13, 26 May 2020 . . . .262n.226
*Munteanu v the Republic of Moldova* no 34168/11, 26 May 2020 . . . . . . . . . . . . . . . . 205–6n.164
*Mustafa Tunç and Fecire Tunç v Turkey* [GC] no 24014/05, 14 April 2015 . . . 128n.25, 139n.91,
143n.118, 150n.156, 151nn.163–66, 168n.274, 169n.277
*Muta v Ukrain* no 37246/06, 31 July 2012. . . . . . . . . . . . . . . . . . . . . . . . . . . . . . .129n.30, 140n.99
*Myumyun v Bulgaria* no 67258/13, 3 November 2011 . . . . . . . . . . . . . . . . . . . . . .98n.17, 157n.212

*Nachova and Others v Bulgaria* no 43577 and 43579/98, 6 July 2005 . . . . . . . 130n.39, 148n.144,
155n.195, 174n.20, 276n.274
*Nada v Switzerland* [GC] no 10593/08, 12 September 2012 . . . . . . . . . . . . . . . . . . . . . . . . .219n.2
*Naït-Liman v Switzerland* [GC] no 51357/07, 15 March 2018. . . . . . . . . . . . . . . . . . . . .286n.324
*Nana Muradyan v Romania* no 69517/11, 5 April 2022. . . . . . . . . . . . . . . . . . . . . . . . . .210n.191
*Nasr and Ghali v Italy* no 44883/09, 23 February 2016. . . . . . . . . . . . . . . . . . . . . . . . . . .163n.247
*N.B. v Slovakia*, no 29518/10, 12 June 2012 . . . . . . . . . . . . . . . . . . . . . . . . . . . . . . . . . . . .145n.127
*N.D. and N.T. v Spain* [GC] no 8675/15, 13 February 2020 . . . . . . . . . .219n.2, 229n.37, 229n.39,
235n.81, 240–41
*Nencheva and Others v Bulgaria* no 48609/06, 18 June 2013 . . . . . . . . . .24n.23, 30n.55, 38n.108,
61n.102, 62, 84n.45
*Nessa and Others v Finland* (dec) no 31862/02, 6 May 2003 . . . . . . . . . . . . . . . . . . . . . .241n.118
*Nevmerkzhitsky v Ukraine* no 54825/00, 5 April 2005 . . . . . . . . . . . . . . . . . . . . . . . . . . . .108n.62
*Nicolae Virgiliu Tănase v Romania* [GC] no 41720/13, 25 June 2019 . . . . . . . . . . . . . . . . 124n.6,
126nn.11–15, 128n.22, 133n.55, 135, 141–47, 156, 157n.209,
158n.223, 173n.16, 182n.67, 205–6n.164, 206n.172, 217n.224
*Nikolova and Velichkova v Bulgaria* no 7888/03, 20 December 2007 . . . . . . . . . . . . . . . .133n.57
*N.P. v Moldova* no 58455/13, 6 October 2015 . . . . . . . . . . . . . . . . . . . . . . . . . . . . . . . . . .120n.114
*Nunez v Norway* no 55597/09, 28 June 2011 . . . . . . . . . . . . . . . . . . . . . . . . . . . . . . . . . . . . .75n.16

*Öcalan v Turkey* [GC] no 46221/99, 12 May 2005. . . . . . . . . . . . . . . . . . . . 235–36, 237, 289n.337
*Odièvre v France* [GC] no 42326/98, 13 February 2003 . . . . . . . . . . . . . . . . . . . . . . . . . . .102n.39
*Oganezova v Armenia* no 71367/12, 17 May 2022 . . . . . . 138n.84, 175n.32, 203n.157, 210n.191
*O'Keeffe v Ireland* [GC] no 35810/09, 28 January 2014. . . . . . . . . . . . 28n.47, 28n.49, 29–30n.52,
31n.65, 47, 55n.64, 56, 69n.140, 73nn.1–3, 132n.46,
132n.54, 140n.99, 149n.145, 173n.17, 183n.76, 217n.225
*Olewnik-Cieplińska and Olewnik v Poland* no 20147/15, 5 September 2019 . . . . . . . . . . .48n.20
*Oliari and Others v Italy* no 187661/11, 21 July 2015 . . . . . . . . . . . . . . . . . . . . . . .86n.60, 174n.18
*Öneryildiz v Turkey* [GC] no 48939/99, 30 November 2004 . . . . . . . . . . .26n.35, 33n.73, 58n.79,
92, 92n.81, 134n.63, 142, 142n.109
*Opuz v Turkey* no 33401/02, 9 June 2009 . . . . . . . . . . . . . . . . . . . . . . 1n.4, 30–31, 38n.104, 47n.11,
82n.41, 99n.18, 118n.112
*Orchowski v Poland* no 17885/04, 22 October 2009 . . . . . . . . . . . . . . . . . . . . . . . . . . . . . .61n.101
*Oruk v Turkey* no 33647/04, 4 February 2014 . . . . . . . . . . . . . . . . . . . . . . . . . . . . . . . . . .144n.122
*Osman v Denmark* no 38058/09, 14 June 2011 . . . . . . . . . . . . . . . . . . . . . . . . . . . . . . . . . . . .11n.35
*Osman v the United Kingdom* [GC] no 23452/94, 28 October 1998 . . . . . . . 23n.18, 25, 38n.104,
40n.119, 79n.30, 99n.18, 171, 203–14
*Ostendorf v Germany* no 15598/08, 7 March 2013 . . . . . . . . . . . . . . . . . . . . . . . . 111n.79, 112n.84
*Otgon v the Republic of Moldova* no 22743/07, 25 October 2016. . . . . . . . . . . . . . . . . . . . .19n.77
*Özel and Others v Turkey* no 14350/05, 15245/05 and 16051 . . . . . . . . . . . . . . . . . . . . . . . . . . . .39

*Pad and Others v Turkey* (dec.) no 60167/00, 28 June 2007 . . . . . . . . . . . . . . . 252–53, 253n.181
*Paduret v Moldova and Russia* no 26626/11, 9 May 2017. . . . . . . . . .233n.68, 234n.71, 279n.289
*Palić v Bosnia and Herzegovina* no 4704/04, 15 February 2011 . . . . . . . . . . . . . . . . . . . .165n.261

## xviii  Table of Cases

*Panaitescu v Romania* no 30909/06, 10 April 2012...............................65n.123
*Paposhvili v Belgium* [GC] no 41738/10, 13 December 2016......................183n.70
*Pârvu v Romania* no 13326/18, 30 August 2022....................................153
*Pavel Shishkov v Russia* no 78754/13, 2 March 2021............... 40n.115, 82n.41, 120n.114
*Paul and Audrey Edwards v United Kingdom* no 46477/99, 14 March 2012.............60n.95
*Pedersen and Others v Norway* no 39710/15, 10 March 2020 ......................120n.114
*Penati v Italy* no 44166/15, 11 May 2021 ...............................137n.80, 148n.141
*Perinçek v Switzerland* [GC] App 27510/08, 15 October 2015 ..... 100n.24, 116n.98, 117, 117n.104
*P.H. v Slovakia* no 37574/19, 8 September 2022 ........................173n.10, 206n.166
*Pisari v the Republic of Moldova and Russia* no 42139/12, 21 April 2015............. 232, 233
*Pisică v the Republic of Moldova* no 23641/17, 29 October 2019....................201n.151
*Placi v Italy no* 48754/11, 21 January 2014........................................62n.110
*Plattform 'Ärzte für das Leben' v Austria* no 10126/82, 21 June 1988............. 2n.12, 10–11,
        14–15n.56, 18n.72
*Polat v Austria* no 12886/16, 20 July 2021 ....................................172–73n.9
*Premininy v Russia* no 44973/04, 10 February 2011 .................. 27n.43, 47n.11, 60n.95
*Prilutskiy v Ukraine* no 40429/08, 26 February 2015 ............................40n.115
*P. and S. v Poland* no 57375/08, 30 October 2012 ...............................199n.140

*Railean v Moldova* no 23401/04, 5 January 2010................................143n.117
*Ramsahai and Others v the Netherlands* [GC] no 52391/99, 15 May 2007...... 152n.170, 152n.175
*Rana v Hungary* no 40888/17, 16 July 2020..................................... 176–77
*Rantsev v Cyprus and Russia* no 25965/04, 7 January 2010 .................. 3n.19, 132n.49,
        153–54nn.184–85, 159–64, 168n.273
*Rasheed Haje Tugar v Italy* (dec.) 22869/93, 18 October 1995..............253, 254, 287n.329
*Ražnatović v Montenegro* no 14742/18, 2 September 2021 ..................98n.15, 210n.191
*Razvozzhayev v Russia and Ukraine* no 75732/12, 19 November 2019 ...............161n.238
*R.B. v Estonia* no 22597/16, 22 June 2021 ...... 141n.102, 156n.204, 157n.211, 169n.280, 175n.28
*R.B. v Hungary* no 64602/12, 12 April 2016........................................141n.102
*Remetin v Croatia (No. 2)* no 7446/12, 24 July 2014 .............................141n.101
*Renolde v France* no 5608/05, 16 October 2008...............................34–35n.84
*Ribcheva and Others v Bulgaria* no 37801/16, 30 March 2021......... 48n.19, 54n.59, 110–11,
        123n.5, 132n.49, 134, 135, 136n.76, 137n.78, 139n.87, 142n.108,
        149–50, 150n.154, 152, 154n.186, 205–6n.164, 207–9, 218n.227
*R.L. and Others v Denmark* no 52629/11, 7 March 2017 .................... 73n.6, 100n.24,
*Roche v The United Kingdom* [GC] no 32555/96, 19 October 2005.........19n.78, 66, 199n.140
*Röman v Finland* no 13072/05, 29 January 2013.....................................73n.6
*Romeo Castaño v Belgium* no 8351/17, 9 July 2019................. 163–65, 261n.222, 262
*R.R. v Poland* no 27617/04, 26 May 2011 .................................73n.8, 174n.20

*S. v Germany* (dec) no 10686/83, 5 October 1984..............................239n.105
*Sabalić v Croatia* no 50231/13, 14 January 2021 .............................156n.204
*Safi and Others v Greece* no 5418/15, 7 July 2022 ............................210n.191
*Sakine Epözdemir and Others v Turkey* no 26589/06, 1 December 2015 ...............31n.63
*Salakhov and Islyamova v Ukraine* no 28005/08, 14 March 2013 ....................47n.10
*Salman v Turkey* [GC] no 21986/93, 27 June 2000 ...............................130n.32
*Sandra Janković v Croatia* no 38478/05, 5 March 2009 .........................140n.100
*Sandu and Others v Moldova and Russia* no 21043/05, 17 July 2018 ................. 298–99
*Sargsyan v Azerbaijan* [GC] no 40167/06 16 June 2015........................ 52nn.49–50
*Saribekyan and Balyan v Azerbaijan* no 35746/11, 30 January 2020..................164n.254
*Sarihan v Turkey* no 55907/08, 6 December 2016..................................41n.121
*Sarishvili-Bolkvadze v Georgia* no 58240/08, 19 July 2018........................148n.139
*S.B. v Romania* no 24453/04, 23 September 2014..................................136n.75

## Table of Cases  xix

*Scripnic v the Republic of Moldova* no 63789/13, 13 April 2021 .................158n.229
*Semache v France* no 36083/16, 21 June 2018 ...................................24n.24
*Šilih v Slovenia* [GC] no 71463/01, 9 April 2009 .................... 126nn.15–16, 132n.51
*Sinim v Turkey* no 9441/10, 6 June 2017........................................ 144–45
*S.H. and Others v Austria* [GC] no 57813/00, 3 November 2012 ...........14n.53, 86, 92–93
*Sousa Goucha v Portugal* no 70434/12, 22 March 2016 ..........................198n.137
*Schembri v Malta* (dec.) no 66297/13, 19 September 2017 .......................241n.118
*Shchiborshch and Kuzmina v Russia* no 5269/08, 16 January 2014.................269n.251
*Schüth v Germany* no 1620/03, 23 September 2010 .............................115n.96
*S.M. v Croatia* [GC] no 60561/14, 25 June 2020 ........... 123n.2, 125, 148n.144, 149n.147,
150n.156, 152n.177, 167nn.267–68, 168nn.272–74, 169
*Smiljanić v Croatia* no 35983/14, 25 March 2021 ............... 1n.2, 18n.74, 38n.109, 47n.9,
59–60, 118n.110, 178n.48, 179, 192n.107, 193n.110, 194n.112, 208n.184, 215n.215
*Söderman v Sweden* [GC] no 5786/08, 12 November 2013 ...................... 68–70, 87,
133nn.59–60, 140n.96, 140n.100, 141n.102, 149n.149,
156n.205, 156n.206, 169n.279, 169nn.280–81, 218n.277
*Solomou and Others v Turkey* no 36832/97, 24 June 2008 ...........................253
*Špadijer v Montenegro* no 31549/18, 9 November 2021 ............... 180n.57, 189, 203n.157
*Stankūnaitė v Lithuania* no 67068/11, 29 October 2019..........................115n.97
*Storck v Germany* no 61603/00, 16 June 2005 ...................... 55n.64, 57n.72, 62n.111
*Stoyanova v Bulgaria* no 56070/18, 14 June 2022 ...............................175n.33
*Stoyanovi v Bulgaria* no 42980/04, 9 November 2010 .............33n.73, 48n.22, 68n.133,
79n.32, 193n.111, 195n.119
*S., V. and A. v Denmark* [GC] no 35553/12, 22 October 2018............... 112–13, 112n.80
*Sudita Keita v Hungary* no 42321/15, 12 May 2020....................... 180, 201–2n.153

*Tagayeva and Others v Russia* no 26562/07, 13 April 2017........................296n.377
*Tagiyeva v Azerbaijan* no 72611/14, 7 July 2022 ............... 152n.174, 210n.191, 215n.213
*Tahsin Acar v Turkey* [GC] no 26307/95, 8 April 2004...................132n.47, 156n.202
*Talpis v Italy* no 41237, 2 March 2017....................1n.4, 27n.44, 31n.64, 34–35n.84,
35n.86, 182n.67, 207, 211n.194, 216n.222
*Tanda-Muzinga v France* no 2260/10, 10 July 2014 ............................199n.140
*Taskin and Others v Turkey* no 46117/99, 10 November 2004..........................65
*Ternovszky v Hungary* no 67545/09, 14 December 2010 ........................173n.14
*Tërshana v Albania* no 48756/14, 4 August 2020 ...................... 155n.195, 214n.207
*Tikhonova v Russia* no 13596/05, 30 April 2014 ..............................206n.166
*Tkhelidze v Georgia* no 33056/17, 8 July 2021 ........................ 137n.77, 206n.174,
210n.192, 212n.201, 213n.205
*T.M. and C.M. v The Republic of Moldova* no 26608/11, 28 January 2014 ............87n.65
*T.P. and K.M v the United Kingdom* [GC] no 28945/95, 10 May 2001 ........... 1n.1, 38n.105
*Traskunova v Russia* no 21648/11, 30 August 2022............... 154, 173n.11, 178n.48, 179,
192n.108, 193n.111, 195–96
*Tunikova and Others v Russia* no 55974/16, 14 December 2021......175n.30, 188–89, 191–92,
206n.172, 213n.205, 216n.223
*Turturica and Casian v Moldova and Russia* no 28648/06,
30 August 2016............................................... 232n.55, 279, 283–84
*Tyrer v the United Kingdom* no 5856/72, 25 April 1978 ...........................11n.34

*Uzbyakov v Russia* no 71160/13, 5 May 2020......... 40n.116, 180n.61, 189n.95, 199n.140, 200n.144

*Valdís Fjölnisdóttir and Others v Iceland* no 71552/17, 18 May 2021 .......... 172n.5, 180–81
*Valeriy Fuklev v Ukraine* no 6318/03, 16 January 2014..........................150n.157
*Valiulienė v Lithuania* no 33234/07, 26 March 2013..............................125n.8

*Vallianatos and Others v Greece* [GC] no 29381/08 and 32684/09, 7 November 2013 .... 183n.71
*Van Colle v the United Kingdom* no 7678/09, 13 November 2012 ..................... 80n.36
*Vanyo Todorov v Bulgaria* no 31434/15, 12 July 2020 ................................. 158
*Vardosanidze v Georgia* no 43881/10, 7 May 2020 .............. 40n.115, 142n.109, 206n.173
*Varnava and Others v Turkey* [GC] no 16064/90, 18 September 2009 ...... 281n.302, 297n.382
*Vasilca v the Republic of Moldova* no 69527/10, 11 February 2014 .................... 132n.48
*Vavřička and Others v the Czech Republic* [GC] no 47621, 8 April 2021 .............. 116n.99
*V.C. v Slovakia* no 18968/07, 8 November 2011 ........................... 145n.127, 146
*Velikova v Bulgaria* 41488/98, 18 May 2000 ...................................... 150n.155
*Veronica Ciobanu v Republic of Moldova* no 69829/11, 9 February 2021 ............. 154n.186
*VgT Verein Gegen Tierfabriken v Switzerland* no 24699/94, 28 June 2001 ............. 180n.59
*Vilnes and Others v Norway* no 52806/09, 5 December 2013 ....... 27n.41, 28n.48, 31, 48, 58, 76, 77
*Vinks and Ribicka v Latvia* no 28926/10, 30 January 2020 ........................ 131n.42
*Vo v France* [GC] no 53924/00, 8 July 2004 .............. 56n.65, 128n.22, 141n.106, 155n.199
*Volodina v Russia* no 41261/17, 9 July 2019 ......................... 120–21n.121, 175n.30
*Volodina v Russia* (no.2) no 40419/19, 14 September 2021 ................ 141n.101, 188–89
*Von Hannover v Germany* (no. 2) [GC] no 40660/08,
    7 February 2012 ......................................... 198n.134, 200nn.143–45
*Vovk and Bogdanov v Russia* no 15613/10, 11 February 2020 .............. 137n.80, 147n.136
*Vrábel v Slovakia* (dec.) no 77928/01, 19 January 2010 .......................... 40n.115

*Waiter v Poland* no 42290/08, 15 May 2012 ....................................... 60n.99
*Weber and Saravia v Germany* (dec.) no 54934/00, 29 June 2006 ................... 289n.337
*Women's Initiative Supporting Group and Others v Georgia* no 73204/13,
    16 December 2021 ................................... 125n.8, 206n.171, 210n.191
*Wunderlich v Germany* no 18925/15, 10 January 2019 ............................. 31n.66

*X. v Germany* (dec.) no 1611/62, 25 September 1965 ........................... 238, 239
*X. v the Former Yogoslav Republic of Macedonia* no 29683/16,
    17 January 2019 .......................................... 181n.64, 201–2n.153
*X. v the United Kingdom* (dec) no 7547/76, 15 December 1977 ............ 238, 239, 241n.119
*X. and Others v Bulgaria* [GC] no 22457/16, 2 February 2021 .......... 123n.1, 132, 139n.92,
                                156n.202, 163n.246, 166, 168n.276, 169n.278,
                                175n.28, 182n.67, 191, 205–6n.164, 206n.172
*X. and Y. v Switzerland* no 7289/75 and 7349/76, 14 July 1977 .................... 247, 249
*X. and Y. v the Netherlands* no 8978/80, 26 March 1985 ........................... 10–11

*Y. and Others v Bulgaria* no 9077/18, 22 March 2022 .................... 210n.192, 216n.221
*Yeter v Turkey* no 33750/03, 13 January 2009 .................................. 157n.217
*Y.G. v Russia* no 8647/12, 30 August 2022 ................................... 136, 140–41
*Young, James and Webster v The United Kingdom* no 7601/76, 13 August 1981 ......... 180n.59
*Y.P. v Russia* no 43399/13, 20 September 2022 ............................. 131n.44, 146

*Z. and Others v the United Kingdom* [GC] no 29392/95,
    10 May 2001 ............................. 1n.1, 74n.11, 85n.53, 107n.57, 158n.227
*Zavoloka v Latvia* no 58447/00, 7 July 2009 ..................................... 40n.115
*Zdanoka v Latvia* [GC] 58278/00, 16 March 2006 ............................... 225n.20
*Zinatullin v Russia* no 10551/10, 28 January 2020 ..................... 144n.120, 158n.223

# Introduction

The development of positive obligations has been one of the hallmarks of the work of the European Court of Human Rights (ECtHR or the Court) in interpreting the European Convention on Human Rights (ECHR). Various issues from various spheres of life have been reviewed by the Court as involving possible breaches of positive obligations. Examples of when these obligations might be triggered include when social service departments decide to take children into care or to refrain from doing so,[1] when highway authorities fail to provide warning signs or to ensure road safety,[2] when authorities fail to ensure safety at public places,[3] when women or children are subjected to domestic violence,[4] when police investigate crimes,[5] when the State has to enforce building regulations,[6] when the police fail to capture a dangerous individual who might commit crimes,[7] when people are harmed due to natural disasters or industrial activities,[8] or when the healthcare system fails to prevent diseases or save lives.[9] The systems designed to protect the public from harm are extensive. Consequently, positive obligations have penetrated all provisions of the ECHR and there are no a priori limits to the situations in which they may arise.[10] What most of these situations have in common is that the immediate cause of the harm that the victim suffered was not an act of the State;[11] it is alleged that the State, nevertheless, ought to have protected the person from harm by, for example, providing a warning of a hazard, controlling a third party, removing the person from a dangerous environment, organizing its healthcare or childcare systems in better ways, investing more

---

[1] *Z. and Others v United Kingdom* no 29392/95, 10 May 2001; *T.P. and K.M. v United Kingdom* no 28945/95, 10 May 2001.
[2] *Fatih Çakır and Merve Nisa Çakır v Turkey* no 54558/11, 5 June 2018; *Smiljanić v Croatia* no 35983/14, 25 March 2021, §67.
[3] *Marius Alexandru and Marinela Ştefan v Romania* no 78643/11, 24 March 2020.
[4] *Opuz v Turkey* no 33401/02, 9 June 2009; *Talpis v Italy* no 41237/14, 2 March 2017.
[5] J Chevalier-Watts, 'Effective Investigation under Article 2 of the European Convention on Human Rights: Security the Right to Life or an Onerous Burden on a State?' (2010) 21(3) European Journal of International Law 701.
[6] *Cevrioğlu v Turkey* no 69546/12, 4 October 2016; *Banel v Lithuanis* no 14326/11, 18 June 2013. More generally the State is an enforcer of various regulations. *Fernández Marínez v Spain* [GC] no 56030/07, 12 June 2014, §114.
[7] *Mastromatteo v Italy* [GC] no 37703/97, 24 October 2002.
[8] *Öneryildiz v Turkey* [GC] no 48939/99, 30 November 2004.
[9] *Lopes de Sousa Fernandes v Portugal* [GC] no 56080/13, 19 December 2017.
[10] J Costa, 'The European Court of Human Rights: Consistency of its Case-Law and Positive Obligations' (2008) 26 Netherlands Quarterly of Human Rights 449, 453.
[11] I use the term 'victim' in a general sense as a person who has sustained harm without prejudice to the determination whether the State can be held responsible under ECHR for this harm.

in training its police officers, or taking generally some more extensive protective measures.

It is rather unclear under which circumstances positive obligations may be triggered and how far-reaching they may be, given how difficult it is to draw the boundaries of state responsibility for omissions. The ECtHR has not proposed a general analytical framework for reviewing when these obligations can be set in motion and how expansive their scope might be. The Court has explicitly refused 'to develop a general theory of the positive obligations which may flow from the Convention'.[12] Perhaps as a consequence, it has been observed that the ECtHR's approach to positive obligations is incoherent or even arbitrary, which is not conducive to certainty and predictability.[13] One is left with the impression that the Court simply makes *in casu* judgments when dealing with positive obligations, and that it is hard to direct and structure these by extracting distinctions as to the analytical steps taken and the principles applied. The quality of the Court's reasoning has also been criticized. It has been noted that the problem with positive obligations is that 'their proper scope appears open-ended' and the Strasbourg court 'does not set general conceptual limitations' for its interventions in developing them.[14] Such an approach, it has been argued, 'put[s] the concept of positive obligations into disrepute'.[15] Such an approach can also have institutional repercussions by feeding concerns about the legitimate role of the Court in that it broadens its review into areas perceived as being within the purview of the national authorities.[16]

Given the wide regulatory functions of the State and, more generally, the manifestation of the State in many aspects of our lives and the enormous breadth of state activities,[17] any harm sustained by an individual could potentially be a basis for making an argument that the State had failed to fulfil its positive human rights obligations, since it failed to prevent or mitigate the harm or the risk of harm. It will often be possible to identify some act, which if the State had taken the person would not have suffered harm, or it would have been less likely for the harm or the risk to materialize. Therefore, the impact of positive obligations is potentially boundless. In addition, it is paradoxical that the more measures the State takes to protect, the more likely it

---

[12] *Plattform 'Ärzte für das Leben' v Austria* no 10126/82, 21 June 1988, §31. The Court generally eschews abstract theorizing. A Mowbray, 'The Creativity of the European Court of Human Rights' (2005) 5(1) Human Rights Law Review 57, 61.

[13] M Hakimi, 'State Bystander Responsibility' (2012) 21 European Journal of International Law 341, 349; P Dijk, '"Positive Obligations" Implied in the European Convention on Human Rights: Are the States Still the 'Masters' of the Convention?' in M Castermans-Holleman and others (eds), *The Role of the Nation-State in the 21st Century* (Kluwer 1998) 17, 22.

[14] D Xenos, *The Positive Obligations of the State under the European Convention of Human Rights* (Routledge 2011) 3 and 178; P Thielbörger, 'Positive Obligations in the ECHR after the *Stoicescu* Case: A Concept in Search of Content?' (2012) European Yearbook on Human Rights 259, 261; J Varuhus, *Damages and Human Rights* (Hart Publishing 2016) 297.

[15] Thielbörger, 'Positive Obligations in the ECHR after the *Stoicescu* Case' (n 14) 259, 261.

[16] M Klatt, 'Positive Rights: Who Decides? Judicial Review in Balance' (2015) 13(2) International Journal of Constitutional Law 354; W Sadurski, 'Supranational Public Reason: On Legitimacy of Supranational Norm-producing Authorities' (2015) 4(3) Global Constitutionalism 396, 413.

[17] C Harlow, *State Liability. Tort Law and Beyond* (Oxford University Press 2004) 6.

becomes that it can be held responsible for not doing enough.[18] The objective of this book is to address these challenges by identifying the key analytical issues that need to be tackled in determining whether a State is responsible under the ECHR for failure to fulfil positive obligations.

The ECtHR has produced a rich body of case law on positive obligations, placing the Court at the centre of many polycentric issues that raise difficult questions about the functioning of societies, the role of the State, and the distribution of resources. This development was initiated in the 1970s and since then the Court has been gradually expanding the adjudication of positive obligations, many times by breaking new ground.[19] Scholarly contributions have addressed this progress by focusing on specific subject areas covered in the case law, such as domestic violence, environmental pollution, or medical negligence.[20] In contrast, this book approaches the topic from the perspective of cross-cutting issues, such as state knowledge, causation, and the reasonableness standard, issues which more generally shape the legal standards and analysis. In this regard, Chapter 1 lays the ground by deconstructing positive obligations, explaining how they correlate to rights and what the references to positive obligations' content, scope, and types actually mean.

This book can be contrasted with the works of Mowbray and Akandji-Kombe that are still regarded as the key sources in this field. Mowbray's and Akandji-Kombe's works are descriptive and not recent, weaknesses that the present book aims to remedy.[21] Dröge's, Xenos', and Lavrysen's contributions are relatively more recent and are more analytical.[22] However, much of the progress on this topic has been achieved in a piecemeal fashion. In contrast, rather than proceeding on a right-by-right basis, this book takes a more general analytical approach. It fills an important gap by studying the analytical questions underlying state responsibility under the ECHR for omissions. It explains the structure of review, namely the analytical steps taken for finding a breach of positive obligations under the ECHR. This book is thus distinct since it isolates the separate analytical elements that are crucial for any analysis of positive obligations under the ECHR and situates the Court's approach to these elements in an intelligible framework of analysis. These elements are state knowledge

---

[18] P Atiyah, *The Damage Lottery* (Hart Publishing 1997) 86.
[19] For example, *Rantsev v Cyprus and Russia* no 25965/04, 7 January 2010.
[20] For example, R McQuigg, 'Domestic Violence as a Human Rights Issue: Rumor v Italy' (2016) 26 European Journal of International Law 1009; A Kenyon, 'Complicating Freedom: Investigating Positive Free Speech' in A Kenyon and A Scott (eds), *Positive Free Speech. Rationales, Methods and Implications* (Hart Publishing 2020); A Kenyon, *Democracy of Expression. Positive Free Speech and Law* (Cambridge University Press 2021).
[21] A Mowbray, *The Development of Positive Obligations under the European Convention on Human Rights by the European Court of Human Rights* (Hart Publishing 2004); J Akandji-Kombe, *Positive Obligations under the European Convention on Human Rights* (Council of Europe Publishing 2007).
[22] C Dröge, *Positive Verpflichtungen der Staaten in der Europäischen Menschenrechtskonvention* (Springer 2003); Xenos, *The Positive Obligations of the State under the European Convention of Human Rights* (n 14); R Lavrysen, 'The Scope of Rights and the Scope of Obligations: Positive Obligations' in E Brems and J Gerards (eds), *Shaping Rights in the ECHR* (Cambridge University Press 2014); R Lavrysen, 'Protection by the Law: The Positive Obligation to Develop a Legal Framework to Adequately Protect the ECHR Rights' in E Brems and Y Haeck (eds), *Human Rights and Civil Rights in the 21st Century* (Springer 2014) 69.

(Chapter 2), causation (Chapter 3), the standard of reasonableness (Chapter 4), and how the latter standard might be affected by competing obligations (Chapter 5). To do this, I situate these analytical elements, identifiable in the ECtHR case law, within the law on state responsibility, which ensures the anchoring of the analysis in general international law. The book's distinctiveness is further strengthened by its engagement with the most recent case law where positive obligations are invoked. Moreover, based on these recent developments, it identifies and explains the different types of positive obligations (Chapters 6 and 7).

The specific role of human rights law in regulating the relationship between the State and the group of individuals organized in the political community represented by this State is at the core of this book. The balance between how intrusive, on the one hand, and how restrained, on the other, the State should be in its regulations aimed at organizing the community provides an important framework of the analysis. This includes a serious appreciation of the dangers that can be associated with positive obligations whose scope might be too expansive or content too intrusive. Here it needs to be mentioned that a formidable corpus of case law and other normative outputs have been developed in justification of positive obligations and in favour of expansion of their scope and content.[23] These outputs have been crucial in transforming human rights law as a source of norms that require much more than freedom from state interference and that necessitate harnessing the power of the State to secure genuine enjoyment of human rights. This book contributes to this transformation by adding much required analytical sophistication concerning the conditions as to when and how this power can be harnessed.

At the same time, this book shows that an account of positive obligations that fails to consider their intrusiveness and power of coercion seriously is incomplete. Risk aversion, one of the main rationales underpinning positive obligations, can come at a price that the particular political community might not be willing to pay, due to the coercion and infringement of personal freedoms implied. The difficulty of finding a balance between, on the one hand, state interventions to prevent risk and protect individuals and, on the other hand, preservation of the individual's sphere of inviolability is a crucial point addressed in the book. I argue that how and where this balance is struck are decisions to be taken by the particular political community, which ultimately reveals the communitarian nature and the political contingency of human rights law. These decisions characterize the specific community and its identity, since they can steer it in different directions. The two extremes that need to be navigated are intrusive statism, where the State is viewed as the pervasive protector, versus

---

[23] S Fredman, *Human Rights Transformed: Positive Rights and Positive Duties* (Oxford University Press 2008); H Shue, *Basic Rights. Subsistence, Affluence, and U.S. Foreign Policy* (Princeton University Press 1996); K Möller, *The Global Model of Constitutional Law* (Oxford University Press 2012); K Möller, 'Two Conceptions of Positive Liberty: Towards an Autonomy-based Theory of Constitutional Rights' (2009) 29(4) Oxford Journal of Legal Studies 757: 'This is part of the trend of interpreting rights as "enabling people to live autonomous lives, rather than *disabling* the State in certain way."'

Introduction 5

unrestrained liberalism, where protection by the State is always viewed as an unnecessary intrusion.

The communitarian nature of human rights law is further taken up in Chapter 8, which offers an examination of the conceptual hurdles arising if positive obligations under the ECHR were to be applied extraterritorially. Authors have raised the issue of extraterritorial application of positive obligations,[24] but the concrete legal analytical questions that such an application implies have not been addressed systematically. A distinctive feature of the analysis offered in Chapter 8 is that it reverses the methodological order that is usually applied to this question. In particular, I first engage with the substance of positive obligations to show the profoundness and embeddedness of the communitarian limitations of human rights law. Only thereafter, I demonstrate how these limitations emerge in the jurisdictional threshold under Article 1 ECHR. It follows that the uniqueness of my approach is that I first engage in detail with the technical and conceptual issues about the scope and content of positive obligations, which shines light on the normative underpinnings of human rights law, that is, its communitarian nature. Only when this is done do I engage with the specific, both technical/conceptual and normative, challenges extraterritoriality poses in relation to positive obligations. In doing so, I justify the requirement for jurisdiction, as a threshold that reflects the existing relationship between individuals as rights holders and a specific State as a bearer of obligations. Notably, I argue that both the technical and the communitarian aspects illustrate the political and communitarian contingency of human rights.

Finally, clarifications as to the methodology used in the book are due. The analysis offered presents the existing law and practice in its best light, despite the awareness that often the method of review adopted by the Court is haphazard, and not conducive to coherence and clarity.[25] Yet these deficiencies are not an insurmountable obstacle for extracting some general principles from the case law and providing an account of what the Court actually does when it adjudicates positive obligations. The book also aims to find the justifications underpinning the review of positive obligations conducted in the practice of the Court. The efforts to do so imply reconstruction of the practice, so as to facilitate its better understanding and shape its future development.[26] The systematic reconstruction of the practice is not done without critique. This critique, however, does not refer to external theoretical standards for the correction of the practice; rather, in accordance with the approach applied here, I maintain that the practice has the resources to reform itself. External standards are only used to

---

[24] M Milanovic, *Extraterritorial Application of Human Rights Treaties* (Oxford University Press 2011); L Raible, *Human Rights Unbound. A Theory of Extraterritoriality* (Oxford University Press 2020); K Larsen, *The Human Rights Treaty Obligations of Peacekeepers* (Cambridge University Press 2012).
[25] S Greer, 'What's Wrong with the European Convention on Human Rights?' (2008) 30(3) Human Rights Quarterly 680, 697.
[26] This method draws from S Besson, 'The Law in Human Rights Theory' (2013) 7(1) Journal of Human Rights 120; S Besson, 'Science without Borders and the Boundaries of Human Rights' (2015) 4 European Journal of Human Rights 462, 467.

identify possible dangers in light of the above-mentioned difficulties in finding a balance between state intrusiveness and restraint.

It follows that the method employed in the book is to both reflect upon and explain the reasoning of the Court. At certain points, however, the book takes a critical approach to the case law. It extends the limits of its descriptive approach in the face of some inconsistencies within the case law and inadequacies as to how the Court has grappled with some analytical issues that demand more serious consideration in future. In this sense, this book contributes to the establishment of more coherent foundations of positive obligations, and more principled and consistent decision-making. By setting out the factors informing the trigger, content, and scope of positive obligations, it offers guidance for policy-making and adjudication of individual rights. In addition, the book aims to encourage the Court to become more aware of its own analysis, the ways that it delimits state responsibility for omission, and the difficulties of establishing causality, knowledge, and reasonableness in this area.

The selection of case law is limited to judgments under Articles 2 (the right to life), 3 (the right not to be subjected to torture, inhuman or degrading treatment or punishment), and 8 (the right to private and family life) of the ECHR. These provisions have formed the basis for a rich judicial output on positive obligations. In light of the importance of the interests reflected in Articles 2 and 3, protection by the State can be easily expected, given the gravity of the harm involved if these interests are affected. In contrast, Article 8, in particular the notion of 'private life', is broad enough to cover a wide variety of interests, including interests of a less serious nature. This denotes distinctiveness, which is captured in the book. In contrast to Articles 2 and 3, Article 8 also embodies a qualified right, which implies a proportionality assessment whose distinctiveness is also appreciated.

As to the selection of judgments, priority is given to those delivered by the Grand Chamber, but Chamber judgments are also covered, including those that herald important developments concerning positive obligations. The main focus is placed on the Court's judicial output from 2010 until 20 November 2022; however, important judgments prior to this time frame are also included. The selected case law is sufficiently representative to allow an exploration of the analytical questions that underpin the determination of state responsibility under the ECHR for failure to fulfil positive obligations. The corpus of case law used has been collected based on the author's regular review of all judgments delivered by the Court since 2010 and search in the HUDOC database based on the term 'positive obligation'. Since the analysis is qualitative, not all collected judgments have been cited. This will in any case be unnecessary since the applicable principles are repeated. The focus is thus on identifying these general principles and any relevant distinctions introduced in subsequent judgments.

# 1
# Deconstructing Positive Obligations

## Introduction

The European Convention on Human Rights (ECHR) embodies general rules of human rights entitlements that are couched in very broad terms and at a very high level of abstraction. The rights in the Convention are also framed in a simple way that is separated from obligations. The apparent simplicity of the rules as framed in the text, however, belies the complex issues that they generate. The effective application of the ECHR norms requires a degree of clarity as to the meaning of the rights and concreteness of the obligations undertaken by States.[1] In order to be transformed into relatively precise, tangible, and certain rules, the obligations corollary to the rights have to be determined,[2] which entails extensive interpretative efforts. Such efforts have been encouraged, given the argument that if we take rights seriously and see them as normative, we must take obligations seriously.[3] As a consequence, there has been increased interest in the so-called supply side of human rights;[4] that is, in the corresponding obligations.[5] In other words, despite the priority of rights as organizational principles, these rights have to be matched with obligations. As will be explained below, these obligations are institutionally mediated through the State; they are characterized by plurality: a right can trigger multiple obligations that at a very general level can be divided into positive and negative, and, despite the clear justifications that promote the imposition of positive obligations, they raise crucial questions about the intrusive role of the State in the particular political community.

---

[1] J Donnelly, 'The Virtues of Legalization' in S Meckled-García and B Çalı (eds), *The Legalization of Human Rights* (Routledge 2006) 67.
[2] M Addo, *The Legal Nature of International Human Rights* (Martinus Nijhoff Publishers 2010) 187; J Montero, 'Global Poverty, Human Rights and Correlative Duties' (2009) 22(1) Canadian Journal of Law and Jurisprudence 79, 87.
[3] O O'Neill, 'The Dark Side of Human Rights' (2005) 81(2) International Affairs 427, 430; H Shue, 'The Interdependence of Duties' in P Alston and K Komasevski (eds), *The Right to Food* (Martinus Nijhoff Publishers 1984) 83, 84.
[4] J Griffin, *On Human Rights* (Oxford University Press 2008) 111.
[5] J Nickel, 'How Human Rights Generate Duties to Protect and Provide' (1993) 15(1) Human Rights Quarterly 77; J Nickel, *Making Sense of Human Rights* (Blackwell 2007) 37–41; S Besson, 'The Bearers of Human Rights' Duties and Responsibilities for Human Rights: A Quiet (R)evolution' (2015) 32(1) Social Philosophy and Policy 244; A Kuper, 'The Responsibilities Approach to Human Rights' in A Kuper (ed), *Global Responsibilities. Who Must Deliver on Human Rights?* (Routledge 2005).

*Positive Obligations under the European Convention on Human Rights*. Vladislava Stoyanova, Oxford University Press.
© Vladislava Stoyanova 2023. DOI: 10.1093/oso/9780192888044.003.0002

## 1.1 The State as an Institutional Mediator

States are the bearers of obligations under international human rights law.[6] The underlying reason is, first, that power resides in state public institutions that claim the legitimate use of force. The objective of human rights law is to regulate the relationship between these institutions and individuals, so that this force is constrained and directed. In this regard, these institutions have the capacity to respect and uphold human rights obligations.[7] Second, there are reasons related to democratic legitimacy and equality.[8] For reasons of 'political equality in the allocation of the burden and cost of human rights' and for reasons of democratic legitimacy, duties are mediated institutionally through the State.[9] State institutions have a mediating role in the allocation and the reallocation of resources and burdens among individuals; they are also meant to protect the equality of all in doing so and 'to ensure the overall legitimacy of the process'.[10] Equality implies that state institutions fulfil their obligations by having equal respect for each individual;[11] these institutions are able to guarantee equality by distributing burdens and benefits in a way that is compatible with the principle of equality.

Democratic legitimacy implies that the State does not act for its own sake but for the sake of pursuing some general goal of the community, and that it reflects all the interests and concerns of all those it represents. This is also reflected in the current international order, where States are the primary subjects of international law, and responsibility under human rights law is a subset of the law on state responsibility.[12]

---

[6] States bear obligations, but so does any international organization, such as for example the EU, that can exercise jurisdiction and is organized democratically. Besson, 'The Bearers of Human Rights' Duties and Responsibilities for Human Rights' (n 5) 244.

[7] Nickel, 'How Human Rights Generate Duties to Protect and Provide' (n 5) 77, 81.

[8] S Besson, 'The Legitimate Authority of International Human Rights—On the Reciprocal Legitimation of Domestic and International Human Rights' in A Føllesdal (ed), *The Legitimacy of Human Rights* (Cambridge University Press 2013) 32; Besson, 'The Bearers of Human Rights' Duties and Responsibilities for Human Rights' (n 5) 244, 252; S Besson, 'Human Rights and Democracy in a Global Context: Decoupling and Recoupling' (2011) 4(1) Ethics and Global Politics 19.

[9] S Besson, 'Human Rights and Constitutional Law' in R Cruft and others (eds), *Philosophical Foundations of Human Rights* (Oxford University Press 2015) 280, 284.

[10] S Besson 'Science without Borders and the Boundaries of Human Rights' (2015) 4 European Journal of Human Rights 462, 472.

[11] There is no conflict between guaranteeing equality, on the one hand, and the specification of human rights obligations with reference to distributive justice and the application of the proportionality/reasonableness standard on the other. If a policy is disproportionate, this implies that the State has attached too little weight to the interests of the right-holder: 'to attach too little weight to someone's interests means to fail to treat his interests equally important as everyone else's interests'. Equality is respected when a policy 'distributes burdens and benefits in a way that respects every affected person's equal importance'. K Möller, 'Dworkin's Theory of Rights in the Age of Proportionality' (2018) 12(2) Law and Ethics of Human Rights 281, 293, and 297. At the same time, this distribution of burdens and benefits can happen only within the political community. See S Meckled-Garcia, 'Giving Up the Goods: Rethinking the Human Right to Subsistence, Institutional Justice, and Imperfect Duties' (2013) 30(1) Journal of Applied Philosophy 73, 74: 'outside the political communal contexts there is no coherent account of what constitutes a justifiable imposition of burdens for any specific agent that will secure the resource claims of all'.

[12] J Crawford and A Keene, 'The Structure of State Responsibility under the European Convention on Human Rights' in A van Aaken and I Motoc (eds), *The European Convention on Human Rights and General International Law* (Oxford University Press 2018) 178.

Concerns about equality and democratic legitimacy are also reflected in the jurisdictional threshold under Article 1, which determines which State is the bearer of human rights law obligations, a point I elaborate upon in Chapter 8.

What follows then is that although human rights are claimed to be universal, there is no corresponding universality of human rights obligations.[13] To understand this, we must attend to the technicalities of human rights law. More specifically, human rights law typically separates the right from the corresponding obligations.[14] These obligations are not universal, and they are certainly not unlimited in scope. Human rights could be thus perceived as paradoxical. They hold the promise of universality,[15] and yet the reality is that human rights are dependent on the State for their protection, implementation, and realization. The state authorities are the guarantor of the rights and must provide the legal infrastructure through which the rights can be affected.[16] There are no universal duty-bearers. Rather, a particular State needs to be designated as a duty-bearer that has the unified power to regulate and to seek fair distribution.[17]

When the State exercises this unified power, it appears as both an entity that has to be 'civilized' and restrained and, at the same time, as the source of institutional solutions.[18] Rights are institutionally referential, and the sovereign State is the preferred institutional solution.[19] Rights are commonly invoked against exploitative, oppressive, and intrusive practices committed by States. At other times, however, rights are invoked to extend state control and power,[20] and to increase the intrusiveness of the State. This exposes an important tension: on the one hand, the State is regarded as the main problem since it can be a source of oppression and, on the other hand, the State is regarded as the solution since it is also a source of protection.[21] These two roles are in a constant reciprocal relationship. The challenge that arises then is how to find the balance between intrusiveness and restraint. Engaging with this challenge is at the core of this book.

---

[13] S Besson, 'The Allocation of Anti-poverty Duties. Our Rights, but Whose Duties?' in K Shefer (ed), *Poverty and the International Economic Legal System* (Cambridge University Press 2013) 408, 419.

[14] M Hakimi, 'Human Rights Obligations to the Poor' in Shefer (ed), *Poverty and the International Economic Legal System* (n 13) 395.

[15] I Balfour and E Cadava, 'The Claims of Human Rights: An Introduction' (2004) 103 The South Atlantic Quarterly 277, 280; W Hamacher, 'The Right to Have Rights (Four-and-a-Half Remarks)' (2004) 103 The South Atlantic Quarterly 343, 349–50.

[16] R Lawson, 'Out of Control. State Responsibility and Human Rights: Will the ILC's Definition of the 'Act of State' Meet the Challenges of the 21st Century' in M Castermans-Holleman and others (eds), *The Role of the Nation-State in the 21st Century. Human Rights, International Organisations and Foreign Policy* (Kluwer 1998) 91, 91.

[17] S Meckled-Garcia, 'On the Very Idea of Cosmopolitan Justice: Constructivism and International Agency' (2008) 16(3) Journal of Political Philosophy 245.

[18] C Reus-Smit, 'On Rights and Institutions' in C Beits and R Goodin (eds), *Global Basic Rights* (Oxford University Press 2011) 26, 27.

[19] ibid 37.

[20] ibid 44.

[21] This protection has been invoked in light of the increasing importance and power of non-state actors in many contexts of modern life. J Thomas, *Public Rights, Private Relations* (Oxford University Press 2015) 9; I Kolstad, 'Human Rights and Assigned Duties: Implications for Corporations' (2009) 10 Human Rights Review 569–82.

## 1.2 Justifications for Positive Obligations

Human rights law has historically focused on limiting state intrusiveness and proscribing abuses committed by the State. The ECHR was conceived as a legal framework to defend individuals against the misuse of power by States.[22] The prevailing idea during the negotiation of the ECHR was providing a safeguard against totalitarianism. The context was marked by the end of the Second World War and emerging tensions of the Cold War.[23]

However, individuals might suffer harm not inflicted by state agents. They can be threatened by other individuals who act as private parties, and whose actions are not attributable to the State. Individuals can be also threatened by other forces and events, such as earthquakes, mudslides, natural disasters, or epidemics. Harm might be also caused by corporations, armed groups, or intergovernmental organizations. Positive human rights obligations have been used as a tool to address these kinds of situation. In these situations, the acts of such private agents do not become acts of the State.[24] However, the State might be in breach of its human rights obligations not directly because of the acts of the private abusers but as a result of omissions of its own that can be linked to the harm. It has to be immediately clarified that positive obligations are pertinent not only in situations when the direct source of harm is a 'natural' event or a private actor. These obligations are equally relevant in the direct relationship between individuals and the State.[25] Given the pervasive role of the State, it might be also difficult to draw fine lines between the roles of different actors and events in causing harm. I return to this point in Section 1.3 when I address the distinction between positive and negative obligations.[26]

The Court has applied an incremental approach in the development of positive obligations.[27] The origins of this development can be traced to the *Belgian Linguistic* case, where with respect to the right to education, the Court held the State might have a positive obligation to ensure this right.[28] Further elaboration was offered in *Marckx v Belgium*.[29] *X. and Y. v the Netherlands* was another breakthrough case because the

---

[22] K Starmer, 'Positive Obligations under the Convention' in J Jowell and J Cooper (eds), *Understanding Human Rights Principles* (Hart Publishing 2001) 139; P van Dijk, 'Positive Obligations Implied in the European Convention on Human Rights: Are the States Still the 'Masters' of the Convention?' in Castermans-Holleman and others (eds), *The Role of the Nation-State in the 21st Century* (n 16) 17, 18.

[23] E Bates, *The Evolution of the European Convention on Human Rights* (Oxford University Press 2010) 6; Bates, 'The Birth of the European Convention on Human Rights and the European Court of Human Rights' in J Christoffersen and M Madsen (eds), *The European Court of Human Rights between Law and Politics* (Oxford University Press 2011) 18.

[24] *Beganovic v Croatia* no 46423/06, 25 June 2009 §69: 'no direct responsibility can attach to Croatia under the Convention for the acts of the private individuals in question'.

[25] *Valiuliene v Lithuania* no 33234/07, 26 March 2013 §73.

[26] See also Section 5.3.3.

[27] K Haijev, 'The Evolution of Positive Obligations under the European Convention on Human Rights—by the ECtHR' in D Spielmann and others (eds), *The European Convention on Human Rights: A Living Instrument* (Bruylant 2011) 207, 208.

[28] Case 'Relating to Certain Aspects of the Laws on the Use of the Languages in Education in Belgium' v Belgium no 1474/62, 23 July 1968.

[29] *Marckx v Belgium* no 6833/74, 13 June 1979 §31.

application of positive obligations was extended to interpersonal relations. The Court held that 'these obligations may involve the adoption of measures designed to secure respect for private life even in the sphere of the relations of individuals between themselves'.[30] *Plattform 'Ärzte für das Leben' v Austria* was another of the early judgments in which the Court developed positive obligations by observing that it was the duty of the State to 'take reasonable and appropriate measures to enable lawful demonstration to proceed peacefully'.[31]

To substantiate this development, the European Court of Human Rights (ECtHR) refers to Article 1 of the Convention, which imposes an obligation upon the Parties not only to respect, but also to secure the rights in the ECHR.[32] The interpretation of the Convention as a 'living instrument', which implies a 'dynamic and evolutive' interpretation, has also been used as a tool.[33] In addition, when examining whether a State has ensured the rights protected in the ECHR, the Court has also noted that 'the Convention is intended to guarantee not rights that are theoretical or illusory but rights that are practical and effective'.[34] The principle of effectiveness therefore has a crucial role for justifying positive obligations and determining their scope.[35] The wording of certain provisions also provides a justificatory basis. For example, Article 2 stipulates that the right to life 'shall be protected by law'.

It is not my aim to provide theoretical justification for these developments, a task which has been successfully achieved by other authors.[36] Rather, the book accepts these developments and the justifications offered by the Court, and focuses on the technical analytical issues that the specification of the positive obligations demands (ie articulation of the circumstances where the obligations are triggered, their content and scope, the factors that determine this content and scope, and the eventual finding of a breach). An important starting point here is that a right can generate a plurality of positive obligations and the Court cannot specify them *ex ante*. It can only review whether in the particular situation that has transpired in the particular case, the obligation has been fulfilled. This implies an *ex post* review and *ex post* specification of the obligation.

---

[30] *X. and Y. v the Netherlands* no 8978/80, 26 March 1985 §23.
[31] *Plattform 'Ärzte für das Leben' v Austria* no 10126/82, 21 June 1988.
[32] J Akandij-Kombe, *Positive Obligations under the European Convention on Human Rights* (Council of Europe Publishing 2007) 8; *A. v the United Kingdom* no 100/1997/884/1096, 23 September 1998 §22; *Medova v Russia* no 25385/04, 15 January 2009 §103.
[33] A Mowbray, 'The Creativity of the European Court of Human Rights' (2005) 5(1) Human Rights Law Review 57, 64; *Christine Goodwin v United Kingdom* [GC] no 28957/95, 11 July 2002 §74.
[34] *Tyrer v the United Kingdom* no 5856/72, 25 April 1978. See J Merrills, *The Development of International Law by the European Court of Human Rights* (Manchester University Press 1993) 102–03.
[35] Although the existence of positive obligations is not controversial, the Court still presents them as an addition to negative obligations. For example, in the context of Article 8, '[b]y way of introduction, the Court notes that the essential object of Article 8 is to protect the individual against arbitrary action by the public authorities. There may in addition be positive obligation inherent in effective "respect" for private and family life.' *Osman v Denmark* no 38058/09, 14 June 2011 §53.
[36] H Shue, *Basic Rights* (Princeton University Press 1996); S Freedman, *Human Rights Transformed* (Oxford University Press 2008); K Möller, *The Global Model of Constitutional Law* (Oxford University Press 2012).

## 1.3 Plurality of Obligations Owed by the State

A human right might provide for the imposition of many obligations that are context specific. Accordingly, a single human right might generate a plurality of duties, and there is not necessary a one-to-one pairing between obligations and rights.[37] The fulfilment of each right involves the performance of multiple kinds of obligations,[38] the specifications of which raise serious challenges. In particular, the question that arises is how to make a principled limitation to the obligations triggered, their scope and content.

Human rights law obligations have been generally divided into positive and negative.[39] The Court's reasoning also reflects this distinction.[40] While the first category requires the State to take action, the second requires that the State refrain from action.[41] The existence of both types of duties is not controversial. However, while the negative duties might be conceptually easier to delineate, given that the correlation between the right and the obligation might be easier to establish, the positive duties raise a whole gamut of difficult conceptual questions. Specifically, the relationship between the duty and the right might not yield itself to one-to-one correlation.[42] This difficulty originates from the variety of ways through which the positive duty might be fulfilled (ie it might have different content).[43] Difficulties also stem from the existence of variables that might determine whether the duty should be triggered in the first place and if triggered, how demanding it should be (ie the scope of the duty). The absence of one-to-one correlation implies that, for example, the right to be protected does not

---

[37] S Besson, 'The Allocation of Anti-poverty Duties. Our Rights, but Whose Duties?' in Shefer (ed), *Poverty and the International Economic Legal System* (n 13) 408, 415; J Raz, 'On the Nature of Rights' (1984) XCIII Mind 194, 200.

[38] Shue, *Basic Rights* (n 36) 52; J Waldron, 'Rights in Conflict' (1989) 99 Ethics 503, 510.

[39] It has been already widely accepted that all rights, civil, political, and socio-economic, impose both negative and positive obligations. Fredman, *Human Rights Transformed* (Oxford University Press 2008).

[40] Often in the context of Article 8, the Court refuses to specify whether it will examine the case as one implicating positive or negative obligations (*Hatton and Others v the United Kingdom* [GC] no 36022/97, 8 July 2003 §98). Wibye has argued that this refusal does not necessary reflect the Court's conception of obligation, but rather its methodology: '[r]ather than getting embroiled in questions of conceptual delineation, the more efficient approach when tackling individual applications is to proceed directly to proportionality review and the ultimate determination of whether the state has struck the right balance between active measures and non-interference'. J Wibye, 'Beyond Acts and Omissions—Distinguishing Positive and Negative Duties at the European Court of Human Rights' (2022) 23 Human Rights Review 479 . See also M Klatt, 'Positive Obligations under the European Convention on Human Rights' (2011) Heidelberg Journal of International Law 691, 694 where it is demonstrated in detail that the Court's position that the distinction does not matter, is mistaken.

[41] M Klatt, 'Positive Rights: Who Decides? Judicial Review in Balance' (2015) 13(2) International Journal of Constitutional Law 354. Judge Martin defined positive obligations in *Gül v Switzerland* no 23218/94, 19 February 1996, as obligations that 'require Member States to take action'.

[42] Alexy frames this as alternativity: 'protective rights have an *alternative* or disjunctive structure, and defensive rights, a conjunctive structure. Unconstitutional (positive) action of the State has a definitive counterpart, which consists in the omission of just that unconstitutional action. The alternative structure implies that unconstitutional omission has no definitive counterpart, but as many possible counterparts as alternatives exist.' R Alexy, 'On Constitutional Rights to Protection' (2009) 3 Legisprudence 1, 5.

[43] For elaboration of the argument that the distinguishing feature of positive obligations is that they have 'multiple fulfillment options', see Wibye, 'Beyond Acts and Omissions' (n 40). See also Klatt, 'Positive Obligations under the European Convention on Human Rights' (n 40) 691.

trigger *any* action on behalf of the State that amounts to protection. There is therefore a disjunction between the right and the obligations since there are many possible alternatives to ensure the right.[44] This is clearly reflected in the practice of the Court that has emphasized that States can choose which alternatives to employ to fulfil their positive obligations.[45] Whichever alternative is chosen, however, it has to be reasonable and strike a 'fair balance' between different interests. The tests of reasonableness and 'fair balance' and the related disjunction between rights and obligations, raise serious conceptual problems that will be addressed in more detail in Chapter 4.

Another difficulty when dealing with the subject of obligations in human rights law stems from the distinction itself between positive and negative obligations and the related difficulty in making the distinction between action and omission, especially when the addressee of these obligations is the State. The contemporary reality is that the State is 'a pervasive regulator and architect of a vast web of social, economic, and political strategies and choices'.[46] Accordingly, the distinction between action and inaction, arguably, 'fails to reflect the distribution of power and the ways in which government can cause harm in the modern welfare state'.[47] It is possible to reformulate inactions as actions and vice versa. The formulation and reformulation are determined by the reigning assumptions and the baselines that a specific society has about the role of the State. These baselines can, for example, affect and disrupt causal chains.[48] As Pogge has observed, the application of the distinction between acts and omissions to collective agents and social institutions, such as the State, is baffling if we do not have 'baseline comparisons'.[49] It follows then that there is no normatively neutral way for advancing *one single* general justification for the distinction in *all possible* situations. Since the distinction between actions and omissions might not be easy to make, a more useful way to understand the distinction between positive and negative obligations might be by focusing on the variety of alternative measures for their fulfilment and on any differences as to how this variety might be limited in the context of negative and positive obligations. As already noted above, positive obligations can be fulfilled through a variety of ways. It can, however, be objected that States also have at their disposal different means of limiting rights and some of these means might be in breach of negative obligations. This implies that the availability of a variety of

---

[44] M Klatt and M Meister, *The Constitutional Structure of Proportionality* (Oxford University Press 2012) 88–89.
[45] V Stoyanova, 'The Disjunctive Structure of Positive Rights under the European Convention on Human Rights' (2018) 87 Nordic Journal of International Law 344–392.
[46] S Bandes, 'The Negative Constitution: A Critique' (1989–90) 88 Michigan Law Review 2271, 2284–85. It is possible to say that family law, welfare law, employment law, or property law causes harm to interests protected by human rights. See L Oette, 'Austerity and the Limits of Policy-induced Suffering: What Role for the Prohibition of Torture and Other Ill-treatment?' (2015) 15 Human Rights Law Review 669; Adler, *Cruel, Inhuman or Degrading Treatment? Benefit Sanctions in the UK* (2018).
[47] Bandes, 'The Negative Constitution' (n 46) 2283.
[48] J Lichtenberg, 'Are There Any Basic Rights?' in Beits and Goodin (eds), *Global Basic Rights* (n 18) 72, 87.
[49] T Pogge, 'Recognized and Violated by International Law: The Human Rights of the Global Poor' (2005) 18(4) Leiden Journal of International Law 717, 728.

alternative means is also relevant in the context of negative obligations. There is, however, still a difference. In particular, *all* means that constitute disproportionate limitations are in breach of negative obligations.[50] As Wibye has noted, once a limitation measure passes the threshold of disproportionality, the only way to comply is to abstain from this measure.[51] One can rebut that States still have a wide range of possible measures at their disposal how to limit rights. However, the normative starting point is that States have to choose the least restrictive measures when they take actions to limit rights.[52] In this way, *their choice of measures is more circumscribed*. In contrast, the Court has never formulated a test to the effect that States have to undertake the most protective measures to ensure the rights.[53] The starting point is rather that States can choose the measures and their failure to choose the best measure for protecting a person (arguably in fulfilment of a positive obligation) does not necessary lead to a breach. In comparison, when the Court adjudicates negative obligations, its starting point is *not* that States have different means of restrictive rights and that even if one restrictive measure is disproportionate, the proportionality of other measures will still be examined. If *one single* measure limiting the right is disproportionate, this measure is straightforwardly in breach of negative obligations.[54]

It then follows that the difference can be understood as one of degree. In particular, it is the *wider* choice of means/alternatives/measures that characterizes compliance with positive obligations in comparison with negative obligations. This makes the finding of breach more difficult because of the need to consider more alternatives and counterfactuals (ie what other means could have been used to ensure the right). As Klatt has observed, 'unlawful omission of an action has no definite opposite'.[55] Here a circularity needs to be acknowledged since the absence of definitive opposites, which implies the availability of multiple options for fulfilment of positive obligations, is premised on the distinction between acts and omissions. This suggests that it is ultimately difficult to separate our conceptualization of obligations and the distinction between positive and negative obligations from the distinction between acts and omissions completely.

Despite all these difficulties, the dichotomy between positive and negative obligations is used by the ECtHR,[56] and this book does not seek to question

---

[50] See Klatt, 'Positive Obligations under the European Convention on Human Rights' (n 40) 694.
[51] Wibye, 'Beyond Acts and Omissions' (n 40).
[52] Notably, the Court does not consistently apply the least restrictive test means test as part of its proportionality review in negative obligations cases. See E Brems and L Lavrysen, 'Don't Use a Sledgehammer to Crack a Nut: Less Restrictive Means in the Case Law of the European Court of Human Rights' (2015) 15 Human Rights Law Review 139; J Gerards, 'How to Improve the Necessity Test of the European Court of Human Rights' (2013) 11(2) International Journal of Constitutional Law 466.
[53] In fact, in the context of Article 8, the Court has even suggested a rejection to search for more protective alternative measures, as part of its review. See *S.H. and Others v Austria* [GC] no 57813/00, 3 November 2011 §106; *Hristozov and Others v Bulgaria* no 47039/11 and 358/12, 13 November 2012 §125; *Evans v United Kingdom* [GC] no 6339/05, 10 April 2007 §91. See Section 4.2.3.
[54] Klatt, 'Positive Obligations under the European Convention on Human Rights' (n 40) 695.
[55] ibid 695.
[56] The delineation criteria have not been clearly articulated in the case law. This failure can be related to the refusal by the Court to 'to develop a general theory of the positive obligations which may flow from the Convention' (*Plattform 'Ärzte für das Leben' v Austria* no 10126/82, 21 June 1988 §31). Neither the

it.[57] Nor does it challenge the designation of a corresponding obligation as positive by the Court. Rather the book's point of departure is that, although problematic, the distinction needs to be maintained because finding responsibility for omissions and delimiting this responsibility raises distinct analytical challenges.[58] More specifically, the State, through its organs, commits a multiplicity of omissions, and it would be absurd to suggest that each one of them should give rise to responsibility. For an omission to be legally relevant, there must be an obligation upon the State to do something in the first place, and in this sense, the State's omission needs to be shown to have been wrongful. The existence of an obligation to do something might have to be proven and justified.[59] Even if this is possible, there might be no clearly prescribed standards against which the omission can be juxtaposed, so that it can be determined whether the State has breached its positive obligation due to the omission (ie whether the omission is actually wrongful). The determination of these standards is shaped by the elements of causation, knowledge, and reasonableness that are at the heart of the analysis in the next chapters.

Besides these analytical challenges that justify the preservation of the distinction between positive and negative obligations, there are additional reasons of a wider normative and societal nature. If the distinction is completely blurred, it might become difficult to discern the different types and sources of harm suffered within the society and in what ways the State has or has not caused them. This in turn is important in navigating the balance between intrusiveness and restraint; that is, between extension of protection and the risk of regulatory (and even coercive) overreach. More specifically, certain harms are directly caused by the State in breach of negative obligations.

---

failure nor the refusal is, however, surprising. The Court does not engage with complex philosophical discourses and in any case, as McMahan notes, the problem of distinguishing causing harm by action versus by omission is persistent. J McMahan, 'Killing, Letting Die, and Withdrawal of Aid' (1993) 103 Ethics 250. Wibye has also demonstrated how there is 'no universally reliable correlation between acts and omission and doing and allowing harm'. Wibye, 'Beyond Acts and Omissions' (n 40).

[57] Moral philosophy has also engaged with this issue and made the point that causing harm by action cannot be equated with causing harm by omission. See Section 5.3.3. S Smet, 'Conflict between Absolute Rights: A Reply to Steven Greer' (2013) 13 Human Rights Law Review 469, 490; W Quinn, 'Actions, Intentions, and Consequences: The Doctrine of Doing and Allowing' (1989) 98 Philosophical Review 287; McMahan, 'Killing, Letting Die, and Withdrawal of Aid' (n 56) 250; J Wibye 'Reviving the Distinction between Positive and Negative Human Rights' (2022) 35(4) Ratio Juris 363. National constitutional law, administrative law, and tort law also have adopted the distinction and developed complex analytical frameworks for examining when state authorities can be held responsible for omissions. See R Alexy, *A Theory of Constitutional Rights* (Oxford University Press 2010) 308–09; Plunkett, *The Duty of Care in Negligence* (2018).

[58] The distinction between acts and omissions is also intelligible for moral reasons: morally we can make a difference between affecting another person for worse and failing to improve his/her position. See T Honore, 'Are Omissions Less Culpable' in P Cane and J Stapleton (eds), *Essays for Patrick Atiyah* (Oxford University Press 1991) 31, 41; McMahan, 'Killing, Letting Die, and Withdrawal of Aid' (n 56) 250. See also Section 5.3.3.

[59] The concept of omission implies a circularity: to know whether the State omitted to do something it is assumed that we know that the State should have done it. The concept of *wrongful* omission seems to be a way of addressing this circularity since it implies that the objective is to ascertain whether the State *legally* should have done something.

Other interests might be harmed by causes beyond reasonable control. Even if causes of harm are within some control, any interventions by the State to prevent the harm or to remedy it might cause attendant harm and repercussions of nature or scale that the society might not be willing to pay.[60] In this context, normative questions about the values cherished by the society also arise. For example, risk aversion, even if feasible, might imply sacrificing and harming the interests of inviolability and freedom of state intrusion that are at the core of human rights law.

## 1.4 Priority of Rights as Organizational Principles

Despite the efforts made in this book to understand how positive obligations are specified through the deployment of causation, knowledge, and reasonableness standards, and in this way to address the concerns about their indeterminacy, the book accepts that determinacy cannot and should not be achieved. In this sense, the insecurity in the case law is understandable since the Court applies an instrument, the ECHR, within which rights have priorities as organizing principles over obligations.[61] To explain this requires a brief foray into the nature of rights.

Rights are intermediaries between interests and duties.[62] The interests and values that justify rights may be recognized and protected before specifying the duties corresponding to them.[63] In addition, rights cover a wide and diverse area of interests and values.[64] Over time new aspects of these interests and values can be discerned, even

---

[60] For elaboration on the notion of 'attendant harm', see Section 5.3.
[61] There are generally two major branches of rights theory. The first one views rights and their correlative duties as an entailed relationship and as logically necessary correlatives. In this view, if there is a right, logically there must be a correlative duty and a duty bearer. See H Steinder, 'Working Rights' in M Kramer (ed), *A Debate Over Rights: Philosophical Enquiries* (Clarendon Press 1998) 233; C Wellman, *Real Rights* (Oxford University Press 1995); W Hohfeld, 'Fundamental Legal Conceptions as Applied in Judicial Reasoning' (1917) 8 Yale Law Journal 710. The other branch is reflected in the interest-based theories and views rights as logically prior to the identification of duties. See J Raz, *The Morality of Freedom* (Clarendon Press 1986). On this account, rights are 'the way interests generate duties'. See J Waldron, *Liberal Rights: Collected Papers 1981–1991* (Cambridge University Press 1993) 214. According to the interest theory of rights, important interests ground duties and rights are conceptually prior to the duties that correspond to them. The ECHR adopts an interest-based conception of rights. See Thomas, *Public Rights, Private Relations* (n 21) 106.
[62] Raz, 'On the Nature of Rights' (n 37) 194, 208: 'the interests are part of the justification of the rights which are part of the justification of the duties. Rights are intermediate conclusions in arguments from ultimate values to duties.' Thomas, *Public Rights, Private Relations* (n 21) 149: 'The nature of rights ... is coherently distinct from that of both interests and duties, and contains some analytical content that allows us to move from the former to the latter.'; S Besson, *The Morality of Conflict: Reasonable Disagreement and the Law* (Hart Publishing 2005) 423.
[63] N MacCormick, 'Rights in Legislation' in P Hacker and J Raz (eds), *Law, Morality and Society: Essays in Honour of H.L.A. Hart* (Clarendon Press 1977) 199–202; Besson, *The Morality of Conflict* (n 62) 422.
[64] There is a debate about how to draw the line between rights and interests, that is between important interests which should be the basis for human rights and other interests. See J Gerards, 'Fundamental Rights and Other Interests. Should it Really Make a Difference?' in E Brems (ed), *Conflicts between Fundamental Rights* (Intersentia 2008) 655–90. This debate does not need to detain us here. It is rather assumed that interests which generate rights have special weight over other interests. S Greer, *The European Convention on Human Rights. Achievements, Problems and Prospects* (Cambridge University Press 2006)

if they are still hidden from our present power of perception.[65] Accordingly, human rights law has a 'dynamic aspect', namely its ability to create new duties, which is fundamental for the understanding of its nature and function.[66] In addition to this dynamism, a rights-based reasoning focuses the attention on the victim and on the harm that he or she has experienced.[67] It follows that the explicit indication of rights accompanied by vague formulation of any corresponding obligations (eg the obligation to ensure rights, without indication of the specific measures that need to be undertaken) has its strengths and weaknesses.

The weakness is that the obligations are difficult to pinpoint in terms of content and scope, both *ex ante* and *post factum*. The obligations vary: they can have different content and scope (ie stringency) depending on the specific context and the harm inflicted on the interest protected by the right. At the same time, however, the imperfection of human rights law, due to the indeterminacy of the corresponding obligations, has its advantages. The strength is that rights, once formulated with reference to fundamental interests, operate like 'a normative resource base from which a whole array'[68] of obligations can be developed. Having rights as organization principles allows flexibility for the emergence of new duties and the adaptation of old duties in the light of context and societal developments.[69] Concurrently with this flexibility and dynamism, rights—as intermediaries between interests and duties—also provide us with 'an intermediary level of agreement' as to 'the superiority of some interests over others', even if we disagree on the content and scope of the corresponding obligations.[70]

In sum, human rights law works from rights as a point of departure towards obligations.[71] Having rights as organizational principles causes conceptual difficulties when these rights need to be matched with obligations. The boundaries of state

---

196, 208–10: 'Convention rights take procedural and evidential, but not conclusive substantive, priority over the democratic pursuit of the public interest.'

[65] J Gerards, 'The Prism of Fundamental Rights' (2008) 8 European Constitutional Law Review 173, 178.
[66] Raz, 'On the Nature of Rights' (n 37) 194, 200.
[67] Rights-based reasoning and duty-based reasoning have different perspectives. If focus is put on the right, interferences with the right are presumed unlawful and it is up for the defender (ie the State) to justify its actions. A duty-based reasoning focuses attention on the putative wrongdoer and it follows that the notion of reasonable conduct and the harm actually caused become central. T Hickman, 'Tort Law, Public Authorities, and the Human Rights Act 1998' in D Fairgrieve and others (eds), *Tort Liability of Public Authorities in Comparative Perspective* (British Institute of International and Comparative Law 2002) 17, 20.
[68] Waldron, 'Rights in Conflict' (n 38) 503, 511.
[69] Report on the Right to Adequate Food as a Human Right submitted by Mr. Asbjørn Eide, E/CN.4/Sub.2/1987/23, 7 July 1987, §47.
[70] Besson, *The Morality of Conflict* (n 62) 424.
[71] This can be contrasted with a legal framework, such as the common law tort of negligence, that works backwards. The starting point is who should bear the burden of compensation, and, in this sense, rights are a 'by-product of the common law's remedial business, rather than its starting point'. J Varuhas, *Damages and Human Rights* (Hart Publishing 2016) 44; V Stoyanova, 'Common Law Tort of Negligence as a Tool for Deconstructing Positive Obligations under the European Convention on Human Rights' (2020) 24(5) The International Journal of Human Rights 632.

responsibility for omissions can thus be difficult to delineate in a more principled and general fashion.

## 1.5 Trigger, Scope, Content, and Types of Positive Obligations

This difficulty can explain the refusal by the Court 'to develop a general theory of the positive obligations which may flow from the Convention'.[72] Despite this refusal, some general important analytical distinctions can be extracted from the case law. Different *types* of positive obligation can be distinguished that can be *triggered* under specific circumstances. The types relate to the *content* of the obligations, which can be expressed at different levels of abstraction and concreteness. Content thus refers to the measures that the State should take (or should have taken if the situation is looked upon retroactively). Besides content, positive obligations have a *scope* that refers to how demanding and stringent they can be (how many measures, or how far reaching these measures should be).[73] Certain *factors/standards* can be identified in the case law (ie state knowledge, causation, and reasonableness) that determine this scope and thus the intensity of the obligation. These factors also determine whether a breach will be found (ie a failure to fulfil the obligation, which leads to state responsibility).[74] These factors are scrutinized in Chapters 2, 3, 4, and 5.

As to the trigger, in the context of Articles 2 and 3, the starting assumption is that the State is permanently under the positive obligation to ensure that individuals within its jurisdiction are not subjected to ill-treatment. Very similarly to French law on administrative liability,[75] the existence of a general *prima facia* obligation is not under question; rather the State is assumed to be under a general obligation to administer competently, which flows from the very nature of state sovereignty.[76] This is, however, an obligation framed at a very general level of abstraction, detached from the concrete facts of the case. At the more concrete level, the Court has distinguished

---

[72] *Plattform 'Ärzte für das Leben' v Austria* no 10126/82, 21 June 1988 §31.
[73] The domestic violence case of *Branko Tomašić and Others v Croatia* no 46598/06, 15 January 2009, §§55–57, can be taken as an example. The Court decided that the scope of the positive obligation included not only placing the abuser in detention but also offering psychological assistance. A wider scope thus implies more measures.
[74] Different terms are used in the judgments to express 'content' and 'scope' and the Court has not adopted a consistent terminology and meaning of the different terms. See, for example, *Bărbulescu v Romania* [GC] §114, where the Court refers to the 'nature and scope of positive obligations' without explaining what more specifically is meant with these terms. See *Smiljanić v Croatia* no 35983/14, 25 March 2021 §70, where the Court refers to the 'extent of the positive obligations'.
[75] C Harlow, 'Fault Liability in French and English Public Law' (1976) 39(5) Modern Law Review 517.
[76] See also N Mavronicola, 'What is an "Absolute Right"? Deciphering Absoluteness in the Context of Article 3 of the European Convention on Human Rights' (2012) 12 Human Rights Law Review 723, 734; N Mavronicola, *Torture, Inhumanity and Degradation under Article 3 of the ECHR. Absolute Rights and Absolute Wrongs* (Hart Publishing 2021) 14: positive obligations corresponding to Article 3 are not displaceable since 'protecting people from proscribed harm is at *all* times obligatory'; however, what these obligations 'encompass in each given situation is a matter of specification'.

three types of positive obligations. First, the obligation to conduct an effective official investigation upon reasonable allegations that harm has materialized. This well-established obligation has been also referred to as the procedural limb of Articles 2 and 3. In addition to this procedural obligation, the rights enshrined in these provisions generate substantive positive obligations. In this respect, we can distinguish two other obligations, namely the obligation to adopt an effective regulatory framework with procedural guarantees so as to prevent harm against the public at large, and finally, the obligation to take such protective operational measures as may be triggered when a specific individual is at 'real and immediate' risk of harm. Each of these types will be examined in detail in Chapters 6 and 7.

The approach to Article 8 and how positive obligations are triggered under this provision is different. Due to the indeterminacy of the notion of private life,[77] the Court first decides whether positive obligations can be generally triggered in the light of the particular case.[78] Therefore, not every claim under Article 8 automatically triggers such obligations at general level.[79] These might have to be initially justified.[80] In this justification, there is a tendency to conflate the definitional threshold analysis under Article 8 with the analysis of whether positive obligations are triggered in the first place.[81] Accordingly, the Court might be faced from the beginning with multiple tasks of appreciation: it decides on the definitional threshold of Article 8 and the related importance of the sphere of private life at stake in the case, and on whether the case should trigger positive obligations. A balancing test might thus determine both

---

[77] G Letsas, *A Theory of Interpretation of the European Convention on Human Rights* (Oxford University Press 2007) 126–30; Dissenting Opinion of Judge Lemmens to *Otgon v the Republic of Moldova* no 22743/07, 25 October 2016.

[78] *Aksu v Turkey* [GC] no 4149/04, 15 March 2012 §59: 'there *may* be positive obligations inherent in the effective respect for private life'; *Christine Goodwin v United Kingdom* [GC] no 28957/59, 11 July 2002 §72; *Roche v United Kingdom* [GC] no 32555/96, 19 October 2005 §157; *Babylonova v Slovakia* no 69146/01, 20 June 2006 §§51–52; *Harroudj v France* no 43631/09, 4 October 2012 §47: '[i]n determining *whether or not a positive obligation exists*, regard must also be had to the fair balance that has to be struck between the general interest of the community and the interests of the individual, the search for which balance is inherent in the whole of the Convention'; *Fadeyeva v Russia* no 55723/00, 9 June 2005 §89: '[i]n these circumstances, the Court's first task is to assess whether the State could reasonably be expected to act as to prevent or put an end to the alleged infringement of the applicant rights'; *Fedotova and Others v Russia* no 40792/10, 13 July 2021, §44: 'While the essential object of Article 8 is to protect individuals against arbitrary interference by public authorities, *it may also* impose on a State certain positive obligations to ensure effective respect for the rights protection by Article 8' (emphasis added).

[79] Some deviations in the framing used by the Court can be also observed. See *Beizaraz and Levickas v Lithuania* no 41288/15, 14 January 2020 §110: 'Positive obligations on the State *are inherent in the right* to effective respect for private life under Article 8; these obligations *may* involve the adoption of measures even in the sphere of the relations of individuals between themselves' (emphasis added).

[80] For a critique of the Court's approach, see L Lavrysen, *Human Rights in a Positive State* (Intersentia 2016), where it is argued that if the definitional threshold of Article 8 is passed, 'the authorities are under a prima facie positive obligations to "protect" and "fulfill" the individual's right'.

[81] For example, *Hudorovič and Others v Slovenia* no 24816/14 and 25140/14, 10 March 2020 §§116–117, where the Court left open the question whether the failure to ensure access to clean water and sanitation to member of Roma communities falls within the definitional scope of Article 8. This question was joined with the question whether the State had failed to fulfil any positive obligations in this context. Even in negative obligation cases, the Court does not follow a strict demarcation between definitional and application stages. J Gerards and H Senden, 'The Structure of Fundamental Rights and the European Court of Human Rights' (2009) 7(4) International Journal of Constitutional Law 619.

whether the claim falls within the definitional limits of private life, and whether there are any positive obligations in this context.[82]

## Conclusion

Human rights, as institutionally mediated through the State that provides the infrastructure for their realization, embody a tension: they are meant to restrain the State and, at the same time, they may require more interventions by the State. This tension needs to be openly acknowledged. It then follows that despite the difficulties in attributing omissions, as opposed to actions, to the State that is a pervasive regulator, the two roles of the State should be distinguished. This distinction can be helpful both in better understanding the different types and sources of harm, and in preventing a too interventionist State. The focus should be on better understanding when State interventions should be forthcoming, how far reaching they should be and what more concrete measures they should imply. These are difficult questions that are at the core of the deconstruction of positive obligations under the ECHR. The ECtHR has tried to address these questions in its rich case law on positive obligations. There are no easy answers, yet certain guiding factors can be clearly identified. The first is knowledge by the State about harm or the risk of harm.

---

[82] For a possible explanation as to why the Court does this, see Stoyanova, 'The Disjunctive Structure of Positive Rights under the European Convention on Human Rights' (n 45) 382.

# 2
# State Knowledge

## Introduction

The Court has consistently reiterated that positive obligations arise when the state authorities knew *or* ought to have known about the risk of harm.[1] This chapter analyses the role of state knowledge in the framework of positive obligations and sets the Court's approach to knowledge within an intelligible framework of analysis. To do so, it is first important to provide an adequate frame of reference. This is achieved by clarifying in Section 2.1 the role of fault in the law of state responsibility more generally. Section 2.2 then clarifies whether fault is a necessary factor for triggering positive obligations under the European Convention on Human Rights (ECHR) or for determining a breach, and what distinctions have been introduced in the case law in this respect. Since fault in the context of these obligations has been framed as actual or putative knowledge by the State of risk of harm, Section 2.3 examines how state knowledge is established in the case law and what principles are used in establishing the knowledge of an abstract organizational entity such as a State. Since the triggering of positive obligations and the determination of a breach are dependent on state knowledge about risk of harm, Sections 2.4–2.7 consider whether any requirements have been imposed as to the nature of this risk. Finally, Section 2.8 examines the role of the victim's contributory fault, and how it relates to state fault.

## 2.1 The Role of Fault in State Responsibility

The starting point for the study of state knowledge is the work of the International Law Commission (ILC) on state responsibility, and in particular on the elements of a wrongful act. The ILC Articles on the Responsibility of States for Internationally Wrongful Acts (ILC Draft Articles)[2] define state responsibility as the attribution to the State of conduct (in the form of an act or omission) that breaches that State's international obligations. Every breach entails responsibility without any additional element such as 'fault'.[3] The ILC Draft Articles thus take an agnostic approach to the

---

[1] *Centre for Legal Resources on Behalf of Valentin Câmpeanu v Romania* [GC] no 47848/08, 17 July 2014 §130.
[2] ILC Yearbook 2001/II(2) 26.
[3] J Crawford, 'Revisiting the Draft Articles on State Responsibility' (1999) 10(2) European Journal of International Law 435, 438.

*Positive Obligations under the European Convention on Human Rights.* Vladislava Stoyanova, Oxford University Press.
© Vladislava Stoyanova 2023. DOI: 10.1093/oso/9780192888044.003.0003

question of fault, since they are based on the principle of 'objective' responsibility.[4] This principle implies that to conclude whether a State is in breach, a comparison needs to be made between the conduct actually performed by the State and the conduct legally prescribed by the relevant primary obligation.[5] This approach was seen as desirable since, first, it might be difficult to identify any subjective element of fault (whether in the form of intent, knowledge, or negligence) of an organizational entity such as a State,[6] and second, it might be equally difficult to prove it.[7]

Although no requirement for fault is imposed *ab extra*, the primary obligations might incorporate such a requirement.[8] This is particularly the case where this primary obligation demands that the State do something (a positive obligation) and the State fails to do it (ie it commits an omission).[9] The ILC Commentaries note that 'it may be difficult to isolate an "omission" from the surrounding circumstances which are relevant for the determination of responsibility'.[10] Such a surrounding circumstance can be fault.[11] By referring to the *Corfu Channel* case, the ILC Commentary gives an example how knowledge as a circumstance combined with omission gave rise to responsibility.[12] In the *Corfu Channel* case, the International Court of Justice (ICJ) held that it was a sufficient basis for Albanian responsibility that it knew, or must have known, of the presence of the mines in its territorial waters and did nothing to warn third States of their presence.[13]

Positive obligations raise particularly challenging questions because an omission is at their core. As a consequence, it might be under question whether there is an obligation upon the State to do something in the first place.[14] Even if there is such an obligation, there might be no clearly prescribed legal standard against which any omission can be compared, so that it can be determined whether because of this omission the State has breached its positive obligation.[15] These challenges can be approached in

---

[4] J Crawford, *State Responsibility. The General Part* (Cambridge University Press 2013) 61; ILC Draft Articles Commentary to Article 2, §10.
[5] ILC Draft Articles Commentary, Article 12, §2. Crawford, *State Responsibility* (n 4) 217.
[6] A Favre, 'Fault as an Element of the Illicit Act' (1964) 52 Georgetown Law Journal 555, 556.
[7] Crawford, *State Responsibility* (n 4) 61.
[8] ibid 219.
[9] A Gattini, 'Smoking/No Smoking: Some Remarks on the Current Place of Fault in the ILC Draft Articles on State Responsibility' (1999) 10(2) European Journal of International Law 397, 398.
[10] ILC Draft Articles Commentary to Article 2, §4.
[11] This explains why certain authors attempt to establish a distinction between breach of international obligations due to omissions versus breach due to actions based on the notion of fault. F Latty, 'Actions and Omissions' in J Crawford and others (eds), *The Law of International Responsibility* (Oxford University Press 2015) 362.
[12] ILC Draft Articles Commentary to Article 2, §4.
[13] *Corfu Channel*, Merits, Judgment, ICJ Reports 1949, page 4, §§22–23.
[14] In the absence of a primary obligation to do something, no omission can be complained of. However, the existence of a primary obligation to do something, might have to be proven or justified. An example to this effect originates from *Case Concerning the Application of the Convention on the Prevention and Punishment of the Crime of Genocide* 27 February 2007, §427, where the ICJ first explained in its reasoning that the obligation to prevent genocide has a 'separate legal existence on its own'.
[15] The State might be called on to take 'appropriate steps', and there cannot be an abstract determination what 'appropriate' actually means. See, for example, *United States Diplomatic and Consular Staff in Tehran*, Judgment, ICJ Reports 1980, §§31–32 and 63–67.

various ways ranging from the so-called strict/absolute liability to failure to exercise 'due diligence', which can be perceived as two ends of a spectrum. 'Strict/absolute' liability implies that once harm materializes, the State is responsible irrespective of any element of state knowledge about the risk of harm. In contrast, failure to exercise 'due diligence' leads to state responsibility only if the State was at fault because it knew (or should have known) about the risk of harm, but failed to take diligent measures to prevent it.[16] Positive obligations under ECHR are of the latter type since they do require fault.

The notion of 'fault' describes a blameworthy psychological attitude of the author of an act or omission. Such attitude can be one of intention (the actor means to cause the harm), knowledge (that actor is aware that an omission might cause harm, but behaves differently from the way that could avoid the harm), or negligence (the author might not know about possible harm or risk, but it should have known and did not act in a diligent manner to avoid the harm).[17] In the context of positive obligations, no issue of intent arises. The Court has explicitly rejected the standard of intentional and wilful disregard of the risk of harm for the purposes of assessing breach of positive obligations.[18]

As to knowledge, it should first be underscored that the State as an organizational entity cannot actually have this psychological and cognitive attitude. Responsibility for omission can then be established by comparing the actual state conduct with such conduct as one could legitimately expect from a normally directed and diligent State.[19] This suggests that the standard of fault is negligence,[20] and the type of negligence applied is objective.[21] However, what conduct can be expected from a diligent

---

[16] See generally Second Report of the International Law Association Study Group on Due Diligence in International Law (2016); A Ollino, *Due Diligence Obligations in International Law* (Cambridge University Press 2022).

[17] G Palmisano, 'Fault', *Max Planck Encyclopedia of Public International Law* (Oxford University Press 2007).

[18] *Osman v the United Kingdom* [GC] no 87/1997/871/1083, 28 October 1998 §116. In *Osman*, the respondent government tried to argue that a failure to take preventive operational measures is present only when there is 'gross dereliction or willful disregard' of the authorities' duty to protect life. Pursuant to this argument, a State can be in breach of its positive obligation to take protective operational measures only if the authorities have manifested gross negligence in handling the situation. Alternatively, the respondent government argued in *Osman* that a State can be in breach of its positive obligation only if its authorities intentionally disregarded the risk to the victim. If these arguments were to be accepted, then the circle of situations when States are under the obligation to act to prevent harm to individuals would be considerably circumscribed. In *Osman*, the ECtHR explicitly rejected the arguments submitted by the United Kingdom: 'The Court does not accept the Government's view that the failure to perceive the risk to life in the circumstances known at the time or to take preventive measures to avoid that risk must be tantamount to gross negligence or wilful disregard of the duty to protect life.'

[19] Favre, 'Fault as an Element of the Illicit Act' (n 6) 561–62.

[20] Palmisano, Fault (n 17) §17, where it is explained that the concept of fault is frequently presented as ' "objective failure" to fulfil the content of an international obligation of conduct, imposing a certain degree of, or standard, of due diligence (or vigilance, or care), rather than as an additional subjective condition of responsibility'. See also S Somers, *The European Convention on Human Rights as an Instrument of Tort Law* (Intersentia 2018) 185, where it is also explained that the positive obligations under the ECHR are 'very akin to negligence'.

[21] Here one can draw a comparative parallel with criminal law. Criminal law scholarship has shown that there is a subjective and an objective negligence. The first type implies that negligence is examined not only objectively, but also with reference to the defendant's individual faculties and qualities. See

State can be dependent on the actual availability of relevant information about risk of harm, which ought to be not only objectively assessed[22] but also subjectively appreciated. It follows that actual knowledge and subjective appreciation of information by specific individuals who are part of the institutional structures of the State might be of relevance.[23]

We shall see how the Court has approached these difficult issues in its abundant case law on positive obligations. A prior clarification is due to the effect that although the Court has referred to the term 'negligently',[24] the consistently used standard is 'knew or ought to have known' about the risk of harm. This standard ('knew') reflects actual knowledge by the State. As an alternative, it also reflects negligence by the State ('ought to have known'), which implies putative knowledge.[25] As will be shown below, the distinction between the two is blurred in the case law. In light of the terminology deployed in the Court's judgments and the blurring of this distinction, in what follows the term 'knowledge' will be used generally to refer to the fault element required in the context of ECHR positive obligations.

## 2.2 Triggering and Breach of Positive Obligations under ECHR

Two initial questions concerning the precise role of state knowledge need to be clarified. First, is state knowledge a necessary precondition for the triggering of a positive obligation? Second, is state knowledge an element relevant in determining whether the obligation has been breached?

In relation to the obligation of taking protective operational measures,[26] the Court has held that

---

T Weigend, 'Subjective Elements of Criminal Liability' in M Dubber and T Hőrnle (eds), *The Oxford Handbook of Criminal Law* (Oxford University Press 2014); G Fletcher, 'The Theory of Criminal Negligence: A Comparative Analysis' (1971) 119(3) University of Pennsylvania Law Review 401; W Seavey, 'Negligence: Subjective of Objective' (1927) 41(1) Harvard Law Review 1.

[22] One can make a parallel with the approach to the appreciation of risk in the ILC Draft Articles on Prevention of Transboundary Harm from Hazardous Activities, in whose commentary it is stated that '[t]he notion of risk is thus to be taken objectively, as denoting an appreciation of possible harm resulting from an activity, which a properly informed observer had or ought to have had'. Commentary to Article 2, §14.

[23] See eg *Nencheva v Bulgaria* no 48609/06, 18 June 2013 §121. A case about severely disabled children held in an institution, who died during the winter. The Court noted how the director of the institution and the city mayor informed high-ranking officials at the Social Ministry about the dire conditions of the children.

[24] See eg *Semache v France* no 36083/16, 21 June 2018 §101.

[25] The existence of any risk of harm has to be analytically separated from the existence of any official knowledge about this risk. A risk can objectively exist even if no one knows about it.

[26] See Section 7.3.

not every claimed risk to life can entail for the authorities a Convention requirement to take operational measures to prevent that risk from materializing. *A positive obligation will arise*, the Court has held, where it has been established that the authorities *knew or ought to have known at the time* of the existence of a real and immediate *risk to the life of an identified individual* or individuals from the criminal acts of a third party and they failed to take measures within the scope of their powers, which judged reasonable, might have been expected to avoid that risk.[27]

It follows that the triggering of the positive obligation of taking protective operational measures to provide 'personal protection of one or more individuals identifiable in advance' requires actual or putative state knowledge. In this sense, knowledge about a particular individual at risk sets in motion the obligation.[28] In the case law, this has been framed as the *Osman* test since *Osman v the United Kingdom* was the Grand Chamber judgment where the Court framed the obligation.[29] Once the obligation is triggered, the determination of a breach is made by reference to the standard of reasonableness.[30] What can reasonably be expected from the State may depend on the actual or putative knowledge about risk of harm the State had, and on the preciseness of this knowledge. Thus, state knowledge also plays a role in determining a breach. This determination entails asking whether the State took reasonable measures to provide individualized protection to the specific individual.

In contrast to the obligation of taking protective operational measures, the obligation upon the State to provide 'general protection to society' is assumed to be applicable at all times.[31] As the Court has framed it, the positive obligation upon the State to 'put in place a legislative and administrative framework designed to provide effective deterrence against threats to the right to life'[32] 'must be construed as applying in the context of any activity, whether public or not, in which the right to life may be at risk'.[33] Knowledge that a particular individual identifiable in advance could be harmed is not required. Rather, the State is required to be aware or to have been aware of the existence of a general problem.[34] A particular applicant in a particular case simply happens to be a representative victim in relation to this general problem. State

---

[27] *Mastromatteo v Italy* [GC] no 37703/97, 24 October 2002 §68 (emphasis added); *Gorovensky and Bugara v Ukraine* nos 36146/05 and 42418/05, 12 January 2012 §32; *Maiorano and Others v Italy* no 28634/06, 15 December 2009; *Choreftakis and Choreftaki v Greece* no 46846/08, 17 January 2012; *Eremia v The Republic of Moldova* no 3564/11, 28 May 2013 §56.
[28] For the uncertainty as to whether knowledge refers to the particular individual at risk, or to the particular actor or source of risk, see Section 7.3.
[29] *Osman v the United Kingdom* [GC] no 23452/94, 28 October 1998 §116.
[30] ibid §116.
[31] *Cevrioğlu v Turkey* no 69546/12, 4 October 2016 §50. See Section 7.1. See also Section 1.5 where a nuance as to the positive obligations triggered under Article 8 was noted.
[32] *Budayeva and Others* no 15339/02, 20 March 2008 §129.
[33] ibid §129; *Öneryildiz v Turkey* [GC] no 48939/99, 30 November 2004 §71.
[34] This distinction is clearly made in many judgments. See *Mastromatteo v Italy* [GC] no 37703/97, 24 October 2002 §§67–79; *Kotilainen and Other v Finland* no 62439/12, 17 September 2020 §§67–69.

knowledge here is relevant for determining whether the State should have acted differently and, accordingly, whether it is in breach of its positive obligation.[35]

It is important first of all to distinguish between the positive obligation of taking protective operational measures and that of providing general protection because they imply state knowledge in relation to different things. The first implies knowledge about a particular individual at a specific type of risk framed as 'real and immediate'. The standard of 'real and immediate' narrows the circumstances when this obligation can be breached. This standard is examined in Section 2.7. The second implies state knowledge of a more general risk. Importantly, an omission by the State can be scrutinized in relation to both substantive positive obligations.[36]

## 2.3 Actual Knowledge versus Putative Knowledge

The determination of a breach of both positive obligations is contingent on actual or putative knowledge. This means that even if the State in fact had no knowledge of the risk of harm, the Court can also ask whether the State should have known or should have foreseen the harm.[37] Actual and putative knowledge are thus provided as alternatives.

### 2.3.1 Different Possible Ways of Assessing Putative Knowledge

The standard of 'ought to have known' has remained unclear. To improve appreciation of it, it is useful to make the following analytical distinctions. In particular, the question whether the State authorities 'ought to have known' of the existence of a risk of harm could be answered with reference to three considerations. First, was the harm objectively or scientifically foreseeable at the relevant point in time, so that the state authorities should have known about it? Second, would the state authorities have correctly assessed the risk of harm based on the information they would have had if they

---

[35] The Court does not necessary determine what exactly the State should have done: 'the choice of means for ensuring the positive obligations under Article 2 is in principle a matter that falls within the Contracting States' margin of appreciation'. *Cevrioğlu v Turkey* no 69546/12, 4 October 2016 §55; *Fadeyeva v Russia* no 55723/00, 9 June 2005 §96; *Budayeva and Others v Russia* no 15339/02, 20 March 2008 §§134–135; *Öneryildiz v Turkey* [GC] no 48939/99, 30 November 2004 §107; *Kolaydenko and Others v Russia* no 17423/05, 28 February 2012 §60. The particular applicant still needs to be affected. See Section 7.1.

[36] As to the procedural obligation to investigate, knowledge is also relevant for its trigger. Information needs to reach the State and this information needs to reach certain level of credibility. Nuances exist depending on the type of harm and its source. These will be, however, explained in detail in Chapter 6.

[37] *D.P. and J.C. v The United Kingdom* no 38719/97, 10 October 2002 §§111–112, where the Court explicitly held that the local authorities did not know about the sexual abuse suffered by the applicants, but then it assessed whether the authorities 'should have been aware that the applicants were suffering sexual abuse from their stepfather'.

had carried out their obligations?[38] Carrying out these obligations might imply consulting scientific studies and taking decisions accordingly. Third, should the state authorities have known of the risk, based on the information that was *actually* before them at that particular point in time?

The Court has not appreciated these three distinctions in its case law. The first alternative might be the most onerous for the state authorities since it implies, for example, *post factum* reference to scientific studies about risks of harm that were generally available at the time when the events were unfolding.[39] A possible problem that might emerge here is that the scientific evidence might have been inconclusive at the time when the State might have had to take protective measures.[40] In light of this uncertainty, it might be unreasonable to expect the State to know about a risk of harm when there was no objective standard against which any knowledge could be measured.[41]

The second alternative (ie the state authorities should have correctly assessed the risk of harm based on the information they would have had if they had carried out their obligations) presupposes that the national authorities were, in fact, under an obligation that they failed to fulfil.[42] This might be a premature conclusion since it might be also contingent on the reasonableness of imposing such an obligation.[43] This obligation might entail taking measures to predict possible risk of harm by drawing on scientific studies or investigating and studying certain phenomenon or events to acquire knowledge.[44] At the same time, if state knowledge is assessed in a way that ignores what information the state authorities would or could have had if they had

---

[38] This approach was applied in *DP v United Kingdom* [2003] 36 EHRR 14, where the local authority did not know about the risk of harm, but the Court held that 'Article 3 will also be engaged if the public authority did not know about the abuse but would have known about it had it made reasonable enquiries and exercised reasonable vigilance'.
[39] This approach was applied in *Brincat and Others v Malta* no 60908/11, 24 July 2014 §106.
[40] The problem of inconclusive scientific evidence has led to the introduction of the principle of precaution in international law. As a principle for managing risk, precaution is based on the idea that scientific uncertainty should not be used as a justification for not taking protective measures. The precautionary principle can be contrasted with the preventive principle. The latter implies avoidance of known risks or risks that should have been known in light of objectively available evidence. For this distinction and its complexities see A Trouwborst, 'Prevention, Precaution, Logic and Law: The Relationship between the Precautionary Principle and the Preventive Principle in International Law and Associated Questions' (2009) 2(2) Erasmus Law Review 105. Given that breaches of positive obligations under the ECHR are assessed against the standard of whether the State knew or ought to have known about the risk of harm, these obligations are underpinned by the logic of the preventive rather than the precautionary principle.
[41] See Partly Dissenting Opinion of Judge Nordén, Joined by Judge Lorenzen in *Vilnes and Others v Norway* nos 52806/09 and 22703/10, 5 December 2013.
[42] This second approach is applied in British common law tort of negligence for assessing liability of public authorities. D Nolan, 'Negligence and Human Rights Law: The Case for Separate Development' (2013) 76(2) Modern Law Review (2013) 286, 306.
[43] An initial assumption that the authorities had duties and therefore ought to have known about risks of harm might be warranted or even taken as self-evident in some specific circumstances. See *Preminiy v Russia* no 44973/04, 10 February 2011 §85, a case about a prisoner who was beaten by other prisoners.
[44] This approach was applied in *Talpis v Italy* no 41237/14, 2 March 2017 §118, where the majority could not conclusively determine that the victim was at an imminent risk, but added that the national authorities should have assessed the risk. See Partly Dissenting Opinion of Judge Spano in *Talpis v Italy*, who is sceptical of the majority's approach that implied that investigative passivity by the national authorities gave rise to putative knowledge. In *Kurt v Austria* [GC] no 62903/15, 15 June 2021 §167, the issue seems to have been resolved in favour of an imposition of a positive obligation of conducting risk assessment. See Section 7.3.3.

carried out their obligations,[45] this might allow the State to use its own faulty omission to excuse itself for the resulting harm.[46]

The third alternative (ie the state authorities should have known of the risk, based on the information that was *in fact* before them at the particular point in time) is the most favourable and the least onerous from the perspective of the State. The reason is that the appreciation of state knowledge is made with reference to the information that was actually before the state authorities, with no regard as to what information could have been available or should have been actively pursued by the authorities.

Although the third alternative might be the least demanding and might imply less likelihood of finding a breach in favour of the victim, it needs to be borne in mind that the State is limited in its capacity to augur potential harms. The existence of relevant knowledge about harms and risks of harm and the accuracy of this knowledge might be contingent on the availability of state resources. Investment of resources might thus be necessary for the State to acquire knowledge and predict harm. Constant vigilance and 'active anticipation'[47] of harm by the State can be costly.[48]

At this juncture, it becomes clear how the approach to state knowledge for the assessment of positive obligations is also intertwined with other considerations, such as reasonableness. The European Court of Human Rights (ECtHR) has consistently reiterated that the scope of positive obligations to protect has to be reasonable and 'to be interpreted in such a way as not to impose an excessive burden on the authorities'.[49] This intertwinement will be further explored in Chapter 4. The important point here is that if the State authorities play a proactive role in taking initiatives to gain knowledge about risks, this might be an arduous task. This is acknowledged by the Court with reference to the reasonableness standard. On the other hand, the Court has also held that the requirement for practical and effective protection of the rights and freedoms in the Convention might necessitate that the authorities act proactively. It follows that inherent in every determination as to whether there is a breach of a positive obligation is the tension between effective protection of individual interests as embodied in the ECHR rights on the one hand, and practical considerations on the other.

---

[45] On many occasions, the Court has found the respondent State to be under a procedural obligation to conduct studies so that relevant information about possible risks of harm is obtained or to consult with such studies. See E Brems, 'Procedural Protection. An Examination of Procedural Safeguards Read into Substantive Convention Rights' in E Brems and J Gerards (eds), *Shaping Rights in the ECHR. The Role of the European Court of Human Rights in Determining the Scope of Human Rights* (Cambridge University Press 2014) 137; V Stoyanova, 'Causation between State Omission and Harm within the Framework of Positive Obligations under' (2018) 18 Human Rights Law Review 309, 335.

[46] For such a warning, see Partly Concurring, Partly Dissenting Opinion of Judge Pinto De Albuquerque in *Fernandes De Oliveira v Portugal* [GC] no 78103/14, 31 January 2019 §24.

[47] L Lavrysen, 'Protection by the Law: The Positive Obligation to Develop a Legal Framework to Adequately Protect the ECHR Rights' in E Brems and Y Haeck (eds), *Human Rights and Civil Rights in the 21st Century* (Springer 2014) 69. Lavrysen refers to the case of *K.U. v Finland* no 2872/02, 2 December 2008 §48. See also *O'Keeffe v Ireland* [GC] no 35810/09, 28 January 2014 §168.

[48] This has been acknowledged by the Court. See *Vilnes and Others v Norway* nos 52806/09 and 22703/10, 5 December 2013 §239: '[the Court] appreciates that scientific research into the matter not only required considerable investment but was also very complex and time-consuming'.

[49] *O'Keeffe v Ireland* [GC] no 35810/09, 28 January 2014 §144.

As Chapter 4 will show, examples of such considerations that trigger assessment of reasonableness include availability of resources, budgetary constraints, or operational choices that need to be made by the national authorities.

## 2.3.2 State Knowledge Necessarily Implies Normative Assessment

Clarity in the 'ought to have known' standard is further obscured by the fact that often the Court does not conclusively establish in its judgments whether the State actually knew about the risk or whether it should have known. It is not clear which of these two standards is actually found fulfilled in the specific case. Consequently, although as a general principle, a distinction is made between actual versus putative knowledge, these two standards are merged when the specific case is analysed by the Court. For example, in *Öneryildiz v Turkey*, the Court first said that it was impossible for the authorities not to have known of the risk that the rubbish tip posed to the people living nearby,[50] a determination that implied that the authorities actually knew. But then the Court proceeded to say '[i]t follows that the Turkish authorities at several levels knew *or ought to have known* that there was a real and immediate risk to the number of persons living near the Ümraniye municipal rubbish tip' (emphasis added).[51] The addition of the expression 'ought to have known' implies that it was not certain whether the national authorities knew, but in any case they should have known.

The above-explained obscurity surrounding the distinction between actual knowledge and the 'ought to have known' standard relates to the fact that the State as an organizational entity does not have awareness in the first place. It cannot know about things and, in this sense, the element of fault can only be inferred. The establishment of this element necessarily implies some normative judgments. These are made when the standards of 'ought to have known' and reasonableness are applied.

## 2.4 Assessment of Knowledge

Despite the inevitability of normative assessments, an attempt can be made to understand how the Court justifies a finding that a State had knowledge. In particular, how does the Court demonstrate in its judgments that an organizational entity such as the State knew or ought to have known?

The adoption of national legislation, sub-laws, and rules to address certain harms might be sufficient to presume that the particular State knew about these harms.[52]

---

[50] *Öneryildiz v Turkey* [GC] no 48939/99, 30 November 2004 §101.
[51] ibid §101; *Frick v Switzerland* no 23405/16, 30 June 2020 §88.
[52] In *O'Keeffe v Ireland* [GC] no 35810/09, 28 January 2014 §168, the GC established that the respondent state was aware in the 1970s of risks associated with sexual abuse of children by adults through, *inter alia*, 'its prosecution of such crimes at a significant rate'. Five judges from the Grand Chamber dissented in *O'Keeffe*

Other standards, however, have also been applied. For example, references to 'objective scientific research'[53] might also be used to conclude that the State had knowledge about harms. The Court has also referred to different national reports that have been prepared.[54] Communication in the form of letters or other documents between various state institutions, for example, has been also used as a reference.[55] The State has wide regulatory functions which involve it in many activities, such as issuing permits. This involvement can also lead to the conclusion that the State knew about harms and risks of harms. For example, in *Cevrioğlu v Turkey*, a case involving a child that drowned in a water pit at a construction site, the respondent State argued that the accident could not have been foreseeable since the construction in question had only recently started. The Court responded by holding that since a permit for the construction had been issued, it could be assumed that the State knew about it.[56]

The nature of the activity within which harm materializes is also of relevance for the assessment of state knowledge. If the activity is inherently dangerous in nature, then there is a normative expectation that the State continuously monitors the operation of that activity, and thus knows, or should know, about risks.[57] Other circumstances, such as protection of children from a family member already convicted of sexual offences, can also imply an expectation from the State to monitor the situation.[58]

It is not clear whether the existence of specific national rules regulating certain activities that might pose risks is sufficient and necessary for the establishment of state knowledge. Do such regulations need to be complemented with, for example, expert reports, so that the Court can conclude that the State knew or ought to have known? For example, in *Öneryildiz v Turkey* the Court placed emphasis on an expert report.[59] However, it also added that it was impossible for the authorities not to have known of the risks 'particularly as there were specific regulations on the matter'.[60]

To what extent do contextual circumstances and general patterns suffice for the purpose of fulfilling the knowledge requirement? Are expert opinions and studies that identify patterns of problems in specific areas enough? For example, in *Opuz v Turkey*, a domestic violence case, the Court explicitly took note of the existence of domestic violence as a general problem in the country and the measures undertaken

---

and questioned this approach. See Joint Partly Dissenting Opinion of Judges Zupancic, Gyulumyan, Kalaydjieva, De Gaetano, and Wojtyczek §13; a similar approach was applied in *Brincat and Others v Malta* no 60908/11, 24 July 2014 §105, where the Court accepted that as early as 1987 laws were adopted to protect employees from asbestos and therefore since that date the State knew about the dangers associated with this substance. See also *Öneryildiz v Turkey* [GC] no 48939/99, 30 November 2004 §§98 and 101.

[53] *Brincat and Others v Malta* no 60908/11, 24 July 2014 §106.
[54] *Öneryildiz v Turkey* [GC] no 48939/99, 30 November 2004 §98.
[55] *Nencheva v Bulgaria* no 48609/06, 18 June 2013 §§121–122.
[56] *Cevrioğlu v Turkey* no 69546/12, 4 October 2016 §68.
[57] See Concurring Opinion of Judge Lemmens in *Cavit Tınarlıoğlu v Turkey* no 3648/04, 2 February 2016; *Cevrioğlu v Turkey* no 69546/12, 4 October 2016 §57: 'inherently hazardous nature' of some activities.
[58] *E. and Others v the United Kingdom* no 33218/96, 26 November 2002 §96.
[59] *Öneryildiz v Turkey* [GC] no 48939/99, 30 November 2004 §§98–100.
[60] ibid §101.

in relation to this problem. This was necessary to set out the context within which the particular applicant had suffered harm.[61] However, for the purposes of establishing whether the authorities could have foreseen the abuse, the Court depicted in detail all the circumstances under which the abusive husband harmed the victims. There was a long history of assaults by the husband, and the victims had informed the authorities of the situation on many occasions, which gave grounds for the Court to conclude that the first limb of the *Osman* test (ie the State 'knew or ought to have known') was fulfilled.[62]

The ECtHR's case law thus leans towards the conclusion that for the purpose of applying protective operational measures, constructive knowledge in the form of general awareness about the existence of general problematic patterns will not suffice.[63] Protective operational measures are activated when the authorities are aware that *a specific* individual could be at risk.[64]

## 2.5 No Benefit of Hindsight

Positive obligations are assessed *ex post facto* by the Court. The problem that arises then concerns the question which point in time should serve as a reference for determining whether the State knew or ought to have known about the risk of harm. Should this be the point in the past at which it might have been expected of the State to fulfil its positive obligations? Should this be the point in the present when the Court made its own assessment about events that happened in the past? The Court has emphasized that state knowledge should be assessed without the benefit of the hindsight,[65] which means that the first of the above-mentioned two questions can be answered in the affirmative. For example, in *Vilnes and Others v Norway*, the Court held that 'regard ought to be had to the knowledge possessed at the material time—an assessment of liability ought not to be based on hindsight'.[66]

---

[61] *Opuz v Turkey* [GC] no 3401/02, 9 June 2009 §132.
[62] ibid §§135–136. Similar approach was taken in *Konrova v Slovakia* no 7510/04, 31 May 2007 §52; *Milanovic v Servia* no 44614/07, 14 December 2010 §89.
[63] This insufficiency clearly emerged in *Sakine Epözdemir and Others v Turkey* no 26589/06, 1 December 2015 §§65–72, a case about the murder of a lawyer of a pro-Kurdish political party against the general background of the 'unknown perpetrators killings' in Turkey. The Court found no violation of Article 2 since the authorities did not know that specifically the lawyer's life was at risk. See Joint Partly Dissenting Opinion of Vučinič and Lemmens who considered that 'it was the authorities' duty to assess the general situation, characterized by a climate of terror against Kurdish leaders, and to draw the appropriate conclusions with respect to the persons belonging to the targeted group'.
[64] This is particularly clear in the domestic violence cases: *Halime Kilic v Turkey* no 63034/11, 28 June 2016 §94; *Talpis v Italy* no 41237/14, 2 March 2017 §111. See Section 7.3
[65] *O'Keeffe v Ireland* [GC] no 35810/09, 28 January 2014 §§143–152; *Kurt v Austria* [GC] no 62903/15, 15 June 2021 §195.
[66] *Vilnes and Others v Norway* no 52806/09 and 22703/10, 5 December 2013 §222; *Association Innocence en Danger and Association Enfance et Partage v France* nos 15343/15 and 16806/15, 4 June 2020 §160; *Wunderlich v Germany* no 18925/15, 10 January 2019 §52: 'The authorities—both medical and social—have a duty to protect children and cannot be held liable every time genuine and reasonably-held concerns about the safety of children vis-à-vis members of their families are proved, retrospectively, to have been misguided'.

## 2.6 Burden of Proof

An important question for determining state knowledge concerns the burden and the standard of proof: which party has to prove that the State knew or ought to have known? Does the Court place the onus upon the victim to prove the foreseeability of harm, or is the burden on the respondent State to plead that the harm was not foreseeable?

Engagement with these questions has to start with the acknowledgement that first, the Convention system is subsidiary to the domestic legal systems where the case has been litigated and evidence submitted;[67] and second, the Court has been in general very flexible in its approach to the burden and the standard of proof.[68] It would be beyond the scope of this section to engage with these issues. It suffices to add that in principle the applicant has the burden of proof and the Court is reluctant to second-guess the findings of fact made at national level.[69] Yet the burden of proof is contingent on the substantive issues in question.[70] The Court has added as a general principle that 'the level of persuasion necessary for reaching a particular conclusion and, in this connection, the distribution of the burden of proof, are intrinsically linked to the specificities of the facts, the nature of allegation made and the Convention right at stake'.[71]

In relation to the burden of proving knowledge, it is important that the Court has allowed flexibility. Although the State is not perceived to be an omniscient entity and thus is not expected to know about all activities that take place under its jurisdiction by the mere fact of the exercise of exclusive sovereignty,[72] the flexibility implies that important inferences are made from the mere fact that the State has control. In *Öneryildiz v Turkey*, the Court held that

> often, in practice, the true circumstances of the death, are, or may be, largely confined within the knowledge of State officials or authorities [references omitted]. In the Court's view, such considerations are indisputably valid in the context of dangerous activities, when lives have been lost as a result of events occurring under

---

[67] M Ambrus, 'The European Court of Human Rights and Standards of Proof' in L Gruszczynski and W Werner (eds), *Deference in International Courts and Tribunals: Standard of Review and Margin of Appreciation* (Oxford University Press 2014) 235.

[68] T Thienel, 'The Burden and Standard of Proof in the European Court of Human Rights' (2007) 50 German Yearbook of International Law 543; J Kokott, *The Burden and Standard of Proof in Comparative and International Human Rights Law* (Kluwer Law International 1998). Rules regarding the standard and burden of proof are not a central preoccupation of international courts.

[69] '[E]xcept in cases of manifest arbitrariness or error, it is not the Court's function to call into question the findings of fact made by the domestic authorities, particularly when it comes to scientific expert assessment, which by definition call for specific and detailed knowledge of the subject.' *Lopes de Sousa Fernandes v Spain* [GC] no 56080/13, 19 December 2017 §199.

[70] Thienel, 'The Burden and Standard of Proof in the European Court of Human Rights' (n 68) 543.

[71] *El Masri v the Former Yugoslav Republic of Macedonia* [GC] no 39630/09, 13 December 2012 §151.

[72] *Corfu Channel* case [1919] ICJ Report 1, p. 18: 'the fact of … exclusive territorial control exercised by a State within its frontiers has a bearing upon the methods of proof available to establish the knowledge of that State as to such events'.

the responsibility of public authorities, which are often the *only entities to have sufficient relevant knowledge to identify and establish the complex phenomena that might have caused such incidents*.[73]

This means that the Court is sensitive as to who might be in a better position to discharge the burden of proof. When the applicant is in a weaker position than the respondent State as regards obtaining evidence, there is a case to be made for transferring the burden of proof. This implies that it might be more realistic to ask the State to prove that it was not negligent than to ask the victim to prove negligence in how the State had managed the situation. An alternative approach, that is possibly more favourable to the State, is to place the evidential burden upon the State, so that it is expected that it should provide an explanation for the omission. In *Fadeyeva v Russia*, a case in which the applicant argued that the operation of a steel plant in close proximity to her home endangered her health in violation of Article 8, the Court clarified that 'the onus is on the State to justify, using detailed and rigorous data, a situation in which certain individuals bear a heavy burden on behalf of the rest of the community'.[74]

## 2.7 The Nature and the Level of Risk

It is clear from the case law that for a State to be in breach of its positive obligations it is enough if it knew or ought to have known about *risk* of harm. State responsibility therefore centres on the concept of risk and how the State anticipates and deals with risks. This section considers whether the Court has imposed any standards as to the nature and the level of this risk.

### 2.7.1 The 'Real and Immediate Risk' Standard

In relation to the positive obligation of adopting an effective regulatory framework, no qualifiers have been added as to the nature of the risk of harm that the State knew or ought to have known about.[75] In contrast, in the context of the positive obligation of taking protective operational measures, the standard repeatedly invoked by the Court is one of 'real and immediate risk'.[76] It follows that the triggering and the

---

[73] *Öneryildiz v Turkey* [GC] no 48939/99, 30 November 2004 §93 (emphasis added); *Stoyanovi v Bulgaria* no 42980/04, 9 November 2010 §63.
[74] *Fadeyeva v Russia* no 55723/00, 9 June 2005 §128; *Cordella and Others v Italy* nos 54414/13 and 54264/15, 24 January 2019 §161.
[75] For example, *Cevrioğlu v Turkey* no 69546/12, 4 October 2016 §51, where the Court referred to 'potential risk to human lives involved'. See Section 7.3.
[76] It should be added that often in the 'General principles' part of the judgment, the Court refers to the 'real and immediate risk' standard, while never mentioning it or explaining whether it is fulfilled in the 'Application of those principles to the present case' part. Often the reason is that the specific case was such that the positive obligation of taking protective operation measures was not relevant, since the issue was

finding of breach of the positive obligation to take protective operational measures depends on whether the State knew or should have known about 'real and immediate risk' of harm.

The Court has never specifically elaborated on the meaning of 'real and immediate risk,' and has never engaged in any in-depth elucidation of the stringency of this standard.[77] 'Real' risk could be understood as risk that is objectively given.[78] The adjective 'real' could also refer to the probability that the risk will materialize. It could be also understood in light of the likelihood the *specific* risk arising.[79] 'Immediate risk' could be understood as risk that is 'present and continuing'.[80] Immediacy could be also more narrowly interpreted to refer to harm that was expected to 'materialize at any time'.[81] It follows that while 'real' can be linked with the probability/likelihood of the harm occurring, 'immediate' can be linked with its closeness, in terms of timing, to a relevant point in time.[82] 'Immediate' can thus express a temporality, a specific time frame within which harm could materialize. 'Real and immediate' has been also interpreted as implying a risk that is 'substantial or significant', 'not a remote or fanciful one', and 'real and ever-present.'[83]

In light of this ambiguity, it is difficult to assess the stringency of the 'real and immediate' risk standard in the Court's case law. In some cases where the Court found it fulfilled, it is clear that the risk was specific, but of questionable imminence.[84] In other

---

rather possible failure by the State to afford general protection to society at large. See *Georgel and Georgeta Stoicescu v Romania* no 9718/03, 26 July 2011 §§51–56.

[77] This has led to a profound misunderstanding of the *Osman* test and different interpretations at national level. See, for example, L Hoyano and C Keenan, *Child Abuse: Law and Policy Across Boundaries* (Oxford University Press 2010) 391–93 describing the *Osman* test as requiring a 'egregious neglect of duty'.

[78] Stoyanova, 'Causation between State Omission and Harm within the Framework of Positive Obligations under the European Convention on Human Rights' (n 45) 339.

[79] *Kotilainen and Others v Finland* no 62439/12, 17 September 2020 §§78-80. According to the Court's reasoning in *Kotilainen* there was a risk that the authorities could have known, but they could not have known that there was 'an actual risk of an attack in the form of a school shooting.' The Court reasoned that 'although ... there were certain factual elements suggesting that the perpetrator might potentially pose a risk of life-threatening acts, the school killing actually committed by him was not reasonably foreseeable'.

[80] Stoyanova, 'Causation between State Omission and Harm within the Framework of Positive Obligations under the European Convention on Human Rights' (n 45) 340. This is how the standard has been understood by some national jurisdictions. See *Re W's Application* [2004] NIQB 67; *Re Officer L* [2007] UKHL 36, Lord Carswell; *Smith v Chief Constable of Sussex* [2008] EWCA Civ 39. See also A Gerry, 'Obligation to Prevent Crime and to Protect and Provide Redress to Victims of Crime' in M Colvin and J Cooper (eds), *Human Rights in the Investigation and Prosecution of Crime* (Oxford University Press 2009) 423, 432.

[81] For a useful outline see F Ebert and R Sijniensky, 'Preventing Violation of the Right to Life in the European and the Inter-American Human Rights Systems: From *Osman* Test to a Coherent Doctrine on Risk Prevention?' (2015) 15 Human Rights Law Review 343, 359.

[82] The concept of imminence has been also linked to the probability of the risk of harm occurring rather than to its temporal closeness to the present. L Duvic-Paoli, 'Prevention in International Environmental Law and the Anticipation of Risk(s): A Multifaceted Norm' in M Ambrus and others (eds), *Risk and Regulation of Uncertainty in International Law* (Oxford University Press 2017) 141, 153.

[83] Dissenting Opinion of Judge Metoc in *Hiller v Austria* no 1967/14, 22 November 2016.

[84] *Talpis v Italy* no 41237/14, 2 March 2017 §122, a domestic violence case where the Court concluded that the risk was real and added that 'the imminent materialization of which [of the risk] could not be excluded'. See Partly Dissenting Opinion of Judge Spano in *Talpis v Italy* §5, where he argued that in light of the timing of the attack, the risk cannot be defined as imminent. See also *Renolde v France* no 5608/05, 16 October 2008 §89, a case about a person who committed a suicide, where the Court observed that

cases, the risk might be assessed as imminent but its source was difficult to perceive.[85] At the same time, the Court has tended to expand the meaning of the term 'immediacy' and to invoke it in cases where one can hardly identify an immediate risk.[86] A question that has also remained open concerns the time frame within which a risk can be considered as imminent. For example, in *Öneryildiz v Turkey*, a case about a methane gas explosion at a garbage collection point that led to loss of life and destruction of property, the Court observed that

> neither the reality nor the immediacy of the danger in question is in dispute, seeing that the risk of an explosion had clearly come into being long before it was highlighted in the report of 7 May 1991 and that, as the site continued to operate in the same conditions, that risk could only have increased during the period until it materialised on 28 April 1993.

It follows that the Court considered the risk of explosion to have been imminent years before the explosion actually happened.[87] This implies a very long time frame of imminent risk.

In other circumstances, the Court has applied a much more restrictive time frame. For example, in *Fernandes de Oliveira v Portugal*,[88] a case about a patient voluntarily hospitalized in a psychiatric hospital who subsequently committed suicide, the Grand Chamber found no violation of Article 2. The reason for this finding was that it has not been established that the authorities knew or ought to have known that there was an immediate risk to A.J.'s life in the days preceding the day when he committed suicide. The absence of immediacy of the risk was key in this case. In rejecting the approach of the Chamber,[89] the Grand Chamber accepted that 'there were no worrying signs in A.J.'s behaviour *in the days immediately* preceding his suicide' (emphasis added).[90]

In his dissent attached to the Grand Chamber judgment in *Fernandes de Oliveira v Portugal*, Judge Pinto de Albuquerque observed that the gap of twenty-six days,

---

'[a]lthough his condition and the immediacy of the risk of a fresh suicide varied, the Court considers that that risk was real and Joselito Renolde required careful monitoring in case of any sudden deterioration'. In *Kurt v Austria* [GC] no 62903/15, 15 June 2021 §§175–176, it was explicitly held that the immediacy standard is applied with flexibility in the context of domestic violence. See Section 7.3.

[85] For an overview of these discrepancies see Ebert and Sijniensky, 'Preventing Violations of the Right to Life in the European and Inter-American Human Rights Systems' (n 81) 343–68.
[86] See Partly Concurring, Partly Dissenting Opinion of Judge Sajo in *Banel v Lithuania* no 14326/11, 18 June 2013, a case about the death of a boy after the collapse of a roof. See also *Talpis v Italy* no 41237/14, 2 March 2017 §122, a domestic violence case, where the Court stated that the national authorities 'should have known that applicant's husband constituted a real risk to her, the imminent materialisation of which could not be excluded'.
[87] *Öneryildiz v Turkey* [GC] §100.
[88] *Fernandes de Oliveira v Portugal* [GC] no 78103/14, 31 January 2019 §131.
[89] The Chamber found that Portugal was under a positive obligation to protect the applicant's son since the State was aware of an immediate risk to his life. *Fernandes de Oliveir v Portugal* [GC] no 78103/14, 28 March 2017 §75.
[90] *Fernandes de Oliveira v Portugal* [GC] §§129, 131–132.

with an episode of serious self-harm, between a failed suicide and a successful one, should have been enough for assessing the risk of harm as immediate.[91] In contrast, the majority of the Grand Chamber preferred to assess immediacy with reference to a shorter time frame, namely 'the days immediately preceding' the successful suicide.

The Grand Chamber's approach in *Fernandes de Oliveira v Portugal* is consistent with the earlier medical negligence judgment of *Lopes de Sousa Fernandes v Portugal*, where the Grand Chamber also invoked the immediacy of the risk to restrict the circumstances leading to responsibility for failure to fulfil positive obligations. In the latter case, the applicant complained under Article 2 ECHR about the death of her husband after a hospital-acquired infection and a series of alleged medical failures. The Grand Chamber accepted that the responsibility of the State for failure to fulfil substantive positive obligations under Article 2 'may be engaged in respect of the acts and omissions of health-care providers' but only in 'very exceptional circumstances'.[92]

To frame these 'exceptional circumstances' the Court invoked the immediacy of the harm as a criterion.[93] Two types of exceptional circumstance were framed: (i) 'where an individual patient's life is knowingly put in danger by denial of access to life-saving *emergency* treatment' (emphasis added),[94] and (ii) 'where a systemic or structural dysfunction in hospital services results in a patient being deprived of access to life-saving *emergency* treatment and the authorities knew about or ought to have known about that risk' (emphasis added).[95] The threshold of immediacy was thus framed as one of emergency, which, if reached, can allow the triggering of a positive obligation upon the States to protect the life of the *particular* patient.[96]

As a response to the Grand Chamber's approach in *Lopes de Sousa Fernandes*, Judge Pinto de Albuquerque argued that in situations revealing structural and systemic deficiencies, no requirement for imminent risk should be imposed. His argument is that 'in situations of systemic or structural dysfunction which are known or ought to have

---

[91] Partly Concurring, Partly Dissenting Opinion of Judge Pinto de Albuquerque Joined by Judge Harutyuyan in *Fernandes de Oliveira v Portugal* [GC] §22.

[92] *Lopes de Sousa Fernandes v Portugal* [GC] no 56080/13, 19 December 2017 §190. Circumstances manifesting 'acts and omissions of health-care providers' were distinguished in the judgment from circumstances of 'alleged medical negligence'. It appears from the Grand Chamber's reasons that in the latter type of circumstances, the substantive positive obligation upon the State is less demanding. The Grand Chamber found that the specific case is one of 'medical negligence' and, therefore, 'Portugal's substantive positive obligations are *limited* to the setting-up of an adequate regulatory framework compelling hospitals, whether private or public, to adopt appropriate measures for the protection of patient's lives' (emphasis added) (§203). Since the regulatory framework in Portugal did not disclose any shortcomings, the respondent State was not found in violation of Article 2 ECHR. See also §182 where the Grand Chamber referred to 'cases which concern allegations of *mere* medical negligence' (emphasis added).

[93] See also *Lopes de Sousa Fernandes v Portugal* [GC] §182 where the Grand Chamber referred to 'denial of immediate emergency care'.

[94] ibid §191.

[95] ibid §192.

[96] My understanding of the Grand Chamber's reasoning is that if the above-mentioned exceptional circumstances are triggered, the positive obligation upon the State will be more demanding since it will include an obligation to protect the specific applicant. In contrast, when the exceptional circumstances are not applicable, but the case is only one of 'mere medical negligence' (§182), the scope of the positive obligation under Article 2 is narrower in that it does not include an individualized protection. The circumstances of Lopes de Sousa Fernandes' husband were found by the Court to be ones of 'mere medical negligence'.

be known to the authorities, the *Osman* test must be qualified, in so far as the requirement of "immediate risk" must be scaled down to one of "present risk".[97] He also suggested reformulating the *Osman* test by scaling it down to 'present risk' in the context of domestic violence.[98] As Section 7.3 will explain in more detail, indeed in *Kurt v Austria*, the GC did modify the test in the specific context of domestic violence.

Judge Pinto de Albuquerque's stance in support of rejecting the immediate risk test might seem appealing, given the haphazard approach of the Court to the 'real and immediate' risk standard, as mentioned above. In particular, the standard has been invoked by the Court to conveniently limit the scope of the positive obligations in areas such as medical negligence.[99] In other cases, it is mentioned, but then it is left unexplained whether and how it is of any relevance.[100]

At the same time, however, Judge Pinto de Albuquerque's position might be hard to understand given that, in situations of systemic and structural dysfunction, the positive obligation of affording general protection might be relevant. In the context of this obligation, no requirement for 'immediate risk' has been raised in principle in the Court's case law. In fact, the Court has not introduced clarifications as to the nature and level of the required risk that the State should know about. This implies a margin of flexibility.[101]

One of the difficulties with finding a breach of the positive obligation of affording general protection to the society, however, is that the applicant has to demonstrate the causal link between the specific harm that he/she sustained and some general systemic or structural deficiencies posing risks the State knew, or ought to have known, about.[102] In contrast, when the victim is identifiable in advance as being at 'real and immediate risk', a situation that might call for protective operational measures of an ad hoc nature, the causal link between the harm sustained by the victim and the failure to

---

[97] Judge Pinto de Albuquerque Dissenting Opinion in *Lopes de Sousa Fernandes v Spain* §91.
[98] Concurring Opinion Pinto de Albuquerque in *Valiuliene v Lithuania* no 33234/07, 26 March 2013, where the following reformulation of the *Osman* test was suggested: 'If a State knows or ought to know that a segment of its population, such as women, is subject to repeated violence and fails to prevent harm from befalling the members of that group of people when they face a present (but not yet imminent) risk, the State can be found responsible by omission for the resulting human rights violations.'
[99] *Lopes de Sousa Fernandes v Portugal* §§182–192.
[100] *Georgel and Georgeta Stoicescu v Romania* no 9718/03, 26 July 2011 §§51–56.
[101] With these two positive obligations the Court seems to address two different types of risk. The obligation of adopting effective regulatory framework is arguably intended to address risks that are 'centrally and mass produced' and broadly distributed'. The obligation of taking protective operational measures, however, is arguably intended to address risks that are 'in relatively discrete units'. For this distinction and further references see M Ambrus, 'The European Court of Human Rights as Governor of Risk' in Ambrus and others (eds), *Risk and Regulation of Uncertainty in International Law* (n 82) 99, 102.
[102] The Court has held that 'the mere fact that the regulatory framework may be deficient in some respects is not sufficient in itself to raise an issue under Article 2 of the Convention. It must be shown to have operated to the patient's detriment'. This means that the applicant has to demonstrate that any deficiencies have concretely affected him/her. See *Fernandes de Oliveira v Portugal* [GC] §§107 and 116. On causation see generally Stoyanova, 'Causation between State Omission and Harm within the Framework of Positive Obligations under the European Convention on Human Rights' (n 45) 309.

take these measures might be easier to discern. In this sense, the immediacy of the risk makes it easier to find a causal connection between harm and failures by the State.[103]

In addition, it might be unreasonable to expect the State to take protective operational measures of an ad hoc nature when a person is not exposed to an immediate risk of harm. This might be the case not only due to practical and financial considerations; concerns as to whether the State might have assumed too intrusive role might also arise. It should be added that protective operational measures by the State might be directed against other individuals (eg the alleged abusers).[104] This might create situations where the State's efforts to protect some individuals limit other individuals' rights, a concern that will be addressed in Chapter 5.[105] One can also imagine situations where the State, by protecting an individual, infringes on his or her own personal autonomy, which can also be controversial.[106] These possibilities add further strength to the argument that the circumstances when protective operational measures are called for should be an object of some constraint. The requirement for 'real and immediate risk', despite its ambiguous contours in the case law, provides such a restraining function.

## 2.7.2 Man-made versus Natural Harms

Besides 'real and immediate risk', another distinction can be discerned in the case law based on the predictability of the risk of harm, namely the one between risks posed by human activities and those posed by natural hazards. In the sphere of 'dangerous activities of a man-made nature',[107] the case law suggests that the risk of harm is assumed to be more predictable and, accordingly, more demanding positive obligations are imposed upon the State.[108] The Court has also noted that some activities are inherently dangerous.[109] This point can be illustrated with reference to *Kotilainen and Others v Finland,* a case about a school shooting where the perpetrator use a gun for

---

[103] For this reason, McBride links the 'real and immediate' risk test with causality. J McBride, 'Protecting Life: Positive Obligation to Help' (1999) 24 European Law Review 43.

[104] A State is expected to fulfil its positive obligations in way that 'fully respects due process and other guarantees which legitimately place restraints on the scope of their action to investigate crime and bring offenders to justice'. *Osman v the United Kingdom* [GC] no 23452/94, 28 October 1998 §116; *Opuz v Turkey* [GC] no 3401/02, 9 June 2009 §129.

[105] This has emerged, for example, in cases involving taking of children into state care. See *T.P. and K.M. v the United Kingdom* [GC] no 28945/95, 10 May 2001, where the taking into care of a child by the national authorities and his separation from his mother lead to violation of the right to private life.

[106] *Fernandes de Oliveira v Portugal* §112.

[107] *Budayeva and Others v Russia* no 15339/02, 20 March 2008 §135.

[108] *Finogenov and Others v Russia* nos 18299/03 and 27311, 20 December 2011 §243: 'the more predictable a hazard, the greater the obligation to protect against it'. *Nencheva and Others v Bulgaria* no 48609/06, 18 June 2013 §122, where the Court emphasized that the deaths of the disabled children did not happen suddenly and under *force majeure* circumstances, under which the State might not be able to react. Rather the deaths happened one after another and over a prolonged period of time.

[109] *Gorgiev v The Former Yugoslav Republic of Macedonia* no 26984/05, 19 April 2012 §73; *Smiljanić v Croatia* no 35983/14, 25 March 2021, §67.

which he had a licence, and which could have been removed from his possession by the police shortly before the shooting. The Court clarified that '[t]he extent of the positive obligations in a given context depends on the *kind of risk* concerned and the possibilities of mitigating them'.[110] It reasoned that there is a *'particularly high risk* to life inherent in any misconduct involving the use of firearms'.[111] This appeared to be the sole basis for finding Finland responsible, given the absence of causation and state knowledge.[112]

In contrast, natural phenomena that are 'beyond human control' are assumed to imply less predictable risks. The reduced predictability might imply less demanding positive obligations to prevent the harm from materializing.[113] In *Özel and Others v Turkey*, a case involving a natural disaster, namely an earthquake that caused the collapse of buildings leading to loss of life, the Court pointed out:

> in connection with natural hazards, that the scope of the positive obligations imputable to the State in the particular circumstances would depend on the origin of the threat and the extent to which one or the other risk is susceptible to mitigation, and clearly affirmed that those obligations applied in so far as the circumstances of a particular case pointed to the *imminence* of a natural hazard that had been *clearly identifiable*, and especially where it concerned a recurring calamity affecting a distinct area developed for human habitation or use.[114]

This quotation suggests that in the context of natural hazards, breach of positive obligations will be found only if the risk is imminent and clearly identifiable. These requirements have a limitative function that makes the finding of a breach less likely. At the same time, pursuant to the above quotation, the recurrence of the harm is perceived as an indication that the 'the natural hazard was clearly identifiable'.

The Court has so far not elaborated the meaning and stringency of the criteria of imminence and identifiability of the natural hazard nor has it resorted exclusively to these criteria in finding no violation. The Court's analysis in *Özel and Others v Turkey* was restricted to the procedural aspect of Article 2. It thus remains to be seen how the Court will approach the criteria of imminence and identifiability in future cases involving natural hazards. The Court might take an approach similar to the one in *Lopes de Sousa Fernandes*, where, as explained in Section 2.7, the immediacy of the harm was rendered of paramount importance for finding a breach in the area of medical negligence.

---

[110] *Kotilainen and Others v Finland* no 62439/12, 17 September 2020 §67 (emphasis added); *Cavit Tınarlıoğlu v Turkey* no 3648/04, 2 February 2002 §90.

[111] *Kotilainen and Others v Finland* §89.

[112] ibid §89 'it could not be held that the decision not to seize the gun was causally relevant to the subsequent killing' and §78 where the Court accepted that the authorities could not have known that the perpetrator would plan a school shooting.

[113] *Kolyadenko and Others v Russia* no 17423/05, 28 February 2012 §161.

[114] *Özel and Others v Turkey* nos 14350/05, 15245/05, and 16051, 17 November 2015 §171 (emphasis added); *Budayeva and Others v Russia* no 15339/02, 20 March 2008 §137.

## 2.8 Contributory Fault of the Victim

The negligent conduct of the victim can be an important factor in the Court's assessment of State responsibility, especially when the victim faced a risk that he or she could appreciate and avoid.[115] The applicant's own inaction might have contributed to the course of events, for which he or she complains.[116] The victim might have assumed risks by voluntarily exposing himself/herself to a known and appreciated risk.[117] In this sense, the victim had an understanding of the dangerous situation and voluntarily encountered it.[118] However, the level of appreciation by the victim might be dubious, which also needs to be taken into account.

It has been a standard assertion in the case law that the conduct of the victim is a relevant factor in the assessment of breach of positive obligation:

> Bearing in mind the difficulties involved in policing modern societies, *the unpredictability of human conduct* and the operational choices which must be made in terms of priorities and resources, the scope of the positive obligation must be interpreted in a way which does not impose an impossible and disproportionate burden on the authorities.[119]

It follows that 'the unpredictability of human conduct', and accordingly the possibility that victims themselves undertake risks, affects the determination whether the finding of a breach would be unreasonable, since it might lead to the imposition of a disproportionate burden on the State. At the same time, the Court's approach is also

---

[115] 'Article 2 of the Convention cannot be interpreted as guaranteeing to every individual an absolute level of security in any activity in which the right to life may be at stake, in particular where the person concerned bears a degree of responsibility for the accident having exposed himself to unjustified danger'. *Gökdemir v Turkey* (dec) no 66309/09, 19 May 2015 §17; *Prilutskiy v Ukraine* no 40429/08, 26 February 2015 §§32–35. The Court is very reluctant to criticize States under the substantive limb of Article 2 in cases involving the victims of sports accidents (*Furdík v Slovakia* (dec) no 42994/05, 2 December 2008; *Molie v Romania* (dec) no 13754/02, 1 September 2009; *Vrábel v Slovakia* (dec) no 77928/01, 19 January 2010; *Koceski v the Former Republic of Macedonia* (dec) no 41107/07, 22 October 2013; *Cavit Tınarlıoğlu v Turkey* no 3648/04, 2 February 2016 §§104–106), of accidents on board boats (*Leray and Others v France* (dec) no 44617/98, 16 January 2001) or of road-traffic accidents (*Zavoloka v Latvia* no 58447/00, 7 July 2009 §39). See also *Mikayil Mammadov v Azerbaijan* no 4762/05, 17 December 2009 §111, where the applicant committed suicide to prevent the eviction of her family; the Court held that this was conduct that the authorities could not reasonably have anticipated. See also *Vardosanidze v Georgia* no 43881/10, 7 May 2020 §61, where the contributory fault of the victim was crucial for finding no violation of Article 2. *Safi and Others v Greece* no 5418/15, 7 July 2022 §165 (sinking of a board with foreign nationals in the Aegean Sea close to the Greece coast); *Pavel Shishkov v Russia* no 78754/13, 2 March 2021 §91 (the applicant's own inaction led to the severance of his ties with his daughter); *Hudorovič and Others v Slovenia* no 24816/14, 10 March 2010 §§151–152 (the applicants themselves did not take steps to connect to the public water supply); *Vardosanidze v Georgia* no 43881/10, 7 May 2020 §61l; *A. and B. v Romania*, no 48442 and 48831/16, 2 June 2020 §§131–135.

[116] *Uzbyakov v Russia* no 71160/13, 5 May 2020 §109 (inaction by the applicant to ensure that he is registered as the father on his children's birth certificates).

[117] D Bederman, 'Contributory Fault and State Responsibility' (1990) 30 Virginia Journal of International Law 335, 336.

[118] ibid 355.

[119] *Osman v the United Kingdom* [GC] no 23452/94, 28 October 1998 §166 (emphasis added).

clear to the effect that the victim's faulty conduct cannot be an excuse for omissions by the State. Victim's fault cannot negate the very fact of the State's omissions, which might constitute the basis of a finding that the State had failed to fulfil its positive obligations.

This is even the case when the victim's contributory fault is engaged in circumstances when he or she participates in unlawful activities leading to harm in this context. For example, in *Öneryildiz v Turkey* the Court held that

> [i]n those circumstances [the State encouraged the integration of the slump, did not react to breaches of town-planning regulations and legitimized the existence of the slump by even taxing its inhabitants], it would be hard for the Government to maintain legitimately that any negligence or lack of foresight should be attributed to the victims of the accident of 28 April 1993, ....[120]

An important nuance, however, is that Turkey itself, the respondent State in *Öneryildiz*, endorsed and did not sanction the unlawful conduct of the victims. When a State reacts to unlawful conduct that might lead to harm and actively tries to prevent it, then a different approach seems warranted.

Another important nuance emerging from *Öneryildiz v Turkey* for assessment of contributory fault concerns state efforts to disseminate information so that individuals can take precautionary measures. If the State has disseminated relevant information enabling individuals to assess the risks that they might run because of the choices that they make, then it is less likely that it will be found in breach of its positive obligations.[121]

Victim's contributory fault can act as an intervening cause of his or her harm. Due to contributory fault by the victim, it might not be possible to prove that the State's omission caused the harm. However, in light of the Court's flexible approach to causation in general (see Chapter 3), this has not been an obstacle for finding States responsible for a failure to fulfil positive obligations. For example, in *Cevrioğlu v Turkey*,

> [t]he Court acknowledges that the primary responsibility for the accident in the instant case lay with H.C. However, the failure of the State to enforce an effective inspection system may also be regarded as a *relevant factor* in these circumstances....[122]

The standard of causation between the harm and any omission by Turkey in this case was framed at a very low level: the omission was simply viewed as 'a relevant factor',

---

[120] *Öneryildiz v Turkey* [GC] §106.
[121] See also *Sarihan v Turkey* no 55907/08, 6 December 2016 §54 (injury due to explosion of a mine in a military zone knowingly entered by the applicant; the zone was marked with signs and the authorities had informed the population).
[122] *Cevrioğlu v Turkey* no 69546/12, 4 October 2016 §67 (emphasis added).

which sufficed for finding a breach. By way of comparison, in the similar case of *Iliya Petrov v Bulgaria*,[123] where a boy was severely harmed after entering a transformer and receiving an electric shock, the Court acknowledged that the boy was very unwise to enter such a dangerous place. At the same time, the Court highlighted that the 'decisive factor' leading to the incident was the inadequate control by the authorities regarding the safety of electric transformers. Thus, the 'decisive factor' appears to be more exacting standard for causation than 'relevant factor'.

Finally, it needs to be highlighted that there might be cases where a submission by the respondent State that the victims knew about the risk of harm can backfire. This happened in *Brincat and Others v Malta*, where the applicants complained about their exposure to asbestos. The respondent State argued that 'anyone in such a work environment would in any case be fully aware of the hazards involved'. The Court responded that this statement is 'in stark contrast to the Government's repeated argument that they (despite being employers and therefore well acquainted with such an environment) were for long unaware of the dangers'.[124]

## Conclusion

Fault is an important element in the assessment of state responsibility for breach of positive obligations under the ECHR. More specifically, the ECtHR has consistently referred to the standard of 'knew or ought to have known' in its analysis, reflecting actual or putative knowledge by the State about risk of harm. This standard is applied to establish a breach of the positive obligation to take operational measures to protect a concrete individual who might have been at 'real and immediate' risk of harm. The standard of 'knew or ought to have known' is also applied for the establishment of a breach of the positive obligation of ensuring an effective regulatory framework aimed at providing general protection. Any deficiencies in this regulatory framework have to be causally linked to the harm sustained by the specific applicant.

Without making a clear and conclusive determination whether the State actually knew or should have known about the risk of harm in the particular case, the Court has referred to various factors to demonstrate actual or putative knowledge such as existence of national regulations, or scientific reports. It has also insisted that state knowledge is assessed with reference to the information possessed at the time when protective measures should have been forthcoming, and applicants cannot benefit from information that might have emerged subsequently. The Court has also clarified that, although the burden of proof is on the applicant to demonstrate state knowledge, in some circumstances the State is in a better position to carry this burden.

Despite these principles that can be observed in the case law, the assessment of state knowledge is imbued with normative considerations. Their initial premise is that the

---

[123] *Iliya Petrov v Bulgaria* no 19202/03, 24 April 2012 §63.
[124] *Brincat and others v Malta* §114.

State as an organizational entity cannot have awareness, and in this sense, it cannot know about anything. 'Ought to have known' is an inherently normative standard. The points of reference in the assessment as to whether the State 'ought to have known' remain unclear. Inevitably, this assessment is intertwined with calculations of any causality between the harm sustained by the victim and any state omissions, an issue explored in detail in Chapter 3. The assessment of whether the State 'ought to have known' is also intertwined with concerns that positive obligations should not impose an unreasonable burden on the State. This concern is addressed in Chapter 4.

# 3
# Causation

## Introduction

Causation implies some nexus between the harm sustained by the applicant (harm that falls within the definitional scope of one of the protected rights) and the alleged omission by the State to ensure the right. Causation is essential for understanding positive obligations and responding to the concerns as to the elusiveness of their scope. Yet while the issue of causation has been extensively addressed in other areas of law, it has been surprisingly neglected in the area of international human rights law.[1] The objective of this chapter is to fill this gap by investigating how the ECtHR finds causal connections between harm and state omissions within the framework of positive obligations.

Any engagement with causation has to start with the awareness that ascribing causality in human society is fraught with complexities.[2] There has been a clear acknowledgment that causality by omission is hard to ascertain. National law has struggled with issues of causality by omission,[3] as indeed has philosophy.[4] A further problem is that causality by omission implies a counterfactual and speculative analysis. It might be possible to identify diverse omissions that might have causal connections to the harm.[5] The role of normativity and policy considerations when determining causality has been also noted.[6] Finally, the issue of causality is fraught with difficulties from an evidential point of view since determining causality might be a highly factual process.

---

[1] D McGrogan, 'The Problem of Causality in International Human Rights Law' (2016) 65 International and Comparative Law Quarterly 615 (with focus on UN monitoring system); F Rigaux, 'International Responsibility and the Principle of Causality' in M Ragazzi (ed), *International Responsibility Today. Essays in Memory of Oscar Schachter* (Martinus Nijhoff Publishers 2005) 81; L Lavrysen, *Human Rights in a Positive State* (Intersentia 2016) 137; V Lanovoy, 'Causation in the Law of State Responsibility' (2022) British Yearbook of International Law 1.
[2] D Ho and D Rubin, 'Credible Causal Interference for Empirical Legal Studies' (2011) 7 Annual Review of Law and Social Science 17.
[3] D Fairgrieve, 'Pushing the Boundaries of Public Authority Liability' in D Fairgrieve and others (eds), *Tort Liability of Public Authorities in Comparative Perspective* (British Institute of International and Comparative Law 2002) 475 at 494; C Booth and D Squires, *The Negligence Liability of Public Authorities* (Oxford University Press 2006).
[4] D Husak, 'Omissions, Causation and Liability' (1980) 30 Philosophical Quarterly 318.
[5] S McGrath, 'Causation by Omissions: A Dilemma' (2005) 123 Philosophical Studies 125.
[6] S Steel, 'Causation in Tort Law and Criminal Law: Unity and Divergence?' in M Dyson (ed), *Unravelling Tort and Crime* (Cambridge University Press 2014) 239; R Fumerton and K Kress, 'Causation and the Law: Preemption, Lawful Sufficiency, and Causal Sufficiency' (2001) 64 Law and Contemporary Problems 83.

The European Court of Human Rights (ECtHR) is certainly confronted with all these challenges, which can be also related to the uncertainties about the scope and the content of the positive obligations generated by the European Convention of Human Rights (ECHR). This chapter shows how the Court approaches these challenges. Section 3.1 will elaborate on the question as to why causation is significant in the context of positive obligations under the ECHR. No clear test has been articulated by the Court for verifying the place of state omissions in the chain of events. Against this backdrop, I suggest that inspiration from other areas of the law on state responsibility could be useful. Section 3.2 thus draws a parallel with the rules on attribution in international law. Since these rules express lines of proximity, it is useful to assess their underlying justifications to improve our understanding of the linkages between harm and state conduct. More specifically, the rules on attribution are founded on the principle that control implies responsibility and the same principle can be extended in the context of positive obligations. Accordingly, the degree of control exercised by the State is essential for assessing lines of causation. This is also reflected in the case law of the Court.

Since the question as to how much control the State should have could imply normative judgments in which the Court might not want to see itself implicated, and since empirical and epistemological uncertainty might hamper assessments of causations, the Court can resort to techniques that avoid the direct resolution of these normative issues and uncertainties. Section 3.3 will identify two such techniques: domestic legality and procedural guarantees. Finally, Section 3.4 will discuss another technique for limiting state responsibility that refers to the distinction between systemic as opposed to incidental failures.

## 3.1 The Role and the Standard of Causation

Identifying the causation between harm and state omission is crucial for finding the respondent State responsible for that omission under the ECHR. This was clearly exemplified in *L.C.B. v United Kingdom*, a case demonstrative of a failure to establish this connection. The applicant sought to attribute her leukaemia to her father's exposure to radiation from atmospheric tests of nuclear weapons during his military service. She claimed that the failure by the State to warn her parents of the possible risk to her health caused by her father's participation in the nuclear tests, and its earlier failure to monitor her father's radiation dose levels, gave rise to violation of Article 2. The Court did not dispute that the respondent State was generally under a positive obligation to protect the right to life; accordingly, it defined its task as determining whether 'given the circumstances of the case, the State did all that could have been required of it to prevent the applicant's life from being avoidably put at risk'. It could not, however, establish a connection between any omission by the State and the disease from which the *particular* applicant suffered: 'it is clearly uncertain whether monitoring of the applicant's health *in utero* and from birth would have led to earlier diagnosis and medical intervention such as to diminish the severity of her disease'.[7]

Since the establishment of a causal connection is crucial, the applicable standard needs to be articulated. This standard has not been framed as requiring an affirmative answer to the question whether 'violation would have been avoided'.[8] Such a proposal would be problematic anyhow since it would be based on the assumption that the cause of the harm is the State's omission, and the consequence of this omission is the harm. These strict causality links are an erroneous reflection of the requirement for causation between the harm and the State's conduct as developed in the case law. The omission by the State might be just one factor contributing role to the occurrence of the harm. The 'but for' test, which means that but for the State's failure, the harm would not have happened, has been explicitly rejected by the ECtHR.[9] From the perspective of the individual who claims to be a victim of a human rights violation, it would be too demanding, and ultimately, it might be impossible to prove that if the State had adopted effective protective measures, the abuse would not have happened.[10] In short, there is no requirement that, but for the omission, harm would not have materialized.

Instead, the Court has formulated the following standard: '[a] failure to take reasonably available measures which could have had a *real prospect* of altering the outcome *or* mitigating the harm is sufficient to engage the responsibility of the State'.[11] Avoidance of the harm and its mitigation are formulated as alternatives, which leads to further relaxation of the standard. In addition, the undertaking of protective measures by the State might only have had a real prospect of avoiding or mitigating the *risk* of harm, which adds further flexibility to the causation analysis. For example, in *O'Keeffe v Ireland*, the enquiry was framed as to whether 'effective regulatory framework of protection in place before 1973 might "judged reasonably, have been expected to avoid, or at least, minimise *the risk or the damage* suffered" by the present applicant'.[12]

---

[7] *L.C.B. v United Kingdom* no 14/1997/798/1001, 9 June 1998, §40.
[8] For such an erroneous proposal, see M Ugrekhelidze, 'Causation: Reflection in the Mirror of the European Convention on Human Rights (A Sketch)' in L Calflisch and others (eds), *Liber Amicorum Luzius Wildhaber Human Rights—Strasbourg Views* (Engel Publisher 2007) 469, 476.
[9] *E. and Others v United Kingdom* no 33218/96, 26 November 2002 §99; *Smiljanić v Croatia* no 35983/14, 25 March 2021 §84. This distinguishes the review of responsibility under the ECHR from other legal inquiries. See A Summers, 'Common-Sense Causation in the Law' (2018) 38 Oxford Journal of Legal Studies 793.
[10] *Salakhov and Islyamova v Ukraine* no 28005/08, 14 March 2013 §181: 'Whether or not the authorities' efforts could in principle have averted the fatal outcome in the present case is not decisive for this conclusion [failure to discharge a positive obligation]. What matters for the Court is whether they did everything reasonably possible in the circumstances, in good faith and in a timely manner, to try to save the first applicant's life.' See also *Karpylenko v Ukraine* no 15509/12, 11 February 2016 §81.
[11] *O'Keeffe v Ireland* [GC] no 35810/09, 28 January 2014 §149 (emphasis added); *Opuz v Turkey* no 33401/02, 9 June 2009 §136; *Preminiy v Russia* no 44973/04, 10 February 2011 §84; *Bljakaj and Others v Croatia* no 74448/12, 18 September 2014 §124; *Kotilainen and Others v Finland* no 62439/12, 17 September 2020 §87.
[12] *O'Keeffe v Ireland* [GC] no 35810/09, 28 January 2014 §166; *E. and Others v United Kingdom* no 33218/96, 26 November 2002 §100.

The Court does not consistently refer to the 'real prospect' test in all of its judgments, though. Note in this respect that the Court uses different expressions in order to refer to the causation between the harm and any omissions. For example, in *Vilnes and Others v Norway* it framed the question as to whether harm is 'caused', 'attributable', or 'imputable to any specific shortcomings for which he [the applicant] criticized the State'.[13] This question was asked without considering the degree of likelihood that the absence of these shortcomings would have mitigated the harm or the risk of harm. Nor are there any concrete standards as to the degree of effectiveness required from any measures that the State should have arguably undertaken, so that the omission of taking these measures can be regarded as relevant.[14]

In *Budayeva and Others v Russia*, the review was framed as whether 'there was a causal link' between the serious administrative flaws that impeded the implementation of the land-planning and emergency relief policies and the death and the injuries sustained by the applicants.[15] The Court has also used the expressions 'direct causal link',[16] 'direct and immediate link',[17] 'strong enough link',[18] 'linked directly',[19] and only 'link'.[20] The term 'nexus' has been also used: '[t]he combination of these factors shows a *sufficient nexus* between the pollutant emissions and the State to raise an issue of the State's positive obligation under Article 8 of the Convention',[21] as have the expressions 'due to'[22] and 'can be linked directly'.[23] In *E. and Others v the United Kingdom*, the Court referred to the standard of 'significant influence': the failings of the relevant authorities disclosed in the case 'must be regarded as having had a significant influence on the course of events'.[24] In contrast, in *Makaratzis v Greece*, it was observed that the deficiencies in the legal and administrative framework had a '*bearing* ... on the way in which the potentially lethal police operation culminating in the applicant's arrest was conducted'.[25] In *Hiller v Austria*, the Court found that 'M.K.'s escape [from psychiatric hospital] and subsequent suicide had not been foreseeable for the hospital and

---

[13] *Vilnes and Others v Norway* no 52806/09 and 22703/10, 5 December 2013 §§225–229.
[14] Some effectiveness is, however, required. See, for example, *Mosley v United Kingdom* no 48009/08, 10 May 2011 §§12–18, where the Court observed that the measure invoked by the applicant (ie legally binding pre-notification order) that in his submission the State should have taken to protect his private life, would not have dissuaded the newspaper from publishing the information about him.
[15] *Budayeva and Others v Russia* no 15339/02, 20 March 2008 §158; *Fernandes de Oliveira v Portugal* [GC] no 78103/14, 31 January 2019 §122, where no causal link was established between the emergency procedure and the death of the applicant's son.
[16] *Dodov v Bulgaria* no 59548/00, 17 January 2008 §97.
[17] *Draon v France* [GC] no 1513/03, 6 October 2005 §106. A clarification as to the application of the 'direct and immediate link' test in the context of Article 8 is due here. The Court seems to use the test to also determine whether the definitional threshold of Article 8 can be engaged in the first place. This can be related to the tendency of collapsing the definitional threshold enquiry, on the one hand, with the enquiry about the triggering and scope of positive obligations, on the other. See Section 1.5.
[18] *Dubetska and Others v Ukraine* no 30499/03, 10 February 2011 §123.
[19] *Ribcheva and Others v Bulgaria* no 37801/16, 30 March 2021 §176.
[20] *Olewnik-Cieplińska and Olewnik v Poland* no 20147/15, 5 September 2019 §130.
[21] *Fadeyeva v Russia* no 55723/00, 9 June 2005 §92 (emphasis added).
[22] *Stoyanovi v Bulgaria* no 42980/04, 9 November 2010 §61.
[23] *Giuliani and Gaggio v Italy* [GC] no 23458/02, 24 March 2011 §253.
[24] *E. and Others v The United Kingdom* no 33218/96, 26 November 2002 §100.
[25] *Makaratzis v Greece* [GC] no 50385/99, 20 December 2004 §63 (emphasis added).

was not therefore attributable to it', a formulation that reflects the interdependence between foreseeability and causation.[26] To express the requirement for causation, the Court has also referred to 'measures ... which might have been expected to avoid the risk'.[27]

It is doubtful whether these various terms reflect any differences in the substance of the analysis, varying scrutiny as to the causation element and different standards of causation. The Court has not developed anything close to a consistent terminology. Overall then, and despite the usage of the 'real prospect' standard that appears to offer a more principled approach, uncertainty pervades the case law.

## 3.2 Control and Causation

### 3.2.1 The Rules on Attribution

Against the backdrop of the above tangle and intricacy in the case law, the question arises whether it is possible to find some structure by drawing inspiration from other areas of the law on state responsibility. Within the framework of state responsibility, issues of causation arise in contexts other than positive obligations.[28] More specifically, the rules of attribution in general international law themselves reflect lines of proximity. Attribution as defined in the International Law Commission (ILC) Draft Articles reflects rules for connecting conduct to the State.[29] The rationale behind these rules is 'limiting responsibility to conduct which engages the State as an organization'.[30] As I will show below, the role of causation in the realm of positive obligations is very similar: limiting the responsibility of the State to circumstances where the State is engaged in the harm as an organization. It needs to be acknowledged, however, that once attribution is established, the causation between state action and harm is evident. In contrast, in the context of positive obligations and claimed omissions, the lines of causation might not be that easily discernible and might raise challenges.

The rules on attribution connect agents and entities to the State. Conduct is attributable to the State when committed by its actual organs[31] and *de facto* organs[32]

---

[26] *Hiller v Austria* no 1967/14, 22 November 2016 §53.
[27] *Kotilainen and Others v Finland* no 62439/12, 17 September 2020 §73.
[28] Another way in which causation matters in human rights law and in international law more generally relates to remedies. In particular, once a violation of a right has been found, causation needs to be established between the violation and any harm for the purposes of awarding damages. See Article 41, ECHR. For an in-depth discussion on causation in the context of Article 41 see M Kellner and I Durant, 'Causation' in A Fenyves and others (eds), *Tort Law in the Jurisprudence of the European Court of Human Rights* (De Gruyter 2011) 449. This is an area of enquiry not pursued here.
[29] J Crawford, *State Responsibility. The General Part* (Cambridge University Press 2013) 113.
[30] Draft Articles on Responsibility of States for International Wrongful Acts with Commentaries, *Yearbook of International Law Commission*, 2001, Vol. II (Part Two), 38 §2.
[31] Articles 4–7 ILC Draft Articles form the hard core of the doctrine of attribution since they deal with organs and agencies of state exercising sovereignty authority: see Crawford, *State Responsibility* (n 29) 115.
[32] Article 4(2) ILC Draft Articles; Crawford, *State Responsibility* (n 29) 126.

or by entities directed and controlled by it.[33] As to the first group of organs, the fundamental principle is that the State is responsible for the actions of its organs, even if they act *ultra vires*[34] and even if they are no longer under its control.[35] That the State controls its organs is a normative assumption; the capacity to control and the actual control are irrelevant. The conduct of state organs thus might give rise to per se responsibility on the part of the State.[36] As the ILC has framed it: '[t]he attribution of conduct to the State as a subject of international law is based on criteria determined by international law and *not on the mere recognition of a link of factual causality*'.[37]

With regard to non-state entities, their actions may be attributable to a State if they act under the instruction, direction, or control of that state. Attribution arises in this context because 'there exists a specific factual relationship between the person or entity engaging in the conduct and the State' and 'a real link between the person or group performing the act and the State machinery'.[38] The ILC Draft Articles do not specify the level of control required, which has led to controversies. The International Court of Justice has applied the test of 'effective control'; while other adjudicative bodies have endorsed the standard of 'overall control'.[39] This debate need not to detain us here.

It might come as a surprise that I mention the rules on attribution in the context of positive obligations. While these rules are certainly of importance in the context of negative obligations, they are generally perceived as irrelevant when the case is formulated as one involving a failure to fulfil positive obligations.[40] The obligation to ensure human rights does not require a determination that the actual harm is attributable to the State in the sense of the ILC Draft Articles on State Responsibility[41] and the previously mentioned rules of attribution. The triggering of positive obligations

---

[33] Article 8 ILC Draft Articles.
[34] Article 7 ILC Draft Articles; *Armed Activities (DRC v Uganda)* ICJ Reports 2005, 162, 242. The difficulty here lay in distinguishing an official, though *ultra vires*, act from a purely private act: see Crawford, *State Responsibility* (n 29) 115.
[35] Draft Articles Commentary, Article 7 §18; ILC Commentary, 43 §7.
[36] I say 'might' because '[a]s a normative operation, attribution must be clearly distinguished from the characterization of conduct as internationally wrongful': see ICL Commentary, 39 §4.
[37] ILC Commentary, 39 §4 (emphasis added).
[38] ILC Commentary, 47 §1.
[39] Contrast *Military and Paramilitary Activities in against* Nicaragua *(Nicaragua v US)* (Merits) [1986] ICJ Reports 14 §§109-115 (requiring effective control) with Case IT-94-1, *Prosecutor v Tadic (Appeal Judgement)*, IT-94-1-A, International Criminal Tribunal for the former Yugoslavia (ICTY), 15 July 1999 §§115–131 (adopting a standard of overall control). See also the confirmation of the effective control test in *Application of the Convention on the Prevention and Punishment of the Crime of Genocide*, ICJ Rep. 2007, pp. 43, 207 and *DRC v Uganda* §226.
[40] International law has accepted the distinction between primary and secondary rules of state responsibility. Primary rules are the substantive obligations in the various subject areas of international law. Secondary rules are those that elaborate on what it means for a State to be held responsible for violations of these duties. The rules on attribution belong to the latter. Positive obligations belong to the former: see Draft Articles on State Responsibility §1.
[41] It needs to be acknowledged, however, that on some occasions the ECtHR is not clear in its judgments as to why the respondent state can be held responsible: is it because harmful conduct is attributable to it or is it because it failed to fulfil its positive obligations? For example, *Cyprus v Turkey* no 25781/94, 10 May 2011 §§69–80. For discussion on the Court's unclear logic, see M Milanovic, 'From Compromise to Principle: Clarifying the Concept of State "Jurisdiction" in Human Rights Treaties' (2008) 8 Human Rights Law Review 411.

and the scope of these obligations are contingent on the primary obligations at stake, which are not a subject of the law on state responsibility as such. However, it is still relevant to engage with attribution, since the rules of attribution under international law articulate lines of proximity. They express relationships of directness and immediacy between the act of the State and the harm. It is meaningful to consider the justifications and the theoretical underpinnings of these relationships, so that we improve our understanding of the linkages between harm and state conduct in the form of omission.

## 3.2.2 The Role of Control and the Extension of the Logic of the Rules on Attribution

The rules on attribution seek to establish a nexus between the State and the *agent* who caused the harm. The status of the agent is thus of importance and the harm caused by him/her is directly attributable to the State. Even if the conduct is in breach of the national legislation or the state agent exceeds the authority granted by national law (*ultra vires* acts),[42] attribution is still established as long as the organ acts *within its capacity*.[43] This must be differentiated from cases 'where the conduct is so removed from the scope of their official functions that it should be assimilated to that of private individuals, not attributable to the State'.[44]

In contrast, Article 8 of the ILC Draft Articles highlights the question of 'direction and control'. It clarifies that 'such control will be attributable to the State only if it [the State] directed or controlled the specific operation and the conduct complaint of was an integral part of the operation'. However, as Evans observes, this is not the way the ECtHR has extended the scope of the obligations under the ECHR. It is rather positive obligations that have served this purpose.[45] For example, there might be situations where it is not really possible to show that the State has directly caused harm through its agents or entities under its control.[46]

Two basic principles follow from the above. First, acts of state organs are attributable to the State and the issue of control seems to be immaterial. Second, when the first principle is not applicable since, for example, none of the requirements in Articles

---

[42] *Ilaşcu and Others v Moldova and Russia* no 48787/99, 8 July 2004 §319.
[43] Report of the ILC A/56/10 (2001) 'Draft Articles' at 44, ('State's authorities are strictly liable for the conduct of their subordinates; they are under a duty to impose their will and cannot shelter behind their inability to ensure that it is respected'). See also *Ilaşcu and Others v Moldova and Russia* no 48787/99, 8 July 2004 §319.
[44] Report of the ILC A/56/10 (2001) Draft Articles at 102.
[45] M Evans, 'State Responsibility and the European Convention on Human Rights: Role and Realm' in M Fitzmaurice and D Sarooshi (eds), *Issues of State Responsibility before International Judicial Institutions* (Hart Publishing 2004) 139, 157.
[46] *Medova v Russia* no 25385/04, 15 January 2009 §95 (disappearance case); *Albekov and Others v Russia* no 68216/01, 9 October 2008 §§80–86 (it was not possible to establish who laid the mines which caused death; the Court did not have to decide on the issue since the respondent state was aware that mines were laid in the area and were under the positive obligation to protect the residents from the risks involved).

4, 5, and 6 of the ILC Draft Articles is fulfilled, the second principle is triggered: control implies responsibility.[47] This principle is not side-lined once a case is framed as involving positive obligations. On the contrary, control by the State (not in the sense of Article 8 of the ILC Draft Articles though, which aims to link the State with a specific *agent*) is still relevant for determining the scope of these positive obligations. Public authorities are established to fulfil prescribed aims and they are conferred powers. They assume control over areas of activity, in this way putting themselves in proximate relationship with harm that might arise in these areas.[48] It follows that control structures lines of causation. The more control, the closer proximity may be expected between state conduct and harm, and accordingly, the positive obligations are more demanding. These positive obligations are thus commensurate with the extent of the control. In this sense, we can see some extension of the logic that applies to the rules on attribution. This normative account fits current practice since, as we will see in this chapter, it is reflected in the case law under the ECHR.

The question which emerges at this junction is what principles apply if the state authorities are out of control. Do States have positive obligations when they do not have control? Can they absolve themselves from responsibility under human rights law by simply saying that they did not have control? Can they decide to relinquish control and free themselves from responsibility? The presumption that operates is that States have control over their territory and therefore continue to be under the obligation to ensure the rights enshrined in the ECHR.[49] This implies that States have to reassert control and take measures to secure these rights *as a matter of principle*.[50] This certainly does not translate into state responsibility for failure to ensure human rights in every concrete case. States might face some practical difficulties in reasserting control and in the degree of control that they can practically exercise; however, these will have to be taken into account in the assessment of the scope of the positive obligations in

---

[47] For this distinction see Lawson, 'Out of Control. State Responsibility and Human Rights: Will the ILC's Definition of the "Act of State" Meet the Challenges of the 21st Century' in M Castermans-Holleman and others (eds), *The Role of the Nation-State in the 21st Century. Human Rights, International Organisations and Foreign Policy* (Kluwer 1998) 91 97.

[48] Similar considerations have been made relevant in the context of claims against public authorities for damages at national level: see D Brodie, 'Compulsory Altruism and Public Authorities' in Fairgrieve and others (eds), *Tort Liability of Public Authorities in Comparative Perspective* (n 3) 541, 551: 'I would suggest that where a public authority is concerned the court should, rather than seeking to identify pure omissions, look to see whether the authority in question has statutory responsibility to control, regulate, or supervise the relevant area of social or economic activity in the community.'

[49] *Sargyan v Azerbaijan* [GC] no 40167/06 16 June 2015 §§128–131; S Besson, 'The Bearers of Human Rights; Duties and Responsibilities for Human Rights: A Quite (R)evolution' (2015) 32 Social Philosophy and Policy 244, 253: 'there is a general human rights' positive duty for States to exercise jurisdiction and hence to incur human rights duties'.

[50] *Sargyan v Azerbaijan* §131. The following clarification is due here. In *Sargyan v Azerbaijan,* the issue under discussion was control for the purpose of establishing jurisdiction under Article 1 ECHR. However, the same logic can be extended in the context of positive obligations. On the use of the notion of 'control' for different purposes (establishing jurisdiction, attribution, and positive obligations), see S Besson, 'Concurrent Responsibilities under the European Convention on Human Rights: The Concurrence of Human Rights Jurisdictions, Duties and Responsibilities' in A van Aaken and I Motoc (eds), *The European Convention on Human Rights and General International Law* (Oxford University Press 2018) 155. See Chapter 8.

the particular case. In addition to issues of practicality and feasibility, certain areas of activities are underpinned with the normative assumption that the State must wield more control. I engage with these areas in more detail in Section 3.2.4. First, however, I turn to circumstances where state agents inflict harm and how the positive obligations in relation to this harm are shaped by the degree of control exercised.

## 3.2.3 Control and Prevention of State-inflicted Harm

Positive obligations are usually analysed in circumstances when private actors cause harm. However, they are just as relevant in circumstances where state agents inflict harm. States are equally under the obligation to structure the relationships between their agents and individuals in such a way that harm is prevented and, if it occurs, is adequately addressed. In this context, the harm caused by failures in these structures is more closely proximate to the State and, accordingly, the obligation to prevent it is more demanding. For these reasons and in relation to the right to life, the Court has observed that '[w]hen lethal force is used within "policing operation" by the authorities, it is difficult to separate the State's negative obligations under the Convention from its positive obligations'.[51] Still, in its analysis the Court distinguishes the two, and to this effect it has established that Article 2 requires careful scrutiny not only as to whether the use of force by state agents was strictly proportionate to the aim of protecting persons against unlawful violence (negative obligation),[52] but also whether the overall operation was 'planned and controlled by the authorities so as to minimize,to the greatest extent possible, recourse to lethal force' (positive obligation).[53]

The intensity of the above positive obligation is influenced by the level of control that the State has over the situation. For example, in *Giuliani and Gaggio v Italy*, the absence of foreseeability as to the course of the events, as well as the ensuing reduced level of control by the State over the situation, were taken into account in determining whether the organization and the planning of the policing operations were compatible with the obligation to protect life.[54] Similarly, in *Isayeva v Russia*, where the applicant's close relatives were killed by indiscriminate bombing by the Russian military, one of the factors considered by the Court was that the military operation conducted by Russia was not spontaneous and therefore, the State had control over the circumstances.[55] Likewise, in *Makaratzis v Greece* the Court did not overlook the fact 'the applicant was injured during an unplanned operation which gave rise to developments to which the police were called upon to react without prior preparation'. In the latter judgment it was also added that if the unpredictability of the events and the

---

[51] *Finogenov and Others v Russia* no 18299/03 and 27311/03, 20 December 2011 §208.
[52] See Article 2(2) of the ECHR which delineates limited circumstances when use of force might be justified.
[53] *McCann and Others v United Kingdom* [GC] no 18984/91, 27 September 1995 §§194.
[54] §§253–262.
[55] *Isayeva v Russia* no 57950/00, 24 February 2005 §188.

resultant reduction of the level of control were not taken into account in the assessment of the positive obligations, this might lead to the imposition of an 'impossible burden on the authorities'.[56]

In the course of assessing the control over the situation and the scope of the positive obligations, the reasons as to why the state authorities did not have control are also of importance. Absence of foreseeability could be one such reason. In *Makaratzis v Greece*, however, it was established that the degeneration of the situation and the ensuing chaos

> was largely due to the fact that at the time neither individual police officers nor the chase, seen as a collective police operation, had the benefit of the appropriate structure which should have been provided by the domestic law and practice.[57]

Since the absence of control was seen as attributable to deficiencies in the national legislation, Greece was found to have failed to protect the right to life. Therefore, despite the unpredictability of the events and the ensuing reduced level of practical control over the circumstances, the normative expectation that police operations are regulated by laws was determinative.

*Finogenov and Others v Russia*, a case involving hostage-taking in a theatre that was stormed by the Russian authorities after the dispersal of an unknown narcotic gas, strongly supports the argument that there is a correlation between the control and the scope of the positive obligations. In *Finogenov and Others v Russia*, the Court modified the well-established *Osman* test,[58] by observing that:

> [t]he authorities' positive obligations under Article 2 of the Convention are not unqualified: not every presumed threat to life obliges the authorities to take specific measures to avoid the risk. A duty to take specific measures arises only if the authorities knew or ought to have known at the time of the existence of a real and immediate risk to life *and if the authorities retained a certain degree of control over the situation*.[59]

The Court delineated a different intensity of obligations and applied a different degree of scrutiny depending on the degree of control that the State had over the situation. It distinguished *Finogenov* from the abovementioned *Isayeva v Russia* since '[t]he hostage taking came as a surprise for the authorities, so the military preparations for the storming had to be made very quickly and in full secrecy'. In addition, the authorities

---

[56] *Makaratzis v Greece* [GC] no 50385/99, 20 December 2004 §69.
[57] ibid §70.
[58] See Section 7.3.
[59] *Finogenov and Others v Russia* nos 18299/03 and 27311/03, 20 December 2011 §209 (emphasis added). See also *Ribcheva and Others v Bulgaria* no 37801/16, 30 March 2021 §167.

were not in control of the situation inside the theatre where the hostages were kept, which was also of material consideration.[60]

In contrast to the storming of the theatre, however, the positive obligations in relation to the subsequent rescue operation were of different intensity since 'no serious time constraint existed and the authorities were in control of the situation'. This justified a different approach when assessing the conduct of the Russian authorities.[61] While the use of the gas and the storming were found not to be disproportionate measures in breach of Article 2, the rescue and evacuation operation were found inadequate. The latter operation was subjected to more thorough scrutiny because it was not spontaneous. In addition, it could be expected from the authorities that they had some general emergency plan and some control of the situation outside the building where the rescue efforts took place. The predictability of the harm also implied a higher level of control and more demanding positive obligations: 'the more predictable a hazard, the greater the obligation to protect against it'.[62]

In conclusion, control over the situation is crucial for a finding of causation, and important for assessing the intensity of the positive obligation. At the same time and as already intimated in the end of Section 3.2.2, positive obligations themselves might require more pervasive control in certain circumstances. Section 3.2.4 will expand on this argument. Prior to this, however, the circularity in the above argumentation needs to be acknowledged. If States have control, they put themselves in closer causal relations with harm that might materialize and the positive obligations invoked in these circumstances are more robust. At the same time, the positive obligations themselves might require more control by the State. Instead of occluding this paradox, it should be rather openly acknowledged. The paradox is part of a much broader issue that ultimately concerns the role of the State in the society and to what extent and under what circumstances this role should be more intrusive.[63]

## 3.2.4 Assumption of Control in the Area of Public Services

A cluster of positive obligations cases involve provision of public services. These services can be provided by public or private bodies. It has been well established in the case law that States are not absolved of their human rights law obligations by delegating certain services to private bodies.[64] The designation of the body is thus not of

---

[60] *Finogenov and Others v Russia* §213.
[61] ibid §214.
[62] ibid §§243. See also *Mikayil Mammadov v Azerbaijan* no 4762/05, 17 December 2009 §§196–119.
[63] This paradox is further exaggerated if one takes into account that human rights are traditionally invoked to circumscribe the exercise of state control (States' negative obligations to refrain), while positive human rights obligations might require more state control. See Section 1.1.
[64] *Costello-Roberts v United Kingdom* no 13134/87, 25 March 1993; *Dodov v Bulgaria* no 59548/00, 17 January 2008 para 80; *Storck v Germany* no 61603/00, 16 June 2005 §103; *O'Keeffe v Ireland* [GC] no 35810/09, 28 January 2014 §150.

significance. For example, the Court has observed that 'in the public-health sphere, these positive obligations require the State to make regulations compelling hospitals, *whether private or public*, to adopt appropriate measures for the protection of patients' lives'.[65] The nature of the activity, however—that is, public services—is of important material consideration since the scope of the positive obligation increases as a function of this nature. The normative assumption that operates in this context is that the State should assume control in relation to these services and, as a consequence, the intensity of the obligation rises.

A question which arises here is how to define public services.[66] The importance of the interest at stake, and also the relational context, can be determinative in delineating the contours of this definition. For example, in relation to education, the Court has emphasized that children have no alternative but to attend school since primary education is obligatory.[67] In *O'Keeffe v Ireland*, the Court went so far as to establish an '*inherent* obligation [of the State] to protect children in this context, of potential risks'.[68] The applicant in this case complained that the system of primary education failed to protect her from sexual abuse by a teacher. In relation to this complaint, the Court held that

> the primary education context of the present case *defines to a large extent the nature and the importance of this obligation*. The Court's case law makes it clear that the positive obligation of protection assumes particular importance in the context of the *provision of an important public service* such as primary education, school authorities being obliged to protect the health and well-being of pupils and, in particular, of young children who are especially vulnerable and are under the exclusive control of those authorities.[69]

Although the school in question was owned and managed by a non-state actor, the Court relied on the fact that education is an importance public service and on the vulnerability of children to determine the scope of the positive obligation.[70]

The importance of the activity in question and the control of the authorities were also emphasized in *Ilbeyi Kemaloglu and Meriye Kemaloglu v Turkey*, a case about

---

[65] *Calvelli and Ciglio v Italy* [GC] no 32967/96, 17 January 2002 §49 (emphasis added); *Vo v France* [GC] no 53924/00, 8 July 2004 §89; *Center for Legal Resources on behalf of Valentin Câmpeanu v Romania* [GC] no 47848/08, 17 July 2014 §130; *Lambert and Others v France* [GC] no 46043/14, 5 June 2015 §140.

[66] One way will be to say that public functions are the ones that the State has historically performed. For a more in-depth discussion, see J Thomas, *Public Rights, Private Relations* (Oxford University Press 2015) 41.

[67] *O'Keeffe v Ireland* [GC] no 35810/09, 28 January 2014 §151. This notion of 'inherent obligation' has not remained unchallenged. In their dissenting opinion, five judges challenged the assumption that there is some inherent risk of sexual abuse in the context of education.

[68] ibid §162; *F.O. v Croatia* no 29555/13, 22 April 2021 §82: 'In the context of provision of an important public service such as education, the essential role of the education authorities is to protect the health and well-being of students having regard, in particular, to their vulnerability relating to their young age.'

[69] *O'Keeffe v Ireland* [GC] no 35810/09, 28 January 2014 §145 (emphasis added).

[70] ibid §157.

the child who froze to death after being left alone by the school authorities in a heavy snow storm:

> the State's duty to safeguard the right to life is also applicable to school authorities, who carry an obligation to protect the health and well-being of pupils, in particular young children who are especially vulnerable and are under the exclusive control of the authorities.[71]

The same principle has been applied to psychiatric institutions, in relation to which 'the State remained under a duty to exercise supervision and control',[72] and nursing homes, which the State is under the obligation to regulate.[73] Similar reasoning underpinned *Iliya Petrov v Bulgaria*, where the Court held that the 'decisive factor' for the incident to occur was the deficient control by the authorities regarding the safety of electric transformers,[74] the latter being a public service in relation to which the State is expected to exercise control. *Cevrioğlu v Turkey* is also illustrative in this respect. The case concerns the death of a boy as a result of falling into a large water-filled hole outside a private building under construction in a residential area. The Court referred to the 'inherently hazardous nature' of construction sites and, accordingly, the expectation that the State controls, inspects, and supervises the activities at these sites.[75] In its reasoning, the Court added that the State 'in the present context had a more compelling responsibility towards the members of the public who had to live with the very real dangers posed by construction work on their doorsteps'.[76]

The above outlined expectation that in certain areas the State assumes control, shapes the approach to causation. For example, in *Cevrioğlu v Turkey*, it was admitted that no causal link may exist between the failings to inspect the construction site and the death of the boy 'for the purposes of civil liability'. However, in the context of state responsibility where the objective is to find the responsibility of a collective, strict causation lines are inappropriate. In this respect, the Court observed that 'proper implementation of an inspection mechanism would undoubtedly have increased the possibility of identifying and remedying the failings which were responsible for the death of the applicant's son'.[77]

---

[71] *Ilbeyi Kemaloglu and Meriye Kemaloglu v Turkey* no 19986/06, 10 April 2012 §35.
[72] *Storck v Germany* no 61603/00, 16 June 2005 §103.
[73] *Dodov v Bulgaria* no 59548/00, 17 January 2008 §§84–86.
[74] *Iliya Petrov v Bulgaria* no 19202/03, 24 April 2012 §63 (basic safety precautions were missing including not locking the door of the transformer located at a park for children).
[75] *Cevrioğlu v Turkey* no 69546/12, 4 October 2016 §57.
[76] ibid §67.
[77] ibid §69.

## 3.2.5 Source of the Harm and the Related Level of Control

The establishment of causation between failures on behalf of the State to take measures and harm is also affected by the source of the harm: whether the source is a natural or a man-made phenomenon. In both contexts, the State is under the general obligation to protect; however, in the event of a harm ensuing from a man-made phenomenon, causality is easier to establish, and the scope of the positive obligations is more demanding.[78]

In situations involving 'dangerous activities', where the harm is perceived as man-made, or in relation to events 'regulated and controlled by the State', it is easier to establish that state omissions are causative to harm. An example to this effect is *Öneryildiz v Turkey*, a case about an explosion at a garbage collection point. In its submissions to the Court, Turkey tried to challenge the extension of positive obligations under Article 2 to all circumstances of unintentional death. The Court, however, emphasized the dangerous nature of the activity and the ensuing expectation that the State regulates it. In this way, it established a causation between the harm and failure by the State to regulate.[79]

In *Vilnes and Others v Norway*, the Court extended this logic to *risky activities* and observed that 'it sees no need to consider in detail the degree of involvement of the respondent State in the hazardous activity in question, since the Convention obligation applies "any activity, whether public or not"'.[80] The same approach was adopted in *Kolyadenko and Others v Russia*, a case about an urgent massive evacuation of water from reservoir, where the Court also emphasized that a reservoir is a man-made industrial facility.[81]

The above analysis is not modified by the nature of the agent that performs the activity. Whether that activity is performed by a public entity or by, for example, private corporations, is immaterial. Thus, the Court's assertion in *Brincat and Others v Malta* that the positive obligation to safeguard lives '*may* apply in cases, such as the present one, dealing with exposure to asbestos at a workplace which was *run by a public corporation owned and controlled by the Government*' is confusing.[82] If consistency in the case law is to be maintained, the public or private nature of the entity that engages in

---

[78] This more demanding scope can be also justified based on the understanding that harm ensuing from a man-made phenomenon might be easier to predict and know about and thus preventive protective measures can be considered as more reasonable. See Section 2.7.2. On the intertwinement between the factors of state knowledge, causation, and reasonableness, see Section 4.1.

[79] Reference was made to the various texts adopted by the Council of Europe in the field of environment and the industrial activities: *Öneryildiz v Turkey* [GC] no 48939/99, 30 November 2004 §§59–62 and 71. Other industrial activities reviewed by the Court are nuclear testing (*L.C.B. v United Kingdom* no 23413/94, 9 June 1998), toxic emission from fertilizer factory (*Guerra and Others v Italy* [GC] no 14967/89, 19 February 1998), and exposure to asbestos at a workplace (*Brincat and Others v Malta* no 60908/11, 24 July 2014).

[80] *Vilnes and Others v Norway* no 52806/09, 5 December 2013 §223.

[81] *Kolyadenko and Others v Russia* no 17423/05, 28 February 2012 §164.

[82] *Brincat and Others v Malta* no 60908/11, 24 July 2014 § 81 (emphasis added).

the activity is not pertinent. As the Court itself has observed, the positive obligation to protect life applies 'in the context of any activity, whether public or not'.[83]

The above cases implicating man-made harm can be distinguished from circumstances where harm is caused by 'natural' disasters. It is more difficult to establish causality, and therefore the positive obligations are not that extensive in cases of natural disasters 'which are as such beyond human control' and 'do not call for the same extent of State involvement'.[84] In *Budayeva and Others v Russia*, a case about a mudslide causing loss of life and destruction of property, the Court observed that '[t]he scope of the positive obligations imputable to the State in the particular circumstances would depend on the origin of the threat and the extent to which one or the other risk is susceptible to mitigation'.[85] It was added that the consideration of not imposing a disproportionate burden on the State 'must be afforded even greater weight in the sphere of emergency relief in relation to a meteorological event, which is as such *beyond human control, than in the sphere of dangerous activities of a man-made nature*'.[86] Still, against the background of the national authorities' omissions in the implementation of land-planning and emergency relief policies in the hazardous area where the mudslide occurred, and the existence of a causal link between these failures and death of the victim, Russia was found to have failed to discharge its positive obligations under Article 2.[87]

Finally, situations need to be distinguished when the source of harm is a specific individual, and in this sense it is a man-made harm. However, variations need to be acknowledged depending on whether this individual, who can generally be called the perpetrator,[88] is within the control of the State. When the person is, then it is more likely that the omission to prevent the harm (or the risk of harm) that he or she has ultimately inflicted, irrespective of the identifiability of any possible victims,[89] is considered causative. There is, however, instability in the case law of the Court as to how being in control of the State is to be understood. Cases such as *Maiorano and Others v Italy*, where prisoners inflicted harm after being released from prison,[90] appear relatively uncontroversial. The same can be said about *Bljakaj and Others v Croatia*, where a person with history of violence, unlawful possession of a firearm, and alcohol abuse committed a murder on the same day when he was initially under the control of the police, but the police failed to take actions to supervise him.[91] The case of *Gorovenko and Bugara v Ukraine*, where a police officer committed a murder with his service gun

---

[83] *Vilnes and Others v Norway* no 52806/09, 5 December 2013 §223 (the Court 'sees no need to consider in detail the degree of involvement of the respondent State in the hazardous activity in question, since the Convention obligation applies to "any activity, whether public or private"').
[84] *Budayeva and Others v Russia* no 15339/02, 20 March 2008 §174.
[85] ibid §137.
[86] ibid §135 (emphasis added).
[87] ibid §§158–159.
[88] This label is without prejudice to the establishment of any individual criminal responsibility.
[89] The Court has referred to 'the obligation to afford general protection to society' to indicate the unidentifiability of the victims. *Kotilainen and Others v Finland* no 62439/12, 17 September 2020 §71.
[90] *Maiorano and Others v Italy* no 28634/06, 15 December 2009 §107.
[91] *Bljakaj and Others v Croatia* no 74448/12, 18 September 2014 §115.

while off duty, can be also added within this category. The Court explicitly based its reasoning on the expectation that when the State equips its police forces, 'the selection of agents allowed to carry such firearms must also be subject to particular scrutiny'.[92] Cases such as *Kotilainen and Others v Finland* and *Smiljanić v Croatia* are, however, more controversial since the perpetrators were not within the control of the State. In this way, the boundaries of state responsibility for omissions seem to have been pushed to questionable limits.[93]

## 3.2.6 Assumption of Control over the Victim

While the preceding sections addressed the issue of state control over certain circumstances, activities and persons who might be sources of harm, this section focuses on control over individuals who are the object of the harm. Once the State has undertaken any special responsibilities in relation to certain individuals, the lines of causation between harm and state omissions solidify. States owe more extensive positive obligations to those with whom they have special ties. The primary example in this respect is prisoners, who are placed under extensive state control.[94] This control implies more demanding positive obligations. These have been considered in various contexts (protection from private violence,[95] protection from suicide,[96] acceptable detention conditions, including prevention of health hazards,[97] and provision of minimum socio-economic assistance). It will suffice to compare the scope of the positive obligations in relation to the provision of healthcare for prisoners with the scope of the positive obligation in relation to provision of healthcare to the population at large.[98] In the latter context, the Court applies a high definitional threshold to find violations of Articles 3 and 8 in the sphere of socio-economic assistance.[99] The Court has not excluded the possibility that violations of Articles 3 and 8 might be found in circumstances characterized with deprivations resulting from, for example,

---

[92] *Gorovenko and Bugara v Ukraine* nos 36146/05 and 42418/05, 12 January 2012 §38.
[93] See Partly Dissenting Opinion of Judge Eicke in *Kotilainen and Others v Finland* and Dissenting Opinion of Judge Wojtyczek in *Smiljanić v Croatia* no 35983/14, 25 March 2021.
[94] *Keenan v United Kingdom* no 27229/95, 3 April 2001 §91; *I.E. v Moldova* no 45422/13, 26 May 2020 §40.
[95] *Paul and Audrey Edwards v United Kingdom* no 46477/99, 14 March 2012 §§57–64 (a detainee was killed by another detainee while held in prison); *Premininy v Russia* no 44973/04, 10 February 2011 §91 (a detainee was systematically beaten by other detainees).
[96] *Keenan v United Kingdom* §90 (the applicant argued that her son died from suicide due to the prison authorities' failure to protect his life).
[97] *Florea v Romania* no 37186/03, 14 September 2010 (protection from passive smoking); *Jashi v Georgia* no 10799/06, 8 January 2013 (provision of adequate care for detainee's mental health).
[98] L Oette, 'Austerity and the Limits of Policy-Induced Suffering: What Role for the Prohibition of Torture and Other Ill-Treatment?' (2015) 15 Human Rights Law Review 669, 681; C O'Cinneide, 'A Modest Proposal. Destitution, State Responsibility and the European Convention on Human Rights' (2008) 5 European Human Rights Law Review 583.
[99] *Waiter v Poland* no 42290/08, 15 May 2012 §§36–42 (access to life-saving drug); *Budina v Russia* no 45603/05 (dec) 18 June 2009.

insufficient welfare benefits; however, such a finding will be made under exceptional circumstances.[100]

The exceptionality approach, however, will be modified if the other elements intervene. As mentioned above, no such approach is applied in relation to prisoners. The Court has taken this very far, since not even financial considerations (eg the argument that the State does not have enough money to maintain prisons) are accepted.[101] There are other circumstances where, due to the special relationship between the State and the victim and more specificity due to the assumption of control by the State over the victim, the logic of exceptionality is displaced. In *Denis Vasilyev v Russia*, the Court observed that the duty to protect is not 'confined to the specific context of the military and penitentiary facilities'.[102] It added that

> [i]t also becomes relevant in other situations in which the physical well-being of individuals is dependent, to a decisive extent, on the actions by the authorities, who are legally required to take measures within the scope of their powers which might have been necessary to avoid the risk of damage to life and limb.[103]

The factual substratum of *Denis Vasilyev v Russia* was underpinned by omissions by police officers. In particular, after finding the applicant unconscious on the street, they left without calling for medical assistance. Despite the important assertion framed by the Court in the above quotation to the effect that the obligation to protect is triggered when the well-being of the individual is dependent on the State, the reasoning in the judgment overall is confusing. The Court pointed to various factors (vulnerability of the person, knowledge about his position, control over him once the State authorities knew about his position, and the requirements under the national legislation to render assistance) to find that the State was in breach of its positive obligations. Overall, the reasoning manifests a heavy emphasis on the requisites of the national legislation to assist the person, which tilted the Court to find a violation of Article 3. In Section 3.3.1, I will discuss the role of domestic legality in more detail.

Here it is pertinent to observe that there might be other situations where the above-mentioned exceptionality might be in place. One such example is where the State has precluded the availability of alternative means of protection and assistance. Such a situation might transpire in relation to asylum-seekers, who might not be allowed to work in the first place, which will inevitably modify the analysis as to whether the

---

[100] J Gerards, 'The ECtHR's Response to Fundamental Rights Issues related to Financial and Economic Difficulties—the Problem of Compartmentalization' (2015) 13 Netherlands Quarterly of Human Rights 274.
[101] *Orchowski v Poland* no 17885/04, 22 October 2009 §153.
[102] *Nencheva v Bulgaria* no 48609/06, 18 June 2013 §119 (severely disabled children held in an institution died during the winter); *Centre for Legal Resources on Behalf of Velentin Campeanu v Romania* [GC] §§134–144.
[103] *Denis Vasilyev v Russia* no 32704/04, 17 December 2009 §§115–116.

absence of socio-economic assistance by the State is causative to harm falling within the scope of Article 3 or 8.[104]

Because of the special relationship between the person and the State that arises in the above-mentioned contexts, the foreseeability of the harm requirement might be loosened.[105] In light of the special position of the victim in relation to the State, it might hardly be possible to argue that the State did not know or ought not to have known about the harm or the risk of harm. Some aspects of the case law, however, cause confusion. For example, in *Nencheva v Bulgaria*, the Court extensively reviewed whether the central national authorities knew about the dire circumstances of the disabled children who were accommodated in a home. In light of the fact that the home in question was under the control of these authorities, one is left to wonder whether the authorities should in any case have known about the risks faced by the children. Even if they did not actually know, there should have been mechanisms for channelling such information.[106] In sum, as observed in Section 2.3, the case law is ambiguous as to which factor has a dominating role: the actual knowledge about harm, on the one hand, or the normative supposition that state authorities should know or necessarily knew about the harm (or risk of harm) to individuals under their control.

One final observation is due in this section. The special position of the victim can be related to the particular vulnerability of certain categories of persons.[107] The Court has recognized various groups as vulnerable: children,[108] asylum-seekers,[109] prisoners and military conscripts,[110] persons with disabilities,[111] victims of domestic violence,[112] and Roma.[113] It is useful, however, to distinguish between the sources of these various vulnerabilities. Some of them might be innate and inherent vulnerabilities (eg children). Others might be related to the social context (eg Roma, religious minorities).[114] In this section, I have drawn attention to a distinctive vulnerability that stems from the specific relationship with the State and, in particular, from the exposure of the person to state power. Prisoners, for example, who due to their detention are exposed to state power and deprived of other sources of help, are placed in a special relationship with the State, which explains the more demanding positive obligations.[115] Certainly, this special relationship could be intimately related to or substantiated by vulnerability stemming from innateness or social context (eg protection

---

[104] See *Adam, R v Secretary of the State for the Home Department* [2005] UKHL 66 (depriving asylum-seekers from social support when they are not allowed to engage in remunerated employment).
[105] *Keller v Russia* no 26824/04, 17 October 2013 §88.
[106] *Nencheva v Bulgaria* no 48609/06, 18 June 2013 §§121–122.
[107] L Peroni and A Timmer, 'Vulnerable Groups: The Promise of an Emerging Concept in European Human Rights Convention Law' (2013) 11 International Journal of Constitutional Law 1056.
[108] *E. and Others v United Kingdom* no 33218/96, 26 November 2002 §88.
[109] *M.S.S. v Belgium and Greece* [GC] no 30696/09, 21 January 2011 §232.
[110] *Placì v Italy* no 48754/11, 21 January 2014 §49.
[111] *Storck v Germany* no 61603/00, 16 June 2005.
[112] *Bevacqua and S. v Bulgaria* no 71127/01, 12 June 2008 §65.
[113] *D.H. and Others v the Czech Republic* [GC] no 57325/00, 3 November 2007 §182.
[114] *Milanovic v Serbia* no 44614/07, 14 December 2010 §89.
[115] One can distinguish this situation from 'pre-existing vulnerabilities.' For a discussion in the context of tort law, see S Green, *Causation in Negligence* (Hart Publishing 2015) 38.

of children in the context of compulsory education) and in this sense, the different sources of vulnerability might be interrelated.

## 3.3 Techniques for Avoiding Causation

So far, this chapter has covered areas where traditionally the State has had an important role, and in this sense, it places itself more easily in closer causal relations with harm that might materialize (eg policing operations, provision of public services, industrial activities, restraints imposed upon individuals). In other areas, however, the intensity of the involvement of the State can be more controversial (eg protection of the environment, regulation of private companies) and the question as to how intrusive its role should be and how much control the State should exercise can be more contentious. Moreover, the establishment of causation between harm and state omissions might be hampered by empirical and epistemological uncertainties. Since the Court might not want to see itself deeply implicated in normative judgments about the role of the State in society more generally, and since the Court might not be in a position to resolve empirical and epistemological uncertainties, it has crafted techniques to avoid making these judgments and resolutions. These techniques also mean that the Court does not have to confront the issue directly as to whether state omission is causative to harm. Two such techniques will be discussed here: domestic legality and procedural protection.

### 3.3.1 Domestic Legality

When an omission is contrary to the national regulatory framework, causation between this omission and the harm amounting to violation of human rights law is easier to assume. In other words, when the national legislation or applicable regulatory standards themselves envisioned the undertaking of certain measures and these were not performed, the Court is more willing to accept that there is a nexus between the non-performance and harm. The underlying assumption is that the national regulatory framework was adopted in order to prevent harm. Once this is transposed at the level of the ECHR, whether or not this is indeed the case (to wit, whether or not generally or in relation to the particular applicant the proper application of the legal framework would have indeed prevented harm or reduced the risk of harm) seems to be less relevant, since the above assumption continues to operate.

How non-compliance with the national legal requirements renders the proximity standard less stringent from the perspective of the applicant was made obvious in *I. v Finland*. The applicant complained that a hospital had failed to guarantee the security of her data against unauthorized access. She worked as a nurse and was diagnosed as HIV-positive. At certain point, she suspected that her colleagues were aware of her illness and soon her contract was not renewed. On the facts, it was not possible to determine whether her records were actually accessed by an unauthorized third person. As a consequence, it was not possible to prove a causal connection between deficiencies in the access rules in this particular hospital (ie not maintaining a log of all persons who had accessed her medical files) and the harm that she had experienced (ie dissemination of information about her medical condition). However, the Court did not find it necessary to prove such causation. Instead, it observed that *'what is decisive* is that the records system in place in the hospital was clearly not in accordance with the legal requirements' in the national legislation and did not hesitate to find a failure on behalf of the State to fulfil its positive obligation under Article 8.[116]

The requirements laid down in the national legislation, including those that require positive measures, establish a baseline. Any deviation from this baseline is suspect and makes it easier to argue that a State's failure to comply with its own baseline is causative of harm. Support for this approach can be found in the context of the right to life and the adequate standard of healthcare.[117] *Lopes de Sousa Fernandes v Portugal* and *Elena Cojocaru v Romania* are judgments in point. The Court observed that it would not speculate on the particular patient's prospects for survival if the measures required by the medical protocols had been actually undertaken. It sufficed for the establishment of state responsibility that there was 'apparent lack of coordination of the medical services and ... delay in administering the appropriate emergency treatment', which 'attest to a dysfunctionality of the public hospital services'.[118] In the reasoning of the majority, this dysfunctionality could be related to non-observance of medical protocols. On the facts, however, it was not entirely clear whether non-compliance with the protocols caused the death of the applicants' relatives. The Court's leniency regarding causality in the above-mentioned two cases prompted Judges Sajó and Tsotsoria to dissent by observing that it is hard to understand 'how an alleged organisational negligence that did not result in death can be construed as the basis of State responsibility for failing to protect life'. In their Joint Dissenting Opinion, they also added that even if there had been a causal relation this is still not enough to find a violation. I will return to this aspect of their argument below, where I address the distinction between incidental and systemic failures. Here it is pertinent to observe that the Grand Chamber in *Lopes de Sousa Fernandes v Portugal* addressed the dissenters' concern by observing that

> the question whether there has been a failure by the State in its regulatory duties calls for a concrete assessment of the alleged deficiencies rather than an abstract one.... Therefore, the mere fact that the regulatory framework may be deficient in some respect is not sufficient in itself to raise an issue under Article 2 of the Convention. It must be shown to have operated to the patient's detriment.[119]

---

[116] *I. v Finland* no 20511/03, 17 July 2008 §44.
[117] *Cyprus v Turkey* [GC] no 25781/94, 10 May 200 §219.
[118] *Lopes de Sousa Fernandes v Portugal* no 56080/13, 15 December 2015 §114 (Chamber judgment); *Elena Cojocaru v Romania* no 74114/12, 22 March 2016 §111.
[119] *Lopes de Sousa Fernandes v Portugal* [GC] no 56080/13, 19 December 2017 §188.

It follows that the Grand Chamber has modified the Chamber's approach. As the above quotation shows, causality needs to be established between the organizational negligence and the condition of the *specific* applicant. This will be further explained in Section 7.1.3. that addresses the different levels of specificity for framing positive obligations.

Using the national regulatory framework as a metric has been applied in other areas of the case law. More specifically, in *A. v Croatia*, a domestic violence case, the failure by the national authorities to implement measures ordered by the national courts was highlighted and led the Court to conclude that the respondent state failed to ensure the victim's right to private life.[120] In *Taskin and Others v Turkey*, the applicant complained that the operation of a gold mine posed risks to their right to life and private life. The respondent government challenged the assertion that the operation of the mine had harmful effects, and in this sense scientific uncertainty permeated the facts. The Court did not find it necessary to engage with the issue as to whether the operation of the mine was indeed contributory to harm, since this operation was contrary to domestic law.[121]

Certainly, the State might have perfectly complied with the existing national legal and regulatory framework and still have failed to fulfil its positive obligations under the ECHR, since deficiencies in this very framework might be causative to harm.[122] On the other hand, even if a failure to take certain protective measures was contrary to the national law and regulation, this is not in itself conclusive that the State has failed to fulfil its positive obligations under the ECHR. The Court might pursue further enquiries into lines of causation.[123] Domestic legality is thus not a conclusive test.[124] This renders the analysis distinctive in comparison with cases framed as implicating negative obligations, where if a measure restricting the right is not 'in accordance with the

---

[120] *A. v Croatia* no 55164/08, 14 October 2010 §79.
[121] *Taskin and Others v Turkey* no 46117/99, 10 November 2004 (the national authorities did not comply with decisions by the national court ordering the closure of a mine); *Giacomelli v Italy* no 59909/00, 2 November 2006 §93 (the State authorities did not comply with domestic legislation on environmental matters and failed to enforce judicial decisions); *Kalender v Turkey* no 4314/02, 15 December 2009 §§43–47 (relatives of the applicants were killed in an accident at a railway station; the Court found a violation of Article 2 in its substantive aspect in view of the significant number and the seriousness of the breaches of the national safety regulations).
[122] See Section 7.1.2.
[123] See, for example, *Panaitescu v Romania* no 30909/06, 10 April 2012 §36. *Kotilainen and Others v Finland* no 62439/12, 17 September 2020 §§88–89, where the omission to seize the gun subsequently used to kill multiple individuals at a school, was established to be contrary to the domestic law. The Court took note of this illegality, but it also added that 'the seizure of the perpetrator's weapon was a reasonable measure of precaution to take under circumstances where doubts had arisen, on the basis of the information that had come to the attention of the competent authority, as to whether the perpetrator was fit to possess a dangerous firearm'.
[124] See Section 7.1. See eg *Fadeyeva v Russia* no 55723/00, 9 June 2005 §98 (after observing that the domestic legality is not a separate and conclusive test, the Court added that it is 'rather one of many aspects which should be taken into account in assessing whether the State has struck a "fair balance" in accordance with Article 8(2)'). The problem with this approach is that the Court combines various factors, including non-compliance with the national legislation, into the general and very elusive standard of fair balance. This makes it impossible to objectively assess the role of and the weight attached to each individual factor, including non-compliance with domestic legislation.

law', this automatically renders the restriction contrary to human rights law.[125] Still, as clarified above, even in the context of positive obligations, domestic legality plays an important role in shaping lines of causality. In addition, the notion of legality does not only have a substantive aspect which, as explicated above, concerns compliance with domestic regulatory frameworks; it also has a procedural aspect, to which I now turn.

### 3.3.2 Procedural Protection

In various fields of its case law on positive obligations, the ECtHR has added a procedural layer to the scope of the Convention rights by requiring States to ensure the availability of effective national procedures. The rationale behind this move is the proposition that procedural guarantees are instrumental for better protection of the substantive guarantees.[126] The task of this section is not to offer a general analysis of the development of procedural protection by the Court, an issue to which I will return in Chapter 7. The focus here is rather the underlying causality, namely the understanding that the substantive harm is less likely to have materialized had the decision-making process at national level been of sufficient quality. The main argument I advance here is that procedural protection offers an avenue for the Court to deal (or rather not to deal) with empirical and epistemological uncertainty. This uncertainty poses challenges in ascertaining the remoteness or the closeness of the harm sustained by the individual and state omissions; procedural protection resolves the difficulty. The Court can eschew conclusive determinations that certain substantive omissions cause harm, and instead can focus on procedural omissions and deficiencies at national level.

The inclusion of a right to access to information in the environment-related judgments delivered by the Court supports the above argument.[127] In *Roche v United Kingdom* there was uncertainty whether the applicant had been put at risk through his participation in chemical tests. This uncertainty did not have to be resolved because the Court framed its task as considering whether

> a positive obligation arose to provide an 'effective and accessible procedure' enabling the applicant to have access to 'all relevant and appropriate information' which would allow him to assess any risk to which he had been exposed during his participation in the tests.[128]

---

[125] See Section 7.1.
[126] Section 7.2.
[127] *Öneryildiz v Turkey* [GC] no 48939/99, 30 November 2004 §§89–90; *Budayeva and Others v Russia* no 15339/02, 20 March 2008 §132; *Hatton and Others v United Kingdom* [GC] no 36022/97, 8 July 1997 §104. See also K Steyn and H Slarks, 'Positive Obligation to Provide Access to Information under the European Convention on Human Rights' (2012) 17 Judicial Review 308.
[128] *Roche v United Kingdom* [GC] no 32555/96, 19 October 2005 §§161–162.

The Court also added that the applicant's uncertainty 'as to whether or not he had been put at risk through his participation in the test carried out at Porton Down, could reasonably be accepted to have caused him substantial anxiety and stress'.[129] Accordingly, the core issue in the case was shaped not as how the tests themselves contributed to the harm falling within the scope of Article 8 but how the denial of access to information about the tests caused harm falling within the scope of Article 8. These are certainly two distinct, although related, types of harm.

Access to information is only one element for assessing procedural protection. As *Hatton and Others v the United Kingdom* shows, the Court can scrutinize more generally the quality of the national decision-making process.[130] In particular, scientific uncertainty underpinned the case since '[t]he position concerning research into sleep disturbance and night flights is far from static'.[131] No finding on this specific point had to be made at the level of the Strasbourg Court, however, because the national decision-making process was found adequate. No fundamental procedural flaws in the preparation of the night flight scheme at Heathrow airport were found.

## 3.4 Technique for Limiting Responsibility when Causation is Present

Besides avenues for avoiding explicit determinations on causal connections between harm and omissions, argumentative techniques for not finding responsibility even when factual causation might be present can be also discerned in the case law. In particular, the reasonableness standard and the 'real and immediate risk' test might affect and mould the assessment of causation. The intertwinement between these tests and standards will be elaborated upon in Chapter 4, where the standard of reasonableness is under consideration. Here the focus will be on another technique used by the Court for limiting state responsibility for omissions, namely the distinction between incidental and systemic failures. *Mastromatteo v Italy* can illustrate the relevance of this technique. An explanation of the outcome in *Mastromatteo v Italy*, where no violation was eventually found, is that the errors on the part of the national authorities appeared incidental and not systematic.[132] In this sense, it might be considered unreasonable to find Italy responsible under ECHR for isolated errors and omissions even if they might have caused harm. This line of reasoning clearly emerges in the context of Article 2 and healthcare:

---

[129] ibid §161.
[130] *Hatton and Others v United Kingdom* [GC].
[131] ibid §128.
[132] See *Mastromatteo v Italy* [GC] no 37703/97, 24 October 2002 §73, where it was observed that the percentage of crimes committed by prisoners on semi-custodial regime was very low.

> [W]here a Contacting State had made adequate provision to secure high professional standards among health professionals and to protect the lives of patients, it cannot accept that matters such as error of judgment on the part of a health professional or negligent coordination among health professionals in the treatment of a particular patient are sufficient of themselves to call a Contracting State to account from the standpoint of its positive obligations under Article 2 of the Convention to protect life.[133]

As pointed out in the Joint Dissenting Opinion in *Lopes De Sousa Fernandes v Portugal*, the majority had set a standard that casual acts of negligence by members of staff would not give rise to a substantive breach of Article 2. The Grand Chamber judgment in *Lopes De Sousa Fernandes v Portugal* not only unequivocally upheld the principle embodied in the above quotation but it added an additional layer of restrictiveness as compared to the approach by the Chamber in the same case.[134] Any deficiencies that might give rise to a substantive violation of Article 2 in medical cases need not only be systemic or structural (and thus not 'a mere error or medical negligence'), but they must also implicate denial of immediate emergency care.[135]

The suggestion that incidental failures might not afford a basis for state responsibility is reminiscent of another test that has been invoked in the case law, namely the 'significant flaw' test. The Chamber invoked this test in precluding responsibility in *Söderman v Sweden*. In particular, it observed that 'only significant flaws in legislation and practice, and their application, would amount to a breach of a State's positive obligations under the said provision [Article 8]'.[136] Subsequently, however, when the Grand Chamber reviewed *Söderman v Sweden*, it partially rejected the 'significant flaws' test:

> [S]uch a significant-flaw test, while understandable in the context of investigations, has no meaningful role in an assessment as to whether the respondent State had in place an *adequate legal framework* [emphasis in the original] in compliance with its positive obligations under Article 8 of the Convention since the issue before the Court concerns the question whether *the law afforded an acceptable level of protection* to the applicant in the circumstances.[137]

---

[133] *Lopes de Sousa Fernandes v Portugal* [GC] no 56080/13, 19 December 2017 §108; *Elena Cojocaru v Romania* no 74114/12, 22 March 2016 §100. Similar reasoning has been endorsed in other contexts too. See *Stoyanovi v Bulgaria* no 42980/04, 9 November 2010 §61.
[134] As opposed to the Chamber in *Lopes de Sousa Fernandes*, which found a substantive violation of Article 2, the Grand Chamber, did not, in this way overruling the Chamber.
[135] *Lopes de Sousa Fernandes v Portugal* [GC] §§ 182-92. In §§191–192 of the judgment, the Grand Chamber explained the circumstances when 'denial of immediate emergency care' will transpire. These circumstances are framed as 'very exceptional circumstances'.
[136] *Söderman v Sweden* [GC] no 5786/08, 12 November 2013 §50.
[137] ibid §91 (emphasis added).

'Acceptable level of protection' is a standard the Court had never used before.[138] What is also interesting about *Söderman v Sweden* is that no reasonableness standard was even invoked: the Grand Chamber was simply not satisfied that the relevant Swedish law, both criminal and civil, as it stood at the time when the applicant's stepfather covertly attempted to film her naked in their bathroom for a sexual purpose, ensured protection of her right to respect for her private life.[139] In particular, the act of filming was not criminalized.

The approach by the Grand Chamber in *Söderman v Sweden* barely squares with the approach in *Mastromatteo v Italy*, or in fact in other judgments where the issue was whether the national legal and administrative framework was effective and where reasonableness was applied as a factor in the delimitation of the scope of the positive obligation.[140] Can any explanations concerning this inconsistency be found? An overview of the case law shows that when criminal legislation is invoked as a means of ensuring the rights,[141] no test of reasonableness is applied and, in fact, the issue of causation seems to be immaterial. As a consequence, it is simply assumed that criminalization (or an interpretation of the national criminal law so that its reach is more expansive) contributes to the better protection of human rights.[142] In contrast, when legal frameworks other than criminal law are at issue, reasonableness and competing interests are included as factors in the analysis. *Mastromatteo v Italy* exemplifies this, since ultimately the issue in this case was whether the national framework regulating prison leave contained sufficient safeguards to protect the general population from prisoners on leave.

The above-described approach, under which the test of reasonableness is not applied when the issue is whether the national criminal law ensures effective protection, is, however, balanced in the following way. Criminalization, as a means of ensuring human rights, is required only where the harm sustained by the victim meets a certain threshold of severity. This will be the case, for example, where Articles 2, 3, or 4 are found applicable,[143] and where 'fundamental values and essential aspects of private life are at stake'.[144]

In sum, it was relatively easy to reject the 'significant flaw' test in *Söderman v Sweden* because the effectiveness of the criminal law lay at the core of the case. In contrast, the healthcare cases seem to raise more challenging issues related to allocation of resources and medical expertise. These cases might prompt the Court to be more

---

[138] Since *Söderman v Sweden* [GC] no 5786/08, 12 November 2013 the standard has not been applied in other cases either.
[139] *Söderman v Sweden* [GC] §117.
[140] *O'Keeffe v Ireland* [GC] no 35810/09, 28 January 2014 §166.
[141] In *Söderman v Sweden*, the applicant invoked the ineffectiveness of not only the national criminal law remedies, but also of the civil law remedies. However, the civil law remedies were contingent on the criminal law remedies.
[142] See Section 7.1.1.
[143] In the circumstances of unintentional killing, the Court has clarified that absence of a criminal law remedy might not be problematic. See Chapter 6.
[144] *Söderman v Sweden* [GC] no 5786/08, 12 November 2013 §82.

cautious in finding a substantive violation of Article 2, since *inter alia* it might be difficult to assess the causal connections between the alleged inappropriate medical treatment and the harm sustained by the specific person. Perhaps for this reason, many of the cases in this area conclude only with a finding of a procedural violation (ie failure to set up an independent judicial system so that the cause of death of patients in the care of the medical profession can be determined and those responsible held accountable).[145] In this way, the Court avoids engagement with difficult questions of causation. The difficulties in establishing causal connections might also invite the Court to maintain the distinction between systemic and incidental failures. When confronted with information about deficiencies of a more systemic nature, the Court might more readily link the concrete case with these general shortcomings.

## Conclusion

No hard-edged legal tests apply to cases invoking positive obligations under the ECHR. This flexibility is similarly applied to the requirement for causation, that is, the linkage between the harm sustained by the individual applicant and state omissions. While certainty is not required that the interposition of a missing action would have prevented the harm, no general threshold has been articulated as to how likely it is that a protective measure would have averted the harm. The Court also merges issues of knowledge, reasonableness, and causation in its assessment of state responsibility in the framework of positive obligations.

Human rights law is thus far from rigid in the assessment of the linkage between state omissions and harm, an approach that can be understood in light of the objective of this body of law, namely assessing the responsibility of a collective (ie the State). This assessment is underpinned by the assumption that the State is the entity tasked to ensure the rights of the individuals within its jurisdiction. As a consequence, the ECtHR's approach wavers between effective protection of human rights on the one hand and not imposing an unreasonable burden on the State on the other. It meanders between on the one hand, concerns about effective protection of important interests that might require a more intrusive state, and on the other, concerns about possible consequences from a too intrusive state role and other interests that might be protected if restraint were exercised. The establishment of causation is influenced by these considerations, which can be ultimately linked with the distribution of costs and protection within the society. The distribution of social goods and costs depends on a wide framework of decisions, action, practices, and institutions that make

---

[145] See Section 6.2. For example *Belenko v Russia* no 25435/06, 18 December 2014 §§84–85; *Burzykowski v Poland* no 11562/05, 27 June 2006 §118; *Dodov v Bulgaria* no 59548/00, 17 January 2008 §98; *Kudra v Croatia* no 13904/07, 18 December 2012 §§106–121; *Bilbija and Blazevic v Croatia* no 62870/13, 12 January 2016 §119.

distribution possible. Within this framework, the identification of which decision is ultimately and definitively responsible and which is not, cannot be a 'coherent idea'.[146]

Still, it would not be satisfactory to simply say that the standard of causation applied oscillates between effectiveness and reasonableness and between intrusiveness and restraint. Analytical rigour demands that we further scrutinize the role of causation in the context of positive obligations. This scrutiny shows that by assuming control over certain activities, the State places itself in closer causal relationships with harm that might arise in relation to these activities even if this harm is not directly attributable to state agents. Control thus implies closer causality and more demanding positive obligations. Paradoxically, in certain areas the absence of sufficient control by the State creates the basis for the finding that the State has failed to fulfil positive obligations. This paradox is perhaps only apparent since these areas are underpinned by the normative assumption that the State should assume control. This shapes the approach to causation by making it less stringent.

Establishing causation between harm and state omission may be fraught with factual and epistemological uncertainty. In these circumstances, a conclusive determination that the nexus between state omission and harm is too attenuated or sufficiently solid to sustain a violation, might be eschewed. Instead, the Court might instead ask whether the omission was contrary to the applicable domestic legal framework. In cases of non-compliance with this framework, the Court is more prepared to find that the omission has contributed to harm. Another avenue for avoiding issues of causality is by focusing on the process at national level leading to a decision that is allegedly contrary to States' positive obligations. If this process is of sufficient quality, the finding of a violation is less likely. The assessment of the quality of the process also includes the availability of procedural guarantees. If these are incorporated at national level, the finding of a violation is also less likely.

Finally, techniques that might limit the finding that the State is responsible have been considered. Although its contours are still uncertain, the distinction between incidental and systemic failures might be one such technique. As a consequence, even if a failure is causative to harm, when the concrete case is representative of a mere incidental failure, no state responsibility might be found. The standard of reasonableness, to which I now turn, might be also determinative and have limiting functions in finding state responsibility for omissions.

---

[146] S Meckled-Garcia, 'Do Transnational Economic Effects Violate Human Rights?' (2009) 2(3) Ethics and Global Politics 259, 265.

# 4
# Reasonableness

## Introduction

As already suggested in Chapter 2, States are not omniscient. It needs to be added that they are not almighty either. Positive obligations need therefore to be interpreted 'in such a way as not to impose an excessive burden on the authorities'.[1] The Court has referred to the requirement of not imposing 'impossible and disproportionate burden'[2] upon the States. It has also framed a standard of reasonableness: States are only expected to undertake 'reasonable steps to prevent ill-treatment of which the authorities had, or ought to have had, knowledge'.[3] In the context of Article 8, the 'fair balance' test has been invoked.[4] No clarifications have been offered in the case law whether excessiveness, disproportionate burden, reasonableness, and 'fair balance' are intended to mean different things. Rather, these standards seem to refer to a similar concern.[5] In particular, the Court has in mind general public interests,[6] including public policy considerations, budgetary concerns,[7] cost-effectiveness and management of resources,[8] some practical obstacles,[9] the multitude of interests that might be affected, and any multidimensional consequences.[10] All these can be

---

[1] *O'Keeffe v Ireland* [GC] no 35810/09, 28 January 2014 §144; *Cevrioğlu v Turkey* no 69546/12, 4 October 2016 §52.
[2] *Budayeva and Others v Russia* no 15339/02, 20 March 2008 §135; *Öneryildiz v Turkey* [GC] no 48939/99, 30 November 2004 §107.
[3] *O'Keeffe v Ireland* §144; *Centre for Legal Resources on behalf of Valentin Campeanu v Romania* [GC] no 47848/08, 17 July 2014, §132.
[4] *López Ribalda and Others v Spain* [GC] no 1874/13 and 8567/13, 17 October 2019 §111.
[5] A Mowbray, 'A Study of the Principle of Fair Balance in the Jurisprudence of the European Court of Human Rights' (2010) 10(2) Human Rights Law Review 289.
[6] Such public interests are indicated in Article 8(2). It has been suggested that these are, however, wider in the context of positive obligations. An example would be the 'general interest of legal certainty'. See *Röman v Finland* no 13072/05, 29 January 2013 §51; *R.L. and Others v Denmark* no 52629/11, 7 March 2017 §40, the Court referred to the general interest of 'legal certainty and finality in family relations'.
[7] For example, *Kapa and Others v Poland*, no 75031/13, 14 October 2021 §163. For how budgetary constraints play a role in the context of positive obligations, see F Bydlinksi, 'Methodological Approaches to the Tort Law of the ECHR' in A Fenyves and others (eds), *Tort Law in the Jurisprudence of the European Court of Human Rights* (De Gruyter 2011) 29 63.
[8] *Öneryildiz v Turkey* [GC] no 48939/99, 30 November 2004§107; *Ilia Petrov v Bulgaria* no 19202/03, 24 April 2012 §64, for the danger of diverting state resources. *R.R. v Poland* no 27617/04, 26 May 2011 §155, where it is suggested that lack of medical equipment or financial resources are relevant consideration in the determination of the scope of the positive obligations.
[9] See *Dodov v Bulgaria* no 59548/00, 17 January 2008 §102.
[10] See *Mosley v United Kingdom* no 48009/08, 10 May 2011 §121 referring to wider negative implication of any pre-notification requirement on reporting and investigative journalism.

factors that compete with the assistance and protection interests of the particular applicant.[11]

It follows, similarly to the conclusions in Chapters 2 and 3, that the establishment of actual or putative knowledge about risk, and of causal links between state omissions and harm, is underpinned by normative considerations, the determination of what can be reasonably expected from the State also implies normative judgments.[12] These might be pulled in different directions by practical considerations, apprehensions about the intrusive role of the State, and considerations of effective protection of competing individual interests as protected by other rights.[13] The standard of reasonableness, the overarching term that will be used in the analysis below, refers to the choices that need to be made in terms of priorities, resources and values in the society.[14] A major normative tension that emerges is the one between the value of protection (of the individual who happened to be an applicant before the European Court of Human Rights (ECtHR) claiming that the State has failed to protect him/her) on the one hand, and the value of freedom from intrusiveness and distribution of resources for other purposes (other than protection as invoked by the applicant) on the other.

It is difficult to frame these priorities concretely in the context of the specific judgment. This might explain why the Court often mentions the test of reasonableness in passing, and it is ultimately hard to assess its importance. Sometimes, reasonableness is simply mentioned at the end of the judgment, and one is left to wonder how it is linked with the preceding analysis. In some judgments, various factors are invoked in assessing the reasonableness of the concrete positive obligation without elaboration as to the weight ascribed to each, and the relationship between the different factors. It seems thus that any consideration can be made relevant for assessing reasonableness, and at the same time, anything can be left out too. Often no explanation is offered

---

[11] See T Hickman, 'The Reasonableness Principle: Reassessing its Place in the Public Sphere' (2004) 63 Cambridge Law Journal 166. For example, in *Z. and Others v the United Kingdom* [GC] no 29392/95, 10 May 2001 §74, the Court referred to 'the important countervailing principle of respecting and preserving family life', which implies that the positive obligations under Article 3 cannot extend to the unreasonable limit of splitting families by taking children into care so that these children can be protected. In the context of Article 8, the legitimate aims framed in Article 8(2) 'may be of certain relevance' in the assessment of any public interests that might compete with the individual interests. See also *Maurice v France* [GC] no 11810/03, 6 October 2005 §114. The public interests might be, however, more widely construed than what the test of Article 8(2) explicitly indicates. See *Hristozov and Others v Bulgaria* no 47039/11, 13 November 2012 §122.

[12] This corresponds to the view that '[t]here is no risk which can even be described without reference to a value.' A Giddens, 'Risk and Responsibility' (1999) 62(1) Modern Law Review 1, 5.

[13] This justifies the concern originally expressed by Judge Wold in his Party Dissenting Opinion in *Case 'Relating to Certain Aspects of the Laws on the Use of the Languages in Education in Belgium' v Belgium* no 1474/62, 23 July 1968: 'And even worse is the interpretation by the majority that the Convention "implies a just balance between the protection of the general interest of the community and the respect due to fundamental human rights". I strongly disagree with this interpretation. In my opinion it carries the Court into the very middle of the internal political question of each Member State, which it has never been the intention that the Court should deal with.'

[14] See Section 7.1.3.2 that addresses the technical role of the standard of reasonableness in the Court's reasoning.

as to the relevance or irrelevance of considerations. Some considerations and factors relevant in the reasonableness standard might also be deduced only implicitly from the reasoning. The standard can be thus characterized as fluid and flexible, hence the difficulty in defining public interests and relating them conceptually with individual rights.[15]

Despite this obscurity, which is in a way justifiable due to the variety of concrete factual circumstances that might arise in different cases,[16] the diversity of priorities and interests in the concrete society and the uncertainty in the ways in which individuals might be effectively protected, some important principles are discernible in the case law. The first is the intertwinement between the assessments of the factors of state knowledge and causation, on the one hand, and standard of reasonableness on the other (Section 4.1). The second is the contingency of the reasonableness standard on the appreciation of alternative measures of protection (Section 4.2), which in turn can be affected by the margin of appreciation applied (Section 4.3). Finally, an important consideration that shapes the reasonableness standard is the relevance of obligations (that can be both negative and positive) corresponding to human rights that might compete with positive obligations. The State might thus face a situation of competing obligations, which raises a whole set of difficulties that will be addressed in Chapter 5.

## 4.1 Intertwinement with Knowledge and Causation

What constitutes reasonable steps in the particular circumstances of the case can be intertwined with considerations about the level and nature of state knowledge about risks of harm and about the causal links between the harm and any omissions by the State.[17] It might be therefore difficult to separate the test of reasonableness and the factors of knowledge and causation. Harm about which the State has comprehensive knowledge, and that might thus be more foreseeable,[18] might call for more protective interventions; accordingly, the test of reasonableness might be applied in a more

---

[15] For a useful outline of this difficulty see A McHarg, 'Reconciling Human Rights and the Public Interest: Conceptual problems and Doctrinal Uncertainty in the Jurisprudence of the European Court of Human Rights' (1999) 62 Modern Law Review 671. For the multidimensional relationship between human rights and public interests, see also R Alexy, 'Individual Rights and Collective Goods' in C Nino (ed), *Rights* (Dartmouth 1992) 169; J Waldron, 'Can Communal Goods be Human Rights?' (1987) 28(2) European Journal of Sociology 296.

[16] The Court has developed some general principles that can guide the balancing of relevant interests in relation to different cluster of cases. Examples include cases concerning limitations on the institution of paternity claims (*Boljevic v Serbia* no 47443/14, 16 June 2020) or cases concerning deportation of family member (*Nunez v Norway* no 55597/09, 28 June 2011).

[17] For a critique of the argument that these elements are intertwined, see L Lavrysen, 'Causation and Positive Obligations under the European Convention on Human Rights: A Reply to Vladislava Stoyanova' (2018) 18 Human Rights Law Review 705. The weakness of this critique is that it is based on certain distinctions in tort law that are not followed in the ECtHR's reasoning.

[18] *Budayeva and Other v Russia* no 15339/02, 20 March 2008 §136–137; *Kolyadenko and Others v Russia* no 17423/05, 28 February 2012 §161.

relaxed way to the benefit of providing more protection. Harm which is more predictable and more immediate might also imply a stronger protection claim.[19] Harm that is more difficult to causally link to state omissions and knowledge about risks might imply less demanding positive obligations upon the State, since it might not be reasonable to expect from the State to act.

## 4.1.1 Weak Causation Counterbalanced by the Reasonableness Standard

How might the reasonableness standard more concretely affect and mould the assessment of causation? *Vilnes and Others v Norway*, for example, suggests that even if the lines of causation between state omissions and harm are tenuous, reasonableness might intervene and buttress a finding of a violation. This case is thus an example where quite wide-ranging assumptions about causal relationships were made,[20] which seems to be counterbalanced by the reasonableness of undertaking protection measures by the State. It thus merits more detailed examination. The applicants, who worked as divers in the North Sea for private companies, complained that Norway did not adopt an effective legal framework of safety regulations to prevent the divers' lives and health being put at risk. While dismissing most of the divers' allegations, the ECtHR still found a failure on behalf of Norway. The underlying reason was that the companies were left with little accountability vis-à-vis the state authorities in relation to the usage of diving tables, which were treated as company business secrets.[21] In other words, Norway allowed a situation in which the divers were not informed about the health and life-related risks pertaining to the usage of diving tables.

There are two types of causality underpinning *Vilnes and Others v Norway* that have to be separated and further clarified. The first relates to the extent to which the rapid decompression tables did in fact contribute to the applicants' medical problems. The standard for assessing this contribution was formulated in the following way by the Court:

> The Court, having regard to the parties' arguments in the light of the material submitted, finds a *strong likelihood* that the applicants' health had significantly deteriorated as a result of decompression sickness, amongst other factors. This state of affairs *had presumably been caused* by the use of too-rapid decompression tables.... Thus, with the hindsight at least, it seems *probable* that had the authorities intervened to forestall the use of rapid decompression tables earlier, they would

---

[19] See Section 7.3, where an argument is formulated that what distinguish the positive obligation of taking protective operational measures that implies intrusive measures against a specific individual, is precisely the immediacy of the harm.
[20] *Vilnes and Others v Norway* no 52806/09, 5 December 2013 §§233–244.
[21] Diving tables relate to the planning and the monitoring of the decompression.

have succeeded in removing more rapidly what appears to have been a major cause of excessive risk to the applicants' safety and health in the present case.[22]

However, as the Court framed the case, the core issue was not that the State had not prevented the use of rapid decompression tables *as such* or that it had not prevented their use earlier. As the Court alluded in the above citation, the conclusion that elimination of the tables would have reduced the risk can be reached only with the benefit of hindsight. At the material time in the past, it was widely believed that diving did not have serious long-term effects in the absence of decompression sickness. A procedural duty was rather placed at the heart of the case, namely the duty of the State to provide information essential for the divers to assess the health risks. Although the risks associated with diving at that time were still disputed, the *raison d'être* of the decompression tables themselves was to provide information essential for the assessment of risk to personal health.[23] As the Court observed, the authorities were aware that the diving companies kept the tables confidential for competitive reasons.[24] The authorities failed to enlighten the divers about the risks, which in the logic of the judgment would have enabled the divers to give informed consent to the taking of such risks.[25]

In light of the above, a second type of causality was brought forward in the judgment: if the State had ensured that the divers could assess the risks to their health and give informed consent to the risks involved, this would have led to the elimination of the use of the rapid tables. The Court frames this in the following way:

> Had they done so [had the authorities ensured that the companies provide information by not keeping the tables confidential] *they might conceivably have helped* to eliminate sooner the use of rapid tables as a means for companies to promote their own commercial interest, potentially adding to the risks to divers' health and safety.[26]

Two comments are pertinent here: first, the standard of 'conceivably have helped' as a test of causation appears to be very low and has not been used before *Vilnes and Others v Norway*. Second, the reasoning in the above quotation leads to contradictions within the judgment. Given the absence of clear expert understanding at the time of the consequences of using decompression tables, as in fact acknowledged by the Court itself, it is hard to maintain that if the divers themselves had had access to the tables, this information would have been of use and led them to change their behaviour.

---

[22] *Vilnes and Others v Norway* no 52806/09, 5 December 2013 §233 (emphasis added).
[23] ibid §240.
[24] ibid §238.
[25] ibid §243.
[26] ibid §244 (emphasis added).

The above analysis is not to suggest that the State was not at fault. The wrong that can be clearly imputed to the State is that it allowed the companies to treat the decompression tables as their business secret and keep them confidential for competitive reasons. How that wrong can be linked with the harm sustained by the particular applicants so that this harm can be translated into international responsibility under the European Convention on Human Rights (ECHR), however, is a separate question. In its response to this question, the Court appeared to be very flexible when assessing causation. Admittedly, this seems to have been counterbalanced with the understanding that it is not reasonable to allow business secrets in relation to issues that raise controversies as to their impact on human health. In other words, it would not have been anything close to an unreasonable burden on the State to demand disclosure of the tables.

## 4.1.2 Strong Causation Counterbalanced by the Reasonableness Standard

Attention to the other end of the spectrum is also warranted. At that end, even if there is clear factual causality between state conduct and harm, the reasonableness standard can influence the determination whether the respondent State is responsible for any omissions and tilt it in favour of no violation. *Mastromatteo v Italy* is illustrative in this respect. A brief summary of the facts is apposite here. The applicant's son was murdered by a gang of criminals. The murder was carried out at a time when the criminals were on special prison leave or benefiting from a regime of semi-liberty. It was undisputed that if the State had not released the criminals, Mastromatteo would not have been murdered. In this sense, one can see a clear causation: failure by the State to keep them in prison resulted in severe harm. The Court, however, observed that

> a mere condition *sine qua non* does not suffice to engage the responsibility of the State under the Convention; it must be shown that the death of A. Mastromatteo resulted from a failure on the part of the national authorities to 'do all that could reasonably be expected of them to avoid a real and immediate risk to life of which they had or ought to have had knowledge', the relevant risk in the present case being a risk to life for members of the public at large rather than for one or more identified individuals.[27]

The Court went on to examine the decision of the national authorities to let the criminals on leave and concluded that

---

[27] *Mastromatteo v Italy* [GC] no 37703/97, 24 October 2002 §74.

there was nothing in the material before the national authorities to alert them to the fact that the release of M.R. or G.M. would pose *a real and immediate threat to life*, still less that it would lead to the tragic death of A. Mastromatteo as a result of the chance sequence of events which occurred in the present case.[28]

In light of the benefits associated with rehabilitation programmes for prisoners, the judgment suggests that it would not have been reasonable to keep M.R. and G.M. in prison when the State did not know that they posed 'real and immediate' risk to harm. The Court thus took note of broader considerations related to reasonableness and the interest of others,[29] namely the benefits associated with letting prisoners on leave for the purpose of social reintegration.

## 4.1.3 Reasonableness and Immediacy of the Risk

Having illustrated how the reasonableness standard interacts with causation and in this way affects the assessment of responsibility, I can proceed to explain the intertwinement between the standard and the factor of state knowledge. The focus can be directed to the role of the 'real and immediate risk' test and how it relates to reasonableness.[30] As explained in Chapter 2, this test is relevant for triggering the positive obligation of taking protective operational measures, since it is required that the State knew or should have known about dangers for a *specific identifiable* individual.[31] This requirement of specificity and identifiability of the victim is warranted, given that it might be unreasonable to expect the authorities to take protective operation measures of an ad hoc nature without some imminence and concreteness of the risk to which a particular individual is exposed. In other words, it would be unreasonable to expect the State to take such measures in relation to an indeterminate group of people.

This can be contrasted with situations where the applicant, who happens to be a representative victim, challenges some general deficiencies in the national regulatory framework and where there is no immediate danger to any specific individual.[32] These situations might call for an obligation upon the State to put in place a general legislative and administrative framework for regulating activities so that harm is prevented. In the assessment of breach of this obligation, the causality between any deficiencies and harm might be given more prominent role (ie more demanding causality standard), which can be offset by the absence of immediacy of the harm. In

---

[28] ibid §76 (emphasis added).
[29] For a useful outline of the interests involved see Partly Dissenting Opinion of Judge Bonello in *Mastromatteo v Italy* [GC] §7.
[30] *Osman v United Kingdom* [GC] no 23452/94, 28 October 1998 §116.
[31] See also Section 7.3.
[32] There are judgments where the Court is very clear about the distinction between circumstances calling for protective operational measures and circumstances requiring general protection of the society. See *Bljakaj and Others v Croatia* no 74448/12, 18 September 2014 §124; *Stoyanovi v Bulgaria* no 42980/04, 9 November 2010 §§59–62; *Mikhno v Ukrain* no 32514/12, 1 September 2016 §126.

comparison, when the positive obligation of taking protective operational measures is triggered, the immediacy of the harm, or the risk of harm, might warrant a more relaxed approach to causation.

The current uncertainty as to the meaning of 'immediate' risk, however, and the threshold of immediacy required, spreads confusion in the case law.[33] The reason for this confusion is not simply the Court's inadequate stringency in the application of the standards, a point already intimated in Chapter 2. There are also broader considerations that need to be seriously considered. In particular, if the State were to take protective actions against any potential risk *regardless of its immediacy*, then we might be confronted with the problem of a too intrusive state. This is a general dilemma that surfaces in the context of positive obligation. It calls for caution when expanding the scope of the positive obligation of putting in place general legislative and administrative framework for regulating activities so that harm is prevented. On a related point, we as a society might have to accept certain levels of risk,[34] and this might militate against expansive construction of positive obligations. This is an argument that bulwarks the proposition that even in cases of clear factual causality, responsibility for omissions should not be found because society has to tolerate and accept certain risks. It needs to be thus openly acknowledged that a possible danger flowing from positive obligations is the encouragement of policies of risk aversion and pre-emptive actions aimed to avert or protect from risks. The challenge that needs to be confronted then is how to delimit positive obligations to resist intrusiveness justified by risk aversion.

## 4.1.4 The Importance and the Justifiability of the Analytical Distinctions

Despite the intertwinement between the standards of reasonableness, state knowledge, and causation, analytical clarity demands their separation and an awareness of their distinct roles.[35] In some circumstances it would make little sense to enquire what measures could have been reasonably taken to prevent harm if the State authorities did not know about the risk of such harm in the first place.[36] In other

---

[33] See Party Concurring and Partly Dissenting Opinion of Judge Sajó in *Banel v Lithuania* no 14326/11, 18 June 2013 (death of a boy after collapse of a roof). See also Section 7.3 for detailed explanations how the *Osman* test has been modified in the case law.

[34] The issue of acceptable level of risk has come to a head in the context of home births and state-imposed regulations as to the conditions under which women can give birth: see Dissenting Opinion of Judges Sajó, Karakas, Nicolaou, Laffranque, and Kellder in *Dubská and Krejzová v The Czech Republic* [GC] nos 28859/11 and 28473/12, 15 November 2016 §29.

[35] See I Plakokefalos, 'Causation in the Law of State Responsibility and the Problem of Overdetermination: In Search of Clarity' (2015) 26(2) European Journal of International Law 471, 478, where the author concludes that more generally in international law, knowledge about harm and foreseeability of harm are presented as causation, and the different elements of causation, knowledge, and foreseeability are not sufficiently clearly distinguished.

[36] *Van Colle v the United Kingdom* no 7678/09, 13 November 2012 §96, where the Court determined that the harm was not foreseeable in the first place. See also *Hiller v Austria* no 1967/14, 22 November 2016 §53.

circumstances, if the State could foresee concrete risks of harm with greater precision, then it is more reasonable to expect it to take protective measures. If the nature of the risk of harm is vaguer and its precise origins more difficult to foresee, then it might be less reasonable to impose positive obligations. There might also be circumstances where even if the State had taken measures, it is questionable whether these could have prevented the harm the specific victim complains of. This might point to an absence of causality between the harm and any omissions by the State.[37]

The analytical distinction between the standards of reasonableness, state knowledge, and causation is all the more important given the challenge of how to resist intrusive positive obligations seen as warranted by the need to avert risk. This challenge can be confronted by better awareness as to how intrusive measures are justified. Are they justified based on the knowledge about harm or the risk of harm? How conclusive or inconclusive is this knowledge? How immediate is the harm? Are intrusive measures justified since they are expected to cause reduction in the risk of harm? How stable is this causality? Even if stable, is it still reasonable to undertake these measures since, for example, they themselves might create other forms of risks for other individuals or groups in the society? The analytical distinction between the standards of reasonableness, state knowledge, and causation, can help us in formulating and isolating such questions.

## 4.2 Consideration of Alternative Protective Measures

The above-discussed intertwinement between reasonableness, knowledge, and causation, and the related flexibility in the determination of breach of positive obligations, is demonstrative of the fluid and adjustable structure of review followed by the ECtHR. The absence of strict correlation between the right and the corresponding positive obligations, as already noted in Chapter 1, also explains this fluidity and adjustability. This absence implies that an omission by the State has no definitive counterpart. There is only a range of reasonable measures and alternatives that might be possible to advance as actions to ensure the right. In the context of the concrete case, this range is proposed so that the alleged omission can become knowable and cognizable. Notably, what is reasonable to expect from the State, and how to strike a 'fair balance' between different interests in the society, cannot be assessed without consideration of this possible range of alternative measures. It follows that whenever the reasonableness of a measure is at issue, the availability of alternative measures and their assessment is germane. This is also crucial for averting the danger of overreach of positive obligations: the existence of alternatives presupposes that there might be measures that sufficiently serve the purpose of fulfilling positive obligations, and at

---

[37] For example, *L.C.B. v United Kingdom* no 14/1997/798/1001, 9 June 1998 §40.

the same time serve other interests, including leaving intact or causing less damage to other human rights and public policy concerns.

In this context, the Court has made the important clarification that

> the choice of means for ensuring the positive obligations under Article 2 is in principle a matter that falls within the Contracting State's margin of appreciation. There are a number of avenues for ensuring Convention rights, and even if the State has failed to apply one particular measure provided for by domestic law, it may still fulfill its positive duty by other means.[38]

Similarly, in relation to Article 3, the ECtHR has stated that it is not its role 'to replace the national authorities and to choose instead of them from among the wide range of possible measures that could be taken to secure compliance with their positive obligations'.[39] Likewise, in the context of Article 8 it has been reiterated that States have different ways and means of meeting their positive obligations.[40] The consistent pronouncement by the Court in relation to cases reviewed under Article 2 that 'it is sufficient for an applicant to show that the authorities did not do *all* that could be reasonably expected of them to avoid a real and immediate risk to life of which they have or ought to have knowledge'[41] does not undermine the discretion that the State has in choosing measures of protection. The reference to '*all* that could be reasonably expected' could imply that if the application can point to one single measure that the State could have done, the latter would be found responsible for the omission. The addition, however, of the qualified 'reasonably expected' affirms that the State has a choice and a failure to fulfil any specific measure does not necessarily lead to a finding of a violation.[42]

Despite the discretion of the State in choosing measures, the analysis of responsibility for breach of positive obligations has to include considerations of what protective measures could have been undertaken, or what measures alterative to the ones actually performed could have been undertaken,[43] otherwise it is difficult to

---

[38] *Cevrioglu v Turkey* no 69546/12, 4 October 2016 §55; *Fadeyeva v Russia* no 55723/00, 9 June 2005 §96; *Budayeva and Others v Russia* no 15339/02, 20 March 2008 §§134–135; *Öneryildiz v Turkey* [GC] no 48939/99, 30 November 2004 §107; *Kolyadenko and Others v Russia* no 17423/05, 28 February 2012 §160; *Lambert and Others v France* [GC] no 46043/14, 5 June 2015 §146.

[39] *Eremia v the Republic of Moldova* no 3564/11, 28 May 2013 §50; *Bevacqua and S. v Bulgaria* no 71117/01, 12 June 2008 §82.

[40] *Hatton and Others v United Kingdom* [GC] no 36022/97, 8 July 2003 §123; *Valiuliene v Lithuania* no 33234/07, 26 March 2013 §85; *Bărbulescu v Romania* [GC] no 61496/08, 5 September 2017 §113.

[41] *Opuz v Turkey* no 33401/02, 9 June 2009 §130 (emphasis added); *A. and B. v Romania* nos 48442/16 and 48831/16, 2 June 2020 § 117. Similar pronouncement has been used in cases involving Article 8. *Pavel Shishkov v Russia* no 78754/13, 2 March 2021 §76: 'The key consideration is whether those authorities have taken *all necessary steps* to facilitate contact as can reasonably be demanded in the special circumstances of each case' (emphasis added).

[42] The Court has observed that 'any presumed threat to life does not oblige the authorities, under the Convention, to take concrete measures to prevent its occurrence'. *Fabris et Parziale v Italy* no 41603/13, 19 March 2020 §75.

[43] For example, *Kurt v Austria* [GC] no 62903/15, 15 June 2021 §192 where the applicant complained about the choice of the measures taken by the authorities to protect her son's life.

perceive and assess an omission as a basis for responsibility. This perception and assessment raise a whole gamut of difficult conceptual questions. First, alternatives could be framed at different levels of abstraction and concreteness (Section 4.2.1). Second, variations can be also observed in the case law as to where in the reasoning of the judgment the alternative is formulated and how it is formulated (Section 4.2.2). Third, variations can be also detected as to the expected standard of protectiveness (ie how much more protective are these alternatives expected to be, in comparison with the measures actually undertaken by the State, if such were in fact undertaken?). This third question is related to the scope of the positive obligation, that is, how demanding should it be to be considered reasonable? (Section 4.2.3) A fourth question, that is more of a procedural nature, is how intense a scrutiny the Court should adopt in searching for and assessing alternatives. The level of scrutiny can be linked with the margin of appreciation doctrine understood as structural deference (ie the principle of subsidiarity) (Section 4.3).

The Court has not systemically, consistently, and explicitly tackled these questions in its judgments. The relevance of all of them, however, can be implicitly identified in the reasoning. Below, I will offer illustrations emerging from different judgments and try to assess the implications from the different ways in which the Court has approached the questions.

## 4.2.1 Levels of Abstraction/Concreteness and the Burden of Proof

As mentioned in Chapter 1, Articles 2 and 3 of the ECHR trigger positive obligations as a matter of principle: once the definitional threshold is passed, these obligations are automatically set in motion. They can be categorized into different types, each of them having particular implications that will be explained in Chapters 6 and 7. The triggering of the *general* obligation to protect necessarily implies that there is a *specific* positive obligation the State has to fulfil (ie a specific measure or range of measures that the State has to undertake) and the related expectation that the State explains what protective measures it has taken. This can be linked to the importance of the rights at stake and the imposition of a burden on the State to show that it has actually taken measures.

At this juncture, the issue as to the burden of proof merits some elaboration: who has the burden to propose the alternatives and to explain that the concrete measures actually taken in terms of content and scope were adequate or not? The Court has not explicitly addressed the issue. It can, however, be observed from the reasoning that the applicant will have to come forward with a *prima facie* case that there are more protective measures that the State could have undertaken, and these will have to be tested against alternatives (including inactions) as supported by the State.[44] Placing

---

[44] See eg *Dordevic v Croatia* no 41526/10, 24 July 2012, where the measures proposed by the Court which could have been taken were very much the same as those proposed by the applicant.

the burden on the applicant to bring forward alternative measures is understandable given that it is an omission that is at the heart of the analysis. The omission becomes knowable when harm materializes and when measures that could have prevented the harm are identified. Once the applicant discharges the burden to forward alternatives, the Court expects the State to provide an explanation as why such alternative measures were not taken.[45]

The general positive obligation to protect as formulated under Articles 2 and 3, has a very open-ended nature and is formulated at a very high level of abstraction. In contrast, the definitive positive obligation is tailored to the specific case. The available measures that can be undertaken to ensure the right thus shrink in relation to the specific case and the arguments of the parties.[46] When the scope of this specific obligation is determined, alternatives have to be weighed, and general and competing interests taken into account.[47]

The analytical distinction between the general positive obligation and the specific one is not clear cut, since it depends on the level of abstraction. In its judgments, the Court formulates concrete positive obligations with different levels of abstraction. Some illustrations can be offered here. In *Öneryildiz v Turkey*, the concrete obligation was framed as to whether the safety regulations in force in Turkey regarding the operation of household-refuse tips and the rehabilitation and clearance of slum areas were sufficient.[48] In *Budayeva and Others v Russia*, the concrete obligation was framed pursuant to the proposal of the applicants as to the alternative protective measures that should have been taken: maintenance of mud-protection engineering facilities and warning infrastructure.[49] In *Budayeva and Others v Russia*, all the suggested measures were in fact envisioned by the national land-planning and emergency relief policies, so the general theoretical problem about the indeterminacy of the measures for ensuring rights was to a certain extent resolved.[50]

As opposed to Articles 2 and 3, the structure of analysis under Article 8 is framed in such a way that no *prima facia* positive obligations are necessarily triggered, as already

---

[45] See *Nencheva and Others v Bulgaria* no 48609/06, 18 June 2013 §124, where the Court emphasized that Bulgaria did not come forward with any explanation as to why it had not taken any measures to prevent the death of the mentally disabled children. *Centre for Legal Resources on behalf of Valentin Campeanu v Romania* [GC] no 47848/08, 17 July 2014 §140, where Romania failed 'to fill in the gaps relating to the lack of relevant medical documents describing Mr Campeanu's situation prior to his death, and the lack of pertinent explanations as to the real cause of his death'. The absence of such explanations can lead to adverse findings. In *Budayeva v Russia* §156, the Court observed that the State is expected to come forward and assert whether it had envisioned 'other solutions to ensure the safety of the local population'.
[46] *Frick v Switzerland* no 23405/16, 30 June 2020 §90-1 where the applicant identified multiple omissions in relation to the failure of the authorities to prevent the suicide of her son while in detention. The Court chose to focus on the omission to equip the cell with video surveillance.
[47] See also Section 7.1.3.1, where three levels of concreteness in the framing of the obligations are identified and addressed. In this Section 4.2.1, the focus is on the third level and on the formulation of the concrete obligation and possible alternatives in this formulation.
[48] *Öneryildiz v Turkey* [GC] no 48939/99, 30 November 2004 §97.
[49] *Budayeva and Others v Russia* no 15339/02, 20 March 2008 §146.
[50] *Budayeva and Others v Russia* §§136–137.

mentioned in Chapter 1.[51] As a consequence, the formulation of a positive obligation (if one is found to generally exist) tends to be more concrete, and to be initially focused on the concrete factual circumstances of the concrete case. In this way, the Court avoids making general structural determinations, as the one consistently made under Articles 2 and 3, that the positive obligations under these provisions 'must be construed as applying in the context of any activity, whether public or not, in which the right to life may be at stake',[52] and requires States 'to take measures designed to ensure that individuals within their jurisdiction are not subjected to torture or inhuman or degrading treatment, including by private individuals'.[53] It instead tailors its findings as much as possible to the specific case under Article 8 and in this way can possibly maintain more space for manoeuvre for future cases. Such space can be justified in light of the indeterminate and wide definitional scope of 'private life'.[54] As to the burden of proof, similarly to what was mentioned above, the expectation is that the applicant has to propose what protective measures the State should have taken.[55]

## 4.2.2 Place and Formulation of the Alternative

Despite the different analytical structure under Articles 2 and 3 as opposed to Article 8, a general pattern can be identified in the case law as to the place and the formulation of the concrete positive obligation (ie the specific content of the obligation: the concrete measures that the State should have arguably undertaken). Three approaches can be delineated as to where in the reasoning of the judgment the alternative is formulated and how it is formulated. First, when the concrete measure that the State should have undertaken is formulated in the beginning of the analysis, and then an assessment is made whether it has been fulfilled. Second, the concrete measure is framed in the beginning, but in a vaguer way by reference to qualifying terms, such as effectiveness, adequacy, and sufficiency. Third, the Court sometimes does not even

---

[51] There are areas in the case law, where the Court has not eschewed the formulation of a general positive obligation under Article 8. For example, it has held that 'Article 8 includes for parents a right that steps be taken to reunite them with their children and an obligation on the national authorities to facilitate such reunion'. *Kuppinger v Germany* no 62198/11, 15 April 2015 §100. See also *Shishkov v Russia* no 78754/13, 2 March 2021 §76. It also needs to be acknowledged that there are judgments where the Court avoids the questions whether Article 8 is applicable, and whether it generally triggers positive obligations. For example, in *Draon v France* [GC] no 1513/03, 21 June 2006 §§110–111, the Court simply observed that irrespective of the answers to these questions, the situation that the applicant complained of does not constitute a breach of Article 8.
[52] *Center for Legal Resources v Romania* [GC] no 47848/08, 17 July 2014 §130.
[53] *E. and Others v the United Kingdom* no 33218/96, 26 November 2002 §88; *Z. and Others v United Kingdom* [GC] no 29392/95, 10 May 2001 §73.
[54] *Hudorovič and Others v Slovenia* no 24816/14 and 25140/14, 10 March 2020 §§116–117, where the Court left open the question whether failure to ensure access to clean water and sanitation to member of Roma communities, falls within the definitional scope of Article 8. This question was joined with the question whether the State has failed to fulfil any positive obligations in this context.
[55] *Hudorovič and Others v Slovenia* §154: 'The Court further notes that the applicants failed to explicitly address the issue of what measures should have been adopted by the State to constitute compliance with its obligation to provide access to basic public utilities.'

frame the concrete positive obligation until the very end of its reasoning, where it concludes whether a fair balance has been struck or whether the conduct of the State was reasonable. The last approach appears to imply the most unpredictability as to the outcome of the judgment.

### 4.2.2.1 Initial formulation of the alternative

The following judgments illustrate the first approach, where the Court frames the concrete positive obligation in the beginning of its analysis and *then* assesses compliance. In *Iliya Petrov v Bulgaria* the concrete positive obligations were initially and specifically framed in the following way: 'the State has the obligation to mark electric facilities with high voltage. The Court has to assess whether the Bulgarian authorities have established adequate regulation regarding this activity'.[56] It then went on to frame the positive obligation at even more concrete level: 'the Court has to assess whether the applicable legislation envisioned regular supervision [over the facilities] for the purpose of taking preventive measures in case of an omission or a signal about omission'.[57]

In *Hämäläinen v Finland*, the concrete obligation was framed as to whether the State had to 'provide an effective and accessible procedure allowing the applicant to have her new gender legally recognized while remaining married'.[58] The issue in this case was not the quality of the procedure in terms of its effectiveness and accessibility but whether such a procedure should generally exist in the first place. Likewise, in *A. B. and C. v Ireland*, the Court asked whether 'there is a positive obligation on the State to provide an effective and accessible procedure allowing the third applicant to establish her entitlement to a lawful abortion'.[59] Similarly to *Hämäläinen v Finland*, the problematic issue in *A. B. and C. v Ireland* was the absence of any domestic procedure. In *S.H. and Others v Austria*, the concrete positive obligation was framed as whether the State had 'to permit certain forms of artificial procreation using either sperm or ova from a third party'.[60] In these examples, the finding that there is such a concrete positive obligation amounts to the finding that this obligation has been breached.[61] This means that the determination that the obligation exists (ie that the State was under the obligation to undertake the concrete measure formulated in the beginning of the reasoning) collapses with the determination that the obligation has been breached. This is due to the fact that it is an omission that is at the basis of the determination.

---

[56] *Iliya Petrov v Bulgaria* no 19202/03, 24 April 2012 §57.
[57] ibid §59.
[58] *Hämäläinen v Finland* [GC] no 37359/09, 16 July 2014 §64.
[59] *A. B. and C. v Ireland* [GC] no 25579/05, 16 December 2010 §246.
[60] *S.H. and Others v Austria* [GC] no 57813/00, 3 November 2012 §88; *Oliari and Others v Italy* nos 18766/11 and 36030/11, 21 July 2015 §164.
[61] See also *Mosley v United Kingdom* no 48009/08, 10 May 2011 §118: 'The question for consideration in the present case is whether the specific measure called for by the applicant, namely a legally binding pre-notification rule, is required in order to discharge that obligation [the positive obligation under Article 8].'

### 4.2.2.2 Initial formulation of a qualified alternative

A variation of the above approach can be observed in judgments where the concrete positive obligation is framed in the beginning but contains some qualifying terms. For example, in *Kolyadenko and Others v Russia*, the Court asserted in the very beginning of the judgment that

> the authorities had positive obligations under Article 2 of the Convention to assess all the potential risks inherent in the operation of the reservoir, and to take practical measures to ensure the *effective protection* of those whose lives might be endangered by those risk.[62]

The insertion of qualifying terms like 'effective protection' denotes uncertainty as to the initial standard against which the subsequent analysis is to be gauged. A similar approach is evident in *Söderman v Sweden*, where the Court set its task to examine whether 'Sweden had an *adequate* legal framework providing the applicant with protection against the concrete actions of her stepfather and will, to this end, assess each of the remedies allegedly available to her'.[63] At no point did the Court clarify how adequacy is to be measured. In the absence of more concrete criteria for defining the required adequacy and sufficiency of the protection to be afforded by the legal framework, it is difficult to make a comparison between the existing measures (that might have been undertaken or the absence of any measures) and the undefined adequate measures (that should have been undertaken).[64] It is difficult to formulate the standard against which any omission is to be measured.

### 4.2.2.3 No initial formulation of an alternative

Finally, in other judgments, the Court does not initially frame the concrete positive obligation at all; rather, in abstract terms it determines that States have to build protective frameworks and then it assesses the different alternatives and their reasonableness. For example, in *Dordevic v Croatia* the enquiry was framed as whether 'the relevant authorities took all reasonable steps in the circumstances of the present case to protect the first applicant [who was a disabled child] from such acts [ongoing harassment by children from the neighbourhood and the school]'.[65] This approach emerges also from *Odievre v France*, where the applicant complained that she could not obtain more information about her biological mother. In its reasoning, the Court initially restated the standard assertion that Article 8 may require measures designed

---

[62] *Kolyadenko and Others v Russia* no 17423/05, 28 February 2012 §166 (emphasis added); see also *Öneryildiz v Turkey* [GC] no 78939/99, 30 November 2004 §97.
[63] *Söderman v Sweden* [GC] no 5786/08, 12 November 2013 §89.
[64] This prompted Judge Kalaydjieva to dissent in *Söderman v Sweden* [GC] no 5786/08, 12 November 2013.
[65] *Dordevic v Croatia* no 41526/10, 24 July 2012 §146; *Eremia v The Republic of Moldova* no 3564/11, 28 May 2013 §58; *Sandra Jankovic v Croatia* no 38478/05, 5 March 2009 §46; *A. v Croatia* no 55164/08, 14 October 2010 §61; *T.M. and C.M. v The Republic of Moldova* no 26608/11, 28 January 2014 §45.

to secure private life. These measures were not concretized from the outset in the light of the particular case. At the end, the Court concluded that the French legislation had struck a fair balance without overstepping the margin of appreciation afforded. When this structure of review is applied, it is assumed that the concrete positive obligation has been fulfilled and its scope does not extend so far as to allow granting the applicant access to information about her biological mother.[66] Similarly to the second approach to the structure of review identified above, when this third approach is applied, it is difficult to formulate the standard against which any omission is to be measured. The third approach, however, implies even more uncertainty given the absence of an initial formulation of any standard against which any omission is to be measured. Rather, the whole analysis as to the existence of an obligation, its scope and its content and its breach, seems to collapse into one overall assessment about reasonableness and fair balancing.

### 4.2.3 The Standard of Protectiveness

Not only does the Court structure its reasoning differently in terms of place and way of framing of the concrete measure that could have been undertaken as an alternative to the omission or the measure actually undertaken. It has also refrained from formulating any standard of protectiveness that this concrete measure has to meet. The question then of how much more protective or more effective any alternatives are expected to be, in comparison with the measures actually undertaken by the State, if such were in fact undertaken, has not been directly addressed. This question is related to the scope of the positive obligation: how demanding should it be to be considered reasonable? Rather, as suggested in the previous section, the Court has used such terms as 'adequate' and 'effective' protection, without elaboration of a test under Articles 2, 3, and 8 for actually measuring the effectiveness and adequacy of the alternative measures.[67]

In addition, no discussion is explicitly present in the judgments as to whether the proposed alternative protective measure (that is the content of the positive obligation invoked) will have to serve any competing general societal interests to the same extent

---

[66] *Odievre v France* [GC] no 42326/98, 13 February 2033 §49. See also Joint Dissenting Opinion of Judges Wildhaber, Bratza, Bonello, Loucaides, Barreto, Tulkens, and Pellonoää §6, where it was suggested that the concrete positive obligation should rather have been framed as whether the French legal system itself allowed balancing of competing interests. This suggestion implies that the positive obligation should have been rather framed as one of a procedural nature.

[67] In the context of policing operations where lethal force is used against individuals by state agents, the Court observes that it is difficult to separate positive and negative obligations and examines whether the operation 'was planned and controlled by the authorities so as to minimie, *to the greatest extent possible*, recourse to lethal force and human losses, and whether *all feasible precautions in the choice of means and methods* of a security operation were taken (emphasis added)'. *Finogenov and Others v Russia* no 18299/03, 20 December 2011 §208. In this context, the Court enquires into alternatives for safeguarding life that are more protective and effective 'to the greatest extent possible'. However, this enquiry is restricted to the context of policing operations.

as the measure already undertaken.[68] This implies that the scope of the alternatives is not strictly restricted by this very criterion.[69] The test of reasonableness, however, serves a general limitative function since the alternative protective measure cannot lead to unreasonable burden on the State. Similarly, no discussion is explicitly present in the judgments as to whether the proposed alternative protective measure will have to serve any relevant third parties' interests (that might compete with the applicant's interests to be protected) *equally* well as the measures actually undertaken by the State (measures that, as the applicant argues, were inadequate). The *tolerable degree* of possible injuriousness upon third party interests might vary depending on the nature of protective measures. The question whether any alternative protective measures (as normally proposed by the applicant who claims to have suffered harm due to the omission of taking these alternatives) should be equally or less injurious to third party interests, seems to be subsumed within the reasonableness standard.

## 4.3 Margin of Appreciation

The question as to the standard of expected protectiveness can be linked with the procedural question as to how deep a scrutiny the Court should apply in searching for and assessing alternatives in terms of their protectiveness. This level of scrutiny can be linked with the margin of appreciation doctrine understood as a structural deference (ie the principle of subsidiarity). It is beyond the scope of this book to engage more generally with the margin of appreciation doctrine. The analysis here is restricted to the relevance of the doctrine to the appreciation of alternatives as a crucial part in the assessment of reasonableness.

### 4.3.1 Delineation between Structural Deference and Appreciation of Alternatives

It is first important to introduce a distinction between the implications from the doctrine, on the one hand, and the choice of means for fulfilling positive obligations, on the other. This choice needs to be analytically demarcated from the margin of appreciation doctrine understood as a qualifier to the intensity of review exercised by the ECtHR as an international human rights court. This separation, however, does not mean that the applied intensity of review does not affect the stringency of the inquiry as to the existence of alternatives and as to how protective these should be.

---

[68] Such a criterion has been formulated in the context of national constitutional law. A Barak, *Proportionality. Constitutional Rights and their Limitations* (Cambridge University Press 2012) 433.
[69] Such a limitation is applicable in relation to negative obligations that also presuppose consideration of alternatives via the application of the less intrusive means test. See E Brems and L Lavrysen, '"Don't' Use a Sledgehammer to Crack a Nut": Less Restrictive Means in the Case Law of the European Court of Human Rights' (2015) 15 Human Rights Law Review 139.

The margin of appreciation, in its structural sense, implies that 'the national authorities are better placed to make the assessment of the necessity and proportionality of measures' affecting rights.[70] As a consequence, the Court will not declare 'a violation or will not fully scrutinize decisions made by national authorities for reasons having to do with the status of the ECHR as an international convention'.[71] The margin of appreciation is thus more a matter of who takes the decision rather than what this decision should be on its substance.[72] It is about limiting the intensity of review due to deference.

In practice, however, when the Court defers to the national authorities, it is likely to allow the national decision to stand, which can in turn be interpreted (arguably incorrectly) as if substantively the correct decision has been taken at the national level.[73] The structural restraint exercised by the Court in practice is thus viewed as having substantive repercussions, since it implies in terms of public and political perceptions that the correct balancing between competing interests has been done at national level. In the context of positive obligations, the perception possibly created when the Court defers to the national authorities leading to a finding of no violation is that the best or the only possible protective measure has been taken. Substantively, however, this might not be the case—there might be alternative protective measures that could have been undertaken that serve and accommodate various relevant interests in a better way. Scrutiny of such alternatives, however, might not be performed at the level of the ECtHR due to structural deference.

The margin of appreciation in its structural sense should not be confused with the choice of means for ensuring the rights as required by Article 1 of the ECHR. This choice implies a scope of discretion that is, in fact, *inevitable* even in the context of protection of constitutional rights at the national level.[74] References to margin in this context simply convey the idea that the Court does not dictate what concrete measures need to be taken for ensuring positive obligations. In the practice of the Court, however, this distinction is blurred. The term 'margin' is used as a referent to both, which causes confusion.[75] A reason that might have partially sown the confusion is that the

---

[70] 'ECtHR Background Paper, Subsidiarity: A Two-Sided Coin?' 30 January 2015, §§16–17.
[71] G Letsas, 'Two Concept of the Margin of Appreciation' (2006) 26(4) Oxford Journal of Legal Studies 705, 707.
[72] M Hutchinson, 'The Margin of Appreciation Doctrine in the European Court of Human Rights' (1999) 48(3) International and Comparative Law Quarterly 638, 640.
[73] E Brems, 'Human Rights: Minimum and Maximum Perspectives' (2009) 9 Human Rights Law Review 349, 353: 'the public and political perception of such an ECHR judgment [where the Court finds no violation since it grants a wide margin of appreciation] in practice is that of a Court clearance of a restrictive practice as such'.
[74] R Alexy, *A Theory of Constitutional Rights* (Oxford University Press 2010) 309; R Alexy, 'On Constitutional Rights to Protection' (2009) 3 Legisprudence 1, 5; Barak, *Proportionality* (n 68) 433; K Möller, *The Global Model of Constitutional Rights* (Oxford University Press 2012) 179.
[75] D Xenos, *The Positive Obligations of the State under the European Convention of Human Rights* (Routledge 2012) 64; J Kratochvil, 'The Inflation of the Margin of Appreciation by the European Court of Human Rights' (2011) 29(3) Netherlands Quarterly of Human Rights 324, 334; S Besson, 'Subsidiarity in International Human Rights Law—What is Subsidiary about Human Rights' (2016) 61(1) The American Journal of Jurisprudence 69, 84; G Letsas, 'The Margin of Appreciation Revisited' in A Etinson (ed), *Human Rights: Moral or Political?* (Oxford University Press 2018) 296.

choice of protective means, and the related uncertainty as to what positive obligations require, invites and facilitates the exercise of judicial deference.[76] Accordingly, there is some excuse for this judicial uncertainty. Still, the two meanings of the margin need to be analytically distinguished.

Due to the predominant focus on negative obligations, little discussion has been generated about this distinction in the context of positive obligations. Besides the general perception that the margin of appreciation in positive obligation cases is wider,[77] a more in-depth analysis has not been offered. To remedy this gap, the first question that needs to be asked is: in what way is the margin wider? If 'margin' is understood to refer to the scope of means for ensuring the rights, it might be indeed wider for reasons already explained in Section 1.3, where it was emphasized that there is no one-to-one correction between the right and the corresponding positive obligations, since the latter can be fulfilled through a variety of means. As to the intensity of review, it is questionable whether generally the ECtHR is more deferential in positive obligations cases involving qualified rights. Accordingly, the formulation of the case as a positive obligation case does not necessarily lead to more structural deference.[78]

The second question that needs to be discussed is how the intensity of review by the ECtHR affects the assessment of the scope of the protective measures for ensuring positive rights and the choice of these measures. In the assessment whether adequate and sufficient measures have been taken, the Court can exercise different scrutiny. In this sense, the structural margin of appreciation can affect the stringency of the search for more protective alternative measures. It can also affect the stringency of the assessment as to how protective these measures should be. The intensity of review could be so low that the Court might not even search for more protective alternatives in the first place. In this sense, the structural margin can be perceived as a factor that affects the stringency of the positive obligations. Since the rigour with which the reasonableness and the fair balance tests are applied corresponds to the width of the margin of appreciation,[79] a narrow margin implies more attention to alternatives. It implies a more careful search for more protective measures. It also implies a heavier burden on the State to justify that the undertaking of more protective measures is unreasonable. A wide margin (ie less scrutiny by the ECtHR) implies more superficial enquiry about the availability of alternatives that might better protect the right.

A clarification is immediately due here. Similarly to what was elucidated above (ie the structural margin is more of a matter of who takes the decision rather than what this decision should be on its substance), the stringency of positive obligations per se is not affected by the structural margin. In practice, however, a wide margin and

---

[76] Y Shany, 'Toward a General Margin of Appreciation Doctrine in International Law?' (2006) 16(5) European Journal of International Law 907, 910.
[77] L Lavrysen, *Human Rights in a Positive State* (Intersentia 2016) 214.
[78] For example, *Dubska and Krejzova v the Czech Republic* [GC] nos 28859/11 and 28473/12, 15 November 2016.
[79] Y Arai-Takahashi, *The Margin of Appreciation Doctrine and the Principle of Proportionality in the ECHR* (Intersentia 2002) 204.

limited international scrutiny leading to a finding of no violation of the ECHR, may be received as an *ex post* confirmation of the domestic determination of the stringency of the obligation.[80]

Finally, the structural margin might not figure at all in the Court's reasoning since, for example, a positive measure might be deemed unreasonable independently of the structural margin. At the same time, it also needs to be underscored that the degree of scrutiny exercised by the ECHR cannot constitute a justification for not taking a protective measure or for not taking a more protective measure *at national level*.

## 4.3.2 Scrutiny in the Appreciation of Alternatives

Having introduced the above general clarifications, we can investigate how the standard of expected protectiveness, as linked with the margin of appreciation, is expressed in concrete judgments. In some judgments under Articles 2 and 3, the Court has indeed linked the test of reasonableness and the assessment of alternatives with the margin of appreciation. In *Öneryıldız v Turkey*, it observed that

> an impossible and disproportionate burden must not be imposed on the authorities without consideration being given, in particular, to the operational choices which they must make in terms of priorities and resources; this results from the *wide margin of appreciation* States enjoy, as the Court has previously held, in difficult social and technical spheres such as the one in issue in the instant case.[81]

It is not entirely clear what the function of the margin of appreciation is here, or what it adds to the test of reasonableness and the scope of discretion that States inevitably enjoy in terms of means for fulfilling their positive obligations. In some positive obligations cases under Articles 2 and 3, the Court never refers to the margin[82] nor specifies its scope.[83] It can be therefore safely assumed that the references to margin simply mean diversity of avenues for ensuring Convention rights and not structural deference.

Turning to Article 8 and the question how scrutinizing the Court is in terms of searching for and assessing alternatives in the context of this qualified right, the following illustrations can be provided. In *Hatton v United Kingdom*, after indicating a wide margin, the Court held that its supervisory function 'being of a subsidiary nature, is limited to reviewing whether or not *the particular* solution adopted can be

---

[80] Besson, 'Subsidiarity in International Human Rights Law' (n 75) 85.
[81] *Öneryildiz v Turkey* [GC] no 48939/99, 30 November 2004 §107; *Kolaydenko and Others v Russia* no 17423/05, 28 February 2012 §§160 and 183; *Budayeva and Others v Russia* no 15339/02, 20 March 2008 §§134–135.
[82] *Centre for Legal Resources on behalf of Valentin Campeanu v Romania* [GC] no 47848/08, 17 July 2014.
[83] *Ilbeyi Kemaloglu and Meriye Kemaloglu v Turkey* no 19986/06, 10 April 2012 §37; *Lambert and Others v France* [GC] no 46043/14, 5 June 2015 §144; *Ciechonska v Poland* no 19776/04, 14 June 2011 §65.

regarded as striking a fair balance'.[84] This signals that the Court will not probe into alternatives. This was framed in even clearer terms in *S.H. and Others v Austria*:

> The Court accepts that the Austrian legislature could have devised a different legal framework for regulating artificial procreation that would have made ovum donation permissible. It notes in this regard that this latter solution has been adopted in a number of member States of the Council of Europe. However, the central question in terms of art 8 of the Convention *is not whether a different solution might have been adopted by the legislature that would arguably have struck a fairer balance*, but whether, in striking the balance at the point at which it did, the Austrian legislature exceeded the margin of appreciation afforded to its under that Article.[85]

The implication of the above is that the availability of a different solution that might be more solicitous to individual interests, and even more considerate of general interests, might not lead to a finding that the State has failed to fulfil its positive obligations under the ECHR. There might be a better alternative to ensure the right (without any added costs to competing general interests), but the one already adopted, although not as protective as the first, might suffice against the ECHR standards *as supervised by the ECtHR*.

Arguably, the approach alters with the shift in the level of judicial scrutiny. This is confirmed by the judicial practice, since more protective alternative analysis has not been *explicitly* rejected in judgments where the margin was not been determined to be wide.[86] In these judgments, it can be expected that States still enjoy the inevitable discretion in terms of choosing protective measures. At the same time, however, it can be also anticipated that the assessment whether a 'fair balance' has been struck includes a consideration of more protective measures.

## Conclusion

Reasonableness is a flexible standard since it implies consideration of various factors that might compete with the interests that favour extension of protection in the form of positive obligations. This flexibility is further evident through the intertwinement of the standard with the factors of state knowledge and causation that were reviewed

---

[84] *Hatton and Others v United Kingdom* [GC] no 36022/97, 8 July 2003 §123 (emphasis added). See also *Sandra Jankovic v Croatia* no 38478/05, 5 March 2009 §46; *Kalucza v Hungary* no 57693/10, 24 April 2012 §63, where the Court noted that 'its task is not to take the place of the competent Hungarian authorities in determining *the most appropriate methods* of protecting individuals from attacks on their personal integrity, but rather to review under the Convention the decision that those authorities have taken in the exercise of their power of appreciation' (emphasis added).

[85] *S.H. and Others v Austria* [GC] no 57813/00, 3 November 2011 §106 (emphasis added); *Hristozov and Others v Bulgaria* no 47039/11, 13 November 2012 §125; *Evans v United Kingdom* [GC] no 6339/05, 10 April 2007 §91.

[86] *A., B. and C. v Ireland* [GC] no 25579/05, 16 December 2010 §§249–266.

in Chapters 2 and 3. As a result, these factors and standards can counterbalance themselves in the reasoning, yet awareness of their distinctiveness is recommendable since it can help in resisting too intrusive positive obligations.

When the reasonableness of positive obligations in terms of their content and scope is at issue, it is necessary to assess the availability of alternative protective measures and their level of protectiveness. The assessment of alternatives poses many challenging conceptual questions. This explains the variations in the case law as to the framing of the alternatives, the expected level of their relative protectiveness, and the level of scrutiny in search for alternatives. Yet awareness of these questions and their distinctness, as shown in this chapter, can be important for averting the danger of positive obligations overreach. In particular, the existence of alternatives presupposes that there might be measures that sufficiently serve the purpose of fulfilling positive obligations, while at the same time also serve other (possibly competing) interests. In other words, there might be positive protection measures that leave intact or cause less damage to competing public interests or individual interests that underpin human rights. Competition with individual interests that base human rights raises distinct issues that are in the focus of the next chapter.

# 5
# Competing Obligations

## Introduction

The choice of protective measures is shaped by the multiplicity of interests involved. As already mentioned, the standard of reasonableness in the Court's reasoning implies concern with interests that might compete with interests that favour protection.[1] These competing interests can be the basis of human rights that in turn generate obligations. Positive human rights obligations therefore can compete, and even conflict, with other human rights obligations, both positive and negative. This is important since protection might lead to diversion of resources, potentially in breach of other positive obligations, and unjustifiable forms and levels of intrusiveness and coercion that might be in breach of negative obligations. The latter can be particularly disturbing in light of the tension between obligations that constrain state power (negative obligations) and obligations that mandate state power or demand its more expansive exercise (positive obligations). These tensions are relevant all the time when positive obligations are at stake, although they are not always explicit in the Court's reasoning. The tensions imply that the more the State protects certain interests, the less it might be able to protect and the more it might interfere with other interests.

Some conceptual distinctions are due from the outset. It is important to differentiate between competition of obligations and conflict of obligations. Both imply a disagreement as to how different interests that ground rights should be protected. The latter is, however, narrower since it implies a dilemma and deadlock: a solution cannot be found without sacrificing a core requirement of one or the other right at stake.[2] The rights at stake thus trigger obligations that give rise to *incompatible* actions. In contrast, competition of obligations implies hard choices among different actions for protection of interests that ground rights. The consequences of the choices can be unduly harsh for the individuals involved.[3]

---

[1] An interest-based theory of rights, as expounded in Chapter 1, accepts that interests that underpin rights can and do conflict. L Zucca, *Constitutional Dilemmas* (Oxford University Press 2007) 57. The interests underlying rights can be outweighed by other important considerations, including collective interests. This interest-based model can be contrasted with the model of rights as 'trumps'. For the latter see, R Dworkin, *Taking Rights Seriously* (Duckworth 1977) 193; R Dworkin, 'Rights as Trumps' in J Waldron (ed), *Theories of Rights* (Oxford University Press 1984); R Nozick, *Anarchy, State and Utopia* (Basil Blackwell 1974) ix; H Steiner, *An Essay on Rights* (Blackwell 1994) 199.

[2] Zucca, *Constitutional Dilemmas* (n 1) 57.

[3] A Bhagwhat, 'Hard Cases and the (D)Evolution of Constitutional Doctrine' (1989) 30 Connecticut Law Review 961, 966.

Although the distinction between competition and conflict of obligations is analytically useful to keep in mind, it should not be overstated.[4] Interests that ground rights and the positive obligations owned by the State that correspond to these rights can be framed differently, with different degrees of specification and different known and knowable alternatives. All of these imply that there might be different degrees of competition and tension, some of which might come close to or reach a level where in a *concrete* situation a dilemma and thus a conflict arises.[5]

There is a body of literature on conflict of rights.[6] The scholarly engagement with conflict of rights has not, however, placed sufficient focus on the issue from the specific perspective of positive obligations and the limits that these obligations should be subjected to given tensions and possible conflicts with other obligations (both positive and negative).[7] Yet the existing scholarly debates concerning conflicts of rights have put forward proposals about how conflicts can be addressed that will be used in the forthcoming analysis.

It should also be mentioned that authors have raised awareness about dangers when criminal law and the associated positive human rights obligations to criminalize and to investigate[8] are mobilized to protect against harm.[9] These warnings are legitimate, given the coercion implied in criminal law,[10] which has serious consequences for the individuals who are the objects of this coercion. The anxiety about possible overreach of positive obligations, however, needs to be extended by exploring their intrusive implications not only in the context of criminalization and criminal law enforcement but

---

[4] This can possibly explain why Smet refers to 'purported conflict' of rights. S Smet, 'Conflicts of Rights in Theoretical and Comparative Perspective' in S Smet and E Brems (eds), *When Human Rights Clash at the European Court of Human Rights. Conflict or Harmony?* (Oxford University Press 2017) 1.

[5] *Evans v United Kingdom* [GC] no 6339/05, 10 April 2007, has been referred to as an example of a case where such a dilemma arises (ie denying maternity versus forcing paternity). See J Bomholl and L Zucca, 'The Tragedy of Ms Evans: Conflicts and Incommensurability of Rights' (2006) 2 European Constitutional Law Review 424. However, a different conceptualization of the relevant positive obligation could have avoided framing the case as one of conflict of obligations. For example, the positive obligation could have been conceptualized as developing a procedure at national level so that an assessment is made whether the frozen embryos should be destroyed. This would have avoided the conflict of the interests involved. On the distinction between conflict of interests and of obligations, see S Besson, 'Human Rights in Relation: A Critical Reading of the ECtHR's Approach to Conflicts of Rights' in Smet and Brems (eds) *When Human Rights Clash at the European Court of Human Rights* (n 4) 23, 28: 'some conflicts of rights may be traced back to conflicts of interests, of course, but they need not and even if they can, this is only part of what is at stake in the conflict'. Besson has explained that 'most of the time, conflict of rights are conflicts of duties'. S Besson, *The Morality of Conflict* (Hart Publishing 2005) 432.

[6] S Smet, *Resolving Conflicts between Human Rights. The Judge's Dilemma* (Routledge 2017); E Brems (ed), *Conflicts between Fundamental Rights* (Intersentia 2008); Zucca, *Constitutional Dilemmas* (n 1).

[7] Instead a lot of focus has been placed, for example, on the conflict between freedom of expression and the right to private life and reputation. See eg *Axel Springer AG v Germany* [GC] no 39954/08, 7 February 2012.

[8] See Chapter 6 and Section 7.1.1.

[9] For a useful overview, see N Mavronicola and L Lavrysen, 'Introducing the Sharp Edge of the European Convention on Human Rights' in L Lavrysen and N Mavronicola (eds) *Coercive Human Rights* (Hart Publishing 2020) 1; K Engle and others (eds), *Anti-Impunity and the Human Rights Agenda* (Cambridge University Press 2017).

[10] F Tulkens, 'The Paradoxical Relationship between Criminal Law and Human Rights' (2011) 9 Journal of International Criminal Justice 577.

more generally.[11] The specific concern of this chapter is then how competing human rights obligations owned by the State need to be taken into consideration in the determination of the scope and the content of positive obligations so that a possible protective overreach can be prevented. The chapter first explains that obligations need to be specified so that tensions and competitions between obligations can be recognized (Section 5.1). Once competing obligations become cognizable, they should be denoted a distinctive and special role (in contrast to competing general public interests) in the assessment of the reasonableness of the positive obligations (Section 5.2). The chapter then discusses considerations that can be relevant to addressing the tension between positive obligations and other (both positive and negative) human rights obligations corresponding to absolute, strictly qualified, and qualified rights (Section 5.3). These considerations include respecting the equal moral status of each affected individual, the relative importance of the affected interests grounding rights as related to the relative importance of the corresponding obligations, whether actions or omissions form the content of the obligations, and the determinacy of the harm and the affected individuals. Finally, while acknowledging the difficulties, it is proposed that the obligations can be framed in such a way in terms of content and scope that accommodation is possible (Section 5.4).

## 5.1 Specification for Tensions to Become Cognizable

The analysis has to start with the acknowledgement that 'conflict of interests lie at the foundation of rights'. The reason is the value and social pluralism that characterizes our societies, and the fact that people have 'different views about what is part of their wellbeing or the common good'.[12] Since human rights involve a complex set of relations that are regulated by the State, when rights are exercised by individuals the risk of competing claims is high.[13]

On a more technical note, conflicting and competing obligations are unavoidable given the dynamic nature of rights. As explained in Chapter 1, this dynamism implies that rights generate a plurality of obligations, each with more or less specific content and scope. This makes the question of competing human rights obligations inevitable and pervasive.[14] Since a right can ground multiple obligations, some of these might conflict or be in tension with other obligations produced by the same right or other rights. These conflicts and tensions might be binary or multipolar (ie multiple

---

[11] For a valuable attempt in this direction, see L Lazarus, 'Preventive Obligations, Risk and Coercive Overreach' in Lavrysen and Mavronicola (eds) *Coercive Human Rights* (n 9) 249.
[12] Besson, *The Morality of Conflict* (n 5) 425–26.
[13] Zucca, *Constitutional Dilemmas* (n 1) 45.
[14] Besson, *The Morality of Conflict* (n 5) 419–56.

interests that ground human rights might be implicated). They might involve obligations corresponding to rights held by the same or by different right-holders.[15]

The conflicts and tensions can become cognizable once the content and the scope of the potentially conflicting or competing obligations become known. A certain level of specification of the obligations is thus necessary to recognize and detect the tensions. Their identification is dependent on the level of abstraction and individualization of the obligations. For example, the abstract positive obligation to protect the right to life is not necessarily in conflict with the abstract positive obligation to ensure the right to private life.[16] However, if the level of abstraction is reduced and the degree of specificity increased, a tension can become more perceivable. For example, protection of the right to life by deployment of more police resources to address gang violence might come at the price of fewer resources for helping victims of domestic violence, which might be in tension with the positive obligation of ensuring their right to private life. Imposition of restrictions (such as closing of schools, gyms, and other facilities, and limits on the possibility for people to gather) might be in fulfilment of the positive obligation to ensure the right to life by preventing the spread of disease. Such restrictions, however, might not only be in tension with the negative obligations corresponding to the right to private life and freedom of assembly; these might also imply less opportunity, for example, for the authorities to detect and prevent child abuse at home, which might make it less likely for a State to fulfil its positive obligations.

Since the competing obligations are more specific in some situations, the Court has acknowledged the tension. For example, it has observed that 'the national authorities *cannot* be expected to discharge their positive obligations under Article 3 of the Convention by acting in breach of the requirements of its Article 7, one of which is that the criminal law must not be construed extensively to an accused's detriment'.[17] In relation to the positive obligation of taking protective operational measures, the

---

[15] Conflicts and tensions might arise between obligations corresponding to rights owned by the same person. Euthanasia emerges as a relevant example. See *Haas v Switzerland* no 31322/07, 20 January 2011 §§53–54, where the issue was whether the State was under a positive obligation under Article 8 to permit a dignified suicide. This issue implied consideration of State's positive obligation under Article 8 for protecting 'vulnerable persons, even against actions by which they endanger their own lives'. For the Court, Article 2 'obliges the national authorities to prevent an individual from taking his or her own life if the decision has not been taken freely and with full understanding of what is involved'. Another example concerns restrictive measures against persons with mental disabilities. See *Fernandes de Oliveira v Portugal* [GC] no 78103/14, 31 January 2019 §112: 'the authorities must discharge their duties in a manner compatible with the rights and freedoms of the individual concerned and in such a way as to diminish the opportunity for self-harm, without infringing personal autonomy. The Court has acknowledged that excessively restrictive measures may give rise to issues under Article 3, 5 and 8 of the Convention'. See also *Fabris et Parziale v Italy* no 41603/13, 19 March 2020 §§77–86 (the obligation to protect detainees from self-harm could lead to excessively restrictive measures that could be problematic with regard to Article 3, 5 and 8). See also *Ražnatović v Montenegro* no 14742, 2 September 2021 §37.

[16] See Section 7.1.3.1, where this is framed as level one of abstraction as the most abstract level of framing the positive obligation.

[17] *Myumyun v Bulgaria* no 67258/13, 3 November 2015 §76 (emphasis added). For the overuse of the criminal justice system *against* the individual, see P Pinto de Albuquerque, 'The Overuse of Criminal Justice in the Case Law of the European Court of Human Rights' in C van Kempen and M Jendly (eds) *Overuse of the Criminal Justice System* (Intersentia 2019) 67.

following limitation to its scope and content has been imposed: the police have to exercise 'their powers to control and prevent crime in a manner which *fully respects* the due process and other guarantees which legitimately place restraints on the scope of their action to investigate and bring offenders to justice, including the guarantees contained in Article 5 and 8 of the Convention'.[18]

## 5.2 The Distinction between General Interests and Interests that Form the Basis of Human Rights

The specification of the positive obligations implies a specification of those individuals whose interests are meant to be protected and of those individuals whose interests might be harmed because of this protection. It is in the context of this specification that the reasonableness of positive obligations, both in terms of their content and scope, can be assessed. Notably, reasonableness here is not, or not only, opposed to general public interests (or other non-human rights considerations), an opposition that was in the focus of Chapter 4. The standard of reasonableness is rather opposed to negative and/or positive obligations corresponding to human rights.[19] It is of normative significance when the extension of protection might be unreasonableness due to competing human rights, as opposed to competing public interests. The reason for this difference can be related to the idea that human rights (including the human rights of, for example, the person who might be the object of an intrusive measure that is arguably necessary for the protection of somebody else) carry a special normative force over non-rights considerations. Since human rights protect certain fundamental interests, they can be considered special superior categories of norms.[20] These norms are meant to impose limits 'on what can be done to individuals for the sake of the greater benefit of others' and 'on the sacrifices that can be demanded from them as a contribution to the general good'.[21] Rights therefore impose limits on utilitarian arguments that involve trade-offs.

The special role of human rights has been also noted by the European Court of Human Rights (ECtHR) in one of its early judgments addressing positive obligations. In the *Belgium Linguistic* case, it was observed that '[t]he Convention therefore implies

---

[18] *Opuz v Turkey* no 33401/02, 9 June 2009 §129 (emphasis added); *Osman v the United Kingdom* [GC] no 23452/94, 28 October 1998 §116.

[19] Here one can make a parallel with the existing scholarly analysis of proportionality in the context of negative obligations. In this context, an argument has been advanced for making a difference when the proportionality test is applied to situations when infringements of relative rights are justified by reference to public interests and situations when such infringements are justified by reference to the need of protecting another person's human rights. For an elaboration of this argument, see S Smet, *Resolving Conflicts between Human Rights. The Judge's Dilemma* (Routledge 2017) 35.

[20] ibid 33; S Greer, *The European Convention on Human Rights – Achievements, Problems and Prospects* (Cambridge University Press 2006) 196, 208–10.

[21] J Waldron, 'Rights in Conflict' (1989) 99 Ethics 503, 508.

a just balance between the protection of the general interest of the Community and the respect due to fundamental human rights *while attaching particular importance to the latter*'.[22] In cases of tension where the specification leads to the identification of competing interests that ground rights, this particular importance should be attached to the interests on both sides of the equation—those that justify protective measures (in fulfilment of positive obligations) and those that might be harmed due to these very measures. This implies that the above-mentioned role of human rights, to impose limits on utilitarian trade-offs, might not be relevant since it is not public interests that act as counterweights but rather other rights.[23] The Court itself has made a distinction between balancing against 'the general interest of the community as a whole' and balancing against 'competing private interests'.[24] Due to the special normative force of human rights that contrast them with public interests (or other non-human rights considerations), these competing interests that underpin human rights and corresponding obligations enter the framework of analysis on a footing equal with the interests of the applicant who claims protection.[25]

Although interests that found rights have some degree of priority over non-rights based interests,[26] a challenge needs to be immediately noted: how to distinguish between competing interests grounding human rights that generate obligations, on the one hand, and competing general public interests on the other? Such a distinction could be suspect, since public interests can be considered as expressing individuals' human rights.[27] In this sense, the rights of others are hidden behind the general interests of, for example, 'public safety', 'economic well-being of the country', or 'protection of health', and thus the human rights law review necessarily includes multipolar competing claims. All these claims could be somehow related to interests that underpin human rights. There is always a possibility that interests that actually ground rights remain 'hidden' behind general interests. As a consequence, any competing obligations corresponding to rights might not be identified and considered.

---

[22] Case 'Relating to Certain Aspects of the Laws on the Use of Languages in Education in Belgium' v Belgium (Merits) no 1474/62, 23 July 1968, 28 (emphasis added).

[23] It is of course possible that public interests might act together with other rights as counterweights.

[24] *R.L. and Others v Denmark* no 52629/11, 7 March 2017 §39. The text of Article 8(2) itself indicates 'protection of the rights and freedoms of others' as an interest separate from the general interests of, for example, 'public safety or the economic well-being of the country'. At the same time, however, 'the rights of others', an expression in Articles 8(2), 9(2), 10(2), and 11(2) ECHR, has been given a wider meaning by the Court since it is not limited to the rights of others *as specifically protected by the ECHR*. See *Fernández Marínez v Spain* [GC] no 56030/07, 12 June 2014 §121; *Perinçek v Sweitserland* [GC] App 27510/08, 15 October 2015 §156.

[25] J Waldron, 'Security and Liberty: The Image of Balance' (2003) 11(2) Journal of Political Philosophy 191, 198: 'Rights versus rights is a different ballgame from rights versus social utility.'

[26] Besson, *The Morality of Conflict* (n 5) 439.

[27] K Möller, *The Global Model of Constitutional Rights* (Oxford University Press 2012) 136: 'We often speak of something being in the public or general interest. This is really a short form of saying that it serves everyone's autonomy interests.' See also P Decoulombier, 'Conflicts between Fundamental Rights and the European Court of Human Rights: An Overview' in Brems (ed), *Conflicts between Fundamental Rights* (n 6) 223; J Gerards, 'Fundamental Rights and Other Interests: Should it Really Make a Difference' in Brems (ed), *Conflicts between Fundamental Rights* (n 6) 655–90.

The challenge to demarcate the province of individual rights from the realm of general (public) interests relates to the difficulties in finding a defensible conception of the public interests and their relationship with individual rights.[28] No attempt is made here to outline the existing theoretical discussions in this area.[29] An understanding that seems most compatible with the interest model of rights is that public interests are one element in the decision-making calculus. They imply a collective, though not necessarily uniform, benefit for *all* members of society rather than one that attaches only to particular individuals or groups.[30] All members of society as equals can benefit from the protection of general interests.[31] These interests permit utilitarian arguments in the assessment of the obligations and quantitative considerations matter.[32] The *basis for the justification* of public interests is therefore utilitarian and quantitative. In contrast, what is distinctive about an interest that grounds a right is that 'the benefit to the individual is seen as the ground of the duty, as a "sufficient reason" for it'.[33] The justification of interests that underpin individual rights is therefore distinctive. Human rights thus imply that the protection of certain interests '*to* or *for* or *from the point of view of* some individual'[34] are given '*qualitative* precedence over the social calculus of interests generally'.[35]

Some complications arise, however, since, as I will explain in more detail below, we can assign different degrees of importance to the obligations generated by the same right. As a result of this, as Waldron has observed, we might begin 'to lose our sense of the qualitative precedence this right—as a source of duties—has over other considerations in morality'.[36] Waldron has framed this contradiction in the following way:

> We want to retain some sense that rights have qualitative priority over considerations of utility and even in regard to one another. But we also want some way of expressing the fact that not all the duties generated by a given right have the same degree of importance.[37]

---

[28] Dworkin, for example, has noted that there is some confusion in the idea of balancing between the interests of the individual versus the interests of the community: 'The interests of each individual are already balanced into the interests of the community as a whole, and the idea of a further balance, between their separate interests and the results of the first balance, is itself therefore mysterious.' R Dworkin, 'Principle, Policy Procedure' in *A Matter of Principle* (Harvard University Press 1985) 73.

[29] A McHarg, 'Reconciling Human Rights and the Public Interest: Conceptual problems and Doctrinal Uncertainty in the Jurisprudence of the European Court of Human Rights' (1999) 62 Modern Law Review 671.

[30] Waldron, 'Rights in Conflict' (n 21) 507: 'one of the important features of rights discourse is that rights are attributed to individuals one by one, not collectively or in the aggregate'.

[31] R Alexy, 'Individual Rights and Collective Goods' in C Nino (ed) *Rights* (Dartmouth 1992) 163, 167: collective goods have non-distributive character: 'it is conceptually, actually and legally impossible to break up the good into parts and to assigned shares to individuals'.

[32] Waldron, 'Rights in Conflict' (n 21) 509. Certain considerations weight in the calculus only because of the numbers involved (eg one life can be sacrificed so that a greater number of lives may be saved).

[33] J Waldron, 'Can Communal Goods be Human Rights?' (1987) 28(2) European Journal of Sociology 296, 313.

[34] ibid 301 (emphasis in the original).

[35] Waldron, 'Rights in Conflict' (n 21) 512 (emphasis added).

[36] ibid 514.

[37] ibid 516.

Waldron argues that this contradiction cannot be solved. He admits that

> [m]any, perhaps most, conflicts—whether between rights and utility or among rights themselves—are best handled in the sort of balancing way that the quantitative image of weight suggests: we establish the relative importance of the interests at stake, and the contribution each of the conflicting duties may make to the importance of the interest it protects, and we try to maximize our promotion of what we take to be important.[38]

He adds, however, that in some situations, qualitative precedence might be possible, and it can offer a solution. These situations arise when 'internal connections' between considerations can be established that denote the importance of the interests that underpin human rights obligations. The idea of 'internal connections' prompts us to ask *deeper and systemic questions* as to why certain interests that ground rights are protected. For example, freedom of expression is protected so that, *inter alia*, received opinions can be challenged and complacency shaken. This implies that any conflicting positive obligation to protect the interests of individuals whose beliefs are challenged can be of a much lesser qualitative significance. The reduction of its importance is thus due to considerations that are *internal* to the right itself. The idea of 'internal connections' implies that we need to ask much more systemic questions as to the kind of society we want to be: one that leans towards a more restrained role of the State or towards more State intrusion for the sake of protection.

Notably and despite the useful guidance offered by the theoretical discussions mentioned above, competing obligations are difficult to reduce to bright-line binary oppositions (eg individual versus individual interests or individual versus public interests). There is a plurality of interests at stake with various degree of specification and determinacy as to their importance and their holders. In the mist of this plurality, however, as already suggested above, an all-penetrating tension arises as to the role of the State. An enhanced role of the State implies more intrusiveness in the name of protection against (known or unknown) risks. It could imply adjusting liberties downward so that protection is achieved. At the same time, if the State does not act, including by negatively affecting rights, this might have protection costs for certain individuals or groups within the society.

The determinacy and the identifiability of the individuals that might be the target of intrusiveness might be a relevant consideration[39] in this tension. Their rights might be at stake when intrusive measures are undertaken against them for the sake of protecting other individuals (ie those that claim to be victims since the State has arguably

---

[38] ibid 518–19.
[39] Besides the competing interests of two parties and any general interests, the interests of more or less specifiable third parties might be also at stake to varying degrees. See *Odièvre v France* [GC] no 42326/98, 13 February 2003 where not only the human rights of the applicant, who wanted to know her biological mother, who chose to give birth anonymously, but the interests of third parties were also involved (eg the adoptive parents, members of the biological mother's family).

failed to protect them). In contrast, when general interests are invoked, the group of any possibly negatively affected individuals might be more indeterminate. Besides determinacy, another relevant and related consideration might be the concreteness and actuality of the burden or intrusiveness that the competing right might need to suffer. This burden and intrusiveness might not be so speculative when a concrete interest that bases a right is invoked. In contrast, when general interests are invoked, their actual preservation (by not extending protection to the applicant or extending only a more limited protection) might be more abstract and speculative.[40] This can be also related to the vagueness of the general interests themselves, which also means that there are many ways in which these interests can be served or disserved.[41] Some of these ways might underpin obligations corresponding to rights, which can give rise to a situation of competing obligations. There might, however, be other ways of serving public interests that do not relate to obligations, in which case the situation might simply be one of balancing public interests with interests that base human rights obligations. This brings us back to the importance of alternatives in the assessment of the reasonableness standard (see Section 4.2).

## 5.3 Addressing the Competition

What can guide the resolution of tensions between obligations? What considerations could be relevant to address the problem that positive obligations meant to prevent harm can actually cause harm to other interests meant to be protected by other obligations, both positive and negative? For the purpose of clarity, the latter form of harm will be framed as attendant harm. As opposed to harm caused by omissions (which could amount to failures by the State to fulfil positive obligations), *attendant harm* arises from the State's conduct in fulfilment of positive obligations.

### 5.3.1 Equal Moral Status

The way in which the individual is treated in terms of his or her equal moral status and status of inviolability is an important consideration for addressing competing obligations.[42] This implies, for example, that an intervention (arguably in fulfilment of a positive obligation) might be necessary to protect life, but this intervention might

---

[40] For the development of this argument from the perspective of invocation of general interests as legitimate objectives pursued for limiting human rights, see Smet, *Resolving Conflicts between Human Rights* (n 19) 51.

[41] Waldron, 'Rights in Conflict' (n 21) 510: 'There are many ways in which a given interest can be served or disserved, and we should not expect to find that only one of those ways is singled out and made the subject matter of a duty.'

[42] S Besson, 'Human Rights in Relation. A Critical Reading of the ECtHR's Approach to Conflicts of Rights' in Smet and Brems (eds) *When Human Rights Clash at the European Court of Human Rights* (n 4) 23, 32.

lead to harming somebody else physically. The latter then might be treated as an object whose equal moral status and status of inviolability is harmed.[43] If this is the case, positive obligations to prevent harm are not acceptable since the attendant harm implies treating individuals as objects.[44] The question as to when individuals are actually treated as objects raises its own challenges, which I return to later in the section. At this stage, it is important that assigning equal moral status is a conclusive criterion in the resolution of tensions between obligations. In contrast, the considerations addressed in Sections 5.3.2–5.3.5 behave more like principles that can be taken into account rather than rules.

## 5.3.2 The Relative Importance of the Interests and the Obligations Triggered

Besides not harming the equal moral status of individuals, considering the importance of the interests in the specific context where the obligations are invoked might be also helpful in addressing competing obligations. Under this understanding, since the interests protected by the right to life are more significant, they might have to be given priority over the interests protected by, for example, the right to private life. Relatedly, when the core of the right to private life is at stake,[45] it might be easier to justify positive obligations to protect this core. A similar argument can be formulated in relation to the so-called absolute rights. Without entering into a detailed discussion as to the nature of 'absolute rights' and what absoluteness actually means,[46] it suffices for present purposes to note that they are meant to reflect interests that protect fundamental values.

It is indeed the case that some rights protect interests of higher importance. However, the argument that the obligations generated by these rights should necessarily and always be given priority in the case of competition is *flawed*. The reason is that a right can trigger multiple obligations, not all of which are 'equally strong in relation to the interests protected by that right they are grounded on'.[47] For instance, the

---

[43] According to the status theory of rights, which can be viewed as a refinement of the interest-based theory of rights, 'rights express the recognition of a person's status as being who has a high, even if not an absolute level of inviolability'. Besson, *The Morality of Conflict* (n 5) 422–23.

[44] A good illustration of this situation originates from the judgment of the German Federal Constitutional Court that declared unconstitutional legislation that empowered the authorities to shoot down a passenger airplane if it could be assumed that this would save the lives of people on the ground. The Court found that the legislation neglected the constitutional status of the individuals in the airplane as subjects with dignity and inalienable rights. They would be treated as objects that can be sacrificed. Bundesverfassungsgericht (BVerfG—Federal Constitutional Court), 59 Neue Juristische Wochenschrift 751 (2006).

[45] For elaboration of the argument that rights have a core of interests that they protect, see I Leijten, *Core Socio-Economic Rights and the European Court of Human Rights* (Cambridge University Press 2018).

[46] Greer, *The European Convention on Human Rights. Achievements, Problems and Prospects* (n 20) 233: it would 'be clearer to avoid the term "absolute" altogether'. For a study on what an absolute right is and what this entails for its interpretation, see N Mavronicola, *Torture, Inhumanity and Degradation under Article 3 of the ECHR. Absolute Rights and Absolute Wrongs* (Hart Publishing 2021).

[47] Besson, *The Morality of Conflict* (n 5) 437–38. See also Waldron, 'Rights in Conflict' (n 21) 515.

right to life triggers the negative obligation upon the State not to kill arbitrarily; it also triggers the positive obligation upon the State to organize its healthcare system so that life is protected; it can also trigger the positive obligation to protect from interpersonal violence. These various obligations cannot always rank equally in comparison to the obligations corresponding to, for example, the right to private and family life.[48] In addition, these obligations can have different content and scope that need to be specified in given circumstances. It cannot be that all more specifically framed positive obligations corresponding to the rights enshrined in Article 3, normally framed as absolute, necessarily take priority over obligations under Article 8. For this reason, Besson has correctly observed that 'the solution to conflicts of rights may have to lie in weighting and balancing the different interests in conflict in a specific case rather than in recognizing the general qualitative priority of one right over another'.[49]

A right that protects important interests does exercise higher constraints in the reasoning in specific cases,[50] and 'there will be a cause to grant it a higher abstract value in the balancing test than the rights which it competes'.[51] However, the higher abstract value that can be assigned to the interests protected by, for example, the right to life does not mean that any measure protecting these interests (or any measure that might protect these interests) ought to be forthcoming. If this were the case, there would be no reasonable limits to the positive obligations corresponding to this right. The undertaking of any protective measures, and their scope, is subject to the tests of knowledge, causation, and reasonableness, including any competing individual or public interests. *Kotilainen and Others v Finland* is a case in point. The applicants were relatives of individuals killed in a school shooting. The perpetrator, a student himself, had serious mental problems and used a weapon he had acquired with a licence granted by the authorities. The applicants argued that Finland failed to protect their relatives' right to life since, *inter alia*, the police authorities failed to obtain the perpetrator's medical and military records to verify data regarding his mental health. The Court responded that

> confidentiality of health data is a vital principle in the legal systems of all the Contracting Parties, and also protected under Article 8 of the Convention. The

---

[48] See *Choreftakis and Choreftaki v Greece* no 46846/08, 17 January 2012 §60: 'the Greek system of conditional release, as it was applied in the present case, did not disturb the fair balance between the objective of social reintegration of Z.L. [the concrete individual in relation to whom the applicants argued that the State should have taken restrictive measures so that their son's life could be protected] and the goal of preventing him from reoffending'.

[49] Besson, *The Morality of Conflict* (n 5) 438.

[50] S Besson, 'Human Rights in Relation. A Critical Reading of the ECtHR's Approach to Conflicts of Rights' in Smet and Brems (eds) *When Human Rights Clash at the European Court of Human Rights* (n 4) 23, 35; Mavronicola, *Torture, Inhumanity and Degradation under Article 3 of the ECHR* (n 46) 53: 'positive obligations to secure the right enshrined in Article 3 should be more onerous than those obligations corresponding to rights that are displaceable, since the latter's infringement can in principle be withstood'.

[51] S Smet 'Conflicts between Human Rights and the ECtHR' in Smet and Brems (eds), *When Human Rights Clash at the European Court of Human Rights* (n 4) 38, 46; Smet, *Resolving Conflicts between Human Rights* (n 19) 148.

Court has acknowledged that respect for such confidentiality is crucial not only for the sake of the patients' sense of privacy but to preserve their confidence in the health service and to ensure that persons are not discouraged from seeking diagnosis or treatment, which would undermine the preventive efforts in health care [reference omitted]. The domestic law must therefore afford appropriate safeguards to prevent any such communication or disclosure of personal health data as may be inconsistent with the guarantees in Article 8 of the Convention.[52]

This reasoning illustrates that tensions between obligations corresponding to the right to life, and those corresponding to the right to private life, are not necessarily resolved in favour of the first. It needs also to be added that the Court in *Kotilainen and Others v Finland* tried to mitigate the tension. One the one hand, it noted that in some situations, despite the possibilities for justified interferences, the stringency of any negative obligations under Article 8 can be quite high: 'access by the police to an individual's medical data *cannot be a matter of routine*'.[53] On the other hand, the Court noted that the scope of any positive obligations under Article 2 can be quite indeterminate given the uncertainties regarding causality and state knowledge: 'even if data on the perpetrator's medical history had been available, it cannot be determined whether or to what extent the assessment of whether the perpetrator posed a risk and imminent risk at the relevant time might have depended on such information'.[54]

The varying strength of obligations can be also illustrated with reference to Article 3. The Court has maintained that Article 3 enshrines 'one of the most fundamental values of democratic societies and prohibits in absolute terms torture and inhuman or degrading treatment'.[55] Indeed, the negative obligations corresponding to this provision are absolute in the sense that they do not compete with other interests that can *limit these obligations*, once it is determined that state agents have inflicted harm that qualifies as torture or inhuman or degrading treatment.[56] In contrast, the positive obligations corresponding to Article 3 are certainly not absolute, since competing interests interfere and can limit these obligations. It follows that in the determination of the *concrete* scope of the positive obligations, competing interests are allowed and can eventually lead to a conclusion of no violation. This statement, however, begs a refinement. As explained in Chapter 1, at a very general level, provisions such as Articles 3 and 2 trigger positive obligations automatically since the State is under the abstract

---

[52] *Kotilainen and Others v Finland* no 62439/12, 17 September 2020 §83.
[53] ibid §83 (emphasis added).
[54] ibid §83. The Court still found a violation of Article 2 since 'the domestic authorities have not observed the special duty of diligence incumbent on them because of the particularly high level of risk to life inherent in any misconduct involving the use of firearms'.
[55] *Gäfgen v Germany* [GC] no 22978/05, 1 June 2010 §107.
[56] There could be competition with interests, but this is performed at the definitional stage of the analysis, where contextualization (and consideration of different interests) is inevitable and where the question is whether the minimum level of ill-treatment has been reached so that Article 3 is engaged. Once this threshold is reached, the negative obligation upon the State is directly violated and in this sense Article 3 is absolute. S Smet, 'Conflict between Absolute Rights: A Reply to Steven Greer' 2013 (13) Human Rights Law Review 469, 476–77.

positive obligation to protect those within its jurisdiction all the time. In this sense, these positive obligations can be framed as absolute. However, when their scope and content need to be determined at a more concrete level, competing interests interfere and *can displace any concrete positive obligations*. In this sense, therefore, they are not absolute.[57]

In conclusion, while the importance of the interests can be a guiding principle, given the variety of obligations and the varying degree of their stringency, tensions between obligations cannot necessarily be resolved with reference to the general qualitative priority of the interests. It might be more helpful if the relative importance of the interest is taken into account, for example the specific aspect of private life that is at stake in the concrete case, together with the contribution that the concrete positive obligation may make to the protection of this aspect, and how competing obligations might affect this aspect. To assess the relative importance of the interests that underpin the right, it might be useful to contextualize the right by asking deeper and systemic questions as to why we have certain rights, as suggested in Section 5.2, and in which direction the society might be pulled (more or less state intrusion) in the light of the obligations that are assigned to this right.

## 5.3.3 Action versus Omission

To understand the varying strength and importance of the different obligations in relation to the interests protected by the right is a crucial analytical insight, yet within this variety, it is relevant to make a distinction between obligations that require the taking of an action (positive obligations) and those that require restraint (negative obligations). Despite the problematic distinction between these two, causing harm by

---

[57] I disagree with Smet's analysis on this point. With reference to *Z and Others v the United Kingdom* [GC] no 29392/95, 10 May 2001 (para 74), Smet notes that the reference in the reasoning to 'countervailing principle of respecting and preserving family life', 'may entice us to conclude that balancing is possible under Article 3 after all. However, upon closer reading of the judgment, such a conclusion becomes untenable. It seems to me that, rather than being read as allowing balancing, the full quote falls to be understood as recognizing that the search for a solution within the family may be worth striving for, but under the—not to be surrendered, because absolute—condition that the abuse is put to an end.... The absolute nature of Article 3, also in its positive dimension, thus seems undeniable.' Smet seems to say that it is an absolute obligation to put the abuse to an end once the State is aware or ought to have been aware. This is, however, hard to accept for at least two reasons. First, the condition triggering the obligation, namely 'ought to have been aware' implies a relative assessment (see Chapter 2). Second, even if accepted that the State knew (or ought to have known) about the abuse, it is not under the obligation to do *everything possibly conceivable* to stop the abuse. Not every possible measure that can stop the abuse is demanded as a matter of positive obligations. If absoluteness is understood as the State having obligations under Article 3 to all the time make efforts to prevent and stop abuse within families, then the absolute nature of positive obligations corresponding to Article 3 can be accepted. However, these obligations are at a very general and abstract level and do not tell us much about what concretely needs to be done and what choices might arise between different alternative measures. See Smet, 'Conflict between Absolute Rights' (n 56) 478–9; S Smet, 'The "Absolute" Prohibition of Torture and Inhuman or Degrading Treatment in Article 3 ECHR' in E Brems and J Gerards (eds) *Shaping Rights in the ECHR. The Role of the European Court of Human Rights in Determining the Scope of Human Rights* (Cambridge University Press 2014) 273, 281.

action (possibly in breach of negative obligations) rather than by omission (possibly by failure to fulfil positive obligations) makes a difference in moral and legal terms.[58] In moral terms, there is a difference between, for example, killing versus letting someone die. The former, unlike the latter, implies direct agency.[59] The distinction between action and omission is thus pertinent in the efforts to disentangle competing obligations. With reference to this distinction and the nature of the protected rights (absolute or qualified) then, various constellations of competing obligations are possible. These will be addressed below.

### 5.3.3.1 Negative obligations compete with positive obligations in the context of Article 3

Mavronicola has addressed a conflict between positive and negative obligations that pertain to absolute rights. In the context of Article 3, she has explained that 'there is no positive duty to act in a way that constitutes a violation of the negative duty encompassed by an absolute right'. Any positive duties therefore have to be delimited 'in a way that excludes taking action that amount to a violation of the negative duty of an absolute right'.[60] For example, the State cannot be under the positive obligation to torture a kidnapper to discover the whereabouts of the child that he had kidnapped, so that the child can be saved.[61] Another example emerges in the context of forced feeding of detainees: there is no positive obligation to force feed them and in this way to subject them to treatment contrary to Article 3 so that their life can be saved.[62] Mavronicola frames this as intra-Convention legality.[63]

### 5.3.3.2 Negative obligations compete with positive obligations in the context Article 2

A competition between negative and positive obligations corresponding to the right to life needs to be an object of a distinctive analysis. This right is not absolute since under certain strictly construed circumstances, deprivation of life by the State can be justifiable.[64] Still, it is a right ranked together with Article 3 'as one of the most important provisions in the Convention'.[65] In the light of this distinctiveness, Smet has argued that 'all other things being equal, the negative obligation not to kill one person

---

[58] Smet, 'Conflict between Absolute Rights' (n 56) 490.
[59] On the distinction between direct versus indirect agency from the perspective of moral philosophy, see W Quinn, 'Actions, Intentions, and Consequences: The Doctrine of Doing and Allowing' (1989) 98 The Philosophical Review 287.
[60] N Mavronicola, 'What is an "Absolute Right"? Deciphering Absoluteness in the Context of Article 3 of the European Convention on Human Rights' (2012) 12 Human Rights Law Review 723, 732.
[61] See *Gäfgen v Germany* [GC] no 22978/05, 1 June 2010 §177.
[62] The Court's analysis focuses on whether the forced-feeding amounts to inhuman or degrading treatment since 'a measure which is of therapeutic necessity from the point of view of established principles of medicine cannot in principle be regarded as inhuman and degrading. The same can be said about force-feeding that is aimed at saving the life of a particular detainee who consciously refuses to take food'. *Nevmerkzhitsky v Ukraine* no 54825/00, 5 April 2005 §94.
[63] Mavronicola, *Torture, Inhumanity and Degradation under Article 3 of the ECHR* (n 46) 54 and 150.
[64] See E Wicks, *The Right to Life and Conflicting Interests* (Oxford University Press 2010).
[65] *Kotilainen and Others v Finland* no 62439/12, 17 September 2020 §65.

trumps the positive obligation to save the life of another person. Therefore, *in principle* the negative obligation weighs heavier than the positive obligation to safe life.'[66] He has, however, also added that 'negative rights can nevertheless, *under certain conditions,* be outweighed by positive rights'. This means that balancing between the two can be allowed, yet Smet adds that there is also a limit to this balancing. By drawing a distinction between direct and indirect agency, he submits that 'balancing cannot be allowed when interference with negative right entails treating a person as a means to an end.'[67] So direct agency that presupposes the usage of individuals as a means is a nullifying factor that cancels any possibility for balancing.[68] If this nullifying factor is not present, however, and thus individuals will not be treated as means, balancing is allowed. This permits the possibility that 'the positive obligation toward the many—at some point—outweigh the negative obligation toward the few'.[69]

Smet's arguments are, however, vulnerable in at least three ways. First, the Kantian formula of treating people not as means but as ends is notoriously unclear, and it has difficulties in offering guidance in concrete situations.[70] Second, Smet's arguments are developed against the backdrop of very *specific* instances where positive and negative obligations conflict. The content of the obligations is therefore specific. The argument is built under the assumption that the action required by the positive obligation (the content of the obligation) is not only very specific but also that alternatives are not possible. The assumption that alternative protective measures are absent seems to work in favour of the conclusion that positive obligations might outweigh negative ones. It might, however, be possible to specify positive obligations in a way that implies actions not in breach of negative obligations. Finally, Smet's arguments draw on moral philosophy, and are thus developed from a perspective that implies that individuals are holders of obligations. Moral philosophy does provide useful guidance; however, the framework needs adjustment to incorporate the State as the holder of obligations.[71]

In relation to the right to life, this adjustment implies at least two things. First, the State is under an absolute negative obligation not to use lethal force for purposes other than those indicated in Article 2(2), and any positive obligations are conclusively limited in this way. Mavronicola's argument, as mentioned above in relation to Article 3, applies here also: there is no positive obligation upon the State to act in a way contrary to Article 2(2) of the Convention (ECHR) with reference to the specific purposes.

---

[66] Smet, 'Conflict between Absolute Rights' (n 56) 490 (emphasis in the original). See also Wicks, *The Right to Life and Conflicting Interests* (n 64) 153.
[67] Smet, 'Conflict between Absolute Rights' (n 56) 472.
[68] ibid 493.
[69] ibid 494.
[70] K Möller, 'The Right to Life between Absolute and Proportionate Protection' in S Bronitt and others (eds) *Shooting to Kill: Socio-Legal Perspectives on the Use of Lethal Force* (Hart Publishing 2012) 47, 53.
[71] Smet expressly notes this specificity here S Smet, 'On the Existence and Nature of Conflicts between Human Rights at the European Court of Human Rights' (2017) 17 Human Rights Law Review 499, 517.

The second implication, when the State is the duty bearer, is that States' negative obligations are qualified: lethal force 'which is no more than absolutely necessary' can be used for three concrete purposes as indicated in Article 2(2) ECHR. The first one, 'in defence of any person from unlawful violence', is particularly interesting, since defending a person from violence could give rise to positive obligations. Both types of obligations in this situation, positive and negative, could arise. On the negative obligations side, the State is obliged to refrain from using lethal force that is no more than absolutely necessary. This can be reformulated in the following way—the State is *allowed* to use force that is absolutely necessary for this concrete purpose ('in defence of any person from unlawful violence'). On the positive obligations side, the State owes positive obligations to *both* the individual who is the object of the lethal force employed by state agents, and the individual(s) who need to be defended from unlawful violence in the sense of Article 2(2)(a). The positive obligation owed to the individual who is the object of the force employed by the State is *more demanding* since this obligation is a reformulation of the negative obligation upon the State not to use lethal force unless 'absolutely necessary'. The standard of 'absolutely necessary' is demanding.[72] In contrast, the positive obligation owned to the individual who needs to be defended from unlawful violence is weaker: its scope and content is shaped by the standard of reasonableness.

The competition between negative obligations and positive obligations, both corresponding to Article 2, came to the fore in *Ribcheva and Others v Bulgaria*, a case about a police officer who was killed during a police operation against an armed dangerous individual. The applicants argued that the State failed to fulfil its positive obligation to take measures under Article 2 to prevent the death of the office, who was shot by the armed individual. The applicants argued that the operation had not been well planned and the officers were not well equipped. The source of the competition was the following—a differently planned operation with heavy armed police officers might imply higher risk to the life of the individual who was the object of the operation.[73] Different planning and the usage of more lethal weapons by the officers are measures that can form the content of the positive obligation to protect the officers' right to life. Notably, although the State has the general positive obligation to protect the officers' life, the standard for assessing compliance is reasonableness. This means that the risk to their life has to be 'reduced to a reasonable minimum'.[74] These measures, however, might be incompatible with the negative obligation owed to the individual, who had to be neutralized during the operation. The standard for assessing

---

[72] *Giuliani and Gaggio v Italy* [GC] no 23458/02, 24 March 2011 §176: 'The use of the term "absolutely necessary" indicates that a stricter and more compelling test of necessity must be employed than that normally applicable when determining whether State action is "necessary in a democratic society" under paragraphs 2 of Articles 8 to 11 of the Convention.'
[73] *Ribcheva and Others v Bulgaria* no 37801/16, 30 March 2021 §173: 'the use of more lethal weapons will normally ensure better protection of the lives of any officers involved in a law-enforcement operation, and at the same time increase the risk to the lives of the targets of that operation'.
[74] *Ribcheva and Others v Bulgaria* §166.

compliance with this negative obligation is strict proportionality. This means that the risk to life has to be reduced to the point of being no more than absolutely necessary.[75]

There are thus two different standards for assessing compliance with the positive and the negative obligations corresponding to Article 2. The standard for assessing the conduct and the planning of police operations so that the Court can review whether the State has complied with its negative obligation (ie state agents not to use lethal force unless no more than absolutely necessary) is a distinctive standard. Although it is as flexible as the standard of reasonableness, the former is clearly more demanding that the latter.

The competition between positive obligations corresponding to Article 2 and negative obligations corresponding also to Article 2 resembles the competition between positive obligations corresponding to Article 2 and negative obligations correspond to Article 5 ECHR (the right to liberty and security). The reason is that Article 5 has a similar structure to Article 2 since it exhaustively indicates certain circumstances when deprivation of liberty is allowed. The competition was explicitly addressed in *Kurt v Austria*, since the applicant formulated an argument that her child's life could have been protected by placing the child's father (who eventually killed the child) into detention.[76] The Court affirmed that any measures entailing deprivation of liberty, even if it was a measure that aimed to serve the purpose of protecting life, 'will have to fulfil the requirements of the relevant domestic law as well as the specific conditions set out in Article 5 and the case-law pertaining to it'.[77] These conditions allow the authorities to detain an individual 'in order to secure the fulfilment of any obligation prescribed by law' (Article 5(1)(b) ECHR) or 'when it is reasonably considered necessary to prevent his committing an offence' (Article 5(1)(c) ECHR). Let's examine each of these two measures that can be framed as the content of positive obligations intended to protect such an important interest as the right to life.[78] The aim of this examination is to understand how they compete with negative obligations (ie the obligation not to deprive individuals of liberty).

As to the first one regulated by Article 5(1)(b) ECHR, the obligation not to commit a criminal offence is an obligation that can justify a preventive detention in the sense of this provision. However, this criminal offence has to be 'specific and concrete', a requirement fulfilled under three conditions. First, 'the place and time of the imminent commission of the offence and its potential victim or victims have been sufficiently specified'.[79] Second, the detainee was 'made aware of the specific act which he or she

---

[75] *Giuliani and Gaggio v Italy* [GC] no 23458/02, 24 March 2011 §§175–176.
[76] *Kurt v Austria* [GC] no 62903/15, 15 June 2021 §118.
[77] ibid §184.
[78] Article 5 ECHR allows detention in other circumstances, however, these two can be most directly regarded as being preventive measures that can be undertaken in fulfilment of positive obligations. Prevention of further offences could be only a secondary effect of pretrial detention allowed by Article 5(1)(c) ECHR.
[79] *Ostendorf v Germany* no 15598/08, 7 March 2013 §93.

was to refrain from committing'. And third, the person 'showed himself or herself not to be willing to refrain from committing the act'.[80]

Detention as a preventive measure arguably in fulfilment of positive obligations could be justified under Article 5(1)(c) ECHR as reasonably considered necessary to prevent the commission of an offence. Similarly to Article 5(1)(b), this will be preventive detention unrelated to criminal proceedings.[81] The above-mentioned requirement regarding the specificity and the concreteness of the offence are similarly applicable, so that such a preventive detention is permissible. As the Court noted in *S., V. and A. v Denmark*, Article 5(1)(c) ECHR 'does no more than afford the Contracting States a means of preventing a concrete and specific offence as regard, in particular, the place and time of its commission and its victim(s)'.[82] A general perception that a person might be dangerous does not suffice. In *S., V. and A. v Denmark*, it was also added that for preventive detention under the terms of Article 5(1)(c) ECHR to be permissible, 'the authorities must show convincingly that the person concerned would in all likelihood have been involved in the concrete and specific offence, had its commission not been prevented by the detention'.[83] This comes close to a 'but for' test, a point in relation to which the preventive detention permissible under the terms Article 5(1)(c) ECHR might be distinguished from the preventive detention permissible under the terms Article 5(1)(b) ECHR. Another distinguishing point is that for detention to be allowed under Article 5(1)(c) ECHR, it is not necessary that the detained persons were given specific orders what to do or not to do.[84] Lastly, another possible distinction between the requirements so that detention is deemed permissible under the two provisions relates to the imminence of the offence. It seems that imminence of the offence is a separate and independent test under Article 5(1)(b) ECHR. In contrast, the requirement for imminence of the offence can be part of the necessity assessment, in other words a relevant consideration in the assessment whether the preventive detention was necessary.[85]

Putting aside all the details and uncertainties as to the distinction between Article 5(1)(b) and Article 5(1)(c), both allowing preventing detention outside the context of criminal proceedings, for the purposes of this chapter, it is important to highlight that the permissibility of the measure of preventive detention depends on strictly construed requirements. These are specificity and imminence of the harm that the measure aims to prevent. These are stricter than the 'real and immediate risk' standard applied in the context of the *Osman* test.[86] This suggests weakening the positive obligations when the concrete measure that these obligations might demand implies

---

[80] *S., V. and A. v Denmark* [GC] no 35553/12, 22 October 2018 §83.
[81] *S., V. and A. v Denmark* [GC] no 35553/12, 22 October 2018 §116. See also §124 of this judgment where the Court referred *inter alia* to the positive obligation of taking protective operational measures under Articles 2 and 3 ECHR, as a justification for such preventive detention.
[82] ibid §89.
[83] Ibid §91.
[84] This was the basis on which *S., V. and A. v Denmark*, §83, was distinguished from *Ostendorf v Germany*.
[85] *S., V. and A. v Denmark* [GC] §§161 and 172.
[86] See Sections 2.7.1 and 7.3.

competition with negative obligations that are specifically regulated (as is the case with deprivation of liberty regulated by Article 5 ECHR). When preventive detention is the content of the positive obligation (ie the concrete measure invoked), the triggering of this obligation and the assessment of breach are thus subject to much stricter requirements related to specificity of the harm and its imminence.

In addition, there is a clear presumption militating against the imposition of such a positive obligation. Any detention, including preventing detention, has to be necessary. As the Court clarified in *S., V. and A. v Denmark*, '[t]he detention of an individual is such a serious measure that it is justified only as a last resort where other, less severe measures have been considered and found to be insufficient'.[87] Detention will not be necessary and thus in breach of negative obligations if less severe measures are sufficient for preventing harm and thus protecting. This implies that the content of the positive obligation to prevent harm cannot include the measure of preventive detention when less intrusive alternatives are available.[88]

### 5.3.3.3 Positive obligations compete with positive obligations in the context of Articles 2, 3, and 8

Having addressed the relationship between positive and negative obligations in the context of Article 3, framed as absolute, and Article 2 that is not absolute but is still framed in a way that imposes very high restraints upon state conduct, the analysis can proceed to the other possible constellations. One of them is when Articles 2 and 3 both trigger different positive obligations, and given that in principle the interests protected by these rights are equally important,[89] competition might be hard to resolve. The resolution will depend on the specification of the obligations against the standards of knowledge, causation, and reasonableness.

Articles 2 and 3 can also trigger positive obligations that compete with positive obligations corresponding to qualified rights, such as Article 8, that in principle protect less important interests. As mentioned above, specification of the obligations is required for addressing this competition since not all of them are equally strong in relation to the interests protected by the right on which they are grounded. This implies that positive obligations under Article 8 can in some situations be stronger than positive obligations under, for example, Articles 2 and 3.

---

[87] *S., V. and A. v Denmark* [GC] no 35553/12, 22 October 2018 §77. Although the reasoning refers to the 'last resort', this standard in practice is not possible to apply since it implies that *all* other possible alternative measures are examined and found inadequate. In practice, measures that are less severe in comparison to detention are considered (§§161–169).
[88] ibid §§161–169.
[89] I have in mind circumstances where Article 2(2) is not relevant and any positive obligations to use lethal force, for example, to protect individuals from unlawful violence, are not an issue.

### 5.3.3.4 Negative obligations under Article 8 compete with positive obligations under Articles 2 and 3

A more challenging scenario might arise when positive obligations corresponding to Articles 3 and 2 compete with negative obligations corresponding to qualified rights such as Article 8. Mavronicola's argument about intra-Convention legality could be invoked again here. This would mean that any positive obligations under Articles 2 and 3 may only extend to measures that amount to necessary and proportionate infringements on qualified rights.[90] In its practice, the Court has also observed that 'for a positive obligation to arise [under Article 2], it must in any event be established that the authorities failed to take measures *within the scope of their powers* which, judged reasonably, might have been expected to avoid that risk'.[91] Measures 'within the scope of their powers' could be interpreted to mean measures allowed under the limitations clauses of qualified rights; that is, measures that are in accordance with the law, pursue legitimate aims, and are necessary and proportionate. This implies that a conflict between positive obligations corresponding to Articles 2 and 3, and negative obligations corresponding to qualified rights, will have to be resolved in favour of the latter. Such a conflict can arise in the unlikely scenario where *the only possible measure* in fulfilment of the positive obligation amounts to an unjustified and disproportionate interference with, for example, rights under Article 8.

This is, however, useful only to a certain degree. The assessment of the scope and content of positive obligations under both qualified and unqualified rights is dependent on the standard of reasonableness. At the same time, the scope and content of negative obligations under Article 8 (ie what the State is under the obligation to refrain from doing) is also subject to proportionality assessment. It follows that on both sides of the possible tension, the flexible standards of reasonableness and proportionality apply. In addition, alternative measures are not only relevant in the assessment of the reasonableness of any positive obligations (ie what measures the State could take that are sufficiently protective without being disproportionately intrusive) but also in the assessment of negative obligations (what measures the State could take that are less or even least intrusive to the right so that it complies with its negative obligations).[92] In sum, a complex assessment of alternatives in the concrete situation has to be made. This assessment implies consideration of alternative measures that can ensure sufficient and better protection (so that the State fulfils its positive obligations) and consideration of alternative measures that are less intrusive (so that the State fulfil its negative obligations by not disproportionally interfering with rights).

*Kurt v Austria* falls within this scenario since the question addressed was how positive obligations corresponding to the right to life (ie protecting the life of a child

---

[90] Mavronicola, *Torture, Inhumanity and Degradation under Article 3 of the ECHR* (n 46) 150.
[91] *Kotilainen and Others v Finland* no 62439/12, 17 September 2020 §73 (emphasis added).
[92] Assessment of alternatives is an element part of the necessity test within the proportionality analysis. See E Brems and L Lavrysen, '"Don't Use a Sledgehammer to Crack a Nut": Less Restrictive Means in the Case Law of the European Court of Human Rights' (2015) 15 Human Rights Law Review 139.

killed by his father) might compete with negative obligations corresponding to the perpetrator's right to private and family life and the right to freedom of movement.[93] The positive obligations 'must remain in compliance with the State's other obligations under the Convention'.[94] The Court in *Kurt v Austria* referred to the principle of proportionality for assessing this compliance:

> The nature and severity of the assessed risk [to the life] will always be an important factor with regard to the proportionality of any protective and prevention measures to be taken, whether in the context of Article 8 of the Convention or, as the case may be, of restrictions of liberty falling under Article 2 of Protocol No. 4, which provides for freedom of movement.[95]

### 5.3.3.5 Negative and positive obligations compete in the context of Article 8

Two final constellations in the context of qualified rights need to be reviewed: first, competition between positive obligations corresponding to qualified rights; and second, competition between positive and negative obligations corresponding to qualified rights. As to the first, no general initial principle can be put forward; rather, the resolution depends on the specification of the obligations in light of the standards of knowledge, causation, and reasonableness.[96] Reference to the relative importance of the interests meant to be protected also offers guidance.[97]

As to the scenario when positive and negative obligations corresponding to qualified rights compete, the starting point here is that positive obligations cannot be extended in a way that implies unjustified infringements of qualified rights. In this sense, negative obligations win. Yet, as already mentioned above, the assessment of whether an infringement is justifiable and proportionate in accordance with Article 8(2) ECHR is a specific and complex one that includes assessment of alternative less intrusive measures. This means that it might be possible for the State to take measures that infringe the right but are *less intrusive* (and thus not in violation of negative obligations) and at the same time, *sufficiently protective* for other interests involved (and

---

[93] Article 2 of Protocol No 4 to the ECHR.
[94] *Kurt v Austria* [GC] no 62903/15, 15 June 2021 §183.
[95] ibid (references omitted).
[96] See *Schüth v Germany* no 1620/03, 23 September 2010 §57 for example, where the issue was framed as 'whether the State was required, in the context of its positive obligations under Article 8, to uphold the applicant's right to respect for his private life against his dismissal by the Catholic Church. Accordingly, the Court, by examining how the German employment tribunal balanced the applicant's right with the Catholic Church's right under Article 9 and 11, will have to ascertain whether or not a sufficient degree of protection was afforded to the applicant.' The Court concluded that the domestic court failed to properly balance the interests involved in accordance with the principle of proportionality.
[97] The Court, for example, has consistently referred to the importance of the interests of the child: 'Article 8 "imposes on the authorities an obligation to take measures to reconcile the conflicting interests of the parties, keeping in mind the paramount interest of the child which, depending on their nature and seriousness, may override those of the parent"'. *Stankūnaitė v Lithuania* no 67068/11, 29 October 2019 §121.

thus in fulfilment of positive obligations). The assessment of alternatives, however, can be shaped by the important principle that limitations upon rights are to be interpreted restrictively.[98] Generally, this implies that actions by the State that harm carry a heavy justificatory burden.[99] The assumption underpinning human rights law is that intrusive measures need to be always and as a matter of principle justified. In contrast, such a principle does not operate in the context of omissions. The Court has never said that the State is under a *general* burden to justify its omissions. Practically, this is simply impossible because omissions are pervasive and might not be even cognizable.[100]

To conclude, negative obligations that are violated when the State acts impose higher restraints and, in some situations, conclusively 'win'. Positive obligations that are violated when the State omits to act might be weaker. The reason is that, in contrast to omissions, actions leading to harm might be more difficult to justify.

In its practice, the Court has been faced with tensions between qualified rights, one of which is framed as triggering negative obligations, while the other positive. The Court has had to rule on cases involving applicants who claimed violation of negative obligations corresponding to their right to freedom of expression, since the State had sanctioned them arguably to protect other individuals affected by the expressions.[101] At the same time, there have also been applicants who claim failure by the State to fulfil its positive obligations under Article 8 due to failures to limit certain expressions.[102] Such tensions, however, have not been framed as tensions between obligations. Although the Court has noted that restrictions upon rights need to be strictly construed and, therefore, '[t]he need for any restrictions must therefore be established convincingly',[103] which would imply some higher importance of negative obligations in abstract, the tension is rather framed as one of interests, which has some implications, as I will explain below. More concretely, the Court has noted that

> [t]he salient question [when faced with the need to strike a balance between two Convention rights: the right to freedom of expression under Article 10 and the right

---

[98] *Demir and Baykara v Turkey* [GC] no 34503/94, 12 November 2008 §146; *Perinçek v Switzerland* [GC] no 27510/08, 15 October 2015 §151: 'Bearing in mind that the context in which the terms in issue were used is a treaty for the effective protection of individual human rights, that clauses, such as Article 10(2), that permit interference with Convention rights *must be interpreted restrictively*, and that, more generally, exceptions to a general rule cannot be given a broad interpretation' (emphasis added).

[99] This can explain the Dissenting Opinion of Judges Martens and Matscher in *Gustafsson v Sweden* [GC] no 15573/89, 25 April 1996 §8: 'The Convention purports to lay down fundamental rights of the individual and to furnish the individual an effective protection against interferences with these rights. Therefore, once it is recognized that Article 11 encompasses a negative as well as a positive freedom of association, the negative freedom should in principle prevail in a conflict between them.' The Dissent, however, adds that '[t]he words "in principle" should be stressed'. See also Dissenting Opinion of Judge Wojtyczek in *Vavřička and Others v the Czech Republic* [GC] no 47621, 8 April 2021 4, where he explains that the State has the burden to justify interferences.

[100] See Section 4.2.1 where it is explained that the applicant has the initial burden.

[101] *Perinçek v Switzerland* [GC] no 27510/08, 15 October 2015.

[102] *Aksu v Turkey* [GC] no 4149/04 and 41029/07, 15 March 2012 §61; *Budinova and Chaprazov v Bulgaria* no 12567/13, 16 February 2021 §87.

[103] *Aksu v Turkey* [GC] §64.

to respect for private life under Article 8] is what relative weight should be ascribed to these two rights, which are *in principle entitled to equal respect*, in the specific circumstances of this case. It requires the Court to examine the comparative importance of the concrete aspects of the two rights that were at stake, the need to restrict, or to protect, each of them, and the proportionality between the means used and the aims sought to be achieved.[104]

The Court has also added that 'no hierarchical relationship exists between the rights guaranteed by the two Articles [Article 8 and 10]'.[105] Since the tension is framed as competition between the interests protected by the rights, the Court has determined different factors relevant to the assessment of the importance of the different interest on the two sides. For example, it has been established that the interests protected by the right to freedom of expression weight heavier when the right holder's speech contributes to a public debate, However, ultimately the issue is about the concrete measures taken, which is nicely reflected in the final statement in *Perinçek v Switzerland*: 'the Court concludes that it was not necessary, in a democratic society, *to subject the applicant to a criminal penalty* in order to protect the rights of the Armenian community at stake in the present case'.[106] The concrete measure taken, that is, the content of the positive obligation, was not considered necessary since alternatives to the usage of criminal penalty were available.

## 5.3.4 Determinacy of the Harm and the Affected Individuals

Another factor that can also guide the approach to competing obligations can be the determinacy of the harm in terms of potentiality and actuality. For example, the claimed protection of the right to life might be only a potentiality. It might be speculative and thus uncertain whether it is actually achievable.[107] In contrast, the attendant harm to interests caused by the interventions undertaken with the aim to protect life, might not be speculative, but certain and concrete,[108] or at least it might be easier to foresee it.

In the context of a concrete case before the ECtHR, the harm suffered by the concrete applicant who invokes positive obligations is usually not speculative. However, any attendant harm that might be caused to other individuals or groups due to the

---

[104] *Perinçek v Switzerland* [GC] §128 (emphasis added); *Budinova and Chaprazov v Bulgaria* §89.
[105] *Aksu v Turkey* [GC] §63 (emphasis added).
[106] *Perinçek v Switzerland* [GC] §280 (emphasis added).
[107] The ECtHR makes a *post factum* assessment in the specific case. In this context, no requirement is raised that the protective measure necessarily would have prevented the harm. See Chapter 3 that addresses causation.
[108] A nuance can be added here as to whether the attendant harm is intended. This harm could be unforeseeable and thus not intended; it could be also foreseeable, but still not intended.

interventions required by the invoked positive obligation might be more speculative. This difficulty is further exacerbated by the fact that these other individuals or groups are not directly involved in the case; it is rather the respondent state that has to represent their interests.

The uncertainty of any attendant harm that might be caused by measures taken in fulfilment of positive obligations is also related to the indeterminacy of the individuals or groups within the society who might have to suffer this harm. This has a quantitative dimension since positive obligations might lead to interventions restricting the interests of multiple individuals, and their number might be difficult to predict. Different groups within this multiplicity might be affected differently, some more seriously, others less so. Some of these individuals and groups might be easier to identify than others. The indeterminacy might also have a qualitative dimension since, for example, some groups might be considered as vulnerable, which in turn might make it more difficult to argue the reasonableness of affecting their interests for the protection of other groups.[109]

There is a risk that the positive obligations are somehow given priority just because they have been invoked by the applicant in the specific case.[110] Since the rights enshrined in the ECHR can be only invoked against a State, a situation that involves competing interests between private individuals is transformed once framed in terms of human rights law obligations.[111] This transformation implies that the conflict becomes one between the applicant who invokes positive obligations and the respondent State that might try to justify its inaction or less demanding positive obligations as necessary to respect its negative obligations owned to others (that are not involved in the proceedings before the Court).[112] The State might also try to justify its inaction or less demanding positive obligations as necessary to, for example, preserve resources so that it can ensure its positive obligations owned to other individuals or groups.

The determinacy of the party on one side of the equation, the concrete applicant, might tilt the reasoning in his or her favour, while any competing obligations might be left in the background. In other words, any attendant harm meant to be avoided or prevented by competing obligations might not be sufficiently highlighted but rather

---

[109] Vulnerability has been normally invoked before the ECtHR in support of more expansive positive obligations owed to individuals or groups considered vulnerable. *Aksu v Turkey* [GC] nos 4149/04 and 41029/07, 15 March 2012 §75; *Berkman v Russia* no 46712/15 1 December 2020 §46.

[110] This has been called 'preferential framing'. O Schutter and F Tulkens, 'Rights in Conflict: The European Court of Human Rights as a Pragmatic Institution' in Brems (ed), *Conflicts between Fundamental Rights* (n 6) 188; Smit, *Conflicts between Fundamental Rights* (n 6) 36 and 127. The Court has noted this risk in the specific context where positive obligations under Article 8 might be in tension with negative obligations under Article 10. See *Perinçek v Switzerland* [GC] no 27510/08, 15 October 2015 §198(i). See also Dissenting Opinion of Judge Wojtyczek in *Smiljanić v Croatia* no 35983/14, 25 March 2021.

[111] C Loven, ' "Verticalized" Cases before the European Court of Human Rights Unravelled' (2020) 38(4) Netherlands Quarterly of Human Rights 246.

[112] A danger also arises that the State might insincerely argue that it had no positive obligations, or it had such obligations but with limited scope, because they would constitute unjustified interferences with individuals' rights. See *Opuz v Turkey* no 33401/02, 9 June 2009 §140, where Turkey tried (unsuccessfully) to defend the absence of a requirement under its domestic law to pursue prosecution when the victim of domestic violence withdraws her complaint.

subsumed under the general standard of reasonableness together with any relevant general interests. Since the effects of intrusive measures (undertaken in fulfilment of positive obligations) might be diffuse and the lines of causality difficult to discern, these effects might not necessarily be framed as infringements of negative obligations. The attendant harm could be rather subsumed under the heading of negative effects upon general interests. Circumstances can also transpire where measures to arguably protect the interests of an applicant (or identifiable groups within the society) lead to withdrawal or non-extension of resources to other unidentifiable individuals or groups in the society. However, due to the indeterminacy of attendant harm and the individuals who might suffer this harm, the withdrawal and non-extension of resources can rather be framed as undermining of general interests.

To conclude, the indeterminacy of individuals that might be affected by the attendant harm and the ensuing difficulty or even absence of more concrete formulation of any competing positive or negative obligations held by them, could be conducive to more expansive positive obligations. It follows that some level of specification is required for the tension between obligations to become cognizable and this specification has to be achieved on both sides of the tension.

## 5.4 Accommodation of Obligations

Given that positive obligations can be specified in different ways and can be thus fulfilled by various measures, it is not likely that the State is confronted with a genuine conflict, that is, it owes obligations that are impossible to simultaneously fulfil. Rather, it would be possible for the State to take measures to comply with its positive obligations in a way that also implies respect for negative obligations and compliance with positive obligations owed to other persons. Given the available choices, it would be possible to find a compromise between the various obligations involved. They might be accommodated with varying sacrifices to their content and scope.

The positive obligation of protecting children by taking them into care so that they are removed from abusive family situations and the negative obligation upon the State not to disproportionately interfere with family life can be used as an illustration. When a child suffers abuse in the family, this could be very serious harm (falling within the definitional scope of Article 3), which justifies more demanding positive obligation that might weigh more heavily against any negative obligation to respect family life.[113] There might also be a risk that the harm would worsen in terms of severity and frequency. At the same time, the separation of the family could be also perceived as a measure causing serious harm. However, the severity of this harm might depend on the time frame (the duration of the separation) and any compensatory measures undertaken by the authorities (eg granting access rights to the parents and

---

[113] *K. and T. v Finland* no 25702/94, 12 July 2001 §269.

subsequent measures for facilitation of family reunification).[114] In light of these compensatory measures, the interests protected by the right to family life that ground any negative obligations might suffer a more limited damage. Meanwhile, any compensatory measures, such as facilitation of the reunion between a child and the parent, might face difficulties that should be also taken into account.[115]

It might, however, be difficult for a single judgment to reflect all the complexities involved in the specification and the accommodation of the obligations.[116] There is also an important structural limitation reflected in the principle of subsidiarity.[117] The outcome of the judgment is also binary—violation due to failure to fulfil the positive obligation in the case of the specific applicant or no violation. This binary outcome can send problematic messages, including higher ranking of positive obligations where responsibility is established. It will be useful then if the Court in its reasoning signals the importance of relating positive obligations with any competing human rights law obligations.[118] The involved human rights obligations have to be given equal respect. As opposed to general interests that are considered within the reasonableness standard, the interests protected by human rights that found obligations have special normative force. This specificity needs to be acknowledged in the reasoning. It might be therefore preferable for the Court to explicitly and early on in its reasoning note the danger of 'regulatory overreach',[119] 'coercive overreach',[120] and of extensive widening of the structures of control in the name of positive obligations.[121] The balancing and

---

[114] *Pedersen and Others v Norway* no 39710/15, 10 March 2020 §68; *K. and T. v Finland* [GC] no 25702/94, 12 July 2001 §268; *N.P. v Moldova* no 58455/13, 6 October 2015 §65; *Pavel Shishkov v Russia* no 78754/13, 2 March 2021 §76: 'Article 8 of the Convention thus imposes on every State the obligation to aim to reunite a natural parent with his or her child.'

[115] *Khusnutdinov and X. v Russia* no 76598/12, 18 December 2018 §80: 'any obligation to apply coercion in this area [ie the obligation upon the State to facilitate the reunion of a child with his/her parents] must be limited since the interests as well as the rights and freedoms of all concerned must be taken into account, and more particularly the best interests of the child and his or her rights under Article 8 of the Convention.'

[116] Admittedly, the Court cannot be expected to explore and theorize the various analytical issues that a single case might raise. '[i]t might sometimes be preferable not to say too much in a judgment when every argument may open up new discussions'. P Lemmens and M Courtoy, 'Deterrence as a Key Factor in the European Court of Human Rights Case Law' in Lavrysen and Mavronicola (eds), *Coercive Human Rights* (n 9) 55, 56.

[117] The mentioned complexity is more appropriate to be addressed by the national legislator, which implies the Court might refuse to perform a concrete proportionality review and an ad hoc balancing of the interest. The assumption rather is that this balancing has been already done by the national legislator. See S Smet, 'When Human Rights Clash in "the Age of Subsidiarity" in P Agha (ed), *Human Rights between Law and Politics: The Margin of Appreciation in Post-National Contexts* (Hart Publishing 2017) 55.

[118] The reasoning in *Kotilainen and Others v Finland* no 62439/12, 17 September 2020 §88, is a useful illustration to this effect: 'The Court also observes that such a measure [seizing the gun from the perpetrator who used is to kill students at a school shooting] would not have entailed any significant interference with *any competing rights* under the Convention, and thus it would not have involved any particularly difficult and delicate balancing exercise (emphasis added).'

[119] Partly Dissenting Opinion of Judge Eicke in *Kotilainen and Others v Finland*: 'a risk of (and perhaps an incentive for) regulatory overreach with the Stated aim of achieving yet greater security for everybody (or at least the impression thereof)'.

[120] L Lazarus, 'Positive Obligations and Criminal Justice: Duties to Protect or Coerce' in L Zedner and J Roberts (eds), *Principles and Values in Criminal Law and Criminal Justice* (Oxford University Press 2012) 135.

[121] Such a danger clearly arises if the position expressed by Judge Pinto in his separate opinion in *Volodina v Russia* no 41261/17, 9 July 2019, were to be followed. Judge Pinto endorsed 'preventive detention

reasonableness analysis has also to reflect the relation between different obligations and any tensions among them expressly.

Recognition of competing obligations is beneficial because it opens a discussion as to the appropriateness of different protective measures and how they serve different interests. Such a discussion can facilitate the search for alternatives that are less detrimental to all (or most) interests involved. It also reveals that ultimately trade-offs are unavoidable and that choices need to be made. There are therefore no tidy solutions. Despite the risk of oversimplification, the choice made will have to be assessed against the broader framework where more protection, that demands more state interventions and intrusiveness, competes, with liberty that calls for more restrained State. The direction taken is reflective of the kind of society that we want to be and how we choose to use our resource.

## Conclusion

Once the content and the scope of positive obligations is specified, it might emerge that their fulfilment might cause attendant harm to interests that underlie human rights. This implies that a positive obligation might stand in competition with other obligations (both positive and negative) intended to prevent such attendant harm. This competition needs to be taken into account so that the content and the scope of positive obligations do not extend unreasonably, and protective overreach is avoided. In the assessment of the reasonableness and for the purpose of preventing such overreach, competing obligations should be assigned a role distinct from the role of competing general public interests. In contrast to the latter, whose justifications are utilitarian and quantitative, the interests that ground competing human rights obligations pertain to single individuals and are meant to have qualitative precedence over utilitarian calculations. When human rights law obligations compete, such qualitative precedence is assigned to both sides of the competition, and the challenge arises how to address it so that protective overreach and the above-mentioned attendant harm are avoided.

Four considerations can guide the response to this challenge. First, positive obligations to prevent harm are not acceptable when these obligations themselves cause attendant harm that implies treating individuals as objects. Second, the importance of the interests on each side of the competition is also a relevant consideration. This, however, does *not* mean a general qualitative priority of one right over another (eg along the lines that the right to life is generally more important that the right to private life and therefore, any positive obligations corresponding to the first 'win out' in cases of competition). The reason is that a right can trigger multiple obligations, and

---

of the perpetrators where this is deemed necessary'. Yet, it needs to be considered how such a detention is compatible with the rights of the 'perpetrators'.

these can stand in different relations to obligations triggered by other rights, in terms of content and scope. Within this multiplicity of competing obligations, it is still relevant to distinguish between positive and negative obligations. This distinction is the third consideration that plays a role in avoiding protective overreach. This distinction can be also further refined since it is also relevant to distinguish whether these competing obligations (positive or negative) correspond to absolute (ie Article 3), strictly qualified (Article 2), or qualified rights (Article 8). One implication from these two distinctions is that the content of positive obligations cannot include actions in breach of negative obligations. A positive obligation whose content includes actions that can be defined as torture, or that go beyond the circumstances indicated in Article 2(2), is conclusively defeated. Even if a positive obligation fits within and serves the purposes under Article 2(2), it is weaker in comparison to the obligation upon the State not to use lethal force unless 'absolutely necessary'. Positive obligations whose content include actions amounting to disproportionate infringement with qualified rights are also precluded. It is indeed difficult to assess whether the action is disproportionate, which makes the resolution of the competition also difficult. A relevant consideration here is that, unlike with omissions, the State is assumed to be under a constant burden to justify its actions as might amount to infringements. Finally, the determinacy of the attendant harm and the affected individuals is another consideration discussed in this chapter that can guide the approach to competing obligations. The higher the determinacy, the more importance can be assigned to the obligations that might compete with positive obligations.

Despite the relevance of the four considerations discussed above, competitions and tensions between obligations are unavoidable given the role of the State in mediating different interests within the society (see Section 1.1). The identification and the acknowledgement of these competitions is helpful since it can promote a choice of protective measures that can accommodate all affected interests, in this way avoiding disproportionate forms of intrusiveness.

Having explained how the protective measures that form the content of positive obligations are shaped by the factors of state knowledge, causation, and reasonableness and by any competing obligations, a closer focus on the measures is warranted. These can be generally divided into *post factum* measures with the objective of investigating harm and preventive measures with the objective of averting the actual harm from materializing. Given these objectives, the former constitute the content of the procedural positive obligation to investigate, addressed in Chapter 6, while the latter constitute the content of substantive positive obligations, addressed in Chapter 7. Chapters 6 and 7 conclude with sections that aim to reflect upon the role of reasonableness explicitly as related to the factors of knowledge and causation, in the trigger and the delineation of the content and the scope of the procedural and the substantive positive obligations.

# 6
# Procedural Positive Obligation to Investigate

## Introduction

Under certain conditions, national authorities are under the positive obligation to conduct effective investigation into allegations that individuals have been harmed. The obligation to investigate has been extensively developed in relation to the right to life and the right not to be subjected to torture, inhumane or degrading treatment or punishment. It has been referred to as a procedural obligation or as the procedural limb of Articles 2 and 3.[1] The Court has also referred to 'the converging principles of the procedural obligation' under these two articles.[2] The content and the scope of the obligation to investigate under Article 8 has been also reviewed by the Court in light of similar principles and requirements,[3] yet the obligation, when reviewed under Article 8, has some specifics that will be noted in the forthcoming analysis.

The above-mentioned provisions impose two types of investigative duties that need to be separated from the start.[4] The content of the first type can be formulated as a general obligation for the state to have an *effective judicial system* so that light can be shed on the course of events that arguably led to harm. This general obligation does not require the State to initiate a particular type of investigation, since any proceedings—criminal, civil, administrative, disciplinary, or combinations of these—can suffice.[5] The second type can be framed as an obligation that has a more specific content since it requires the State to initiate a specific type of investigation, namely an *official criminal investigation*. These two types (ie the general obligation to have an effective judicial system, on the one hand, and the more specific and more demanding obligation to conduct official criminal investigation) have produced distinct lines of case law as

---

[1] *X and Others v Bulgaria* [GC] no 22457/16, 2 February 2021 §178.
[2] *S.M. v Croatia* [GC] no 60561/14, 25 June 2020 §309; *Mocanu and Others v Romania* [GC] no 10865/09, 17 September 2014 §§216–217.
[3] *Botoyan v Armenia* no 5766/17, 8 February 2022 §91. K Kamber, *Prosecuting Human Rights Offences* (Martinus Nijhoff Publishers 2017) 339.
[4] K Kamber, 'Substantive and Procedural Criminal Law Protection of Human Rights in the Law of the European Convention on Human Rights' (2020) 20(1) Human Rights Law Review 75, 78.
[5] *Ribcheva and Others v Bulgaria* no 37801/16, 30 March 2021 §139: 'It cannot be said that there should be one unified procedure satisfying all requirements: the tasks of fact-finding and ensuring accountability may be shared between different authorities, as long as the procedures as a whole provide for the necessary safeguards in an accessible and effective manner.' *Anna Todorova v Bulgaria* no 23302/03, 24 May 2011 §74: 'Article 2 did not necessarily call for a criminal-law remedy. The Court must then take a comprehensive look at the procedures that were available to the applicant in relation to her son's death.'

*Positive Obligations under the European Convention on Human Rights*. Vladislava Stoyanova, Oxford University Press.
© Vladislava Stoyanova 2023. DOI: 10.1093/oso/9780192888044.003.0007

to when they are triggered and how they can be fulfilled. While the two types of obligations might impose similar requirements in terms of independence, thoroughness, promptness, public oversight, and victim involvement, this is not always the case. For this reason, it is important to categorize which obligation is triggered under what circumstances, which will be done in Section 6.1.

Section 6.2. will then clarify these requirements, in this way explaining the content of the procedural obligation. As it will show, the content varies depending on the source of the harm (ie harm inflicted by state actors, by non-state actors, or linked with arguable omissions). These variations also affect how the proceedings at national level ought to be initiated. Section 6.2 will also explain when these proceedings can be considered effective and when they might demand cooperation with other States. The Conclusion will link this chapter with Chapters 2 to 5 by reflecting upon the role of causation, knowledge, and reasonableness in the trigger and the articulation of the content and scope of the obligation to investigate.

Before this, two more introductory remarks are due. The first one concerns the distinction between the conditions that *trigger the review by the Court* as to whether the State was under the obligation to investigate, on the one hand, and the conditions that *trigger the obligation to investigate*, on the other. The latter issue will be addressed in Section 6.1 and refers to the actual assessment by the Court of whether, at the relevant point in time, the obligation was triggered (ie whether the obligation was engaged and existed) for the national authorities. In contrast, the first issue is of a more general nature since it concerns the *ratione materiae* compatibility of the applicant's complaints. In other words, it concerns the definitional scope of the rights as a necessary preliminary question that needs to be resolved before the Court can even proceed to review any obligations corresponding to the rights.[6] Normally, the Court will first assess whether the harm invoked by the applicant affects interests covered by the definitional scope of the relevant right. In case of a positive determination, the Court will continue to review compliance with obligations corresponding to the rights whose definitional scopes have been already found to be engaged. In the context of the procedural obligation, however, this two-stage review can cause complications.[7] The reason is that it might not be possible or very difficult to perform the first stage properly, because there was no investigation of the facts by the national authorities, or the investigation was ineffective. The question that arises then is whether, when faced with this difficulty, the Court should ignore the definitional stage and move directly to the second stage (ie the review of whether the obligation to investigate was triggered).

---

[6] See eg *Nicolae Virgiliu Tănase v Romania* [GC] no 41720/13, 25 June 2019 §§115–145, where the complaint was incompatible *ratione materiae* with Articles 3 and 8, but it could be examined under the definitional scope of Article 2. A complaint could be declared incompatible based on other grounds, such as incompatibility *ratione loci*. See Chapter 8.

[7] For the two-stage review, see J Gerards and E Brems, 'Introduction' in E Brems and J Gerards (eds), *Shaping Rights in the ECHR. The Role of the European Court of Human Rights in Determining the Scope of Human Rights* (Cambridge University Press 2014) 1.

## Introduction 125

In many judgments under Article 3, the Court has first determined whether the minimum definitional threshold of Article 3 is met and only then has it reviewed whether the State has lived up to its positive obligations, including its procedural obligation.[8] In *S.M. v Croatia*, however, the problem arising from this approach came to the fore. The national authorities investigated and there were criminal proceedings. The national courts however concluded that there was insufficient evidence for convicting the individual. If the European Court of Human Rights (ECtHR) were to rely on these factual findings (that were at the end found inadequate by the Court) without questioning their thoroughness it might not be able to decide whether the definitional scope of the right is engaged. If the two-stage approach were therefore to be strictly followed, this would imply that breach of obligations cannot be assessed. In *S.M. v Croatia* the Court avoided the definitional stage: it never determined whether indeed the harm alleged by the applicant fell within the definitional scope of the relevant right. It directly assessed compliance with the procedural obligation. The Court noted that when the applicant's complaint is 'essentially of a procedural nature'

> a conclusion as to whether the domestic authorities' procedural obligation arose has to be based on the circumstances prevailing at the time when the relevant allegations were made or when the prima facia evidence of treatment contrary to Article 4 was brought to the authorities attention and *not on a subsequent conclusion reached upon the completion of the investigation of the relevant proceedings*. This is particularly true when there are allegations that such conclusions and the relevant domestic proceedings were marred by significant procedural flaws. Indeed relying on such domestic findings and conclusions would entail *a risk of creating a circular reasoning* resulting in a case concerning an arguable claim or prima facie evidence of treatment contrary to Article 4 remaining outside the Court's scrutiny under the Convention.[9]

While this approach might be understandable given the objective of the procedural obligation to investigate (ie fact finding), it is not without its challenges. At least three can be identified. First, the Court risks taking the role of fact finder.[10] Second, the approach suggests a differentiation between the standards that trigger the review by the

---

[8] *Denis Vasilyev v Russia* no 32704/04, 17 December 2009 §95; *C.A.S. and C.S. v Romania* no 26692/05, 20 March 2012; *Valiulienė v Lithuania* no 33234/07, 26 March 2013 §73; *Koky and Others v Slovakia* no 13624/03, 12 June 2012 §§216–225; *Women's Initiative Supporting Group and Others v Georgia* no 73204/13, 16 December 2021 §61. See, however, *Beganović v Croatia* no 46423/06, 25 June 2009 §68, where the Court only established that 'the applicant's allegations of ill-treatment were "arguable" and capable of "raising a reasonable suspicion" so as to attract the applicability of Article 3 of the Convention'.

[9] *M.S. v Croatia* [GC] no 60561/14, 25 June 2020 §§324–325 (emphasis added). Although this is an Article 4 case, the Court refers to the 'converging principles of the procedural obligation under Articles 2 and 3' and how these actually inform the procedural obligation under Article 4.

[10] The Court has warned that 'it must be cautious in taking on the role of a first-instance tribunal of fact where this was not rendered unavoidable by the circumstances of a particular case'. *Bouyid v Belgium* [GC] no 23380/09, 28 September 2015 §85.

Court, depending on the obligations invoked.[11] Third, human rights as expressions of fundamental interests might risk being trivialized if the Court's review avoids an assessment of how these interests have been specifically harmed (ie avoidance of the definitional stage).[12] These challenges might vary for the different rights. In the context of Article 2, normally the harm is easy to identify since there is physical evidence of death or life-threatening injuries.[13] In the context of Article 3, there is normally some physical evidence of harm and, in addition, the Court has developed certain presumptions.[14] This is certainly, however, not the case for Article 8, given its wide definitional scope. It can therefore be concluded that the easier it is to demonstrate the physical manifestation of the harm, the less poignant the three challenges might be.

The second introductory remark also concerns the trigger of the review by the Court as to whether the State was under the obligation to investigate. As clarified above, the Court might avoid the definitional stage and directly review the triggering of and compliance with the procedural obligation. A question that also arises is whether the triggering of and compliance with the procedural obligation can be also reviewed without any prior determination by the Court that the State has breached any of its substantive obligations. In the context of Articles 2 and 3, it has been explicitly determined that the obligation to investigate is an independent and autonomous obligation that can arise without an actual *or* an arguable breach by the State of its substantive duties.[15] In other words, it is not necessary to first demonstrate that the State bears responsibility for harm through acts or omissions (ie actual breach of substantive negative or positive obligations), so that the Court assesses whether the obligation to investigate arises. Neither is it necessary that the applicant formulates a claim before the Court that the State has breached any of its substantive obligations (ie an arguable breach). A breach of the procedural obligation under Article 2 has been alleged and reviewed by the Court in the absence of any complaint regarding the substantive limb of the provision.[16]

---

[11] See eg *Nicolae Virgiliu Tănase v Romania* [GC] no 41720/13, 25 June 2019 §133, where the Court formulated its task as determining 'whether the facts of the instant case fall under the procedural limb of Article 2', not as whether the facts fall within the scope of Article 2. In fact, the formulation used by the Court in this citation is nonsensical since the facts cannot fall within the procedural obligation or within any obligation for that matter.

[12] In *Nicolae Virgiliu Tănase v Romania* [GC] §§115–132, this risk was avoided by a detailed engagement with the definitional scopes of Articles 3 and 8 and, specifically, with the question whether the harm to the applicant's interests corresponded to the interests meant to be protected by these two provisions.

[13] *Nicolae Virgiliu Tănase v Romania* [GC] §144 has complicated the definitional threshold of Article 2 since it added not only 'seriously life-threatening injuries' but also putting the life of the person 'at real and immediate risk' in the context of activities that are dangerous by their nature.

[14] The Court has found some techniques to address evidential issues in some situations. For example, the absence of physical evidence may be excused when the person has been under the authority and control of the State that alone was in a position to know or establish the facts complained of. *Ibrahimov and Mammadov v Azerbaijan* no 63571/16, 13 February 2020 §89.

[15] *Šilih v Slovenia* [GC] no 71463/01, 9 April 2009 §156; *Nicolae Virgiliu Tănase v Romania* [GC] no 41720/13, 25 June 2019 §138; *Armani Da Silva v United Kingdom* [GC] no 5878/08, 30 March 2016 §231.

[16] *Armani Da Silva v the United Kingdom* [GC] §231; *Šilih v Slovenia* [GC] §158; *Calvelli and Ciglio v Italy* [GC] no 32967/96, 17 January 2002 §§41–57.

The independent and autonomous nature of the obligation implies that investigations are considered to have an intrinsic value. They are meant to elucidate the factual circumstances as a whole. The scope of these circumstances is wide since it is not limited to those that might suggest wrongdoing (in the form of acts or omissions) by the State. In addition, it is not possible to know whether there were such wrongdoings prior to an investigation that aims to elucidate the facts.[17]

The procedural obligation under Article 8 has not been explicitly characterized as 'separate and autonomous'. This can be related to the general ambiguity as to the trigger of positive obligations under this provision, as explained in Section 4.2.1. In addition, the distinction between substantive obligations and the general procedural obligation of having an effective judicial system might not be straightforward. As Chapter 7 will show, the first one includes adoption of effective regulatory framework with effective procedural safeguards. The procedural obligation of having effective judicial system can be regarded as an implementation of this very regulatory framework, which blurs the distinction between the two obligations.

## 6.1 Conditions that Trigger the Obligation

Although, as clarified above, an arguable breach of any substantive obligations might not be necessary for triggering the procedural obligation, there still needs to be a *threshold* that determines when this obligation had arisen for the national authorities at the time when the relevant events were unfolding.[18] This threshold reflects the conditions under which the obligation is triggered (eg an arguable claim of ill-treatment),[19] which will be explained in this section. Here it is relevant to note that a State can be found in breach since it failed to conduct an investigation. This failure leads to a breach because the obligation was found to be triggered by the Court in light of the *post factum* assessment of the circumstances of the specific case. And yet the national authorities did not investigate at the relevant time.[20] The State can be also found in breach since although it actually conducted an investigation, the latter did not comply with the qualitative standards as developed by the Court. This means that

---

[17] *M.H. and Others v Croatia*, no 15670/18 and 43115/18, 18 November 2021 §165. The case concerned the death of a child hit by a train after an alleged denial of an opportunity to seek asylum in Croatia by Croatian police officers and ordered to return to Serbia by following the train tracks. In the absence of an effective investigation, the Court could not conclude if Croatia violated its substantive obligation under Article 2 (ie whether the denial to seek asylum and the push back to Serbia by the Croatian police officers could be causality link with the death).

[18] *Lopes de Sousa Fernandes v Portugal* [GC] no 56080/13, 19 December 2017 §222: 'the applicant had *arguably grounds to suspect that her husbands' death could have been the result of medical negligence*. The respondent State's duty to ensure compliance with the procedural obligations arising under Article 2, in the proceedings instituted with regard to her husband's death, is therefore engaged in the present case' (emphasis added).

[19] Note that this threshold does not correspond to an arguable claim that the responsibility of the State is engaged due to breach of any substantive obligations.

[20] See eg *J.I. v Croatia* no 35898/16, 8 September 2022 §91.

the content or the scope of the obligation is found by the Court to be more demanding or wider in comparison with the investigative measures actually undertaken by the national authorities at the relevant time. The content and the scope of the obligation will be addressed in Section 6.2.

Applicants have argued that national investigations and responses by national judicial systems are ineffective in a wide variety of factual circumstances. It is useful to categorize the case law into different groups for at least three reasons: first, the conditions that trigger the obligation might be different for the different groups; second, there might be nuances as to how the trigger of the obligation is justified; and third, the content and the scope of the obligation might be different for the different groups of cases. This section will clarify the first two, while the third will be covered in Section 6.2.

The cases can be divided into three groups. Section 6.1.1 will cover cases where harm has been inflicted by state actors. Section 6.1.2 will focus on cases where harm has been inflicted by non-state actors. Finally, Section 6.1.3 will addresses cases where harm has been linked with arguable omissions.[21] These last cases have been also characterized as negligence cases. To make these differentiations, the Court has referred to the mental state of the actor: intention (ie intentional infliction of harm by an actor in the first two groups) and negligence that can be manifested by state authorities or by private actors.[22] The meaning attached to these concepts (ie intention and negligence) in the case law has, however, remained vague. For this reason, multiple questions have remained unanswered. For example, if intention is invoked, a question that arises concerns the required level of intention: is it *dolus intent*, where the actor intends to cause the specific harm, or is it intention understood as knowledge about the harm?[23] Another question that can be asked is intention in relationship to what? Is it about the actor's intention to kill or about his or her intention to inflict harm more generally that might inadvertently lead to a lethal outcome?[24] In addition, the actor's mental state might be unknown without an investigation.[25] In the context of Article

---

[21] I use the words 'harmful conduct' and 'actor of harm' without prejudice regarding whether the conduct actually caused the harm and without prejudice to whether this actor is responsible under human rights law (relevant to state actors) or under national criminal, civil, or administrative law (relevant to both state and non-state actors).

[22] Other terms are also used: 'carelessness', 'reckless disregard' (*Öneryildiz v Turkey* [GC] no 48939/99, 30 November 2004 §71); 'fault' (*Lopes de Sousa Fernandes v Portugal* [GC] no 56080/13, 19 December 2017§215); 'unintentional' (*Nicolae Virgiliu Tănase v Romania* [GC] no 41720/13, 25 June 2019 §158); 'intentionally' (*Öneryildiz v Turkey* [GC] §92); 'unintentional negligence' (*Vo v France* [GC] no 53924/00, 8 July 2004 §86); 'negligence' (*Kotilainen and Others v Finland* no 62439/12, 17 September 2020 §91); 'sphere of negligence' (*Mastromatteo v Italy* [GC] no 37703/97, 24 October 2002 §90); 'direct official action' (*Bakanova v Lithuania* no 11167/12, 31 May 2016 §67); 'mere fault, omission or negligence' (*Jeronovičs v Latvia* [GC] no 44898/10, 5 July 2016 §76); 'gross medical negligence' (*Denis Vasilyev v Russia* no 32704/04, 17 December 2009 §53).

[23] These are concepts borrowed from criminal law. See Section 2.1.

[24] *McCann and Others v the United Kingdom* [GC] no 18984/91, 27 September 1995 §148, where it is explained that Article 2(2) 'describes the situations where it is permitted to "use force" which may result, as an unintended outcome, in the deprivation of life'. The Court noted that it must 'subject deprivation of life to the most careful scrutiny, particularly where deliberate lethal force is used'. Based on these quotations, the following distinction can be made: first, intention in relation to outcome (ie death), and second, intention in relation to the actor's action (ie the action itself was deliberately undertaken by the actor).

[25] *Mustafa Tunç and Fecire Tunç v Turkey* [GC] no 24014/05, 14 April 2015 §133.

3, is intention to specifically humiliate or degrade relevant?[26] In the alternative, is the actor's awareness of his or her harmful conduct sufficient for a case to fall within the first two groups of cases? Does awareness refer to harmful consequences of a conduct or is it limited to awareness of the breach of, for example, some safety rules?[27]

The same vagueness surrounds the concept of negligence as used in the case law. For example, in *Kotelnikov v Russia* the Court referred to 'negligent behaviour of a private individual',[28] however no particular meaning was attached to the term 'negligent'. In *Öneryildiz v Turkey*, different levels of negligence attributable to state agents were distinguished.[29] A related question that arises is how to differentiate between, on the one hand, actions without a specific intention but with some awareness about risks from, on the other hand, negligence.[30]

Admittedly, the terms intention and negligence have their own definitional challenges, gradations of seriousness, and nuances as used in the national legal orders. It might not be feasible to expect from the Court to take them all into consideration. The Court rather uses these terms in vague ways, which makes the ensuring categorization and distinctions open to challenges, yet intention and negligence are used in the Court's reasoning as criteria for differentiating cases and, correspondingly, for introduction of differentiations as to the triggering, the scope, and the content of the procedural obligation. The following analysis is therefore structured accordingly.

## 6.1.1 Harm Inflicted by State Actors

Historically, the obligation to investigate was first formulated in circumstances involving use of force by state agents. In *McCann and Others v The United Kingdom*, the Court formulated the obligation of conducting 'effective official investigation when individuals have been killed as a result of use of force by, inter alios, agents of the State'.[31] Whether the outcome (ie actual death or life-threatening injury) of the state agents' actions was intended or not is irrelevant for the trigger of the obligation. However, these are clearly situations where the state agents intended the use of force.

---

[26] *Nicolae Virgiliu Tănase v Romania* [GC] no 41720/13, 25 June 2019 §117: 'the absence of an intention to humiliate or debase the victim cannot conclusively rule out a finding of a violation of Article 3'.
[27] See eg Dissenting Opinion of Judge Bošnjak in *Mažukna v Lithuania* no 72092/12, 11 April 2017, a case about an accident at a workplace reviewed under Article 3, where it was noted that '[t]he offender's intent relates to the violation of safety or health requirements and not to the consequences, which in the present case was the serious bodily harm suffered by the applicant'.
[28] *Kotelnikov v Russia* no 45104/05, 12 July 2016 §95.
[29] *Öneryildiz v Turkey* [GC] no 48939/99, 30 November 2004 §93: 'error of judgment or carelessness' versus negligence but with 'fully realizing the likely consequences and disregarding the powers vested in [the state actors]'.
[30] See eg *Muta v Uktrain* no 37246/06, 31 July 2012, a case about a child being hit with a stone by another child, leaving the first child blind in his eye, where it was not possible to know whether the act was intentional or negligent. Despite this uncertainty, the Court applied the same standards to an investigation concerning an act by a private individual.
[31] *McCann and Others v The United Kingdom* [GC] no 18984/91, 27 September 1995 §161.

The outcome (ie actual death or life-threatening injury) might be possible to causally link with omissions (eg omissions as to the planning of the police operation) that must be also an object of the investigation. This, however, does not change the standard for triggering the obligation, namely the mere fact that an individual has been killed as a result of use of force. As the Court has noted the mere knowledge of the killing on the part of the authorities gives rise *ipso facto* to an obligation under Article 2 to carry out an effective investigation into the circumstances surrounding the death.[32]

In contrast, Article 3 requires 'an arguable claim' of ill-treatment so that the procedural obligation is triggered

> where an individual raises an arguable claim that he has been seriously ill-treated by the police or other such agents of the State unlawfully and in breach of Article 3, that provision, read in conjunction with the State's general duty under Article 1 of the Convention ... requires by implication that there should be an effective official investigation.[33]

In addition to 'arguable claim', 'credible assertion' and 'reasonable suspicion' have been also used as triggers.[34] Similarly to the standard developed under Article 2, no formal complaint is required for the obligation to be triggered.[35] Whether the state actors intended anything beyond the ill-treatment (eg extraction of confession) is not relevant for the trigger of the obligation under Article 3.[36]

The main reasons invoked under Articles 2 and 3 to justify the imposition of the procedural obligation have been effectiveness and accountability. The Court has observed that 'a general legal prohibition of arbitrary killing by the agents of the State would be ineffective, in practice, if there existed no procedure for reviewing the lawfulness of the use of force by State authorities'.[37] If there were no official criminal investigation, 'the general legal prohibition of torture and inhuman and degrading treatment and punishment, despite its fundamental importance, would be ineffective in practice'.[38] As to accountability, the Court has clarified that the purpose of the investigation is to ensure 'accountability for deaths and ill-treatment occurring under their [the authorities] responsibility'.[39] This implies that the investigation has to be capable not only of finding relevant facts but also identification and punishment of

---

[32] *Salman v Turkey* [GC] no 21986/93, 27 June 2000 §105.
[33] *Assenov and Others v Bulgaria* no 24760/94, 28 October 1998 §102; *El-Masri v the former Yugoslav Republic of Macedonia* [GC] no 39630/09, 13 December 2012 §82.
[34] *Mocanu and Others v Romania* [GC] no 10865/09, 17 September 2014 §317.
[35] *El-Masri v the former Yugoslav Republic of Macedonia* [GC] no 39630/09, 13 December 2012 §186.
[36] It is, however, relevant to the content and the scope of the procedural obligation, since the investigation has to also reveal whether there were any specific intentions. See Section 6.2.3.
[37] *McCann and Others v The United Kingdom* [GC] no 18984/91, 27 September 1995 §161.
[38] *Mocanu and Others v Romania* [GC] no 10865/09, 17 September 2014 §316; *Al-Skeini and Others v the United Kingdom* [GC] no 55721/07, 7 July 2011 §163; *El-Masri v the former Yugoslav Republic of Macedonia* [GC] no 39630/09, 13 December 2012 §182; *Bouyid v Belgium* [GC] no 23380/09, 28 September 2015 §116.
[39] *Nachova and Others v Bulgaria* [GC] no 43577/98, 6 July 2005 §110; *Bouyid v Belgium* [GC] no 23380/09, 28 September 2015 §117.

those who might be responsible.[40] This in turn explains why only official criminal investigation is considered as capable of complying with the procedural obligation in cases of harm inflicted by state agents. This will be further clarified in Section 6.2.1.

Having explained the procedural limb of Articles 2 and 3 when state actors inflict harm, the procedural obligation under Article 8 can be addressed. When state actors infringe the interests protected by Article 8, this triggers a review whether the interference was 'in accordance with the law' and pursued a legitimate aim and was proportionate. Domestic proceedings and their quality, including ability to clarify factual circumstances, might be demanded as part of the assessment whether the 'in accordance with the law'[41] or the 'necessary in a democratic society' requirements[42] are met. The different structure of Article 8 (formulation of the right in the first paragraph and then a general limitation clause in the second) might therefore explain why explicit procedural limb of this provision has been barely developed;[43] the focus has rather been on the substantive limb (ie breach of negative obligations).[44] It was for the first time in *Basu v Germany*, where the Court explicitly held that Article 8 has a procedural limb. The applicants claimed that they were subjected to racial profiling by the police during identity check on a train. The Court held that

> an obligation to investigate should even less be excluded in the context of Article 8 in relation to acts of State agents if the applicant makes an arguable claim that he has been targeted on account of specific physical or ethnic characteristics.[45]

As the quotation shows, similarly to the standard under Article 3, the threshold for triggering the obligation was framed as 'an arguable claim'.

## 6.1.2 Harm Inflicted by Non-state Actors

The positive obligation to investigate also arises in circumstances where harm is not inflicted by state authorities. These can be situations where the actors of harm might

---

[40] *Labita v Italy* [GC] no 26772/95, 6 April 2000 §131.
[41] *Azer Ahmadov v Azerbaijan* no 3409/10, 22 July 2021 §§63–74.
[42] *Vinks and Ribicka v Latvia* no 28926/10, 30 January 2020 §116; *Ageyevy v Russia* no 7075/10, 18 April 2013 §128: 'whilst Article 8 contains no explicit procedural requirements, the decision-making process involved in measures of interference must be fair and such as to afford due respect to the interest safeguarded by Article 8'.
[43] Such a procedural limb needs to be distinguished from the procedural safeguards addressed in Section 7.2.
[44] *Y.P. v Russia* no 43399/13, 20 September 2022 §§49 and 57–58, a case of sterilization without consent, where it was determined that access to proceedings for obtaining compensation is part of the positive obligation under Article 8. However, the judicial response in connection with the infringement of Article 8 rights was not assessed separately, but as part of the overall determination that there has been a violation of Article 8.
[45] *Basu v Germany* no 215/19, 18 October 2022 §32.

be private persons,[46] unknown actors,[47] or circumstances of self-inflicted harm.[48] The Court has observed that

> [t]he State's obligation under Article 2 § 1 of the Convention to protect the right to life requires by implication that there should be an effective official investigation when an individual has sustained life-threatening injuries *in suspicious circumstances*, even when the presumed perpetrator of the attack is not a State agent.[49]

The Court has also added that '*the mere knowledge of the killing* on the part of the authorities gave rise *ipso facto* to an obligation under Article 2 of the Convention to carry out an effective investigation into the circumstances surrounding the death'.[50] The Court has also used the following formulation: 'When an intentional taking of life is alleged, the mere fact that the authorities are informed that a death had taken place gives rise *ipso facto* to an obligation under Article 2 to carry out an effective official investigation.'[51]

As to Article 3, the procedural obligation is triggered 'where an individual claims on arguable grounds to have suffered acts contrary to Article 3'. The Court has added that '[s]uch an obligation cannot be considered to be limited solely to cases of ill-treatment by State agents'.[52] For example, in *X and Others v Bulgaria*, the Court concluded that

> the Bulgarian authorities were faced with 'arguable' claims, for the purposes of the case law, of serious abuse of children in their charge, and that they had a duty under Article 3 of the Convention to take the necessary measures without delay to assess the credibility of the claims, clarify the circumstances of the case and identify those responsible.[53]

The threshold of 'arguable claim' is important[54] since it implies some level of substantiation of the claim and quality of the underlying evidence. No formal complaint is,

---

[46] For example, *M.C. v Bulgaria* no 39272/98, 4 December 2003; *O'Keeffe v Ireland* [GC] no 35810/09, 28 January 2014.
[47] As in cases of suspicious deaths and disappearances. For example, *Tahsin Acar v Turkey* [GC] no 26307/95, 8 April 2004 §226.
[48] *Vasilca v the Republic of Moldova* no 69527/10, 11 February 2014 §28.
[49] *Ribcheva and Others v Bulgaria* no 37801/16, 30 March 2021 §125 (emphasis added); *Mustafa Tunc and Fecire Tunc v Turkey* [GC] no 24014/05, 14 April 2015 §§169–182; *Rantsev v Cyprus and Russia* no 25965/04, 7 January 2010 §234.
[50] *Ergi v Turkey* no 23818/94, 28 July 1998 §82 (emphasis added).
[51] *Šilih v Slovenia* [GC] no 71463/01, 9 April 2009 §156.
[52] *X and Others v Bulgaria* [GC] no 22457/16, 2 February 2021 §184; *Beganovic v Croatia* no 46423/06, 25 June 2009 §66; *C.A.S. and C.S. v Romania* no 26692/05, 20 March 2012 §69; *Milanović v Serbia* no 44614/07, 14 December 2010 §§85–86; *M. and Others v Italy and Bulgaria* no 40020/03, 31 July 2012 §§101–103.
[53] *X and Others v Bulgaria* [GC] no 22457/16, 2 February 2021 §201.
[54] In some Article 3 judgments, the Court does not invoke the trigger of 'arguable claim'. It rather observed that 'the procedural obligation arises once a matter has been brought to the attention of the authorities'. *O'Keeffe v Ireland* [GC] no 35810/09, 28 January 2014 §173; *I.E. v Moldova* no 45422/13, 26 May 2020 §42.

however, required: 'once the matter has come to the attention of the authorities, this gives rise *ipso facto* to an obligation under that Article [Article 3] that the State carries out an effective investigation'.[55] Although neither Article 2 nor Article 3 demand a formal complaint, the trigger of the obligation under these provisions has been formulated differently: Article 3 demands an 'arguable claim'. This variation is due to the practical difference in the harm: in the context of Article 2, normally the victim is deceased, and the initiative must rest on the State to start an investigation when faced with this very fact.[56]

As to the justifications invoked by the Court for the trigger of the procedural obligation under Articles 2 and 3, they are similar to the ones mentioned in Section 6.1.1, namely effectiveness and accountability. A relevant nuance that can be added here is that the investigation is essential for 'maintaining public confidence in state authorities' adherence to the rule of law and in preventing any appearance of collusion or tolerance of unlawful acts'.[57]

As to Article 8, the Court has held that the positive obligation upon States to safeguard the individual's physical integrity *may* extend to questions relating to the effectiveness of investigations.[58] No standard has been framed in the case law for triggering such a procedural obligation. The reasoning in judgments where the Court has reviewed the effectiveness of the investigations under Article 8 is based on the assumption that there was such an obligation.[59] No triggers similar to those under Article 2 and 3 (eg 'suspicious circumstances' or 'arguably claim') have been explicitly formulated.[60] This avoidance of a specific formulation of the trigger is related to the absence of certainty that Article 8 as a matter of principle has a procedural limb, as suggested by the usage of the word 'may' in italics above. Procedural requirements under Article 8 can be rather imposed implicitly within the assessment whether the State has complied with its substantive positive obligation to develop an effective regulatory framework to safeguard the right,[61] or when Article 8 is applied in combination with the right to effective remedy enshrined in Article 13 of the Convention.[62]

---

[55] *Nicolae Virgiliu Tănase v Romania* [GC] no 41720/13, 25 June 2019 §115.
[56] *Ilhan v Turkey* [GC] no 22277/93, 27 June 2000 §§91–92: 'although the victim of an alleged breach of this provision [Article 3] may be in a vulnerable position, the practical exigencies of the situation will often differ from cases of use of lethal force or suspicious deaths'.
[57] The Court has invoked the same justification in cases of harm by state actors (*Nikolova and Velichkova v Bulgaria* no 7888/03, 20 December 2007 §57). However, preventing the appearance of collusion and tolerance seems to be a more relevant justification when non-state actors inflict harm. In cases of harm by state actors, there is no collusion, since the state actors themselves cause the harm.
[58] *M.C. v Bulgaria* no 39272/98, 4 December 2003 §52; *C.A.S. and C.S. v Romania* no 26692/05, 20 March 2012 §72; *Moldovan and Others v Romania (no. 2)* no 41138/98 and 64320/01, 12 July 2005 §96; *Burlya and Others v Ukraine* no 3289/10, 6 November 2018 §§161–170.
[59] *Söderman v Sweden* [GC] no 5786/08, 12 November 2013 §§80–89; The same assumption is present in *K.U. v Finland* no 2872/02, 2 December 2008, where an investigation was initiated at national level. However, the perpetrator could not be identified due to the applicable legislation that protected his identity. See also *C v Romania* no 47358/20, 30 August 2022 and *Craxi v Italy (no. 2)* no 25337/94, 17 July 2003 §§74–75;
[60] Dissenting Opinion of Judge Kalaydjieva in *Söderman v Sweden* [GC] no 5786/08, 12 November 2013.
[61] See Section 7.2.
[62] For both approaches see *Jansons v Latvia* no 1434/14, 8 September 2022 §75.

## 6.1.3 Harm Linked with Arguable Omissions

In addition to circumstances of intentional infliction of harm, the procedural obligation can also be triggered when harm can be linked with negligent omissions. The case law has been clear to the effect that the State has the obligation to investigate its own omissions. The procedural obligation is thus triggered when harm materializes (due to a natural disaster or an accident,[63] or when a non-state actor intentionally or unintentionally inflicts harm), and the State must investigate *its own omissions* that could have arguably prevented the harm.[64] This situation emerged in *Ribcheva and others v Bulgaria*, where a police officer was killed during an operation against a dangerous individual. The Court held that the procedural limb of Article 2 was triggered 'when lives have been lost in circumstances potentially engaging the responsibility of the State due to an alleged negligence in discharging its positive obligations under Article 2'. The State had a duty to investigate its own omissions that have arguably 'directly contributed to' death.[65] This investigation does not, however, need to be in the form of criminal investigation since other proceedings may be sufficient, a point that will be further addressed in Section 6.2.

The procedural positive obligation is also triggered where an actor (irrespective of whether it is a state or a non-state actor, since it might not be clear in the first place) inflicts harm arguably due to his or her negligent conduct, and the object of the proceedings is this negligent conduct.[66] This has been applied in the context of health care, where the Court has interpreted

> the procedural obligation of Article 2 in the context of health care as requiring States to set up an effective and independent judicial system so that the cause of death of patients in the care of the medical profession, *whether in the public or the private sector*, can be determined and those responsible made accountable.[67]

As to the threshold for triggering the obligation, the standard of 'arguable grounds to suspect' has been applied. In *Lopes de Sousa Fernandes v Portugal*, the following formulation was used by the Court:

---

[63] *Öneryildiz v Turkey* [GC] no 48939/99, 30 November 2004 §91; *Budayeva and Others v Russia* no 15339/02, 20 March 2008 §§129 and 138.

[64] *Fergec v Croatia* no 68516/14, 9 May 2017 §34–37; *Ribcheva and Others v Bulgaria* no 37801/16, 30 March 2021 §§128–130.

[65] *Ribcheva and Others v Bulgaria* §128.

[66] *Banel v Lithuania* no 14326/11, 18 June 2013 §70: 'an issue of State responsibility under Article 2 of the Convention might arise in the event of inability on the part of the domestic legal system to secure accountability for negligence acts endangering or resulting in loss of human life'. The son of the applicant died after a roof collapsed and it was not clear which authority or person might have been responsible for the maintenance of the building. See also *Fergec v Croatia* no 68516/14, 9 May 2017 §34 that concerned 'the negligence behavior of a private individual which resulted in serious bodily harm', and *Bakanova v Lithuania* no 11167/12, 31 May 2016 §68 that concerned death possibly caused by hazardous working conditions on a private cargo ship.

[67] *Lopes de Sousa Fernandes v Portugal* [GC] no 56080/13, 19 December 2017 §214.

[T]he Court considers that the applicant had *arguable grounds to suspect* that her husband's death could have been the result of medical negligence. The respondent State's duty to ensure compliance with the procedural obligations arising under Article 2, in the proceedings instituted with regard to her husband's death, is therefore engaged in the present case.[68]

The positive obligation to investigate is also triggered when an omission of a non-state actor has arguably led to harm. These situations do not raise any issues as to possible omissions by the State that might have contributed to harm, as, for example, in the above-mentioned *Ribcheva and others v Bulgaria*. The object of the investigation are the omissions (ie negligent conduct) of a non-state actor. This was relevant, for example, in *Nicolae Virgiliu Tănase v Romania*, a case about 'an alleged act of negligence within the context of a road traffic accident in which the applicant was injured'.[69] In this judgment, the Court noted that

> [i]n the event of death the Court has held that where it is not clearly established from the outset that the death has resulted from an accident or another unintentional act, and where the hypothesis of unlawful killing is at least arguable on the facts, the Convention requires that an investigation attaining the minimum threshold of effectiveness be conducted in order to shed light on the circumstances of the death. The fact that the investigation ultimately accepts the hypothesis of an accident has no bearing on this issue, since the obligation to investigate is specifically intended to refute or confirm one or other hypothesis. In such circumstances, the obligation of an effective official investigation exists even where the presumed perpetrator is not a State agent. In the Court's view, the above ought to apply also in cases involving life-threatening injuries.[70]

In *Nicolae Virgiliu Tănase v Romania,* the Court also observed that 'as soon as the authorities become aware of the incident' the procedural obligation is triggered. It clarified that 'once such a matter has come to the attention of the authorities, this imposes on the State *ipso facto* an obligation under Article 2 to carry out an effective investigation'.[71] The existence of an arguable hypothesis of an unlawful killing triggers the more demanding positive obligation of criminal investigation, as Section 6.2.1.3 will explain further.

---

[68] *Lopes de Sousa Fernandes v Portugal* [GC] §222. In other similar cases, no references to the 'arguably grounds to suspect' standard can be found. See eg *Ciechońska v Poland* no 19776/04, 14 June 2011 §71, where the Court held that 'an issue of State responsibility under Article 2 of the Convention may arise in the event of the inability of the domestic legal system to secure accountability for any negligent acts endangering or resulting in the loss of human life'.
[69] *Nicolae Virgiliu Tănase v Romania* [GC] no 41720/13, 25 June 2019 §133.
[70] *Nicolae Virgiliu Tănase v Romania* [GC] §161.
[71] *Nicolae Virgiliu Tănase v Romania* [GC] §§145 and 162.

## 136  Procedural Positive Obligation to Investigate

The procedural obligation has also been found to be triggered under Article 3 in circumstances of alleged negligence. *Gorgiev v former Yugoslav Republic of Macedonia* is an example.[72] The applicant, while serving a prison sentence, was injured by a bull. A violation was found on account of the State's failure to carry out 'an effective official investigation' into the applicant's allegations that no preventive measures have been taken despite the prison authorities' awareness that the bull was aggressive.

Article 8 can also trigger an obligation upon the State to investigate its own omissions that have arguably led to harm. This can be illustrated with *Y.G. v Russia*, a case about authorities' failure to adequately protect the confidentiality of applicant's health data and to investigate the data's disclosure through a database sold at the market. The Court first found breach of the substantive obligation, since the authorities, 'who had access to the data in question, had failed to prevent a breach of confidentiality, as a result of which that data had become publicly available'.[73] It can be inferred from the reasoning in *Y.G. v Russia* that this in turn triggered the procedural obligation upon the authorities to investigate this breach, in other words to investigate the state omissions. It needs, however, to be noted that the two positive obligations (ie the substantive and the procedural) are merged in the reasoning into one general positive obligation to 'ensure adequate protection of the applicant's right to respect for his private life'.[74] For this reason and, as already noted in Sections 6.1.1 and 6.1.2, it is ambiguous whether Article 8 as a matter of principle and in all circumstances triggers a separate procedural obligation.[75] Given the wide range of interests that it protects, this might depend on the type of interests invoked and how they have been affected in each case.

This overview of the case law demonstrates that the State can be under the obligation to investigate its own omissions under Articles 2, 3, and 8. For this obligation to arise, however, is it necessary that these omissions are arguably in violation of any substantive positive obligations? In other words, for the procedural obligation to be triggered, is it necessary that the responsibility of the State could be *potentially* engaged *for any omissions*? A positive answer will undermine the independent and autonomous nature of the procedural obligation. For this reason, a requirement for arguable breach of substantive positive obligations has never been explicitly formulated in the case law, yet it has been stated that investigation is required when 'lives have been lost in circumstances potentially engaging the responsibility of the State due to an alleged negligence in discharging its positive obligations under Article 2'.[76] Further uncertainty exists, since in some cases, the Court first reviews compliance

---

[72] *Gorgiev v former Yugoslav Republic of Macedonia* no 26984/05, 19 April 2004.
[73] *Y.G. v Russia* no 8647/12, 30 August 2022 §47.
[74] ibid §52.
[75] *S.B. v Romania* no 24453/04, 23 September 2014, is, however, an example of a negligence case, where the procedural response by the national authorities, was the sole basis for finding a violation of Article 8.
[76] *Ribcheva and Others v Bulgaria* no 37801/16, 30 March 2021 §129; *Mastromatteo v Italy* [GC] no 37703/97, 24 October 2002 §§89–90 and 94–96; *Branko Tomašić and Others v Croatia*, no 46598/06, 15 January 2009 §64; *Maiorano and Others v Italy* no 28634/06, 15 December 2009 §§127–812; *Kotilainen and Others v Finland* no 62439/12, 17 September 2020 §91; *Mikayil Mammadov v Azerbaijan* no 4762/05, 17 December 2009 §§101 and 122.

with substantive positive obligations and only then with the procedural obligation,[77] while in other cases, the review order is reversed.[78] At the same time, compliance with substantive positive obligations, does not preclude finding of a breach of the procedural obligation.[79] There have also been cases where, although any allegations of breach of substantive positive obligations were declared inadmissible or not examined at all, the obligation to investigate omissions by state authorities, was found to have been triggered.[80]

If arguable breach of substantive positive obligations is not required for the trigger of the procedural obligation, then the following question arises: what should be the object of the investigation be? In other words, which facts should the investigation aim to discover and clarify? These need to be facts that are causally relevant to the harm and facts that are causally relevant to the prevention of the harm. In this way, the investigation can more widely reconstruct the factual circumstances, including any structural and systemic problems or any conduct of private parties that might be possible to causally link with the harm. If no arguable breach of substantive positive obligations is required, these problems and possibilities for prevention that the investigation more widely should aim to reveal need not be a matter of the European Convention on Human Rights' (ECHR) substantive obligations. This also explains why the trigger of the obligation to investigate has been also extended to circumstances of harm caused by the negligent conduct of private actors. The State has been found to be in breach of its procedural obligation due to its failure to investigate such conduct in cases where no arguments are raised about breaches of any substantive obligations owned by the State.[81] This relates to the justifications invoked in the Court's reasoning as to why an investigation should be conducted. Besides effectiveness that has been generally used to justify any positive obligations, the following justifications have been used in the context of Article 2: determining the cause of death and accountability for those that might be responsible.[82] Accountability is understood in a wide sense, certainly not limited to criminal responsibility. Similarly, the determination of the cause is not limited to causes that might make States' positive obligations relevant.

---

[77] *Öneryildiz v Turkey* [GC] no 48939/99, 30 November 2004; *Tkhelidze v Georgia* no 33056/17, 8 July 2021.
[78] *Gorgiev v former Yugoslav Republic of Macedonia* no 26984/05, 19 April 2004; *Ribcheva and Others v Bulgaria* no 37801/16, 30 March 2021.
[79] *Kalicki v Poland* no 46797/08, 8 December 2015 §50: 'The absence of any direct State responsibility for the death of an individual does not exclude the applicability of Article 2.'
[80] *Penati v Italy* no 44166/15, 11 May 2021 §154; *Vovk and Bogdanov v Russia* no 15613/10, 11 February 2020; *Kalicki v Poland* no 46797/08, 8 December 2015 §51.
[81] *Kotelnikov v Russia* no 45104/05, 12 July 2016 §§99–101; *Anna Todorova v Bulgaria* no 23302/03, 24 May 2011 §74.
[82] *Calvelli and Ciglio v Italy* [GC] no 32967/96, 17 January 2002 §49.

## 6.2 Content and Scope of the Obligation

The distinctions between the three groups of cases introduced in Section 6.1 are important not only because the conditions that trigger the procedural obligation might be different and that there might be nuances as to the justifications invoked by the Court to motivate the obligation, but the content and the scope of the obligation might also vary.[83] In other words, the requirements for assessing an investigation as effective might diverge. Admittedly, the Court has noted the similarity of these requirements,

> whereas the general scope of the State's positive obligations might differ between cases where the treatment contrary to the Convention has been inflicted through the involvement of State agents and cases where violence is inflicted by private individuals, the procedural requirements are similar.[84]

And yet some important differences have been consistently applied since it is not reasonable that the standards for investigating, for example, police brutality are the same as those applied to private harm or alleged negligence.[85] The most important difference concerns the type of proceedings that the procedural obligation requires, which will be addressed in Section 6.2.1. How and who initiates the proceedings are also important questions that might have different answers depending on the actors of harm, as Section 6.2.2 will show. Irrespective of these actors, however, the proceedings must be effective. Section 6.2.3 will therefore explain the complexities revolving around the standard of effectiveness. Finally, Section 6.2.4 zooms into cross-border situations and the challenges that they produce for conducting effective proceedings.

### 6.2.1 Type of Proceedings

As already mentioned at the beginning of this chapter, two types of investigative duties can be identified in the case law: first, the general obligation to have an effective judicial system, and second, the more specific and more exacting obligation to conduct official *criminal* investigation. The second one is more exacting since it demands a specific form of the investigation (ie official criminal investigation) and, in this way, more seriously limits the discretion of States how to fulfil their positive obligation.[86] The procedural obligation of having an effective judicial system might also include a

---

[83] *Bakanova v Lithuania* no 11167/12, 31 May 2016 §66; *Y v Bulgaria* no 41990/18, 20 February 2020 §83.
[84] *Beganovic v Croatia* no 46423/06, 25 June 2009 §69; *Denis Vasilyev v Russia* no 32704/04, 17 December 2009 §100; *S.M. v Croatia* [GC] no 60561/14, 25 June 2020 §312; *Oganezova v Armenia* no 71367/12, 17 May 2022 §84.
[85] See Concurring Opinion of Judges Sajó, Tsotsoria, Wojtyczek, and Kucsko-Stadlmayer in *Kraulaidis v Lithuania* no 76805/11, 8 November 2016 §2.
[86] *Lopes de Sousa Fernandes v Portugal* [GC] no 56080/13, 19 December 2017 §216. On States' discretion, see Section 4.3.

requirement for official investigation (ie investigation conducted by the state authorities);[87] this, however, does not necessarily have to be criminal in nature. Yet, given the actual practices of States, it is often the case that precisely the trigger of criminal proceedings enables official investigation. This explains why, in many judgments, the Court assesses the effectiveness of such proceedings, although they might not be demanded as a matter of positive obligations under the ECHR.[88]

### 6.2.1.1 Harm inflicted by state actors

Official criminal investigation is required in cases of harm examined under Articles 2 and 3 and inflicted by state actors.[89] There are two reasons for this enhanced procedural obligation. First, where harm has been caused by state actors, 'the procedural obligation cannot be fulfilled by merely awarding damages', which, in principle, is the objective of civil proceedings.[90] The Court has further clarified that

> if the authorities could confine their reaction to incidents of willful ill-treatment by, *inter alia,* State agents to the mere payment of compensation, while not doing enough to prosecute and punish those responsible, it would be possible in some cases for agents of the State to abuse the rights of those within their control with virtual impunity, and the legal prohibition on taking life, despite its fundamental importance, would be ineffective in practice.[91]

Second, civil proceedings need to be initiated by the victims and they depend on evidence gathered by the victim. This is problematic, since 'often, in practice, the true circumstances of the death in such cases [cases where harm has been inflicted by state actors] are largely confined within the knowledge of State officials or authorities' and therefore 'the bringing of appropriate domestic proceedings, such as a criminal prosecution, disciplinary proceedings and proceedings for the exercise of remedies available to victims and their families, will be conditioned by an adequate official investigation'.[92] It follows that official criminal investigations ensure strong safeguards

---

[87] *Ribcheva and Others v Bulgaria* no 37801/16, 30 March 2021 §125.

[88] Kamber has argued that in this way the ECHR lowers the level of protection since the Court assesses the effectiveness of procedures (eg civil or administrative) that the national legislation itself does not consider as appropriate. The national legislation rather envisions criminal proceedings as the best procedural response. Kamber's concern is not entirely valid given that the effectiveness of other proceedings is still assessed by the Court and when this effectiveness *depends* on criminal investigation, the dependence is taken into account. Kamber *Prosecuting Human Rights Offences* (n 3) 250–51. In addition, it is questionable whether the case law 'gives precedence to the civil or administrative remedies', as Kamber, suggests. The Court rather tries to respect States' discretion as to the type of proceedings and has concerns as to the risk of overcriminalization. On this risk, see also Section 7.1.1.

[89] See Section 6.1.1 for the delineation of the type of cases where harm has been arguably inflicted by state actors.

[90] *Al-Skeini and Others v the United Kingdom* [GC] no 55721/07, 7 July 2011 §165.

[91] *Mustafa Tunç and Fecire Tunç* [GC] no 24014/05, 14 April 2015 §130.

[92] *Makaratzis v Greece* [GC] no 50385/99, 20 December 2004 §73; *X and Others v Bulgaria* [GC] no 22457/16, 2 February 2021 §184.

for elucidating the facts.[93] In addition, under national legislation, killing or serious bodily harm normally gives rise to criminal liability.

Official criminal investigation is not required under Article 8. Given that Article 8 covers wide aspects of human interactions, States have wide discretion in how to regulate these interactions.[94] States have at their disposal different ways for ensuring respect for private and family life, which implies wide flexibility as to the scope and the content of the corresponding obligations.[95] This flexibility has, however, been limited since 'the nature of the State's obligation will depend on the particular aspect of private life that is at issue'.[96] This is a suggestion that in some situations, where state authorities interfere with a particularly important aspect of private life, criminal investigation might be required as a matter of ECHR positive obligations.[97] The requirement for such an investigation and its quality might be also reviewed under Article 13 in conjunction with Article 8.[98]

### 6.2.1.2 Harm inflicted by non-state actors

Official criminal investigation is also required in cases of harm inflicted by non-state actors and examined under Articles 2 and 3.[99] The reason for this enhanced procedural obligation is the importance of the interests protected by these provisions. Irrespective of whether it is a state or a non-state agent, the harm covered by the definitional scopes of Articles 2 and 3 is of severe nature, which justifies the requirement for official criminal investigation.

Similarly to the content and scope of the obligation when state agents interfere with interests protected by Article 8, when harm inflicted by non-state actors reaches only the severity threshold of Article 8, official criminal investigation is *not* necessarily required.[100] Two clarifications are, however, due here. First, in some situations of private

---

[93] *McKerr v the United Kingdom* no 28883/95, 4 May 2001 §134: 'In the normal course of events, a criminal trial, with an adversarial procedure before an independent and impartial judge, must be regarded as furnishing the strongest safeguards of an effective procedure for the finding of facts and the attribution of criminal responsibility'. See *Movsesyan v Armenia* no 27524/09, 16 November 2017 §66 for an illustration how the absence of criminal investigation negatively affected the quality of the fact finding.

[94] *Bărbulescu v Romania* [GC] no 61496/08, 5 September 2017 §108.

[95] *F.O. v Croatia* no 29555/13, 22 April 2021, a case that concerned verbal abuse by a schoolteacher, where the Court did not consider 'in the circumstances of the present case that the recourse to criminal avenue was critical to fulfill the State's obligations under Article 8'.

[96] *Söderman v Sweden* [GC] no 5786/08, 12 November 2013 §79

[97] See *Ageyevy v Russia* no 7075/10, 18 April 2013 §§196–200, where the applicants complained about unauthorized communication of confidential information about a minor's adoption. Criminal investigation was required since 'the applicants acting on their own, without the benefit of the State's assistance in the form of an official inquiry, had no effective means of establishing the perpetrators of these acts, proving their involvement and successfully bringing proceedings against them in the domestic courts'.

[98] *Bagiyeva v Ukraine* no 41085/05, 28 April 2016.

[99] See Section 6.1.2 for the delineation of the type of cases where harm has been arguably inflicted by non-state actors. See *O'Keeffe v Ireland* [GC] no 35810/09, 28 January 2014 §172; *Muta v Uktrain* no 37246/06, 31 July 2012 §59; *Buturugă v Romania* no 56867/15, 11 February 2020 §61; *Bălşan v Romania* no 49645/09, 23 May 2017 §68.

[100] *Söderman v Sweden* [GC] no 5786/08, 12 November 2013; *Jansons v Latvia* no 1434/14, 8 September 2022 §80; *Sandra Janković v Croatia* no 38478/05, 5 March 2009 §50; *Bevacqua and S. v Bulgaria* no 71127/01, 12 June 2008 §82.

violence, where important interests are at stake, civil proceedings are inadequate and instead, the possibility for private criminal prosecution must be available so that the State complies with its positive obligation.[101] Second, in other situations, neither civil proceedings nor private prosecutions are considered adequate, and the requirement for official criminal investigation might be imposed.[102] *Y.G. v Russia* is an example to this effect. Two justifications supported the imposition of the more demanding procedural obligation in this case. The first one refers to the severity of the harm: 'grave acts, where fundamental values and essential aspects of private life are at stake, requires efficient criminal-law provisions and their application through effective investigation and prosecution'.[103] The second justification is the weaker position of the person and the possibility to access relevant evidence:

> In the face of such a major privacy breach, in practical terms, the applicant acting on his own, without the benefit of the State's assistance in the form of an official inquiry, had no effective means of establishing the perpetrators of these acts, proving their involvement and bringing proceedings against them in the domestic courts.[104]

It follows that regardless of the article invoked and the actors of the harm implicated, the better position of the State in terms of gathering evidence and accessing relevant information to clarify facts is a relevant consideration for the Court to impose the more demanding obligation of official criminal investigation and to conclude that alternative proceedings are inadequate.

### 6.2.1.3 Harm linked with arguable omissions

In cases of harm linked with arguable omissions,[105] the State is under the general obligation to have an effective judicial system.[106] This system might offer criminal, civil, administrative, or disciplinary proceedings. Each one of them on its own, or in a combination, can suffice.[107] This applies irrespective of whether the harm can be linked

---

[101] *Bevacqua and S. v Bulgaria* no 71127/01, 12 June 2008 §82; *Sandra Janković v Croatia* no 38478/05, 5 March 2009 §§50–58; *Remetin v Croatia (No. 2)* no 7446/12, 24 July 2014 §§95–96 and 103–113; *Volodina v Russia (no 2)*, no 40419/19, 14 September 2021 §§49 and 57: 'the acts of cyberviolence in the instant case were sufficiently serious to require a criminal-law response on the part of the domestic authorities'.

[102] *R.B. v Estonia* no 22597/16, 22 June 2021 §79; *Söderman v Sweden* [GC] no 5786/08, 12 November 2013 §§82–83; *R.B. v Hungary* no 64602/12, 12 April 2016 §§78–85 where it was established that harassment motivated by racism requires criminal investigation.

[103] *Y.G. v Russia* no 8647/12, 30 August 2022 §43.

[104] ibid §49.

[105] See Section 6.1.3 for the delineation of the type of cases where harm has been arguably inflicted by omissions that could be attributable to both state and non-state actors.

[106] *Öneryildiz v Turkey* [GC] no 48939/99, 30 November 2004 §92; *Vo v France* [GC] no 53924/00 8 July 2004 §90; *Calvelli and Ciglio v Italy* [GC] no 32967/96, 17 January 2002 §51.

[107] *Nicolae Virgiliu Tănase v Romania* [GC] no 41720/13, 25 June 2019 §159; *Lopes de Sousa Fernandes v Portugal* [GC] no 56080/13, 19 December 2017 §§215 and 225 (the question was framed as whether 'the legal system as a whole dealt adequately with the case at hand').

with omissions by state or non-state actors.[108] The Court has, however, carved out certain exceptions when criminal proceedings are still necessary under Articles 2 and 3. The rest of this section will explain the scope of these exceptions.

*Explicit exceptions under Article 2 where criminal proceedings are required*
Exceptions have been explicitly introduced under Article 2. It is possible to identify three exceptions where the procedural limb of Article 2 demands official criminal investigation in cases of negligence. These exceptions apply in the circumstances of, first, 'dangerous activities'; second, 'seriously life-threatening' injuries where there is an 'arguable hypothesis of unlawful killing'; and third where individuals (even private actors) recklessly disregard their legal duties. Admittedly, the lines between these circumstances can be blurred since, as shown below, the criteria used by the Court to delineate the exceptions are not entirely clear.

The *first* one applies in the context of 'dangerous activities', as held for the first time in *Öneryildiz v Turkey*:

> Where it is established that the negligence attributable to State officials or bodies on that account goes beyond an error of judgment or carelessness, in that the authorities in question, fully realising the likely consequences and disregarding the powers vested in them, failed to take measures that were necessary and sufficient to avert the risks inherent in a dangerous activity, the fact that those responsible for endangering life have not been charged with a criminal offence or prosecuted may amount to a violation of Article 2, irrespective of any other types of remedy which individuals may exercise on their own initiative.[109]

The justification for the imposition of the more demanding obligation is that 'lives have been lost as a result of events occurring under the responsibility of the public authorities'.[110] This implies that the circumstances are confined within these authorities' knowledge. It is precisely they that 'have sufficient relevant knowledge to identify and establish the complex phenomena that might have caused' the harm.[111]

A *second* exception was carved out with *Nicolae Virgiliu Tănase v Romania*, a case that involved a car accident between private parties. It was noted that the procedural obligation 'entails an obligation to carry out an effective official investigation when

---

[108] *Ribcheva and Others v Bulgaria* no 37801/16, 30 March 2021 §§128–131. The issue in this case was not the proceedings against the person that actually killed the applicant's relative. As clarified in Section 6.2.1.2, these proceedings must be criminal in nature. The issue was rather 'whether the authorities were additionally required to investigate whether negligent acts or omissions on the part of officials had also directly contributed to Mr Sharkov's death, and if so, whether the investigations carried out in this case, … were sufficient to discharge this duty'. After determining that investigation was required, the Court noted that it did not have to be criminal in form.
[109] *Öneryildiz v Turkey* [GC] no 48939/99, 30 November 2004 §93; *Vardosanidze v Georgia* no 43881/10, 7 May 2020 §56.
[110] *Öneryildiz v Turkey* [GC] §93.
[111] ibid §93.

individuals have been killed as the result of the use of force, but *may extend to accidents* where an individual has been killed'.[112] The GC continued to identify two situations where the State is under the obligation to carry official criminal investigation in the context of accidents and alleged negligence. The first one is a confirmation of the exception mentioned above and introduced with *Öneryildiz v Turkey*: 'if the activity involved was dangerous by its nature and put the life of the applicant at real and imminent risk'.[113] The more demanding positive obligation of conducting official criminal investigation also applies when 'the injuries the applicant had suffered were seriously life-threatening'.[114] The importance of the protected interests was therefore invoked as a justification in *Nicolae Virgiliu Tănase v Romania*.

As to the situation of 'seriously life-threatening' injuries, where according to *Nicolae Virgiliu Tănase v Romania* the exception applies, the GC tried to narrow the exception by observing that it applies particularly 'where a high-risk private activity is regulated by a detailed legislative and administrative framework whose adequacy and sufficiency for the reduction of the risk for life is beyond doubt or not contested'.[115] The exception introduced with this judgment seems to have been further narrowed down with the requirement that serious life-threatening injuries in the context of highly regulated high-risk private activity demand official criminal investigation only if there is also an *arguable hypothesis of unlawful killing* (including by a non-state actor).[116] In this sense, the death or the life-threatening injuries can be considered as suspicious,[117] and criminal investigation is thus required to confirm or reject the hypothesis of unlawful killing.[118]

Overall, it is difficult to understand the role of the different requirements for the exception introduced with *Nicolae Virgiliu Tănase v Romania* to apply. Not only is the reasoning confusing as to the role of the different factors that condition the exception, but relatedly, the meaning of the different terms used to delineate the exception is

---

[112] *Nicolae Virgiliu Tănase v Romania* [GC] no 41720/13, 25 June 2019 §138 (emphasis added).

[113] Admittedly, this quotation suggests that in addition to the dangerousness of the activity, real and immediate risk is also required. This shows the difficulty in identifying the exact criteria in the case law as to when the more demanding procedural obligation is triggered.

[114] *Nicolae Virgiliu Tănase v Romania* [GC] no 41720/13, 25 June 2019 §144.

[115] ibid §144.

[116] ibid §161–3: 'once it has been established by the initial investigation that death or life-threatening injury has not been inflicted intentionally', there might be no reasons to continue the criminal investigation and civil proceedings might suffice.

[117] See *Asiye Genc v Turkey* no 24109/07, 27 January 2015 §69–73. In this case, the death was regarded as suspicious since the authorities 'put an individual's life at risk through the denial of health care they have undertaken to make available to the population in general'. In *Railean v Moldova* no 23401/04, 5 January 2010 §31, the death was considered as suspicious since it occurred in the context of a hit-and-run car accident, which justified the requirement for criminal investigation. In *Bakanova v Lithuania* no 11167/12, 31 May 2016 §68, the procedural limb of Article 2 demanded criminal investigation since there was a suspicion that the death might have been caused by hazardous working conditions.

[118] *Nicolae Virgiliu Tănase v Romania* [GC] no 41720/13, 25 June 2019 §§160–164: 'where it is not clearly established from the outset that the death [or life-threatening injuries] has resulted from an accident or another unintentional act, and where the hypothesis of unlawful killing is at least arguable on the facts', 'the obligation of an effective official investigation exists even where the presumed perpetrator is not a State agent'. *Mustafa Tunç and Fecire Tunç v Turkey* [GC] no 24014/05, 14 April 2015 §133.

vague.[119] In addition, the GC never explicitly stated that the specific car accident that led to the applicant's injuries actually demanded criminal investigation.[120]

*Sinim v Turkey* can be viewed as having introduced the *third* exception. The case was not about negligence by state officials or bodies that 'goes beyond an error of judgment or carelessness', as in *Öneryildiz v Turkey*. Neither was it about arguable unlawful killing by a non-state actor, as the criteria invoked in *Nicolae Virgiliu Tănase v Romania*. *Sinim v Turkey* was about negligence by non-state actors that was assessed by the Court as going beyond mere accident caused by negligence or carelessness, since it involved 'a deliberate disregard of the relevant rules on the transportation of dangerous goods'. In *Sinim v Turkey*, private parties showed 'voluntary and reckless disregard of their legal duties under the relevant national legislation', as opposed to committing 'a simple omission or human error'. This distinguished *Sinim v Turkey* from cases of non-intentional death where civil remedies are in principle considered sufficient.[121]

In all the three judgments mentioned above (*Öneryildiz v Turkey*, *Nicolae Virgiliu Tănase v Romania*, and *Sinim v Turkey*), where the content of the procedural obligation was expanded to include the requirement for official criminal investigation, the contentious question at the core of the analysis is whether the severity of the harm should be a *sufficient* requirement for this expansion. If not, what additional criteria should be taken into account so that the more demanding procedural positive obligation is imposed? In *Öneryildiz v Turkey*, three other criteria were distinguished: the nature of the activity (ie 'dangerous activity'),[122] negligence by state authorities that goes beyond carelessness,[123] and access to evidence by the state authorities to elucidate

---

[119] The GC refers to the requirement that there needs to be a hypothesis of unlawful killing that is 'at least arguable on the facts', so that criminal investigation is required under Article 2. However, the term 'unlawful killing' remains vague. Is it 'unlawful' in the sense of the Convention? Is it 'unlawful' in the sense of the domestic criminal law? Does 'unlawful killing' include death due to negligence by private actors? It is 'unlawful' in the sense of the national legislation that regulates driving?

[120] *Nicolae Virgiliu Tănase v Romania* [GC] no 41720/13, 25 June 2019 §§179–180: the national authorities conducted criminal proceedings and the Court only noted that 'if deemed effective, such proceedings were by themselves capable of meeting that obligation'. See also *Zinatullin v Russia* no 10551/10, 28 January 2020 §41, another case where the Court did not make it clear whether the more demanding positive obligation applies.

[121] *Sinim v Turkey* no 9441/10, 6 June 2017 §63. The Court added that the activity performed by the private actors (ie transportation of certain categories of dangerous goods without the permission of the competent authorities) was a criminal offence under the national legislation. The Court's reasoning can be therefore understood to the effect that since the national legislation *anyway* required criminal proceedings, such proceedings should be also required as a matter of ECHR positive obligations.

[122] In other cases where criminal investigation was demanded, the dangerous nature of the activity was considered in combination with other criteria. *Oruk v Turkey* no 33647/04, 4 February 2014 §§ 50–65 concerned children killed by the explosion of a rocket near a military firing range. Criminal investigation was required since the authorities had precise knowledge of the risks and the site was under their control.

[123] In other cases, negligence by state authorities that goes beyond carelessness and error of judgment, was the *sole* criterion (in addition to the severity of the harm) invoked in the reasoning to justify the imposition of the more demanding procedural obligation. See *Lopes de Sousa Fernandes v Portugal* [GC] no 56080/13, 19 December 2017 §215, a medical negligence case where the criterion was not found fulfilled. In contrast, in *Asiye Genç v Turkey* no 24109/07, 27 January 2015 §73, where neo-natal care was denied, the Court held that 'in so far as it is shown that the authorities of a Contracting State put an individual's life at risk through the *denial of health care* they have undertaken to make available to the population in general', criminal investigation is required.

how life had been lost.¹²⁴ In *Nicolae Virgiliu Tănase v Romania*, a case about a car accident between private actors, the criterion emphasized by the Court was that the activity was an object of detailed national regulation. In *Sinim v Turkey*, the regulation of the activity was important, but the reasoning also underscores the deliberate disregard of this regulation by the private parties.¹²⁵ It is not clear whether these criteria are cumulatively applied or each one of them on its own might be necessary and sufficient.¹²⁶

Despite these exceptions whose boundaries remain vague, the starting point under Article 2 is that in cases where harm is *not* deliberately inflicted by state or non-state actors, the procedural obligation demands effective judicial system that does not necessarily include criminal proceedings. The same starting point applies to Article 3.¹²⁷ A relevant question here is whether the Court has carved out any exceptions under Article 3 similar to those explained above under Article 2.

*Definitional specificities of Article 3 that affect the carving of similar exceptions*
To respond to this question, it needs to be first noted that Article 3 raises some definitional specifics. These relate to the question of whether harm *not* inflicted intentionally by an actor can be defined as treatment in the sense of Article 3. In *Nicolae Virgiliu Tănase v Romania*, the GC seems to have replied in the negative, which would imply that the claim does not fall within the definitional scope of Article 3 (ie it is not compatible *ratione materiae*) and the question of any obligations under this provision does not even arise. This reply, however, is far from unambiguous for the following reasons. The GC noted that 'an array of factors, each of which is capable of carrying significant weight' are to be taken into account for assessing the definitional threshold (ie the minimum level of severity) under Article 3. It added that '[a]ll these factors presuppose that the treatment to which the victim was "subjected" was the

---

¹²⁴ This criterion is of crucial importance in cases of medical negligence in prison, where criminal investigation is required since evidence will be difficult to obtain by the victims (*Mitkus v Latvia* no 7259/03, 2 October 2012 §§76–77). However, medical negligence in the context of psychiatric internment does not necessarily require criminal investigation (*Dvořáček v the Check Republic* no 12927/13, 6 November 2014 §§110–114). In contrast to prisons, facilities for psychiatric internment are not necessarily closed and inaccessible. It is therefore not equally difficult to obtain evidence and will therefore be 'easier to argue a case of medical negligence related to psychiatric internment before the civil courts than it would be the case with the allegation of medical negligence in the prison context'. Kamber, *Prosecuting Human Rights Offences* (n 3) 243.
¹²⁵ The same factor was distinguished in *Smiljanić v Croatia* no 35983/14, 25 March 2021 §88, a car accident case, where the Court held that criminal investigation was necessary 'in case of an alleged voluntary and reckless disregard by a private individual of his or her legal duties under the relevant legislation'.
¹²⁶ Further uncertainty is caused by the invocation of some additional criteria in the reasoning. For example, in *Öneryildiz v Turkey* [GC] no 48939/99, 30 November 2004 §93, the GC referred to certain developments in relevant European standards to the effect that 'any allegation of such an offence normally gives rise to criminal liability'. This means that the national legislation and, in particular, whether it criminalizes the relevant conduct, can be a relevant point of reference to determine whether criminal proceedings should be demanded as a positive obligation under the ECHR.
¹²⁷ See the cases under Article 3 for alleged medical negligence. *V.C. v Slovakia* no 18968/07, 8 November 2011 §§256; *N.B. v Slovakia*, no 29518/10, 12 June 2012 §84; *I.G. and Others v Slovakia* no 15966/04, 13 November 2012 §129; *Dvořáček v Czech Republic* no 12927/13, 6 November 2014 §111.

consequence of an intentional act'.[128] Importantly, however, intention can be not only at different levels but can be also directed at different things.[129]

These differences came to the fore in *Y.P. v Russia*,[130] as compared to the other involuntary sterilization case of *V.C. v Slovakia*.[131] In the former, Court held that 'the doctors had not acted in bad faith, let alone with an intent of ill-treatment or degrading her'. For this reason, the complaint under Article 3 was found incompatible *ratione materiae*. At the same time, to distinguish *Y.P. v Russia* from *V.C. v Slovakia*, the majority suggested that *Y.P. v Russia* did not reveal any racial motivations, since the woman was not of Roma origin. It follows then that race-related intentions and motivations suffice for treatment to fall within the scope of Article 3. At the same time, as the Partly Dissenting Opinion of Judge Pavli shows, while *intention to specifically degrade the applicant* in *Y.P. v Russia* might be absent, her case was not one of medical negligence either. The doctors did act deliberately to sterilize her in violation of national standards, which makes her case one of intentional ill-treatment.

This nuance has not escaped the attention of the Court since in *Nicolae Virgiliu Tănase v Romania* and in *Y.P. v Russia* it was added that 'the absence of an intention to humiliate or debase the victim cannot conclusively rule out a finding of a violation of Article 3'.[132] With this addition, however, the GC seems to contradict its statement in the very same judgment that 'treatment' under Article 3 has to be a consequence of an intentional act. An alternative interpretation of this addition is that the Court wants to preserve a leeway as to what levels and kinds of intention might be relevant for passing the threshold of Article 3. As noted above, this leeway allowed *Y.P. v Russia* to be distinguished from *V.C. v Slovakia*.

Overall, however, *Nicolae Virgiliu Tănase v Romania* and *Y.P. v Russia* show that the current approach of the Court is to keep the definitional threshold of Article 3 restricted by requiring an actor of harm with intention. If this threshold is passed and the complaint is compatible *ratione materiae*, the procedural limb of Article 3 triggers the more demanding positive obligation of addressing the harm via criminal proceedings (see Sections 6.2.1.1 and 6.2.1.2).

An alternative approach would be relaxing the definitional scope so that any serious harm, even harm linked with omissions (without intentions), could be covered by Article 3. It is, however, questionable whether in these situations of omissions, the demanding requirement for criminal proceedings is all the time warranted. If indeed not warranted under all circumstances even if the harm is serious,[133] this alternative

---

[128] *Nicolae Virgiliu Tănase v Romania* [GC] no 41720/13, 25 June 2019 §121.
[129] See also the beginning of Section 6.1, where the ambiguous ways in which the Court uses terms such as 'intention' and 'negligence' was noted.
[130] *Y.P. v Russia* no 43399/13, 20 September 2022 §37.
[131] *V.C. v Slovakia* no 18968/07, 8 November 2011 §120.
[132] *Nicolae Virgiliu Tănase v Romania* [GC] no 41720/13, 25 June 2019 §117; *Y.P. v Russia* no 43399/13, 20 September 2022 §35.
[133] Caution might be warranted since other types of proceedings might be also appropriate in cases of harmful treatment without this specific intention. See Concurring Opinion of Judge Elósegui in *Y.P. v Russia* no 43399/13, 20 September 2022 §§13–17, where she warns that '[i]f Article 3 is applied to all these

approach could be combined with a relaxation of the corresponding procedural positive obligation. The relaxation would imply that the obligation more generally requires an effective judicial system, where civil, administrative, and other proceedings might suffice. If this road chosen, however, the Court might have to carve out exceptions where Article 3 demands criminal proceedings even in cases of negligence, since there might be different levels of negligence. Given the difficulties in delineating the exceptions, as the above analysis in relation to Article 2 showed, the current approach under Article 3 (ie stricter definitional threshold, but clarity that once the threshold passed criminal proceedings are a necessary requirement as a matter of ECHR positive obligations) might be preferable.

The current approach is by no means set in stone. The reason is that in contradiction to the determination made by the GC in *Nicolae Virgiliu Tănase v Romania* regarding Article 3, there have been judgments where the procedural limb of Article 3 was interpreted as requiring official criminal investigation where the harm was not intentional but was rather linked with arguable omissions by non-state actors. Relevant illustrations include *Kraulaidis v Lithuania* that involved a car accident[134] and *Mažukna v Lithuania* that involved an accident at work.[135]

*Concerns if criminal proceedings are a necessary requirement under Articles 2 and 3*

Despite all the above-described ambiguities, the case law does contain examples where the procedural limb under both Articles 2 and 3 has been expanded to include a requirement for criminal investigation in situations of unintentional harm.[136] This is problematic for at least four reasons. First, the expansion implies that the State is under the positive obligation to criminalize negligent conduct. The ECHR is thus interpreted as giving priority to criminalization and criminal proceedings, which might in some circumstances be counterproductive.[137] Second, the expansion might not only undermine the discretion of States to choose the means for fulfilling positive obligations,[138] it might also ignore the effectiveness of civil remedies. There might be situations (even in the absence of any intent) the door will be open to all kinds of accusations against health personnel by criminal avenues,' which will be contrary to the idea that 'criminal law is the last resort'.

---

[134] *Kraulaidis v Lithuania* no 76805/11, 8 November 2016 §57.

[135] *Mažukna v Lithuania* no 72092/12, 11 April 2017.

[136] For arguments in favour of the expansion of the procedural obligation to include a requirement for criminal proceedings even in cases of negligence, see Joint Concurring Opinion of Judges Pinto de Albuquerque and Elósegui in *Vovk and Bogdanov v Russia* no 15613/10, 11 February 2020, where they note the significance of criminal investigations for discovering the truth and establishment of responsibility. Criminal investigation might be also essential for the effective operation of other proceedings. See *Banel v Lithuania* no 14326/11, 18 June 2013 §71.

[137] *Botoyan v Armenia* no 5766/17, 8 February 2022 §108: 'the authorities must also have regard to counter-considerations, such as the risk of unjustifiably exposing medical practitioners to liability, which can compromise their professional morale and induce them to practice, often to the detriment of their patients, what has come to be known as 'defensive medicine''.

[138] The choice of means for ensuring positive obligation is 'in principle a matter that falls within the Contracting State's margin of appreciation'. *Nicolae Virgiliu Tănase v Romania* [GC] no 41720/13, 25 June 2019 §169. See Section 4.3.

procedural or substantive obstacles for concluding that a defendant is criminally responsible. However, it might be possible to find responsibility in civil proceedings.[139] Third, any expansion of the content of the procedural obligation to include criminal proceedings as a necessary requirement might be difficult to square with the principle that the ECHR does not confer a right to have somebody prosecuted.[140] Fourth, cases of intentional harm are materially different from cases where there is no suspicion of intentional misconduct.[141] The latter normally implicate some structural and systemic problems. It is these general structures and systems that need to be investigated. It is doubtful whether criminal proceedings that narrowly focus on individual responsibility can achieve a review of such structural issues. When it comes to systemic and structural issues, facts can be ascertained through other investigative channels.

Finally, it needs to be noted that although in situations of harm linked with omissions, criminal proceedings might not be necessary for a State to comply with its procedural obligation under the ECHR, such proceedings might still be available under the national legislation. If they are, they would be capable of satisfying the procedural obligation if assessed as effective.[142] This means that States can make choices as to how to fulfil their positive obligation in cases of harm linked with omissions. Whatever choices are made at national level however, national proceedings must operate effectively in practice.[143] This ultimately means that criminal proceedings themselves can be deemed ineffective if they cannot reveal facts about systemic and structural problems.

## 6.2.2 Initiation of the Proceedings

Irrespective of their type, proceedings must be effective to comply with the ECHR. Their effectiveness depends on how the national legislation regulates their initiation. In cases of harm inflicted by state actors and non-state actors that falls within the definitional scope of Articles 2 and 3, where official criminal investigation is necessarily required, the proceedings must be initiated by the State. In other words, the state authorities need to start the proceedings on their own motion (ie *proprio moto*) and carry the burden of the investigation.[144] There might be an official complaint; however, bringing credible allegations to the attention of the authorities suffices for

---

[139] For example, *Sarishvili-Bolkvadze v Georgia* no 58240/08, 19 July 2018 §87, where no individual criminal responsibility was found in the course of the criminal proceedings, but medical negligence was established as part of separate civil proceedings.
[140] See Section 6.2.3.3.
[141] The Joined Partly Dissenting and Party Concurring Opinion in *Penati v Italy* no 44166/15, 11 May 2021.
[142] *Lopes de Sousa Fernandes v Portugal* [GC] no 56080/13, 19 December 2017 §232.
[143] *Civrioğlu v Turkey* no 69546/12, 4 October 2016 §83; *Lopes de Sousa Fernandes v Portugal* [GC] no 56080/13, 19 December 2017 §216.
[144] *Nachova and Others v Bulgaria* [GC] no 43577/98, 6 July 2005 §111; *Bouyid v Belgium* [GC] no 23380/09, 28 September 2015 §119; *S.M. v Croatia* [GC] no 60561/14, 25 June 2020 §314.

the latter to be under the obligation to initiate proceedings.[145] This implies that the national authorities have to gather evidence, including by asking for expert opinions,[146] follow lines of inquiry on their own initiative, and should not 'depend on an initiative of the applicant to take responsibility for the conduct of any investigatory procedures'.[147] Since the prosecuting authorities are better placed than the victim to conduct the investigation, 'any action or lack of action on the part of the victim cannot justify a lack of action on the part of the prosecuting authorities'.[148] The *proprio moto* proceedings are linked with their nature as criminal proceedings. They imply that the State carries the burden to explain and justify any omissions in the course of the investigation.

As explained in Section 6.2.1, upon the infliction of harm that falls within the definitional scope of Article 8, criminal proceedings are not necessarily required and, relatedly, *proprio moto* proceedings are not necessary for the State to fulfil its positive obligation.[149] Neither are such proceedings required in cases of harm linked with arguable omissions reviewed under Articles 2 and 3.[150] However, *proprio moto* proceedings might be required, since by way of exceptions criminal proceedings are necessary in some situations of harm linked with omissions under Articles 2 and 3, as explained in Section 6.2.1.3.

The national authorities might also be under the obligation to initiate investigative proceedings on their own motion, even if these are *not* criminal in nature. *Ribcheva and Others v Bulgaria* is an example to this effect. An officer was shot by an armed person during a police operation that aimed to disarm the person. The procedural obligation under Article 2 was relevant not in relation to the harm caused by the armed person but in relation to the harm caused by the arguable omissions of the state authorities in the planning of the police operation.[151] Given the object of the investigation (ie omissions), it did not have to be criminal in nature, yet the internal investigation by the Ministry of Internal Affairs was found to be flawed since it was not launched by the ministry of its own motion but only in response to a complaint by the officer's relatives. The Court reasoned that the launching of the investigation cannot be left to the initiative of the relatives, particularly in cases 'where the true circumstances of the death are largely confined within the knowledge of State

---

[145] Kamber, *Prosecuting Human Rights Offences* (n 3) 289. See also *El-Masri v the former Yugoslav Republic of Macedonia* [GC] no 39630/09, 13 December 2012 §186; *O'Keeffe v Ireland* [GC] no 35810/09, 28 January 2014 §173.
[146] *M. and Others v Italy and Bulgaria* no 40020/03, 31 July 2012 §105 (no medical examination was ordered by the investigating authorities despite the claims that the applicant was beaten and raped).
[147] *S.M. v Croatia* [GC] no 60561/14, 25 June 2020 §336.
[148] ibid §336.
[149] *Söderman v Sweden* [GC] no 5786/08, 12 November 2013.
[150] *Lopes de Sousa Fernandes v Portugal* [GC] no 56080/13, 19 December 2017 §220: 'Unlike in cases concerning the lethal use of force by State agents, where the competent authorities must of their own motion initiate investigations, in cases concerning medical negligence where the death is caused unintentionally, the States' procedural obligations may come into play upon the institution of proceedings by the deceased's relatives.'
[151] *Ribcheva and Others v Bulgaria* no 37801/16, 30 March 2021 §128.

officials or authorities'.[152] It can by analogy be argued that where such a confinement occurs, *proprio moto* proceedings might be required even if they are not criminal in nature.[153]

### 6.2.3 Effectiveness

Besides the manner of the initiation, five additional criteria have been developed in the case law for assessing the effectiveness of the national proceedings.[154] These are independence, promptness, thoroughness that includes capability of leading to the establishment of the facts and identification of those responsible, involvement of the victim, and public scrutiny. The criteria apply irrespective of the type of proceedings that Articles 2, 3, and 8 might demand. The criteria are therefore equally valid irrespective of the source of harm (ie state actor, non-state actor, or omissions). For example, even if civil proceedings suffice, they still need to be assessed as effective in accordance with these five criteria so that the State complies with its procedural obligation.

Although the Court has developed these *prima facie* criteria, they are open to interpretation and each situation is judged on a case-by-case basis. The Court has thus cautioned against their general applicability.[155] It has clarified that '[t]hese elements [the criteria] are inter-related and each of them, taken separately, does not amount to an end in itself. They are criteria which, taken jointly, enable the degree of effectiveness of the investigation to be assessed.'[156] The Court does not review in abstract whether the available national proceedings meet the criteria but rather whether the proceedings as applied in the concrete case can be considered as effective in light of the criteria.[157]

The concrete review of whether the investigation has been effective implies that the application of the five criteria is very much contingent on the circumstances in the specific case, and yet the Court has more generally observed that '[w]here suspicious death has been inflicted at the hands of a State agent, *particular stringent scrutiny* must be applied by the relevant domestic authorities to the ensuing investigation'.[158] In *Bakanova v Lithuania*, a case characterized as one of death 'not caused by use of

---

[152] ibid §145.
[153] In *Ribcheva and Others v Bulgaria* the absence of *proprio moto* investigation by the ministry was only the first flaw that prevented the proceedings from complying with the procedural limb of Article 2. The other flaw was lack of publicity and of involvement of the applicants. It is not therefore clear whether the first flaw in itself could have been sufficient for finding a violation. See, however, *Mikayil Mammadov v Azerbaijan* no 4762/05 17 December 2009 §§ 102–103, where it is suggested that the state authorities are under the obligation to launch an investigation of whatever mode on their own motion where 'a person dies in suspicious circumstances in which the State's positive obligation under Article 2 is at stake'.
[154] *Ribcheva and Others v Bulgaria* §139.
[155] *Velikova v Bulgaria* 41488/98, 18 May 2000 §80: 'It is not possible to reduce the variety of situations which might occur to a bare check list of acts of investigation or other simplified criteria.'
[156] *S.M. v Croatia* [GC] no 60561/14, 25 June 2020 §319. On this basis the procedural limb of Articles 2, 3, and 8 can be distinguished from the obligations imposed by Article 6. Under the latter provision, independence is an end in itself. *Mustafa Tunç and Fecire Tunç v Turkey* [GC] no 24014/05, 14 April 2015 § 225.
[157] *Valeriy Fuklev v Ukraine* no 6318/03, 16 January 2014 §67.
[158] *Armani Da Silva v the United Kingdom* [GC] no 5878/08, 30 March 2016 §234 (emphasis added).

force or similar direct official action', it was noted that 'the standard against which the investigation's effectiveness is to be assessed may be less exacting'.[159] The variations as to how much more or less stringently the five criteria are applied, depending on the types of cases, as outlined in Section 6.1, have not been explicitly developed by the Court. Importantly, all five criteria are relevant across Articles 2, 3, and 8 in the different groups of cases distinguished in Section 6.1, and in this sense, there are no conceptual differences.[160] Section 6.2.3.1 therefore offers a general clarification of the criteria without distinguishing the relevant article or the different types of cases.

### 6.2.3.1 Independence, promptness, victim involvement, and public scrutiny

Starting with the criterion of independence, not only lack of hierarchical or institutional connection between those involved in the events and the persons responsible for the investigation is required but practical independence is also called for.[161] While this requirement might not be crucial in the context of interpersonal abuses, it is of particular significance when the State has to investigate the implication of its own agents in abuses.[162] The Court undertakes a concrete examination of the independence of the investigation rather than an abstract one. On this basis, the procedural limb is distinguishable from the requirements imposed by Article 6 ECHR.[163] In addition, no 'absolute independence' is demanded under the procedural limb; rather, those undertaking the investigation must be 'sufficiently independent of the person and structures whose responsibility is likely to be engaged'.[164] Judicial review of investigative decisions is not necessarily required.[165] This flexible approach can linked with the requirement for effectiveness which is also flexible:

> Where an issue arises concerning the independence and impartiality of an investigation, the correct approach consists in examining whether and to what extent the disputed circumstance has compromised the investigation's effectiveness and its ability to shed light on the circumstances of the death and to punish those responsible.[166]

Similar flexibility applies to the criteria of promptness. The investigation has to proceed with 'reasonable expedition', which also means that any difficulties that might

---

[159] *Bakanova v Lithuania* no 11167/12, 31 May 2016 §67.
[160] Kamber, *Prosecuting Human Rights Offences* (n 3) 243.
[161] *Turlueva v Russia* no 63638/09, 20 June 2013 §109.
[162] 'What is at stake here is nothing less than public confidence in the State's monopoly on the use of force.' *Armani Da Silva v the United Kingdom* [GC] no 5878/08, 30 March 2016 §232.
[163] *Mustafa Tunç and Fecire Tunç v Turkey* [GC] no 24014/05, 14 April 2015 §222. Here the Court compared the requirement for independence under Article 6 versus the procedural limb of Article 2. The first one is about abstract review of independence. What distinguishes Article 6 is that '[t]he question whether the body presents an appearance of independence is also of relevance'.
[164] *Mustafa Tunç and Fecire Tunç v Turkey* [GC] no 24014/05, 14 April 2015 §223.
[165] *Hanan v Germany* [GC] no 4871/16, 16 February 2021 §220.
[166] *Mustafa Tunç and Fecire Tunç v Turkey* [GC] no 24014/05, 14 April 2015 §224.

prevent progress need to be also considered.[167] And yet, promptness might be crucial in some situations since delays might in practice mean impossibility to actually establish the facts.[168] Promptness can be also important due to more general considerations, such as preventing similar errors.[169]

The criterion of public scrutiny is also applied with flexibility since the degree of public scrutiny required varies from case to case.[170] In addition, competing interests need also to be taken into account since disclosure of materials to the public can affect private individuals.[171] The effectiveness of the investigation is also assessed in the light of the involvement of the victim: '[t]he victim or the next-of-kin must be involved in the procedure to the extent necessary to safeguard their legitimate interests'.[172] For example, in *Ribcheva and others v Bulgaria*, the Court found that the relatives were not involved 'to the extent necessary to safeguard their legitimate interests' and there was no 'sufficient degree of public scrutiny'.[173] These flaws, together with the flaw that the investigation was not initiated by the authorities on their own motion, led the Court to conclude that Bulgaria breached the procedural limb of Article 2. This finding was therefore justified with reference to two of the five criteria. This shows more generally the flexibility not only in terms of the meaning attached to the different criteria. It is also illustrative of how the criteria can be applied independently, which entails that failure to meet one of them might be necessary and sufficient for finding a breach,[174] or in different combinations. When applied in combinations, the failure to meet one of the criteria might not necessarily undermine the overall effectiveness of the proceedings.

### 6.2.3.2 Thoroughness

It might be difficult to distinguish the overarching standard of effectiveness from the criterion of thoroughness.[175] The latter, however, is more narrowly used to characterize the object of the investigation; in particular, what the investigation should aim to discover. As the Court has noted 'the authorities must always make a serious attempt to find out what happened, and should not rely on hasty or ill-founded conclusions to close their investigation'.[176] The authorities must take 'reasonable steps available to them secure the evidence concerning the incident'.[177] They need to establish the facts

---

[167] *Armani Da Silva v the United Kingdom* [GC] no 5878/08, 30 March 2016 §237.
[168] *Antonov v Ukraine* no 28096/04, 3 November 2011 §50.
[169] *Lopes de Sousa Fernandes v Portugal* [GC] no 56080/13, 19 December 2017 §218.
[170] *Ramsahai and Others v the Netherlands* [GC] no 52391/99, 15 May 2007 §353; *Giuliani and Gaggio v Italy* [GC] no 23458/02, 24 March 2011 §304; *Al Nashiri v Romania* no 33234/12, 31 May 2018 §641.
[171] *Giuliani and Gaggio v Italy* [GC] no 23458/02, 24 March 2011 §304.
[172] *Ribcheva and Others v Bulgaria* no 37801/16, 30 March 2021 §§146–7.
[173] ibid §§146–7.
[174] *Tagiyeva v Azerbaijan* no 72611/14, 7 July 2022 §74 (ineffectiveness solely on the basis of the inadequate involvement of the deceased person's family).
[175] The term 'adequacy' has been also used. *Ramsahai and Others v the Netherlands* [GC] no 52391/99, 15 May 2007 §324.
[176] *Butolen v Slovenia* no 41356/08, 26 April 2012 §74.
[177] *Koky and Others v Slovakia* no 13624/03, 12 June 2012 §215; *Beganović v Croatia* no 46423/06, 25 June 2009 §75; *S.M. v Croatia* [GC] no 60561/14, 25 June 2020 §313; *Volv and Bogdanov v Russia* no 15613/10, 11 February 2020 §65.

so that it becomes possible to identify the cause of harm and who might be responsible for this harm. Failures to comply with the requirement of thoroughness have been found for multiple reasons (eg not collecting relevant evidence, not establishing identities, not questioning witnesses, or not consulting experts). They are all context dependent, and no further enumeration and description will be offered here.[178] It is important, however, to underscore that the object of the investigation and thus the facts that the investigation must aim to clarify are different in the different types of cases distinguished in Section 6.1.

When harm has been inflicted by state agents, thoroughness in the establishment of the facts implies *inter alia* that the investigation must be capable of leading to a determination of whether the force used was actually justified in the sense of Article 2(2) ECHR,[179] which means that the State must investigate alleged breaches of the substantive limb of Article 2.[180] The planning and the control of police operations must also be within the object of the investigation. For example, in *Pârvu v Romania*, where state agents killed a person mistakenly thought to be a fugitive, to meet the standard of thoroughness, the investigation was expected to explain why the intervention was necessary and whether

> any special measures had been planned in advance in order to ensure the proper identification of the suspect to be arrested, or to cope with the specific situation of a possible uncertainty or error regarding the identification of the suspect.[181]

In contrast to Article 2, Article 3 is formulated differently since its text does not allow for justifications as to when state actors can use ill-treatment, and yet the question of whether harm falls within the definitional scope of Article 3 can require an assessment of whether the way state agents treated a person was made 'strictly necessary by his own conduct'.[182] Therefore, to be assessed as thorough, the investigation must be not only capable of identifying perpetrators but it must also clarify wider factual circumstances so that an evaluation of whether the test of 'strictly necessary' has been met, can be performed. Notably, these wider factual circumstances might not be possible to discover and evaluate in criminal proceedings, due to their narrow focus.[183]

Similar questions of justifications are not relevant when harm is inflicted by non-state actors. Yet in these cases, establishing the immediate cause of, for example, death does not suffice; the context in which it happened might be also relevant for the investigation to be assessed as thorough.[184] In the context of private harm, where

---

[178] Kamber, *Prosecuting Human Rights Offences* (n 3) 310–326.
[179] *Armani Da Silva v the United Kingdom* [GC] no 5878/08, 30 March 2016 §233.
[180] *Jabłońska v Poland* no 24913/15, 14 May 2020 §61.
[181] *Pârvu v Romania* no 13326/18, 30 August 2022 §97.
[182] *Bouyid v Belgium* [GC] no 23380/09, 28 September 2015 §88; *Corsacov v Moldova* no 18944/02, 4 April 2006 §69.
[183] *McKerr v the United Kingdom* no 28883/95, 4 May 2001 §137; *Al-Skeini and Others v the United Kingdom* [GC] no 55721/07, 7 July 2011 §174.
[184] *Rantsev v Cyprus and Russia* no 25965/04, 7 January 2010 §234: 'the investigation was required to consider not only the immediate context of Ms Rantseva's fall from the balcony but also the broader context

conflicting evidence or conflicting statements emerge, such contradictions need to be thoroughly clarified.[185]

In situations where harm is arguably causally linked with omissions, the alleged omissions need to be an object of an investigation.[186] Any causal links between omissions and harm need to be therefore investigated.[187] The required scope of the investigation in these cases of omissions can be quite far reaching. *Asiye Genç v Turkey* exemplifies this. The case was about the death of a prematurely born baby after multiple transfers between hospitals due to absence of a neo-natal care units. The Court held that the obligation to investigate should also include establishment of the reasons for the lack of basic facilities in neo-natal units, including the reasons why incubators were out of order. These additions to the scope of the investigation were justified with reference to the public interests at stake and the importance of rectifying possible shortcomings in the health services.[188] *Traskunova v Russia* offers another example. It involved the death of a participant in a clinical trial of a new drug. For the investigation to be thorough, it should have included an examination of whether the clinical trials had been conducted in compliance with the relevant national legal framework.[189]

Given that in cases of omissions, the facts that need to be investigated might be not only quite far-ranging but also related to institutional structures and complex organizational issues, it is easy to understand that criminal investigation might not be able to meet the standard of thoroughness. Criminal proceedings narrowly focus on the criminal responsibility of specific individuals and do not encompass fact-finding as to wider structural problems.[190] Given their object, administrative proceedings, for example, might be better placed.[191]

---

of Ms Rantseva's arrival and stay in Cyprus, in order to assess whether there was a link between the allegations of trafficking and Ms Rantseva's subsequent death'.

[185] *Rantsev v Cyprus and Russia* no 25965/04, 7 January 2010 §236; *M.C. v Bulgaria* no 39272/98, 4 December 2003 §178.
[186] *Ribcheva and Others v Bulgaria* no 37801/16, 30 March 2021 §§128–130; *Mikayil Mammadov v Azerbaijna* no 4762/05, 17 December 2009 §101 and 122; *Veronica Ciobanu v Republic of Moldova* no 69829/11, 9 February 2021 §40.
[187] *Ciechońska v Poland* no 19776/04, 14 June 2011 §75; *Bakanova v Lithuania* no 11167/12, 31 May 2016 §68: 'the investigation was required to consider not only the immediate circumstance of V.B.'s heart attack but also the broader context of V.B.'s working conditions on the *Vega*, in order to assess whether there was a link between the allegations of hazardous working conditions and V.B.'s death'.
[188] *Asiye Genç v Turkey* no 24109/07, 37 January 2015 §86. See the Concurring Opinion of Judges Lemmans, Spano, and Kjølbro in *Asiye Genç v Turkey*, who expressed concerns that the obligation to investigate was interpreted in such an expansive way.
[189] *Traskunova v Russia* no 21648/11, 30 August 2022 §85.
[190] *Lopes de Sousa Fernandes v Portugal* [GC] no 56080/13, 19 December 2017 §233; *Botoyan v Armenia* no 5766/17, 8 February 2022 §115.
[191] *Lopes de Sousa Fernandes v Portugal* [GC] no 56080/13, 19 December 2017 §§235–238, where although the Court stated that administrative proceedings were 'capable of providing the most appropriate redress', they were not thorough since they did not include an overall examination about the origin of the bacterium that caused the applicant's husband to contract meningitis.

In terms of thoroughness, in some situations the Court has required that the investigation must aim to discover specific facts. For example, in the case of assassinations, the scrutiny of the domestic authorities must go beyond the identification of the hitman and also include the intellectual author of the crime.[192] In case of killing of a journalist, the investigation must also aim to discover any possible links between the killing and the journalist's professional activities.[193] In case of violence underpinned by possible discriminatory motives, the state authorities must make efforts to unmask such motives.[194] To be assessed as thorough, the investigation must aim to discover whether there were any gender or race related motives for the harm.[195] In addition, individuals, who belong to certain groups (eg women subjected to domestic violence, racial minorities, children) have been characterized as vulnerable,[196] which might also lead to more demanding obligation to investigate.[197] More diligence in conducting a thorough investigation is required also when the harm happened in a general climate conducive to the specific type of violence.[198]

A final note is due regarding disciplinary proceedings and whether they can be considered as thorough and effective. The Court has referred to them as a possible alternative in negligence cases, in this way not excluding the possibility that disciplinary proceedings can on their own satisfy the procedural obligation.[199] However, given their limited object, they might not lead to a sufficiently thorough elucidation of all relevant facts. Disciplinary proceedings are likely to be limited to the employment relationship and might fail to inquire into wider but still relevant factual circumstances.[200] If disciplinary proceedings are not able to offer compensation for both pecuniary and non-pecuniary damages, it is also questionable whether they can meet the standard of effectiveness. This brings me to the question of how the outcome of the proceedings, including any actual compensation, is pertinent in the assessment of their effectiveness.

### 6.2.3.3 Prosecution, trial, sentencing, and compensation

As already shown, the standard of effectiveness has been applied with flexibility. Flexibility is further achieved with the addition of considerations pertaining to the

---

[192] *Mazepa and Others v Russia* no 15086/07, 17 July 2018 §75–79.
[193] ibid §73.
[194] *Genderdoc-M and M.D. v Moldova* no 23914/15, 14 December 2021 §§37 and 45.
[195] *Tërshana v Albania* no 48756/14, 4 August 2020 §160; *Gjikondi and Others v Greece* no 17249/10, 21 December 2017 §118; *Nachova and Others v Bulgaria* [GC] no 43577/98, 6 July 2005 §160; *Abdu v Bulgaria* no 26827/08, 11 March 2014 §44 (for ill-treatment inflicted by a private party).
[196] *Milanović v Serbia* no 44614/07, 14 December 2010 §89; *Koky and Others v Slovakia* no 13624/03, 12 June 2012 §239; *C.A.S. and C.S. v Romania* no 26692/05, 20 March 2012 §81.
[197] *J.I. v Croatia* no 35898/16, 8 September 2022 §84: 'special diligence' in domestic violence cases.
[198] *Tërshana v Albania* no 48756/14, 4 August 2020 §156.
[199] *Calvelli and Ciglio v Italy* [GC] no 32967/96, 17 January 2002 §51; *Vo v France* [GC] no 53924/00 8 July 2004 §90.
[200] *Botoyan v Armenia* no 5766/17, 8 February 2022 §127, where the Court concluded that the available disciplinary remedies were 'connected to employment regulation rather than the establishment of medical malpractice as such', which rendered them ineffective.

result of the proceedings, as relevant.[201] Such an addition seems to be hard to square with the consistently repeated statement in the case law that the positive obligation to investigate is one of means, not of result.[202] Yet the achievement of certain results (ie whether those identified as possibly responsible have been prosecuted, tried, and sentenced, and whether victims have received compensation proportionate to the harm suffered) can be indicative of whether the investigation was in practice effective. Furthermore, the general framing of the obligation as an obligation of having 'effective judicial system' also suggests that its scope and content incorporates measures beyond the investigative stage. The Court has accordingly observed that

> the requirements of Article 2 go beyond the stage of the official investigation, where this has led to the institution of proceedings in the national courts: the proceedings as a whole, including the trial stage, must satisfy the requirements of the positive obligation to protect lives through the law.[203]

The same approach is applicable under Article 3.[204] In the context of cases examined under Article 8 concerning 'serious acts', the Court has also suggested that 'the possibility of obtaining reparation and redress' is also part of the review as to whether the investigation has been effective.[205]

The above does not mean that the State is necessarily under the concrete obligation to prosecute or to convict specific individuals.[206] Such a concrete result is not within the scope and the content of the procedural obligation. Rather, the prosecuting authorities and the national courts are under the obligation to submit the case to

> the careful scrutiny required by Article 2 of the Convention, so that the deterrent effect of the judicial system in place and the significance of the role it is required to play in preventing violations of the right to life are not undermined.[207]

---

[201] The inclusion of some form of substantive redress, as the result of the proceedings, in the assessment of the breach of the obligation, implies that the obligation is not purely procedural anymore. M Reiertsen, *Effective Domestic Remedies and the European Court of Human Rights* (Cambridge University Press 2022) 5. This blurs the lines between substantive and procedural positive obligations. On this point, see also Section 7.2.

[202] *Tahsin Acar v Turkey* [GC] no 26307/95, 8 April 2004 §223; *X and Others v Bulgaria* [GC] no 22457/16, 2 February 2021 §186; *Hanan v Germany* [GC] no 4871/16, 16 February 2021 §210: 'To date, the Court has not faulted a prosecutorial decision which flowed from an investigation which was in all other respects Article 2 compliant, or required the competent domestic court to order a prosecution if that court had taken the considered view that application of the appropriate criminal legislation to the known facts would not result in a conviction.'

[203] *Öneryildiz v Turkey* [GC] no 48939/99, 30 November 2004 §95; *Smiljanić v Croatia* no 35983/14, 25 March 2021 §90.

[204] *R.B. v Estonia* no 22597/16, 22 June 2021 §81; *Sabalić v Croatia* no 50231/13, 14 January 2021 §97.

[205] *Söderman v Sweden* [GC] no 5786/08, 12 November 2013 §83.

[206] *Öneryildiz v Turkey* [GC] no 48939/99, 30 November 2004 §96; *Giuliani and Gaggio v Italy* [GC] no 23458/02, 24 March 2011 §306; *Jeronovičs v Latvia* [GC] no 44898/10, 5 July 2016 §07; *Söderman v Sweden* [GC] no 5786/08, 12 November 2013 §83.

[207] *Öneryildiz v Turkey* [GC] no 48939/99, 30 November 2004 §96.

In *Önerlyildiz v Turkey*, the GC also referred to the judicial authorities' determination to sanction those responsible.[208] The domestic legal system therefore must demonstrate both willingness and capacity to apply the criminal law, yet a decision not to prosecute when the investigation has been thorough, does not suffice for finding of breach.[209] If prosecution was, however, launched and there was a trial, the Court can review the substantive crime for which the alleged perpetrators were tried. If this crime does not reflect the severity of the harm inflicted upon the specific interests meant to be protected by the Convention, the trial proceedings might be assessed as inadequate.[210] Inadequacy can also be found due to problematic national procedural rules that undermine the ability of the trial court to reach a verdict.[211]

Even if the investigation and the trial proceedings were effective, breach can be found due to 'manifest disproportion between the gravity of the act and the punishment imposed'.[212] Breach can be also found when because of the authorities' inactivity, statutory limitations for criminal liability are triggered, which in turn leads to termination of proceedings.[213] For statutory limitation periods to be compatible with the Convention,[214] the national legislation might have to allow for their suspension.[215] Inflexible limitation periods that admit no exceptions, can lead to a breach.[216] In some situations, limitation periods are outright incompatible with the Convention. The Court has held that 'in cases concerning torture or ill-treatment inflicted by State agents, criminal proceedings ought not to be discontinued on account of a limitation period, and also that amnesties and pardons should not be tolerated in such cases'.[217] This is an illustration of how the procedural obligation can be more demanding depending on the actor and the severity of the harm. States are thus expected 'to be all the more stringent when punishing their own agents for the commission of serious life-endangering crimes than they are with ordinary offenders'.[218]

The scope of the procedural obligation includes not only a review as to whether a sentence has been imposed and whether it is of a proportionate gravity but also whether it is actually executed: 'the enforcement of a sentence imposed in the context

---

[208] ibid §115.
[209] *Nicolae Virgiliu Tănase v Romania* [GC] no 41720/13, 25 June 2019 §185.
[210] *Öneryildiz v Turkey* [GC] no 48939/99, 30 November 2004 §116.
[211] *R.B. v Estonia* App no 22597/16, 22 June 2021 §102.
[212] *Armani Da Silva v the United Kingdom* [GC] no 5878/08, 30 March 2016 §§238 and 285; *Smiljanić v Croatia* no 35983/14, 25 March 2021 §88; *Myumyun v Bulgaria* no 67258/13, 3 November 2011 §67.
[213] *Association '21 December 1989' and Others v Romania* no 33810/07, 24 May 2011 §144.
[214] *Mocanu and Others v Romania* [GC] no 10865/09, 17 September 2014 §326.
[215] *Mazukna v Lithuania* no 72092/12, 11 April 2017 §86.
[216] *Mocanu and Others v Romania* [GC] no 10865/09, 17 September 2014 §326. This principle has been extended to harm by private parties, particularly, when it is of serious nature. See *E.G. v the Republic of Moldova* no 37882/13, 13 April 2021 §43.
[217] *Abdülsamet Yaman v Turkey* no 32446/96, 2 November 2004 §55; *Yeter v Turkey* no 33750/03, 13 January 2009 §70; *Association '21 December 1989' and Others v Romania* no 33810/07, 24 May 2011 §144.
[218] *Makuchyan and Minasyan v Azerbaijan and Hungary* no 17247/13, 26 May 2020 §157. The justification for this more demanding obligation is that 'what is at stake is not only the issue of the individual criminal-law liability of the perpetrators but also the State's duty to combat the sense of impunity the offenders may consider themselves to enjoy by virtue of their very office'.

of the right to life must be regarded as an integral part of the procedural obligation of the State under Article 2'.[219] Amnesties,[220] 'unreasonable leniency' shown towards the convicts by their early release,[221] and unjustified delay in the enforcement of custodial sentence,[222] can all be incompatible with the procedural obligation.

Besides enforcement of punishments, the award of compensation and its type and amount are also relevant for assessment of breach of the procedural obligation. The procedural obligation demands a judicial system that must not only be capable of promptly establishing the facts and holding perpetrators accountable but that also provides appropriate redress to the victim.[223] The sole absence of redress can lead to a breach of the procedural obligation in all three types of cases distinguished in Section 6.1.[224]

Compensation can be provided in different ways and different national systems can be organized differently (eg compensation within criminal proceedings, civil in parallel with criminal proceedings, or constitution of the victim as a civil party within the criminal proceedings). The ECHR allows States to make different choices.[225] Regardless of the specific national choice, compensation for both pecuniary and non-pecuniary damages must be available.[226] For example, in *Vanyo Todorov v Bulgaria*, the Court held that despite the effective criminal investigation of the death of the applicant's brother, who was killed by a neighbour, the national judicial system was not effective since it did not allow the possibility for the brother to receive compensation for the immaterial damages that he incurred in relation to the death.[227] Similarly, in *Sarishvili-Bolkvadze v Georgia*, a medical negligence case, the question of compensation was exclusively at stake. The domestic law unconditionally excluded the award of non-pecuniary damages and on this count alone, the procedural obligation under Article 2 was found breached.[228] If the amount of compensation awarded within the civil proceedings is disproportionate, this in itself can also be a basis for the conclusion that the State failed to fulfil its procedural obligation to have an effective judicial system.[229]

---

[219] *Makuchyan and Minasyan v Azerbaijan and Hungary* no 17247/13, 26 May 2020 §50.
[220] *Marguš v Croatia* [GC] no 4455/10, 27 May 2014 §127.
[221] *Enukidze and Girgvliani v Georgia* no 25091/07, 26 April 2011 §§269 and 275.
[222] *Kitanovska Stanojkovic and Others v Macedonia* no 2319/14, 13 October 2016 §33.
[223] *Nicolae Virgiliu Tănase v Romania* [GC] no 41720/13, 25 June 2019 §§137 and 169; *Zinatullin v Russia* no 10551/10, 28 January 2020 §45.
[224] As noted in Section 6.1, Article 8 does not necessary trigger a separate procedural obligation, which might imply that the absence of compensation might need to be combined with other shortcomings for a breach to be found. See *Georgel and Georgeta Stoiescu v Romania* no 9718/03, 26 July 2011 §62.
[225] As long as the procedure chosen is effective in practice. *Lopes de Sousa Fernandes v Portugal* [GC] no 56080/13, 19 December 2017 §216.
[226] *Jeronovičs v Latvia* [GC] no 44898/10, 5 July 2016 §104.
[227] *Vanyo Todorov v Bulgaria* no 31434/15, 12 July 2020 §67; *Movsesyan v Armenia* no 27524/09, 16 November 2017 §74; *Z and Others v the United Kingdom* [GC] no 29392/95, 10 May 2001 §109.
[228] *Sarishvili-Bolkvadze v Georgia* no 58240/08, 19 July 2018 §§94–8.
[229] *Scripnic v the Republic of Moldova* no 63789/13, 13 April 2021 §§43–48. See also *Firstov v Russia* no 42119/04, 20 February 2014 §35 where breach was found since the applicant received an award for non-pecuniary damages that was disproportionately lower than the award that the Court generally awards in comparable cases.

## 6.2.4 Cooperation with Other States in Cross-border Contexts

Individuals might suffer harm in cross-border situations where investigative measures by more than one State are necessary so that the circumstances are clarified, perpetrators identified, and compensation becomes available. Due to the specific challenges that arise in cross-border situations, States might be not only under the obligation to investigate but also under the obligation to cooperate with other States. After clarifying how this obligation was initially imposed by the Court in *Rantsev v Cyprus and Russia*, I will explain how it was further developed in *Güzelyurtlu and Others v Cyprus and Turkey* as a corollary of the procedural obligation to investigate. Finally, I will address the relationship between the obligation to cooperate, as a positive obligation under the ECHR, and external legal frameworks regulating cooperation between States.

### 6.2.4.1 The imposition of a free-standing obligation to cooperate and assist another State

The first time when the application of the procedural obligation in a cross-border situation came to the fore and the Court substantively engaged with it was in *Rantsev v Cyprus and Russia*. This case illustrates a scenario where death happens on the territory of one State (ie the territorial investigating State); however, in light of the cross-border nature of the case, another State might be deemed by the Court to have a human rights law jurisdiction in the sense of Article 1 ECHR, which can in turn trigger the latter's procedural obligation. In this scenario, the second State has *not* exercised its criminal jurisdiction by its own initiative.[230] In particular, in *Rantsev v Cyprus and Russia* a woman was arguably killed by a non-state actor in Cyprus. However, she was of a Russian nationality, which made the case under Article 2 of a cross-border nature. The Court held that since the death took place in Cyprus, 'the obligation to ensure an effective official investigation applies to Cyprus *alone*'.[231] Russia, therefore, had no 'free standing obligation' to investigate the death,[232] since Article 2 does not require 'States' criminal laws to provide for universal jurisdiction in cases involving the death of one of their nationals'.[233] The Court, however, added that a departure from this general approach might be warranted when the case has 'special features'. The fact that the victim holds the nationality of a State is not such a 'special feature'. Which features

---

[230] For the distinction between having a jurisdiction in the sense of Article 1 ECHR and initiation of criminal jurisdiction, see Section 8.4.1.1.
[231] *Rantsev v Cyprus and Russia* no 25965/04, 7 January 2010 §243 (emphasis added); *M. and Others v Italy and Bulgaria* no 40020/03, 31 July 2012 §126.
[232] *Rantsev v Cyprus and Russia* no 25965/04, 7 January 2010 §244.
[233] *Rantsev v Cyprus and Russia* §244. The approach under Article 4 ECHR was different since the case was defined as one of human trafficking of cross-border nature. See V Stoyanova, 'Dancing on the Borders of Article 4: Human Trafficking and the European Court of Human Rights in the Rantsev Case' (2012) 30(2) Netherlands Quarterly of Human Rights 163.

will, however, be special enough to justify departure from the general approach remained unaddressed in this judgment, an issue that I will return to below.

Although Russia had no 'free-standing obligation to investigate', was Russia under an obligation to assist Cyprus in the latter's authorities' investigative efforts? As I will show, the question of whether and how assistance by Russia was a matter of any ECHR positive obligations remained without a clear answer in *Rantsev v Cyprus and Russia*. First, it is relevant to distinguish the following two aspects of this question: one pertaining to the preliminary issue of Russia's jurisdiction in the sense of Article 1, and another one pertaining to the substantive issue as to the separate nature of any obligation to assist. As to Article 1, without any elaboration, the Court simply accepted that Russia had jurisdiction tailored to the procedural obligation.[234] As to the nature of this obligation, the Court framed 'a duty on the State where evidence is located to render any assistance within its competence and means sought under a legal assistance request'.[235] The Court's reasoning does not explain whether such a duty was specifically triggered for Russia in the case, in this way avoiding a determination of whether this was a duty separate from the obligation to investigate. However, since Russia, as explained above, had no obligation to investigate in the first place, and since the Court determined that Russia actually 'made extensive use of the opportunities presented by mutual legal assistance agreements', the reasoning suggests that the obligation to assist another State is *separate* from the obligation to investigate. This is a point that will also be revisited below.

The Court in *Rantsev v Cyprus and Russia* introduced an important limitation as to the scope of the obligation to assist: '[i]n the absence of a legal assistance request, the Russian authorities were not required under Article 2 to secure the evidence themselves'. It follows that formal legal channels and international agreements are key for delineating the scope of the obligation. States might not be required as a matter of their ECHR positive obligations to assist investigations by other State by undertaking measures that go beyond those demanded by formal agreements for mutual assistance.

The limitation was also highlighted by the Court when it considered the procedural obligation upon Cyprus to investigate the death of Ms Rantseva. One criteria used by the Court for assessing the effectiveness of the investigation was whether Cyprus sought assistance from Russia using the procedure set out in the Mutual Assistance Convention and a bilateral Legal Assistance Treaty.[236] This criterion was framed in this way: 'for an investigation to be effective, member States must take such steps as are necessary and available in order to secure relevant evidence, whether or not it is located in the territory of the investigating State'.[237] Contrary to the approach to

---

[234] *Rantsev v Cyprus and Russia* no 25965/04, 7 January 2010 §105–108. This is a manifestation of the divided and tailored approach to jurisdiction, see Chapter 8.
[235] *Rantsev v Cyprus and Russia* no 25965/04, 7 January 2010 §245.
[236] ibid §241.
[237] ibid §241.

Russia however, cooperation for securing evidence was not framed as a separate obligation upon Cyprus but only as one of the criteria for assessing Cyprus' compliance with the obligation to investigate (ie for addressing the question whether the investigation was effective).

### 6.2.4.2 The obligation to cooperate as a corollary of the procedural obligation to investigate

*Güzelyurtlu and Others v Cyprus and Turkey* offers a more detailed explanation of the nature of the obligation to cooperate in cross-border cases.[238] In particular, the judgment frames the obligation as a corollary of the procedural obligation to investigate, which seems to limit the relevance of the obligation to cooperate to contexts involving States that are *Parties to the ECHR*.

*Güzelyurtlu and Others v Cyprus and Turkey* involved a scenario different from *Rantsev v Cyprus and Russia* in that there were *parallel investigations*. Both States, Cyprus on whose territory the killings by private actors were committed and 'TRNC'/Turkey where the suspects escaped, launched investigations on their initiatives. Two issues arose here. First, were Cyprus and Turkey actually required as a matter of their ECHR positive obligations to initiate investigations? Second, how does cooperation between them relate to such obligations?

The imposition of the procedural obligation upon Cyprus was not controversial since the killings happened on its territory. Given that the killings did not happen on the territory of 'TRNC', an entity under the effective control of Turkey,[239] the Court had to address the question of whether Turkey had any procedural obligations at all. This was framed by the Court as a question of Turkey's jurisdiction in the sense of Article 1 ECHR. The question received an affirmative answer on two independent grounds (ie each one of them would suffice for reaching the conclusion that Turkey had a procedural obligation). The first was framed in the following way:

> [I]f the investigative or judicial authorities of a Contracting State initiate their own criminal investigation or proceedings concerning a death which has occurred outside the jurisdiction of that State, by virtue of their domestic law (e.g. under provisions on universal jurisdiction or on the basis of the active or passive personality principle), the institution of that investigation or those proceedings is sufficient to establish a jurisdictional link for the purposes of Article 1 between that State and the victim's relatives who later bring proceedings before the Court.[240]

---

[238] See also *Razvozzhayev v Russia and Ukraine* and *Udaltsov v Russia* no 75732/12, 19 November 2019 §157, where it is explicitly clarified that the principles formulated in *Güzelyurtlu and Others v Cyprus and Turkey* in relation to Article 2, are also applicable to Articles 3 and 5.
[239] See Section 8.3.
[240] *Güzelyurtlu and Others v Cyprus and Turkey* [GC] no 36925/07, 29 January 2019 §188.

This means that if a State itself has triggered a *criminal* investigation about harm that had materialized outside its territory, this investigation is no longer only a matter of national law but it is a matter of ECHR obligations and can be reviewed against the standards developed by the Court regarding effectiveness. There is thus a circularity here: since 'TRNC'/Turkey itself launched a criminal investigation, this triggered an obligation to do so under the ECHR.

Even if 'TRNC'/Turkey had not launched a criminal investigation however, given the 'special features' of the case, 'TRNC'/Turkey would still have been under an obligation to investigate. The existence of 'special features' was therefore the second ground on which Turkey's procedural obligation was found to have been triggered. These special features narrowly pertain to the distinct situation in Cyprus, where the Republic of Cyprus is unable to fulfil its Convention obligations in northern Cyprus, where the suspects fled.[241]

The parallel investigations by the two respondent States were assessed as adequate by the Court; the crux of the problem in *Güzelyurtlu and Others v Cyprus and Turkey* was rather 'the existence and scope of a duty to cooperate as a component of the procedural obligation under Article 2'.[242] It was clarified that 'the failure to cooperate was only one aspect among others in the Court's examination of the effectiveness of the investigation'.[243] The requirement for cooperation *as a component* of the procedural obligation is relevant only when the procedural obligation is triggered in the first place. If cooperation is only a component, how can this be squared with the finding in *Rantsev v Cyprus and Russia*, explained in the previous section, that Russia had no free-standing obligation to investigate but still had an obligation to cooperate with Cyprus for the investigation of the death? In *Güzelyurtlu and Others v Cyprus and Turkey*, the Court resolved this inconsistency by reasoning that

> in cases such as *Rantsev* where a Contracting State has no free-standing obligation to investigate under Article 2, the obligation to cooperate of that State *can only be triggered by a cooperation request made by the investigating State*, which would be required to seek such cooperation of its own motion if relevant evidence or the suspects are located within the jurisdiction of the other State.[244]

All of the above leaves us with two situations. The first transpires when a Contracting State is under the obligation to investigate: it has a 'free-standing obligation' irrespective of the basis on which such an obligation is triggered.[245] Requesting

---

[241] ibid §§193–195.
[242] ibid §221.
[243] ibid §229.
[244] ibid §230. The inconsistency was not entirely resolved since the facts in *Rantsev v Cyprus and Russia* no 25965/04, 7 January 2010 showed that Cyprus never actually requested cooperation from Russia, yet the obligation upon Russia to cooperate was still found triggered and reviewed by the Court.
[245] The harm occurred within its jurisdiction in the sense of Article 1 ECHR or the State itself has exercised its criminal jurisdiction irrespective of the location of the harm, which is enough to establish 'a jurisdictional link for the purposes of Article 1'. *Güzelyurtlu and Others v Cyprus and Turkey* [GC] no 36925/07, 29 January 2019 §188.

cooperation from other States is one of the criteria for assessing the effectiveness of the investigation and therefore for assessing compliance with this obligation.[246] Whether these other States are parties to the ECHR is not relevant since their conduct is not an object of the human rights law review anyway.[247] The second situation emerges when a Contracting State has no 'free-standing obligation' to investigate; however, within its jurisdiction there are suspects or evidence relevant to the investigation initiated by another State. *Since this other State requests cooperation*, this triggers the obligation of the requested Contracting State *to cooperate*, not to investigate.

In relation to the second situation, where the requested State's obligation to cooperate is *not* a component of the obligation to investigate, some ambiguities remain. Is it necessary that the requesting State be a Party to the ECHR? Even if this question is answered in the affirmative, a second question arises: is it necessary that the requesting State is found to be under an obligation demanded by the ECHR to investigate, a component of which is seeking cooperation, so that its request actually triggers the obligation upon the requested State to cooperate?[248] The reasoning in *Güzelyurtlu and Others v Cyprus and Turkey* suggests a positive answer to these questions. The GC justified cooperation by noting 'the Convention's special character as a collective enforcement treaty' entailing 'in principle an obligation on the part of the States concerned to cooperate effectively'.[249] The GC also characterized cooperation as 'a two-way obligation' of seeking and affording assistance.[250] Cooperation has been also characterized as a corollary of the procedural obligation of the investigating State.[251]

### 6.2.4.3 The relationship between the obligation to cooperate under the ECHR and external legal frameworks regulating cooperation

As a corollary, the obligation to cooperate follows from the obligation to investigate under the ECHR, which more generally reveals the regional character of the cooperation and the related obligations. This regional character manifested itself also in *Romeo Castaño v Belgium*. This was the second case after *Rantsev v Cyprus and Russia*, where the Court found that the respondent State was under the independent obligation to cooperate. Similarly to *Rantsev v Cyprus and Russia*, *Romeo Castaño v Belgium* also involved two Parties to the ECHR. The applicant complained about the failure of Belgium to cooperate with Spain so that a suspected murderer, who had fled to Belgium, can be tried in Spain. Belgium's failure arguably consisted of its refusal to surrender the suspect due to risk of her being subjected to human rights law violations if she were to be detained in Spain. The 'special features' that triggered Belgium's

---

[246] See *X and Others v Bulgaria* [GC] no 22457/16, 2 February 2021 §217–219.
[247] See *Nasr and Ghali v Italy* no 44883/09, 23 February 2016 §272, where Italy failed to fulfill its procedural obligation under Article 3 due to *inter alia* its failure to seek extradition from the United States.
[248] Procedurally, this will imply that the requesting State is also a party to the proceedings before the Court as a respondent State.
[249] *Güzelyurtlu and Others v Cyprus and Turkey* [GC] no 36925/07, 29 January 2019 §232.
[250] ibid § 233.
[251] *Rantsev v Cyprus and Russia* no 25965/04, 7 January 2010 §245.

**164** Procedural Positive Obligation to Investigate

obligation to cooperate were that Belgian authorities were informed of 'the Spanish authorities' intention to institute criminal proceedings against N.J.E., and were requested to arrest and surrender her'. This happened 'in the context of the mutual undertakings given by the two States in the sphere of cooperation in criminal matters, in this instance under the European arrest warrant scheme'.[252]

While the answers to the questions concerning the relationship between the ECHR obligations of the requesting and the requested State (as framed in the last paragraph of Section 6.2.4.2) remain yet to be resolved, *Romeo Castaño v Belgium* makes it clear that the obligation to cooperate, as both a separate obligation and as a component of the obligation to investigate, is dependent on existing legal frameworks that States have created to cooperate. These frameworks consist of treaties other than the ECHR. The motivation is that cooperation cannot be performed in a legal vacuum.[253] For this reason,

> the procedural obligation to cooperate will only be breached in respect of a State required to seek cooperation if it has failed to trigger the proper mechanisms for cooperation under the relevant international treaties; and in respect of the requested State, if it has failed to respond properly or has not been able to invoke a legitimate ground for refusing the cooperation requested under those instruments.[254]

As this paragraph suggests, the content of the obligation imposed upon the requested State to cooperate includes two measures: a response and a motivation. First, not responding properly to a request in itself leads to a breach.[255] Second, if the response is negative (as it was in *Romeo Castaño v Belgium*), the refusal has to be based on a legitimate ground.

As to the possibility of the requested State to invoke 'a legitimate ground' to refuse cooperation, *Romeo Castaño v Belgium* made it clear that there are two aspects against which the legitimacy of the ground can be assessed. The first relates to whether the ground for refusal is legitimate *from the perspective of the ECHR*. In *Romeo Castaño v Belgium* the Court held that

> from the standpoint of the Convention, a risk to the person whose surrender is sought of being subjected to inhuman or degrading treatment on account of the conditions of detention in Spain may constitute a legitimate ground for refusing

---

[252] *Romeo Castaño v Belgium* no 8351/17, 9 July 2019 §41.
[253] *Güzelyurtlu and Others v Cyprus and Turkey* [GC] no 36925/07, 29 January 2019 §235.
[254] ibid §236. In some special situations, though, 'informal or *ad hoc* channels of cooperation' outside formal cooperation channels as regulated by international treaties, might be also reasonably expected. ibid §238. See also *Saribekyan and Balyan v Azerbaijan* no 35746/11, 30 January 2020 §73: 'The lack of diplomatic relations does not absolve a Contracting State from the obligation under Article 2 to cooperate in criminal investigations.'
[255] *Güzelyurtlu and Others v Cyprus and Turkey* [GC] no 36925/07, 29 January 2019 §265.

execution of the European arrest warrant and thus for refusing cooperation with Spain.[256]

It is interesting here that the Court did not invoke the legal frameworks that regulate the cooperation between States, to assess the legitimacy of the grounds for refusal. Despite all the emphasis on the importance of these frameworks for the content of the obligation to cooperate, the Court did not use them as a point of reference. Note needs also to be taken of the usage of the term 'a legitimate ground' to refuse cooperation, as opposed to 'a legal ground' or a ground explicitly allowed by legal frameworks specifically regulating cooperation. This suggests that refusals might be assessed as legitimate based on wider considerations.

In addition to its legitimacy, the ground for refusal must be factually substantiated: 'given the presence of third-party rights, the finding that such a risk [risks for ill-treatment after extradition] exists must have a sufficient factual basis'.[257] This requirement was not fulfilled in *Romeo Castaño v Belgium*, since the ground used by the Belgium courts to refuse surrender of the suspect, to the detriment of the applicant's rights, did not have a sufficient factual basis.[258]

The requirement for factual substantiation, as justified by the Court, reveals how when cooperation is no longer only a matter of State-to-State relations but also a matter of a positive obligation under the ECHR, the interests of individuals gain importance. Cooperation as a positive obligation under the ECHR is meant to protect the interests of victims of harm caused by alleged crimes. The State, however, has to also ensure any competing interests (eg the interests of the suspect).[259] The content and the scope of the positive obligation to cooperate therefore has to be framed in a way that accommodates competing interests of individuals.[260]

The interests of victims might not be a core consideration of international treaties regulating cooperation between States. These treaties might allow States discretion as to the modes of cooperation and possibilities for refusal to cooperate. This might lead to situations where States are not obliged to undertake certain measures under these treaties,[261] but such measures might be key for discovering relevant facts, obtaining evidence or sentencing. This might lead to tensions between the discretion allowed by the treaties and compliance with the positive obligations under the ECHR. As a response to this tension, the Court has observed that the obligation to cooperate implies 'as far as possible a combined and harmonious application' of the ECHR and these treaties, 'which should not result in conflict or opposition between them'.[262] For

---

[256] *Romeo Castaño v Belgium* no 8351/17, 9 July 2019 §85.
[257] ibid §85.
[258] ibid §90.
[259] ibid §92.
[260] See Chapter 5.
[261] *Palić v Bosnia and Herzegovina* no 4704/04, 15 February 2011 §65 (the main suspect, a Serbian national, could not be extradited from Serbia).
[262] *Güzelyurtlu and Others v Cyprus and Turkey* [GC] no 36925/07, 29 January 2019 §236.

example, in *Güzelyurtlu and Others v Cyprus and Turkey*, the second respondent State was found in breach of its obligation to cooperate not because it did not extradite the suspects as requested by Cyprus, which was in any case not a measure necessarily obliged to take under the relevant treaties. Breach was found on the narrow ground that Turkey did not provide a motivated reply to the requested extradition. Such a reply was actually required under the relevant extradition treaty.[263]

Treaties that regulate cooperation might also contain provisions worded in very abstract terms. This in turn might be used by the Court as an interpretative tool for suggesting different concrete measures that can be arguably deduced from these treaties' abstract provisions, for the purpose of better protecting victims' interests. It might be questionable, however, whether these concrete measures are actually required under the treaties. *X and Others v Bulgaria* is illustrative since the Court proposed very concrete measures that Bulgaria could have undertaken to seek cooperation from Italy. The case was about children, who prior to their adoption and departure to Italy, lived in an orphanage in Bulgaria, where they were allegedly subjected to sexual abuses. The Court reasoned that the Bulgarian authorities, '*guided by the principles set out in the international instruments* ... could have travelled to Italy in the context of mutual legal assistance or requested the Italian authorities to interview the applicants again'.[264] Another concrete measure invoked in the reasoning was requesting from Italy 'in the context of international judicial cooperation' that the applicants undergo a medical examination.[265] The Lanzarote Convention, among other instruments, was invoked to support these concrete investigative measures.[266] However, given its abstract framing, it can be questioned whether this Convention can give such a concrete content to the obligation to cooperate. Admittedly, cooperation with Italy was only a component of the obligation upon Bulgaria to investigate, which might explain the absence of a more stringent assessment by the Court as to what concrete measures treaties of cooperation actually require.

To summarize, the content and the scope of the obligation to cooperate under the ECHR are shaped by external frameworks regulating cooperation. These frameworks, however, are mainly designed to regulate State-to-State relations. In contrast, the obligation to cooperate under the ECHR corresponds to rights conferred upon individuals, which might favour more expansive cooperative measures to the benefit of individuals aho are victims of crimes. These different perspectives might cause tensions, which the Court will seek to address by 'combined and harmonious application'. The standard of reasonableness which, as Chapter 4 clarified, affects all positive obligations, can also play a role in addressing any tensions and shaping the scope and the content of the obligation to cooperate.

---

[263] ibid §265.
[264] *X and Others v Bulgaria* [GC] no 22457/16, 2 February 2021 §216 (emphasis added).
[265] ibid §219.
[266] Article 38, Council of Europe Convention on the Protection of Children against Sexual Exploitation and Sexual Abuse CETS No 201.

# Conclusion

The standard of reasonableness has a role in all the aspects covered in Chapter 6. By way of a conclusion, this final section of the chapter thus aims to reflect explicitly upon this role in the trigger and in the delineation of the content and the scope of the positive obligation to investigate. Since, as already clarified in Chapters 2, 3, 4, and 5, reasonableness is related to the standards of knowledge and causation, the role of these two standards will be also explained.

The starting point in this explanation is that States are only required to undertake 'reasonable steps' to investigate.[267] The Court has also observed that 'the procedural obligation must not be interpreted in such a way as to impose an impossible or disproportionate burden on the authorities'.[268] The scope and the content of the procedural obligation is more specifically delimited by the standard of reasonableness in at least three ways. *First*, the mere requirement that the obligation *needs to be triggered first*, as explicated in Section 6.1, suggests that States have no investigative duties all the time in relation to everything that happens within their jurisdiction. States need to know about harm and the information needs to reach certain level of credibility. In some situations (ie harm inflicted by state agents), it is reasonable to assume knowledge. In these situations, the obligation to investigate is very closely related to States' negative obligations. Just as importantly, the assessment of compliance with negative obligations is contingent on compliance with the obligation to investigate.[269] The assessment of breach of negative obligations is dependent on the elucidation of the facts, and it is not reasonable to allow the State to avoid review of how it used its coercive powers by benefiting from its own omissions (ie not investigating).[270]

*The second way* in which the standard of reasonableness has a delimiting role relates to the *tailoring of the content and the scope of the obligation to the source and actor of harm*, as explained in Section 6.2.1. This tailoring has happened gradually in the case law. The procedural obligation was first framed in the context of the use of lethal forced by state actors. In this context, certain requirements were developed as reasonable investigative measures that the State has to undertake. These requirements have been subsequently transposed to other contexts. The transposition has happened in the case law in a fragmented fashion and with adaptations and modifications. In particular, when harm reaches a certain gravity (as the harm covered by Articles 2 and

---

[267] *Hanan v Germany* [GC] no 4871/16, 16 February 2021 §204; *Georgia v Russia* (II) [GC] (merits) no 38263/08, 21 January 2021 §326; *S.M. v Croatia* [GC] no 60561/14, 25 June 2020 §316; *Mocanu and Others v Romania* [GC] no 10865/09, 17 September 2014 §320.

[268] *S.M. v Croatia* [GC] no 60561/14, 25 June 2020 §315.

[269] Review of compliance with substantive positive obligations is also similarly dependent on compliance with the obligation to investigate (see eg *Aftanache v Romania* no 999/19, 26 May 2020 §73). There is, however, an important difference. If the facts show that the coercive powers used reach the minimum threshold of Article 3, violation automatically follows. If the facts show that the coercive powers used do not comply with the standard of 'absolutely necessary' under Article 2, violation automatically follows. See Section 8.4.1.2.

[270] Kamber, 'Substantive and Procedural Criminal Law Protection of Human Rights in the Law of the European Convention on Human Rights' (n 4) 99.

3) and is intentionally inflicted by an actor (even if a non-state actor), the content and the scope of the obligation has necessarily to include official criminal investigation.

It has not, however, been considered reasonable to require official criminal investigation in situations of harm linked with negligence. At least three reasons can be advanced for limiting the scope of the positive obligation in this way. First, criminalization of negligent conduct might be problematic.[271] Second, official criminal investigation is resource-demanding, and it is questionable whether these resources should be invested, for example in private disputes about negligence. Third, other proceedings might be better placed to elucidate structural and systemic problems that normally arise in cases of negligence.

And yet, certain exceptions have been carved out in the case law when official criminal investigation might be required even in cases of negligence. As Section 6.2.1 demonstrated, the Court has been struggling to delineate the precise boundaries of these exceptions. It is clear thought that state knowledge plays an important role here. When the State is better placed to know the facts or to access information relevant to the elucidation of the facts, it is reasonable that the State bears the burden of the investigation and, for this reason, an official criminal investigation is demanded.

*The third way* in which the standard of reasonableness has a delimiting role concerns the nature of the obligation to investigate *as an obligation of efforts*. More specifically, since the content and the scope of the obligation can only include 'reasonable steps' to investigate, the Court reviews the capacity of the investigation to lead to the establishment of relevant facts[272] and secure relevant evidence.[273] For this reason, the obligation is not an obligation of result but of means.[274] This characterization of the obligation implies that it is an obligation of best efforts and, as a starting point, States have discretion as to the efforts (ie the concrete investigative measures and the evidence needed).[275] In addition, the Court has repeated that 'it cannot replace the domestic authorities in the assessment of the facts of the case'.[276]

Since the Court's review focuses on the efforts, it is relevant to ask the following question: to what extent should any omissions to undertake certain investigative measures contribute to the undermining of the capacity of the investigation to clarify

---

[271] The requirement for official criminal investigation necessarily implies that the domestic law criminalizes the harm. In this sense, the purpose of the procedural obligation is the application of the national substantive criminal law.

[272] *S.M. v Croatia* [GC] no 60561/14, 25 June 2020 §313; *Koky and Others v Slovakia* no 13624/03, 12 June 2012 §215.

[273] *Rantsev v Cyprus and Russia* no 25965/04, 7 January 2010 §241.

[274] 'the failure of any given investigation to produce conclusions does not, by itself, mean that it was ineffective: an obligation to investigate "is not an obligation of result, but of means"'. See *Mikheyev v Russia* no 77617/01, 26 January 2006 §§107–109; *S.M. v Croatia* [GC] no 60561/14, 25 June 2020 §315; *Mustafa Tunç and Fecire Tunç v Turkey* [GC] no 24014/05, 14 April 2015 §173; *Lopes de Sousa Fernandes v Portugal* [GC] no 56080/13, 19 December 2017 §221.

[275] *Beganović v Croatia* no 46423/06, 25 June 2009 §78: 'The Court must grant substantial deference to the national courts in the choice of appropriate measures, while also maintaining a certain power of review …'. *Lopes de Sousa Fernandes v Portugal* [GC] no 56080/13, 19 December 2017 §216.

[276] *M. and C. v Romania* no 29032/04, 27 September 2011 §113; *X and Others v Bulgaria* [GC] no 22457/16, 2 February 2021 §86.

Conclusion   169

factual circumstances? This is a question about the causation between the efforts and the result. More specifically, it is a question about the causation between the failures to make some effort (ie failure by the authorities to undertake certain investigative measures) and the elucidation of the facts. A causation standard has not been explicitly addressed in the case law, as more generally explained in Chapter 3. Rather, as detailed in Section 6.2.3, the Court refers to the general standard of effectiveness. Section 6.2.3 also indicated that five criteria for assessing effectiveness have been developed. Their causative role, the weight attached to each one of them, and the relationships between them, are however, difficult to assess.

Relevant to the question of causation are the pronouncements that the omissions have to imply failings to follow 'an obvious line of inquiry' that 'undermines to a decisive extent the investigation's ability to establish the circumstances of the case and the identity of those responsible'.[277] It has been also noted that omissions have to imply manifest failures by the national authorities to take into account relevant elements.[278] The Court has also held that its 'task is to examine whether or not the alleged shortcomings in the investigation had such *significant flaws* as to amount to a breach of the respondent State's positive obligations'.[279] All these pronouncements suggest some level of seriousness of the impact of the investigative omissions.

So far, however, 'significant flaws' has not been applied as a separate test but possibly as a way of saying that the Court 'is not concerned with allegations of errors or isolated omissions in the investigation',[280] but only with 'significant shortcomings in the proceedings and the relevant decision-making process'.[281] All of this advocates that omissions to take investigative measures or to discover evidence that do not significantly contribute to the reconstruction of the facts, are not relevant to the finding of breach. The reasoning in concrete cases is, however, far from clear on whether the omissions identified by the Court are significant and to what extent they are contributory (ie to what extent they undermine the achievement of the desired result of fact finding).

A final point is due regarding the nature of the procedural obligation as an obligation of efforts. This point concerns the inclusion of results such as actual prosecution, trial, sentencing and compensation, as relevant factors in the assessment of breach. As Section 6.2.3 mentioned, these inclusions have been justified with reference to the flexible standard of effectiveness. At the same time, the Court has been adamant in its

---

[277] *S.M. v Croatia* [GC] no 60561/14, 25 June 2020 §316; *Mustafa Tunç and Fecire Tunç v Turkey* [GC] no 24014/05, 14 April 2015 §175.
[278] *X and Others v Bulgaria* [GC] no 22457/16, 2 February 2021 §186.
[279] *M. and C. v Romania* no 29032/2011, 27 September 2011 §112 (emphasis added); *M.C. v Bulgaria* no 39272/98, 4 December 2003§167; *Söderman v Sweden* [GC] no 5786/08, 12 November 2013 §91; *S.M. v Croatia* [GC] no 60561/14, 25 June 2020 §318.
[280] *M. and C. v Romania*, no 29032/04, 27 September 2011 §§112; *M.C. v Bulgaria* no 39272/98, 4 December 2003 §168; *C.A.S. and C.S. v Romania* no 26692/05, 20 March 2012 §78; *Söderman v Sweden* [GC] no 5786/08, 12 November 2013 §90; *R.B. v Estonia* no 22597/16, 22 June 2021 §89; *Armani Da Silva v the United Kingdom* [GC] no 5878/08, 30 March 2016, §242.
[281] *S.M. v Croatia* [GC] no 60561/14, 25 June 2020 §318; *Söderman v Sweden* [GC] no 5786/08, 12 November 2013 §§90–91.

repetitions that the ECHR does not confer a right to have third parties prosecuted or sentenced for a criminal offence.[282] Indeed, it does not seem reasonable to expand the scope of the obligation in this way for at least two reasons. First, the lines of causation between omissions, on the one hand, and prosecution and sentencing, on the other, might be more tenuous in comparison with the lines of causation between omissions and fact-finding. Second and relatedly, the interests of third parties intervene in more serious ways when questions of prosecution and conviction are at stake.[283] This places the State in the difficult position of accommodating competing obligations.[284]

---

[282] *Öneryildiz v Turkey* [GC] no 48939/99, 30 November 2004 § 96.

[283] F Tulkens, 'The Paradoxical Relationship between Criminal Law and Human Rights' (2011) 9 Journal of International Criminal Justice 577

[284] Traditionally in criminal proceedings, the focus is on the relationship between the State and the accused. Victims can have the possibility to participate; however, their participatory rights are accessory to the efforts in exercising the public-prerogative of criminal prosecution. Allowing victims 'to have a functional say in the process, may not only impair the rights of defendants but also disturb the conceptual foundation of criminal procedure'. Kamber, *Prosecuting Human Rights Offences* (n 3) 8 and 13. On competing obligations, see Chapter 5.

# 7
# Substantive Positive Obligations

## Introduction

Besides the procedural positive obligation to investigate, the Court has developed 'two distinct albeit related' substantive positive obligations.[1] Section 7.1 will first examine the positive obligation upon the State to put in place effective regulatory frameworks. As part of this obligation, the Court also examines whether national regulatory frameworks contain certain procedural guarantees that are in some respects similar to those discussed in Chapter 6. Although these guarantees are not detachable from the substantive positive obligation of adopting effective regulatory framework, their importance warrants a detailed examination. This will be performed in Section 7.2. Finally, Section 7.3 will focus on the second substantive positive obligation, the obligation upon the State to take preventive operational measures to protect an identified individual in certain circumstances, originally introduced in *Osman v the United Kingdom*.[2] Explaining the distinctiveness of this obligation will be one of the main preoccupations of Section 7.3.

## 7.1 Obligation to Develop Effective Regulatory Frameworks

The text of the Convention explicitly demands the adoption of rules at national level: limitations of rights will automatically amount to breach of negative obligations, if the measure limiting the right is not 'in accordance with the law' or 'in accordance with a procedure prescribed by law'.[3] Legality, the existence of a domestic legal framework allowing the limitations, is a conclusive test for establishing responsibility for breach of negative obligations. The legality requirement, however, cannot be applied in the same way where responsibility for omissions is invoked. If it were, this would imply that for any omission to be justified and viewed as permissible (and thus not in breach of positive obligations), it needs to be regulated by being based on a legal provision.[4] While it is correct that in some situations, the national regulatory framework

---

[1] *Fernandes de Oliveira v Portugal* [GC] no 78103/14, 31 January 2019 §103.
[2] *Osman v the United Kingdom* [GC] no 23452/94, 28 October 1998.
[3] See eg Articles 5(1), 8, 9, 10, and 11 ECHR.
[4] For authors in favour of this idea see A Barak, *Proportionality. Constitutional Rights and their Limitations* (Cambridge University Press 2012) 429–34; L Lavrysen, *Human Rights in a Positive State* (Intersentia 2016) 317.

might regulate or even mandate omissions,[5] it needs to be highlighted that more generally, omissions are not regulated. Omissions might not even be knowable, let alone regulated, even less so in a way that can be expected to meet all the qualitative requirements within the legality test developed in the context of negative obligations.[6]

The above discussion also relates to the assumption that the State, its institutions, and its agents need to have an explicit mandate (ie an authorization) for their actions, so that these can always and as a matter of principle be tested again the legality requirement in human rights law, as part of the assessment whether the State has complied with its negative obligations. In contrast, individuals and private parties are free to choose their conduct. While this conduct can also be an object of regulation (via eg criminal or civil law), these regulations are specific and not pervasive. If they were, this would imply that all aspects of individuals' lives would be regulated, which would lead to an intrusive statism.

Not only can legality not be a conclusive test when the invoked basis for state responsibility is omission but the challenged omission might be precisely the absence of national regulatory frameworks.[7] In this context, it makes little sense to check state responsibility against an initial and conclusive standard of domestic legality. Instead, the need to adopt relevant rules will be at the heart of the assessment of the reasonableness as related to the causation and knowledge standards, which in turn can lead to the conclusion whether state responsibility can be established.

In addition, as the Court has stated, States have discretion as to how to fulfil their positive obligations, which implies that adoption of a national regulatory framework might be just one option at their disposal. The Court has noted that '[t]here are different avenues to ensure "respect for private life", and even if the State has failed to apply one particular measure provided by domestic law, it may still fulfill its positive duty by other means'.[8] This reasoning means that even if an omission is contrary to national law and has caused harm, this per se is not sufficient for finding a failure to fulfil positive obligations.[9] In addition, States also have a choice as to the form of

---

[5] See eg *Valdís Fjölnisdóttir and Others v Iceland* no 71552/17, 18 May 2021 §75 the national regulatory framework did not allow the registration in the Registers Iceland of a parent–child relationship between non-biological parents and a child born in the United States via surrogacy.
[6] For these qualitative requirements, see J Gerards, *General Principles of the European Convention on Human Rights* (Cambridge University Press 2019) 198.
[7] For example, *A., B. and C. v Ireland* [GC] no 25579/05, 16 December 2010 §264; *Sari and Colak v Turkey* no 42596/98 and 42603/98, 4 April 2006 §37. See Section 7.1.2.1.
[8] For example, *Fadeyeva v Russia* no 55723/00, 9 June 2005 §96. See Section 4.2.
[9] For example, *Kapa and Others v Poland* no 75031/13, 14 October 2021 §153, where heavy traffic near the applicants' home exposed them to severe nuisance. The noise caused by the traffic was beyond the statutory norms. This was relevant, but not sufficient for finding a violation. See also *Lozovyye v Russia* no 4587/09, 24 April 2018 §§40–42, where the legal framework was found deficient since 'there was no explicit obligation on the domestic authorities under Russian law to notify relatives of an individual who had died as a result of a criminal act'. This was, however, 'not sufficient in itself to find a violation of the respondent State positive obligations under Article 8 of the Convention'. The Court examined whether the authorities took any practical steps to inform the relatives of the death. Such were found to lack 'reasonable diligence' and on this basis failure to fulfill positive obligations was found. For the same approach see *Polat v Austria* no 12886/16, 20 July 2021 §§111–2, where the Court held 'there appears to be no clear rule under Austrian law governing the extent of information that must or must not be given to close relatives of a deceased person

the regulatory framework: laws adopted by the national parliament or other forms of regulations. In its case law, the Court has reviewed different forms of regulations, including decrees[10] and protocols.[11]

The above clarifications show that the requirement for domestic regulatory frameworks operates differently in the context of establishing breach of positive and negative obligations. In relation to the former, first, States have different fulfilment options,[12] and second, the very existence of a framework regulating the *specific* matter might be at the core of the whole analysis as to whether breach should be found. And yet, very abstractly, the Court has formulated the general positive obligation of developing an effective regulatory framework,[13] so that the rights in the Convention can be ensured, as required by Article 1 of the Convention (ECHR). In the context of the right to life, this has also been based on the text of the provision since Article 2 says that the right to life 'shall be protected by law'. The principle of effectiveness has also justified the need for 'a positive regulatory environment', which means that States must adopt legal rules to ensure that the individuals can enjoy their rights.[14]

The adoption and implementation of regulatory frameworks at national level guarantee that individuals are provided with legal protection in their relationships with state institutions, state agents, and private individuals.[15] The Court has thus held that Article 2 imposes

> a primary duty to have in place a legislative and administrative framework designed to provide effective deterrence against threats to the right to life, and applies in the context of any activity, public or not, in which the right to life may be at stake.[16]

Compliance with Article 3 is also tested in light of State's frameworks of laws designed to ensure that individuals are not subjected to ill-treatment, including by private individuals.[17] Article 8 also imposes a 'positive obligation to establish a legal framework

---

in respect of whom a post-mortem has been performed'. The Court ruled that 'this lack of clear rule is not sufficient in itself to find a violation'.

[10] For example, *P.H. v Slovakia* no 37574/19, 8 September 2022 §114, which involved the police's failure to comply with an internal degree for ensuring the safety of persons under their custody.
[11] For example, *Traskunova v Russia* no 21648/11, 30 August 2022 §76.
[12] See Section 1.3, where it was noted that what distinguishes positive obligations is that they have different fulfillment options.
[13] See Section 7.1.3, where the different levels of abstractions in the framing of the positive obligation are explained.
[14] Concurring Opinion of Judges Sajó and Tulkens in *Ternovszky v Hungary* no 67545/09, 14 December 2010.
[15] L Lavrysen, 'Protection by the Law: The Positive Obligation to Develop a Legal Framework to Adequately Protect the ECHR Rights' in E Brems and Y Haeck (eds), *Human Rights and Civil Rights in the 21st Century* (Springer 2014) 69.
[16] For example, *Nicolae Virgiliu Tănase v Romania* [GC] no 41720/13, 25 June 2019 §135.
[17] For example, *O'Keeffe v Ireland* [GC] no 35810/09, 28 January 2014 §§144–152.

guaranteeing the effective enjoyment of the rights guaranteed' by this provision.[18] The Court has also added that positive obligations under Article 8 are 'not adequately fulfilled unless it [the State] secures respect for private life in the relations between individuals by setting up a legislative framework taking into consideration the various interests to be protected in the particular context'.[19]

The positive obligation of adopting an effective regulatory framework can be examined with reference to various contexts where harm might materialize (eg domestic violence, medical negligence, road traffic, etc). Section 7.1.1 takes note of this diversity while drawing attention to criminal law as a regulatory regime whose specificity needs to be highlighted. Section 7.1.2 then identifies the type of deficiencies in national regulatory frameworks that can lead to a breach. Finally, Section 7.1.3 examines how these deficiencies are reviewed by the Court: is it an abstract or a concrete review?

## 7.1.1 Diversity of Regulatory Spheres and the Role of Criminal Law

The regulatory frameworks under review in different cases can pertain to various regulatory spheres. Very diverse national regulations have given rise to breaches under Articles 2, 3, and 8.[20] For example, in *O'Keefe v Ireland*, the Court asked whether 'the State's framework of laws, and notably its mechanism of detection and reporting, provided effective protection for children attending a National School against the risk of sexual abuse'.[21] In the context of healthcare, States are under the obligation to 'put in place an effective regulatory framework compelling hospitals, whether private or public, to adopt appropriate measures for the protection of patients' lives'.[22] In the context of labour law, the Court has examined the legal framework for protecting the employee's private life and correspondence 'in the context of his professional relationship with a private employer'.[23]

The Court's role is not to determine what domestic legal framework is the most appropriate for ensuring the rights,[24] rather it reviews whether the regulatory

---

[18] For example, *Fedotova and Others v Russia* no 40792/10, 13 July 2021 §44; *Oliari and Others* no 187661/11, 21 July 2015 §185.
[19] For example, *Bărbulescu v Romania* [GC] no 61496/08, 5 September 2017 §115.
[20] See *Marckx v Belgium* no 6833/74, 13 June 1979 §31, where it was held that the right to family life implies 'the existence in domestic law of legal safeguards that render possible as from the moment of birth the child's integration in his family'. *Nachova and Others v Bulgaria* [GC] no 43577/98 and 43579/98, 6 July 2005 §§99–102, where in relation to the right to life, the ECtHR found that the national legal framework on the use of firearms by the police has to contain clear safeguards to prevent the arbitrary deprivation of life. *R.R. v Poland* no 27617/04, 26 May 2011 §188, where in relation to the right to private life, the Court ruled that '[c]ompliance with the State's positive obligation to secure to their citizens their right to effective respect for their physical and psychological integrity may necessitate, in turn, the adoption of regulations concerning access to information about an individual's health'.
[21] *O'Keefe v Ireland* [GC] no 35810/09, 28 January 2014 §152.
[22] *Lopes de Sousa Fernandes v Portugal* [GC] no 56080/13, 19 December 2017 §§ 166–189.
[23] *Bărbulescu v Romania* [GC] no 61496/08, 5 September 2017 §116.
[24] For example, *Hristozov and Others v Bulgaria* nos 47039/11 and 358/12 §105. See Section 4.2.

framework provided the national authorities with different options of measures.[25] This can be illustrated by *C.E. and Others v France*, where the applicants complained that the French law did not allow an adoption of a child by the former partner of the child's biological mother. Neither did it allow the issuance of a document attesting to the legal relationship between a child and the former partner of the child's biological mother. France was found not to have failed to fulfil its positive obligation under Article 8 since the French legislation allowed for other legal possibilities for enabling the relationship between the children and the former partners of the children's biological mothers.[26]

Despite this diversity and choices left to States, distinctive attention needs to be directed to the national substantive criminal law as a distinctive regulatory framework against which compliance with the positive obligation is reviewed. While in many situations, civil law, administrative law, or professional avenues for supervision might suffice to regulate,[27] in other situations characterized with more severe forms of harm, criminalization of harmful conduct is considered necessary.[28] In these situations, failure to criminalize or to interpret the domestic criminal law in a more expansive way might lead to a failure to fulfil the positive obligation.[29] The Court does not necessarily pronounce how specifically the national criminal law must be worded. For example, it has observed that 'domestic violence may be categorized in the domestic legal system as a separate offence or as an aggravating element of other offences'.[30] Similarly, in the context of hate speech, the Court has refused 'to rule on the constituted elements of the offence of incitement of hatred and discrimination'.[31] However, the choice made by the national authorities as to the legal characterization of the crime could lead to breach.[32] The failure to characterize the crime with reference to aggravating factors can also lead to a breach.[33]

Criminalization, including its expansion, as a necessary measure for fulfilling positive obligations raises challenging questions about the interaction between human rights and criminal law,[34] including concerns that the former is used to expand the

---

[25] For example, *Fernandes de Oliveira v Portugal* [GC] no 78103/14, 31 January 2019 §117.
[26] *C.E. and Others v France* no 29775/18 and 29693/19, 24 March 2022.
[27] For example, *F.O. v Croatia* no 29555/13, 22 April 2022 §93, a case that involved a verbal abuse of a pupil by a schoolteacher.
[28] For example, *X. and Others v Bulgaria* [GC] no 22457/16, 2 February 2021 §179; *R.B. v Estonia* no 22597/16, 22 June 2021 §79; *Kurt v Austria* [GC] no 62903/15, 15 June 2021 §157.
[29] For example, *M.C. v Bulgaria* no 39272/98, 4 December 2003 §150.
[30] *Tunikova and Others v Russia* no 55974/16, 14 December 2021 §86; *Volodina v Russia* no 41261/17, 9 July 2019 §79.
[31] *Association Accept and Others v Romania* no 19237/16, 1 June 2021 §103.
[32] For example, *Oganezova v Armenia* no 71367/12, 17 May 2022 §103: 'while the arson attack was formally investigated and the perpetrators convicted, the legal assessment of the crime took no account of the hate motive of the arson attack, effectively rendering this fundamental aspect of the crime invisible and of no criminal significance'.
[33] For example, *Stoyanova v Bulgaria* no 56070/18, 14 June 2022 §73.
[34] A Ashworth, *Positive Obligations in Criminal Law* (Hart Publishing 2013) 196–211; F Tulkens, 'The Paradoxical Relationship between Criminal Law and Human Rights' (2011) 9 Journal of International Criminal Justice 577; V Stoyanova, 'Article 4 of the ECHR and the Obligation of Criminalising Slavery, Servitude, Forced Labour and Human Trafficking' (2014) 3 Cambridge Journal of International and Comparative Law 407.

coercive power of the State.[35] The Court has observed that criminal sanctions 'could be invoked only as an *ultima ration* measure'.[36] At the same time, it has maintained that only criminal law can ensure adequate protection and deterrence against certain *serious* harms.[37] The case law is permeated by the assumption that criminalization ensures deterrence and in this sense, has preventive functions. Criminal law is therefore not only invoked for the purposes of better elucidation of facts, establishment of accountability, and redress, as clarified in Chapter 6, but also as a means of prevention. Yet, and again similarly to the concerns expressed in Chapter 6 about whether criminal law should be a tool necessary demanded as a matter of ECHR positive obligations, the preventive role of criminal law as a necessary tool for ensuring rights can also be problematic. For this reason, the Court has invoked a certain level of seriousness of the harm to delimit this role. Beyond these delimitations, various other regulatory frameworks can be relevant.

### 7.1.2 Types of Deficiencies in the Regulatory Framework

Although various regulatory spheres could come under scrutiny, the deficiencies in the regulatory frameworks can be grouped into four general types: (i) absence of a regulatory framework, (ii) qualitative deficiencies of the framework, (iii) ineffective implementation, and (iv) adoption of a problematic framework. While the reduction to these four types is a simplification, since it might be difficult to draw strict demarcation lines between them, it is useful to distinguish them to improve an understanding of the content of the positive obligation.

#### 7.1.2.1 Absence of a relevant national regulatory framework

In multiple cases, the absence of relevant national rules to regulate certain activities has been the basis for finding a breach. For example, in *Arskaya v Ukraine*, the Court found a violation of Article 2 since there was a lack of appropriate rules for establishing patients' decision-making capacity, including their informed consent to treatment.[38] *Mehmet Şentürk and Bekir Şentürk v Turkey* exposed that the domestic law did not have any provisions capable of preventing the failure to give the patient the medical treatment she had required on account of her condition.[39] The regulatory gap exposed in *Aydoğdu v Tukey* was the lack of rules for hospitals to ensure protection of

---

[35] N Mavronicola, 'Coercive Overreach, Dilution and Diversion: Potential Dangers of Aligning Human Rights Protection with Criminal Law (Enforcement)' in L Lavrysen and N Mavronicola (eds), *Coercive Human Rights* (Hart Publishing 2020) 184.
[36] *Association Accept and Others v Romania* no 19237/16, 1 June 2021 §102. See also Concurring Opinion of Judge Tulkens in *M.C. v Bulgaria* no 39272/98, 4 December 2003: 'I consider that criminal proceedings should remain, both in theory and in practice, a last resort or subsidiary remedy and that their use, even in the context of positive obligations, calls for a certain degree of "restraint".'
[37] For example, *Association Accept and Others v Romania* no 19237/16, 1 June 2021 §102.
[38] *Arskaya v Ukraine* no 45076/05, 5 December 2013 §§84–91.
[39] *Mehmet Şentürk and Bekir Şentürk v Turkey* no 13423/09, 9 April 2013.

the lives of premature babies.[40] In *Fedotova and Others v Russia*, the Court acknowledged that Russia had a margin of appreciation to 'choose the most appropriate form of registration of same-sex unions taking into account its specific social and cultural context (for example, civil partnership, civil union, or civil solidarity act)'. In this case, however, Russia has 'overstepped that margin, because no legal framework capable of protecting the applicants' relationships as same-sex couples has been available under domestic law'.[41] Similarly, in *Rana v Hungary*, there was a gap in the relevant legislation 'in that there was no statutory basis allowing for recognition of gender reassignment and access to the name-changing procedure for lawfully settled non-Hungarian citizens'.[42] Likewise, the applicant in *Boljević v Serbia* had no legal way to reopen proceedings regarding the establishment of his paternity:

> After the expiry of the deadline in question, domestic law did not therefore allow for the relevant elements of the applicant's specific situation to be taken into account or for a balancing of the relevant interests to be carried out.[43]

The deficiency in *Boljević v Serbia* could be understood as an absence of a regulatory framework, but it could also be presented as a deficient framing of this framework due to its rigidity. It did not allow exceptions and balancing of competing interests. This illustrates the fluidity of the types of deficiencies, distinguished at the beginning of Section 7.1.2.

It is also important to note that in some cases, like *Boljević v Serbia*, the absence of a legal framework was one primary consideration in the reasoning leading to the establishment of breach. Other considerations that might be of a more general nature (ie absence of procedural safeguards in the regulatory framework),[44] or of a more specific nature characterizing the particular situation of the applicant, can also be relevant. For example, in *Boljević v Serbia* the purported biological father was dead, on which basis the Court emphasized the applicant's 'very specific circumstances'.[45] Similarly, in *Rana v Hungary* the Court narrowed down its reasoning by noting that the relevant authorities did not take into account the fact that the applicant had been recognized as a refugee precisely because he had been persecuted on grounds of being transgender in his country of origin. This narrowing implies that the finding of a violation does not mean that the national legislation must change to the effect that everybody in Hungary irrespective of their migration status should have access to the relevant procedure. More generally, failure to fulfil the positive obligation of adopting an effective regulatory framework due to a regulatory gap does not mean that the State has to close this gap in any specific way. The State retains its discretion in this respect.[46]

---

[40] *Aydoğdu v Turkey* no 40448/06, 30 August 2016.
[41] *Fedotova and Others v Russia* no 40792/10, 13 July 2021 §56.
[42] *Rana v Hungary* no 40888/17, 16 July 2020 §37.
[43] *Boljević v Serbia* no 47443/14, 16 June 2020 §54.
[44] See Section 7.2.
[45] *Boljević v Serbia* no 47443/14, 16 June 2020 §56.
[46] See Sections 4.2 and 4.3.

## 7.1.2.2 Deficiencies in the framing of the regulatory framework

Besides regulatory gaps, the national regulatory framework could be deficient since the existing rules do not comply with certain qualitative standards. For example, the rules might not be sufficiently clear, predictable, and comprehensive.[47] The rules might not be specific enough or not 'geared to the special features of the activity' that they intend to regulate.[48] The expected qualitative standards, however, cannot be as stringent as those normally applied to assess compliance with the 'in accordance with the law' requirement in the context of negative obligations. This was explicitly clarified in *Fernandes De Oliveira v Portugal*, a case about a psychiatric patient who, while in voluntary hospitalization, committed suicide. The applicant argued that the national regulatory framework was deficient since there were no *written* guidelines about restraint measures applicable to psychiatric patients. The GC did not see the absence of written guidelines as a deficiency since it held that there is a distinction

> between the quality of law requirements under Articles 3, 5 and 8 of the Convention where the negative aspect of the respective right is at stake and the duty to have a regulatory framework in place under Article 2 to protect a person from harm inflicted by third parties or by themselves. Quality of law under Article 5(1) implies that where a national law authorises deprivation of liberty it must be sufficiently accessible, precise and foreseeable in its application, in order to avoid all risk of arbitrariness. The purpose of the regulatory framework requirement under Article 2 being different, namely providing the necessary tools for the protection of a patient's life, the lack of a written policy on the use of restraint measures is not determinative of its efficiency and does not in itself warrant a finding that Article 2 was breached.[49]

The above quotation suggests more flexibility in the assessment of any qualitative deficiencies when the positive obligation of adopting effective regulatory framework is under review.

## 7.1.2.3 Ineffective implementation of the regulatory framework

The relevant national regulatory frameworks might be adequately framed. The basis for finding a violation might rather be the national authorities' failure to implement them. In this regard, the Court has emphasized that

---

[47] For example, *Gross v Switzerland* no 67810/10, 14 May 2013 §§65–69, where the ECtHR found that the absence of clear and comprehensive guidelines on whether and under which circumstances an individual should be granted the ability to acquire a lethal dose of medication, violated the applicant's right to private life.

[48] For example, *Traskunova v Russia* no 21648/11, 30 August 2022 §73. In the context of 'dangerous activities', States are obliged to adopt rules governing 'licensing, setting up, operation, security and supervision of the activity'. Regulations needs to be also geared with regard to the level of the potential risk. See also *Smiljanić v Croatia* no 35983/14, 25 March 2021 §67.

[49] *Fernandes de Oliveiri v Portugal* [GC] no 78103/14, 31 January 2019 §19.

the States' obligation to regulate must be understood in a broader sense, which includes the duty to ensure the effective functioning of that regulatory framework. The regulatory duties thus encompass necessary measures to ensure implementation, including supervision and enforcement. Thus, the States' positive obligation under the substantive limb of Article 2 extends to a duty to ensure the effective functioning of the regulatory framework adopted for the protection of life.[50]

Failure to implement means that the legal framework is not practically effective.[51] Absence of such practical effectiveness was the reason for the Court to find a violation in *Smiljanić v Croatia*: the State failed to enforce the domestic legal framework regulating road traffic.[52] *Traskunova v Russia* offers another example. The relevant protocols required that the applicant undergo a medical check-up prior to participation in the trial of a new drug. However, 'in breach of the rules and safeguards created by the domestic system itself', such a check-up was not performed.[53] *Monteanu v Moldova* is another relevant example: the domestic authorities failed to implement the protection orders against the applicant's abusive husband.[54]

The question of whether the national regulatory framework was effectively implemented may raise issues as to the correct interpretation of national laws and regulations. When faced with this issue, the Court's starting point is that '[i]n light of the principle of subsidiarity, it is not for the Court to substitute its views for those of the national authorities and to interpret and apply the domestic law'.[55] However, the State might be expected to explain discrepancies between the meaning of the domestic law and the measures actually undertaken by the authorities in implementation of this law. For example, in *Jivan v Romania*, an elderly disabled person complained that he had been denied a personal assistant when this option was actually provided by the Romanian law. The Court observed that in their decisions the domestic courts did not explain

> the apparent discrepancies between the applicant's particular situation of a lack of autonomy and support, and the finding that he was not entitled, under the domestic law, to a personal assistant.[56]

It follows that although the domestic courts are the ones who interpret the domestic regulatory framework for the purposes of its implementation, defects in

---

[50] For example, *Kotilainen and Others v Finland* no 62439/12, 17 September 2020 §66; *Lopes de Sousa Fernandes v Portugal* [GC] no 56080/13, 19 December 2017 §189.
[51] *Loste v France* no 59227/12, 3 November 2022 §§96–104; *A. and B. v Georgia* no 73975/16, 10 February 2022 §48; *F.O. v Croatia* no 29555/13, 22 April 2022 §97.
[52] For example, *Smiljanić v Croatia* no 35983/14, 25 March 2021 §§66 and 77.
[53] *Traskunova v Russia* no 21648/11, 30 August 2022 §76.
[54] *Monteanu v Moldova* no 34168/11, 26 May 2020 §71. See also *Cuence Zarzoco v Spain* no 23383/12, 16 January 2018 that concerned failure to enforce a city ordinance for reduction of noise pollution.
[55] *Jivan v Romania* no 62250/19, 8 February 2022 §47.
[56] *Jivan v Romania* no 62250/19, 8 February 2022 §49.

these interpretations can be relevant in the assessment of state responsibility under the ECHR.

Finally, it needs to be observed that a failure to comply with the relevant domestic regulations is not conclusive to find that the State has failed to fulfil its positive obligation. The Court reviews whether the implementation of the national legal framework was 'defective to the point of constituting a violation' of the positive obligation.[57] For example, in *Jansons v Latvia*, the applicant complained that the national authorities failed to protect him against private actors who forced him out of his home. There was no formal eviction order as required by the domestic legislation prior to his removal. This was an important but not a conclusive factor in the Court's reasoning that the authorities did not take appropriate measures to secure the applicant's respect for his home. The Court considered additional omissions by the authorities.[58]

### 7.1.2.4 Adoption of problematic regulatory framework

In some situations, the identified omissions by the State do not concern inadequacies in the framing of the legal framework or its ineffective implementation; rather the rules imposed by the framework might be problematic. Adoption of rules that *allow* certain activities or conduct by different actors could therefore also lead to breach of the positive obligation of adopting effective regulatory framework. In these cases, the responsibility of the State might be engaged because the national regulatory framework makes certain treatment or certain situations lawful.[59] In other words, the framework contains certain conditions or restrictions that can be causally linked with harm. *Sudita Keita v Hungary* is an example to this effect. A stateless person complained that he could not make his status regular. In particular, the national legislation required a 'lawful stay' to be recognized as a stateless person, a requirement that he could not fulfil.[60] This judgment demonstrates that rigid rules that do not allow any exceptions, consideration of individual circumstances, or flexibility as to their implementation, can lead to a finding of a breach.[61]

Adoption and implementation of problematic regulatory frameworks could be interpreted as a breach of a negative obligation, not as a failure to fulfil a positive obligation. The reason is that if the national regulatory framework contains certain restrictions or imposes certain conditions, it can be argued that the State has intervened via the adoption of these rules.[62] One can also argue that at this point the division

---

[57] For example, *Špadijer v Montenegro* no 31549/18, 9 November 2021 §101, a case that concerned harassment at the workplace.
[58] *Jansons v Latvia* no 1434/14, 8 September 2022 §78.
[59] For example, *Young, James and Webster v The United Kingdom* no 7601/76, 13 August 1981 §489; *VgT Verein Gegen Tierfabriken v Switserland* no 24699/94, 28 June 2001 §45.
[60] *Sudita Keita v Hungary* no 42321/15, 12 May 2020 §39
[61] For example, *Uzbyakov v Russia* no 71160/13, 5 May 2020 §123: 'automatic application of inflexible legal provisions in that field [family life and best interests of the child] amounted to failure to respect' family life'.
[62] P van Dijk, 'Positive Obligations Implied in the European Convention on Human Rights: Are the States still the 'Masters' of the Convention?' in M Castermans-Holleman and others (eds), *The Role of the Nation State in the 21st Century: Human Rights, International Organizations and Foreign Policy* (Kluwer 1998) 17, 25.

between negative and positive obligations collapses. As already discussed in Section 1.3, the division is based on certain baselines and assumptions that might vary in different cases. Here it can be added that if it is a non-state actor that has intervened, even if allowed to do so and sanctioned to do so by the national regulatory framework and courts, the case is likely to be examined as a positive obligation case.[63] In other cases, other baselines can be considered relevant by the Court. *Valdís Fjölnisdóttir and Others v Iceland* offers an illustration. The national regulatory framework did not allow the registration in the Registers Iceland of a parent–child relationship between non-biological parents and a child born in the United States via surrogacy. This could have been framed as a positive obligation case since the applicants in practice asked for a change in the law so that such a registration could be possible. The reason the Court chose to frame the case as a negative obligation was that the child already had a birth certificate issued in the United States indicating the applicants as the parents.[64]

## 7.1.3 Concrete or Abstract Reasonableness Review of the Regulatory Framework

Regardless of the types of deficiencies that the regulatory framework might suffer from, when an applicant argues that the national regulatory framework is deficient, this claim relates to general failures by the State that have affected him or her. In this sense, the applicant is a representative victim affected by general regulatory deficiencies, a point in relation to which the positive obligation of adopting effective regulatory framework can be distinguished from the positive obligation of taking protective operational measures. As Section 7.3 will explain, the content of the latter obligation includes concrete, individually targeted, and, as its name suggests, operational protection. In contrast, when the Court reviews compliance with the positive obligation of adopting an effective regulatory framework, the applicant is arguably a representative victim of general regulatory deficiencies.

In this case, the Court can take different approaches to its review. One approach is to limit its review to assessing *the reasonableness of the specific measure or decision* that, although based on the generally applicable national regulatory framework, concretely affected the applicant. This will imply a *concrete review* since the Court assesses the reasonableness of the measure or the decision for the concrete applicant in light of his/her concrete situation. An alternative approach that the Court could take is to review *the reasonableness of the national regulatory framework in more abstract terms*. This *abstract review* implies that the Court ventures to assess more generally

---

[63] For example, *Bărbulescu v Romania* [GC] no 61496/08, 5 September 2017 §111.
[64] *Valdís Fjölnisdóttir and Others v Iceland* no 71552/17, 18 May 2021 §75. No breach was found since the law allowed other legal possibilities for regularizing the parent–child relationship and the applicants faced no practical hindrances to enjoy the relationship. Contrast this with *X. v the Former Yugoslav Republic of Macedonia* no 29683/16, 17 January 2019 §64.

## 182  Substantive Positive Obligations

the national regulatory framework by identifying any general, structural, and systemic deficiencies.

The choice between concrete and abstract review affects the judicial reasoning and the finding of a breach.[65] The reason is that the positive obligation can be framed with different levels of abstractness/generality and, accordingly, with different levels of concreteness/specificity (Section 7.1.3.1). Relatedly, as I will also show below, the choice between abstract and concrete review affects the role of the Court. Specifically, the choice shapes whether its role is limited to rule-implementer, or whether it also becomes a rule-maker. When the Court reviews the national regulatory framework in more abstract terms and identifies its deficiencies, it might come very close to exercising the role of a rule-maker since its reasoning might suggest how rules should be formulated at the national level. The choice between abstract and concrete review also affects the type of justice the Court delivers, individual versus constitutional. More abstract review suggests a stronger focus on constitutional justice. The choice between concrete and abstract review is also revealing of the function of the reasonableness standard (Section 7.1.3.2). Finally, although concrete review is the starting point, I will show how in its reasoning, the Court meanders between the concrete and the abstract since it seeks to assert the roles of both rule-implementer and rule-maker and to deliver both of the above-mentioned types of justice (Section 7.1.3.3).

### 7.1.3.1  Levels of concreteness in the framing of the obligations

To understand the complexities regarding the type of review, it is relevant to explain that the Court has framed the positive obligation of adopting an effective regulatory framework at three levels of specificity.[66] In its reasoning, it starts with the first level that is the most general and abstract. It is reflected in the standard general formulation that States are under the obligation to set up an effective regulatory framework to ensure the rights (see Section 7.1.1).[67] At this level, no determination of breach

---

[65] For an analysis in relation to negative obligations, see J Gerards, 'Abstract and Concrete Reasonableness Review by the European Court of Human Rights' (2020) 1 European Convention on Human Rights Law Review 218.

[66] See also Section 4.2.1, where two levels are analysed for the purpose of understanding the role of alternatives in the reasoning. As I will further explain in Section 7.1.3.1, only in some specific contexts (eg domestic violence, protection of children) an intermediate second level of specificity can be identified. Therefore, it most situations there are indeed only two levels. See also V Stoyanova, 'Framing Positive Obligations under the European Convention on Human Rights: Mediating between the Abtract and the Concrete' (2023) 23(3) Human Rights Law Review.

[67] In its judgments, the Court distinguishes between the step of articulating general standards and the step of applying the standards to the concrete facts, where the question of breach arises. The first step (that I frame as the first level) is reflected in the section of the judgments entitled 'General principles'. The second step is reflected in the section of the judgment entitled 'Application of the above principles in the instant case' or 'Application to the present case'. See for example *Kurt v Austria* [GC] no 62903/15, 15 June 2021 §§157–210; *Lopes de Sousa Fernandes v Portugal* [GC] no 56080/13, 19 December 2017 §§164–167 and 197–205; *Fernandes de Oliveira v Portugal* [GC] no 78103/14, 31 January 2019 §§104–132; *Kotilainen and Others v Finland* no 62439/12, 17 September 2020 §§65–90; *X and Others v Bulgaria* [GC] no 22457/16, 2 February 2021 §§176–193; *Nicolae Virgiliu Tănase v Romania* [GC] no 41720/13, 25 June 2019 §§157–172; *Talpis v Italy* no 41237, 2 March 2017 §§95–107; *Hudorovič and Others v Slovenia* no 24816/14 and 25140/14, 10 March 2020 §§139–159.

is made and, accordingly, no reasonableness review is undertaken, rather the Court aims to articulate some general principles regarding the objective of preventing loss of life and ill-treatment and respecting private and family life.[68] This can be related to the constitutional role of the Court[69] to formulate some general standards for state conduct.[70] The level of abstractness of these formulations is high and they are detached from the facts of the case.

Yet it is not the role of the Court 'to examine *in abstracto* the compatibility of national legislative or constitutional provisions with the requirements of the Convention'.[71] This relates to the Court's primary objective to provide individual rather than constitutional justice,[72] which is also reflected in the admissibility requirement that the applicant must be a victim of an alleged violation.[73] The latter means that he or she has to be specifically affected. The starting point is therefore that the Court cannot perform a purely abstract review. This starting point expresses the idea that human rights justice is centred on the individual. Human rights justice is therefore placed 'not in the abstraction of general situations which law-makers have regard for, but in the concreteness of particular cases, irreducible in their singularity'.[74] In this sense, the Court does not directly review national regulatory frameworks. It can only do it indirectly once these frameworks have affected a concrete individual, who in the proceedings before the Court, has a standing as a victim.[75]

In some areas, the Court has further made concrete the general positive obligation of adopting an effective regulatory framework, for which reason it is possible to identify a *second level of specificity* in the articulation of the obligation. This has been done, for example, in the area of domestic violence and the protection of children.[76] *Kurt v Austria* is illustrative. The Court affirmed that 'special diligence is required from the authorities when dealing with cases of domestic violence'.[77] Given the Court's

---

[68] The specifics regarding Article 8 are ignored here since they were explained in Section 4.2.
[69] J Christoffersen, 'Individual and Constitutional Justice: Can the Power Balance of Adjudication be Reversed?' in J Christoffersen and M Madsen (eds), *The European Court of Human Rights between Law and Politics* (Oxford University Press 2011) 181.
[70] 'Although the primary purpose of the Convention system is to provide individual relief, its mission is also to determine issues on public-policy grounds in the common interests, thereby raising the general standards of protection of human rights and extending human rights jurisprudence throughout the community of Convention States.' *Paposhvili v Belgium* [GC] no 41738/10, 13 December 2016 §130.
[71] *McCann and Others v The United Kingdom* [GC] no 18984/91, 27 September 1995 §153; *Marckx v Belgium* no 6833/74, 13 June 1979 §27. For further references, see Partly Concurring, Partly Dissenting Opinion of Judge Pinto de Albuquerque in *Vallianatos and Others v Greece* [GC] no 29381/08 and 32684/09, 7 November 2013.
[72] On the interplay between these objectives see S Greer, 'Constitutionalizing Adjudication under the European Convention on Human Rights' (2003) 23 Oxford Journal of Legal Studies 405.
[73] Article 34 ECHR.
[74] F Tulkens and S Van Drooghenbroeck, 'La Cour de cassation et la Cour européenne des droits de l'homme. Les voies de la banalisation' in *Imperat Lex. Liber Amicorum Pierre Marchal* (Larcier, 2003) 133 cited in F Tulkens, 'Different Standards of Judicial Review. The Nature and Object of the Judgment of the European Court of Human Rights'.
[75] Gerards, 'Abstract and Concrete Reasonableness Review by the European Court of Human Rights' (n 65) 226.
[76] *O'Keeffe v Ireland* [GC] no 35810/09, 28 January 2014 §146.
[77] *Kurt v Austria* [GC] no 62903/15, 15 June 2021 §166.

constitutional role, this affirmation seems to send a signal that more demanding positive obligations might be formulated in this area. The reference to 'special diligence' can also mean that each individual case of domestic violence that might raise an issue of state responsibility for omissions is examined in light of the wider societal problem of domestic violence. As the Court framed it: '[t]he issue of domestic violence—which can take various forms ... transcends the circumstances of an individual case'.[78] This might imply that the reasoning is more contextual and abstract, not exclusively focused on the concrete factual circumstances and on the concrete causal links between specific omissions and harm. Such a contextualization and abstraction of the reasoning might imply an easier finding of a breach when the case fits within some wider problems perceived as structural in society. Similarly to the first level, this second level of specificity in the formulation of the positive obligation does not include a determination of breach and no reasonableness review is undertaken.

Such a review is only undertaken when the Court must determine breach in the concrete case, which reflects the *third level*. In its approach to reasoning therefore the Court moves from the general to the specific. When this third level of specificity is reached, the question that arises is whether the Court formulates the specific positive obligation (ie the specific measure that should have been undertaken) with which the State has to comply, so that a review of whether the obligation has been breached can be performed. As already explained in Section 4.2, varying more or less concrete formulations of the obligation is possible and various ways of specifying the obligation can be identified in the case law. The reason for these variations is that arguable omissions are at the core of the analysis and States have discretion as to how to address the omissions (ie what measures to undertake as counterparts to these omissions).[79] As a result, the whole review collapses into an assessment about reasonableness; in other words, the whole review about state responsibility collapses into an assessment of breach of an obligation that has barely been more specifically articulated besides with reference to the standard of reasonableness. The requirement for causation (ie how the protective measure concretely could have prevented the harm or reduced the risk for the concrete victim) that can be expected to help in making concrete the specific obligation, and thus in making concrete the review, cannot entirely serve these aims, given the flexible way in which it is applied, as explained in Chapter 3.

States' discretion implies that it is States that adopt regulatory frameworks (ie States are the rule-makers), and the Court's task is to review whether the respondent State has done what can be reasonably expected. The starting point that States have discretion as to how to fulfil their positive obligations concretely (ie how to formulate their national regulatory frameworks so that protective measures can be undertaken) affects the degree of abstractness in the reasoning. It increases it. The discretion implies that the Court more generally examines the choices made at national level and

---

[78] *Kurt v Austria* [GC] no 62903/15, 15 June 2021 §161.
[79] See Section 1.3. On discretion, see also Section 4.3.

their reasonableness.[80] The starting point that States have discretion as to the concrete measures to ensure the rights (ie the concrete formulation of the regulations) pulls the reasoning towards more abstractness since the review is limited to the determination as to whether the national choice (ie the existing regulatory framework) is reasonable. The review does not necessarily extend to include concretely how the regulatory framework should have been framed so that the applicant's rights can be ensured. Moonen and Lavrysen have also added that 'the ECtHR's reasoning will become more abstract, in order to better take into account the broader consequences that may result from its judgment, and in particular, to avoid overly reducing the ability of other states to provide their own answers in future cases'.[81] Including wider considerations as part of the reasonableness assessment therefore increases the level of abstractness in the reasoning. General considerations as to whether certain rules should be in place or how they should be formulated presuppose speculation about the various affected interests in the society. This increases the level of abstractness in the reasoning since it is difficult to predict these interests and make them concrete,[82] based on the concrete facts of the concrete case. Normally, prediction and consideration of the multiplicity of affected interests is performed by the national legislator.

That said, what is reasonable is always dependent on facts. The standard of reasonableness has no initial and independent content. It cannot exist independently of the concrete facts, which further explains the collapse of the two analytical steps (ie imposition of an obligation and determination of breach) in the reasoning. The invocation of the standard of reasonableness also explains the concrete review performed by the Court.[83] In this review, various national decisions and measures (or the absence of such decisions and measures) are assessed with reference to the particular concrete situation of the applicant, and the validity of this balancing (ie the validity of the conclusion on the balancing) is limited to the specific case. Simultaneously, however, and as already suggested above, the invocation of reasonableness also allows an increase in the level of abstraction.

### 7.1.3.2 Functions of the standard of 'reasonable' in the review

It is pertinent here to dwell upon the invocation of reasonableness so that the review performed by the Court is better understood. In contrast to Chapters 4 and 5 that engaged substantively with the meaning of reasonableness (ie how considerations such as competing obligations or financial constraints are relevant in the application of the

---

[80] J Gerards, 'Pluralism, Deference and the Margin of Appreciation Doctrine' (2011) 17(1) European Law Journal 80, 106.
[81] T Moonen and L Lavrysen, 'Abstract but Concrete, or Concrete but Abstract? A Guide to the Nature of Advisory Opinions under Protocol No 16 to the ECHR' (2021) 21(3) Human Rights Law Review 752, 771.
[82] See Chapter 5.
[83] Reasonableness as a legal standard 'has to deal with situations of great factual complexity, where the circumstances of the various cases are so manifold that a single rule could not do justice to the situations likely to arise.... It is normatively relatively poor, allowing the legal operator to shape the legal answer with full regard to the varying circumstances of the case.' O Corten and R Kolb, 'Reasonableness in International Law' *Max Planck Encyclopedia of International Law* (Oxford University Press 2021).

standard), the objective here is to clarify the role that the invocation of 'reasonableness' has. In particular, what functions does reasonableness serve in the human rights law review and reasoning? How does it enable the review to operate?

Corten has identified two functions that the notion of 'reasonable' serves in the judicial reasoning, 'technical' and 'ideological'.[84] The invocation of reasonableness serves the technical function of adaptivity and flexibility, an application of a rule to a dynamic social reality. It enables judges to 'present their decisions and motivation, often of their own creation, as perfectly in line with the intention of States' and to 'provide a reasoning in the absence of more precise criteria'. When there is no single solution, 'judges will draw upon the notion of "reasonable" in order to avoid declaring a *non liquet*'. Corten adds that '[t]he notion of "reasonable" is thus served to fill legal lacunae'. These explanations are more than relevant to the ECHR context. As already noted, the Court does not initially formulate the concrete positive obligation so that it can subsequently review breach. It does not conclusively rule how the national regulatory framework should be concretely formulated so that the State complies with its positive obligation. This reveals the absence of precise initial criteria in the review. The Court's reasoning instead meanders between the concrete and the abstract, between the concrete facts and some abstract standards, such as, for example, 'special diligence'.[85]

This meandering does not resolve the tension between the discretion that States have to choose their legal frameworks and measures of protection (ie how to fulfil their positive obligation) on the one hand, and the Court's intervention in this discretion so that a judgment is delivered (ie breach or no breach of an obligation is found) on the other. As explained in Chapter 4, the finding of a breach or no breach necessitates that alternative formulations of the legal framework are taken into account. The operation of formulating such alternatives implies formulation of proposals as to how the national legal framework could be framed or what concrete measures of protection could have been undertaken which could be perceived as intrusive. This brings me to the second function that the notion of 'reasonable' serves. Corten has named it ideological, 'the notion of "reasonable" is used in order to legitimize an assertion which is, by definition, subject to challenge'. It then follows that by labelling the formulated alternatives as reasonable so that a breach is found, or by asserting that the existing national legal framework is actually reasonable so that no breach can be found, the Court tries to legitimize its judgment. Such legitimization is necessary given the binary nature of the conclusion in the judgment (ie only two options are possible for the Court: finding of a violation or no violation),[86] when in fact various

---

[84] O Corten, 'The Notion of "Reasonable" in International Law: Legal Discourse, Reason and Contradictions' (1999) 48(3) International and Comparative Law Quarterly 613.
[85] *Kurt v Austria* [GC] no 62903/15, 15 June 2021 §166.
[86] Brems has framed this 'border control human rights monitoring'. See E Brems, 'Human Rights: Minimum and Maximum Perspectives' (2009) 9(3) Human Rights Law Review 349.

solutions are possible. This variety of solutions justifies the discretion that States have to choose their legal frameworks and measures of protection.

To explain further the ideological function that the notion of 'reasonable' serves, Corten has added that the invocation of reasonableness aims at masking the values that stand behind the judgment 'by elaborating a solution apparently based solely on reason'. Reverting to the example concerning the requirement for 'special diligence' in the context of domestic violence as formulated in *Kurt v Austria*, there are indeed certain values that the Court seeks to promote.[87] In other contexts, other values work at the background. *Kotilainen and Others v Finland*, a case about mass shooting at a school, is also illustrative. No failures by Finland could be identified by the Court for allowing the perpetrator to own a gun in accordance with the domestic legislation and for not taking operational measures to protect the victims since the killings perpetrated by the gun owner, were not foreseeable.[88] Yet by formulating a 'special duty of diligence incumbent on them [the national authorities] because [of] the particularly high level of risk to life inherent in any misconduct involving the use of firearms',[89] Finland was still found in violation of Article 2. Certain values stand behind this formulation, which prompted the Court to increase the level of abstractness in its reasoning by observing that 'the seizure of the perpetrator's weapon was a reasonable measure of *precaution*', despite the acknowledgement that the concrete decision not to seize the gun was not causally relevant to the subsequent shooting.

In sum, the invocation of the standard of 'reasonableness', first enables the human rights law review to oscillate between the abstract and the concrete and second, preserves state discretion even though the Court might find a violation. This oscillation is also enabled by the different levels of concreteness used by the Court to frame the positive obligation of adopting an effective regulatory framework. As explained above, level one and two are abstract, and they allow the Court to develop some general standards by which the Court assumes a constitutional function and the role of a rule-maker, yet such a role is not that controversial since the framing of the rules is very general ('general standards') and no decision on breach is delivered on these levels. Such a role becomes more controversial when the obligation needs to be framed in more concrete terms (ie what I framed as level three) and the question of breach conclusively resolved with a judgment. The controversy arises since the resolution of the question of breach (ie violation or no violation) necessitates that alternative *concrete* formulations of the legal framework are considered and assessed. At this point, the invocation of the standard of reasonableness is useful to raise again the level

---

[87] These values have been, for example, expressed in the Council of Europe Convention on preventing and combating violence against women and domestic violence No 210 that the Court cites in *Kurt v Austria* [GC] no 62903/15, 15 June 2021.
[88] See Section 7.3.
[89] *Kotilainen and Others v Finland* no 62439/12, 17 September 2020 §§84–89. See V Stoyanova, 'Specification of Positive Obligations by the European Court of Human Rights and the Roles of Reasonablness, Prevention and Precaution' in A Ollino and I Papanicolopulu (eds) *The Concept of Obligation in International Law* (Oxford University Press, forthcoming).

**188** Substantive Positive Obligations

of abstractness and communicate the message that a resolution in favour of a breach does not necessarily undermine States' discretion. Section 7.1.3.3 will illustrate more explicitly how these shifts are performed in the case law in that the Court meanders between the concrete and the abstract.

### 7.1.3.3 Meandering between the concrete and the abstract

Four approaches can be identified in the case law as to how the Court's reasoning meanders between more abstract and more concrete review of any deficiencies in the national legal frameworks. These are (i) mixing abstract and concrete review, (ii) only concrete review, (iii) only abstract review, and (iv) two-step approach with abstract review as an initial threshold.

*Mixing abstract and concrete review*
The formulation of the positive obligation of adopting an effective regulatory framework in general terms (what in Section 7.1.3.1 I framed as levels one and two) implies that the Court's reasoning includes some abstract determinations as to whether there is a relevant national regulatory framework. At this general level, the framework might be found satisfactory, which implies that in the abstract the framework has adequately balanced different interests and, in this sense, it is reasonable. The Court then moves on to examine the application of the framework in the concrete case. The review might go back and forth between the abstract and the concrete in relation to different aspects. An example of this approach is *Hudorovič and Others v Slovenia*, a case about access to safe drinking water and sanitation for Roma communities. Slovenia's public utility infrastructure was an object of comprehensive regulatory framework that generally recognized the vulnerability of the Roma community. The reasoning included additional general pronouncements to the effect that 'non-negligible proportion of the Slovenian population living in remote areas do not have access to the public water supply system' and 'considerable part of the population in Slovenia does not yet benefit from a public sewage system'. At the same time, the Court also reviewed the actions concretely applied to the applicants, which were also found reasonable.[90]

In other cases, the regulatory framework might be assessed as satisfactory on a general level, however the concrete case may reveal an unreasonable hardship for the specific applicant.[91] This can be contrasted with cases where the regulatory framework is generally assessed as problematic. However, this is not sufficient for finding a violation, and the Court still considers the harm caused to the specific applicant. *Volodina v Russia (no 2)*, a case about cyber domestic violence, is illustrative of how the Court includes both general pronouncements about the regulatory framework and assessment of the specific situation of the applicant. To this effect, in *Volodina v Russia (no 2)*, the Court held that the Russian legislation 'does not provide victims of domestic violence with any comparable protection [in the form of "restraining" and

---

[90] *Hudorovič and Others v Slovenia* no 24816/14 and 25140/14/14, 10 March 2020.
[91] For example, *M.A. v Denmark* [GC] no 6697/18, 9 July 2021.

"protection" orders]. The respondent Government did not identify any effective remedies that the authorities could have used to ensure the applicant's protection against recurrent acts of cyberviolence.'[92] Similarly, the reasoning in *Tunikova and Others v Russia* combines abstract and concrete review. The Court first described the general flaws in the national regulatory framework (ie absence of criminalization of domestic violence) and then noted how these have affected the concrete applicants:

> The legislative framework did not equip the authorities with legal tools to deal with early warning signs of domestic violence unless and until the aggressive behaviour of a perpetrator has escalated into causing of physical injuries, which is what happened in the case of Ms Gracheva who had been mutilated by her husband.[93]

The absence of a relevant national regulatory framework, like that in *Tunikova and Others v Russia*,[94] or rigid national regulations without possibilities for flexible application increase the level of abstractness in the reasoning. *Špadijer v Montenegro*, a case about bullying by colleagues at work, is illustrative. The Court identified some general deficiencies: 'the applicant did not receive protection because the courts required proof of incidents occurring every week for six months'. The Court held that

> [d]espite the margin of appreciation enjoyed by Contracting States in devising protection mechanisms in respect of acts of harassment at work, the Court finds it difficult to accept the adequacy of such an approach in the instant case. The Court considers that complaints about bullying should be thoroughly examined on a case-by-case basis....

This could be viewed as an example of an inflexible regulatory framework. The Court assessed it by mixing abstract and concrete review in its reasoning.[95]

In some areas, the Court has developed general criteria as to how competing interests should be balanced,[96] which also brings an element of abstractness in the reasoning. Having outlined the criteria, as a next step, the Court verifies whether the domestic authorities have assessed the case in light of these criteria. In this way, as will be further explained in Section 7.2, the Court limits itself to a procedural review. Here it is relevant to underscore that this procedural approach tends to lead to 'a reasoning that is less tailored to the determination of the specific substantive issues at stake in a particular case'.[97] As Moonen and Lavrysen have also explained, the procedural

---

[92] *Volodina v Russia* (no 2) no 40419/19, 14 September 2021 §58.
[93] *Tunikova and Others v Russia* no 55974/16, 14 December 2021 §89.
[94] For another relevant example, see *Fedotova and Others v Russia* no 40792/10, 13 July 2021 that concerned lack of legal recognition of same-sex relationships.
[95] For another relevant example, see *Uzbyakov v Russia* no 71160/13, 5 May 2020 §§120–123, that concerned inflexible grounds for revocation of an adoption order.
[96] For example, *Axel Springer AG v Germany* [GC] no 39954/08, 7 February 2012 §§89–95; *Bărbulescu v Romania* [GC] no 61496/08, 5 September 2017 §123
[97] Moonen and Lavrysen, 'Abstract but Concrete, or Concrete but Abstract?' (n 81) 771.

review aims to incentivize States 'to ensure the provision of procedural justice at a more structural level'.[98] The procedural approach clearly preserves the margin of appreciation enjoyed by States since it does not lead to a substantive determination of how the competing interests should be concretely balanced.

Yet despite its procedural approach, the Court's reasoning can include substantive assessment relevant to the concrete applicant.[99] When the Court mixes abstract and concrete review, it combines considerations that refer generally to the legal framework with considerations about its effects on the specific applicant. It is difficult to distinguish distinctive and conclusive steps (eg first abstract and only then concrete review). This can be confusing since it might not be clear whether violation is found due to some general deficiencies (ie general omissions) or due to concrete omissions (ie the concrete application of the laws to the specific applicant).

*Only concrete review*

Some judgments include only concrete review. This can be illustrated with reference to *C.E. and Others v France*. The core of the complaint in this case was the absence of legal recognition of a child–parent relationship between children and their biological mothers' former partners. The Court did not engage in an abstract review; it refused to make some general pronouncements about the reasonableness of this lacuna in the national legislation. The Court performed only a concrete review by holding that the concrete applicants could enjoy family life in practice and resort to other forms of legal protection, as a result of which no violation of Article 8 was found.[100]

*Botoyan v Armenia* is another example. It was clear that there was no regulatory framework regarding 'the surgical specialisms of general surgery and traumatology and orthopaedics or regarding the procuring of orthopaedic appliances'. It was also clear from the facts of the case that the doctor who operated on the applicant, who subsequently suffered from serious complications resulting in her disability, had no relevant specialization. This general regulatory gap, however, was not assessed due to absence of causation:

> [t]he experts [ ... ] concluded that her surgery had generally been performed correctly and that the complications which had arisen at the post-operative stage were *not directly linked* to the fact that she had not been operated on by a relevant specialist.[101]

The Court's reasoning thus relied on causation, when the required standard of causation is generally fluid, as extensively shown in Chapter 3, and when epistemologically

---

[98] ibid 771.
[99] See Section 7.2.
[100] *C.E. and Others v France* no 29775/18 and 29693/19, 24 March 2022.
[101] *Botoyan v Armenia* no 5766/17, 8 February 2022 §102 (emphasis added).

any causal links might not have been addressed via scientific evidence. All of this demonstrates the flexibility that the Court can apply in its reasoning.

*Only abstract review*

The flexibility in the reasoning is even more obvious given that in the very same judgment of *Botoyan v Armenia*, the Court chose to review only in abstract the regulatory framework regarding access to information about risks and informed consent about medical treatment. This shows how different approaches can be adopted in the same judgment. In particular, the reasoning in *Botoyan v Armenia* includes the general statement that States have the obligation to adopt the necessary regulatory measures so that patients give their informed consent to medical procedures to assess risks. Reviewed in the abstract, the regulatory framework for obtaining a patient's informed consent was not found defective.[102] The actual implementation of this framework to the specific applicant was, however, ignored in the reasoning pertaining to the substantive positive obligation.

This was perhaps offset with the finding of a procedural violation of Article 8. The Court observed that 'at no point during the investigation or court proceedings were the applicant's complaints with regard to the absence of her informed consent to the surgery and its possible risks examined'.[103] It follows that the Court could not know whether the applicant in *Botoyan v Armenia* concretely consented, since this fact was not clarified at national level. For this reason, the Court's reasoning remained at an abstract level with focus on the question whether the national regulatory framework for obtaining informed consent was *in general* sufficient. Due to the procedural failures of the national authorities, the Court could not assess the concrete application of this framework to the applicant.

*X. and Others v Bulgaria* is another example of a review limited to abstract assessment of the regulatory framework, where its general adequacy was enough for not finding a breach. The GC examined the regulatory mechanisms for preventing and detecting ill-treatment of children who are in the care of public institutions. The review was at an abstract level since no examination is present in the Court's reasoning as to whether and how these mechanisms affected the specific victims. Similarly to what was explained above in relation to *Botoyan v Armenia*, the reason for the absence of such a review was that the Court did not have the relevant information. As it noted in *X and Others v Bulgaria*: 'the information in the case file does not enable it to confirm or refute the factual findings contained in the reports of the relevant services which inspected the orphanage as regards the implementation of these measures'.[104]

The above shows that any concrete review is dependent on proper fact-finding at domestic level, which justifies the importance of the autonomous procedural positive obligation to investigate, whose trigger, content, and scope were clarified in Chapter 6.

---

[102] ibid §104.
[103] ibid §112
[104] *X and Others v Bulgaria* [GC] no 22457/16, 2 February 2021 §§195–196

## 192  Substantive Positive Obligations

This also justifies the importance of the procedural standards developed by the Court as part of its assessment of breach of the positive obligation of adopting an effective regulatory framework (Section 7.2). In some cases, however, the general deficiencies in the national regulatory framework are so obvious that the review of the Court remains exclusively abstract. For example, in *Tunikova and Others v Russia*, a domestic violence case, the deficiencies in the national regulatory framework regarding barring orders were so obvious that the Court did not even have to review how they specifically affected the applicant. It held that it needed to be satisfied that

> *from a general point of view*, the domestic legal framework is adequate to afford protection against acts of violence by private individuals in each particular case. In other words, the toolbox of legal and operational measures available must give the authorities involved a range of sufficient measures to choose from, ... Russia ... has remained among only a few member States whose national legislation does not provide victims of domestic violence with any equivalent or comparative measures of protection [ie restraining orders or barring orders].

This led to the general conclusion that 'no form of protection orders has been made available to victims of domestic violence in Russia'.[105]

*Two-step approach with abstract review as an initial threshold*
In the examples provided so far, no suggestion can be identified in the reasoning that the abstract or the concrete review necessarily act as separate and conclusive threshold steps. Such a suggestion, however, can be discerned in some areas of the case law. These areas include cases implicating medical negligence,[106] road traffic accidents,[107] and dangerous activities.[108] In these cases, abstract deficiencies in the regulatory framework seem to be demanded as an initial threshold, so that the Court proceeds to assess how the concrete applicant has been affected. Specifically, in *Lopes de Sousa Fernandes v Portugal* the GC formulated the following standard:

> [I]n the context of alleged medical negligence, the States' substantive positive obligations relating to medical treatment *are limited* to a duty to regulate, that is to say, a duty to put in place an effective regulatory framework compelling hospitals, whether public or private, to adopt appropriate measures for the protection of patients' lives.

---

[105] *Tunikova and Others v Russia* no 55974/16, 14 December 2021 §95–96 (emphasis added).
[106] *Lopes de Sousa Fernandes v Portugal* [GC] no 56080/13, 19 December 2017 §§186–187; *Fernandes de Oliveira v Portugal* [GC] no 78103/14, 31 January 2019 §106.
[107] *Smiljanić v Croatia* no 35983/14, 25 March 2021 §70; *Marius Alexandru and Marinela Ştefan v Romania* no 78643/11, 24 March 2020 §100.
[108] *Traskunova v Russia* no 21648/11, 30 August 2022 §73; *Kotilainen and Others v Finland* no 62439/12, 17 September 2020 §§67–68.

> *Even in cases where medical negligence was established*, the Court would *normally* find a substantive violation of Article 2 *only* if the relevant regulatory framework failed to ensure proper protection of the patient's life. The Court reaffirms that where a Contracting State has made adequate provision for securing high professional standards among health professionals and the protection of the lives of patients, matters such as an error of judgment on the part of a health professional or negligent coordination among health professionals in the treatment of a *particular patient are not sufficient* of themselves to call a Contracting State to account from the standpoint of its positive obligations under Article 2 of the Convention to protect life.[109]

In the context of road traffic accidents, the Court has reformulated the above in the following way:

> where a State has adopted an overall legal framework and legislation tailored to the protective requirements in the specific context, matters such as an error of judgment on the part of an individual player, or negligent coordination among professionals, whether public or private, *could not be sufficient of themselves* to make the State accountable from the standpoint of its positive obligation under Article 2.[110]

In the context of 'dangerous activities', like clinical trials of drugs, the following reformulation has been used:

> Whenever a State undertakes or organises dangerous activities, or authorises them, it must ensure through a system of rules and through sufficient control that the risk is reduced to a reasonable minimum. If nevertheless damage arises, it will *only* amount to a breach of the State's positive obligations if it was due to insufficient regulations or insufficient control, but not if the damage was caused through the negligent conduct of an individual or the concatenation of unfortunate events.[111]

These pronouncements are suggestive of an exclusive abstract review. They are, however, followed by the following statements that in turn suggest a concrete review:

> For the Court's examination of a particular case, the question whether there has been a failure by the State in its regulatory duties calls for *a concrete assessment of*

---

[109] *Lopes de Sousa Fernandes v Portugal* [GC] no 56080/13, 19 December 2017 §§186–187 (emphasis added); *Fernandes de Oliveira v Portugal* [GC] no 78103/14, 31 January 2019 §106.
[110] *Smiljanić v Croatia* no 35983/14, 25 March 2021 §70 (emphasis added).
[111] *Traskunova v Russia* no 21648/11, 30 August 2022 §73 (emphasis added); *Stoyanovi v Bulgaria* no 42980/04, 9 November 2010 §61; *Binişan v Romania* no 39438/05, 20 May 2014 §72.

*the alleged deficiencies rather than an abstract one. In this regard, the Court reiterates that its task is not normally to review the relevant law and practice in abstracto, but to determine whether the manner in which they were applied to, or affected, the applicant gave rise to a violation of the Convention. Therefore, the mere fact that the regulatory framework may be deficient in some respect is not sufficient in itself to raise an issue under Article 2 of the Convention. It must be shown to have operated to the patient's detriment.*[112]

Interpreted in combination, all these quotations denote a two-step approach, which, for the sake of simplicity, I will label the *Fernandes de Oliveira v Portugal* test/approach to review. The question asked at the first step is whether the State has adopted an overall legal framework tailored to the protective requirements in the specific context. If yes, and if there are no 'systemic or structural dysfunctions',[113] the review will *not* proceed further and no breach of the positive obligation will be found. For example, in *Lopes de Sousa Fernandes v Portugal*, the analysis was limited to this abstract step since the respondent State had a legal framework and no sufficient evidence of 'systemic or structural dysfunction' were adduced.[114]

Only if no tailored legal framework exists *or* only if the existing one suffers from 'systemic or structural dysfunctions' will the Court's review proceed to a necessary second step. This second step entails a concrete review. The GC in *Lopes de Sousa Fernandes v Portugal* even suggested the standard of causation for the purposes of the concrete review: the deficiencies in the legal framework must contribute *decisively* to the death of the specific victim.[115]

It is relevant to note that the mere absence of a relevant regulatory framework or the mere structural deficiencies in the existing one (the first step) does not directly lead to a violation. The Court's review does not remain only at the abstract level since the establishment of a violation requires that the applicant be concretely affected. The abstract review, as formulated by the GC in *Lopes de Sousa Fernandes*, seems therefore to act like *an initial threshold* so that the Court proceeds to the second step, the concrete review.

Such a strict two-step approach (ie first abstract review and *only* if general deficiencies found can the concrete situation of the application be reviewed), is not however consistently followed.[116] In *Fernandes de Oliveira v Portugal*, another case of alleged

---

[112] *Lopes de Sousa Fernandes v Portugal* [GC] no 56080/13, 19 December 2017 §188 (emphasis added and references omitted); *Smiljanić v Croatia* no 35983/14, 25 March 2021 §72;
[113] *Lopes de Sousa Fernandes v Portugal* [GC] §§201–205.
[114] ibid.
[115] ibid.
[116] Judges have also opposed it. See Partly Dissenting Opinion of Judge Serghides in *Lopes de Sousa Fernandes v Portugal* [GC] no 56080/13, 19 December 2017 §12: 'I do not support this view, because in no situation, other than health-care situations, in which there is a serious risk threatening life and which triggers a substantive positive obligation on the part of the State to protect life, does the Court's case-law require *a systemic problem as a precondition* for a possible violation of Article 2 of the Convention' (emphasis added).

medical negligence concerning a suicide during voluntary hospitalization, the GC mixes elements of concrete and abstract review, while initially noting concrete review as its guiding parameter.[117] For example, it assessed the Mental Health Act in some more abstract terms and then it assessed how it provided the necessary means to address the needs of the specific patient (ie the applicant's son).[118]

The inconsistent application is not that surprising, given the logical fallacy in the standard. To explain, let me repeat the following sentence:

> If nevertheless damage arises, it will *only* amount to a breach of the State's positive obligations if it was due to insufficient regulations or insufficient control, but not if the damage was caused through the negligent conduct of an individual or the concatenation of unfortunate events.[119]

The sentence assumes two oppositions that exclude each other. Such an assumption cannot be correct for the following reasons. The first part of the sentence implies no breach if sufficient general regulations and control are in place. The second part of the sentence implies no breach if harm is caused through 'the negligent conduct of an individual or the concatenation of unfortunately events'. There might, however, be various situations that fit neither within the first scenario nor the second. In addition, both parts contain vague terms such as 'insufficient' and 'negligent',[120] which further undermines their distinctiveness and the assumption that they are useful for categorically framing two different scenarios (ie damage due to insufficient general regulations versus damage due to concrete individual negligence). At the end of the day, therefore, the Court has rhetorically framed abstract review as an initial threshold to possibly assuage any concerns about its intrusive role. Yet, on a closer analysis, the Court has still preserved sufficient flexibility in the manoeuvring between the abstract and the concrete in its review of whether the State has complied with its positive obligation of adopting an effective regulatory framework.

The reasoning in *Traskunova v Russia* can be helpful to explain the manoeuvring more concretely. The case was about the death of a participant in the clinical trial of a new medical product. The respondent State was found to have failed to fulfil its positive obligation under Article 2 since the national legal framework was not implemented in practice. In particular, the relevant protocols required that the participants in the clinical trial undergo a comprehensive medical check-up. The applicant's daughter was not subjected to such a check-up. Neither did she receive full information to enable

---

[117] *Fernandes de Oliveira v Portugal* [GC] no 78103/14, 31 January 2019 §116.
[118] ibid §117.
[119] *Traskunova v Russia* no 21648/11, 30 August 2022 §73 (emphasis added); *Stoyanovi v Bulgaria* no 42980/04, 9 November 2010 §61; *Binişan v Romania* no 39438/05, 20 May 2014 §72. Admittedly, this very sentence has not been repeated by the GC in the judgments of *Lopes de Sousa Fernandes v Portugal* [GC] §186 and *Fernandes de Oliveira v Portugal* [GC] no 78103/14, 31 January 2019 §106. These GC judgments contain less categorical formulations by using the words 'normally' and 'not sufficient'.
[120] See also the beginning of Section 6.1, where it was explained that the meaning attached to concepts such as intention and negligence has remained vague in the case law.

her to assess the trial's potential risks and make an informed choice about her participation in it. The Court's reasoning, however, does not show any concern about whether these omissions were due to the negligence of a specific doctor (which could have precluded the finding of a violation if the *Fernandes de Oliveira v Portugal* test is followed) or due to some more general structural deficiencies.[121] This shows the detachment between the *Fernandes de Oliveira v Portugal* test developed at an abstract level on the one hand, and the reasoning on the concrete facts on the other hand.[122]

The question that is relevant to ask here is why the GC has suggested an abstract review as an initial threshold to the effect that general deficiencies in the regulatory framework need to first be *necessarily* demonstrated, so that the Court proceeds to concretely review how these deficiencies 'operated to the patient's detriment'. The Court has not offered justifications. A possible answer is that isolated or operational omissions (even though it is possible to causally link these to harm) should not lead to the responsibility of the State as an organizational entity. The justification is therefore limiting the boundaries of state responsibility for omissions. Operational omissions might be more appropriate to examine through the lens of the positive obligation of taking protective operational measures, whose trigger is an object of specific limitations. These will be explained in Section 7.3.

Another possible answer relates to fact-finding and epistemological uncertainty. The first step in the *Lopes de Sousa Fernandes* test, the abstract review, is less dependent on fact-finding. The Court has access to existing national regulatory frameworks and can assess their reasonableness in abstract, in this way taking the opportunity to make some relevant general pronouncements about general standards, without necessarily finding a substantive violation in the specific case. The latter requires a concrete review, which is dependent on the fact-finding performed by the national authorities.[123] At this stage, the Court can easily choose to apply a procedural turn, framing the review as being one about the procedural obligation, and avoiding pronouncements regarding breach of the substantive obligation in the specific case.[124]

In sum, the *Fernandes de Oliveira v Portugal* approach to review facilitates the achievement of at least two objectives. First, it helps in the development of general

---

[121] See also *Kotilainen and Others v Finland* no 62439/12, 17 September 2020 where the Court found a violation of Article 2 because of an *individual* error, ie the gun used by the perpetrator of a mass shooting was not seized by the police because the responsible police officer decided not to do so. To find a violation by circumventing the *Fernandes de Oliveira v Portugal* test, the Court created another positive obligation: taking of 'reasonable measure of precaution' in the protection of public safety (§§84–89).

[122] In some other judgments, the Court only invokes that part of the *Fernandes de Oliveira v Portugal* test that requires that the regulatory framework operated to the applicant's detriment. See *Gvozdeva v Russia* no 69997/11, 22 March 2022 §33; *Khudoroshko v Russia* no 3959/14, 18 January 2022 §36. See also *Botoyan v Armenia* no 5766/17, 8 February 2022 §92, where the part of the test as to how individual error and individual negligence cannot give rise to state responsibility for breach of the positive obligation, is not mentioned. Rather, no violation is found in *Botoyan v Armenia* due to lack of causality.

[123] For example, the answer to the question how a national regulation operated specifically to the detriment of the applicant or whether the specific harm to the specific applicant was caused by error of judgment or individual negligence, requires fact-finding.

[124] See *Marius Alexandru and Marinela Ștefan v Romania* no 78643/11, 24 March 2020 §§104–107. See Section 7.2.

and abstract *substantive* standards, so that the Court serves its constitutional role and acts as a rule-maker, without intruding into States' discretion as to how rules should be formulated specifically and applied to concrete cases. Second, it helps in the development of *procedural* obligations. It is precisely this latter development that will be examined in more detail in Section 7.2.

## 7.2 Obligation to Develop Effective National Procedures

Protection by the legal framework requires States to develop not only substantive but also procedural guarantees. Procedures contribute to the effective application of the substantive guarantees. In other words, fair procedures are arguably more likely to lead to fairer results.[125] The ECHR imposes some explicit procedural obligations.[126] Chapter 6 addressed the autonomous positive procedural obligation that is triggered under certain conditions and that is relevant *post factum*, after the harm has materialized. In contrast, the procedural guarantees discussed in this chapter are meant to apply *ex ante* since their rationale is to prevent harm (eg to prevent an arguably harmful decision by the national authorities). As opposed to the procedural obligation addressed in Chapter 6, the procedural guarantees addressed here do not have an autonomous and self-standing role since, as Brems has explained, 'procedural shortcoming is not necessarily conclusive for the finding of a violation; in many cases it is one among several factors that contribute to such a finding'.[127] Arnardóttir has also clarified how 'procedural elements' are invoked 'among the balance of reasons when the Court pronounces on the substantive merits and assesses the proportionality or reasonableness of a measure'.[128] Gerards has also observed how the Court 'has woven procedural elements into its substantive reasonableness review'.[129] Gerards has also added that '[p]rocedural arguments are supportive, i.e. as part of the overall set of arguments to be taken into account in building a "narrative" leading up to' a judgment.[130]

The non-self-standing role of the procedural guarantees needs further elaboration, which will be offered in Section 7.2.1. Given this role that implies a mixture of

---

[125] B Çali, 'Balancing Human Rights? Methodological Problems with Weights, Scales and Proportions' (2007) 29(1) Human Rights Quarterly 251, 267; E Brems, 'The "Logics" of Procedural-Type Review by the European Court of Human Rights' in J Gerards and E Brems (eds), *Procedural Review in European Fundamental Rights Cases* (Cambridge University Press 2017) 17, 18.
[126] Articles 5, 6, and 13 of the ECHR and Articles 1, 2, 3, and 4 of Protocol 7.
[127] E Brems, 'Procedural Protection. An Examination of Procedural Safeguards Read into Substantive Convention Rights' in Brems and Gerards (eds), *Shaping Rights in the ECHR. The Role of the European Court of Human Rights in Determining the Scope of Human Rights* (2014) 137, 158.
[128] Arnardóttir, 'The "Procedural Turn" under the European Convention on Human Rights and Presumptions of Convention Compliance' (2017) I CON 9, 14.
[129] J Gerards, 'Procedural Review by the ECtHR: A Typology' in Gerards and Brems (eds), *Procedural Review in European Fundamental Rights Cases* (n 125) 127, 129.
[130] ibid 149.

procedural and substantive arguments in the determination of a breach, it is relevant also to reflect upon how this role and mixture affect the actual content of the positive obligation, which will be done in Section 7.2.2.

## 7.2.1 Not a Self-standing Positive Obligation

A clarification of the non-self-standing role of the procedural guarantees developed in the case law requires first, understanding the state conduct of which the applicant complains. This conduct is a result of *decisions* taken at the national level, not least because the applicant needs to exhaust domestic remedies for the claim before the Court to be admissible. These could be decisions by the national legislator or by administrative or judicial bodies.[131] If it is a decision by the national legislator or by the government,[132] its formulation will be more abstract since the decision is of a general nature. An example emerges from *Hatton and Others v the United Kingdom*, where the issue was the general state policy on night flights at Heathrow airport.[133] If it is a decision by administrative or judicial bodies, it might be more tailored to the situation of the applicant. Illustrative examples include a refusal by the national courts to grant an injunction against publication of certain materials;[134] a refusal by the national courts to declare unlawful the termination of an employment contract;[135] a confirmation by the national courts of dismissal from employment;[136] or a decision to dismiss the applicant's defamation proceedings.[137]

It is possible to distinguish between the outcome of the decisions and the process as to how the decisions were taken. The *outcome* refers to the content/substance of the decisions taken at national level where different interests have been balanced in a particular way. The *process*, on the one hand, refers to the steps taken at national level to reach these decisions (ie to reach the particular balancing of the competing interests).[138] As the Court noted in *Hatton and Others v the United Kingdom*,

> there are two aspects to the inquiry which may be carried out by the Court. First, the Court may assess the substantive merits of the government's decision, to

---

[131] Often the harm caused by these decisions is formulated as covered by Article 8, a provision that has been referred to as 'a laboratory for procedural justice issues'. E Brems and L Lavrysen, 'Procedural Justice in the Human Rights Adjudication: The European Court of Human Rights' (2013) 25 Human Rights Quarterly 176.

[132] For example, *Animal Defenders International v the United Kingdom* [GC] no 48876/08, 22 April 2013 §108; *Maurice v France* [GC] no 11810/03, 6 October 2005 §121; *M.A. v Denmark* [GC] no 6697/18, 9 July 2021 §§147–50. See also M Saul, 'The European Court of Human Rights' Margin of Appreciation and the Process of National Parliaments' (2015) 15 Human Rights Law Review 745.

[133] *Hatton and Others v the United Kingdom* [GC] no 36022/97, 8 July 2003.

[134] For example, *Von Hannover v Germany* (no. 2) [GC] no 40660/08, 7 February 2012.

[135] For example, *Bărbulescu v Romania* [GC] no 61496/08, 5 September 2017.

[136] For example, *López Ribalda and Others v Spain* [GC] no 1874/13 and 8567/13, 17 October 2019 §109.

[137] For example, *Sousa Goucha v Portugal* no 70434/12, 22 March 2016.

[138] L Huijbers, *Process-based Fundamental Rights Review* (Intersentia 2019) 113.

ensure that it is compatible with Article 8. Secondly, it may scrutinize the decision-making process to ensure that due weight has been accorded to the interests of the individual.[139]

For example, in *Bărbulescu v Romania* that concerned termination of an employment contract after secret surveillance of an employee, the outcome is the termination of the contract. The process refers to the procedures followed at national level by the applicant to challenge this termination.

The Court has developed in its reasoning certain procedural *standards* for assessing the national procedures. These can include access to the procedure; its overall quality, promptness, and effectiveness; its independence; the extent to which affected individuals have been involved; or the extent to which decisions are motivated.[140] These procedural standards can play a different role in the reasoning of the Court. This role can be more or less important and in a different relationship with the outcome (ie the reasonableness of the decision). All of this makes it very difficult to insulate the standards (each one in isolation or all of them as a combination) as self-standing positive obligations.[141] Rather, they are elements/aspects in the reasoning. At a more abstract level, however, it is possible to say that States are under the positive obligation to develop effective national procedures to ensure the rights.

As to the relationship between the process and the outcome (ie the substance of the decision that has affected the applicant), in its reasoning the Court often assesses the reasonableness of both. In this way, the Court's argumentation might not contain a distinction between the analysis as to whether the national decision (ie the outcome) was reasonable or whether the national process leading to this decision was of sufficient quality. In some situations, the Court can draw negative inferences from the absence of procedural guarantees, as a consequence of which the outcome is viewed as more suspect. In other situations, the observance of procedural guarantees at national level makes it more likely that the Court can accept the outcome as reasonable.[142] In this latter case, the Court itself is less likely to rebalance the interests at stake in a different way to reach a conclusion that the outcome (ie the national decision where

---

[139] *Hatton and Others v the United Kingdom* [GC] no 36022/97, 8 July 2003 §99.
[140] For example, ibid §104; *Roche v The United Kingdom* [GC] no 32555/96, 19 October 2005 §§162–167; *A., B. and C v Ireland* [GC] no 25579/05, 16 December 2010 §267; *Gaskin v the United Kingdom* no 10454/83, 7 July 1989 §49; *Uzbyakov v Russia* no 71160/13, 5 May 2020 §106; *P. and S. v Poland* no 57375/08, 30 October 2012 §111; *Tanda-Muzinga v France* no 2260/10, 10 July 2014 §82.
[141] A similar problem was identified in Section 6.2.3 about the autonomous procedural positive obligation to investigate. The important difference is, however, that the procedural guarantees addressed in Section 6.2.3, although in different possible combinations and with different importance attached to them in different cases, as a combination do have a self-standing role.
[142] Brems has assessed as problematic when the Court 'draws positive substantive inferences from the observance of procedural' guarantees. Brems, 'Procedural Protection' (n 127). See also O Arnardóttir, 'The "Procedural Turn" under the European Convention on Human Rights and Presumptions of Convention Compliance' (2017) 15(1) International Journal of Constitutional Law 9, 15, who has noted that positive inferences are more controversial since their role can be so far reaching as to eliminate the Court's substantive engagement with the reasonableness of the outcome.

interests have been balanced) was not reasonable and, therefore, the State has failed to fulfil its positive obligations. All this leads to a more abstract review—the Court does not closely scrutinize the actual solutions offered by the national decisions since given the subject matter (eg socio-economic policy, ethical moral dilemmas, involvement of various possible competing private interests, etc) it is difficult to have one single right answer/outcome.

In some areas of its case law, the Court has elaborated the standards that the national decision-making bodies need to take into account. For example, the Court has formulated the standards as to how private life and freedom of expression need to be balanced,[143] and reviews if the national courts are following these standards.[144] However, as already noted above, the Court's review still contains arguments about the reasonableness of the outcome. For example, the review does not only assess whether the national authorities have taken into account whether the publication contributed to the public debate, but the Court itself assesses whether the publication contributed to a debate of general interest.[145] The Court does not only consider whether the domestic courts have provided a substantiation for a certain finding but also assesses whether this finding can actually be justified based on the facts. In this way, the Court also assesses whether the finding of the domestic courts is substantively flawed.[146]

## 7.2.2 The Content of the Obligation

Given the above-described argumentation in the judgments where procedural and substantive aspects are mixed, the following question arises: what is the actual content of the obligation imposed upon the State? The Court has articulated its task as reviewing whether the decisions the domestic authorities have taken pursuant to their margin of appreciation are in conformity with the standards laid down in the Court's case law.[147] The positive obligation then can be formulated as an obligation to balance interests in accordance with the criteria developed by the Court. The content of the obligation is therefore about the process of decision-making and in this sense it can be considered as a procedural obligation.

Yet the finding that the obligation has been fulfilled has substantive repercussions. No violation implies that the national authorities have fulfilled their positive obligation to balance interests in accordance with the criteria developed by the Court, and

---

[143] For example, *Von Hannover v Germany (no. 2)* [GC] no 40660/08 and 60641/08 §§95–113; *Axel Springer AG v Germany* [GC] no 39954/08, 7 February 2012 §78–95.

[144] Other areas include, for example, employees' interests to private life (*Bărbulescu v Romania* [GC] no 61496/08, 5 September 2017; *Lópoez Ribalda and Others v Spain* [GC] no 1874/13, 17 October 2019) and taking of children into care (*Uzbyakov v Russia* no 71160/13, 5 May 2020).

[145] For example, *Von Hannover v Germany (no. 2)* [GC] no 40660/08, 7 February 2012 §118; *Dupate v Latvia* no 18068/11, 19 November 2020 §53; *Khadija Ismayilova v Azerbaijan (no 3)* no 35283/14, 7 May 2020 §70; *Hájovsky v Slovakia* no 7796/16, 1 July 2021 §36.

[146] For example, *Dupate v Latvia* no 18068/11, 19 November 2020 §74.

[147] For example, *Bărbulescu v Romania* [GC] no 61496/08, 5 September 2017 §127.

therefore the outcome is acceptable from the perspective of the Convention. A finding of a violation can, on the one hand, be expected not to communicate anything about the outcome (ie how the interests ought to be balanced). Rather, the national authorities are under the obligation to perform another balancing act by following the procedural standards. However, since the Court includes substantive elements in its reasoning, the outcome of any new balancing might be also predictable from the Court's reasoning.[148] This depends on the role of these substantive elements, which as suggested above, can have varying importance. A finding of a violation is therefore inconclusive as to the outcome. It is conceivable that the national authorities might take the same decision, that is, the same outcome could be reached as the one originally challenged before the Court; this time, however, by following the correct decision-making process.

Besides the margin of appreciation, that is, the flexibility the national authorities have as to what decisions to take to solve various problems,[149] which might explain the willingness of the Court to focus on procedural guarantees and to eschew substantively balancing the affected interests,[150] there are further related reasons that explain the focus on procedural guarantees in the reasoning. These include the impossibility for the Court to know the facts.[151] In addition, in some cases, it is precisely the absence of a procedure or the absence of an effective procedure that is the omission formulated by the applicant.[152] In the latter situation, one can say that there is a gap in the regulatory framework. However, the distinguishing feature here is that the framework is one about procedure.[153] The content of the obligation then is to have a national procedure, and the outcome of this procedure is not part of the content of the obligation.

---

[148] See eg *Behar and Gutman v Bulgaria* no 29335/13, 16 February 2021 §105, a case that concerned anti-Semitic statements by a leader of a political party. The Court held that '[a]lthough they recognized the tension between the two rights, the courts cannot be said to have *property* weighted their relative importance in the circumstances.... By in effect ascribing considerable weight to Mr Siderov's right to freedom of expression..., the Bulgarian courts failed to carry out the requisite balancing exercise in line with the criteria laid down in the Court's case-law.'

[149] Subsidiarity, understood as structural deference (see Section 4.3), has been the avenue through which the quality of the national decision-making process is of relevance to the ECHR review. To use Legg's terms, the quality of the national decision-making processes is a factor external to the merits, but it is a factor that influences the Court's review on the merits. A Legg, *The Margin of Appreciation in International Human Rights Law: Deference and Proportionality* (Oxford University Press 2012) 18. Although it is related, analytically it is an issue separated from what this section is concerned with. This section is rather about the margin of appreciation as a normative flexibility in the substantive reasonableness review performed by the Court. The question here is how procedural elements are taken into account in the reasonableness review, and not on the role of these elements as an external factor.

[150] Huijbers, *Process-based Fundamental Rights Review* (n 138) 295.

[151] For example, *Pisică v the Republic of Moldova* no 23641/17, 29 October 2019 §76.

[152] For example, *Drašković v Montenegro* no 40597/17, 9 June 2020, where there was gap in the national legal framework since it did not envision mechanisms for balancing of the competing interests and for recognizing the applicant's legal interest.

[153] For example, *Sudita Keita v Hungary* no 42321/15, 12 May 2020 §32, where the relevant positive obligation imposed upon the State was to 'provide an effective and accessible procedure or a combination of procedures enabling the applicant to have the issue of his status in Hungary determined with due regard to his private-life interests under Article 8 of the Convention'. See also *Darboe and Camara v Italy* no 5797/17, 21 July 2022, where the applicant did not benefit from minimum procedural guarantees based on his status as an asylum-seeker who claimed to be a child; *X. v the Former Yugoslav Republic of Macedonia* no 29683/16, 17 January 2019 §70, where the Court observed that 'the current legal framework... does not provide

The focus on procedural guarantees in the reasoning does not only imply that the reasonableness of the decisions/the outcome as such might either not be addressed or be addressed only indirectly, it also implies that the causation between the harm claimed by the applicant and the alleged substantive omissions by the State is of less import. An example will be helpful to clarify this point. In *Bărbulescu v Romania*, the harm invoked by the applicant was the termination of an employment contract after secret monitoring of his communication by the employer. The invoked state omission was the failure by the national courts to reverse this termination since it was arguably in breach of the applicant's private life and correspondence. The reasonableness of this omission as such was not at the heart of the Court's reasoning. Rather the Court framed its task as reviewing the process leading to this omission: how the national courts assessed the reasonableness. This review led to the following conclusion by the Court:

> [I]t appears that the domestic courts *failed to determine*, in particular, whether the applicant had received prior notice from his employer of the possibility that his communications on Yahoo Messenger might be monitored; nor did they *have regard* either to the fact that he had not been informed of the nature or the extent of the monitoring, or to the degree of intrusion into his private life and correspondence. In addition, they *failed to determine*, firstly, the specific reasons justifying the introduction of the monitoring measures; secondly, whether the employer could have used measures entailing less intrusion into the applicant's private life and correspondence; and thirdly, whether the communications might have been accessed without his knowledge.[154]

The failures to determine and to consider these factors are hard to link causally with the harm claimed by the applicant (ie termination of a contract after surveillance of this communication). Even if the national courts determined and considered all of the above-mentioned factors, these courts could have still refused to invalidate the termination of the contract. The human rights law review then does not centre on omissions as causally linked to harm, that is, 'on primary issues relating to rights'.[155] It rather centres on the margin of appreciation of the national authorities, the limited fact-finding role of the Court, and its limited expertise in deciding on complex polycentric issues. These procedural elements operate in tandem with primary issues relating to rights since, for example, the Court still invokes the severity of the harm and as already mentioned, the Court can still add other substantive elements in its

---

"quick, transparent and accessible procedures" for changing on birth certificates the registered sex of transgender people'.

[154] *Bărbulescu v Romania* [GC] no 61496/08, 5 September 2017 §140 (emphasis added).
[155] T Poole, 'Legitimacy, Rights and Judicial Review' (2005) 25(4) Oxford Journal of Legal Studies 697, 709.

reasoning. Yet when the Court's review is about the national process, the actual harm and its causes are in the background.

In sum, the national legal framework must incorporate procedural guarantees so that decisions harmful to interests protected by human rights can be prevented. It is hard to isolate these guarantees as self-standing positive obligations whose content is strictly limited to having national procedures that comply with certain qualitative standards. The reason is that the Court still tends to incorporate an assessment of the actual outcome (ie the actual decision) reached at domestic level without necessarily exclusively focusing on assessing the domestic process followed to reach this outcome. This is understandable since it will be too formalistic to base a judgment exclusively on the question of whether the national authorities have followed a certain procedural guarantee[156] without any consideration of the actual outcome as causally related to the actual harm invoked by the applicant.

## 7.3 Obligation to Take Protective Operational Measures

Substantive and procedural protection ensured via regulatory frameworks with effectively applied procedural guarantees is of crucial importance for general prevention of harm. In addition to this general prevention, States are under the positive obligation, originally developed in *Osman v the United Kingdom*, to take protective operational measures to prevent harm against a specific individual who is at real and immediate risk (referred to below also as the *Osman* obligation).[157] The purpose of this section is to show how the test for reviewing compliance with the obligation has undergone transformations in the case law since the qualifications that characterize it have been destabilized. Consequently, the test has been invoked in scenarios beyond its original conception, which has led to an expansion of the obligation and blurring of its boundaries. Due to these invocations of the *Osman* test, it has been fragmented in the case law into subtests so that it can be adapted to and made to fit in different scenarios. As a result, it might be currently difficult to find its coherent logic. This in turn challenges the independence of the obligation as a separate and specific obligation triggered

---

[156] Gerards, 'Procedural Review by the ECtHR: A Typology' (n 129) 155, where it is noted that it is 'too "empty" to base a judgment on procedural reasons only'.
[157] *Osman v the United Kingdom* [GC] no 23452/94, 28 October 1998. Most of the cases where this obligation has been found triggered have been examined under Article 2. The obligation is also relevant to Article 3 cases (eg *Oganezova v Armenia* no 71367/12 and 72961/12, 17 May 2022 §83). In the context of Article 8, it is less clear whether the positive obligation of taking protective preventive operational measures, is directly relevant. See *Association Accept and Others v Romania* no 19237/16, 1 June 2021 §101; *F.O. v Croatia* no 29555/13, 22 April 2021; *Špadijer v Montenegro* no 31549/18, 9 November 2021 §87. It cannot be precluded that the *Osman* obligation might be also directly applied to Article 8 (see *Malagić v Croatia* no 29417/17, 17 November 2022 §57). Given the wide meaning of private life, the immediacy standard that characterizes the *Osman* obligation might, however, appear not entirely relevant.

under certain conditions and with a specific content. Suggestions as to how the independence of the obligation can be preserved will also be proposed.

To achieve this objective, Section 7.3.1 will first explain the obligation as originally developed in *Osman v the United Kingdom*. This ensures that the forthcoming analysis has an initial analytical standard against which to assess any subsequent developments. Section 7.3.2 will then focus on developments that have led to modifications of the elements of the *Osman* test concerning the source/actor of harm, the object of the harm (ie the victim), and the type of risk (ie the immediacy of the risk). Section 7.3.3 will explain another adjustment of the test pertaining to the knowledge of the State about risk and more specifically, whether absence of knowledge can be assumed when no risk assessment has been performed.[158] Section 7.3.4 will address other possible adjustments of the test with reference to harm-related, temporal, and geographical specifications. Section 7.3.5 will focus on the content and scope of the obligation—what protective measures ought to be forthcoming given the adjustments and the specifications discussed in the previous sections. This final section will also reflect upon the distinctiveness of the *Osman* obligation in light of its content and scope.

## 7.3.1 The Test as Originally Developed in *Osman v the United Kingdom*

In brief, *Osman v the United Kingdom* concerned a teacher who wounded Ahmed Osman, his former student, after developing an obsessive emotional attachment to him, and killed the student's father. Prior to the lethal incident, the teacher destroyed the family's property and participated in other similar threatening incidents. The family claimed that the State failed to protect the right to life of Ahmed and his father. After noting that States are generally under the positive obligation 'to take steps to safeguards the lives of those within its jurisdiction', the GC added that Article 2 'may also imply in certain *well-defined circumstances* a positive obligation on the authorities to take preventive operational measures to protect an individual whose life is at risk from the criminal acts of another individual'.[159] The circumstances are well-defined since

> it must be established to its [the Court's] satisfaction that the authorities knew or ought to have known at the time of the existence of a real and immediate risk to the life of an identified individual or individuals from the criminal acts of a third party and that they failed to take measures within the scope of their powers which, judged reasonably, might have been expected to avoid that risk.[160]

---

[158] The focus on these elements is justified given that in Section 2.7.1 the actual test of 'real and immediate' risk was already discussed.
[159] *Osman v the United Kingdom* [GC] no 23452/94, 28 October 1998 §115 (emphasis added).
[160] ibid.

As Chapter 2 already noted, the distinguishing feature of this positive obligation is the specifics of the individual who is the object of protection (ie the victim of harm) and the specifics of the risk of harm to which he or she might be exposed. Section 2.7.1 explained that this risk must be 'real and immediate' so that the obligation of taking protective operation measures is triggered. Section 4.1.3 clarified how the requirements for a specific identified individual who is the object of protection, and for immediacy of the risk of harm, relate to the standards of causation and reasonableness. In particular, given that the victim is identified and that the risk is immediate, it might be easier to accept that it is reasonable to take protective measures targeted for the specific victim and respectively intrusive restrictive measures against individuals who are the actors of harm.[161] Given the targeted nature of the measures, it is easier to accept that they contribute causally to the prevention of the harm.

All of this reveals how the positive obligation of taking protective operational measures, originally developed in *Osman v the United Kingdom*, is characterized by certain qualifications.[162] First, the requisite risk that triggers the obligation is qualified since it is specific in kind (ie 'real and immediate'). Second, the object of protection is qualified since a specific individual identified in advance is targeted for protection by the State. Third, the required preventive measures (ie the content and the scope of the obligation) are also qualified in relation to the nature of the risk and the object of protection. The first two of these qualifications were clearly applied in *Osman*, where the GC found no violation since it considered that the police neither knew nor ought to have known about a real and immediate lethal risk against the specific members of the Osman family.[163] The third qualification was not relevant since given the absence of knowledge, the content of the obligation was not reviewed. The third qualification can be better understood with reference to subsequent case law, which will be done in Section 7.3.5. Prior to addressing the measures required under the *Osman* test, the modifications and the adjustments of the first two qualifications observable in the post-*Osman* case law, will be explained.

## 7.3.2 Modifications of the Test Regarding the Actors of Harm, the Objects of Harm, and the Immediacy of the Risk

After *Osman v the United Kingdom*, the test has been invoked many times and the Court has multiple times confirmed that this is a positive obligation different from the positive obligation addressed in Section 7.1; state responsibility therefore can be tested against both positive obligations.[164] Yet the case law is also confusing since the

---

[161] See Chapter 5 on competing obligations.
[162] Concurring Opinion in *Kurt v Austria* [GC] no 62903/15, 15 June 2021 §§8–10.
[163] See Section 2.3 for the distinction between 'knew or ought to have known'.
[164] See eg *Nicolae Virgiliu Tănase v Romania* [GC] no 41720/13, 25 June 2019 §§135–136; *X and Others v Bulgaria* [GC] no 22457/16, 2 February 2021 §§181–183; *Fernandes de Oliveira v Portugal* [GC] no

*Osman* test seems to be invoked not only in circumstances where a non-state actor has inflicted harm but also where the harm cannot be directly attributed to a specific actor,[165] where individuals under the custody[166] or the responsibility[167] of the State suffer harm, or where individuals in healthcare institutions suffer harm,[168] to provide few examples.[169] Scenarios where the victim herself is the actor of harm have been also included.[170] The actors of the harm have been thus distanced from the *Osman*-type scenarios.

Similar expansion can be noted regarding the object of the harm, that is, the victim or the potential victim that needs to be protected.[171] On the one hand, the obligation flowing from the *Osman* test has been limited to 'preventive operational measures to protect an identified individual from another individual',[172] which has justified its label as 'a duty of *personal* protection'.[173] On the other hand, the obligation has been also invoked in circumstances where while the actors are identified,[174] this can hardly be said about their victims. *Mastromatteo v Italy* is a case at point. It involved prisoners who while on leave killed a random individual. In *Mastromatteo v Italy* the Court invoked the *Osman* test and observed that 'the relevant risk in the present case

---

78103/14, 31 January 2019 §103; *Derenik Mkrtchyan and Gayane Mkrtchyan v Armenia* no 69736/12, 30 November 2021 §§50–57; *Munteanu v the Republic of Moldova* no 34168/11, 26 May 2020 §62. These references make it clear that actual or putative knowledge about real and immediate risk triggers specifically the positive obligation of taking operational measures to protect a specific person. See also *Ribcheva and Others v Bulgaria* no 37801/16, 30 March 2021 §157, where it was observed that the obligation to have in place legislative and administrative framework 'is not in issue in the present case'.

[165] *Dodov v Bulgaria* no 59548/00, 17 January 2008 §100.
[166] *Keenan v United Kingdom* no 27229/95, 3 April 2001 (suicide of a prisoner); *Tikhonova v Russia* no 13596/05, 30 April 2014 (suicide during compulsory military service); *P.H. v Slovakia* no 37574/19, 8 September 2022 (fall through the window of the police station); *I.E. v The Republic of Moldova* no 45422/13, 26 May 2020 (ill-treatment in prison).
[167] *Centre for Legal Resources on Behalf of Velntin Câmpeanu v Romania* [GC] no 47848/08, 17 July 2014 §130.
[168] *Fernandes de Oliveira v Portugal* [GC] no 78103/14, 31 January 2019.
[169] See F Ebert and R Sijniensky, 'Preventing Violations of the Right to Life in the European and the Inter-American Human Rights System: From the *Osman* Test to a Coherent Doctrine of Risk Prevention?' (2015) 15 Human Rights Law Review 343.
[170] *Fernandes de Oliveira v Portugal* [GC] no 78103/14, 31 January 2019 §108: 'Article 2 may imply, in certain well-defined circumstances, a positive obligation on the authorities to take preventive operational measures to protect an individual from another individual or, in particular circumstances, from himself.'
[171] For reference to 'potential victims', see *Women's Initiative Supporting Group and Others v Georgia* no 73204/13, 16 December 2021 §68.
[172] *Nicolae Virgiliu Tănase v Romania* [GC] no 41720/13, 25 June 2019 §136; *X and Others v Bulgaria* [GC] no 22457/16, 2 February 2021 §§181–183. See also *Tunikova and Others v Russia* no 55974/16, 14 December 2021 §78: 'specific individual against a risk'; *Kotilainen and Others v Finland* no 62439/12, 17 September 2020 §70: the obligation to take preventive operational measures has been established for situations where 'the real and immediate risk from criminal acts of a third party concerns the life of one or more *identified or identifiable individuals*' (emphasis added).
[173] *Kotilainen and Others v Finland* no 62439/12, 17 September 2020 §81 (emphasis added); *Vardosanidze v Georgia* no 43881/10, 7 May 2020 §53.
[174] See *Tkhelidze v Georgia* no 33056/17, 8 July 2021 §52, where rather than asking whether the victim was identifiable, the Court asked 'whether a real and immediate danger emanating from an *identifiable* individual existed'.

being a risk to life for members of the public at large rather than for one or more identified individuals'.[175]

All of the above suggests that there is uncertainty in the case law as to the applicability of the criteria regarding the specificity of the victim and the specificity of the actors of harm.[176] When the victim is identified or identifiable (ie the State knew or ought to have known that a specific person is at risk),[177] this presupposes some *special relationship of proximity* between the victim and the State,[178] which in turn can be invoked as a justification for the imposition of the positive obligation.[179] However, this proximity might be possible to accept on other bases, including identification and thus specification of the actors of harm, as reflected in *Mastromatteo v Italy*. Other bases are also discernible in the case law. An example is when the actor of harm had been under the control of the State shortly before causing harm to the victim, as in *Talpis v Italy*.[180] A less solid basis is perhaps when the actor of harm himself was in contact with the authorities, in this way opening opportunities for the authorities to take preventive measures, as in *Bljakaj and Others v Croatia*.[181] Another possible basis is when the actor of harm had a gun issued in breach of the existing domestic legislation, as in *Gorovensky and Bugara v Ukrain*.[182] It could be argued that by not complying with its own legislation, the State placed itself in a closer proximate relationship with the harm.[183]

What has not remained unnoticed is the uncertainty in how to conceptualize the proximity between the State and the harm so that responsibility of the State is not categorically denied in all circumstances where the victim is an unknown member of the public with no prior connection with the authorities. In *Ribcheva and Others v*

---

[175] *Mastromatteo v Italy* [GC] no 37703/97, 24 October 2022 §74.
[176] There is another source of confusion in the case law. In some judgments, the *Osman* test has been invoked for testing compliance with the positive obligation addressed in Section 7.1. See eg *Centre for Legal Resources on Behalf of Velentin Câmpeanu v Romania* [GC] no 47848/08, 17 July 2014 §130, where it seems to be assumed that all positive obligations under Article 2 are subject to the *Osman* test. As to the specific case, the harm that led to Velentin Câmpeanu's death was present for a prolonged period of time, which made the notion of 'immediate' irrelevant and therefore, the pertinence of the *Osman* obligation questionable.
[177] The victim is 'identified' when it can be established that the State knew about the risk to him or her. The victim is 'identifiable' when the State ought to have known about the risk. As clarified in Section 2.3, in its reasoning the Court often fails to specify which of these two standards is actually met in the particular case.
[178] This is comparable to one of the requirements under tort law of negligence, where there is no liability for omissions unless there is a special relationship of proximity between the public authority and the claimant. T Hickman 'Tort Law, Public Authorities, and the Human Rights Act 1998' in D Fairgrieve and others (eds), *Tort Liability of Public Authorities in Comparative Perspective* (British Institute of International and Comparative Law 2002) 17, 42. Where the claimant is an unknown member of the public, with no prior connection with the public authority, the national courts have tended to hold that no duty of care is owned. C Booth and D Squires, *The Negligence Liability of Public Authorities* (Oxford University Press 2006) 332.
[179] See Chapter 1 where it is explained that the State cannot be generally expected to protect unknown members of the public against all possible harms. If it were, this can lead to authoritarian statism.
[180] See Separate Opinion of Judge Eicke in *Talpis v Italy* no 41237/14, 2 March 2017 §10. See Section 3.2.2 where an argument is developed that by exercising control the State places itself in proximate relationships.
[181] *Bljakaj and Others v Croatia* no 74448/12, 18 September 2014 §115.
[182] *Gorovensky and Bugara v Ukraine* nos 36146/05 and 42418/05, 12 January 2012 §39.
[183] Section 7.1 explains the role of legality in establishing breach of positive obligations.

*Bulgaria*, in an attempt to find some consistency, the Court reasoned that the obligation to take preventive operational measures actually implies two types of obligations. The *first* one is relevant when the authorities must take steps to protect an *identified* individual, which can be viewed as classical *Osman*-type scenarios. The *second* is 'to take steps to protect members of the public who cannot be identified in advance from a real and immediate risk of lethal acts emanating from such people'.[184] The reference to 'such people' in the quotation suggests that this second obligation is still somehow qualified in terms of the specifics of the actors of harm. However, the actors of harm were not specified in a principled manner, which could have been helpful for clarifying more generally when this second obligation is triggered so that guidance for future cases might be forthcoming. Rather, to specify the actors, the Court in *Ribcheva and Others v Bulgaria* enumerated the scenarios that have already arisen in previous judgments, thus leaving open the question of whether this second positive obligation is limited only to these scenarios.[185] The scenarios, as enumerated in *Ribcheva and Others v Bulgaria*, were limited to three examples:

> (a) the release of violent prisoners on leave or on licence, (b) the supervision of a mentally disturbed person known to be predisposed to violence, and (c) a terrorist group suspected of preparing to attack unknown civilian targets in a given area....[186]

Interestingly, the facts in *Ribcheva and Others v Bulgaria* did not fit any of these three scenarios. Neither did they fit within what was framed as a first type *Osman* obligation. The case was about a police officer who was shot dead by a dangerous individual during a police operation organized to disarm the latter. The Court noted that 'the authorities clearly knew that Mr Sharkov's life could be at risk from Mr P.P. [the dangerous individual who shot] if he took part in an operation to arrest him'.[187] While the actor of harm was identified, any police officer in the operation was at risk. Whether the risk was 'real and immediate' was a question that the Court failed to consider; rather it directly started to assess compliance. This failure was, on the one hand, understandable since, as the Court itself observed, the police operation was inherently dangerous and the police officers by virtue of their duties were exposed to risks, which made the 'real and immediate' risk standard irrelevant to the case. On the other hand, however, the failure by the Court to invoke the standard of 'real and immediate' further distanced the case from the original standards developed in *Osman v the United*

---

[184] *Ribcheva and Others v Bulgaria* no 37801/16, 30 March 2021 §158. See also *Kotilainen and Others v Finland* no 62439/12, 17 September 2020 §§70–72 and the Dissenting Opinion of Judge Wojtyczek in *Smiljanić v Croatia* no 35983/14, 25 March 2021.

[185] See also *Kotilainen and Others v Finland* no 62439/12, 17 September 2020 §§70 and 84, where the Court also invoked the second positive obligation.

[186] *Ribcheva and Others v Bulgaria* no 37801/16, 30 March 2021§158 (with relevant references). Admittedly, this is not a GC judgment, although it is marked as being a key case.

[187] *Ribcheva and Others v Bulgaria* no 37801/16, 30 March 2021§160.

*Kingdom*. This more generally challenges the specificity of the obligation of taking protective operational measures as a separate obligation.

Indeed, what was at issue in assessing compliance in *Ribcheva and Others v Bulgaria* was the organization of the operation and, in particular, whether any failings in the organization were sufficiently causally linked with the officer's death. The absence of sufficiently strong causal links was key for the finding that Bulgaria did *not* breach Article 2. This reliance on clear causal links in the reasoning, given the irrelevance of the standard of real and immediate risk to a specific identified individual (as required by the original *Osman* test), is in synchrony with the argument advanced in Section 4.1.3. It was observed therein that what distinguishes the positive obligation of taking protective operational measures, *as triggered* upon 'real and immediate' risk against an identified individual, is that causality can play a less important role. What also distinguishes this obligation is that its content implies concrete protective measures for this specific identified individual, a point to which I will return in Section 7.3.5.

To recap, the analysis of *Ribcheva and Others v Bulgaria* reveals that the Court explicitly modified the obligation of taking protective operational measures. The modification implied disregarding the requirements for 'real and immediate risk' and for an identified victim. This modification was, however, counterbalanced by a stronger reliance in the reasoning on causality. Given its role, the Court can certainly perform such modifications that adjust the original test, yet this does raise questions about the independent role of the obligation as originally introduced in *Osman v the United Kingdom*.

While in *Ribcheva and Others v Bulgaria* the 'real and immediate risk' standard was irrelevant, in *Kurt v Austria* it was explicitly modified. This was a domestic violence case, where the applicant alleged that the Austrian authorities had failed to protect a mother and her children from her violent husband, and that this resulted in him murdering their son. The GC in *Kurt v Austria* held that in the context of domestic violence 'the application of the immediacy standard ... should take into account the specific features of domestic violence cases, and the ways in which they differ from incident-based situations such as that in *Osman*'. Given the 'consecutive cycles of domestic violence' and the tendency of the violence to escalate, the word 'immediate' 'refers to any situations of domestic violence in which harm is imminent *or has already materialised and is likely to happen again*'.[188] This means that the immediacy of the harm is not a requirement for the State to be under the positive obligation of taking protective operational measures. Rather, the likelihood for the harm to happen again suffices in the specific context of domestic violence. The Court clarified that the standard of immediacy needs to be applied

---

[188] *Kurt v Austria* [GC] no 62903/15, 15 June 2021 §175.

in a more flexible manner than in traditional *Osman*-type situations, taking into account the common trajectory of escalation in domestic violence cases, even if the exact time and place of an attack could not be predicted in a given case.[189]

The implications from this modified standard did not became visible when concretely applied to the facts in *Kurt v Austria*. The GC found that 'no lethality risk to the children was discernible at the time', since on the basis of the information available to the authorities at the relevant time, 'it did not appear likely that E. would obtain a firearm, go to his children's school and take his own son's life in such a rapid escalation of events'.[190] This reasoning demonstrates how even though one element of the test might be relaxed (ie the immediacy of the risk), other elements might be used to restrain the finding of breach. These elements were the specific type of the risk (ie lethality risk) and the specific location of the risk (ie the school). Section 7.3.4 will further explain the role of these specifications.

Going back to the modification of the immediacy standard and its impact, two explanations are relevant. First, the modification is limited to cases of domestic violence, which suggests a fragmentation of the *Oman* test depending on the context, thus leading to subtests. The standard of 'real and immediate risk', which as clarified in Section 2.7.1 has been in any case interpreted in a flexible manner, continues to apply more generally.[191] Second, the domestic violence case law following *Kurt v Austria* does not show that this modification in particular has had a huge impact.[192] The reason is that the focus has rather been placed on the obligation upon the authorities to assess the risk rather than on the outcome of any such assessment (ie was the risk actually likely to happen again).[193] The addition of this obligation as part of the *Osman* test will be examined in Section 7.3.3.

---

[189] ibid §76. The same reasoning is applied to Article 3. See *De Giorgi v Italy* no 23735/19, 16 June 2022 §70; *M.S. v Italy* no 32715/19, 7 July 2022 §117.

[190] *Kurt v Austria* [GC] no 62903/15, 15 June 2021 §§207–209.

[191] See the following judgments delivered after *Kurt v Austria* [GC], *Gvozdeva v Russia* no 69997/11, 22 March 2022 (suicide of a conscript); *Khudoroshko v Russia* no 3959/14, 18 January 2022 (suicide of a conscript as a result of hazing practices); *Loste v France* no 59227/12, 3 November 2022 (sexual abuse of a child by her foster father); *Lyubov Vasilyeva v Russia* no 62080/09, 18 January 2022 §61 (failure to protect the life of conscript who committed suicide during military service); *Nana Muradyan v Romania* no 69517/11, 5 April 2022 (suicide of a conscript); *Oganezova v Armenia* no 71367/12, (failure to protect an LGBT bar owner from attacks); *Safi and Others v Greece* no 5418/15, 7 July 2022 (sinking of a boat carrying migrants); *Tagiyeva v Azerbaijan* no 72611/14, 7 July 2022 (stabbing of a well-known writer); *Derenik Mkrtchyan and Gayane Mkrtchyan v Armenia* no 69736/12, 30 November 2021 (death of a child at school after being beaten by schoolmates); *Ražnatović v Montenegro* no 14742/18, 2 September 2021 (suicide of a patient at psychiatric hospital); *Women's Initiatives Supporting Group and Others v Georgia* no 73204/13, 16 December 2021 (homophobic attacks during an LGBT rally).

[192] See *Landi v Italy* no 10929/19, 7 April 2022 (see §78 where the Chamber summarized *Kurt v Austria* [GC]); *M.S. v Italy* no 32715/19, 7 July 2022; *A. and B. v Georgia* no 73975/16, 10 February 2022; *Y and Others v Bulgaria* no 9077/18, 22 March 2022; *De Giorgi v Italy* no 23735/19, 16 June 2022. See, however, *Tkhelidze v Georgia* no 33056/07, 8 July 2021 §53: 'Where there is a lasting situation of domestic violence, there can hardly be any doubt about the immediacy of the danger posed to the victim.'

[193] In addition to risk assessment, a measure whose relationship with the *Osman* test is not clear (see Section 7.3.3), the GC in *Kurt v Austria* §165, framed 'the requirement to respond immediately to allegations of domestic violence'. This requirement has nothing to do with the assessment of any risk as such. Neither is it related to the *Osman* test. It is rather an introduction of a separate specific positive

## 7.3.3 Adjustment of the Test by Adding Risk Assessment as an 'Integral Part'

Despite the above-described modifications of the test, actual or putative knowledge about a risk is crucial so that the obligation of taking protective operational measures is triggered. Although, as explained in Chapter 2, the standard of 'real and immediate' has remained ambiguous, the demonstration that the State had actual *or* putative knowledge of risk is key. Chapter 2 also suggested that the assessment of putative knowledge (ie the State 'ought to have known') raises the question whether state passivity in assessing risks should suffice for assuming putative knowledge for the purpose of triggering the *Osman* obligation.[194] As a response to possible negative consequences from state passivity, risk assessment has been introduced as 'an integral part of the duty to take preventive operational measures'.[195] As this section will show, however, how and in what way risk assessment is 'an integral part' has remained unclear. Therefore, the above question cannot be clearly answered.

The innovation of adding risk assessment to the *Osman* test, was introduced with *Kurt v Austria*:

> [T]he assessment of the nature and level of risk constitutes an integral part of the duty to take preventive operational measures where the presence of a risk so requires. Thus, an examination of the State's compliance with this duty under Article 2 must comprise an analysis of both the adequacy of the assessment of risk conducted by the domestic authorities and, where a relevant risk triggered the duty to act was or ought to have been identified, the adequacy of the preventive measures taken.[196]

This quotation can be understood to the effect that a procedural positive obligation has been added to assess risks,[197] as part of the *Osman* test. In contrast to the modification of the 'immediacy' standard, this addition has general relevance, since it does not seem restricted to the domestic violence context.[198] The quoted paragraph, however, does not help in clarifying the relationship between this procedural positive obligation and the substantive positive obligation of taking protective operational

---

obligation—any allegation of domestic violence demands an immediate response. This demand is imposed without any requirement that these authorities initially assess whether there is 'real and immediate risk'.

[194] See also Partly Dissenting Opinion of Judge Spano in *Talpis v Italy* no 41237/14, 2 March 2017 §7.
[195] *Kurt v Austria* [GC] no 62903/15, 15 June 2021 §159.
[196] ibid.
[197] This will be very similar to how the Court has developed different procedural guarantees as part of the assessment of breach. See Section 7.2.
[198] Risk assessment is framed in §159 of *Kurt v Austria* [GC] no 62903/15, 15 June 2021 as being applicable in all contexts, not limited to domestic violence. §159 is in the part of the judgment entitled 'General principles'. See also *Derenik Mkrtchyan and Gayane Mkrtchyan v Armenia* no 69736/12, 30 November 2021 §50 that concerned the death of a child at school after being beaten by schoolmates.

measures. It suggests that the first is 'an integral part' of the second, which implies that risk assessment is *not* a separate obligation.[199] It is unclear, though, how the nature and level of risk can be assessed, if there is no obligation to assess risk in the first place. In addition, a conclusion that risk assessment is not a separate obligation is not supported by paragraph 168 of *Kurt v Austria*, where the GC specified the obligation as an obligation to conduct 'lethality risk assessment' and added that

> in order to be in a position to know whether there is a real and immediate risk to the life of a victim of domestic violence, the authorities are under a duty to carry out a lethality risk assessment which is autonomous, proactive and comprehensive.[200]

This quotation seems to speak in favour of an independent obligation.[201] When applied to the concrete facts, however, it is part of the *Osman* test. In particular, it was part of the assessment whether the authorities knew or ought to have known that there was a real and immediate risk to the life of the applicant's son. More specifically, the GC observed in paragraph 205 that

> [w]hile it is true that *no separate risk assessment* was explicitly carried out in relation to the children, the Court considers that on the basis of the information available at the relevant time *this would not have changed the situation*....[202]

This reasoning means that since there was no separate positive obligation to conduct a risk assessment regarding threats to the life of the children, the question of breach did not need to be engaged with. It also means that even if a risk assessment in relation to the children had been carried out, 'this would not have changed the situation'. In other words, even if the authorities had conducted a separate risk assessment, the result would have been the conclusion that the children were *not* at risk. The Court clarified that

> [t]he authorities could legitimately assume that the children were protected in the domestic sphere from potential non-lethal forms of violence and harassment by their father to the same extent as the applicant, through the barring and protection

---

[199] Framing risk assessment as 'part of the duty' might be illogical. How could 'part' of the duty be risk assessment, when *the duty itself is triggered* upon knowledge about risk? How could the State already have a duty (whose content is arguably the assessment of the risk), when it is not yet clear whether the State was under the obligation to take protective operational measures?

[200] *Kurt v Austria* [GC] no 62903/15, 15 June 2021 §168.

[201] See also the post-*Kurt v Austria* [GC] judgments of *Landi v Italy* no 10929/19, 7 April 2022 §78; *M.S. v Italy* no 32715/19, 7 July 2022 §116; *A. and B. v Georgia* no 73975/16, 10 February 2022 §42; *Y and Others v Bulgaria* no 9077/18, 22 March 2022 §89; *De Giorgi v Italy* no 23735/19, 16 June 2022 §69, where the Court in the part of the judgments entitled 'General principles' formulated risk assessment as an independent obligation. See, however, *Tkhelidze v Georgia* no 33056/07, 8 July 2021, where risk assessment was not included in the part about the general principles.

[202] *Kurt v Austria* [GC] no 62903/15, 15 June 2021 §205 (emphasis added).

order. There were no indications of a risk to the children at their school let alone a lethality risk.[203]

Indeed, given the facts of the case, it seems correct that there were no indications that could make the national authorities aware that the children might be exposed to a lethal risk. However, this refers to the result of the risk assessment, not to the question of whether the national authorities conducted a risk assessment in relation to the children. It was clear that they did not.[204] Any separate obligation to undertake a risk assessment was watered down by making the result a relevant consideration. The overall reasoning thus includes ambiguities as to the nature and content of the obligation and its relationship with the obligation of taking protective operational measures. The post-*Kurt v Austria* case law has not been helpful in resolving this ambiguity.[205]

In sum, the precise role of risk assessment as 'an integral part of the duty to take preventive operational measures' remains to be clarified.[206] The requirement for risk assessment appears to be a useful procedural tool to relieve the Court of making the substantive determination as to whether the State really knew or ought to have known about the risk. At the same time, finding a breach merely on this procedural ground appears too formalistic, which explains why the Court still considers the outcomes (ie was there actual or putative knowledge about risk). The *Osman* test indeed demands consideration and a conclusion as to whether the authorities had actual or putative knowledge. It would be therefore problematic if mere state passivity in assessing risks would suffice for establishing putative knowledge, without any consideration of the outcomes.

---

[203] ibid §206.
[204] See Joint Dissenting Opinion in *Kurt v Austria* [GC] §8–12.
[205] An approach similar to *Kurt v Austria* [GC] was applied in *Landi v Italy* no 10929/19, 7 April 2022 §§90–91, since when the obligation of conducting risk assessment was applied to the facts, it was made dependent on the result. In *Landi v Italy*, the result was the conclusion that there was actually a risk and therefore, among other failures, the authorities were found to have failed to carry out a risk assessment. See also *M.S. v Italy* no 32715/19, 7 July 2022 §125 and *De Giorgi v Italy* no 23735/19, 16 June 2022 §78. The reasoning in *X. and Others v Bulgaria* no 9077/18, 22 March 2022 §§98–105 seems to be different since the Court focused on the *efforts* by the authorities to perform risk assessment and only when it moved to review breach of the *Osman* test, it noted that '[h]ad the authorities carried out a proper risk assessment, in particular on 17 August 2017, it is likely that they would have appreciated—based on the information available to them at that time—that Mr V., ... could pose a real and immediate risk to her life, as those notions are to be understood in the context of domestic violence'. See also *Tunikova and Others v Russia* no 55974/16, 14 December 2021 §108 that suggests that breach of the obligation to conduct risk assessment, is not dependent on the result (ie the conclusion whether there was risk or not): 'It is immaterial that there was no recurrence of violence in Ms Tunikova's case, as in order to determine whether this obligation has been fulfilled, the authorities must be able to shown that they have undertaken a proactive and autonomous risk assessment....' See, however, *Tkhelidze v Georgia* no 33056/07, 8 July 2021 §54, where risk assessment was clearly not formulated as a separate obligation. Risk assessment was rather mentioned as a measure that the authorities should have taken to fulfil their obligation to take protective operational measures (ie the *Osman* test).
[206] In *Malagić v Croatia* no 29417/17, 17 November 2022 §65, there is a reference to 'risk assessment at regular intervals'. How such *regular* risk assessment relates to the *Osman* obligation, is another issue begging clarifications.

## 7.3.4 Adjustment of the Test by Adding Harm-related, Temporal, and Geographical Specifications

So far, I have explained how the elements of the *Osman* test pertaining to the actor of harm, the object of harm, the type of risk, and the knowledge about the risk, have been modified and adjusted. The focus in this section will be on choices for further adjustments by specifying the nature of the harm, the time frame within which the harm might materialize, and the location where it might materialize. In its reasoning, the Court can choose whether to apply such specifications, which affects the finding of a breach of the positive obligations. These specifications can be related to the assertion in the case law that the authorities are under the obligation to take preventive operational measures 'in certain well-defined circumstances'.[207] The specifications help in the definition of the circumstances.

To start with, in *Osman v the United Kingdom* the Court specified the risk as a lethality risk. It assessed the risk with reference to concrete dates so that it could conclude whether there was 'any decisive stage in the sequence of the events leading up to the tragic shooting when it could be said that the police knew or ought to have known that the lives of the Osman family were at real and immediate risk from Paget-Lewis'.[208] Similar harm-related specifications were used in *Kurt v Austria*:

> [T]he Court agrees with the Government that, on the basis of what was known to the authorities at the material time, there were no indications of a real and immediate risk of further violence against the applicant's son *outside the area* for which a barring order had been issued, let alone *a lethality risk*.[209]

These words suggest a harm-related specification, since the risk was not framed more generally as risk of harm but as lethality risk. A geographical specification of the risk was also used in the formulation of the obligation, since it was noted that '[t]here were no indications of a risk to the children *at their school*'.[210] The reference to certain areas and to 'private or public spaces' also suggests a geographical framing of the risk.[211]

It follows that the risk could be circumscribed to specific locations (geographical specification and delimitation of the risk), and/or to specific timing (temporal specification and delimitation of the risk), and/or as being of specific kind/severity/ category (category specification and delimitation).[212] The utilization of such specifications in the formulation of the obligation is analytically necessary so that the Court can apply the positive obligation to the specific facts. The important point here is that

---

[207] *Osman v the United Kingdom* [GC] no 23452/94, 28 October 1998 §115. The expression 'in appropriate circumstances' has been also used *Tërshana v Albania* no 48756/14, 4 August 2020 §147.
[208] *Osman v the United Kingdom* [GC] no 23452/94, 28 October 1998 §121.
[209] *Kurt v Austria* [GC] §209 (emphasis added).
[210] ibid §206 (emphasis added).
[211] ibid §209.
[212] The category specification is related to the ECHR provision invoked.

when the Court applies the *Osman* test, it can choose which specifications to use when it articulates the obligation and, accordingly, which aspects to highlight. In *Kurt v Austria*, for example, the obligation was articulated narrowly with reference to the above-mentioned geographical and harm-related specifications, which made it easier to conclude that there was no breach. In *Fernandes de Oliveira v Portugal*, a temporal specification played a crucial role, since it could not be established that the authorities knew or ought to have known that 'there was an immediate risk to A.J.'s life *in the days preceding* 27 April 2000'.[213] Such specifications depend on the facts in each case. Importantly, which time frames or locations to foreground is a matter of choice, which also reveals the flexibility that the Court has in the framing of the content and the scope of the obligation.

## 7.3.5 Content and Scope of the Obligation—the Operational Measures

The focus in this section is on the content and scope of the obligation: the protective measures that ought to be forthcoming, given the adjustments and the specifications discussed in the previous sections. As observed in *Osman v the United Kingdom* and consistently repeated thereafter, the measures have to be within the scope of the authorities powers, reasonable, and expected to avoid the risk.[214] These requirements refer to the standards of reasonableness and causation that were extensively addressed in Chapters 3, 4, and 5. In this section, it needs additionally to be highlighted how the measures that form the content and the scope of the positive obligation are *individually targeted operational* measures. This distinguishes them from the content and the scope of the positive obligation addressed in Section 7.1. The latter also requires actions by the State that need to be causally linked to the prevention of the specific harm to the specific individual and, as clarified in Section 7.1.3.3, the starting point is that the Court does not review regulatory frameworks in abstract. Yet general measures form the content and the scope of the positive obligation of adopting an effective regulatory framework.[215]

The *Osman* obligation, as a separate and specific obligation triggered under certain conditions, also needs to have a specific and distinguishable content.[216] It is distinguishable in that *individually targeted operational* measures form its content.[217] They

---

[213] *Fernandes de Oliveira v Portugal* [GC] no 78103/14, 31 January 2019 §131 (emphasis added). See also *Tagiyeva v Azerbaijan* no 72611/14, 7 July 2022 §63.
[214] *Osman v the United Kingdom* [GC] no 23452/94, 28 October 1998 §116.
[215] See Dissenting Opinion of Judge Wojtyczek in *Smiljanić v Croatia* no 35983/14, 25 March 2021.
[216] Despite all the modifications and adjustments discussed in Section 7.3, at the beginning of Section 7.3.2 it was also noted how the Court in principle continues to conceptually separate the positive obligation of taking protective operational measures from the positive obligation of adopting effective regulatory framework. This implies that there needs to be a justificatory basis for this separation.
[217] This distinction came to the fore, for example, in *Loste v France* no 59227/12, 3 November 2022 §§96–104. Breach was found due to the failure of the State to implement the national legislation regarding the protection of children placed with foster families. This was therefore a breach of the positive obligation of

are targeted since the *Osman* obligation entails preventive restrictions on individually identified persons (ie the actors and the objects of harm).[218] The intrusiveness of these restrictions can be easier to consider as reasonable since it is an identified person at real and immediate risk that needs to be protected, not the public more generally. Imposition of individually targeted preventing restrictions (some of which might compete with negative obligations)[219] might be more difficult to consider as reasonable, when the risk is diluted, and it is risk to the public at large.[220]

Given the immediacy of the risk, the measures that form the content of the obligation can also be expected to be of an immediate character, which relates to their operational nature. Here, a distinction needs to be made between the immediacy of the risk and the immediacy of the preventive measures.[221] The first triggers the obligation. The latter forms the content of the obligation, yet given the immediacy of the risk, measures that are capable of immediate protection can be expected to form the content of the obligation. Breach of the obligation should be therefore limited to situations where the authorities had (or should have had) at their disposal measures with immediate effects that meet the above-mentioned standards of legality and reasonableness.[222] Such measures might be unavailable due to some general deficiencies in the regulatory framework,[223] which might also justify review of these deficiencies from the perspective of the positive obligation addressed in Section 7.1. This shows that the two positive obligations can be related. They are both also similarly subjected to the standard of reasonableness.

---

adopting effective regulatory framework (see Section 7.1). France, however, tried to invoke the *Osman* test by arguing that it did not know and could not know about the abuses the applicant was subjected to by her foster father. The Court said that France could not rely on the absence of knowledge since 'there was a manifest deficiency in the regular monitoring of the application *as provided for by the legal provision then in force*' (emphasis added). This shows that the *Osman* obligation was not the relevant one.

[218] In cases of suicides, the actor and object of harm coincide.
[219] See Chapter 5 on competing obligations.
[220] Notably, when the risk to the public is very high and there is a risk that many people may be harmed, preventive restrictions might be also considered reasonable. See *Kotilainen and Others v Finland* no 62439/12, 17 September 2020 §§84–90 that concerned school shooting. Yet, the Court found no violation of the obligation of taking protective operational measures in this case. It rather argued that 'the domestic authorities have not observed the special duty of diligence incumbent on them because of the particularly high level of risk inherent in any misconduct involving the use of firearms'. It follows then that in *Kotilainen and Others v Finland*, the Court framed a new positive obligation that does not fit within those addressed in Sections 7.1 and 7.2. See Partly Dissenting Opinion of Judge Eicke in *Kotilainen and Others v Finland*.
[221] In its post-*Kurt v Austria* [GC] case law, the Court makes a separate assessment whether the authorities have 'respond[ed] immediately to allegation of domestic violence'. See *Y and Others v Bulgaria* App no 9077/18, 22 March 2022 §89; *De Giorgi v Italy* no 23735/19, 16 June 2022 §69; *Landi v Italy* no 10929/19, 7 April 2022 §78; *M.S. v Italy* no 32715/19 §116. See Separate Opinion of Judge Sabato in *Landi v Italy*, where he appeals for a distinction between the verification on the one hand, of the immediacy of the risk, and on the other hand, of the immediacy of the authorities' reaction.
[222] See Dissenting Opinion of Judge Spano in *Talpis v Italy* no 41237/14, 2 March 2017: 'It is unclear what Convention-compliant measures the police could have taken on the night in question on avoid the ultimate tragic outcome.... the majority fails both to specify the minutiae as well as to explain the feasibility of maintaining adherence to due process and Convention guarantees in the deployment of such measures.'
[223] For example, *Tunikova and Others v Russia* no 55974/16, 14 December 2021 §§108–110, where the national legislation did not allow the possibility for issuing protection orders for victims of domestic violence.

# Conclusion

Similarly to the last section in Chapter 6, the concluding section in this chapter also aims to summarize the analysis by reflecting upon the role of reasonableness in the trigger and in the delineation of the content and the scope of the substantive positive obligations. Since, as already clarified in Chapters 2, 3, 4, and 5, reasonableness is related to the standards of knowledge and causation, the role of these two standards will also be explained.

A connecting thread emerging from Chapter 7 is that the role of these standards is related to the level of specificity used to frame the positive obligation. The obligation upon the State to 'take appropriate steps to safeguard the lives of those within its jurisdiction'[224] and 'to take measures designed to ensure that individuals within their jurisdiction are not subjected to torture or inhuman or degrading treatment',[225] is framed at a very high level of abstraction.[226] It tells us nothing about the concrete measures that this obligation might entail, and the standards of causation, knowledge, and reasonableness have no role since the question of breach is not addressed at this high level of abstraction. In its case law, the Court has specified this abstract obligation by developing three positive obligations: the procedural positive obligation upon States to investigate, addressed in Chapter 6; the substantive positive obligation to develop effective regulatory frameworks with effective procedures, addressed in Sections 7.1 and 7.2; and the substantive positive obligation to take protective operational measures (ie the *Osman* obligation), addressed in Section 7.3. The last two were examined in this chapter, therefore the forthcoming analysis concentrates on them. Since, as explained in Section 7.2, it is difficult to separate the development of effective national procedures from the obligation of developing effective regulatory frameworks, the focus will be on the latter.

To start with, the *Osman* obligation is more specific than the obligation to develop effective regulatory frameworks. As Section 7.3 clarified, the *Osman* obligation is characterized by certain initial qualifications and specifications pertaining to the risk (ie 'real and immediate') and the object of protection (ie an identified victim). True, inconsistencies can be identified in the case law as to the application and the delimitation of these specifications, yet the Court continues to insist on the distinctive nature of this obligation as one about 'personal protection'. It is triggered only upon a certain specific threshold (actual or putative knowledge about certain type of risk). Given that the operational measures are targeted to protect a specific individual who is an object of a 'real and immediate risk', the causation between the measures and the prevention of this specific harm might be easier to discern and, accordingly, the measures might

---

[224] *Nicolae Virgiliu Tănase v Romania* [GC] no 41720/13, 25 June 2019 §134 (further relevant reference in the same paragraph).
[225] *O'Keeffe v Ireland* [GC] no 35810/09, 28 January 2014 §144.
[226] For the specifics of Article 8, see Sections 1.5 and 4.2.

be easier to consider as reasonable. This can be contrasted with situations where protection needs to be ensured for unidentifiable members of the public.

As Section 7.1 explained, in these situations, the pertinent obligation is the positive obligation to develop effective regulatory frameworks that aim at general prevention. The applicant might be a representative victim of certain deficiencies in these frameworks. In contrast to the *Osman* obligation, no threshold regarding knowledge by the State of a specific risk (ie immediate risk) to a specific individual is necessary to trigger the obligation. To determine breach, however, any deficiencies must be causally linked to the harm claimed by the applicant, as explained in Chapter 3. In addition, to determine breach and to identify any lines of causation, the obligation needs also to be further specified. Section 7.1.3 clarified the levels of specificities that could be identified in the Court's reasoning. It emphasized that the final level (that I framed as level three) is the crucial one, since at this level the question of breach needs to be determined. To move to this level of specificity so that the question of breach is decided, the content and the scope of the obligation (ie the specific measures) that the State should have arguably undertaken need to be made concrete. As explained in Section 4.2, this requires articulations of alternative *concrete* formulations of the legal framework and an assessment of these alternatives. These concrete articulations might be hard to square with the starting position, as consistently confirmed in the case law, that States have discretion as to how to fulfil their positive obligations and, accordingly, how to frame their national regulatory frameworks. To mediate this tension, the Court qualifies the more concrete formulations of alternatives with the standard of reasonableness.[227] This qualification increases the level of abstractness in the reasoning and implies that there is no one single correct solution. This in turn helps in preserving the discretion of States.

It was also added in Section 7.1.3.1 that the invocation of reasonableness as a standard in the framing of the concrete obligation masks certain values that stand behind the judgment. The role of normative considerations and value-related assumptions was similarly highlighted in the previous chapters, where these assumptions were also linked with the communitarian nature of human rights law. Their importance can be made even more lucid by engaging with the application of positive obligations in extraterritorial circumstances, where the communitarian structures are disrupted.

---

[227] Besides 'reasonable', the Court refers to other malleable terms like 'sufficient', 'adequate', or 'effective' to characterize the measures that form the content of the positive obligation. For example, *Kurt v Austria* [GC] no 62903/15, 15 June 2021 §209; *Öneryildiz v Turkey* [GC] no 48939/99, 30 November 2004 §108; *Söderman v Sweden* [GC] no 5786/08, 12 November 2013 §117; *Ribcheva and Others v Bulgaria* no 37801/16, 30 March 2021 §180.

# 8
# Extraterritorial Positive Obligations

## Introduction

This chapter addresses the challenging analytical issues triggered if positive obligations under the ECHR should apply in extraterritorial circumstances. These issues arise if States bear obligations in relation to individuals located beyond their territorial limits.[1] A distinctive feature of the analysis is that it reverses the methodological order that is usually applied to this question. Specifically, I first engage with the substance of positive obligations to show the profoundness and embeddedness of the communitarian limitations of human rights law. Only thereafter do I demonstrate how these limitations emerge in the jurisdictional threshold under Article 1 of the European Convention on Human Rights (ECHR). The existing literature tends to address jurisdiction as a separate and preliminary issue, which is indeed understandable since it is an initial threshold question.[2] This threshold is meant to answer the question of whether a State can be assigned obligations in the first place. This is a question that precedes any analysis on the merits, namely whether positive obligations can be triggered and what is their scope and content, if triggered.

Yet my reverse path illuminates the interconnectedness between the analysis on the merits and the jurisdictional threshold. The threshold cannot be understood without first understanding the principles that underpin the reasoning on the merits regarding the content and scope of human rights obligations.[3] I argue that any conceptualization

---

[1] I am not concerned here with the type of positive obligations invoked by the Court in *Ilascu and Catan and Others v Moldova and Russia* [GC] no 43370/04, 19 October 2012 §110. These are independent positive obligations invoked in respect to the ECHR as a whole, not positive obligations invoked in relation to a specific right. M Milanovic and T Papic, 'The Applicability of the ECHR in Contested Territories' (2018) 67 International and Comparative Law Quarterly 779, 788.

[2] For jurisdiction as a 'threshold criterion', see *Al-Jedda v the United Kingdom* [GC] no 27021/08, 7 July 2011 §74; *H.F. and Others v France* [GC] no 24384/19, 14 September 2022 §184; *Al-Skeini and Others v the United Kingdom* [GC] no 55721/07, 7 July 2011 §130; *Nada v Switzerland* [GC] no 10593/08, 12 September 2012 §118; *Catan and Others v the Republic of Moldova and Russia* [GC] no 43370/04, 19 October 2012 §103; *N.D. and N.T. v Spain* [GC] no 8675/15, 13 February 2020 §102: 'The exercise of "jurisdiction" *is a necessary condition* for a Contracting State to be able to be held responsible for acts or omissions imputable to it which give rise to an allegation of the infringement of rights and freedoms set forth in the Convention.' In *M.N. and Others v Belgium* (dec) no 3599/18, 5 May 2020 §97, jurisdiction was referred to as a condition *sine qua non* for a State to be held responsible.

[3] For this reason my approach differs from Raible's. In L Raible, *Human Rights Unbound. A Theory of Extraterritoriality* (Oxford University Press 2020) 81, Raible maintains that an account of jurisdiction to be considered successful should meet the following criteria: 'it should tie the relationship to the part of the theory of human rights that concerns the justification of the allocation of obligations to a specific duty bearer *rather than, say, the process of specification of the content of the obligations*' (emphasis added). See also A Vandenbogaerde, *Towards Shared Accountability in International Human Rights Law* (Intersentia 2016) 239, where it is also argued that factors for determining responsibility (ie whether the State has failed to

and evaluation of the requirement of jurisdiction has to be preceded by a profound understanding of the communitarian nature of positive obligations in human rights law, and the related conceptual issues that they raise on the merits. In this way, this chapter offers the first examination of the conceptual difficulties that arise if positive obligations are to be applied extraterritorially. In addition, my particular focus on positive obligations sheds lights more generally on problems related to extraterritoriality that have been overlooked.

There have been discussions about the interconnectedness between the jurisdictional threshold and any obligations that the State of extraterritorial jurisdiction might have. These discussions have tended to favour relaxation of the jurisdictional requirement under Article 1 ECHR as a threshold, so that any obligations can be easily assigned, with subsequent resolution of any difficult analytical issues on the merits (ie when determining the triggering, the scope, and the content of the obligations).[4] This resolution implies tailoring the scope and content of the obligations to extraterritorial settings.

In contrast, I aim to demonstrate that there are certain preconditions that enable the analysis on the merits, and the jurisdictional threshold under Article 1 ECHR is meant to ensure these preconditions. The clarification of the principles that underpin the analysis of positive obligations in domestic/territorial settings helps in understanding these preconditions and offers the foundations for exploring the conceptual challenges that might arise in extraterritorial settings.

The main argument that emerges is that the analysis on the merits—which aims to answer the question whether the State is to be found responsible for omissions that have arguably led to harm—cannot be performed without reference to a political community and its interests. This analysis therefore presupposes decision-making within a specific political community, where political institutions claim authority over individuals and where this authority is imbued with legitimacy. The analysis accordingly presupposes a normative relationship between the State and the individual. The normativity comes from this relationship of political authority within the political community.

After outlining these communitarian presuppositions that underpin the reasoning regarding positive obligations, I show that these presuppositions justify the jurisdictional threshold in human rights law. It then follows that the threshold, if it is to serve a purpose, is meant to reflect the political and legal relationship between the State and the affected individuals. It also follows that this threshold cannot be explained without reference to this political and legal relationship. Jurisdiction as a threshold is then of fundamental importance for human rights law in that it unites individuals,

---

fulfil its positive obligations) should *not* be used for determining whether the State should be assigned obligations (ie whether it has jurisdiction in human rights law).

[4] M Milanovic, *Extraterritorial Application of Human Rights Treaties* (Oxford University Press 2011) 103; C Ryngaert, 'Extraterritorial Obligations under Human Rights Law' in M Lattimer and P Sands (eds), *The Grey Zone: Civilian Protection Between Human Rights and the Laws of War* (Hart Publishing 2018) 273.

## Introduction 221

as holders of human rights, and the State, as a bearer of obligations corresponding to these rights.[5] Jurisdiction reflects this important relational nature.

It should be clear from the beginning that I do not aim to put forward any proposals as to how jurisdiction in human rights law should be generally interpreted. Nor do I aim to pick out elements from different European Court of Human Rights (ECtHR) judgments in order to argue which ones should or should not matter; this has been done by others.[6] Nor yet do I aim to propose how the ECtHR case law on the issue could be made more predictable and more consistent. It is clear that the reasoning of the Court in this area is often ambiguous and sometimes even straight-out contradictory.[7] I rather want to explain the inherent challenges that arise if positive obligations are applied extraterritorially. These challenges relate to the innate characteristics of human rights law as a body of law meant to regulate the relationship between individuals organized in a political community. Since the focus is on the challenges, the forthcoming analysis provides a justification for the jurisdictional threshold in human rights law, and for the difficulties faced by the Court in achieving consistency. It explains why it is necessary to initially ask the question of whether a particular state should hold obligations corresponding to rights invoked by certain individuals.

Despite the extensive literature on the extraterritorial application of the ECHR, the scholarly engagement with the justifications underpinning the jurisdictional threshold and with their manifestations in the context of positive obligations has been very limited. An important exception in this respect is Besson, who has argued that jurisdiction in the sense of Article 1 ECHR is a normative threshold. She has explained that the implication from the jurisdictional clause in Article 1 ECHR is that it 'conditions the applicability of those rights and duties on political and legal circumstances where a certain relationship exists between rights-holder and state parties'.[8] Besson asserts that 'given those ties between human rights and political authority through jurisdiction, it should come as no surprise that the ECtHR takes political concerns seriously when deciding cases of extraterritorial application of the Convention'. She

---

[5] This understanding is contrary to the position that 'jurisdiction' in human rights law is an empty concept. See M Scheinin, 'Just Another Word? Jurisdiction in the Roadmaps of State Responsibility and Human Rights' in M Langford and others (eds), *Global Justice, State Duties: The Extraterritorial Scope of Economic, Social and Cultural Rights in International Law* (Cambridge University Press 2013) 212.

[6] T Altwicker, 'Transnationlizing Rights: International Human Rights Law in Cross-Border Contexts' (2018) 29(2) European Journal of International Law 581, 590 (proposal that the jurisdictional test should be based on 'control of (harmful) circumstances'); V Tzevelekos, 'Reconstructing the Effective Control Criterion in Extraterritorial Human Rights Breaches: Direct Attribution of Wrongfulness, Due Diligence, and Concurrent Responsibility' (2014) 36 Michigan Journal of International Law 129; V Moreno-Lax, 'The Architecture of Functional Jurisdiction: Unpacking Contactless Control On Public Powers, S.S. and Others v Italy and the "Operational Model"' (2020) 21 German Law Journal 385.

[7] Lord Rodger, *Al Skeini* [2007] UKHL 26 §67: 'the judgments and decisions of the European Court do not speak with one voice'; Concurring opinion of Judge Bonello in *Al Skeini and Others v the United Kingdom*: 'patch-work case-law at best'.

[8] S Besson, 'The Extraterritoriality of the European Convention on Human Rights: Why Human Rights Depend on Jurisdiction and What Jurisdiction Amounts to' (2012) 25 Leiden Journal of International Law 857, 860.

describes this as a normative threshold ('normative relationship that *unites* state parties to their subjects').[9]

Besson adds that jurisdiction is also a practical threshold, since it provides the conditions for the corresponding duties to be feasible.[10] Concerns about the practicality and feasibility of imposing obligations cannot be therefore disregarded. An exclusive focus on these concerns and on facticist elements that imply limiting the jurisdictional analysis to whether a state act or omission factually caused any harm to individuals wherever located, is, however, inconclusive. It ignores the normative aspects of the jurisdictional threshold that Besson links to membership in a democratic political community that has an egalitarian basis (ie equal moral status of individuals). In contrast to Besson, whose analysis is quite abstract, I explain more concretely which normative considerations are at play and demonstrate in concrete terms how these considerations play out specifically in the context of positive obligations. This is necessary since it is not entirely helpful to refer to 'the normative dimension' of jurisdiction, as Besson does, without elaborating how this normative dimension manifests itself more concretely. The site of manifestation chosen is positive obligations, which also adds distinctiveness to the analysis performed in this chapter.

To achieve the chapter's objectives, the following path will be followed. Section 8.1 explains the normative presuppositions that need to be present so that it can be determined whether a State is to be found responsible under ECHR for failure to fulfil positive obligations. To do this, I draw on the previous chapters of this book to show the interrelated preconditions that need to be present so that the analysis on the merits, which aims to address the triggering, the scope, and the content of positive obligations, can be performed. In brief, these preconditions are three: a bounded political order where decisions as to the role of the State can be taken, interdependencies of stakes and interests within the bounded political community, and a democratically constituted sovereign. I also highlight how in the light of these normative preconditions, responsibility for failure to fulfil positive obligations is not exclusively assessed against the standard of actual capacity and practical feasibility. This does raise serious doubts as the appropriateness of an exclusive facticist approach to jurisdiction under Article 1 ECHR. Section 8.2 then shows whether and how these normative preconditions are reflected in the meaning of jurisdiction as developed by the Court. Section 8.3 explains the implications from an approach where the meaning of jurisdiction is adapted and made relative depending on the rights and obligations invoked on the merits. Finally, Section 8.4 engages with the question of what conceptual challenges emerge if a State owes positive obligations to persons located beyond its borders, given the absence of the preconditions explained in Section 8.1.

---

[9] ibid 863
[10] ibid 863.

## 8.1 Positive Obligations' Normative Preconditions

The previous chapters of this book, through an examination of the standards of knowledge, causation, and reasonableness, enable us to understand the normative presuppositions that underpin positive obligations. The first of these is that these obligations are contingent on normative positions about the role of the State in the specific society (Section 8.1.1). Second, these obligations presuppose democratic legitimacy of the decisions taken within the bounded society (Section 8.1.2). Bounded political and legal order, interdependent stakes of the individuals belonging to this order, and balancing of interests that are institutionally channelled through a democratically constituted sovereign, are important because they build the set of preconditions that permit and enable the analysis on the merits. Finally, it needs to be underscored that in the light of the two preconditions mentioned above, the triggering, content, and scope of positive obligations is far from exclusively determined by mere actual capacity to fulfil them (Section 8.1.3). It then follows that the assessment of breach is not limited to the requirement for feasibility.[11]

These three normative preconditions, which will be explained in detail below, equip the Court with the conceptual tools for performing the analysis on the merits. These tools serve to determine the triggering, the scope, and the content of positive obligations. The assessment of knowledge, reasonableness, and causation is done in the light of these normative preconditions. If jurisdiction in the sense of Article 1 ECHR is indeed a threshold meant to have a meaning (a starting assumption that I endorse), then it can be expected that its purpose is to ensure this set of preconditions that enable the analysis on the merits. For this reason, Section 8.4 will offer an understanding as to what these preconditions imply if positive obligations should be applied extraterritorially.

---

[11] In the existing literature in the field of extraterritorial application of the ECHR, there seems to be an assumption that it is only actual capacity that determines the imposition, the content, and the scope of positive obligations. This assumption is connected with the understanding that the jurisdictional threshold is also only about actual capacity and control. See Milanovic, *Extraterritorial Application of Human Rights Treaties* (n 4) 119 'jurisdiction is conceived of only territorially, but where that threshold criterion applies only to the positive obligation of States to secure or ensure human rights, because it is only when States possess a sufficient degree of control over territory that these obligations can be realistically kept'. See also R Lawson, 'Life After Bankovic: On the Extraterritorial Application of the European Convention on Human Rights' in F Coomans and M Kamminga (eds), *Extraterritorial Application of Human Rights Treaties* (Intersentia 2004) 83, 84, who has proposed a 'gradual approach to the notion of jurisdiction': 'the extent to which Contracting parties must secure the rights and freedoms of individuals outside their borders is commensurate with their ability to do so—that is: the scope of their obligations depend on the degree of control and authority that they exercise'. See also Tzevelekos, 'Reconstructing the Effective Control Criterion in Extraterritorial Human Rights Breaches' (n 6) 163 ('Effectiveness, therefore, is crucial to due diligence; it inherently operates as an element that allows the assessment of state fault and the expected standard of diligence.').

## 8.1.1 The Role of the State in Society

The analysis in Chapters 2 to 7 demonstrates that human rights law is far from rigid in the assessment of the linkage between omissions and harm. This flexibility is understandable in the light of the objective of human rights law, namely assessing the responsibility of a collective (the State) that is meant to be instrumental since it does not act for its own sake but for the sake of pursing some general goals of the particular community. As a member of this community and part of the decision-making processes therein, it is easy to understand why this particular State, which represents the particular community, can be identified as the relevant bearer of obligations vis-à-vis its members. It is this State that has to respond to human rights law claims and shoulder positive obligations.

The analysis also reveals that the review of breach of positive obligations is shaped by normative considerations concerning the role of the State in the particular political community and how intrusive or restrained this role should be. The relational nature of human rights law also becomes clear and with it the difficult task of the State to balance different interests within the community. This balancing can be pulled in different directions by practical concerns and considerations about effective protection of individual interests. Questions about allocation of burdens, costs, resources, and benefits within the society matter. Where resources are an issue, choices about the balancing between collective and individual interests need to be made. Positive obligations thus reveal the relational aspects of rights, and the interdependency of the interests of different individuals within society. In some circumstances, some individuals have to bear a burden for the benefit of others, in others the former might be the beneficiaries while the latter might have to accept more disadvantageous positions.

The question about the role of the State in the particular society is thus pivotal. It also follows that positive obligations are about the distribution of power within the society, and about reigning assumptions and baselines in the society. Any baselines used can affect and disrupt causal chains and determine the approach to state knowledge and to the standard of reasonableness. All this confirms Koskenniemi's observation that human rights do not exist outside the structures of political deliberation.[12] Positive obligations are thus derived 'from the will representation of a particular political community organized in a nation-state with delimited territory'[13] and are 'a by-product of the particular kind of society'.[14]

As suggested in Chapter 4 under the discussion of the margin of appreciation, an important assumption underpinning the Court's reasoning is that the content of

---

[12] M Koskenniemi, 'Human Rights, Politics and Love' (2001) 4 Mennesker og Rettigheter 33, 38.
[13] G Noll, 'The Exclusionary Construction of Human Rights in International Law and Political Theory' IIIS Discussion Paper (2003) 10.
[14] C Brown 'Universal Human Rights: A Critique' (1997) 1 International Journal of Human Rights 41, 58–59. For an account that explains how human rights are political and at the same time justified by a natural-law approach based on dignity, see L Valentini, 'In What Sense are Human Rights Political?' (2012) 60 Political Studies 180.

positive obligations is specified at national level. This specification happens through an egalitarian procedure in which all can participate (if the ideal of democracy is fulfilled) or, at least, those affected can participate.[15] The specification of the content of positive obligations at national level through democratic and egalitarian procedures raises challenges in extraterritorial settings, where those affected are not part of the specification procedure, a point I return to in Section 8.4. The specification implies that there are no clear initial standards against which any omission can be juxtaposed. Rather the standards are gauged in light of the particular case, and the analysis is submerged into the determination of a breach. This implies that the question as to the existence of a positive obligation is fused with the question of whether the obligation has been breached, which creates uncertainty in the case law. The absence of concrete initial standards and the ensuring uncertainty can be more generally linked with the analytical challenges when determining state responsibility based on omissions.[16] To wit, the State constantly commits omissions, and whether any of these omissions should give rise to responsibility can only be assessed with reference to the normative understandings about the role of the State in the particular society.

## 8.1.2 Democratic Legitimacy and Territorial Boundedness

Positive obligations are closely related to issues of democratic legitimacy, political equality,[17] and territorial boundedness. Human rights are tied to political membership,[18] which echoes Hannah Arendt's claim that the first thing that we distribute to ourselves is membership in a community. Territory is to a certain extent a proxy of this community, since 'people living on the same territory, ... are the most likely to share not only roughly equal, but also interdependent stakes across a broad range of issues in life'.[19] Democracy, the political model envisioned by the ECHR,[20] and democratic

---

[15] S Besson, 'Subsidiarity in International Human Rights Law—What is Subsidiary about Human Rights' (2016) 61(1) American Journal of Jurisprudence 69.
[16] See more specifically Sections 4.2 and 7.1.3.
[17] S Besson, 'The Legitimate Authority of International Human Rights – On the Reciprocal Legitimation of Domestic and International Human Rights' in A Føllesdal (ed), *The Legitimacy of Human Rights* (Cambridge University Press 2013) 32; S Besson, 'The Bearers of Human Rights' Duties and Responsibilities for Human Rights: A Quiet (R)evolution' (2015) 32(1) Social Philosophy and Policy 244, 252; S Besson, 'Human Rights and Democracy in a Global Context: Decoupling and Recoupling' (2011) 4(1) Ethics and Global Politics 19; S Besson, 'Human Rights and Constitutional Law' in R Cruft and others (eds), *Philosophical Foundations of Human Rights* (Oxford University Press 2015) 280, 284.
[18] Besson, 'Human Rights and Democracy in a Global Context' (n 17) 19.
[19] S Besson, 'Why and What (State) Jurisdiction. Legal Plurality, Individual Equality and Territorial Legitimacy' in J Klabbers and G Palombella (eds), *The Challenge of Inter-Legality* (Cambridge University Press 2019) 91, 121.
[20] *Zdanoka v Latvia* [GC] 58278/00, 16 March 2006 §98. Article 2 together with Article 3 'enshrine one of the fundamental values of democratic societies making up the Council of Europe', which implies an understanding that democracy is the 'framework in which human rights may best be demanded, fostered and protected'. S Skinner, *Lethal Force, the Right to Life and the ECHR. Narratives of Death and Democracy* (Hart Publishing 2019) 64.

legitimacy require territorial governance since 'shared inhabitation of a territory is the most fundamental basis of political constituency'.[21] A shared physical world, a shared territory, implies sharing of interests and articulation of a self-governing constituency.[22] In this way, a shared territory establishes a link between the demos and its governance.[23] It ensures a shared public space with relatively clear lines of authorization and accountability, where collective interests can be deliberated.[24] A shared territory that is bounded also presupposes a certain degree of predictability as to the group of people affected whose interests need to be taken into account. This also enables the balancing of these interests for the purpose of determining the content and the scope of any positive obligations upon the State.

It also explains why positive obligations are formulated with reference to a territorial institutional infrastructure in mind. They might require the adoption of new or the modification of existing national regulatory frameworks, as Section 7.1 showed. They might also require the incorporation of procedures with certain procedural safeguards, clarified in Section 7.2. All this is a reflection of the nature of human rights law: 'the subject of human rights norms are emplaced within a concrete and bounded legal order, … and presumed to exist within the legal and political relationship that constitute that order'.[25] As Besson has also argued, the context of a political community of equals enables public institutions to specify and allocate human rights obligations.[26]

The account echoes Hanna Arendt's insight that membership in a political community is determinative for the 'right to have rights'.[27] No doubt, this insight, as supported by my account of positive obligations, sits uneasily with a central tenet often invoked in human rights law, namely the universality of human rights. However, the tenet that individuals have human rights purely by virtue of being humans does not hold if we are to be true to the legal positivism tools and the legal technicalities for triggering and assessing breach of obligations.[28] The operation of these technicalities is enabled by the political contingency of human rights and their communitarian/'social-contractarian' nature.[29] In this chapter, I will return to the appeal to universality since

---

[21] A Jurkevics, 'Democracy in Contested Territory: On the Legitimacy of Global Legal Pluralism' (2019) 25(2) Critical Review of International Social and Political Philosophy 1, 3.
[22] Ibid 11.
[23] ibid.
[24] R Bellamy, 'The Democratic Legitimacy of International Human Rights Convention: Political Constitutionalism and the European Convention on Human Rights' (2015) 25(4) European Journal of International Law 1019, 1030.
[25] N Bhuta, 'The Frontiers of Extraterritoriality—Human Rights Law as Global Law' in N Bhuta (ed), *The Frontiers of Human Rights. Extraterritoriality and its Challenges* (Oxford University Press 2016) 1, 8.
[26] S Besson, 'The Egalitarian Dimension of Human Rights' (2013) 136 Beiheft, Archiv für Rechts- und Sozialphilosophie 19–52; Besson, 'The Bearers of Human Rights' Duties and Responsibilities for Human Rights' (n 17) 248–57.
[27] H Arendt, 'The Decline of the Nation State and the End of the Rights of Man' in *The Origins of Totalitarianism* (Meridian Books 1958)
[28] Noll, 'The Exclusionary Construction of Human Rights in International Law and Political Theory' (n 13) 9.
[29] ibid 10: 'The technical and the social-contractarian aspects are but two sides of the same coin, both illustrating various dimensions in the political contingency of human rights.'

it has had a central role in the arguments how expansive the jurisdictional threshold under Article 1 should be.[30]

Territorial boundedness implies the existence of a structured relationship over a period of time. This temporal dimension needs to be also acknowledged. For this purpose, it is relevant to highlight that when the Court assesses compliance with substantive positive obligations, it extends the factual and temporal scope of its assessment by including events and state conduct prior to the specific harmful incident in question. This is very clear in the context of the positive obligation of adopting effective regulatory framework. An extension of the factual and temporal frame of reference also implies an expansion of the range of possible causal factors that can be deemed relevant, thus enlarging the time frame under consideration. Overall, this expansion of the scope of the analysis and of the scope of the causality narrative allows identification of some structural problems,[31] and the diagnosis of such problems is precisely at the core of the positive obligation of adopting effective regulatory framework. The expansion of the factual and temporal scope of the assessment and the evaluation of legal structures is possible due to the existence of a structured relationship over a period of time between the State and individuals concerned. In extraterritorial circumstances, such a relationship might be absent or at a very rudimentary level. The time factor might be also absent. I return to these specifics in Section 8.4.

For the relationship to be structured, it might also have to be formal, regulated by a legal framework, which brings us to the issue of domestic legality and the existence of relevant domestic procedures and their role in the assessment of causal links between omissions and harm. While domestic legality, domestic regulatory, and procedural standards are not definitive tests, they do have decisive roles since they are used as important referents for identifying relevant omissions.[32] When harm caused by omissions, arguably imputable to a State of extraterritorial jurisdiction, materializes in a context where there is no structured formal relationship between this State and the affected individuals regulated by law, there might be no referents to help in finding causation. When a State and the affected individuals are not necessarily connected by common decision-making structures, legal standards and procedures that can serve as referents for assessing omissions might not be available. Even if certain procedures are available, these might be without guarantees and without reason-giving. These gaps will be further explored in Section 8.4.

---

[30] See, in particular, Sections 8.4.1.5, 8.4.2.1, and 8.4.2.3.
[31] For an analysis about the right to life, see Skinner, *Lethal Force, the Right to Life and the ECHR* (n 20) 83.
[32] Sections 3.3.1 and 7.1.

## 8.1.3 Not Contingent Exclusively on Actual Capacity

Another important conclusion from the analysis of positive obligations performed in the previous chapters is that their triggering, content, and scope are not contingent only on actual capacity of the State to perform them. Rather, normative and political questions as to how intrusive the role of the State should be and how to relate and balance different interests within the community play vital roles. It is thus crucial to highlight that the tests of reasonableness, knowledge, and causation are not only about, respectively, actual capacity, actual knowledge, or factual cause-and-effect links (links that might be in any case difficult to conclusively prove). For example, the State might have the capacity in a given situation to take protective operational measures, and indeed such measures might contribute to prevention of harm, but it might not be desirable to do so since the society risks intrusive measures that it might not be willing to tolerate.[33] Another reason why actual capacity is not the exclusive reference point for understanding positive obligations is that in many situations it might be clear that the State had no actual capacity or had limited capacity; despite this, state responsibility for failure to fulfil positive obligations might be established. The reason for this is the normative understanding that the State should have had this capacity or, at least, have made efforts to build the capacity or a procedure.[34] This reveals a paradox that characterizes positive obligations: on the one hand, their content and scope is contingent on capacity, while on the other hand, positive obligations themselves might demand more capacity for the State to act.[35] This paradox is related to the role of the State in society as an institutional structure within which different but interdependent and interrelated interests are channelled and deliberated. The State also reflects the structures within which decisions are made as to which risks are worth taking and what measures can be taken for the prevention or the mitigation of other risks.

## 8.2 Deconstructing Jurisdiction

The question that arises is whether and how the meaning of jurisdiction, as developed in the case law of the Court, actually reflects the preconditions outlined in Section 8.1. Does jurisdiction as interpreted in the case law actually serve the purpose of ensuring these preconditions?[36] Put differently, how are legality, interdependence of stakes and interests, and democratic legitimacy reflected in the developed meaning of jurisdiction? These are the questions at the core of this section. The questions whether and

---

[33] See eg *Hiller v Austria* no 1967/14, 22 November 2016 §§50–57, where the Court did not agree that the State should have further restricted the freedom of movement of a person with mental disability to prevent him from taking his own life. See Chapter 5 on conflicting obligations.
[34] See eg Section 7.3.3 on the procedure of risk assessment as an 'integral part' of the *Osman* obligation.
[35] See Section 3.2.3.
[36] A separate question is whether Article 1 *should* serve this purpose, or it should rather serve purposes other than enabling the analysis on the merits.

how positive obligations *could* be conceptualized, operationalized, and applied in circumstances where the normal preconditions do not obtain, and what challenges accordingly arise will be addressed in Section 8.4.

This section is built upon an analysis of relevant ECtHR judgments that address Article 1 of the ECHR. The structure therefore reflects the models of extraterritorial jurisdiction framed in the case law. Since in some respects the judgments are inconclusive, ambiguous, and openly contradictory, references to other sources (eg academic scholarship) that have attempted to reconstruct the case law will be also made. It also needs to be borne in mind that when the meaning of jurisdiction is constructed based on the case law, this meaning is necessarily limited. Although the Court has attempted to clarify some general principles, the meaning is ultimately shaped by the specifics of the factual scenarios in the cases and the particular legal issues raised in each case. This opens the possibility for speculation regarding how the principles might be applied in circumstances that have not transpired in already-adjudicated cases. It also explains the caution that characterizes the forthcoming analysis. In addition, the absence of consistency in the case law can channel the analysis into selectivity. Cautiousness is thus also warranted to avoid this as much as possible.

## 8.2.1 The Territorial Paradigm

As a starting point, the Court has underlined the inherently territorial nature of jurisdiction and maintains a presumption against extraterritorial application of the Convention.[37] As positive obligations are framed with reference to a territorial institutional infrastructure in mind, grounding jurisdiction (as an initial threshold) primarily on territory appears understandable. This reflects the territorial paradigm that structures human rights law, a paradigm related to issues of democratic legitimacy and distribution of resources within the political community, as suggested in Section 8.1.

The Court has not justified this starting assumption by directly invoking democratic legitimacy and communitarian arguments; rather, it has invoked state sovereignty and possible clash between sovereign entitlements.[38] In particular, it has held that the meaning of jurisdiction in the sense of Article 1 ECHR needs to be informed by the meaning of jurisdiction in public international law.[39] As the Court has reasoned, 'the jurisdictional competence of a State is primarily territorial' and the exercise

---

[37] *N.D. and N.T. v Spain* [GC] no 8675/15, 13 February 2020 §103; *M.N. and Others v Belgium* [GC] (dec) no 3599/18, 5 May 2020 §98. For a theoretical defence of the territorial limitation of human rights law, see S Ratner, *The Thin Justice of International Law* (Oxford University Press 2015) 271.

[38] *H.F. and Others v France* [GC] no 24384/19, 14 September 2022 §185. Still, the reference to the ECHR as 'a constitutional instrument of European public order' is suggestive of communitarianism. See *Bankovic and Others v Belgium and Others* [GC] (dec) no 52207/99, 12 December 2001 §80; *Carter v Russia* no 20914/07, 21 September 2021 §134.

[39] *N.D. and N.T. v Spain* [GC] no 8675/15, 13 February 2020 §109; *H.F. and Others v France* [GC] no 24384/19, 14 September 2022 §184.

of jurisdiction extraterritorially (based on the accepted principles such as nationality, passive personality, effect or universality) is 'as a general rule, defined and limited by the sovereign territorial rights of other relevant States'.[40] It has also added that 'the Convention does not govern the actions of States not parties to it, nor does it purport to be a means of requiring the Contracting States to impose Convention standards on other States'.[41] These pronouncements expose concerns about the *territorial* State's sovereignty in its external (ie coexistence and cooperation between States as distinct and equal sovereign entities) and internal (ie authority over all political and legal matters) dimensions.[42] The jurisdiction threshold is thus invoked by the Court to protect 'interests and values of the political community *qua* sovereign equals to others' and the 'democratic autonomy'[43] of the territorial state.

Yet these concerns are not pre-eminent, and human rights jurisdiction beyond the territorial paradigm is not entirely rejected. It can occur in exceptional circumstances that require 'special justification'.[44] The exceptionality test, as invoked by the Court, suggests a restrained approach that does not necessarily respond to the empirical reality where state conduct can in many situations affect individuals located outside the state territory. Here it is useful to distinguish between first, circumstances where the State acts through its agents abroad (and in this way it might exercise control over foreign territory or control over persons located extraterritorially), and second, circumstances where the State's domestic conduct has effects outside the territory.[45]

Typical examples that fall within the first type of circumstances are military interventions, occupation of foreign territory, arrest and detention by state officials abroad, or administration of detention facilities abroad. The meaning of jurisdiction in the Court's case law, and in the academic literature, has been predominantly developed against the backdrop of these circumstances. They include elements of force and direct control. They also refer to situations that are not only very distanced from some sort of commonality and political and legal unity between the State and the affected individuals but are often 'predicated on relations of mutual hostility'.[46] These circumstances are reflected in the leading judgment of *Al-Skeini and Others v the United Kingdom*,[47] where the Court has attempted to more generally introduce some clarity

---

[40] *Bankovic and Others v Belgium and Others* [GC] (dec) no 52207/99, 12 December 2001 §§59 and 61; *H.F. and Others v France* [GC] no 24384/19, 14 September 2022 §185.
[41] *Bankovic and Others v Belgium and Others* [GC] (dec) no 52207/99, 12 December 2001 §66; *Medvedyev and Others v France* [GC] no 3394/03, 29 March 2010 §63.
[42] On these two dimensions, see S Besson, 'Sovereignty' in R Wolfrum (ed), *Max Planck Encyclopedia of International Law* (Oxford University Press 2011) §§72–73.
[43] On these functions and values behind state sovereignty, see ibid §§109 and 139.
[44] *Bankovic and Others v Belgium and Others* [GC] (dec) no 52207/99, 12 December 2001 §§61 and 80; *Medvedyev and Others v France* [GC] no 3394/03, 29 March 2010 §64; *H.F. and Others v France* [GC] no 24384/19, 14 September 2022 §185.
[45] For the introduction of this distinction, see L Bartels, 'The EU's Human Rights Obligations in Relation to Policies with Extraterritorial Effect' (2014) 25(4) European Journal of International Law 1071; see also A Ollino, 'Justifications and Limits of Extraterritorial Obligations of States: Effects-based Extraterritoriality in Human Rights Law' (paper on file with the author), on the distinction between extraterritorial conduct of a State and extraterritorial effects of a state conduct.
[46] Bhuta, 'The Frontiers of Extraterritoriality' (n 25) 12.
[47] *Al-Skeini and Others v United Kingdom* [GC] no 55721/07, 7 July 2011.

regarding Article 1 of the ECHR by outlining different models of extraterritorial jurisdiction. The following analysis will be organized based on the models in *Al-Skeini*, and where relevant their application in other judgments (Sections 8.2.2–8.2.5). After clarifying the *Al-Skeini* models and what they imply for positive obligations, Section 8.2.6 will turn to the circumstances where the domestic conduct of a State has effects outside its territory, a situation that seems to fall outside the *Al-Skeini* models. Finally, Section 8.2.7 will examine how the existence of procedural links has been constituted as a separate and specific basis for jurisdiction.

## 8.2.2 Effective Control over an Area

### 8.2.2.1 Trigger

In *Al-Skeini*, the Court clarified that extraterritorial jurisdiction could be triggered when

> as a consequence of lawful or unlawful military action, a Contracting State exercises effective control of an area outside the national territory. The obligation to secure, in such an area, the rights and freedoms set out in the Convention, derives from the fact of such control, whether it be exercised directly, through the Contracting State's own armed forced, or through a subordinate local administration.[48]

*Jaloud v the Netherlands* clarified that 'the status of "occupying power" … or lack of it, is not *per se* determinative'.[49] What is decisive is the fact that the State has control over an area outside its national territory. In *Georgia v Russia* (II), it was decided that such a control was absent 'during the active phase of hostilities in the context of an international armed conflict'.[50]

The leading cases where the 'control over an area' model (ie the spatial model) was applied involve the situation in Northern Cyprus, with *Loizidou v Turkey* being one of the most important judgments.[51] The substantive analysis in this judgment involved breach of the negative obligation not to interfere with the right to property unjustifiably.[52] Another example is *Cyprus v Turkey*,[53] where, *inter alia*, a violation of the procedural limb of Article 2 was found, since Turkey did not conduct an effective investigation to clarify the fate of the missing persons.

---

[48] ibid §§138–140; *Georgia v Russia (II)* [GC] no 38263/08, 21 January 2021 §116.
[49] *Jaloud v the Netherlands* [GC] no 47708/08, 20 November 2014 §142.
[50] *Georgia v Russia (II)* [GC] no 38263/08, 21 January 2021 §138.
[51] *Loizidou v Turkey* (preliminary objections) no 15318/89, 23 March 1995 §62.
[52] *Loizidou v Turkey* (Merits) [GC] no 15318/89, 18 December 1996 §64. For the purposes of the substantive analysis no balancing between competing interests was performed in the reasoning of the Court since the respondent state never sought to justify the interference, which made the finding of a violation easy.
[53] *Cyprus v Turkey* [GC] no 25781/94, 10 May 2001 §77. See also *Manitaras and Others v Turkey* (dec) no 54591/00, 3 June 2008 §27.

Another group of judgments where the 'control over an area' model has been applied concerns the situation in the 'Moldovan Republic of Transdniestria'.[54] What distinguishes these cases is that rather than physical control over the region of Transdniestria, the Court has highlighted the 'effective control and decisive influence' of Russia over the separatist regime in the region.[55] Yet, in *Al-Skeini*, the Court did not make any distinction between its approaches to the situations in Northern Cyprus and Transdniestria; it instead referred to both as examples of extraterritorial jurisdiction based on control over an area.[56] In *Georgia v Russia* (II), both Russia's physical control (ie military presence) and influence through economic and political support were invoked.[57]

Besides Northern Cyprus, the Transdniestria and the South Ossetia/Abkhazia situations, there are other judgments where 'control over an area' has been invoked. An example is *Issa and Others v Turkey*, concerning the arrest, detention, and killing of the applicants' relatives in the course of a military operation by Turkish forces in northern Iraq. In *Issa*, the Court invoked the 'control over an area' model as follows: 'if there is a sufficient factual basis for holding that, at the relevant time, the victims were within that specific area [where Turkey had effective overall control], it would follow logically that they were within the jurisdiction of Turkey'.[58] Such a factual basis was found lacking in the particular case and, for this reason, the applicants were found not to be within the jurisdiction of Turkey.

Two other relevant examples emerge from *Pisari v the Republic of Moldova and Russia* and *Jaloud v the Netherlands*. The first judgment involved the killing of a person by a Russian soldier at a military checkpoint in the territory of Moldova. The Court observed that 'the checkpoint in question, situated in the security zone, was manned and commanded by Russian soldiers', which implied that Russia had control over the area. Since the victim was within this area, Russia's obligations were triggered.[59] The substantive question was whether the use of force against the person complied with the 'absolute necessary' standard under Article 2(2) ECHR. The Court reached a conclusion that it did not. A violation of the procedural limb of Article 2 was also found since Russia did not involve the victim's relatives in the investigation of the circumstances of the killing.[60]

---

[54] See eg *Chiragov and Others v Armenia* [GC] no 13216/05, 16 June 2015 §170.
[55] The Court seems to be placing an emphasis on the decisive military, political and economic influence of Russia and on the Russian control over the Transdniestrian authorities. *Catan and Others v Moldova* [GC] no 43370/04, 19 October 2012 §122; *Ilaşcu and Others v Moldova and Russia* no 48787/99, 8 July 2004; *Mozer v the Republic of Moldova and Russia* [GC] no 11138/10, 23 February 2016 §110; *Ivantoc and Others v Moldova and Russia* no 23687/05, 15 November 2011 §§116–120; *Turturica and Casian v Moldova and Russia* no 28648/06, 30 August 2016 §33; *Mangîr and Others v Moldova and Russia* no 50157/06, 17 July 2018 §§28–31.
[56] *Al-Skeini and Others v United Kingdom* [GC] no 55721/07, 7 July 2011 §§138–139.
[57] *Georgia v Russia (II)* [GC] no 38263/08, 21 January 2021 §§165–175.
[58] *Issa and Others v Turkey* no 31821/96, 16 November 2004 §74.
[59] *Pisari v the Republic of Moldova and Russia* no 42139/12, 21 April 2015 §33.
[60] ibid §59.

*Jaloud v the Netherlands* involved a situation very similar to *Pisari*: Dutch troops opened fire at a military checkpoint in occupied Iraq, as a result of which a person was shot dead.[61] He was found to be within the jurisdiction of the Netherlands since the State had 'authority and control over persons passing through the checkpoint'.[62] The question on the merits in *Jaloud* was whether the respondent State complied with its procedural obligation to conduct an investigation under Article 2. The Court answered in the negative,[63] and in the same way as in *Pisari*, it invoked the standards normally applied to the procedural limb of Article 2 in domestic circumstances.[64] It did mention though that reasonable allowances need to be made for 'the relatively difficult conditions under which the Netherlands military and investigators had to work'.[65]

### 8.2.2.2 How does the model reflect the preconditions?

Having explained the trigger of the spatial model of jurisdiction, that is, 'the effective control of an area', as developed in the case law of the Court, the question whether the model actually reflects the preconditions outlined in Section 8.1, can be addressed. First, it is relevant to note that in the Northern Cyprus cases, the Court accepts that the State with extraterritorial jurisdiction (ie Turkey) has both procedural[66] and substantive[67] positive obligations. This acceptance is based on the assumption that the whole conduct (in the form of actions or omissions) of the authorities of Northern Cyprus is attributable to Turkey. No distinction is therefore made in the Court's reasoning between the conduct of Turkey and the conduct of the Northern Cypriot authorities.

A similar approach is applied to the Transdniestria cases. The Court accepted that there was no direct involvement by Russia in the actions taken by the authorities in Transdniestria.[68] Yet the Court assumed that since Russia had jurisdiction understood as control over the area, the conduct of the authorities of the 'Moldovan Republic of Transdniestria' was attributable to it. As a consequence, Russia was found in breach of negative obligations under Article 2, Protocol 1 in *Catan and Others v The Republic of Moldova and Russia*,[69] under Articles 5 and 3 in *Mozer v the Republic of Moldova and Russia*[70] and under Article 1, Protocol 1 (the right to property) in

---

[61] *Jaloud v the Netherlands* [GC] no 47708/08, 20 November 2014.
[62] ibid §152.
[63] ibid §§208, 211, 216, 220, and 227.
[64] ibid §§188 and 199.
[65] ibid §226.
[66] *Cyprus v Turkey* [GC] no 25781/94, 10 May 2001 §136 (breach of the procedural obligation under Article 2 due to absence of an effective investigation to clarify the fate of the Greek-Cypriot missing persons).
[67] *Manitaras and Others v Turkey* (dec) no 54591/00, 3 June 2008 §§62 and 72 (the positive obligation of taking protective operational measures was found not triggered since there was no information that the victim's life was at risk).
[68] *Catan and Others v the Republic of Moldova and Russia* [GC] no 43370/04, 19 October 2012 §§114 and 149; *Paduret v Moldova and Russia* no 26626/11, 9 May 2017 §§35–37.
[69] *Catan and Others v the Republic of Moldova and Russia* [GC] no 43370/04, 19 October 2012 §150.
[70] *Mozer v the Republic of Moldova and Russia* [GC] no 11138/10, 23 February 2016 §§156–158 (regarding the applicant's detention) and §184 (regarding the conditions of detention in which the applicant was kept).

*Paduret v Moldova and Russia*.[71] Any positive obligations of Russia were not invoked in this cluster of cases.

A conclusion that could be drawn is that the State that exercises extraterritorial jurisdiction because it has control over an area can own both positive and negative obligations corresponding to the rights of the individuals within this area.[72] Since the 'control over an area' model can be considered an extension of the starting assumption that jurisdiction flows from territory,[73] it can be expected that some of the presuppositions that normally operate within the national territory exists even when a State controls an area beyond its territory. For example, the State might have the capacity—flowing from its control—to prevent harm.

However, the other presuppositions discussed in Section 8.1 might not be present, such as a bounded political and legal order, interdependent stakes of the individuals belonging to this order, or balancing of interests that are institutionally channelled through a democratically constituted sovereign. In none of the cases where the 'control over an area' model was found applicable has the Court grappled with the difficult questions, raised by the substantive positive obligations of taking protective operational measures and of an adoptive effective regulatory framework, as discussed in Section 8.1. These difficulties are solved in the context of political and legal unity. In contrast, the circumstances in the cases discussed here can be characterized as absence of commonality and political and legal unity between the affected individuals and the respondent States as bearers of human rights obligations. In some cases, such as *Jaloud*, the relationship between the population, of which the affected individuals form part, and the respondent State can be even described as one of mutual hostility.[74]

It is interesting that in its reasoning, the Court tries to represent some commonality and mutual interests between the respondent States as bearers of human rights obligations and the population. In the Transdniestria cases, the Court places emphasis on the decisive military, political, and economic influence of Russia, as if the Transdniestrian and Russian authorities converge. In *Jaloud*, the Court mentioned that the checkpoint that was under Dutch command had been set up 'to restore conditions of stability and security conductive to the creation of an effective administration in the country',[75] which could imply that the Dutch presence was in the interest of the local population.[76]

---

[71] *Paduret v Moldova and Russia* no 26626/11, 9 May 2017 §§35–37.
[72] *Al-Skeini and Others v United Kingdom* [GC] no 55721/07, 7 July 2011 §138.
[73] When a State has control of an area, it 'takes on responsibilities on a governmental scale and the circumstances are in many ways analogous to the State's own territory'. N Lubell, *Extraterritorial Use of Force against Non-State Actors* (Oxford University Press 2011) 211.
[74] Bhuta, 'The Frontiers of Extraterritoriality' (n 25) 12.
[75] *Jaloud v the Netherlands* [GC] no 47708/08, 20 November 2014 §152.
[76] The invocation of such communality and mutuality between the interests of the State with extraterritorial 'territorial control', and the population of another state, is not uncontroversial. The reason is that 'it comes very close to giving priority, in the name of human rights protection to quasi-governmental effectivity over democratic legitimacy and hence condoning forms of illegal long-term occupation provided they respect human rights'. S Besson, 'International Courts and the Jurisprudence of Statehood' (2019) 10(1) International Legal Theory 30, 49.

## Deconstructing Jurisdiction

The spatial model might guarantee the capacity of the State of extraterritorial jurisdiction to ensure positive obligations, and, at the same time, the Court has also invoked in some judgments forms of commonality between the interests of this State and the local population; nevertheless uncertainty prevails, since the role of these invocations is not clear. Further uncertainty is caused by the oscillation between the 'control over an area' and the 'control over persons' models in the case law. As explained by Milanovic, the spatial model is conflated with the personal once applied to smaller areas and objects such as checkpoints or buildings.[77] This conflation is evident in the case law of the Court. The Court often does not specify which model it actually applies and fluctuates between the 'control over an area' and the 'control over persons' models. An example to this effect emerges from *Jaloud*. Although the case was presented above as an illustration of the 'control over an area' model, the reasoning is confusing. In particular, the Court first established that whether or not a State had control over an area did not depend on that State's status as an occupying power (it was the United Kingdom, not the Netherlands, that was the formal occupying power in the region).[78] Establishing this suggested a reliance on the spatial model. In addition, the Court observed that 'the Netherlands assumed responsibility for providing security in that *area*',[79] which also hinted at reliance on the spatial model. However, in its reasoning the Court also confusingly referred to 'control over persons passing through the checkpoint'.[80] In this regard, the case law refers not only to control over persons and areas as reference points, but also to control over 'events' that can give rise to jurisdiction,[81] which is also confusing.

### 8.2.3 Physical Power and Control over a Person

#### 8.2.3.1 Trigger

In *Al Skeini*, the Court explained that 'the use of force by a State's agents operating outside its territory may bring the individual thereby brought under control of the State's authorities into the State's Article 1 jurisdiction'.[82] The leading judgments where jurisdiction was found established based on the 'control over a person' model are *Öcalan v Turkey*,[83] *Isaak v Turkey*,[84] *Medvedyev and Others v*

---

[77] Milanovic, *Extraterritorial Application of Human Rights Treaties* (n 4) 171.
[78] *Jaloud v the Netherlands* [GC] no 47708/08, 20 November 2014 §142.
[79] ibid §149.
[80] ibid §152.
[81] *N.D. and N.T. v Spain* [GC] no 8675/15, 13 February 2020 §111: 'Accordingly, the *events* giving rise to the alleged violations fall within Spain's "jurisdiction" within the meaning of Article 1 of the Convention' (emphasis added).
[82] *Al-Skeini and Others v the United Kingdom* [GC] no 55721/07, 7 July 2011 §136; *Georgia v Russia (II)* [GC] no 38263/08, 21 January 2021 §117.
[83] *Öcalan v Turkey* [GC] no 46221/99, 12 May 2005.
[84] *Isaak and Others v Turkey* (dec) no 44587/98, 28 September 2006: 'even if the acts complained of took place in the neutral UN buffer zone, the Court considers that the deceased was under the authority and/or

*France*,⁸⁵ and *Hassan v the United Kingdom*.⁸⁶ In *Al Skeini*, the Court tried to clarify the model by adding that

> [t]he Court does not consider that jurisdiction in the above cases arose *solely* from the control exercised by the Contracting State over the buildings, aircraft or ship in which the individuals were held. What is *decisive* in such cases is the exercise of *physical power and control over* the person in question.[87]

This clarification is valuable since it suggests that control over physical environment where persons might be located is not necessary. This can help to distinguish the 'control over the person' and the 'control over an area' models. At the same time, however, the above quotation does leave some ambiguity as to whether the exercise of physical power and control over the person in itself will suffice, without any control of any physical environment. Physical control over the person might be decisive, but the question left open is whether it is sufficient.[88] The word 'solely' leaves open the possibility of requiring some form of control over the space where the affected individuals are, so that the personal model is triggered.[89]

A relevant question is also whether and how state agents can control a person without having any control of the physical environment where that person is located. This could happen, for example, by simply and directly shooting him or her. The implication, however, is that without the requirement for some spatial control over the physical environment, the 'control over the person' model might collapse into a cause-and-effect model.[90] The latter has been rejected by *Bankovic*, a rejection that *Al-Skeini* has not challenged, as I will explain in Section 8.2.6.

In its analysis of the specific facts, the Court in *Al-Skeini* did not directly invoke control over an area, but it did invoke 'the exercise of some of the public powers normally to be exercised by a sovereign government' to supplement the control over the

> effective control of the respondent State through its agents. It concludes, accordingly, that the matter complained of in the present application fall within the "jurisdiction of Turkey".

---

[85] *Medvedyev and Others v France* [GC] no 3394/03, 29 March 2010 §67.

[86] *Hassan v the United Kingdom* [GC] no 29750/09, 16 September 2014 §76 (taking an individual into custody).

[87] *Al-Skeini and Others v United Kingdom* [GC] no 55721/07, 7 July 2011 §136 (emphasis added).

[88] In *Medvedyev and Others v France* [GC] no 3394/03, 29 March 2010 §67, the Court referred to both control over the ship and its crew: 'as this was a case of France having exercised full and exclusive control over the *Winner* and its crew, at least *de facto*, from the time of its inception, in a continued and uninterrupted manner until they were tried in France, the applicants were effectively within the France's jurisdiction for the purposes of Article 1 of the Convention'.

[89] M Milanovic, '*Al-Skeini* and *Al-Jedda* in Strasbourg' (2012) 23(1) European Journal of International Law 121, 128.

[90] Milanovic has proposed that a possible way to limit the personal model so that it does not lose its meaning 'since it simply collapses into the position that a State has human rights obligations whenever it can actually violates the rights of the individual concerned', is by restricting it to circumstances where 'only physical custody over an individual could satisfy' it. However, he ultimately rejects this limitation as arbitrary. See Milanovic, *Extraterritorial Application of Human Rights Treaties* (n 4) 119 and 173.

individuals.[91] It was in these circumstances characterized by the exercise of public powers that the respondent state exercised control over the individuals. This invocation is also an indication that mere control over an individual might not suffice.

### 8.2.3.2  How does the model reflect the preconditions?

The invocation of 'public powers' in *Al-Skeini* is suggestive of the preconditions mentioned in Section 8.1, a point that will be further discussed in Section 8.2.5, where the 'public powers' model of jurisdiction is addressed. If this invocation is ignored, however, the exercise of mere physical power over a person, without consideration of the context in terms 'public powers' or spatial control, is a very different situation from the circumstances where positive human rights obligations are normally applied. This might explain the reluctance of the Court to assert the independent existence of the 'control over a person' model and instead to invoke additional factors in its analysis under Article 1 ECHR (such as 'public powers' in *Al-Skeini*, control over the ship in *Medvedyev*,[92] de jure control of the Italian authorities over the applicants in *Hirsi*,[93] or the regional nature of the ECHR regime and the 'legal space of the Convention' as in *Carter v Russia*).[94]

In none of the cases where jurisdiction was found based on 'control over a person' model did the Court raise the difficult issues surrounding positive obligations, as outlined in Section 8.1. Rather, it was the procedural limb of Article 2, namely the obligation to investigate, that was at the core of *Al-Skeini*. In *Isaak v Turkey*, it was fairly straightforward that the use of force against the victim by the Turkish or Turkish-Cypriot forces could not be justified under Article 2(2) of the Convention.[95] Similarly, it was easy to find a violation of the procedural limb of Article 2 since Turkey failed to produce any evidence that an investigation had been carried out into the circumstances of the victim's death.[96] In *Öcalan v Turkey*, most of the obligations invoked were relevant when the applicant was already in Turkey.[97] As to *Carter v Russia*, once the jurisdictional threshold passed, it was fairly straightforward to apply on the merits the standards regarding the obligation to investigate and the negative obligation not to kill arbitrary under Article 2.[98]

---

[91] *Al-Skeini and Others v United Kingdom* [GC] no 55721/07, 7 July 2011 §149.
[92] *Medvedyev and Others v France* [GC] no 3394/03, 29 March 2010 §67.
[93] *Hirsi Jamaa and Others v Italy* [GC] no 27765/09, 23 February 2012 §81.
[94] *Carter v Russia* no 20914/07, 21 September 2021 §§128–130 and 134: 'Targeted violations of the human rights of an individual *by one Contracting State in the territory of another Contracting State* undermine the effectiveness of the Convention both as a guardian of human rights and as a guarantor of peace, security and the rule of law in Europe' (emphasis added).
[95] *Isaak and Others v Turkey* (dec) no 44587/98, 28 September 2006 §119.
[96] *Isaak v Turkey* §124–125.
[97] Articles 6 and 5(3) ECHR were invoked in *Öcalan v Turkey* [GC] no 46221/99, 12 May 2005.
[98] The Court rather faced evidentiary challenges. These were, however, addressed by shifting the burden to Russia.

## 8.2.4 Acts of Diplomatic and Consular Agents

### 8.2.4.1 Trigger

In *Al Skeini*, the Court explained that 'it is clear that acts of diplomatic and consular agents, who are present on foreign territory in accordance with provisions of international law, may amount to an exercise of jurisdiction when these agents exert authority and control over others'.[99] Two issues need to be clarified in relation to the 'acts of diplomatic and consular agents' model so that we can understand whether and how the model reflects the normative preconditions outlined in Section 8.1. The first is the relevance of the nationality of the affected persons. Nationality clearly reflects the preconditions discussed in Section 8.1, since it implies a normative relationship between the affected individuals and the agents representing these individuals' state of nationality. The second issue concerns the role of the diplomatic and consular agents' acts in the causal chain of events leading to harm. Here a controversial issue is whether mere physical power over non-nationals, without regard to other considerations, would suffice for triggering this model of jurisdiction.

### 8.2.4.2 How does the model reflect the preconditions?
*Nationality*

When the 'acts of diplomatic and consular agents' model is applied in relation to nationals, there is a clear commonality that unites the diplomatic and consular agents and the affected individuals. In early decisions issued by the Commission, where the model was applied, nationality was explicitly made a relevant factor. For example, in *X v Germany*, the Commission observed that

> in certain respects, *the nationals of a Contracting State* are within its 'jurisdiction' even when domiciled or resident abroad; whereas, in particular, the diplomatic and consular representatives of their country of origin perform certain duties with regard to them which may, in certain circumstances, make that country liable in respect of the Convention.[100]

*X v the United Kingdom* also concerned a national, who was however physically present in her own state. The applicant, a British national, complained that the British consulate in Jordan did not fulfil its positive obligation to ensure the return of her child from Jordan. The Commission easily accepted in this case that the jurisdictional threshold was fulfilled:

> [T]he Commission is satisfied that even though the alleged failure of the consular authorities to do all in their power to help the applicant occurred outside

---

[99] *Al-Skeini and Others v the United Kingdom* [GC] no 55721/07, 7 July 2011 §134; *H.F. and Others v France* [GC] no 24384/19, 14 September 2022 §186.
[100] *X. v Germany* (dec) no 1611/62, 25 September 1965.

the territory of the United Kingdom, it was still 'within the jurisdiction' within the meaning of Article 1 of the Convention.[101]

There have been cases, however, where nationality of the affected person was without any relevance. In *M. v Denmark*, for example, the applicant was a German national. He complained about the actions of the Danish ambassador in the German Democratic Republic. Without much discussion, the Commission accepted that he was within the jurisdiction of Denmark: 'the acts of the Danish ambassador complained of affected persons within the jurisdiction of the Danish authorities within the meaning of Article 1 of the Convention'.[102]

The inadmissibility decision of the Grand Chamber in *M.N. and Others v Belgium* has introduced some further clarity on the relevance of nationality.[103] The applicants were a married couple and their two minor children, all Syrian nationals, who travelled to the Belgian embassy in Beirut to submit applications for visas. These were refused since the applicants had the intention to lodge asylum applications on arrival. They complained to the Strasbourg Court that the refusal had exposed them to a situation incompatible with Article 3 ECHR.[104] In first addressing the preliminary issue as to whether the applicants were within the jurisdiction of Belgium, the Court introduced the following distinction. It distinguished between 'State's nationals or their property', on the one hand, and 'certain persons' over whom a State exercises *physical* power and control, on the other. The above-mentioned cases of *X. v Germany* and *X. v the United Kingdom* belong to the first group.[105] Since these cases concerned nationals, no requirement was raised for actual physical control over the individuals by the diplomatic and consular agents.[106] In contrast, *M. v Denmark* fell within the second group of non-nationals. For jurisdiction to arise in relation to them, diplomatic or consular officials have to 'exercise physical power and control'.

As the Court highlighted, the applicants in *M.N. and Others v Belgium* did not belong to the first group (ie they were not Belgian nationals). Nor did the diplomatic

---

[101] *X. v the United Kingdom* (dec) no 7547/76, 15 December 1977. See also *S v Germany* (dec) no 10686/83, 5 October 1984 where the applicant complained about of alleged failures of the German diplomatic authorities in Morocco. The Commission seemed to assume that the applicant was within the jurisdiction of Germany, but still declared the application inadmissible since the ECHR confers 'no right to diplomatic intervention vis-á-vis a third State'.

[102] *M. v Denmark* (dec) no 17392/90, 14 October 1992 (inadmissible since the treatment complained of was attributable to the authorities of the German Democratic Republic). See also *Treska v Albania and Italy* (dec) no 26937/04, 29 June 2006, where the nationality of the applicants was not a relevant consideration in the examination of the question whether they fell within the jurisdiction of Italy.

[103] See *M.N. and Others v Belgium* [GC] (dec) no 3599/18 5 May 2020 §106.

[104] They also argued that Belgium was in violation of Article 6 (the right to fair trial) since they could not pursue the execution of the national court's judgment that instructed Belgium to actually issue them with visas. The Grand Chamber found that Article 6 was not applicable since issues of entry, residence, and removal of aliens, as 'every other decision relating to immigration' do not engage civil rights within the meaning of Article 6. *M.N. and Others v Belgium* §137.

[105] In *M.N. and Others v Belgium* [GC] (dec) no 3599/18, 5 May 2020 §106 the Court also referred to *S. v Germany* (dec) no 10686/83, 5 October 1984.

[106] See below in this section where *H.F. and Others v France* [GC] no 24384/19, 14 September 2022 is analysed due to the nuances added regarding the issue of control and nationals.

agents exercise '*de facto* control' over them.[107] The mere 'administrative control' of Belgium over its embassies was found insufficient.[108] The fact that the applicants brought proceedings at domestic level to ensure their entry in the country was also found insufficient to bring them within the Belgian jurisdiction.[109] On this point, the Court had to distinguish the case from other judgments where 'procedural' control was found sufficient.[110] The basis for the distinction was that, as opposed to other judgments where 'procedural' control triggered Article 1,[111] an application for a visa is a unilateral choice of the individual. As the Court noted, such a choice cannot create a jurisdictional link.[112]

This ultimately meant that foreign nationals who apply for visas at embassies with the intention to seek protection do not fall within the jurisdiction of the ECHR State Parties in the sense of Article 1. As a consequence, the protection from *non-refoulement* under Article 3 cannot be triggered since the affected individuals cannot be constituted as holders of rights. This conclusion needs to be juxtaposed against the Grand Chamber's reasoning in *N.D. and N.T. v Spain*, which appears to be based on the premise that foreigners who apply for protection at embassies and consulates of a State Party are within the latter's jurisdiction.[113] The applicants in this case argued that they were subjected to a collective expulsion after their immediate return to Morocco. The Court found that the applicants were under Spanish jurisdiction since they were on Spanish territory, and that they were indeed subjected to an 'expulsion' within the meaning of Article 4 Protocol 4. The final issue that had to be resolved was whether the 'expulsion' was 'collective'. The Court made the answer to this question dependent on whether there were 'genuine and effective means of legal entry',[114] such as border procedures and visa applications at embassies and consulates,[115] that the applicants could effectively make use of. While a stronger emphasis was placed on the availability of border procedures, the Court in *N.D. and N.T. v Spain* also reasoned that the applicants could have taken advantage of existing procedures for claiming international protection at Spanish embassies and consulates.[116] This gave the basis for the Court eventually to conclude that the absence of individual identification and assessment of the applicants' circumstances could be justified, and was thus not 'collective' in

---

[107] *M.N. and Others v Belgium* [GC] (dec) no 3599/18, 5 May 2020 §§118–119.
[108] *M.N. and Others v Belgium* [GC] §119.
[109] *M.N. and Others v Belgium* [GC] §§121–123.
[110] See Section 8.2.7.
[111] See eg *Güzelyurtlu and Others v Cyprus and Turkey* [GC] no 36925/07, 29 January 2019.
[112] *M.N. and Others v Belgium* [GC] (dec) no 3599/18, 5 May 2020 §123. On this point, the Court followed its approach in *Abdul Wahab Khan v the United Kingdom* (dec) no 11987/11, 28 January 2014 §§28 (inadmissible).
[113] *N.D. and N.T. v Spain* [GC] no 8675/15, 13 February 2020 §§ 222–228. Note also that in *M.N. and Others v Belgium* [GC] (dec) no 3599/18, 5 May 2020 §126, the Grand Chamber observed that the negative in this case 'does not prejudice the endeavours made by States Parties to facilitate access to asylum procedures through their embassies and/or consular representations'.
[114] *N.D. and N.T. v Spain* [GC] no 8675/15, 13 February 2020 §201.
[115] *N.D. and N.T. v Spain* [GC] §§212–222.
[116] *N.D. and N.T. v Spain* [GC] §§223–228.

violation of the prohibition of collective expulsion, since the applicants had not taken advantage of existing legal entry procedures.

In light of this finding, the issue that emerges is how to square the reasoning in *M.N. and Others v Belgium* with *N.D. and N.T. v Spain*. The two are indeed reconcilable given the clarifications that follow. If procedures for humanitarian visas are available, this can be used to the applicants' detriment in the assessment of the prohibition on 'collective expulsions'. This is despite the fact that the availability of such procedures (and any relevant procedural safeguards) is not a matter of individual rights corresponding to ECHR obligations since the affected individuals are not within the States' jurisdiction in the sense of Article 1 ECHR. The facilitation of access to asylum procedures through embassies and/or consular representations is accordingly a matter of state discretion, and not one of individual human rights. If this discretion is exercised, it becomes relevant in the legal analysis under Article 4 Protocol 4.

*M.N. and Others v Belgium* introduced another important distinction regarding non-nationals who apply to diplomatic and consular agents for visa and permits to be allowed entry. Circumstances like those of the applicants in *M.N. and Others v Belgium*, where they sought entry to be protected from *non-refoulement* under Article 3, were distinguished from circumstances where non-nationals apply for visas and residence permits for the purposes of family reunification. Circumstances involving family reunification 'contained an international element' but 'did not involve extraterritoriality for the purposes of Article 1 of the Convention', since 'the jurisdictional link resulted from a pre-existing family or private life that this State [the addressee of a family reunification visa] had a duty to protect'.[117] In circumstances of visa applications for family reunification, the link with the State in question is present, since the applicant lives there and wishes to be joined by family members, or the applicant's family lives in this State and the applicant wishes to join them.[118]

## Causation

The distinction between nationals and non-nationals introduced in *M.N. and Others v Belgium*, and the related requirement that the latter have to be under the *de facto* control exercised by the State's diplomatic agents so that they are under this State's jurisdiction, has important implications for the causation question. In particular, it has implications for the role that the diplomatic and consular agents' conduct needs to play in the causal chain of events allegedly leading to harm.

The extent to which this conduct may affect 'State's nationals or their property' is still an open issue. It can be assumed, though, that the relaxed causation standard as normally applied in positive obligation cases in domestic settings might be applicable (see Chapter 3).[119] Relatedly, no requirement seems to be imposed for *physical* power

---

[117] *M.N. and Others v Belgium* [GC] (dec) no 3599/18, 5 May 2020 §109.
[118] See *Nessa and Others v Finland* (dec) no 31862/02, 6 May 2003; *Schembri v Malta* (dec) no 66297/13, 19 September 2017.
[119] *X v the United Kingdom* (dec) no 7547/76, 15 December 1977 can be used as an illustration.

and control, so that nationals affected by their own countries' diplomatic and consular agents fall within the jurisdiction of the State of nationality. *H.F. and Others v France* warrants some scrutiny at this juncture, since the GC directly engaged with these issues. The applicants in the case were the parents of two women who travelled to Syria with their partners to join the Islamic State in the Levant (ISIL). After the fall of the Islamic Statehe women together with their children, all French nationals, were detained in inhumane conditions in camps in Syrian Kurdistan. The applicants argued that France by not repatriating the women and the children, violated Article 3 and Article 3(2) of Protocol 4 to the ECHR ('No one shall be deprived of the right to enter the territory of the State of which he is a national').

On the question of jurisdiction, the GC in *H.F. and Others v France* dismissed the applicants' argument that

> the French nationality of their family members constitutes a sufficient connection with the State in order to establish a jurisdictional link between them and that State, as such a position would be tantamount to requiring the State to comply with Article 3 of the Convention despite the fact that it has no "control", within the meaning of its case-law, over the camps in north-eastern Syria where the impugned ill-treatment is allegedly being inflicted.[120]

The GC concluded that

> the applicants cannot validly argue that the mere decision of the French authorities not to repatriate their family members has the effect of bringing them within the scope of France's jurisdiction as regards the ill-treatment to which they are subjected in Syrian camps under Kurdish control.[121]

This decision was placed in a normative context: 'neither domestic law nor international law ... requires the State to act on behalf of its nationals and to repatriate them'. This illustrates how legality plays a role in the conceptualization of jurisdiction, a point that will be elaborated upon in Section 8.4.1.

As to the jurisdiction link for the purposes of Article 3(2) of Protocol 4 to the ECHR,[122] a provision that specifically concerns nationals, the GC noted:

> While nationality is a factor that is ordinarily taken into account as a basis for the extraterritorial exercise of jurisdiction by a State (see *Banković*, cited above, § 59), *it cannot constitute an autonomous basis of jurisdiction*. The protection by France of the applicants' family members would in the present case, as indicated by

---

[120] *H.F. and Others v France* [GC] no 24384/19, 14 September 2022 §198.
[121] *H.F. and Others v France* [GC] §203.
[122] See Section 8.3 where the question how jurisdiction can be triggered differently for different rights and obligations is addressed.

the domestic courts, require negotiation with the Kurdish authorities which are holding them, or even an intervention on Kurdish-administered territory.[123]

Nationality is therefore necessary, but insufficient. The Court held that in addition to the 'legal link between the State and its nationals', 'special features' need to be present.[124] Such features were present in *H.F. and Others v France* given *inter alia* the 'real and immediate threat' to the lives and well-being of the relevant individuals, the vulnerability of the children, inability to leave the camps and Kurdish authorities' willingness to cooperate.[125]

In sum, the Court in *H.F. and Others v France* avoided a determination that *under all circumstances* nationals who wish to enter their State of nationality and rely on the right to enter, fall within the jurisdiction of this State.[126] It did also clarify that 'effective control' is, not required due to the subject matter of the specific right: '[i]f the right to enter secured by that provision were limited to nationals already in the territory of that State or under its effective control, the right would be rendered ineffective'.[127] The jurisdictional threshold was therefore tailored to the specific right, which will be explored in more detail in Section 8.3. As to non-nationals, according to the reasoning in *M.N. and Others v Belgium*, '*de facto* control' and 'physical power' over them is a precondition, so that jurisdiction can be triggered. It remains to be seen how this requirement will operate in future cases.[128] It also remains to be better elucidated in the Court's case law how the requirement for '*de facto* control' in the 'acts of diplomatic and consular agent' model is different from the 'physical power and control over a person' model of jurisdiction (Section 8.2.3). In addition, it remains to be tested whether any requirements additional or alternative to mere physical control might be introduced by the Court, as for example, in *Al-Skeini*, where 'public powers' were invoked. For example, non-nationals might participate in proceedings initiated by the State that the diplomatic or consular agents represent, which might suggest an exercise of some form of 'public powers' over these non-nationals.[129] Finally, one might observe that in *M.N. and Others v Belgium*, the immigration control powers of the respondent state played a crucial role and shaped the Court's approach to jurisdiction under Article 1.[130] Such powers might not be at issue in other circumstances

---

[123] *H.F. and Others v France* [GC] no 24384/19, 14 September 2022 §206 (emphasis added). See Section 8.4.1.4 where the question of coordination of sovereignties is addressed.
[124] *H.F. and Others v France* [GC] §213.
[125] ibid §213.
[126] ibid §212.
[127] ibid §209.
[128] To justify its finding that the diplomatic agents exercised no *de facto* control over the applicants, the Court reasoned that they 'freely chose to present themselves at the Belgian Embassy in Beirut, and to submit their visa applications there—as indeed they could have chosen to approach any other embassy; they had then been free to leave the premises of the Belgium embassy without any hindrance'. If a case emerges where these circumstances differ, there might be an opening for a different approach.
[129] See Section 8.2.5.
[130] *M.N. and Others v Belgium* [GC] (dec) no 3599/18, 5 May 2020 §124.

where decisions by diplomat and consular agents affect individuals. An approach more favourable to the applicants might thus be considered warranted.

## 8.2.5 Exercise of Public Powers

### 8.2.5.1 The autonomy of the model

Prior to explaining how the 'public powers' model of jurisdiction might be triggered, it needs to be discussed whether it can be actually considered an autonomous model under Article 1 of the ECHR. Pursuant to the general principles outlined in *Al-Skeini*, the exercise of 'public powers' is a separate basis for jurisdiction.[131] A confusion has arisen, however, as to the precise role of 'public powers' because of how the Court invoked these powers in its assessment of the particular facts in *Al-Skeini*.[132] More specifically, the Court established that the United Kingdom 'assumed in Iraq the exercise of some of the public powers normally to be exercised by a sovereign government'. Then it added that the United Kingdom 'exercised authority and control' over the individuals. In this way, two models of extraterritorial jurisdiction (the 'public powers' and 'physical power and control over the person') were simultaneously applied to the specific facts, which creates doubts as to the independent existence of each one of them.

As a consequence, different interpretations of *Al-Skeini* have emerged. Besson, for example, considers that the public power requirement is one of the three constitutive elements of jurisdiction in *all* models.[133] This relates to her argument that the jurisdictional clause in Article 1 ECHR 'conditions the applicability of ... rights and duties on political and legal circumstances where a certain relationship exists between rights-holder and state parties'.[134] Jurisdiction as a threshold is meant to ensure the tie between the individuals as rights holders and political authority as bearer of obligations.

---

[131] *Al-Skeini and Others v United Kingdom* [GC] no 55721/07, 7 July 2011 §135.
[132] ibid §149.
[133] Besson, 'The Extraterritoriality of the European Convention on Human Rights' (n 8) 873. A similar reconstruction of the judgments delivered before *Al-Skeini* has been offered in S Miller, 'Revisiting Extraterritorial Jurisdiction: A Territorial Justification for Extraterritorial Jurisdiction under the European Convention' (2010) 20 European Journal of International Law 1223, 1236 where an argument is formulated that extraterritorial jurisdiction is 'predicated on a state's functional exercise of sovereignty', which implies 'exercising functions in another state's territory which are normally associated with the acts of a sovereign state on its own territory'. The latter acts imply some 'administrative or regulatory powers'. Moreno-Lax also appears to endorse the position that the exercise of public powers is a constitutive element of jurisdiction in *all* models. However, her interpretation as to when 'public powers' are exercised, and thus trigger the jurisdiction threshold, is extremely (indeed unjustifiably) wide: 'If ... there is a piece of legislation enacted, a policy plan implemented, and/or a court decision enforcing the legislation or the policy plan in relation to said famine in said remote land, there should be no obstacle to consider such action as one demonstrative of state jurisdiction.... the jurisdictional nexus ... exists ... through the planning and execution of policy and/or operational conduct over which the State exerts effective (if not exclusive) control.' She argues that when the State exercises 'situational' control that is 'determinative of the material course of events', the State exercises jurisdiction in the sense of Article 1 ECHR. Moreno-Lax, 'The Architecture of Functional Jurisdiction' (n 6) 397 and 403.
[134] Besson, 'The Extraterritoriality of the European Convention on Human Rights' (n 8) 860.

This tie can be guaranteed when public powers are exercised by public authorities that claim legitimacy. This understanding corresponds to the analysis in Section 8.1 where the argument was formulated that the triggering and the analysis as to the content and scope of positive obligations do presuppose such a tie, a structured relationship between the rights holders and the State, as a bearer of obligations. I will return to this point below.

Raible's position seems to be in alignment with Besson's to a certain extent. Raible develops the argument that 'political power' is 'the underlying concept that best captures jurisdiction'.[135] While she does acknowledge the connection of this argument with the reference in *Al-Skeini* to 'public powers', Raible instead aims generally to develop a whole separate theoretical model as to the meaning of jurisdiction in human rights law. She defines 'political power' as 'the power of public institutions to transform individual powers with an outcome of control of human activities through the application of rules'.[136] 'Political power', according to her account, implies 'a capacity of the public institutions to apply principles and rules of their choice'.[137] The imposition of a regulatory framework seems to be crucial in the determination of whether 'political power' is present.[138] She adds that 'institutions with political power provide the backdrop against which the equal moral status of individuals—which is the value underpinning human rights—can be safeguarded'.[139] She rejects the notion that jurisdiction means power over a person or power over an area; instead, she posits that 'to establish jurisdiction, it is sufficient that certain areas of an individual's activity are under the control of a State, as long as this control is rooted in political power, that is power to transform powers held by an institution'.[140] The test that she develops is as follows: if a State has political power over an area of activity and 'of a kind that a public institution is able to transform powers of individuals in this area, then the institution must extend equal concern and respect to the affected individuals in this area of activity'.[141] The extension of equal concern implies that the State can be constituted as a duty bearer.

An alternative position to that taken by Besson and Raible is that the exercise of public powers is a necessary constitutive element in the *spatial model* of extraterritorial jurisdiction. This position is supported by *Bankovic and Others v Belgium and Others*. Therein the Court reasons that through effective control over an area and

---

[135] Raible, *Human Rights Unbound* (n 3) 5 and 101: 'pervasive political power as a potential'.
[136] ibid 134.
[137] ibid 139. In her account, these rules have to be applied to the individuals in question since 'a touch of their consequences is not enough' (p. 207). For this reason, she rejects the proposition that when the EU subsidizes its farmers who, as a consequence, can sell their products at lower prices, with which farmers in third countries cannot compete, the EU owes human rights obligation to the latter group of farmers. She explains that '[s]ubsidies and the rules that implement them are applied only to producers who are eligible to receive them in the first place. Producers abroad are not, and are thus not within the jurisdiction of the subsidizing state.'
[138] Raible, *Human Rights Unbound* (n 3) 192.
[139] ibid 135.
[140] ibid 143.
[141] ibid 146.

'its inhabitants', the State exercises 'public powers', a situation which in its entirety amounts to jurisdiction in the sense of Article 1 ECHR.[142] Yet in *Loizidou v Turkey* and *Cyprus v Turkey*, one of the leading cases under the spatial model, no explicit references to public powers are made. One can, however, attempt the argument that the reasoning in these judgments contains an implicit understanding that the respondent state had such powers because, as explained in Section 8.2.1, the conduct of the subordinate administration was viewed as converging with the conduct of Turkey.

In contrast to *Bankovic*, *Al-Skeini* supports the argument that the public power requirement is relevant to the *personal model* of extraterritorial jurisdiction.[143] In the reasoning to the particular facts in *Al-Skeini*, the exercise of 'public powers' appears to be an additional requirement that needs to be fulfilled to trigger the personal model.[144] Milanovic has observed that based on how the Court referred to 'public powers' when applying the principle to the specific facts in *Al-Skeini*, 'it seems the idea was to add a specification to the personal model that would preserve its role as a delimiting criterion of extraterritoriality'.[145] The Court needed to invoke such an criterion since, as mentioned in Section 8.2.3, one problem with the personal model is that it is hard to delimit, and consequently might simply collapse into a cause-and-effect model.

The inadmissibility decision in *M.N. and Others v Belgium* seems to support the understanding that the exercise of 'public powers' cannot be an independent model without any additional elements of personal or territorial *physical* control or relationship of nationality. In this decision, the Grand Chamber openly observed that 'in ruling on the applicant's visa applications, the Belgian authorities took decisions concerning the conditions for entry to Belgian "territory"' and, in so doing, exercised a public power.[146] However, this did not suffice for passing the jurisdictional threshold. This is so, even though the requirements for triggering the 'public powers' model indicated in *Al-Skeini*,[147] namely consent of the territorial state, an agreement and exclusive attribution, would be likely to be fulfilled in the case of embassies and consulates. If the applicants had been found to be under Belgian jurisdiction, as the Court continued to reason, this would have led to a situation where decisions taken at national

---

[142] *Bankovic and Others v Belgium and Others* [GC] (dec) no 52207/99, 12 December 2001 §71: 'In sum, the case-law of the Court demonstrates that its recognition of the exercise of extra-territorial jurisdiction by a Contracting State is exceptional: it has done so when the respondent State, through the effective control of the relevant territory and its inhabitants abroad as a consequence of military occupation or through the consent, invitation or acquiescence of the Government of that territory, exercises *all or some of the public powers* normally to be exercised by that Government' (emphasis added).
[143] Milanovic, '*Al-Skeini* and *Al-Jedda* in Strasbourg' (n 89) 131; see also *Georgia v Russia (II)* [GC] no 38263/08, 21 January 2021 §117–118.
[144] *Al-Skeini and Others v the United Kingdom* [GC] no 55721/07, 7 July 2011 §149. In *Hassan v the United Kingdom* [GC] no 29750/09, 16 September 2014 §75, the Court clarified that the facts in *Al-Skeini* 'tended to demonstrate that the United Kingdom was far from being in effective control of the south-eastern area which is occupied' in this way confirming that the 'control over an area' model was not relevant *Al-Skeini*.
[145] Milanovic, '*Al-Skeini* and *Al-Jedda* in Strasbourg' (n 89) 130.
[146] *M.N. and Others v Belgium* [GC] (dec) no 3599/18, 5 May 2020 §112.
[147] *Al-Skeini and Others v the United Kingdom* [GC] no 55721/07, 7 July 2011 §135.

level that have an impact on non-nationals abroad would render these persons rights holders under the ECHR. This was a situation the Court could not accept.

Nor does the part of the reasoning in *M.N. and Others v Belgium* where the ECtHR recapitulated general principles regarding jurisdiction seem to support an understanding that the 'public powers' can be a separate model. Rather, in the recapitulation of its case law, the Court assumed that since a State had control over an area, it exercised public powers: 'a State was exercising its jurisdiction extraterritorially, when, in an area outside its national territory, it exercised public powers such as authority and responsibility in respect of the maintenance of security'.[148] Somehow inconsistently, this statement is followed by references to *X. and Y. v Switzerland* and *Drozd and Janousek v France and Spain*, where no issue of control over an area arise, and to *Al-Skeini and Others*, where the core issue was arguably control over the persons.

### 8.2.5.2 Trigger

Overall, the case law pertaining to the 'public powers' model is limited and many questions remain unresolved, including the relevance of the elements of spatial and personal control and their interaction.[149] The autonomy of this model is therefore yet to be fully tested. Nonetheless, this should not prevent an analysis of the requirements mentioned in *Al-Skeini* that need to be fulfilled so that the model is triggered.[150] These were formulated in the following way:

> [T]he Court has recognized the exercise of extraterritorial jurisdiction by a Contracting State when, through the consent, invitation or acquiescence of the Government of that territory, it exercises all or some of the public powers normally to be exercised by that Government. Thus, where, in accordance with custom, treaty or other agreement, authorities of the Contracting State carry out executive or judicial function on the territory of another State, the Contracting State may be responsible for breaches of the Convention thereby incurred, as long as the acts in question are attributable to it rather than to the territorial State.[151]

Two elements from this quotation beg clarification: first, the requirement for a consent by the territorial state and for an agreement between the two relevant States, and second, the requirement for attribution.

---

[148] *M.N. and Others v Belgium* [GC] (dec) no 3599/18, 5 May 2020 §104.
[149] The 'public powers' model as framed in *Al-Skeini* has been also considered as a 'halfway house' between the spatial and personal models of jurisdiction. Elements of both of these models would thus need to be present. A Cowan, 'A New Watershed? Re-evaluating *Bankovic* in Light of *Al-Skeini*' (2012) 1 Cambridge Journal of International and Comparative Law 224.
[150] *Al-Skeini and Others v the United Kingdom* [GC] no 55721/07, 7 July 2011 §135.
[151] *Al-Skeini and Others v the United Kingdom* §135; *H.F. and Others v France* [GC] no 24384/19, 14 September 2022 §186.

## The requirements for a consent and an agreement

The requirements for 'consent, invitation or acquiescence' by the territorial state, and for an agreement between the two States, imply some form of a *legal* entitlement of the State of extraterritorial jurisdiction to act.[152] The latter presupposes the existence of certain applicable norms that could potentially enable the analysis on the merits that pertains to breach of any obligations.[153] If it is accepted that in *Al-Skeini* the Court did actually apply the 'public powers' model (or at least some elements of it), then it needs to be observed that the United Kingdom did not assume public powers in Iraq with the consent, at the invitation, or with the acquiescence of Iraq. Nor was there an agreement with Iraq.[154] However, it could be argued that the United Kingdom had legal entitlement and was allowed to exercise 'public powers' based on relevant UN Security Council Resolutions.[155] This would mean that international law sources could be invoked within the 'public powers' model for satisfying the elements of consent and agreement of the territorial state.

## The requirement for exclusive attribution

The quotation from *Al-Skeini* where the Court generally outlined the elements that need to be fulfilled for triggering the 'public powers' model seems to suggest that the concrete measure that is challenged ('the acts in question') must be attributable solely to the State of extraterritorial jurisdiction.[156] A requirement for exclusive and sole attribution might, however, be excessive: an alternative interpretation of the 'public powers' model as outlined in *Al-Skeini* might also be possible. In particular, the expression 'the acts in question are attributable to it [the State of extraterritorial jurisdiction] rather than to the territorial state' could mean more attributable to the former state, not exclusively attributable to it. Notably, the reasoning of the Court in *Al-Skeini* to the particular factual circumstances of the case is not helpful for resolving this uncertainty in the interpretation.

---

[152] This reveals a connection between jurisdiction as an authority of the State to regulate conduct as circumscribed by the sovereignty of other States, on the one hand, and jurisdiction in the sense of Article 1 ECHR, on the other. The Court has been criticized for eliding the two. See Milanovic, *Extraterritorial Application of Human Rights Treaties* (n 4) 22. Without prejudice to the autonomy of each concept, there seems nonetheless to be a connection between them. See Section 8.4.1.

[153] See Section 7.1.

[154] This has given basis for arguments that 'jurisdiction vis-a-vis public powers is determined by a *factual assessment* of whether a State is exercising "all or some of the public powers normally exercised by that Government"' (emphasis added). L Halewood, 'Avoiding the Legal Black Hole: Re-evaluating the Applicability of the European Convention on Human Rights to the UK's Targeted Killing Policy' (2019) 9(2) Göttingen Journal of International Law 301, 323; see also I Park, *The Right to Life in Armed Conflict* (Oxford University Press 2018) 79.

[155] *Al-Skeini and Others v the United Kingdom* [GC] no 55721/07, 7 July 2011 §§146–148.

[156] The last sentence from the quotation from §135 from *Al-Skeini and Others v the United Kingdom* [GC] no 55721/07, 7 July 2011 (ie 'the Contracting State may be responsible for breaches of the Convention thereby incurred, as long as the acts in question are attributable to it rather than to the territorial State') might anticipate that the Contracting State and the territorial State might both reasonably be candidates for attribution, but that the Contracting State's jurisdiction might be deemed present *if and only if* the acts in question are attributable solely to the Contracting State.

The Court in *Al-Skeini* referred *X. and Y. v Switzerland*, a case that might be of some assistance for better understanding of the 'public powers' model and the attribution requirement. *X. and Y. v Switzerland* concerned the exercise of immigration powers by one country on the territory of another.[157] The Swiss authorities were competent in the matter of immigration enforcement in Lichtenstein according to a bilateral treaty. Due to violations of immigration laws, the applicant was prohibited from entering Lichtenstein, leading *inter alia* to breach of his right to family life. Switzerland argued that the jurisdictional requirement under Article 1 ECHR was not fulfilled. The Commission noted that Lichtenstein 'had delegated to Switzerland most of its sovereign rights in the field of aliens' police' and concluded that 'it is *exclusively* the Swiss authorities which have acted, although with effect in the territory of Lichtenstein' (emphasis added). It follows that *X. and Y. v Switzerland* supports an exclusive attribution of the act to the State of extraterritorial jurisdiction.[158] If this is indeed the generally applicable standard, it can be observed that a requirement for exclusive attribution might be very difficult to fulfil in scenarios where States cooperate and the role of each state might be difficult to disentangle.

Under the 'public powers' model as formulated in *Al-Skeini*, 'the acts in question', acts that cause harm to an interest protected by human rights law, need to be linked to the State of extraterritorial jurisdiction. In this sense, attribution could be more generally understood as causation, and not necessarily in the narrow sense as envisioned by the rules of attribution in public international law.[159] The requirement that arguably demands the complete exclusion of the attribution to the territorial state seems to ensure the *close factual causality* between the State of extraterritorial jurisdiction and the 'acts in question' that have produced the harm.

Such close factual causality might be particularly difficult to achieve when the 'acts in question' take the form of omissions. The exercise of 'public powers' might imply the assumption of tasks that are normally performed by the territorial state, or could be even normally within the prerogative of this State. Any omissions in the context of the exercise of these powers might thus be omissions attributable to the territorial state. A causal link between omissions and the State of extraterritorial jurisdiction might therefore be difficult to demonstrate.

### 8.2.5.3 How does the model reflect the preconditions?

As shown above, uncertainty clouds the 'public power' model regarding its autonomous standing and the actual requirements it raises. This uncertainty is also due to the

---

[157] *X. and Y. v Switzerland* nos 7289/75 and 7349/76, 14 July 1977.
[158] The same distinction applies in relation to *Drozd and Janousek v France and Spain* no 12747/87, 26 June 1992, that was also mentioned in *Al Skeini* as an example of the 'public powers' model. In particular, French and Spanish judges acted extraterritorially in Andorra. However, in contrast to *X. and Y. v Switzerland*, where exclusive attribution to the extraterritorially acting state was established, in *Drozd and Janousek* the judges' acts were attributable to Andorra, not to France and Spain, which, as the applicants argued, acted extraterritorially.
[159] See Articles on the Responsibility of States to Internationally Wrongful Acts, 2001 YILC Vol II (Part Two) 26.

## 250   Extraterritorial Positive Obligations

fact the model has been applied only in few exceptional and idiosyncratic cases,[160] yet it can be observed that this model reflects the preconditions discussed in Section 8.1. As clarified above, it does imply some sort of formal legal context that structures the relationship between the State and the affected individuals.

The requirement of exclusive attribution can be also understood as a confirmation of the specificity of human rights law, given its communitarian character, as preoccupied with the vertical political and legal relationship between a State and a group of individuals.[161] The conceptual underpinnings of the rules that characterise human rights law (including the jurisdictional threshold) need to cater for communitarian interests and democratic legitimacy.[162] The exclusive attribution requirement for making the 'public powers' model applicable can be thus related to the clarification that, although as a matter of fact state jurisdiction might not be exclusive (and thus it might be 'concurrent'),[163] it claims to be exclusive.[164] Human rights law assumes absence of coextensive or competing sovereignties (ie legal and political authorities).[165] Accordingly, although in practice two States might be exercising human rights jurisdiction, dual democratic legitimacy and dual democratic justifications for limiting rights or imposing positive obligations might be hard to operationalize.

### 8.2.6   Extraterritorial Effects

The spatial and the personal models of jurisdiction presuppose that state agents of the extraterritorially acting state exercise *physical control* over an area or over persons located outside the state territory, which implies some form of physical contact. In contrast, the other two models already discussed above (ie acts of diplomatic and consular agents and the exercise of 'public powers') seem to be predominantly constructed on

---

[160] *X. and Y. v Switzerland* and, in particular, the Switzerland–Lichtenstein context, is idiosyncratic.

[161] For the specificity of this vertical relationship see M den Heijer and R Lawson, 'Extraterritorial Human Rights and the Concept of "Jurisdiction"' in L Malcom (ed), *Global Justice, State Duties* (Cambridge University Press 2013)153, 154.

[162] Human rights are coupled with a specific state community. See Section 8.1. See also Noll, 'The Exclusionary Construction of Human Rights in International Law and Political Theory' (n 13). For the mutual relationship between human rights and democracy, see Besson, 'Human Rights and Democracy in a Global Context' (n 17) 19.

[163] The position in *Ilaşcu and Others v Moldova and Russia* no 48787/99, 8 July 2004, namely that both respondents had jurisdiction in relation to the same events, supports the understanding that jurisdiction can be exercised at the same time by two States in relation to the same events. For a detailed analysis, including indication of existing contradictions in the case law, see O de Schutter, 'Globalization and Jurisdiction' (2006) 6 Baltic Yearbook of International Law 185, 226.

[164] Besson, 'The Extraterritoriality of the European Convention on Human Rights' (n 8) 869. See also G Noll, 'Theorizing Jurisdiction' in A Orford and F Hoffmann (eds), *The Oxford Handbook of the Theory of International Law* (Oxford University Press 2016) 600, 606, who also concludes in his analysis that to understand jurisdiction in human rights law 'the power to exclude or supplant other, potentially competing powers, appears to be decisive'.

[165] This explains why the jurisdictional threshold might 'render nugatory some of the principles of the law on state responsibility that have been developed with a view to accommodate the involvement of multiple entities'. M den Heijer, 'Shared Responsibility before the ECtHR' (2013) 60(3) Netherlands International Law Review 411, 436.

the basis of *legal entitlement*.[166] A State can, however, affect persons located beyond its borders in ways that do not strictly fit within the physical control and the legal entitlement paradigm. This is despite the insecurity that clouds the boundaries of these two paradigms and how they relate to each other. Such situations are characterized by mere effects and can arise when, for example, multinational corporations registered in one State operate in other States,[167] or when a State provides funds,[168] equipment, weapons, intelligence, or more widely assistance that are then used by other States or actors in harmful ways. Trade and investment regimes and finance also have global repercussions.[169] Another example emerges from scenario when a State provides subsidies for domestic production or incentives for production of certain crops such as biofuels, which may have global effects on livelihood and environment.[170] Certain domestic policies might thus have negative repercussions for food security in other countries.[171] The question here is whether States hold human rights obligations in relation to individuals located beyond their borders who suffer the detrimental *effects* of these States' policies.[172]

These policies tend to be reviewed from the perspective of economic and social rights,[173] and in this context, much scholarly attention has been devoted to harm

---

[166] I say predominantly since in *M.N. and Others v Belgium* [GC] (dec) no 3599/18, 5 May 2020 in relation to foreign nationals, the Court did impose a requirement for physical control, so that acts of diplomatic and consular agents affecting *foreigners* can be defined as an exercise of jurisdiction (see Section 8.2.4). As to the 'public powers' model, given the requirement for attribution so that this model can be applied, some physical contact between the agents of the State of extraterritorial jurisdiction and the affected individuals, might also be required.

[167] D Augestein, 'The Crisis of International Human Rights Law in the Global Market Economy' (2013) 44 Netherlands Yearbook of International Law 41.

[168] A Barros, *Governance as Responsibility: Member States as Human Rights Protectors in International Financial Institutions* (Cambridge University Press 2019).

[169] Linarelli and others (eds), *The Misery of International Law: Confrontations with Injustice in the Global Economy* (Oxford University Press 2018) 226.

[170] H Haugen, 'International Obligations and the Right to Food: Clarifying the Potentials and Limitation in Applying a Human Rights Approach when Facing Biofuels Expansion' (2012) 11(3) Journal of Human Rights 405.

[171] J Mowbray, 'The Right to Food and the International Economic System: An Assessment of the Rights-Based Approach to the Problem of World Hunger' (2007) 20(3) Leiden Journal of International Law 545.

[172] Jurisdiction based only on extraterritorial effects has been favoured by Principle 8(a) of the Maastricht Principles on Extraterritorial Obligations of States in the Area of Economic, Social and Cultural Rights, 28 September 2011. There has been also a scholarly debate on the issue: A Berkes, 'Extraterritorial Responsibility of the Home States for MNCs Violations of Human Rights' in Y Radi (ed), *Research Handbook on Human Rights and Investment* (Edward Elgar Publishing 2018) 304; D Augunstein and D Kinley, 'When Human Rights 'Responsibilities' Become Duties': The Extra-territorial Obligations of States that Bind Corporations' in D Bilchiz and S Deva (eds), *Human Rights Obligations of Business: Beyond the Corporate Responsibility to Respect* (Cambridge University Press 2013) 271; I Kanalan, 'Extraterritorial State Obligations beyond the Concept of Jurisdiction' (2018) 19 German Law Journal 43; A Khalfan, 'Development Cooperation and Extraterritorial Obligations' in M Langford and A Russell (eds), *The Human Right To Water: Theory, Practice and Prospects* (Cambridge University Press 2017) 396; M Craven, 'The Violence of Dispossession: Extra-territoriality and Economic, Social and Cultural Rights' in M Baderin and R McCorquodale (eds), *Economic Social and Cultural Rights in Actions* (Oxford University Press 2007) 75.

[173] Langford and others (eds), *Global Justice, State Duties* (n 5); A Vandenbogaerde, 'Attributing Extraterritorial Obligations under the International Covenant on Economic, Social and Cultural Rights' (2015) 9 Human Rights and International Legal Discourse 6. See also CESCR General Comment 23(2016) on the right to just and favourable conditions of work, UN Doc. E/C.12/GC/23, §69; Guiding Principles on Human Rights Impact Assessment of Economic Reforms, 19 December 2018, UN Doc. A/HRC/40/

by multinational corporations. The possibility of framing the harm as falling within the definitional scope of the right to life, the right not to be subjected to torture, inhuman or degrading treatment, and the right to private and family life,[174] is not precluded, however. An assessment as to whether these rights are violated could be made through the framework of positive obligations, since arguments could be formulated that, for example, the State has not regulated private entities sufficiently well, or it has failed to ensure that the assistance provided to other States does not harm individuals located beyond its borders. What is typical here is that the conduct—including any omissions—that arguably leads to negative effects is performed within the territory of the State. While the effects might be extraterritorial, the conduct itself is not.

### 8.2.6.1 Rejection of the model in the case law

A paucity of ECtHR case law in this area can be observed. The Court has made the general statement that 'the responsibility of Contracting States can be involved by acts and omission of their authorities which produce effects outside their own territory'.[175] This can happen 'only in exceptional circumstances'.[176] In *Bankovic*, however, the Court clearly rejected the cause-and-effect notion of jurisdiction. It precluded that

> anyone adversely affected by an act imputable to a Contracting State, wherever in the world that act may have been committed or its consequences felt, is thereby brought within the jurisdiction of that State for the purpose of Article 1 of the Convention.[177]

This was confirmed in *Georgia v Russia* (II).[178] It follows that the preclusion of adverse consequences for individuals cannot be framed as a matter of human rights obligations.[179]

Despite this rejection, there have been judgments where state jurisdiction was triggered by the mere negative effect of a state act.[180] For example, in *Pad and Others v*

---

57, 4; Guiding Principles on Human Rights Impact Assessment of Trade and Investment Agreements, 19 December 2011, UN Doc. A/HRC/19/59 Add 5 §5; CESCR General Comment 24 on the Nature of State Parties' Obligations in the Context of Business Activities, 10 August 2017, UN Doc. E/C.12/GC/24 §27.

[174] The definitional scope of these rights is open to wide interpretation. The absence of a strict division between socio-economic and civil rights can be also noted. See I Leijten, *Core Socio-Economic Rights and the European Court of Human Rights* (Cambridge University Press 2017).

[175] *Loizidou v Turkey* (merits) [GC] no 15318/89, 18 December 1996 §52; *Loizidou v Tukey* (preliminary objections) no 15318/89, 23 March 1995 §62; *Issa and Others v Turkey* no 31821/96, 16 November 2004 §68.

[176] *Georgia v Russia (II)* [GC] no 38263/08, 21 January 2021 §123.

[177] *Bankovic and Others v Belgium and Others* [GC] (dec) no 52207/99, 12 December 2001 §75.

[178] *Georgia v Russia (II)* [GC] no 38263/08, 21 January 2021 §124.

[179] *Abdul Wahab Khan v the United Kingdom* no 11987/11, Decision 28 January 2014 §26 'Nor is there any support in the Court's case-law for the applicant's argument that the State's obligations under Article 3 require it to take this Article into account when making adverse decisions against individuals, even when those individuals are not within its jurisdiction.'

[180] For scholarship that pleas for cause-and-effect understanding of jurisdiction, see generally Ryngaert, 'Extraterritorial Obligations under Human Rights Law' (n 4) 273.

*Turkey*, a case that involved the killing and torture by Turkish forces of Iranian citizens on Iranian territory, the Court considered that

> it is not required to determine the exact location of the impugned events, given that the Government had already admitted that the fire discharged from the helicopters had caused the killing of the applicants' relatives, who had been suspected of being terrorists.[181]

Similar reasoning was applied in *Solomou and Others v Turkey*, where the finding that the bullet that hit the victim had been fired by members of the Turkish-Cypriot forces was enough for the Court to decide that Turkey had jurisdiction.[182] Similarly, in *Andreu v Turkey*, where the applicant was injured by bullets fired from the Turkish Republic of Northern Cyprus while she was in the UN buffer zone, the Court observed that the act of opening fire was 'the direct and immediate cause' of her injuries, which brought her within the jurisdiction of Turkey.[183]

Although the positive findings in *Pad*, *Solomou*, and *Andreu* are hard to square with the result in *Bankovic*, where the firing of the missiles was also 'the direct and immediate cause' for the injuries, the circumstances in the former judgments involve some *physical* contact and a physical act (eg firing of a bullet) that was a direct cause.[184] In contrast, the circumstances described in the beginning of this section do not necessarily include acts causing direct and immediate harm, but rather arguable omissions that might be elements of wider structures and chains with multiple actors involved, both state and non-state.

The admissibility decision in *Tugar v Italy* reveals this problem. *Tugar v Italy* concerned a mine clearer who lost his leg in Iraq after stepping on an anti-personnel mine of Italian origin.[185] The applicant argued that Italy—having omitted to regulate the private company that supplied Iraq with the lethal weapon—failed to protect him by means of an effective transfer licensing system and, as a consequence, Italy did not comply with its positive obligations under Article 2 ECHR. In declaring the application inadmissible, the European Commission on Human Rights reasoned that

> the applicant's injury cannot be seen as a *direct consequence of the failure* of the Italian authorities to legislate on arms transfers. There is *no immediate relationship* between the mere supply, even if not properly regulated, of weapons and the

---

[181] *Pad and Others v Turkey* (dec) no 60167/00, 28 June 2007 §54.
[182] *Solomou and Others v Turkey* no 36832/97, 24 June 2008 §50.
[183] *Andreou v Turkey* (dec) no 45653/99, 3 June 2008.
[184] A clarifying note is due here regarding *Kovačič v Slovenia* [GC] no 44574/98, 3 October 2008, a case not involving a physical contact, but negative extraterritorial effects of the Slovenia's legislation, as a result of which foreign currency depositors in Croatia were prevented from withdrawing funds from their accounts in the Croatian branch of the Slovenian bank. The depositors were found to be within the Slovenian jurisdiction. The case can be viewed in the specific context related to the break-up of the Federal Republic of Yugoslavia.
[185] *Rasheed Haje Tugar v Italy* (dec) 22869/93, 18 October 1995 (inadmissible).

possible "indiscriminate" use thereof in a third country, the latter's action constituting the direct and decisive cause of the accident which the applicant suffered. It follows that the 'adverse consequences' of the failure of Italy to regulate arms transfers to Iraq are 'too remote' to attract the Italian responsibility. [emphasis added]

Pursuant to this reasoning, there were important intervening acts that hampered the causation between the harm and the alleged failure by Italy. First, it was an Italian private company that delivered the weapons—subsequently found guilty of illegal arms trafficking to Iraq by an Italian court. Second, it was Iraq that mined the area. Third, this mining was done in an indiscriminate way. In this sense, there was no conduct by the respondent state that 'may directly expose a particular individual to a particular and immediate risk'.

Admittedly, the Commission's reasoning in *Tugar v Italy* lacks clarity because it seems to conflate the threshold issue of jurisdiction with issues pertaining to the analysis on the merits, such as causation in the context of positive obligations. Nonetheless, it does make clear that mere negative effects of alleged omissions cannot satisfy the triggering of the jurisdictional threshold under Article 1 ECHR.[186] The inadmissibility decision in *M.N. and Others v Belgium* has further confirmed in explicit terms that jurisdiction cannot be triggered simply based on negative extraterritorial effects: 'The mere fact that decisions taken at national level had an impact on the situation of persons resident abroad is also not such as to establish the jurisdiction of the State concerned over those persons outside its territory.'[187]

### 8.2.6.2 Parallels with complicity

Despite this, attempts have been also made to extend the *Soering* principle by arguing that States that facilitate (by sharing intelligence, selling equipment, or providing technical support) and thus are complicit in harm sustained by individuals located in other States, hold human rights obligations because of the foreseeable consequence of the facilitation.[188] It has been also added that the State can and is allowed to control third parties (eg multinational companies) registered on its territory, and therefore scenarios of extraterritorial negative effects do not implicate extraterritorial obligations at all, since the conduct contributing to and facilitating negative effects is performed on the territory of the State.[189]

---

[186] See also *Mohammed Ben Al Mahi and Others v Denmark* no 5853/06, 11 December 2006, where the applicants who were in Morocco, claimed that Denmark had breached the ECHR by allowing the publication of cartoons considered to be offensive to Muslims. The Court held that there was no jurisdictional link between the applicants and Denmark.

[187] *M.N. and Others v Belgium* [GC] (dec) no 3599/18, 5 May 2020 §112.

[188] Jackson has framed these as cases of 'extraterritorial complicity'. M Jackson, 'Freeing *Soering*: The ECHR, State Complicity in Torture and Jurisdiction' (2016) 27(3) European Journal of International Law 817, 824. In *M.N. and Others v Belgium* [GC] (dec) no 3599/18, 5 May 2020 §120, the Grand Chamber rejected such an analogy with the *Soering* principle by noting that 'individuals in cases involving removal from a State's territory are, in theory, on the territory of the State concerned—or at its border'.

[189] C Ryngaert, 'EU Trade Agreements and Human Rights: From Extraterritorial to Territorial Obligations' (2018) 20 International Community Law Review 374, 384–89.

The weakness of all these arguments is that they ignore the specificity of human rights law as a body of law meant to regulate the relationship between a State and individuals as right-holders, and the role of jurisdiction as reflective of this relationship. In this sense, jurisdiction refers to the relationship with the right-holder, not with a third party (eg a company) or with the source of harm more generally.[190] It is thus the location of the potential right holders that is determinative as to whether any correlative obligations can be framed as extraterritorial.[191]

A State may have jurisdiction *under international law* to regulate certain activities, and in this sense, it might be permitted to regulate, for example, third parties such as companies. However, this permission does not necessarily imply that the same State is a holder of obligations under human rights law vis-à-vis the individuals affected by these activities.[192] There might be situations where by exercising activities based on permitted basis of jurisdiction under international law, a State brings individuals within its human rights law jurisdiction.[193] However, still the jurisdictional threshold in human rights law has to be separately and independently passed.[194] Most importantly, there might be a normative and political relationship between the State and the third party (eg a company incorporated in its territory that causes extraterritorial harm). This does not mean that there is such a relationship with the individuals affected by this harm, and this is precisely what the jurisdiction threshold is meant to test.

---

[190] The Court's case law manifest confusion as to the points of the jurisdictional link. The answer to the following question is not clear: link *in relationship to what*? Is it about a link between a State and individuals (*Georgia v Russia (II)* [GC] no 38263/08, 21 January 2021§295)? Is it about a link between a State and events/facts (*Georgia v Russia (II)* [GC] §162 and 175; *H.F. and Others v France* [GC] no 24384/19, 14 September 2022 §190: 'particular facts')? Is it about a link between a State and a complaint (*Georgia v Russia (II)* [GC] §332)? Is it about a link between a State and territory (*H.F. and Others v France* [GC] §208 where the question of France jurisdiction is framed as simultaneously both 'jurisdiction *ratione loci* and *ratione personae*')?

[191] See also the definition of extraterritorial application of human rights treaties in Milanovic, *Extraterritorial Application of Human Rights Treaties* (n 4) 8: 'at the moment of the alleged violation of his or her rights the individual concerned is not physically in the territory of the State party in question, a geographical area over which the State has sovereignty or title'.

[192] For a development of this flawed argument see S Skogly and P Osim, 'Jurisdiction—A Barrier to Compliance with Extraterritorial Obligations to Protect against Human Rights Abuses by Non-State Actors' (2019) 13(2) Human Rights and International Legal Discourse 99. Similarly, see C Ryngaert, *Selfless Intervention. Exercising Jurisdiction in the Common Interest* (Oxford University Press 2020) 59 where an argument is formulated that positive human rights obligations might require States to exercise prescriptive jurisdiction in this way regulating activities beyond their borders. It overlooks, however, that the existence of such obligations is initially contingent on jurisdiction in the sense of Article 1 ECHR.

[193] Situations can be also imagined where since the human rights jurisdiction of a State is found triggered, this particular State is under a positive obligation to exercise prescriptive criminal jurisdiction by, for example, criminalizing certain activities.

[194] Ollino, 'Justifications and Limits of Extraterritorial Obligations of States' (n 45): 'States may exercise enforcement jurisdiction abroad pursuant to international agreements on cooperation and assistance among States in criminal matters, and be required to respect the human rights of people in the exercise of such jurisdiction.' C O'Brien, 'The Home State Duty to Regulate the Human Rights Impacts of TNCs Abroad: A Rebuttal' (2018) 3 Business and Human Rights 47, 61: It is a mistaken view that 'because States are not precluded under general international law from enacting legislation with extraterritorial scope, they have an obligation, under human rights law, to do this'.

Besides the above-mentioned weakness concerning the relational nature of human rights law, another problem arises if jurisdiction is approached solely on the basis of effects and the possibility to influence events outside borders, namely that there are no limits on responsibility. This relates to the conceptual difficulties revolving around responsibility based on omissions. Conduct consisting of an omission can always be attributed to a State. A State is constantly committing omissions or being complicit in omissions that might have multiple and unlimited repercussions. For any omission to be legally relevant in human rights law, however, there needs first to be an obligation to act. As clarified in Section 8.1, the existence of such an obligation is based on normative considerations that are grounded in the relational nature of human rights law.

### 8.2.6.3 Parallels with due diligence

An argument can, however, be anticipated that it is possible to find criteria for imposing limits on responsibility. In particular, only certain omissions can be made legally relevant by imposing knowledge, foreseeability, causality, and reasonableness tests.[195] Pursuant to this argument, if the State knew and/or could foresee that extraterritorial harm could materialize, but failed to take preventive measures, then the omission can become legally relevant, and should be a basis for the formulation of an obligation.[196] From the perspective of causality, the argument can be framed in the following way: if a direct and immediate link can be established between the omission and the extraterritorial harm, then the omission should provide a basis for the framing of an obligation.[197] As to reasonableness, Ryngaert argues that a reasonableness test should gauge whether the connection between the State and the activity to be regulated is sufficiently close.[198]

There are two problems with this set of arguments. First, they defeat the purpose of having a jurisdictional threshold.[199] More specifically, they conflate positive obligations in human rights law with general due diligence standards under public international law.[200] The latter are directly based on foreseeability, reasonableness, and causality *without* an initial threshold, such as the jurisdictional threshold that

---

[195] For such an approach, see CESCR General Comment No 24 §27; HRC General Comment No 36 §22.
[196] Jackson, 'Freeing *Soering*' (n 188) 824.
[197] Lawson, 'Life After Bankovic' (n 11) 104.
[198] C Ryngaert, 'Jurisdiction. Towards a Reasonableness Test' in Langford and others (eds), *Global Justice, State Duties* (n 5) 192, 196–201. The closeness of the connection can be tested against the following standards: whether the State has effective control over the multinational corporation that caused the harm, or whether the State has decisive influence over the corporation or against the mere fact of incorporation in the State.
[199] This problem was also highlighted by the Court in *Bankovic and Others v Belgium and Others* [GC] (dec) no 52207/99, 12 December 2001 §75.
[200] This is very apparent in the following statement, 'the due diligence standard is the appropriate standard in determining a State's jurisdiction'. Ryngaert, 'Jurisdiction. Towards a Reasonableness Test' (n 198) 210. See also Partly Concurring Opinion of Judge Serghides in *Georgia v Russia (II)* [GC] no 38263/08, 21 January 2021, who seems to argue that the ECHR can impose obligations independently from the jurisdictional restraint imposed by Article 1.

importantly distinguishes human rights law as a body of law.[201] This distinction cannot simply be ignored.[202]

Second, what unites all these arguments is that purely factual considerations are proposed to delimit responsibility in human rights law, and any normative dimensions are made irrelevant. The arguments are therefore insensitive to the nature of analysis that human rights law triggers on the merits. In particular, foreseeability, reasonableness, and causality in human rights law are assessed with reference to certain normative presuppositions that operate within the bounded political community,[203] an argument forcefully made in Section 8.1.[204] This can be also related to the inherent characteristic of omissions as a basis for searching for responsibility. As clarified in Section 8.1, omissions can become legally relevant only when some context of accepted standards exists against which such omissions can be juxtaposed.

In conclusion, the constitution of individuals as rights holders by the mere fact that they are harmed by policies conducted by foreign States or third parties located in these States poses many conceptual and normative problems. If jurisdiction is to serve the purpose as a threshold that reflects the relational normative nature of human rights law, these individuals cannot be constituted as rights holders. It might not be possible to frame a relationship between them and these States that fits within and corresponds to the normative and relational paradigm that underpins human rights law.

## 8.2.7 Procedural Link

Having explained the *Al-Skeini* models and rejected extraterritorial effects as a basis for triggering jurisdiction under Article 1 of the ECHR, an appreciation of one more jurisdictional basis is due. It can be framed as a 'procedural link' since it reflects situations where a State establishes a *legal* link with individuals by initiating or making available proceedings at domestic level. This procedural legal link may suffice in establishing a 'jurisdictional link' for the purposes of Article of the 1 ECHR.

---

[201] Positive human rights law obligation and the due diligence obligations differ not only due to the existence of a jurisdictional threshold in relation to the former. They also differ substantively, since not every positive human rights law obligation is an obligation of due diligence, that is, an obligation of conduct. For a detailed comparison see V Stoyanova, 'Due Diligence versus Positive Obligations: Critical Reflections on the Council of Europe Convention on Violence against Women' in J Niemi and others (eds), *International Law and Violence against Women: Europe and the Istanbul Convention* (Routledge 2020) 95.

[202] See also Raible, *Human Rights Unbound* (n 3) 106, who shows that jurisdiction in human rights law refers to 'pre-existing relationship' that 'is logically and normatively prior to any violations because it justifies allocating obligations that need to be present in order to be violated'.

[203] In this sense I disagree with Ollino that foreseeability, reasonableness, and causation are purely factual criteria. Ollino, 'Justifications and Limits of Extraterritorial Obligations of States' (n 45).

[204] By way of clarification, the assessment of foreseeability, reasonableness, and causality *is not done only* with reference to normative presuppositions. As showed in Section 8.1, it is also done with reference to factual criteria: eg the control that the State has over the source of harm or the affected individuals or the extent to which there was objective knowledge about risk of harm. The fulfilment of these factual criteria might face some specific challenges in effects-based extraterritorial situations. For example, knowledge about risk of harm might be limited.

The leading cases are *Markovic and Others v Italy*[205] and *Güzelyurtlu and Others v Cyprus and Turkey*.[206] The facts of the first relate to the same events as those considered in *Bankovic*. However, this time the applicants brought civil proceedings before the Italian courts for compensation for damages (specifically, the death of their relatives) sustained as a result of the NATO air strikes on Belgrade. These proceedings were terminated since the Italian Court of Cassation ruled that the domestic courts had no jurisdiction to examine the claim for compensation. The applicants complained in Strasbourg that the termination precluded them from securing a decision on the merits of their claim, which they claimed was in violation of Article 6 ECHR (the right to fair trail). The respondent state argued that the applicants were not within its jurisdiction in the sense of Article 1 of the ECHR, because it would be 'absurd' to suggest that while Italy had no obligations to protect the right to life (since pursuant to *Bankovic* the jurisdiction threshold was not triggered), it did have any obligations to protect related procedural rights arising from Article 6 of the ECHR.

The Court did not agree with this suggestion, and thus refused to follow the argument by Italy that 'the subsequent institution of proceedings at the national level does not give rise to any obligation on the part of the State towards the persons bringing the proceedings'.[207] It clarified that

> [e]*verything depends on the rights which may be claimed under the law of the State concerned*. If the *domestic law recognizes a right to bring an action* and if the right claimed is one which prima facie possesses the characteristics required by Article 6 of the Convention, the Court sees no reason why such domestic proceedings should not be subjected to the same level of scrutiny as any other proceedings brought at national level.[208]

This implies that domestic courts can hear civil actions that have their origins in extraterritorial events. These origins cannot preclude outright the applicability of Article 6 ECHR: 'If civil proceedings are brought in domestic courts, the State is required by Article 1 of the Convention to secure in those proceedings respect for the rights protected by Article 6'.[209] Without saying that the applicants in *Markovic* were *generally* within the Italian jurisdiction, the Court held that there was a 'jurisdictional link' between them and the respondent State based on the domestic civil proceedings *as allowed under the domestic law*.

The Court then applied its usual analysis to Article 6 of the ECHR. It first affirmed that the domestic proceedings implicated a dispute about an arguable 'civil right',[210]

---

[205] *Markovic and Others v Italy* [GC] no 1398/03, 14 December 2006 §§54–56;
[206] *Güzelyurtlu and Others v Cyprus and Turkey* [GC] no 36925/07, 29 January 2019 §187.
[207] *Markovic and Others v Italy* [GC] no 1398/03, 14 December 2006 §53.
[208] ibid §53 (emphasis added).
[209] ibid §53; *H.F. and Others v France* [GC] no 24384/19, 14 September 2022 §188.
[210] *Markovic and Others v Italy* [GC] no 1398/03, 14 December 2006 §101. The dispute was arguable because this was the first time when the domestic courts were called upon to examine the issue.

which made Article 6 applicable. It then examined whether the requirements under Article 6 were complied with. This was answered affirmatively since the inability to sue the State was based on the limitative conditions imposed by the domestic civil law.[211]

It is important to reflect upon the limitations of *Markovic*. The judgment does not support a general proposition that any proceedings allowed by the domestic law, and subsequently initiated by individuals, can establish a 'jurisdictional link'.[212] Such a link is contingent on the applicability of Article 6, which means that the proceedings have to concern a dispute related to determination of 'civil rights and obligations or of any criminal charge'. This limitation became very clear in *M.N. and Others v Belgium*, where the Court rejected the assertion that the initiation of domestic proceedings to challenge visa refusals brought the applicants within the jurisdiction of Belgium for the purpose of Article 1.[213] The particular proceedings in *M.N. and Others* did not involve civil rights and obligations.[214]

With *Güzelyurtlu and Others v Cyprus and Turkey*, however, the Court has affirmed that proceedings not necessarily covered by Article 6 can also serve as a basis for the existence of a 'jurisdictional link'. It is thus important to examine the implications of this judgment. *Güzelyurtlu* involved the murder of three Turkish Cypriots committed on the territory of the Republic of Cyprus, in relation to which the State opened a criminal investigation. The identified suspects fled to the Turkish Republic of Northern Cyprus (TRNC), which arrested them and also opened an investigation. The proceedings in both countries, however, came to a deadlock when the TRNC refused to surrender the suspects to Cyprus and the latter, for its part, refused the transfer the case file to the TRNC authorities. As a result, the victims' relatives complained under the ECHR that both Cyprus and Turkey were in violation of the procedural limb of Article 2 (ie the obligation to conduct an effective investigation).

While the case is key from the perspective of the positive obligations upon States to cooperate addressed in Section 6.2.4, the analysis here is limited to the jurisdictional challenge. Turkey argued, in particular, that it had no 'jurisdictional link' with the applicants. The Court rejected this position and took the opportunity to establish the following general principles. It introduced two scenarios: first, when proceedings are

---

[211] *Markovic and Others v Italy* [GC] §103–115. Here it should be reminded that Article 6 ECHR does not in itself guarantee any particular content for civil rights and obligations in national law.

[212] Based on *Markovic and Others v Italy*, it has been argued that '[i]f a victim of corporate-related human rights violations located outside the State's territory attempts to bring civil proceedings in the domestic courts of that state, she comes under the latter's human rights jurisdiction within the meaning of Article 1 ECHR'. See D Augenstein, 'Torture or Tort? Transnational Tort Litigation for Corporate-Related Human Rights Violations and the Human Right to a Remedy' (2018) 18 Human Rights Law Review 593, 609. This argument is, however, hard to accept for at least two reasons. First, such proceedings have to be allowed by the domestic law. Second, there needs to be a dispute related to determination of civil rights. If the domestic law is clear that there is no right, there is no dispute, and Article 6 is not applicable.

[213] *M.N. and Others v Belgium* [GC] (dec) no 3599/18, 5 May 2020 §122; *H.F. and Others v France* [GC] no 24384/19, 14 September 2022 §188.

[214] *M.N. and Others v Belgium* [GC] (dec) no 3599/18, 5 May 2020 §137.

initiated by the State despite the fact that the events did not take part on its territory, and second, when the case manifests 'special features'.

In relation to the first scenario, the Court held that

> if the investigative or judicial authorities of a Contracting State initiate their own criminal investigation or proceedings concerning a death which has occurred outside the jurisdiction of the State, by virtue of their domestic law (e.g., under provisions on universal jurisdiction or on the basis of the active or passive personality principle), the institution of that investigation or those proceedings is sufficient to establish a jurisdictional link for the purposes of Article 1 between the State and the victim's relatives who later bring proceedings before the Court.[215]

To justify this approach, the Court immediately referred to the nature of the analysis on the merits. In particular, it highlighted that the obligation to investigate has 'evolved into a separate and autonomous obligation' and '[i]n this sense it can be considered to be a detachable obligation arising out of Article 2 and capable of binding the State even when the death occurred outside its jurisdiction.'[216] Therefore, as was indicated above in relation to *Markovic* and Article 6, there is an intertwinement between the nature of the procedural obligation invoked and the possibility for establishing a 'jurisdictional link', so that compliance with this specific procedural obligation is assessed on the merits.[217] The limits flowing from this intertwinement emerged in *M.N. and Others v Belgium*, which involved administrative proceedings brought at the initiative of the applicants. These were contrasted with criminal proceedings opened by the state authority in the context of the State's procedural obligation under Article 2.[218]

In *Güzelyurtlu*, however, the Court did not limit the possibility for establishing a 'jurisdictional link' to circumstances where the State *itself* has initiated criminal proceedings based on its domestic law in relation to death that occurred outside its territory. It developed a second scenario, where such an initiation is absent but when the Court will still decide whether in any event a 'jurisdictional link' arises by virtue of some 'special features'. Such features can justify a departure from the approach that the procedural obligation under Article 2 is in principle triggered only for the State under whose jurisdiction the deceased was found at the time of death.[219] The reasoning in *Güzelyurtlu* contains no general guidance as to these 'special features' since

---

[215] *Güzelyurtlu and Others v Cyprus and Turkey* [GC] no 36925/07, 29 January 2019 §188 (emphasis added).

[216] *Güzelyurtlu and Others v Cyprus and Turkey* §189.

[217] This intertwinement was the reason for the GC to *reject* that the applicants' relatives were within the jurisdiction of France based on the existence of a procedural link (ie France having opened criminal proceedings against the applicants' daughters) in *H.F. and Others v France* [GC] no 24384/19, 14 September 2022 §194. These criminal proceedings had nothing to do with the obligations that the Court had to assess on the merits. See Section 8.3.

[218] *M.N. and Others v Belgium* [GC] (dec) no 3599/18, 5 May 2020 §122.

[219] *Güzelyurtlu and Others v Cyprus and Turkey* [GC] no 36925/07, 29 January 2019 §190.

these 'will necessary depend on the particular circumstances of each case and may vary considerably from one case to the other'.[220]

In the specific case of *Güzelyurtlu*, the 'special features' were found to have been fulfilled in relation to Turkey.[221] A special feature was the recognition that Turkey is an occupying power and the absence of recognition of the TRNC as a State by the international community. The second special feature was that there was an Interpol notice and the suspects were detained for a period of time by the TRNC authorities.[222] Crucially, in its finding in *Güzelyurtlu* that the applicants had a 'jurisdictional link' with Turkey, the Court added that

> [a]ny other finding would result in a vacuum in the system of human-rights protection in the territory of Cyprus, which falls within the 'legal space of the Convention', thereby running the risk of creating a safe haven in the 'TRNC' for murderers fleeing the territory controlled by Cyprus and therefore impeding the application of criminal laws put in place by the Government of Cyprus to protect the right to life of its citizens and, indeed of any individual within its jurisdiction.[223]

The reference to the 'legal space of the Convention' is notable. It suggests that a procedural link (in the form of initiation of proceedings at national level) will lead to the establishment of a 'jurisdictional link' only in relation to States that are parties to the ECHR.[224] This is further confirmed by the reasoning in *Güzelyurtlu* on the merits, where the Court clarified its approach to the 'obligation of Contracting States to co-operate in transnational cases under the procedural aspect of Article 2' and 'the obligation to cooperate in transnational cases involving a Contracting State and a de facto entity being under the effective control of another Contracting State'.[225] As the quotations suggest, obligations were framed under the assumption that it is States that are Parties to the ECHR that hold these obligations. Subsequent judgments that built

---

[220] *Güzelyurtlu and Others v Cyprus and Turkey* [GC] §190.
[221] The first scenario was also independently applicable to Turkey since the TRNC authorities initiated their own criminal investigation. *Güzelyurtlu and Others v Cyprus and Turkey* [GC] §§191–196.
[222] *Güzelyurtlu and Others v Cyprus and Turkey* [GC] §§192–194. Besides *Güzelyurtlu*, another case where the 'special features' were found fulfilled is *Romeo Castaño v Belgium*, where the issue under consideration was a procedural obligation upon Belgium to cooperate by executing an European arrest warrant in relation to a suspect who committed a murder in Spain, but subsequently fled to Belgium. *Romeo Castaño v Belgium* no 8351/17, 9 July 2019 §42.
[223] *Güzelyurtlu and Others v Cyprus and Turkey* [GC] no 36925/07, 29 January 2019 §195.
[224] The Court has used the reference to 'the legal space (*espace juridique*) of the Contracting States' to limit the extraterritorial application of the ECHR. *Bankovic and Others v Belgium and Others* [GC] (dec) no 52207/99, 12 December 2001 §80; *Hanan v Germany* [GC] no 4871/16, 16 February 2021 §135: 'If the mere fact of instituting a domestic criminal investigation into any death which has occurred anywhere in the world were sufficient to establish a jurisdictional link, without any additional requirements, this would excessively broaden the scope of application of the Convention.' For arguments regarding how the regional character of the ECHR as an instrument of European public space should determine the approach to Article 1, see Partly Dissenting Opinion of Judge Grozev in *Georgia v Russia (II)* [GC] no 38263/08, 21 January 2021.
[225] *Güzelyurtlu and Others v Cyprus and Turkey* [GC] no 36925/07, 29 January 2019 §§229–238 (emphasis added).

upon *Güzelyurtlu* and the principle that a procedural link leads to a 'jurisdictional link' for the purposes of Article 1, even though the investigation and request for cooperation concerned events having occurred outside the state territory, also involve States that are parties to the ECHR.[226]

It is also important to clarify that cases like *Güzelyurtlu v Turkey* and *Romeo Castaño v Belgium* did not implicate any extraterritorial investigatory duties. The procedural measures that Turkey and Belgium were required to undertake had to be performed on their own territory. Turkey had to transfer the suspects from the TRNC, where it is an occupying power, to Cyprus. In *Romeo Castaño v Belgium*, Belgium had to provide a reasoned response to Spain justifying the refusal to surrender the perpetrator, and to base the refusal on legitimate grounds. In addition, these measures involved criminal investigations as opposed to other types of proceedings.

In conclusion, individuals can be constituted as right holders when they are legally and procedurally tied to the State by bringing judicial proceedings (if such are allowed by the domestic law) that trigger the application of Article 6. Their rights are, however, limited in terms of scope and content. These are procedural, not substantive rights, under the ECHR. Individuals can be also constituted as right holders when they are legally and procedurally tied to the State by virtue of criminal proceedings whose effectiveness require the cooperation of this State. Any rights are, however, again limited to procedural guarantees.

More generally, the approach to Article 1 ECHR described in this section implies a relativization of the jurisdictional threshold. The determination whether the threshold is passed is made relative to the specific rights and obligations invoked. While, as Section 8.3 will demonstrate, such a relativization is more generally problematic, the Court has clearly applied it to Article 6 and to the procedural limb of Article 2. Crucially, however, both situations reflect a legal mandate as the conceptual underpinning of jurisdiction. In addition, in relation to the procedural limb of Article 2, the Court has clearly invoked communitarian underpinnings by limiting the triggering of the 'jurisdictional link' to circumstances involving States that are Parties to the ECHR.

A final note is due regarding *Hanan v Germany*, where on the one hand, these communitarian underpinnings were confirmed, while on the other hand, 'special features' justified German's jurisdiction 'outside the legal space of the Convention'.[227] The applicant argued that Germany had not conducted an effective investigation under the procedural limb of Article 2, into an air strike ordered by a German commander in 2009 in Afghanistan that led to multiple deaths, including the applicant's sons. The GC held that

---

[226] *Romeo Castaño v Belgium* no 8351/17, 9 July 2019 (murder in Spain and refusal by Belgium to extradite the suspect); *Mukuchyan and Minasyan v Azerbaijan and Hungary* no 17247/13, 26 May 2020 §§47–52 (murder in Hungary and conviction of the perpetrator in Hungary, but subsequent failure by Azerbaijan to enforce the prison sentence after transfer of the perpetrator).

[227] *Hanan v Germany* [GC] no 4871/16, 16 February 2021 §136.

[i]f the mere fact of instituting a domestic criminal investigation into any death which has occurred anywhere in the world were sufficient to establish a jurisdictional link, without any additional requirements, this would excessively broaden the scope of application of the Convention.[228]

This is a confirmation of the communitarian underpinnings. Yet, the 'jurisdictional link' was found to have been triggered and, in this way, the procedural obligation under Article 2 to investigate deaths was brought into effect, even though the deaths occurred in Afghanistan, a State falling outside 'the legal space of the Convention'.[229] The Court invoked the 'special features' of the case to substantiate this finding. Importantly, all of these were based on a *legal mandate*: first, Germany had an obligation under customary international law to investigate the air strike that led to the deaths; second, the Afghan authorities were, for legal reasons, prevented from instituting a criminal investigation against the military commander who ordered the air strike; and third, German law demanded the initiation of a criminal investigation.[230] This combination of legal mandates was found sufficient to trigger the jurisdiction of Germany *only* in relation to the procedural obligation under Article 2. While Section 8.3 will additionally explore the implications from tailoring the criteria for triggering jurisdiction depending on the type of the obligations invoked on the merits, Section 8.4.1 will further explain the importance of legal mandate as a basis for triggering jurisdiction.

## 8.2.8 Conclusion

The core question under review in this section has been whether and how the preconditions that enable the analysis on the merits regarding the triggering, the content, and the scope of positive obligations are reflected in the meaning of jurisdiction as developed in the Court's case law. As Section 8.1 showed, actual capacity and factual control might be just one of these preconditions. Other crucial preconditions are bounded political and legal order, legal mandate, interdependency of the stakes, and democratically constituted sovereign. These can be generally framed as normative preconditions.

The overall conclusion is that the Court is certainly sensitive to these normative preconditions. This sensitivity has not, however, crystallized with clarity and consistency. Rather, the judgments, and the models of jurisdiction endorsed therein, meander

---

[228] ibid §135.
[229] Joint Partly Dissenting Opinion in *Hanan v Germany* [GC] §11. See also *Georgia v Russia (II)* [GC] no 38263/08, 21 January 2021 where even though the deaths that Russia had to investigate, were within 'the legal space of the Convention', this feature was not invoked in the reasoning.
[230] *Hanan v Germany* [GC] §§137–142.

between a facticist approach and a normative approach. In some of the models, the normative preconditions are more tangible than in others. The 'public powers' model, for example, reflects them in a noticeable way through the requirement for consent of the territorial state, which implies some democratic sanctioning, and the requirement for an agreement between the two relevant States (the one that might have extraterritorial jurisdiction and the other one on whose territory the negatively affected individual are located). The requirement for an agreement and for a legal mandate implies some legal order within which the conduct of the State of extraterritorial jurisdiction could be structured. Since the facticist approach is not exclusive, the possibility is left open that the presence of normative preconditions (expressed, for example, through nationality, legal competence, or legal procedural link) might suffice in justifying the assignment of obligations. Once this tension between the facticist approach and the normative approach and the oscillation between the two is acknowledged, it might be easier to understand why it is so difficult to construct a coherent conceptual underpinning of the jurisdictional threshold under Article 1 ECHR and why the case law is not stable.

It can be expected that this instability will continue. The Court is likely to continue to develop a case-by-case approach while trying to maintain an impression that the cases fit within the models and there is consistency among them (eg by gradually introducing distinctions between different scenarios).[231] At the same time, the Court will keep the normative preconditions in mind without necessarily explicitly formulating them all the time in its reasoning.[232] This might be justified on the grounds that it is too difficult to capture these preconditions by framing them expressly as requirements so that jurisdiction is triggered. In terms of judicial technique, it seems easier to rather use them in an implicit way and when the specific case might demand it. Undoubtedly, this is not conducive to predictability.

However, an approach that implies ignoring the normative preconditions (by discarding the jurisdictional threshold or interpreting it in a very wide fashion), and instead applying an exclusively facticist approach and merging all (or most) considerations at the merits stage, might be equally uncertain and difficult.[233] The difficulties

---

[231] For a confirmation of this casuistic approach, see *M.N. and Others v Belgium* [GC] (dec) no 3599/18, 5 May 2020 §102: 'it was with reference to the specific facts that the Court assessed whether there existed exceptional circumstances justifying a finding by it that the State concerned was exercising jurisdiction extraterritorially'.

[232] See *Big Brother Watch and Others v the United Kingdom* [GC] no 58170, 25 May 2021 §§323, 333, 497, 504, and 513, where the respondent State did not raise objections as to the jurisdictional threshold under Article 1 and this issue was ignored by the Court. Yet in its judgment, the Court multiple times refers to 'citizens' to frame its reasoning.

[233] The academic literature has overwhelmingly supported a position advocating for an expansive extraterritorial application of the ECHR and complementing this with a caution in the application of the actual obligations at the merits stage. See Milanovic, *Extraterritorial Application of Human Rights Treaties* (n 4) 103; Ryngaert, 'Extraterritorial Obligations under Human Rights Law' (n 4) 273, 287. This will require developing separate standards for assessing compliance with human rights law obligations in extraterritorial circumstances. These separate standards will imply compromising and accommodating the analysis normally applied by the Court on the merits. Bhuta has noted that this accommodation will lead

that would arise if extraterritorial positive obligations were to be adjudicated on their merits will be addressed in Section 8.4. Prior to this, however, Section 8.3 will address the proposals for adapting the criteria for determining whether the jurisdictional requirement is fulfilled (or the absence of such a requirement) to the merits stage (in terms of relevant rights and obligations and their scope). This relates to the argument that a different jurisdictional requirement can be applied depending on the rights and the obligations implicated in the analysis on the merits.

## 8.3 Adapting Jurisdiction to the Obligations?

If jurisdiction in the sense of Article 1 ECHR is a threshold, as in fact held by the Court, it would be determinative as to whether a State is a bearer of obligations or not, irrespective of the rights and the corresponding obligations invoked. Yet proposals have been forwarded for breaking this threshold approach and instead showing some flexibility by adapting the jurisdictional requirement to the types of rights and obligations under consideration at the merits stage. The questions that such flexibility raises are as follows: should there be an interdependence between the relevant model of jurisdiction and the type of rights and obligations that could be triggered? Should the State in question be held responsible for all substantive rights and obligations, or should there be a way of delimiting which obligations should apply depending on the model of jurisdiction found relevant? Has the Court referred to such an interdependence in its case law? An affirmative answer to these questions might imply that certain rights and certain obligations might be triggered only when a particular model of jurisdiction is found applicable.

To address these questions, I will first clarify certain pronouncements by the Court that confirm that different rights and obligations could be relevant under the different models of jurisdiction. This is framed as the 'dividing and tailoring' approach (Section 8.3.1). On the one hand, the approach supports the idea that jurisdiction in the sense of Article 1 ECHR is meant to ensure the preconditions for performing the analysis on the merits, since it illustrates the interconnectedness between the preliminary question of jurisdiction and the questions that need to be resolved on the merits. On the other hand, however, this interconnectedness risks being reduced to a complete convergence (Section 8.3.2). This undermines the integrity of jurisdiction as a threshold where certain *general normative questions* should be resolved rather than the specifics of concrete cases. Jurisdiction therefore risks becoming not simply unstable since it generally oscillates between practical feasibility and normativity, it risks being disintegrated and made reducible to the concreteness of single cases.

---

to the establishment of 'a law of extraterritorial human rights', 'one in which human rights norms become flexible abstract principles' adapted to extraterritorial settings. Bhuta, 'The Frontiers of Extraterritoriality' (n 25) 17.

## 8.3.1 Dividing and Tailoring

The origins of the proposal for flexible adaptation of the jurisdiction threshold to the types of the obligations under consideration at the merits stage can be traced back to *Bankovic*. The applicants argued that 'the extent of the positive obligation under Article 1 of the Convention to secure Convention rights would be proportionate to the level of control exercised' in the given extra-territorial situation.[234] This argument would imply that since NATO's control was limited in scope, 'the Article 1 positive obligations could be similarly limited'.[235] The applicants were thus in favour of a lenient approach towards the jurisdiction threshold, thus making it easier to surpass it to the point of having no threshold at all. This leniency, as they argued, could be compensated by a more rigid approach towards the analysis on the merits, making it more difficult to find a breach of the obligations.

The applicants' argument has its basis in the flexibility that characterizes positive obligations, as described in the previous chapters of this book. This flexibility does imply that the scope of the obligations, understood as to how demanding the obligations can be, is adaptable to the particular circumstances in which the obligations have been triggered. The adaptability can be dependent, *inter alia*, on the level of control that the state authorities have over the situation, or, as clarified in Chapter 3, on the level of control that the state authorities *should* have had. However, it is important to highlight that this flexibility and adaptability pertain to the analysis on the merits, not to the preliminary issue of jurisdiction.[236]

In *Bankovic*, the Court responded to the applicants' argument by stating that

> the wording of Article 1 does not provide any support for the applicants' suggestion that the positive obligation in Article 1 to secure "the rights and freedom defined in Section I of this Convention" can be divided and tailored in accordance with the particular circumstances of the extra-territorial act in question.[237]

It has been argued that in *Al-Skeini*, the Court departed from the position expressed in the above quotation from *Bankovic*.[238] Specifically, in *Al-Skeini*, after clarifying the 'physical power and control over a person' model, the Court added that

---

[234] *Bankovic and Others v Belgium and Others* [GC] (dec) no 52207/99, 12 December 2001 §46.
[235] ibid §52.
[236] A source of confusion is that control is a relevant factor for the establishment of jurisdiction as an initial threshold, and for the analysis on the merits as to the trigger and scope of any positive obligations. However, this should not imply that the two (ie the threshold question and the merits) can be merged in the way proposed by the applicants in *Bankovic*.
[237] *Bankovic and Others v Belgium and Others* [GC] (dec) no 52207/99, 12 December 2001 §75.
[238] M Milanovic, 'Jurisdiction and Responsibility. Trends in the Jurisprudence of the Strasbourg Court' in A van Aaken and I Motoc (eds), *The European Convention on Human Rights and General International Law* (Oxford University Press 2018) 97, 98; I Papanicolopulu, *International Law and the Protection of People at Sea* (Oxford University Press 2018)195; Park, *The Right to Life in Armed Conflict* (n 154) 69; S Wallace, *The Application of the European Convention on Human Rights to Military Operations* (Cambridge University Press 2019) 62; C Mallory, *Human Rights Imperialists. The Extraterritorial Application of the European Convention on Human Rights* (Hart Publishing 2020) 168, 189, and 195.

whenever the State, through its agents, exercises control and authority over an individual, and thus jurisdiction, the State is under an obligation under Article 1 to secure to that individual the rights and freedoms under Section I of the Convention *that are relevant to the situation of that individual. In this sense,* therefore, the Convention rights can be 'divided and tailored' (compare *Bankovic and Others*, cited above, para 75).[239]

Despite the cross-references and the use of the same language, it could be argued that the Court is saying two different things in these two quotations. The meaning of the first, from *Bankovic*, is that there cannot be different obligations and different scopes of these obligations depending on different degrees of jurisdiction because there cannot be different degrees of jurisdiction in the first place.[240] This also means that at an abstract level, there cannot be different obligations depending on the different basis (ie models) on which jurisdiction is established (control over area, control over a person, etc), not to mention that the distinctions between the models are blurred. Rather, once jurisdiction is established, all rights and all obligations might be relevant *at an abstract level.* The rights and the corresponding obligations that are *concretely* relevant depend on the concrete situation of the applicants, which is always the case even in domestic settings.

It follows that while jurisdiction cannot be relative,[241] obligations are always relative and concretely tailored.[242] This relativity and tailoring means that the applicants need to challenge a particular action or inaction by the State, then the obligations can be made concrete. The applicants also need to demonstrate how they have been 'directly affected' by this action or inaction that they complain of, so that they have the status of a victim (this being one of the admissibility requirements). This status entails that the person has been directly affected by the act or omission; and that the human rights claim cannot be based on an abstract situation. Rather, the claim has to be based on specific facts affecting specific rights.[243]

Another consideration that undermines the argument that jurisdiction is relative, and that the obligations can be preliminarily adapted to the model of jurisdiction, is that it is not possible to determine *in advance* which type of obligations a State might have and their scope. If the standard of jurisdiction is made contingent on the types of

---

[239] *Al-Skeini and Others v the United Kingdom* [GC] no 55721/07, 7 July 2011 §137 (emphasis added); *Hirsi Jamaa and Others v Italy* [GC] no 27765/09, 23 February 2012 §74; *H.F. and Others v France* [GC] no 24384/19, 14 September 2022 §186.
[240] Besson (n 8) 878: 'jurisdiction is an all-or-nothing matter and not a matter of degree'.
[241] For scholarship that defends the position that jurisdiction should be relative, see Lawson, 'Life After Bankovic' (n 11) 103: 'towards a gradual and context-related approach to jurisdiction'; Ryngaert, 'Jurisdiction. Towards a Reasonableness Test' (n 198) 192, 210 (for an argument that jurisdiction should be perceived as a continuum); W Vandehole, 'Extraterritorial Human Rights Obligations: Taking Stock, Looking Forward' (2013) 1(5) European Journal of Human Rights 827: 'the extent of the obligations attributed to the extraterritorial State may vary in light of the degree of jurisdiction exercised'.
[242] See Sections 4.2 and 7.1.3.1 for the different levels of specifying positive obligations.
[243] See Section 7.1.3, where it is clarified that the Court does not engage in abstract review of omissions.

obligations, this will amount to disruption of the analytical order, in other words preemptively considering the obligations before even considering whether they exist.

The meaning of the above quotation from *Al-Skeini* could be that *once jurisdiction established*, and by implication once a State can be constituted as a bearer of obligations, the content and the scope of these obligations is tailored to the specific situation. This tailoring is related to the above-mentioned flexibility of positive obligations and to the fact that they are context specific. While rights are formulated in abstract terms, obligations have to be made concrete and, in this sense, divided and tailored in the light of the specific case. This dividing and tailoring happens all the time in domestic cases. As demonstrated in the previous chapters of the book, different positive obligations can be triggered in different circumstances and their scope is tailored by different factors (knowledge, reasonableness, and causation).

Once extraterritorial jurisdiction is established, the same dividing and tailoring of obligations takes places depending on the action or inaction challenged by the applicant. This also implies that the concrete extraterritorial circumstances can manifest some specificities as a result of which knowledge, causation, and reasonableness might be more difficult to establish, which might in turn make the finding of a breach less likely.

*Al-Skeini* has, however, caused further confusion on the issue, since when the Court explained the 'control over an area' model of jurisdiction, it added that '[t]he controlling State has the responsibility under Article 1 to secure, within the area under its control, *the entire range of substantive rights* set out in the Convention and those additional Protocols which it has ratified'.[244] This is a pronouncement taken from *Cyprus v Turkey*.[245] It could possibly be interpreted to the effect that, in contrast to 'control over a person' model, when jurisdiction is established based on the 'control over an area' model, the entire range of rights and obligations, including positive obligations, is of relevance.[246] This interpretation could be challenged on the following ground. What the Court sought to clarify in this paragraph from *Al-Skeini* is that when a State has jurisdiction because it controls an area *through a subordinate local administration*, it is not necessary to establish that each act of this administration is specifically attributable to the State of extraterritorial jurisdiction.[247] Nor it is necessary to determine whether, for example, the Turkish forces in Northern Cyprus, actually exercised control in each specific situation.[248] Rather, '[t]he fact that the local administration survives as a result of the Contracting States' military and other support entails that State's responsibility for its policies and actions'.[249] This means that the State

---

[244] *Al-Skeini and Others v United Kingdom* [GC] no 55721/07, 7 July 2011 §138; *H.F. and Others v France* [GC] no 24384/19, 14 September 2022 §187.
[245] *Cyprus v Turkey* no 25781/94, 10 May 2001 §77.
[246] Wallace, *The Application of the European Convention on Human Rights to Military Operations* (n 238) 63–64.
[247] Attributable in the sense of the ILC Draft Articles.
[248] For the same interpretation, see Lawson 'Life After Bankovic' (n 11) 98.
[249] *Al-Skeini and Others v United Kingdom* [GC] no 55721/07, 7 July 2011 §138.

of extraterritorial jurisdiction could be held responsible for the local administration's conduct *as a whole*.

As mentioned in Section 8.2.2, in the reasoning adopted in the cases pertaining to Northern Cyprus and 'the Moldovan Republic of Transdniestria', the Court assumes that the local administration's conduct is entirely attributable to Turkey and Russia respectively. It follows that once jurisdiction is established because a State controls an area 'through a subordinate local administration', no distinction is made in the reasoning between the conduct of the local administration and the conduct of the State of extraterritorial jurisdiction. As also alluded to in Section 8.2.2, one implication from this is that the analysis on the merits focuses on negative obligations (ie how the measures undertaken by the local administration constitute interferences),[250] rather than on how the State of extraterritorial jurisdiction failed to control, regulate, or influence this administration so as to prevent it from taking measures of interference (ie how these failures might constitute breaches of positive obligations of the extraterritorially acting state).

*Once jurisdiction is established* based on the 'control over an area' model, the content and the scope of any obligations is tailored to the specific situation. The applicant will invoke those rights and obligations that are relevant to the specific circumstances based on the specific state conduct challenged. Setting aside the uncertain distinctions between the different models, and the questions surrounding their independent existence (as exposed in Section 8.2), the same is valid once jurisdiction is established based on the 'control over a *person*' model: the applicant will invoke those rights and obligations that are relevant to the specific circumstances. It should be noted that when a State controls a person by killing, detaining, or directly imposing some other restrictions, it would be negative obligations that are most likely of relevance because of the nature of the State conduct, namely actions of interference. When a State controls a person, in this way possibly triggering the personal model of jurisdiction, any positive obligations are likely to be closely related to the negative ones, such as the obligation to investigate the interferences or to apply force in compliance with the requirements of Article 2(2) of the ECHR.[251] This intertwinement between the model of jurisdiction and the relevant obligations on the merits follows from the nature of the state conduct necessarily involved when a particular model is found applicable.

---

[250] Hypothetically positive obligations can be also triggered if a private individual harms another individual in the area, and an argument is made that the local administration failed to protect the latter. Since no distinction is made between conduct of the local administration and conduct of the extraterritorially acting state, this failure will also be attributed to the extraterritorially acting state.

[251] When state agents inflict harm, it might be artificial to consider positive and negative obligation independently: 'When lethal force is used with a "policing operation" by the authorities it is difficult to separate the State's negative obligations under the Convention from its positive obligations.' *Finogenov and Others v Russia* no 18299/03, 20 December 2011 §208; *Shchiborshch and Kuzmina v Russia* no 5269/08, 16 January 2014 §206.

## 8.3.2 Dividing the Tailoring Brought to a Breaking Point

So far, I have demonstrated that it is doubtful whether *Al-Skeini* generally supports the proposal that rights and obligations can be 'divided and tailored' to the effect that only certain rights and obligations can be relevant *at an abstract level* depending on the model of jurisdiction.[252] This doubt, however, seems to have been resolved in favour of such a proposal with the cases of *Hanan v Germany* and *H.F. and Others v France*.[253] This demands a more detailed engagement with these judgments. The facts were already clarified in respectively Sections 8.2.7 and 8.2.4.

In *Hanan v Germany*, the applicant's complaint was exclusively under the procedural limb of Article 2 about the criminal investigation into the air strike that killed his sons. As noted in Section 8.2.7, the Court relied on the 'special features' of the case, all of them based on a legal mandate, to substantiate its finding that the investigative acts by Germany 'are capable of giving rise to the responsibility of Germany under the Convention'.[254] The Court also emphasised that

> it does not follow from the mere establishment of a jurisdictional link in relation to the procedural obligation under Article 2 that the substantive act falls within the jurisdiction of the Contracting State or that the said act is attributable to that State.[255]

The procedural and substantive obligations under Article 2 are therefore divided and the jurisdictional link tailored to the first one. The link is further tailored to the 'special features' of the case, which ultimately implied that the jurisdiction threshold as already tailored to the procedural limb of Article 2, is reducible to the concreteness of the single case.

The division was possible since, as explained in Chapter 6, the procedural obligation to investigate is detachable and independent from the substantive obligations under Article 2. Despite this independence, 'the substantive act' that needs to be investigated still matters for the procedural obligation, since the purpose of the investigation is *inter alia* to establish whether use of force was contrary to Article 2.[256] It thus follows that the dividing and tailoring approach poses some serious conceptual challenges in that it undermines the interconnectedness of obligations in terms of their justifications and scope. This approach that ultimately serves the objective of allowing

---

[252] Here I do not address the deviation that can be observed in the judgments concerning Transdniestria and the positive obligations of Moldova based on its sovereign title over the region. See *Ilascu* and *Catan and Others v Moldova and Russia* [GC] no 43370/04, 19 October 2012 §110.

[253] See also *Georgia v Russia (II)* [GC] no 38263/08, 21 January 2021 §114, where the Court indicated that one of the evolutions since *Bankovic* is that 'the rights under the Convention could be "divided and tailored"'.

[254] *Hanan v Germany* [GC] no 4871/16, 16 February 2021 §144.

[255] ibid §143.

[256] See Section 6.2.3.2.

some scrutiny by the Court by declaring the application admissible, might also undermine the obligations themselves, a point that will be explored in Section 8.4.

The limits of the dividing and tailoring approach were pushed even further in *H.F. and Others v France*, where it was upfront observed that 'the present case requires the Court to address the possibility, as it has previously accepted, that the State's obligation under Article 1 to recognise Convention rights may be "divided and tailored"'.[257] This possibility was actualized in the following way. The reasoning invokes some of the jurisdictional models for finding that the applicant's daughters and grandchildren were *not* within the jurisdiction of France *for the purposes of Article 3*.[258] The reasoning invokes *other* models for concluding that the relatives detained in the camps were within the State's *jurisdiction for the purposes of the right to enter* enshrined in Article 3(2) Protocol 4.[259] The approach to Article 1 was therefore divided for the two rights invoked. It was also tailored since different models were invoked for the different rights. The models were additionally tailored to the specific right since, for example, in relation to the right to enter, it was held that it was not appropriate to apply a requirement that the person was under the effective control of the State.[260]

The Court however did not stop here in how it tailored jurisdiction. It added that

> [i]n the light of the foregoing, it cannot be excluded that certain circumstances relating to the situation of individuals who wish to enter the State of which they are nationals, relying on the rights they derive from Article 3 § 2 of Protocol No. 4, *may give rise to a jurisdictional link with that State for the purposes of Article 1 of the Convention. However, the Court does not consider that it has to define these circumstances in abstracto* since they will necessarily depend on the *specific features of each case* and may vary considerably from one case to another.[261]

The tailoring, therefore, all comes down to the 'special features' of the case. These were indeed features unique to the specific case that can be summarized as including official requests for repatriation, 'real and immediate threat' to life and well-being in the camps, inability to leave the camps to reach French borders, and Kurdish authorities' willingness to help in the repatriation. The level of specificity of the features and the specificity of their combination is, however, so particular and detailed that any principled approach to jurisdiction is made close to impossible. As a consequence, the threshold risks being bereft of meaning. The same features were invoked on the

---

[257] *H.F. and Others v France* [GC] no 24384/19, 14 September 2022 §189.

[258] ibid §§198–203. First, France had no control over the area, ie the camps where the women and the children were located. Second, cause-and-effect as a basis for jurisdiction could be rejected. Third, France had no international law obligations to act to repatriate the women and the children. Fourth, importance was attached to the fact that France had to coordinate with another sovereign.

[259] ibid §§198–203. While France did not exercise 'public powers', the women and the children were French nationals and, as the Court reasoned, applying a requirement for 'effective control' in the context of the right to enter, is not appropriate.

[260] ibid §209.

[261] ibid §212.

merits to support the finding that there are 'exceptional circumstances' in the case,[262] which in turn warranted the imposition of a positive obligation upon France to 'surround the decision-making process, concerning the requests for repatriation, by appropriate safeguards against arbitrariness'.[263] Interestingly, however, if these specific applicants had not sent official requests for repatriation, it seems that they would not be within the jurisdiction of France. This illustrates how the tailoring of the jurisdiction threshold is brought to a point where the threshold is reducible to the concreteness of single cases.

Once jurisdiction triggered in the divided and tailored way described above, a procedural obligation was placed at the heart of the analysis on the merits in *H.F. and Others v France*. As already mentioned, France was under the positive obligation to 'surround the decision-making process, concerning the requests for repatriation, by appropriate safeguards against arbitrariness'.[264] Indeed as explained in Section 7.2, procedural positive obligations have been developed. However, the procedural standards that these obligations imply are linked to some substantive outcomes. True, achievement of outcomes is not determinative, yet the outcomes matter, which demonstrates the interconnectedness of procedural and substantive obligations in terms of their justifications and scope. Which was then the substantive outcome that mattered in the reasoning in *H.F. and Others v France*? The only reasonable candidate was actual repatriation. This was explicitly rejected,[265] since the Court was adamant that the possibility of reviewing decisions to refuse repatriation 'would not necessary mean that the court in question would then have jurisdiction to order, if appropriate, the requested repatriation'.[266] The interconnectedness of obligations in terms of their justifications and scope is thus undermined and the question arises as to the meaning of having a review (ie a national procedure for reviewing refusals), when the outcome of this review is not required to be actual repatriation. The Court therefore almost went full circle: it scrutinized the complaint by applying the divided and tailored approach to jurisdiction at the admissibility stage; the actual obligations were however so tailored to be point of being almost meaningless. Section 8.4 will further explore this meaninglessness.

---

[262] ibid §§264–271. Other circumstances were also added (ie the situation in the camps 'verges on a legal vacuum'; the issuance of arrest warrants against the women; and the cooperation between Turkey and France that could be of help to those who can reach Turkey).
[263] For a detailed argumentation as to how it is problematic when the *same* features are invoked for determining whether jurisdiction in human rights is triggered and for determining the content of obligations, see A Ollino, 'The "Capacity-impact" Model of Jurisdiction and its Implications for States' Positive Human Rights Obligations' (2021) 82 Questions of International Law 81.
[264] *H.F. and Others v France* [GC] no 24384/19, 14 September 2022 §172.
[265] ibid §259: 'French citizens being held in the camps in north-eastern Syria cannot claim a general right to repatriation on the basis of the right to enter national territory under Article 3 § 2 of Protocol No. 4.'
[266] ibid §282.

## 8.3.3 Conclusion

The Court has made the jurisdictional threshold relative by tailoring it to the rights and the obligations that would be considered on the merits. This is in itself an acknowledgment that the threshold cannot be understood without understanding the questions that need to be engaged with in the analysis on the merits. However, *Hanan v Germany* and *H.F. and Others v France* manifest a tendency of bring the 'divide and tailor' approach to a breaking point. This seems to deprive the threshold of any meaning since the tendency is to adjust it (so that an impression is created that there is a threshold) as much possible to the specific case. As a consequence, the problem is not anymore only that the Court's case law fluctuates between a facticist (feasibility) and normative approaches to jurisdiction (as shown in Section 8.2). Another problem also emerges: the singularity of specific cases would govern, and no general coherent approach would be attempted.

Another consequence of the 'divide and tailor' approach is that the interconnectedness of obligations in terms of their justifications and scope might be undermined. It could be objected that this interconnectedness is not that important since, for example, procedural obligations can be independent and separated from any substantive outcomes. The approach, however, that ultimately serves the objective of allowing some scrutiny by the Court, might also undermine the obligations themselves, a point that will be explored in the following section.

## 8.4 Deconstructing Extraterritorial Positive Obligations

Despite the uncertainties that characterize the case law pertaining to the jurisdictional threshold under Article 1 ECHR, Section 8.2 demonstrated that the threshold has been made (although not always consistently and explicitly) sensitive to the objectives and the normative presuppositions of human rights law, namely its communitarian and relational nature. Human rights law is indeed based on a relation between individuals as holders of rights and a State as a holder of obligations corresponding to these rights. If jurisdiction in the sense of Article 1 ECHR is to serve a purpose, it has to reflect this relational character, thus preserving the coherence of human rights law as a distinctive body of law. Section 8.1 explained how this relational character justifies positive obligations and enables the determination of their scope, content, and breach. The objective of the present section is to reflect what challenges and conceptual problems might arise for the triggering of positive obligations, determining their content, scope, and breach in extraterritorial circumstances, where the normal presuppositions (as described in Section 8.1) do not hold; that is, where the relational nature between the State and the affected individuals is disrupted.

More specifically, since political equality, democratic legitimacy, and questions about the role of the State in the particular political community underpin positive obligations, it can be expected that the same issues will have to be seriously taken into account in any discussion of the extraterritorial application of these obligations. Actual capacity to exercise influence and control is not the only factor that determines the triggering, the content, and the scope of positive obligations; other normative considerations also play a decisive role. Engagement with these considerations in extraterritorial circumstances is thus also necessary. The question that arises then is whether and how positive obligations could be conceptualized, operationalized, and applied in circumstances where the normal presuppositions do not obtain. How to perform the usual analysis regarding triggering, scope, content, and factors that determine breach (eg knowledge, causation, and reasonableness) in extraterritorial circumstances where the normative considerations that normally serve as reference points in the analysis might not be present?

Careful engagement with these questions is important, given the clear tendency to advocate for expanding the meaning of jurisdiction (including via the divide and tailor approach, as shown in Section 8.3) by ignoring the relational nature of human rights law, and the related argument that instead of imposing a preliminary threshold, the hard questions in human rights law should be resolved on the merits. As the latter argument goes, 'there is ample room for various forms of deference and flexibility on the merits. This is where these disputes are to be resolved, and where the hard questions lie.'[267] It has been also added that '[w]here the extraterritorial context *can* matter is on the merits, by adding some flexibility to rules that were originally developed for purely domestic application.'[268] Is it, however, possible to have such a flexibility and how can this flexibility be achieved?[269] Is there a price to be paid for this flexibility? Could it be the case that such a flexibility might undermine the coherence of human rights law as a distinctive body of law, whose distinctiveness lies in its communitarian nature?

To respond to these questions, I will examine how the factors that are relevant to the determination of breach, content, and scope of positive obligations could possibly be applied in extraterritorial circumstances. What conceptual challenges does such an application imply? Is it actually possible to afford deference and flexibility without falling into the danger of automatically finding a breach and/or not having the conceptual tools to perform the substantive analysis, or rendering the positive obligation

---

[267] Milanovic, *Extraterritorial Application of Human Rights Treaties* (n 4) 103. For a similar proposal, see Mallory, *Human Rights Imperialists* (n 238) 212–16.
[268] Milanovic, *Extraterritorial Application of Human Rights Treaties* (n 4) 107.
[269] An example where the Court has shown such a flexibility is *Jaloud v the Netherlands* [GC] no 47708/08, 20 November 2014 §226, in relation to the obligation to investigate: the Court 'is prepared to make reasonable allowances for the relatively difficult conditions under which the Netherlands military and investigators had to work. In particular, it must be recognized that they were engaged in a foreign country which had yet to be rebuilt in the aftermath of hostilities, whose language and culture were alien to them, and whose population ... clearly included armed hostile elements.' The Court then assessed that the failings in the investigation were not 'inevitable', which seems to be a demanding standard from the perspective of the State. See N Quénivet, 'The Obligation to Investigate after a Potential Breach of Article 2 ECHR in an Extra-territorial Context: Mission Impossible for the Armed Forced' (2019) 37(2) Netherlands Quarterly of Human Rights 119.

meaningless, as already suggested in Section 8.3? The path for answering these questions is determined by the factors for determining breach of positive obligations: legality, the test of reasonableness, and causality.[270]

## 8.4.1 Legality and Legal Competence

The examination starts with the legality requirement as related to the issue of competence to regulate conduct. It is important to reflect upon the challenges that might arise if responsibility is based on omissions and the harm materializes in a context where there might not be a structured formal relationship regulated by law between the State and the affected individuals who are located extraterritorially. This reflection starts with the observation that the ECtHR case law meanders between legal entitlement and factual control as theoretical underpinnings of jurisdiction (Section 8.4.1.1). While this does create insecurity, at the same time, the avoidance of a categorical rejection of legal entitlement as relevant to the jurisdictional threshold is understandable. The reason is that legality, which can be ensured when the State has legal entitlement, has an important role for the analysis on the merits of both positive and negative obligations (Section 8.4.1.2). Another reason is that compliance with positive obligations presupposes that the State has the entitlement and the competence to regulate activities. Since such entitlement and competence might be absent in relation to individuals located extraterritorially, assessment of compliance with positive obligations cannot be made (Section 8.4.1.3). A third reason is that the imposition of *de facto* regulation that has extraterritorial effects, without the consent of the States where these effects materialize, might be viewed as an imposition of such norms on these States as do not originate from their sovereign taken decisions (Section 8.4.1.4). This raises serious issues regarding the democratic legitimacy of such norms (Section 8.4.1.5).

### 8.4.1.1 Meandering between legal entitlement and factual control

The Court has constantly reiterated its position that jurisdiction in the sense of Article 1 ECHR should be informed by the concept of jurisdiction in general international law.[271] This could imply that only when a State has an entitlement to act

---

[270] These factors mirror the ones discussed in Chapters 3 and 4. The analysis of positive obligations in domestic settings did not include a separate chapter on legality; rather, legality was examined throughout the chapters where relevant (eg Section 7.1). However, due to its central role for the jurisdiction threshold, Section 8.4 starts with legality. A clarification is also due to the effect that Section 8.4 does not include a separate section on state knowledge that could be viewed as corresponding to Chapter 2. The reason is that state knowledge has not been invoked as a factor triggering jurisdiction in the sense of Article 1 of the ECHR.

[271] *Bankovic and Others v Belgium and Others* [GC] (dec) no 52207/99, 12 December 2001 §§59–61; *H.F. and Others v France* [GC] no 24384/19, 14 September 2022 §§184–185.

extraterritorially can jurisdiction for the purposes of Article 1 of the ECHR be established.[272]

*Critique of legal entitlement*

The limitation entailing that the jurisdictional threshold is dependent on legal entitlement has been an object of critique. In particular, it has been explained that jurisdiction understood as 'the authority of the State, based in and limited by international law, to regulate the conduct of persons, both natural and legal, by means of its own domestic law'[273] has nothing to do with the concept of jurisdiction in human rights law treaties.[274] For jurisdiction in the sense of Article 1 ECHR to depend on the entitlement of States to regulate conduct through their national legislation would be an error.[275] It has been thoroughly explained that jurisdiction in public international law aims to set out 'limits on the domestic legal orders of States, so that they do not infringe upon the sovereignty of others'.[276] In this sense, jurisdiction in public international law aims to organize the coexistence of States when their jurisdictions overlap in extraterritorial circumstances. In contrast, jurisdiction in human rights law has a different purpose, namely to determine whether a State can be constituted as a holder of obligations in relation to an individual. It should also be added that jurisdiction in international law is based on permissive principles: States might be authorized, but not necessarily required, to exercise jurisdiction. In contrast, once it is determined that a State has jurisdiction in the sense of Article 1 ECHR, the State has obligations.

Commentators have also identified the ensuing problems if jurisdiction under Article 1 ECHR were to be understood with reference to legal entitlement, legal competence, or some form of legal relationship between the affected individuals and the State.[277] Specifically, such an understanding would imply that if a State affects individuals beyond its borders by acting beyond its legal competence or by exceeding its competence, its conduct could not be scrutinized against the ECHR standards. It has been argued that this situation needs to be avoided and, to this end, international human rights law should be 'agnostic towards the question of whether a State acts lawfully, or whether it respects the sovereignty of other States in "exercising" its jurisdiction'.[278] Jurisdiction in human rights law should then be 'the *actual exercise* of that

---

[272] M Duttwilder, 'Authority, Control and Jurisdiction in the Extraterritorial Application of the European Convention on Human Rights' (2012) 30(2) Netherlands Quarterly of Human Rights 137, 138.
[273] Milanovic, *Extraterritorial Application of Human Rights Treaties* (n 4) 23.
[274] ibid 26; Mallory, *Human Rights Imperialists* (n 238) 27.
[275] Milanovic, *Extraterritorial Application of Human Rights Treaties* (n 4) 40. D Augenstein, 'Paradise Lost: Sovereign State Interest, Global Resource Exploitation and the Politics of Human Rights' (2016) 27(3) European Journal of International Law 669, 685.
[276] Milanovic, *Extraterritorial Application of Human Rights Treaties* (n 4) 29.
[277] H King, 'The Extraterritorial Human Rights Obligations of States' (2009) 9(4) Human Rights Law Review 521, 536; De Schutter, 'Globalization and Jurisdiction (n 163) 197; Lawson, 'Life After Bankovic' (n 11) 104: 'it would be too restrictive to require a formal legal relationship, or some kind of structured relationship existing over a period of time'. Duttwilder, 'Authority, Control and Jurisdiction in the Extraterritorial Application of the European Convention on Human Rights' (n 272) 140.
[278] L Raible, 'Title to Territory and Jurisdiction in International Human Rights Law: Three Models for a Fraught Relationship' (2018) 31 Leiden Journal of International Law 315, 321.

power, whether lawfully or unlawfully'.[279] It has been added that jurisdiction cannot coherently also be the entitlement to exercise this power. Formal considerations, such as jurisdictional competence and sovereignty, should not therefore matter under Article 1 ECHR.[280]

*Legal entitlement as an additional and sufficient basis*
In contrast to the above position, which rejects the relevance of States' legal entitlements as regulated by the international law rules of jurisdiction, another group of commentators have advocated that these entitlements should rather be viewed as an *additional* basis for passing the jurisdictional threshold under human rights law. In this sense, the *de facto* exercise of power and control should still trigger the threshold, but it is just one sufficient possibility. Another separate and *sufficient* alternative should transpire when States are allowed to exercise powers under some international law rules of jurisdiction. This entitlement arguably *on its own* also triggers the threshold and constitutes States as holders of human rights obligations.[281] Competence thus would automatically lead to human rights law jurisdiction and possibly imposition of positive obligations.[282] The rationale behind this position is that States should have human rights law obligations even when they do not have *de facto* control over persons and areas.[283] This position has therefore been developed to remedy some weaknesses of the facticist approach to jurisdiction.

Objections can, however, be raised against favouring legal entitlement as a sufficient trigger of human rights law jurisdiction. First, the international law rules of jurisdiction are permissive rules: States are allowed, but not obliged, to undertake certain measures. Categorically transforming all of these rules into human rights law obligations appears problematic. Second, these rules are meant to regulate relationships between States, not the relationship between a State and individuals. As a consequence, they do not cater for the communitarian nature of the latter relationship.

---

[279] Milanovic and Papic, 'The Applicability of the ECHR in Contested Territories' (n 1) 795 (emphasis in the original). *Issa and Others v Turkey* no 31821/96, 16 November 2004 §71 confirms this approach.

[280] Milanovic and Papic, 'The Applicability of the ECHR in Contested Territories' (n 1) 795.

[281] Papanicolopulu, *International Law and the Protection of People at Sea* (n 238) 150–54, 205: 'in all cases in which the law of the sea or general international law provides that a State has jurisdiction over a person, a maritime zone, a vessel or a platform, then that State is obliged to observe its human rights obligations towards that person or persons in that zone or indeed those on the vessel or platform'. (Papanicolopulu's analysis based on selective reading of the case law); Vandenbogaerde, 'Attributing Extraterritorial Obligations under the International Covenant on Economic, Social and Cultural Rights' (n 173) 6; Vandenbogaerde, *Towards Shared Accountability in International Human Rights Law* (n 3) 244.

[282] Such an approach might be acceptable under EU law and the conditions governing the application of the EU Charter, where there is no provision similar to Article 1 ECHR. See Stoyanova, 'The Right to Life under the EU Charter and Cooperation with Third States to Combat Human Smuggling' (2020) 21(3) German Law Journal 436.

[283] Papanicolopulu, *International Law and the Protection of People at Sea* (n 238) 154.

### 8.4.1.2 The role of legality in the assessment of obligations

The judgments analysed in Section 8.2 do not unequivocally reflect either of the above described two positions. Rather, the ECtHR case law seems confusingly to meander between legal entitlement and factual physical power as conceptual underpinnings of jurisdiction.[284] As Noll has noted, jurisdiction in human rights law is 'inherently unstable' and lacks 'coherent conceptual underpinnings' since it is based on 'two dominant and competing ideas working under the surface of concrete court cases': jurisdiction as legal mandate and jurisdiction as actual exercise of powers. Legal entitlement and *de jure* power by the State continue to be invoked by the Court as important elements so that jurisdiction is established.[285] Accordingly, the question of whether the State exercises powers within some legal confines has not been categorically rejected as irrelevant. This corresponds to the argument formulated throughout this chapter that jurisdiction cannot be reduced to mere factual power and factual capability; other normative considerations are also at play.

The instability in the case law regarding the role of legal competence in the jurisdiction threshold cannot be understood without a more profound consideration of the issues that need to be tackled in the analysis on the merits regarding the obligations. In particular, due regard need to be paid to the institutionally referential nature of human rights law. This body of law relies on domestic public institutions and on the national legal system. It is therefore in need of some linkage with a legal framework. To show this linkage in more detail, I will first address it in the context of negative obligations, before proceeding with positive obligations. Given that, as argued in Section 8.3, obligations are interdependent, the linkage needs to be considered in the context of both obligations. The intertwinement between the two types of obligations justifies the inclusion of negative obligations in the analysis.

*Negative obligations*

In the context of negative obligations, an interference is automatically contrary to human rights law if it does not comply with the 'in accordance with the law' requirement. Compliance with this requirement, also framed as legality, is initially assessed against the domestic legislation and legal standards. Legality also implies compliance with the quality of the law requirement,[286] in terms of accessibility, foreseeability, and

---

[284] Noll, 'Theorizing Jurisdiction' (n 164) 613 and 616.
[285] *Assanidze v Georgia* no 71503/01, 8 April 2004 §137; *Hirsi Jamaa and Others v Italy* [GC] no 27765/09, 23 February 2012, where the Court started to reason on the jurisdictional threshold by referring to the principle in international law that 'a vessel sailing on the high sea is subject to the exclusive jurisdiction of the State of the flag it is flying' and this State has *de jure* control (§77). It added that 'in the period between boarding the ships of the Italian armed forces and being handed over to the Libyan authorities, the applicants were under the continued and exclusive *de jure* and *de facto* control of the Italian authorities' (§81); *H.F. and Others v France* [GC] no 24384/19, 14 September 2022 §201: 'the Court observes that neither domestic law nor international law ... requires that State to act on behalf of its nationals and to repatriate them'. See, however, *Medvedyev and Others v France* [GC] no 3394/03, 29 March 2010 §67, where the Court referred only to *de facto* control over the ship by France.
[286] *M. and Others v Bulgaria* no 41416/08, 26 July 2011 §69.

availability of adversarial proceedings.[287] Therefore, human rights law imposes an initial demand that state conduct is undertaken within some legal confines and in a context regulated by legal frameworks. If this initial demand is not fulfilled, an automatic violation follows without consideration of other factors, such as the aims pursued or the reasonableness of the measure of interference.

It could be the case that the quality of the law standard might be modified to make it less demanding in extraterritorial circumstances. However, it would hardly be possible to completely jettison it. If the threshold question of jurisdiction is entirely and exclusively based on factual power, the legality requirement is not likely to be fulfilled in this way, rendering the finding of a substantive violation of the ECHR inevitable. As a consequence, the finding of jurisdiction in the sense of Article 1 would automatically lead to a finding of a violation of negative obligations, a development that the proponents of the factual power model actually resist.[288]

This is exactly what happened, for example, in *Turturica and Casian v Moldova and Russia*,[289] where the applicants' cars were confiscated by the Transdniestrian authorities, as a result of which they complained to the ECtHR that their right to property has been violated. After finding that this right has been interfered with, the Court concluded that

> [i]n so far as the lawfulness of the interference is concerned, no elements in the present case allow the Court to consider that there was a legal basis for interfering with the rights of the applicants guaranteed by Article 1 of Protocol 1.

No discussion was initiated by the Court as to which national legislation (Moldavian, Russian, or Transdniestrian) could or should be used as a reference point. It was clear that the measures of interference were not provided for by the domestic laws of Moldova or Russia. The legal system of Transdniestria was ignored in the judgment.[290] The interference was thus found not lawful, leading automatically to the

---

[287] See *Medvedyev and Others v France* [GC] no 3394/03, 29 March 2010 §§94–100 for the demanding standards for meeting 'in accordance with the law' requirement even in the context of international cooperation.

[288] The extraterritorial application of human rights treaties 'will rest on a principled basis only if courts are persuaded that a finding of such application as a preliminary matter would not *ipso facto* lead to a loss for the government on the merits (as indeed mostly has been the case so far)'. Milanovic, *Extraterritorial Application of Human Rights Treaties* (n 4) 111; R Lawson, 'Really Out of Sight?' in A Buyse (ed), *Margins of Conflict: The ECHR and Transitions to and from Armed Conflict* (Intersentia 2010) 57.

[289] *Turturica and Casian v Moldova and Russia* no 28648/06, 30 August 2016 §§49–50; see also *Paduret v Moldova and Russia* no 26626/11, 9 May 2017 §29–30 (the applicant's van and merchandise were confiscated by the Transdniestrian authorities on account of their having allegedly failed to register the vehicle), where the similar approach was applied. See also *Cotofan v Moldova and Russia* no 5659/07, 18 June 2019 §§28–29 (seizure of property and imposition of a fine in violation of Article 1 Protocol 1).

[290] '[T]he Court does not recognize the existence of the Transdniestrian legal system as a whole. This allows the Court to find a violation of the Convention by the Russian Federation automatically, without any legal analysis.' Dissenting Opinion of Judge Dedov in *Turturica and Casian v Moldova and Russia* no 28648/06, 30 August 2016.

conclusion that Russia, the State of extraterritorial jurisdiction, was responsible for the violation.[291]

Besides the right to property, another example can be provided regarding the right to liberty. Important legality standards adhere to this right as enshrined in Article 5 of the ECHR. Article 5(1) ECHR requires that any detention must be in accordance with a procedure prescribed by law. *Medvedyev and Others v France* illustrates how the absence of jurisdiction under international law (ie a legal entitlement upon the State to act) might automatically lead to non-compliance with the legality standard.[292] The French authorities intercepted a Cambodian vessel suspected of drug smuggling and confined the crew on board until the arrival at a French port. The crew, who were eventually convicted of drug smuggling, filed an application to the ECtHR challenging, *inter alia*, the legality of their detention on the ship. French law could not provide a legal basis for the detention. Notably, the Court confirmed that besides national laws, other legal standards that can be derived from international law could be used for assessing legality. The UN Convention on the Law of the Sea could not authorize France since Cambodia, the flag state, was not a party to it. A diplomatic note issued by Cambodia did authorize the French authorities to intercept the ship; however, as the Court held, the diplomatic note did not clearly authorize the arrest and the detention of the crew members. Nor did it meet the 'foreseeability' requirement. This led the Court to conclude that the detention had no legal basis and was contrary to Article 5(1) ECHR.[293]

*Hassan v the United Kingdom* provides another illustration of how other standards of international law can be resorted to in assessing the legality of detention in extraterritorial circumstances. In contrast to *Medvedyev and Others v France*, however, such external standards were present and they were derived from international humanitarian law. This allowed the Court to hold that 'deprivation of liberty pursuant to powers under international humanitarian law must be "lawful" to preclude a violation of Article 5(1)'.[294] *Hassan* was about the arrest of a person during active hostilities in Iraq on the suspicion that he might have been combatant or a civilian posing a threat to security. The British army released him once it was established that these suspicions were unfounded. It is of key importance in *Hassan* that the detention of combatants as prisoners of war and of civilians as a prevention without the intention to bring criminal charges is not allowed by the text of Article 5(1) of the ECHR.[295] The Court

---

[291] The Court has taken a different approach to the legality requirement in judgments involving Turkey and the Turkish Republic of Northern Cyprus. The latter's legal and judicial system has been accepted as operating on a 'constitutional and legal basis' reflecting traditions compatible with the ECHR. *Cyprus v Turkey* [GC] no 25781/94, 10 May 2001 §231.
[292] *Medvedyev and Others v France* [GC] no 3394/03, 29 March 2010 §§82–103.
[293] The legal entitlement that France had to undertake the measures was not mentioned by the Court as a relevant factor in the determination whether the crew was within French jurisdiction in the sense of Article 1 ECHR. This determination appears to be based entirely on *de facto* control.
[294] *Hassan v the United Kingdom* [GC] no 29750/09, 16 September 2014 §105.
[295] M Milanovic, 'A Norm Conflict Perspective on the Relationship between International Humanitarian law and Human Rights Law' (2010) 14(3) Journal of Conflict and Security Law 458, 477.

in *Hassan*, however, decided to 'accommodate', 'as far as possible', Article 5(1) to the standards regarding 'the taking of prisoners of war and the detention of civilians who pose a risk to security under the Third and Fourth Geneva Conventions'.[296]

The invocation of such external standards, such as the above-mentioned Geneva Convention, does, however, imply serious modifications of the *normal* human rights law standards.[297] This can explain why the Court in *Hassan* still tried to preserve the (rather vague) relevance of the protection against arbitrariness under Article 5(1) ECHR, even if detention is allowed by international humanitarian law.[298] The Court additionally limited this modification to circumstances of international armed conflict 'where the taking of prisoners of war and the detention of civilians who pose a threat to security are accepted features of international humanitarian law'.[299] The conferral by international humanitarian law of such powers to detain is far less clear in the context of non-international armed conflict,[300] where controversial issues of extraterritoriality, and of whether States are conferred with legal entitlements to undertake certain measures, can also arise.

There are further problems when other branches of international law, and the entitlements that these branches might confer on States, are invoked in assessing legality under human rights law. These problems emerge with even greater seriousness in relation to the right to life. International humanitarian law has been invoked as a source offering external standards for the assessment of whether deprivation of life qualifies as a violation of the right to life. The simultaneous application of human rights law and international humanitarian law standards to loss of life has been the object of extensive scholarly attention.[301] The Court itself has also confirmed the relevance of international humanitarian law to the interpretation of Article 2 of the ECHR.[302] No general analysis is accordingly attempted here. Rather, the enquiry is limited to the lawfulness requirement incorporated not only in Article 2(1) of the ECHR, but also in each of the three subparagraphs of Article 2(2). These subparagraphs enumerate circumstances when deprivation of life might be justifiable: defending a person from '*unlawful* violence', effecting a '*lawful* arrest', and 'action *lawfully* taken' for quelling a riot or insurrection.[303]

The three subparagraphs of Article 2(2) of the ECHR specify exhaustively the circumstances where deprivation of life might not violate the ECHR, provided that the

---

[296] *Hassan v the United Kingdom* [GC] no 29750/09, 16 September 2014 §104.
[297] See Partly Dissenting Opinion of Judge Spano in *Hassan v the United Kingdom* [GC] §16–18.
[298] *Hassan v the United Kingdom* [GC] §105.
[299] ibid §104.
[300] W Abresch, 'A Human Rights Law of Internal Armed Conflict: The European Court of Human Rights in Chechnya' (2005) 16(4) European Journal of International Law 741, 747: 'the humanitarian law of internal armed conflicts is quite spare and seldom specific'.
[301] See for relevant references Park, *The Right to Life in Armed Conflict* (n 154). See also Concurring Opinion of Judge Keller and the Joint Partly Dissenting Opinion of Judges Yudkivska, Pinto de Albuquerque, and Chanturia in *Georgia v Russia (II)* [GC] no 38263/08, 21 January 2021.
[302] *Varnava and Others v Turkey* [GC] no 16064/90, 18 September 2009 §185.
[303] Emphasis added.

use of force 'is no more than absolutely necessary'.[304] These circumstances reflect the limited number of aims that can justify the State resorting to potentially lethal force. To be justifiable, all of these aims are linked with a requirement for lawfulness. The aims thus have to be legal and legitimate. The Court accordingly has to ask whether the State actually pursued any of these three legitimate aims,[305] and whether the measures were suitable for the achievement of the aims. Then the analysis under Article 2 ECHR can move to the 'absolutely necessary' stage, where the Court assesses whether the force used, whose intended or unintended outcome is loss of life, is 'strictly proportionate to the achievement of the permitted aims'.[306]

International humanitarian law also implies some form of proportionality, which also includes an aim in the calculus. But this is the military strategic aim of the attacking party. It is an aim in a very narrow sense restricted to targeting a military objective.[307] Crucially, international humanitarian law is agnostic to the legality and legitimacy of the aims themselves since '[i]t is beyond the laws of war to determine whether it is necessary, or legitimate, for a State to bend another's will, or to conquer'.[308] As a consequence, international humanitarian law has 'no concept of "permitted aims"'.[309] If it had, this would imply consideration of *jus ad bellum* and, accordingly, an entanglement between *jus in bello* and *jus ad bellum*. This is hard to accept since the separation between these two is axiomatic for international humanitarian law.[310]

If the ECtHR is then to consider external standards stemming from international humanitarian law to assess legality for the purposes of Article 2 of the ECHR, it might have to follow this axiom and show indifference to the cause of the conflict and the legitimacy of the aims. In the context of Article 2(2)(c) of the ECHR, which does not preclude use of force that is no more than absolutely necessary 'in action *lawfully* taken for the purpose of quelling a riot or insurrection', indifference would imply overlooking the term 'lawfully' and the legitimacy of the aim pursued with the use of force. Alternatively, the ECtHR might ignore the limitations flowing from the axiom

---

[304] The standard of 'no more than absolutely necessary' will be examined below, where the issue of balancing is covered.

[305] For example, in *Isayeva v Russia* no 57950/00, 24 February 2005 §180–91, the Court held that the aim pursued by the military operation may have been legitimate: 'The presence of a very large group of armed fighters in Katyr-Yurt, and their active resistance to the law-enforcement bodies ... *may have justified use of lethal force* by the agents of the State, thus bring the situation within paragraph 2 of Article 2 (emphasis added).' However, given the 'caution expected from a law-enforcement body in a democratic society', a narrow military aim could not be accepted by the Court. It added that '*the primary aim* of the operation should be to protect lives from unlawful violence' (emphasis added). It can be thus concluded that an operation that gives priority to the aim of killing the armed fighters rather than to the protection of the residence of the town, cannot be accepted under the terms of Article 2(2).

[306] *Isayeva v Russia* no 57950/00, 24 February 2005 §173.

[307] W Schabas, '*Lex Specialis*? Belt and Suspenders? The Parallel Operation of Human Rights Law and the Law of Armed Conflict, and the Conundrum of *Jus Ad Bellum*' (2007) 40(2) Israeli Law Review 592, 607.

[308] A Eide, 'The Laws of War and Human Rights—Differences and Convergences' in C Swinarski (ed), *Studies and Essays on International Humanitarian Law and Red Cross Principles in Honour of Jean Pictet* (Martinus Nijhoff Publishers 1984) 675, 681.

[309] Abresch, 'A Human Rights Law of Internal Armed Conflict' (n 300) 765.

[310] ibid 743.

and enquire whether the killing in wartime amounts to deprivation of the right to life contrary to the ECHR, by including in the enquiry an examination whether the perpetrator acted lawfully (ie whether the use of force was compatible with *jus ad bellum*). So far, the Court has not taken a position on this precise issue.[311] The reasoning in *Georgia v Russia* (II) hints that the Court would rather avoid the issue by invoking the jurisdictional threshold.

The above-mentioned alternatives bring to light a profound problem that might arise when external standards for assessing legality under human rights law are invoked. These standards, just like international humanitarian law, are not necessarily designed to regulate the relationship between the political community and the State, the entity meant to have instrumental functions and thus presumed to act in the general interest of this community. This is rather the task of human rights law, which explains the importance of 'the degree of caution expected from a law-enforcement body in a democratic society'[312] in the assessment of the violation of the right to life. As Abresch has observed, the effect from the shift to human rights law 'is to permit only the general interest of society, rather than the interests of the State *per se*, to weight against the individual's unfettered enjoyment of his or her rights, including the right to life'.[313] As opposed to international humanitarian law, human rights law does not presuppose two opposing parties in a conflict, but instead communality. Therefore, external norms such as those coming from international humanitarian law do not necessarily fit with the presuppositions of human rights law and, in particular, with its communitarian nature. This mismatch can make the operationalization of such external norms difficult, including in assessing the standard of legality under human rights law.

To conclude on the role of legality in the context of negative obligations, the absence of domestic laws or authorization based on international law, as referents in the human rights law analysis on the merits, leads automatically to a finding of a violation. *Turturica and Casian* and *Medvedyev and Others* reveal this. Admittedly, such a categorical result might be avoided by using legal frameworks external to human rights law, such as international humanitarian law, as referents for assessing legality. This, however, might lead to serious modification of the human rights law standards, as showed by *Hassan* in relation to the right to liberty. The utilization of external legal frameworks might be also problematic since their conceptual underpinnings might

---

[311] I do not think that the issue is resolved if a State decides to derogate from Article 2 ECHR. The derogation clause in Article 15 ECHR confirms the relevance for the human rights law analysis of the legality of the resort to force. Among other criteria, derogations from Article 2 are permitted 'in respect of deaths resulting from *lawful* acts of war'. It is possible to argue that what is lawful is determined by reference to international humanitarian law and without any regard to *jus ad bellum*. However, such a limitation does not necessarily follow from the text of Article 15 ECHR. For a different position see Wallace, *The Application of the European Convention on Human Rights to Military Operations* (n 238) 76, where it is argued that once a State derogates from Article 2 ECHR, the Court can establish that the acts of the State were legal under international humanitarian law, which would prevent responsibility under the ECHR.
[312] *Isayeva v Russia* no 57950/00, 24 February 2005 §191.
[313] Abresch, 'A Human Rights Law of Internal Armed Conflict' (n 300) 766.

be hard to reconcile with those of human rights law, as shown in relation to the right to life.

*Positive obligations*

Admittedly, the legality requirement does not have such a strict function in the context of positive obligations since it is not a definitive test. State responsibility for failure to perform positive obligations is not assessed against an initial and conclusive standard of legality. The reason is that positive obligations can be performed through various means, and adoption of national regulatory framework could be just one of these. Equally important, the challenged omission might be precisely the absence of a regulatory framework. In this sense, as Chapter 7 has shown, a failure to perform a positive obligation might lead to responsibility precisely because the State has not regulated certain matters through legislation at all, or the existing regulation is somehow deficient. Yet this does not make regulations and legislation completely irrelevant when assessing state responsibility for failure to perform positive obligations. While domestic legality and regulatory standards are not definitive tests, they do have decisive roles to play in the determination of breach of positive obligations for at least four reasons.

First, as Chapter 3 shows, legality has a role in the assessment of causal links between omissions and harm, since it can be an important referent for identifying *relevant* omissions. Such identification is crucial, otherwise responsibility for omissions is limitless. When harm, arguably caused by omissions imputable to the State that purportedly has extraterritorial jurisdiction, materializes in a context where there is no structured formal relationship between this State and the affected individuals, there might be no referents or standards for the identification of relevant omissions and their assessment.[314]

Second and relatedly, as the case law on positive obligations in domestic settings shows, national legislation, standards, and regulations serve as benchmarks against which alternatives measures are proposed and assessed.[315] As Chapter 4 has shown, the identification and assessment of such alternatives are important to reach a conclusion as to what was reasonable to expect from the State in terms of protective measures. For example, in the context of Article 8, domestic legality could be an important factor in determining which measures strike a fair balance between different pertinent interests. In the context of Article 2, legality is 'also directly relevant' in the proportionality assessment.[316] In extraterritorial circumstances, where there might be no

---

[314] This can explain why a failure to repatriate could not be a *relevant* omission in *H.F. and Others v France* [GC] no 24384/19, 14 September 2022 §259.

[315] Section 4.2. See eg *Gorovensky and Bugara v Ukrain* no 36146/05, 12 January 2012 §§39–40 (breach of positive obligations under Article 2 since a police officer, who shot two persons with his police gun, was issued with the gun in breach of the existing domestic regulations); *Keller v Russia* no 26824/04, 17 October 2013 §89.

[316] *Isayeva v Russia* no 57950/00, 24 February 2005 §199: 'The Court agrees with the applicant that the Government's failure to invoke the provisions of any domestic legislation governing the use of force by the army or security forces in situations such as the present one, whilst not in itself sufficient to decide on a violation of the State's positive obligation to protect the right to life, is, in the circumstances of the present case,

relevant rules, or rules originating from different countries, identification and assessment of reasonable alternatives and of measures that are proportionate and strike a fair balance might be a challenge.

Third, legality is central to enforcement. Failure to fulfil a positive obligation might be found due to ineffective application and enforcement of national regulations.[317] It follows that the assumption underlying the reasoning in positive obligations cases in normal settings is that the State—in the sense that it has the competence—is entitled to and can enforce these laws and regulations. This assumption might not apply in all extraterritorial settings.[318] In Section 8.4.1.3 I will further elaborate on this issue of competence, which is directly relevant to enforcement.

Fourth, litigation before the Court is contingent on the exhaustion of domestic remedies. This is an important admissibility requirement that is applied 'without excessive formalism';[319] yet, if it were to be fulfilled, this would imply that the State had to open its courts to victims irrespective of their location or where the harm occurred. Such an opening could be possibly linked to the right to an effective remedy as protected by Article 13 ECHR, a right that underpins the whole ECHR protection system. What I would like to highlight here is that the availability of remedial national procedures and the findings therein are crucial for the analysis on the merits performed by the Court.

Given the contingency of the right to effective remedy on the jurisdiction threshold under Article 1, it is highly questionable whether Article 13 can be invoked in imposing an *obligation* upon the State to actually open its courts.[320] States might choose to do so by, for example, offering civil remedies (eg tort law litigation), but this is a matter that falls within their discretion.[321] As the Court clarified in *M.N. and Others v Belgium* and *H.F. and Others v France*, bringing proceedings at national level does not necessarily trigger the jurisdictional threshold under Article 1.[322] Even if such national proceedings exist, this does not mean that their availability is a matter of obligations under the ECHR.[323] The Court has also clarified that the refusal of national

---

also directly relevant to the Court's considerations with regard to the proportionality of the response to the attack.'

[317] Section 7.1.2.3.
[318] Territoriality is central to enforcement. A Hertogen, 'Letting Lotus Bloom' (2015) 26(4) European Journal of International Law 901, 920. Enforcement and prescription of rules (ie prescriptive jurisdiction in international law) are interrelated. In determining whether to prescribe rules that affect persons and activities located beyond national borders, States take into consideration any 'restrictions on the possibility of effectively enforcing national laws or judgments'. A Mills, 'Rethinking Jurisdiction in International Law' (2014) 84(1) The British Yearbook of International Law 187, 195.
[319] B Rainey and others, *The European Convention on Human Rights* (Oxford University Press 2021) 34.
[320] J Kapelańska-Pręgowska, 'Extraterritorial Jurisdiction of National Courts and Human Rights Enforcement: Qua vadis justitia?' (2015) 17 International Community Law Review 413, 420.
[321] Many civil claims for human rights violations have been brought against transnational corporations. ibid 430.
[322] *M.N. and Others v Belgium* [GC] (dec) no 3599/18, 5 May 2020 §123; *H.F. and Others v France* [GC] no 24384/19, 14 September 2022 §195. See also Section 8.2.7 for clarifications when such proceedings can trigger jurisdiction.
[323] *M.N. and Others v Belgium* [GC] (dec) no 3599/18, 5 May 2020 §140. See Section 8.2.6.

courts to examine a civil claim for compensation for damage caused in the territory of another State, and to which the forum State has no connection, is not in violation of the right to access to court under Article 6 ECHR.[324]

What significance do all these clarifications have for positive obligations? First, it would appear paradoxical if States had *no* obligation under human rights law to make domestic proceedings available where claimed omissions could be identified and scrutinized, yet States were to owe positive human rights obligations to prevent these omissions. It is also paradoxical, as my analysis of *H.F. and Others v France* in Section 8.3.2 already suggested, if States were to owe some limited procedural positive obligations to review omissions,[325] yet they own no positive obligation to prevent the actual omission. *Hanan v Germany*, addressed in Section 8.3.2, reveals a similar paradox: the State had an obligation to investigate the killing, but not necessary an obligation to prevent it. Second, the analysis of positive obligations in terms of scope and content is contingent on the litigation of the case at national level. This litigation has important implications when the case is considered by the ECtHR on its merits. It reveals the different pertinent interests, their relationship to each other and the omissions invoked. This procedural history has important role for the merits, since it facilitates the analysis that requires the identification of relevant omissions and the reasonableness of any measures that the State should have undertaken. The domestic litigation also reveals the quality of the national procedure and, relatedly, the procedural safeguards offered, which can be crucial in assessing whether the State should be found responsible under the ECHR for omissions.[326]

To conclude on the role of legality in the context of positive obligations, the absence of legal frameworks and related national procedures as referents does have serious implications for the human rights law analysis on the merits. Such frameworks and procedures can be important for the assessment of causality, reasonableness, and enforcement, all of which are crucial elements in determining whether a State has failed to fulfil positive obligations.

### 8.4.1.3 Competence

The issue of legality is related to the issue of state competence. In domestic situations, the assumption is that the State has the competence to regulate everything and to legislate accordingly. This becomes a problematic point in extraterritorial situations

---

[324] *Naït-Liman v Switzerland* [GC] no 51357/07, 15 March 2018. (The Court accepted the applicability of Article 6 to the circumstances of extraterritorial harm, which implied that the applicant had a right of access to a court. This right was restricted when the Swiss courts held that they did not have the jurisdiction to entertain his claim on the merits. However, the Court held that this restriction pursued a legitimate aim and was proportionate.)

[325] Limited since in *H.F. and Others v France* [GC] no 24384/19, 14 September 2022, the weak standard of arbitrariness was invoked. At §155, the GC stated that there was no need to examine the complaint under Article 13 since such a complaint was encompassed by the analysis of the procedural obligation of the State in the context of a refusal to repatriate. Given the procedural standards developed under Article 13, this statement is hard to accept.

[326] See Section 7.2 on implied procedural obligations.

since it is not necessarily the case that the State has the competence (ie the entitlement under general international law) to regulate certain activities that take place beyond its borders. Without this competence, the linkage with a legal framework might be lacking, which is problematic given the institutionally referential nature of human rights law and its reliance on the national legal system.

This problem has been recognized, and it has been observed that a State should not 'be held responsible under the Convention for failing to take actions when it did not have the legal authority to do so'.[327] It has been also noted that '[e]xcept where a state has legal competence to act, it should rarely own positive duties'.[328] At the same time, given the awareness that this might lead to 'responsibility gaps', an argument has been advanced that if the State has the competence to regulate the *source of harm or the actor of harm*, the legality requirement is not a problem and human rights law obligations can be assigned. For example, if a company is incorporated and registered in a State, this State has the competence to regulate the company's conduct, regardless of where the individuals affected by this conduct are located. It would then follow that if the State of incorporation has the competence, an obligation to regulate so that harm is prevented should be assigned to it as a matter of human rights law.[329]

The problem with this argument is that it assumes that competence to regulate a third party causing harm (eg a company), or the source of harm, amounts to control over the individuals (who might be indeed negatively affected), in this way rendering them right holders vis-à-vis the State that has this competence. This assumption is contrary to the understanding that jurisdiction in human rights law reflects a relationship between a State and individuals. Such an assumption also implies that the mere causal link between a state omission (eg the omission to regulate the company) and extraterritorial harm amounts to jurisdiction, and allows the assignment of human rights obligations. As clarified in Section 8.2.6, a mere causal link has been rejected as a basis for jurisdiction under Article 1 of the ECHR. Mere competence to influence the source of harm does not reflect the normative nature of the jurisdictional threshold, as reflective of the relationship between the State as holder of obligations and individuals as rights-holders.

### 8.4.1.4 Coordination of sovereignties

Another reason that might explain the rejection of the cause-and-effect notion of jurisdiction (a notion that is centred on factual considerations) relates to the issue

---

[327] E Roxstrom and others, 'The NATO Bombing Case (Bankovic et al. v Belgium et al.) and the Limits of Western Human Rights Protection' (2005) 23 Boston University International Law Journal 55, 88. See also *Hanan v Germany* [GC] no 4871/16, 16 February 2021 §224, where the Court noted that 'the German civilian prosecution authorities did not have legal powers undertake investigative measures in Afghanistan'.
[328] King, 'The Extraterritorial Human Rights Obligations of States' (n 277) 538.
[329] Vandenbogaerde, 'Attributing Extraterritorial Obligations under the International Covenant on Economic, Social and Cultural Rights' (n 173) 19. In relation to *Tugar v Italy*, the author argues that since Italy had the *de jure* capacity to influence the company through regulation of the arms trade, contrary to the decision of the European Commission, it should have been assigned an obligation to protect. See also HRC General Comment 36 on the Right to Life, 30 October 2018 CCPR/C/GC/36 §22.

of sovereignty and the organization of the coexistence of States when their activities overlap in extraterritorial circumstances.[330] Positive obligations require the adoption of measures, including regulations and legislation, that could imply the need to regulate activities and effects that take place on the territory of other States.[331] Imposition of norms on other States that do not originate from sovereign decisions taken by these States but from external sources can be viewed as problematic[332] because they are forms of interventions.[333]

One can say that external regulations might be favourable and positive for the local population, and in this sense, it might not be problematic to impose external standards. One can also add that the sovereignty of the territorial State has in any case been undermined, since another State (ie the State that arguably has extraterritorial jurisdiction) *de facto* exercises some form of control and influence over the former and its population, and in this sense sovereignty should not be an issue at all.[334] So why not

---

[330] See *Bankovic and Others v Belgium and Others* [GC] (dec) no 52207/99, 12 December 2001 §59: 'a State may not actually exercise jurisdiction on the territory of another without the latter's consent, invitation or acquiescence, unless the former is an occupying State in which case it can be found to exercise jurisdiction in that territory, at least in certain respects'. *M.N. and Others v Belgium* [GC] (dec) no 3599/18, 5 May 2020 §99: 'while international law does not exclude a State's extraterritorial exercise of its jurisdiction, the suggested bases of such jurisdiction (including nationality and flag) are, as a general rule, defined and limited by the sovereign rights of other relevant States'.

[331] This problem can be looked at from another perspective, namely whether the State on whose territory any negative effects have been observed, or whose population has suffered (the affected state), has jurisdiction (in the sense of an entitlement) under international law to regulate the issue, in this way potentially affecting actors and activities located in another state (eg the State where the company is incorporated). Since the locus of the effects is in the territory of the affected State, it is this State that is 'the appropriate locus for political decision making' and it should be permissible to exercise jurisdiction by regulating. See Hertogen, 'Letting Lotus Bloom' (n 318) 921.

[332] See S Skogly and M Gibney, 'Transnational Human Rights Obligations' (2002) 24(3) Human Rights Quarterly 781, 797; Ryngaert 'Jurisdiction: Towards a Reasonableness Test' (n 198) 208: 'a State should not be obliged … to protect individuals located in a foreign State from ESC [economic, social and cultural rights] violation, if, through such protection, it violates the principle of non-intervention'; C Ryngaert, 'Litigating Abuses Committed by Private Military Companies' (2008) 19(5) European Journal of International Law 1035: 'If the idea is regulating, jurisdiction in the PIL sense and its limits will have to be of relevance.' CESCR Statement on the Obligations of States Parties Regarding the Corporate Sector E/C.12/2011/1, 12 July 2011 §5; Vandenbogaerde, 'Attributing Extraterritorial Obligations under the International Covenant on Economic, Social and Cultural Rights' (n 173) 16; De Schutter, 'Globalization and Jurisdiction' (n 163) 191. See also *Case Concerning the Application of the Convention on the Prevention and Punishment of the Crime of Genocide (Bosnia and Herzegovina v Serbia and Montenegro)* Judgment ICJ Reports 2007 p. 43, 26 February 2007 §430: 'The State's capacity to influence *must be assessed by legal criteria*, since it is clear that every State may only act within the limits permitted by international law.'

[333] *Bankovic and Others v Belgium and Others* [GC] (dec) no 52207/99, 12 December 2001 §66: the ECHR does not 'purport to be a means of requiring the Contracting States to impose Convention standards on other States'. *Medvedyev and Others v France* [GC] no 3394/03, 29 March 2010 §63. On how the projection of state regulations abroad can be viewed as a form of abuse and hegemony, see Ryngaert, *Selfless Intervention* (n 192) 36–46.

[334] This undermining can vary in degree, and therefore distinctions might need to be considered between different contexts (eg occupation of a foreign state as opposed to extraterritorial harmful effects by the operation of a company). In the business context, 'violations do not occur in a jurisdictional "black hole" but in another state, which has laws, courts, regulators, a civil society and human rights obligations on its own, even if these might appear imperfect from the point of view of advocates of extraterritoriality, or from the perspective of victim'. C O'Brien, 'The Home State Duty to Regulate the Human Rights Impacts of TNCs Abroad: A Rebuttal' (2018) 3 Business and Human Rights 47, 55–56.

scrutinize this *de facto* control against the substantive human rights law standards without *any* regard to issues of legal competence under general international law? Disregarding the sovereignty of the territorial state would raise fundamental questions about the international legal order and the democratic underpinnings of national legal orders.[335] It is very doubtful whether such questions should be resolved within the framework of human rights law. In this sense, the jurisdictional hurdle posed by Article 1 of the ECHR could be perceived as a filter excluding these broader questions from the realm of human rights law.[336]

And yet if the proposal in favour of scrutinizing *de facto* control against substantive human rights law standards without regard to issues of legal competence *within the jurisdiction threshold* were to be followed, it might be possible to resolve any problematic analytical issues regarding coordination of sovereignties *on the merits*. In this way, the problem of coordination of sovereign competences does not have to serve as a justification for the jurisdictional threshold. How could this possibility be utilized more specifically? For example, when an assessment is made whether a measure that interferes with private life is in accordance with the law, the rules of public international law pertaining to jurisdiction can be included. If these rules are not followed and, as a consequence, the sovereignty of a foreign state is somehow breached or disregarded, the legality requirement under human rights law would not be fulfilled.[337] This failure would lead directly to the finding of a violation for breach of a negative obligation. It follows then that excluding concerns about coordination of sovereignties and competences from the threshold under Article 1 seems to lead to an easy finding of a violation on the merits in the context of negative obligations. The reason is that the legality requirement is *not* met when the State of extraterritorial jurisdiction had no competence.[338] It should be added here that answers to the questions of whether a particular State has a legal competence, and how this is coordinated with the competences of other States, might not be easily forthcoming. The reason is that public international law may not provide clear answers as to the legality of any interventions by the State.[339] This implies that the answer to the question whether the measure of interference is 'in accordance with the law' might also not be easily forthcoming.

---

[335] On the purpose and value of sovereign autonomy of States, see S Besson, 'Sovereignty, International Law and Democracy' (2011) 22(2) European Journal of International Law 373.

[336] This does not mean that such questions are irrelevant for the human rights discourse more generally. For the distinction of these discourses from human rights *law* in a narrow sense, see H Hannum, 'Reinvigorating Human Rights for the Twenty-First Century' in D Akande and others (eds), *Human Rights and 21st Century Challenges* (Oxford University Press 2020) 13.

[337] *Weber and Saravia v Germany* (dec) no 54934/00, 29 June 2006 §§87–88. The applicants who lived in Uruguay complained about secret surveillance of communication. Although Germany objected that they were within its jurisdiction, the Court did not rule on the issue since in anyway considered the application inadmissible on other grounds. As part of the legality assessment under Article 8(2), the Court required 'proof in the form of concordant inferences that the authorities of the respondent State have acted extraterritorially in a manner that is inconsistent with the sovereignty of the foreign State and therefore contrary to international law'. See also *Öcalan v Turkey* [GC] no 46221/99, 12 May 2005 §90.

[338] *Medvedyev and Others v France* [GC] no 3394/03, 29 March 2010 §102.

[339] R Chambers, 'An Evaluation of Two Key Extraterritorial Techniques to Bring Human Rights Standards to Bear on Corporate Misconduct' 2018 (14)2 Utrecht Law Review 22.

How could the possibility of resolving any problematic issues regarding coordination of sovereignties on the merits stage of the analysis be utilized in the context of positive obligations? As already mentioned, legality does not have such a conclusive role in the context of positive obligations. It nonetheless has a role. We should therefore engage with the question whether and how it might be possible to address the issue of coordination of sovereignties in the analysis of positive obligations on the merits. Such an analysis might include as a relevant omission, for example, the failure to conclude an international law agreement with the State where the harmed individuals are located, where to have done so might have contributed to the prevention of harm. Such an analysis could also imply using the national legislation or any national standards of the territorial state as relevant reference points in the identification and assessment of relevant omissions by the State that arguably has extraterritorial jurisdiction.[340] Despite these possibilities, it can be asked whether questions broached upon engagement with the issue of coordination of sovereignties are appropriate within the realm of the human rights law analysis. It might be better if these questions are excluded and left for other branches of international law.

### 8.4.1.5 Democratic legitimacy

By having consistently confirmed that jurisdiction under Article 1 may include considerations about legal competence and entitlements, the Court has inserted an element of legitimacy into the jurisdictional threshold. This means that the conduct of the State of extraterritorial jurisdiction might initially have to be cloaked with legal authority denoting its legitimacy for it to be scrutinized on the merits. For example, the legitimacy of the conduct of the State of extraterritorial jurisdiction can be based on the consent of the territorial state in one form or another. Legitimacy implies that democratic processes have been followed in taking decisions that affect individuals. Why should democratic legitimacy matter as a pertinent consideration within the jurisdictional threshold? What could be the implications for the analysis on the merits, if this consideration were to be ignored?

When States become bearers of human rights law obligations abroad, they are arguably supplanting the regulatory and enforcement choices that might have been made by the territorial State. As mentioned above, positive obligations might require regulatory penetration into the territorial State, which might in turn limit the local population's democratic choices.[341] Sovereign interests that have presumably been identified through democratic deliberations might be affected.[342] For example,

---

[340] For such a proposal see Ryngaert, *Selfless Intervention* (n 192) 125.

[341] Besson also mentions that it may prevent the State of territorial jurisdiction from fulfilling its obligations. She also adds that the existence of concurrent and potentially competing obligations of different States might be 'counterproductive in the long run for its [the State of territorial jurisdiction's] democratic development'. S Besson, 'Concurrent Responsibilities under the European Convention on Human Rights' in van Aaken and Motoc (eds), *The European Convention on Human Rights and General International Law* (n 238) 155, 169.

[342] This presumption can be challenged in the light of the democratic deficit in many countries. In addition, individuals and groups can have interests that diverge from the interests of the State that represents them.

better regulation of companies by their state of incorporation might be in conflict with the policies of the States where these companies operate. Normally, the latter group of States try to attract investment by lowering standards (ie low safety rules, no labour inspections, etc),[343] in this way increasing their competitiveness against other States.[344] It then follows that unilateral regulatory actions by the State of incorporation can cause distributive effects across States and shifts of resources within the affected State. Such effects and shifts might lack legitimacy.

Similar concerns have been also voiced in the context of occupation, where a rights-based relationship between the occupant and the occupied people might confer some legitimacy on the hostile occupation. This might happen if the occupying State tries to justify legal and institutional changes as being necessary for it to perform its human rights law obligations.[345]

The above arguments justifying the jurisdiction threshold based on democratic legitimacy have also been critiqued. *First*, it has been objected that in any case the local population might have never participated in any democratically meaningful way in the taking of such decisions by its State as have had negative effects.[346] *Second*, it has been noted that 'regulatory risks of private human rights harm' have been relegated to host countries of corporate operations that 'are ill-equipped to prevent and redress violations'.[347] As a consequence, 'the distinction between the "territorial" and "extraterritorial" that was once premised on the equal sovereignty entitlements and responsibilities of state to protect human rights within their territory frees global market forces from the constraints of international law'.[348] *Third*, it has been added that concerns about democratic legitimacy and non-intervention can be dismissed, since human rights law reflects international and universal standards. Ryngaert, for example, has noted that 'insofar as the extraterritorially acting state, including the occupying state, does not export its own national or regional interpretations of human rights law but adheres to internationally recognized human rights interpretations, the

---

[343] This could be framed as interference in the economic policies of other States. Ryngaert, 'Towards a Reasonableness Test' (n 198) 195.
[344] A Peters, 'Global Constitutionalism. The Social Dimension' in R Suami and others (eds), *Global Constitutionalism from European and East Asian Perspectives* (Cambridge University Press 2018) 277, 281.
[345] Ryngaert, 'Extraterritorial Obligations under Human Rights Law' (n 4) 273, 285.
[346] This argument has been made, for example, in relation to decisions of taking sovereign debt and restructuring of debts, which can have serious human rights implications. See S Joseph, 'Sovereign Debt and Civil/Political Rights' in I Bantekas and C Lumina (eds), *Sovereign Debt and Human Rights* (Oxford University Press 2018) 303, 304. On democratic deficit, see also M Salomon, 'State of Play and the Road Ahead. A World of Poverty and Human Rights' in Akande and others (eds), *Human Rights and 21st Challenges* (n 336) 214.
[347] Augenstein, 'The Crisis of International Human Rights Law in the Global Market Economy' (n 167) 60. A related argument is that host countries do not tend to protest when 'the home state merely provides a forum for litigation against its "own" corporation (albeit in respect of extraterritorial business activities)'. See Ryngaert, *Selfless Intervention* (n 192) 187. The initiation of litigation, however, does imply the existence of some substantive regulatory standards. These might have distributive effects without legitimacy, and thus be an object of protest.
[348] Augenstein, 'The Crisis of International Human Rights Law in the Global Market Economy' (n 167) 60.

danger of intervention could be considered lessened'.[349] Similarly, it has been added that human rights law in any case is meant to impose limits on state sovereignty and the matters that it regulates do not exclusively belong to the national jurisdiction of the territorial State in any case. It therefore seems unlikely that many instances of 'extraterritorial jurisdiction or other measures will give rise to a breach of the sovereignty of a State'.[350]

These three points, which buttress the argument that democratic legitimacy should be irrelevant in the conceptualization of the jurisdiction threshold in human rights law, merit more detailed attention.[351] The first two draw on general problems whose scope goes far beyond the confines of human rights law. Specifically, it is hard to expect that the imposition of human rights law obligations upon some States should be the solution to the democratic deficit in other States.[352] If any solutions were to be found, they do not necessarily have to be within the realm of international human rights law.[353] As to the third point, as noted by Ryngaert, it overlooks the nature of human rights law. True, universalist standards and global values can be invoked.[354] It cannot be overlooked, however, that substantive human rights law standards are set against the backdrop of the specific political community.[355] This is also true in the context of negative and positive obligations that trigger a legal analysis of balancing

---

[349] Ryngaert, 'Extraterritorial Obligations under Human Rights Law' (n 4) 273, 286. See also Ryngaert, *Selfless Intervention* (n 192) 17 for an argument that States 'can unilaterally extend their (prescriptive) jurisdiction' to address 'globally undesirable situations'. To support this argument, Ryngaert (p. 25) invokes 'internationally shared values', including human rights.

[350] Vandenbogaerde, 'Attributing Extraterritorial Obligations under the International Covenant on Economic, Social and Cultural Rights' (n 173) 25.

[351] The critique of the concerns about sovereignty and democratic legitimacy has been supplemented with a proposal as to how the problem of absence of democratic legitimacy could be remedied. In particular, if the affected persons are involved in the decision-making process and their interests are taken into account, even though they are located extraterritorially, concerns about absence of legitimacy can be alleviated. Such proposals have, however, moral basis and will not be explored further here. See E Benvenisti, 'Sovereigns as Trustees of Humanity: On the Accountability of States to Foreign Stakeholders' (2013) 107 American Journal of International Law 295 (States are *morally* required to take foreigners' interests into account. Benvenisti underscores that any voice given to foreigners is 'without any political power: they have the right to offer their perspectives but not to participate in the actual vote'). See also Ryngaert, *Selfless Intervention* (n 192) 109–25.

[352] International human rights might be used as an argumentative technique to instigate positive changes at domestic level, but this is different from the technical legal analysis that human rights law demands. In addition, any tension between popular sovereignty and human rights 'ought to be resolved within the domestic context where democracy and human rights are in a mutual relationship'. Besson, 'Sovereignty' (n 42) §132.

[353] Human rights claims are made in different contexts. Some of them do not identify legal entitlements and concrete obligations at all, but rather general political goals. G Letsas, *A Theory of Interpretation of the European Convention on Human Rights* (Oxford University Press 2007) 23–24. Each of these contexts can be important.

[354] Another possible problem with the third point, as pointed out by Ryngaert, is that values and interests, although universally accepted as important, might be in tension with each other. The question then is how such tensions could possibly be resolved at a global level.

[355] One can also ask what universality means. It can be contended that 'international human rights laws are only universal in the sense of framing the social, economic and political questions that all (democratic) societies must address, ie the relationship between private autonomy (individual self-determination) and the rights and interests of others, including the interests of society more generally'. S Wheatley, *The Democratic Legitimacy of International Law* (Hart Publishing 2010) 111.

competing interests within this political community.[356] As Section 8.1 shows, this balancing can be linked with the distributive justice that underpins human rights law. It is questionable whether it is 'appropriate to apply social-distributive justice to the actions of States in their external relations',[357] a point that will be examined in detail in the next section, which addresses balancing.

## 8.4.2 Reasonableness and Balancing of Interests

The conceptual framework of human rights law presupposes balancing individual interests with collective public interests. As Chapter 4 shows, this observation is limited to negative obligations corresponding to qualified rights, and to positive obligations corresponding to all rights.[358] For this balancing to be operationalized, there are two important preconditions. First, there needs to be clarity as to which political community is to be used as a point of reference (Section 8.4.2.1). Second, the balancing implies a unity between the individuals and the political community. In other words, the balancing presupposes a communality between the individuals and the political entity (ie the State) whose interests would be used as referents in that balancing (Section 8.4.2.2). After clarifying these two preconditions, I turn to the question of whether and how balancing could be operationalized in extraterritorial settings (Section 8.4.2.3).

### 8.4.2.1 Whose interests are the reference point?

A difficulty that arises in extraterritorial settings concerns the question as to which political community (ie which State) should be taken as a reference point for assessing the balancing of interests and the reasonableness of any positive protective measures. For the balancing and reasonableness assessment to be made operational, there needs to be clarity as to whose interests are to be used as referents. Despite the invocations of the universality of human rights, the reality is that there is no universal community

---

[356] Another possible problem with the third point advanced by Ryngaert can be noted here. It might be correct that all States, including the 'receiving' (ie those that receive the laws of the State externalizing its regulations) might have agreed to some abstract global values. This consent, however, does not necessarily extend to the procedure and method of enforcement. True, the receiving state might not object to some victims getting compensation from a company registered in the home State; but they might object to general preventive regulations. A related problem is that even if the interests protected by universal human rights law are generally acknowledged, and even if it can be assumed that there is some agreement on corresponding negative obligations, this is not the case with positive obligations and the *concrete* measures that they require. Ryngaert, *Selfless Intervention* (n 192) 103) ('What matters and may suffice is that international law has *proscribed* certain conduct' (emphasis in the original). The reference to proscribed conduct implies negative obligations and ignores positive obligations and the concrete measures that they might demand.

[357] S Meckled-Garcia, 'Do Transnational Economic Effects Violate Human Rights?' (2009) 2(3) Ethics and Global Politics 259, 273.

[358] Negative obligations corresponding to unqualified rights, such as those enshrined in Article 3 ECHR, are not an object of the same type of balancing. See V Stoyanova, *Human Trafficking and Slavery Reconsidered* (Cambridge University Press 2017) 279.

with a universal interest that can be used as the standard for analytical correctness. The standard has to be rather the interests of the community that is framed as the holder of human rights obligations, namely the State of extraterritorial jurisdiction. It is the interests of this State (not of the territorial State) that might possibly be of relevance since it is this State that should arguably be constituted as a holder of obligations. This implies dismissing any interests of the territorial State, which in itself might be problematic. Even if not completely dismissed, it might be difficult to understand how the interests of the two political communities relate to each other. It could be equally difficult to incorporate the relationship of interests of different States in the human rights law analysis.

### 8.4.2.2 Sharing and commonality

*Bounded community as a precondition for the operationalization of balancing*

Assuming that it is the interests of the State of extraterritorial jurisdiction that are relevant, additional challenges arise if we consider the second precondition that allows the balancing in human rights law. Specifically, the balancing analysis implies a unity between the individuals and the political community or entity (the State) whose interests are used as referents. In this sense, the State can be identified with the society: it is the organizational form of the society. The State does not have interests on its own, it rather has an instrumental value for this society. The jurisdictional threshold in human rights law (understood as a normative threshold) can ensure these preconditions that enable the operationalization of the balancing between interests within the society.

More specifically, the structure of human rights, and the ensuing balancing analysis, are underpinned by the assumption that these rights are exercised in relation to a political community where there is political equality,[359] and in relation to the circumstances of the interdependent parties, namely those whose interests are infringed and those whose interests benefit from the infringement.[360] The balancing test presupposes decision-making within a community,[361] where there is a crucial element of sharing and commonality.[362] The execution of the balancing presupposes that it is possible to make rational judgments about 'first, [the] intensity of interference [and by analysis, the intensity of harm if no positive protective measures are extended], second, [the] degrees of importance [of the public interest], and third, their relationship to each other'.[363]

---

[359] A Barak, 'Proportionality and Principled Balancing' (2010) 4 Law and Ethics of Human Rights 1, 3; Besson, 'The Egalitarian Dimension of Human Rights' (n 26) 23.

[360] K Möller, 'Proportionality: Challenging the Critics' (2012) 10(3) International Journal of Constitutional Law 709, 716.

[361] The proportionality framework rests on the existence of a democratic community. R Alexy, *A Theory of Constitutional Rights* (Oxford University Press 2010) 417–18.

[362] M Kumm, 'The Idea of Socratic Contestation and the Right to Justification' (2010) 4(2) Law and Ethics of Human Rights 140, 143.

[363] R Alexy, 'The Construction of Constitutional Rights' (2010) 4(1) Law and Ethics of Human Rights 20, 28.

The operation of the balancing framework is therefore intimately related to the boundedness of the community.[364] Political equality that depends on the existence of a political community is conditioned on 'the common subjecthood to decisions and laws, and the interdependence of stakes and the rough equality of those stakes among the members' of the community.[365] This commonality, interdependence, rough equality of stakes, and sharing are crucial for the operation of the balancing framework as an analytical tool in deciding when state conduct (act or omission) amounts to a violation of human rights law. They allow the operation of the balancing test. As Möller explains, balancing is 'about the sacrifice that can legitimately be demanded from one person for the benefit of another person or the public'.[366] The legitimacy of such sacrifice as might be allowed under the balancing test is plausible only if it is 'justifiable to those burdened by it in terms that free and equals can accept'.[367] Kumm adds that

> [i]t must be morally plausible to imagine even those addressees most burdened by a law to have hypothetically consented to it. Even those left worst off and most heavily burdened by legislation must be conceivable as free and equal *partners* in a joint enterprise of law-giving.[368]

Those burdened by the measures 'must be able to interpret the legislative act as a reasonable attempt to specify what citizens—all citizens, including those on the losing side—owe to each other as free and equals'.[369] This equal participation in the political community is important for establishing some commonality between the competing interests that need to be balanced. The equal participation is what relates the interests and enables comparison and equitable sharing.[370] For this reason Meckled-Garcia has observed that if a claim to 'subsistence goods' is 'not against a given social scheme [shared state institutions], no plausible principle exists for defining what counts as a reasonable burden'.[371]

In addition, the normative presuppositions in human rights law (ie a democratic society that provides the context where interests are related and balancing enabled) have not only a qualitative but also a quantitative dimension. In particular, when

---

[364] Barak, 'Proportionality and Principled Balancing' (n 359) 3; Besson, 'The Egalitarian Dimension of Human Rights' (n 26) 23.
[365] Besson, 'The Egalitarian Dimension of Human Rights' (n 26) 31.
[366] Möller, 'Proportionality' (n 360) 716.
[367] Kumm, 'The Idea of Socratic Contestation and the Right to Justification' (n 362) 143.
[368] ibid 168.
[369] ibid 168.
[370] 'Just as a comparison of two weights requires a scale, proportionality and equality presuppose something that enables comparison and equitable sharing.' G Noll, 'Analogy at War: Proportionality, Equality and the Law of Targeting' (2013) 43 Netherlands Yearbook of International Law 205, 206.
[371] S Meckled-Garcia, 'Giving Up the Goods: Rethinking the Human Right to Subsistence, Institutional Justice, and Imperfect Duties' (2013) 30(1) Journal of Applied Philosophy 73, 74: 'outside the political communal contexts there is no coherent account of what constitutes a justifiable imposition of burdens for any specific agent that will secure the resource claims of all'.

balancing of interests is performed within the bounded community, there is certain predictability as to the group of individuals affected on both sides of the scale. This predictability is less likely in cases of boundlessness, where the consequences of measures are not limited to the bounded community. More specifically, the number of individuals affected or the number to be protected might be hard to identify and estimate.

*Balancing without communality*

It needs to be acknowledged that balancing has been used as a legal analytical tool in circumstances not characterized by communality and sharing, notably in relation to loss of life. More specifically, the proportionality principle in international humanitarian law prohibits attacks that may be expected to lead to an excessive loss of life in relation to the value of the military target.[372] Given the arguments that proportionality as understood in international humanitarian law should inform proportionality in human rights law,[373] and more specifically the test under Article 2(2) of the ECHR as to whether any use of force has been 'not more than absolutely necessary',[374] it is crucial to highlight the fundamental difference between the proportionality tests in these two bodies of law (human rights versus international humanitarian law). This difference puts into sharp relief the preconditions (ie communality and sharing) that underpin human rights law.

Article 2 ECHR imposes a positive obligation to protect life; this obligation has been applied in various kinds of circumstances, including planning and execution of police/law enforcement and military operations, hostage taking, battles involving insurgents,[375] artillery attacks, and aerial bombardment.[376] To comply with this positive obligation, any use of force has to be 'no more than absolutely necessary', a test that implies a proportionate relation between the aim pursued by the State and the measures taken.[377] It is central that in comparison with proportionality under international humanitarian law, the proportionality test under Article 2 ECHR is based on different criteria with different considerations on each side of the scales.

---

[372] Article 57(2)(a), Protocol Addition to the Geneva Conventions of 12 August 1949, and relating to the Protection of Victims of International Armed Conflict (Protocol I), 8 June 1977. The following analysis is limited to international armed conflicts since 'humanitarian law leaves the planning and execution of attacks essentially unregulated in internal conflicts'. Abresch, 'A Human Rights Law of Internal Armed Conflict' (n 300) 761–62.

[373] For literature that assumes or argues that these tests are similar or can be reconciled, see Park, *The Right to Life in Armed Conflict* (n 154) 106 and 112, where it is also suggested that the necessity test from international humanitarian law (IHL) should overrule the one from human rights law: there will be 'no violation of a state's substantive right to life obligations where the applicable international humanitarian law principles for the use of lethal force were adhered to'.

[374] *Nachova and Others v Bulgaria* no 43577 and 43579/98, 6 July 2005 §94.

[375] *Ergi v Turkey* no 66/1997/850/1057, 28 July 1998.

[376] *Isayeva, Yusupova and Bazayeva v Russia* no 57947/00, 24 February 2005; *Isayeva v Russia* no 57950/00, 24 February 2005.

[377] The Court has allowed some flexibility in the application of the test, but the essential elements of the test are the same. *Finogenov and Others v Russia* no 18299/03, 20 December 2011 §211; *Tagayeva and Others v Russia* no 26562/07, 13 April 2017 §481.

If we first look at one side of the scale, it is important to note that any aims allowed to be included in the calculus need to be legitimate; such aims are exhaustively enumerated in Article 2(2) ECHR.[378] If these legitimate aims are removed from the calculus and replaced with military exigencies,[379] which is what the proportionality test in international humanitarian law entails, the calculus cannot imply the same type of proportionality as that applied under Article 2 of the ECHR.

If we then look at the other side of the scale, and in particular at the effects of the measures taken, the question that emerges is whose lives matter. In human rights law, *any life matters* and anybody's life is of importance in the balancing. There is no starting assumption that a person can be targeted with lethal force based on his/her status. This is not the case in international humanitarian law, with its heavy emphasis on categorization of individuals into different statuses,[380] where no necessity to kill needs to be shown in respect of combatants or civilians taking a direct part in hostilities.[381] As a consequence, their lives are not placed in the scale.[382]

The considerations that matter on both sides of the human rights law scales can be explained in light of the guiding principle in the application of the proportionality under Article 2 ECHR. This principle has been expressed as the 'caution expected from a law-enforcement body *in a democratic society*'.[383] It reflects the assumption that there are no two competing parties in a conflict, but rather unity, and that the State, the only entity that has the legitimate entitlement to use force, tries to control the situation to the benefit of *all*, including those that might be the object of lethal measures. The 'democratic society' is the element that relates the scales and the factors placed on each side. This is in stark contrast to the assumptions underpinning international humanitarian law.[384] Here lie the origins of the difference between the proportionality tests in these two bodies of law. Overall, then, it follows that although

---

[378] See also Section 5.3.3.2 where the legitimate aims under Article 2(2) were more extensively covered. See also Section 8.4.1.2.

[379] Schabas argues that where force is used with a legitimate aim, IHL can be of use in the human rights law analysis since it is a more sophisticated and developed regime. Schabas, '*Lex Specialis?*' (n 307) 610.

[380] This categorization enables the operation of the principle of distinction in IHL.

[381] Milanovic, 'A Norm Conflict Perspective on the Relationship between International Humanitarian law and Human Rights Law' (n 295) 479.

[382] This can explain why the Court has noted that 'Article 2 must be interpreted *in so far as possible* in light of the general principles of international law, including the rules of international humanitarian law (emphasis added)'. *Varnava and Others v Turkey* [GC] no 16064/90, 18 September 2009 §185.

[383] *McCann and Others v United Kingdom* [GC] no 18984/91, 27 September 1995 §212 (emphasis added); *Isayeva v Russia* §180. The Court has also added that '[t]he circumstances in which deprivation of life may be justified must ... be strictly construed'. *Saribekyan and Balyan v Azerbaijan* no 35746/11, 30 January 2020 §59.

[384] These assumptions explain the reluctance of the States to concede the application of international humanitarian law. In circumstances of internal conflict, conceding the applicability of the Protocol Addition to the Geneva Convention (Protocol I), 8 June 1977, might be interpreted as an admission by the State that 'it is exercising alien occupation or colonial domination against the will of the people'. 'Conceding the applicability of Protocol II further entails acknowledging that a group other than the government exercises control over portions of the State's territory'. Abresch, 'A Human Rights Law of Internal Armed Conflict' (n 300) 756.

balancing has been applied without communality, it serves different principles that are not, and should not be, transposable to human rights law.

### 8.4.2.3 Extraterritorial balancing?

Could then balancing be operationalized in extraterritorial circumstances where there is no communality between the State whose conduct has negative effects and the individuals who have suffered these effects, and where these individuals are possibly unidentifiable?[385] How could this State 'do justice' to these individuals if they are not its parts, but 'stand outside communication'?[386] How to perform balancing when the State has not and does not seek to justify its conduct to affected individuals located extraterritorially, and the latter have never participated in communicative processes where it might be possible to express consent? In other words, is it possible to perform 'extraterritorial balancing', and if so, how?

When sharing and commonality are shaken, as in extraterritorial circumstances, the difficulties that ensue regarding the balancing framework are yet to be truly appreciated by the Court. In the existing judgments where extraterritorial jurisdiction was found, the ECtHR has not yet striven to apply the proportionality test in the determination of breach of negative obligations corresponding to qualified rights. The reason is that the issues on the merits have instead been about the duty to investigate,[387] and the negative obligations corresponding to the right to life[388] and the right to liberty.[389] In contrast, the qualified right to education was invoked in *Catan and Others v Moldova and Russia*, where no evidence was submitted by the respondents that the measures taken in relation to the schools actually pursued any legitimate aims.[390] Similarly, the substantive issues in *Sandu and Others v Moldova and Russia*[391] were *easily* resolved since the respondents did not submit any arguments that there might be a legal basis for the interference with the applicants' right to property. The same happened in *Loizidou v Turkey*.[392] In a similarly easy way the Court in *Chiragov*

---

[385] Difficulties arise in relating the competing interests (ie weighing different gains and losses) in the balancing assessment even when no issues of extraterritoriality arise. See A da Silva, 'Comparing the Incommensurable: Constitutional Principles, Balancing and Rational Decision' (2011) 31(2) Oxford Journal of Legal Studies 273. However, the resolution to these difficulties rests on arguments about democracy and democratic legitimacy. In contrast, in circumstances of extraterritorial harm, the individuals affected are likely not part of the demos.
[386] G Teubner, 'Transnational Fundamental Rights: Horizontal Effect' (2011) 40 Rechtsfilosofie and Rechtstheorie 191, 214.
[387] *Al-Skeini and Others v United Kingdom* [GC] no 55721/07, 7 July 2011; *Jaloud v the Netherlands* [GC] no 47708/08, 20 November 2014.
[388] *Andreou v Turkey* no 45653/99, 27 October 2009. Even if the issue under Article 2 is framed as implicating positive obligations, as for example in *Georgia v Russia II* [GC] no 38263/08, 21 January 2021 §§216–220, since Russia exercised effective control over South Ossetia, 'it was also responsible for the actions of the South Ossetian forces in those territories, without it being necessary to provide proof of "detailed control" of each of those actions'.
[389] *Hassan v the United Kingdom* no 29750/09, 16 September 2014; *Al-Jedda v the United Kingdom* [GC] no 27021/08, 7 July 2011.
[390] *Catan and Others v the Republic of Moldova and Russia* [GC] no 43370/04, 19 October 2012 §144.
[391] *Sandu and Others v Moldova and Russia* no 21043/05, 17 July 2018 §81.
[392] *Loizidou v Turkey* no 16318/89, 18 December 1996 §64.

*and Others v Armenia* found that no aim had been indicated that could justify the interference with the applicants' rights to property and private and family life.[393] In easily finding a violation, the Court in *Chiragov* ignored the complexities of the extraterritorial circumstances that are relevant for the purposes of deciding on the lawfulness and proportionality of the restrictions.[394]

Although the case law has not provided insights into 'extraterritorial balancing', it has been suggested that even in extraterritorial settings, balancing is possible. Milanovic notes that the balancing and proportionality tests can be tweaked 'a bit to accommodate extraterritorial application'.[395] This tweaking implies that 'the scales would weigh somewhat more heavily in favour of state interests than they would otherwise'.[396] This proposal, however, does not solve the above-discussed conceptual problem that the State does not have an interest on its own, but that its interests are rather meant to serve the particular society's interests, and these interests need to be related to the affected individual's interests (ie there needs to be communality). This means that it might make little sense to place more weight somewhere when there is no connection in the first place between the two 'scales' that are to be weighed against each other. The absence of a connection is reflective of the absence of interdependence of stakes that is required for political equality and democracy.

Milanovic also notes possible dangers if the tweaking proposal were to take place. In particular, since state interests would weigh more heavily, the finding of a violation would be less likely. As a consequence, harm against human beings might not only be lawful, 'but lawful in a nice, human rights-friendly sort of way'.[397] In defence of his proposal for 'tweaking' the proportionality test, however, he first notes that it is not possible to predict how balancing could be performed in every given factual scenario. Second, he adds that even if any dangers materialize (ie less likelihood of finding a violation and thus establishing state responsibility), 'the extraterritorial application of the human rights regime would still be worth having with regard to torture, fair trial, or arbitrary deprivations of liberty or life'.[398]

The second point brings us back to the issue of 'dividing and tailoring'. As Section 8.3 showed, the Court has already accepted that jurisdiction as a threshold can be relativized and thus divided and tailored. The tweaking in *Hanan v Germany* led to finding of no violation since the procedural duty under Article 2 had to be applied 'realistically' given the 'active hostilities in an (extraterritorial) armed conflict'.[399] The standard of reasonableness, that is reflective of the operation of balancing of relevant

---

[393] *Chiragov and Others v Armenia* no 13216/05, 16 June 2015 §201; *Ivantoc and Others v Moldova and Russia*, no 23687/05, 15 November 2011 §141–143, where Russia did not invoke any legal basis and justifications for the interference.
[394] See Dissenting Opinion of Judge Pinto de Albuquerque in *Chiragov and Others v Armenia* [GC] no 13216/05, 16 June 2015 §48.
[395] Milanovic (n 4) 112.
[396] ibid 112.
[397] ibid 113.
[398] ibid 114.
[399] *Hanan v Germany* [GC] no 4871/16, 16 February 2021 §200.

interests,[400] was indeed invoked for determining the scope and the content of the procedural duty.[401] It was, however, 'tweaked' by ignoring the very justification for this positive obligation that *united* it with the substantive obligation not to kill unless absolutely necessary in pursuant of the specific aims as indicated in Article 2 ECHR.[402] The 'tweaking' of the reasonableness did not help the applicant; it reflected how the victims' lives themselves still 'stand outside communication'[403] in that the justifications for the actual killings did not matter.[404] The 'divide and tailor' approach to jurisdiction therefore does not and cannot change the fundamental absence of communality between the affected individuals and the political entity; instead it challenges the interconnectedness of human rights in terms of their justifications and scope and content of corresponding obligations.

The implications from *H.F. and Others v France* are similar. As Section 8.3 showed, after dividing and tailoring jurisdiction, any obligations owed also had to be tailored to the point of holding that the only positive obligation owed was subjecting a rejection of a request for repatriation 'to an appropriate individual examination, by an independent body, separate from the executive authorities of the State, but not necessary by a judicial authority'.[405] Similarly to *Hanan v Germany*, this procedural obligation had to be *detached from any justifications that can unite the obligation with the pursuant of any substantive outcome* (ie actual repatriation). An argument that this detachment was necessary *solely* because there is no right to be repatriated is simply not convincing, given how the Court has developed positive obligations more generally in domestic settings. Indeed, there might be no right to be repatriated as such, in the same way as there is no right to have somebody prosecuted as such.[406] However, positive obligations are obligations of means, which means that the efforts are placed at the heart of the assessment of breach.

Again similarly to *Hanan v Germany*, the detachment inevitably affected any determination as to what is reasonable and how balancing in this context could be performed, since the outcome (ie actual repatriation) could not be a relevant consideration in *H.F. and Others v France*. In anticipation of an argument that I might contradict myself since in the very paragraph above I highlighted that it is the process of efforts that matter, not the outcome, for determination of breach of positive obligations, the following clarification is relevant here. For the efforts to be meaningful, they

---

[400] Chapters 4 and 5.
[401] *Hanan v Germany* [GC] no 4871/16, 16 February 2021 [GC] §204.
[402] Joint Partly Dissenting Opinion of Judges Grozev, Ranzoni, and Eicke in *Hanan v Germany* [GC] §12: 'we are concerned that that the majority are now stretching the detachable nature of the procedural obligation beyond breaking point, by abandoning any connection with an underlying substantive Convention obligation under Article 2'.
[403] Teubner, 'Transnational Fundamental Rights' (n 386) 214.
[404] See Section 8.4.1.2 for an analysis how human rights law and humanitarian law address deprivation of life.
[405] *H.F. and Others v France* [GC] no 24384/19, 14 September 2022 §276.
[406] Section 6.2.3.3.

have to be related to the pursuit of certain outcomes. In simple terms, if there is no outcome *in view*, it does not make sense to make efforts.[407]

However, in any case, the usual standards of reasonableness and balancing are snubbed in *H.F. and Others v France* and replaced with 'arbitrariness'. The GC held that

> [i]n sum, there must be a mechanism for the review of decisions not to grant requests for a return to national territory through which it can be ascertained that there is no arbitrariness in any of the grounds that may legitimately be relied upon by the executive authorities, whether derived from compelling public interest considerations or from any legal, diplomatic or material difficulties.[408]

One could say that 'arbitrariness' is the tweaked version of the standard of reasonableness and the balancing of interests that the latter presupposes. One could also say that the above paragraph suggests that the interests of the women and their children in the camps in Syria have to be balanced in a non-arbitrary way against 'compelling public interest considerations' and grounds related to 'any legal, diplomatic or material difficulties'. The requirement for justifications (ie legal, diplomatic, or material difficulties) seems to be crucial here since it can be understood as ensuring the relation between the individuals and France. As already explained, to perform balancing the interests on the two sides need to be related so that there is a communality. Yet the justifications, as applied in *H.F. and Others v France*, hardly create communality, given the rejection in the Court's reasoning of any meaningful substantive outcome (ie actual repatriation). It can be also added that the justifications themselves (ie the public interests or any difficulties) are not elaborated upon. Nobody therefore knows what can be placed on the French State's side of the scale. As to the women's and their children's side of the scale, if a refusal to repatriate them is found arbitrary and unjustified, what interests are actually there to protect? None, given the rejection of the substantive outcome (ie repatriation). To recap, the 'divide and tailor' approach to jurisdiction led to a finding of a violation based on a very narrow ground (ie the national review of the refusals to repatriate was arbitrary). This, however, does not change the fundamental absence of communality between the affected individuals and the political entity, France, that permeates the whole judgment. Here it could be also finally added that France simply did not want the detainees in the camps back as members of its community.

As to the first point that Milanovic puts forward to defend the proposal for tweaking balancing, it is correct that balancing is always fact specific. However, the crucial question that needs to be addressed is whether it might be possible to reconstruct the balancing analysis so that it can respond to claims of human beings regardless of their location and formal membership in a political community, without at the same time completely jettisoning the jurisdictional threshold. The answer might be that if we

---

[407] For a more detailed analysis on the interaction between efforts and outcomes, see Sections 6.2.3.3 and 7.2.
[408] *H.F. and Others v France* [GC] no 24384/19, 14 September 2022 §276.

take the universality of human rights and the interests that they protect as a normative starting point (a point that proposals for expanding the meaning of jurisdiction heavily rely upon),[409] then we need to identify the universal community with relevant general *universal* interests and in some way to universalize the satisfaction and the non-satisfaction of these general interests among States.[410] This could mean, for example, spreading non-satisfaction through burden sharing and solidary mechanisms.

It is beyond the scope of this book to further explain these mechanisms, the complexities that they imply and the reluctance of States to actually undertake them. Suffice to note that universal general interests are hard to identify, given the social and cultural diversity.[411] It is as hard to propose how their satisfaction or non-satisfaction should be spread among States. And in any case, it might be equally hard to distil concrete positive obligations upon some States as opposed to others.[412] Extraterritorial balancing implies international democracy, whose development and operationalization raise very difficult issues.[413] Indeed, States might cooperate and assist each other, which might be suggestive of burden sharing and solidarity. However, this cooperation and assistance is not considered to be a matter of human rights law obligations.[414] In general terms, the question of global distributive justice is outside the realm of human rights law,[415] and concerns have been voiced about the consequences if it is actually framed as a matter of human rights law. Specifically, it might not only undermine the distinctiveness of this body of law but also 'crowds out other ways of understanding harm and recompense'.[416]

---

[409] Milanovic (n 4) 80 and 171: 'universality is no longer just one of many competing ideological viewpoints—universality is the law', the 'normative pull of universality'. Mallory, *Human Rights Imperialists* (n 238) 200–02; Vandenbogaerde, *Towards Shared Accountability in International Human Rights Law* (n 3) 228. Although Raible does not invoke universality, which distinguishes her from other authors, she invokes equality: 'Jurisdiction is about capturing the relationship between the individual and a state that puts the latter in a position to guarantee equal respect and concern. It is this position that acts as a justification for the allocation of duties and thus as a threshold criterion for the application of human rights treaties.' Raible *Human Rights Unbound* (n 3) 10. Raible does not explain, however, equality in relation to whom, or how equality could be operationalized outside the political community. This creates the impression that the way she invokes equality collapses into universality.
[410] The identification of such a universal international community is not unproblematic. See Ryngaert, *Selfless Intervention* (n 192) 28.
[411] Even in the context of the right to life, interventions into other States to protect life are problematic.
[412] Burden sharing and solidarity are suggestive of the appeals to global distributive justice. Such appeals are often framed and justified in terms of human rights. Raible has convincingly demonstrated why this framing, which implies a conflation of global distributive justice and human rights entitlements, is incorrect. Raible, *Human Rights Unbound* (n 3) 7 and 31.
[413] For some initial insights see Besson, 'Sovereignty' (n 42) §§147–149. See also Wheatley, *The Democratic Legitimacy of International Law* (n 355) 311.
[414] Raible, *Human Rights Unbound* (n 3) 72. See also Meckled-Garcia, 'Giving Up the Goods' (n 371) 80: 'In such cases it makes more sense to speak of *imperfect duties* rather than human rights. By imperfect duties I mean duties to incorporate concern for others' wellbeing in our lives with no stipulation as to the degree of contribution' (emphasis in the original).
[415] S Meckled-Garcia, 'On the Very Idea of Cosmopolitan Justice: Constructivism and International Agency' (2008) 16(3) Journal of Political Philosophy 245.
[416] D Kennedy, 'International Human Rights Movement: Part of the Problem?' (2005) 15 Harvard Human Rights Journal 101, 108.

Finally, it also needs to be acknowledged that these complexities are further compounded when a historical perspective is added in determining how to universalize the satisfaction and non-satisfaction of interests among States. In particular, the situation in some countries can be viewed in the light of distributive and corrective justice claims raised in the light of a colonial legacy and subordination.[417] If approached from this perspective, the argument that the interests of the developed countries should be prone to greater non-satisfaction gathers force.

## 8.4.3 Causation

Having discussed the issues of legality, competence, and balancing of interests that cause concerns of conceptual and normative nature if they were to be applied in extraterritorial circumstances, this section turns to the issue of causation, which tends to be viewed as having a factual nature. Causation has been considered as a factual and empirical issue because when the State has physical *de facto* control over an individual or over an area (as in the personal and the spatial models of jurisdiction discussed in Sections 8.2.2 and 8.2.3), the factual causation between harm and state conduct might appear relatively easy to establish. In contrast to circumstances of a physical *de facto* control, the causation between state conduct and extraterritorial harmful consequences (as those described in Section 8.2.6), might raise more serious challenges of a factual and empirical nature.[418] I will show, however, that irrespective of whether the circumstances expose *de facto* control or mere extraterritorial effects, causation is not a pure factual test (Section 8.4.3.1). It is rather assessed against the backdrop of normative considerations based on democratic legitimacy. Such normative considerations are also determinative in the assessment of causation when various States and other actors are involved (Section 8.4.3.2). Ultimately, I show that even if these normative considerations are ignored and the approach to causation is framed as being exclusively factual, there might be very little benefit in the eventual assignment of obligations (Section 8.4.3.3).

### 8.4.3.1 Causation is not a pure factual test

Empirical challenges as to how to establish causal links between omissions and harm generally arise so that state responsibility can be established. Crucially, however, the approach to these challenges is not based on a pure factual and empirical test. Causation is instead also assessed against certain normative considerations based on the relational nature of human rights law, as demonstrated in Chapter 3. This can also

---

[417] For the specific context of migration and the rights of migrants, see T Achiume, 'Migration as Decolonization' (2019) 71 Stanford Law Review 1509, 1533).
[418] Authors have taken note of these factual challenges. See 'Introduction' in Langford and others (eds), *Global Justice, State Duties* (n 5) 1, 7; Vandenbogaerde, 'Attributing Extraterritorial Obligations under the International Covenant on Economic, Social and Cultural Rights' (n 173) 29.

explain why, even in the personal and spatial models of jurisdiction, the Court has also introduced (admittedly, inconsistently) normative elements ('public powers') that can ultimately affect the issue of causation.

In addition, as Chapter 4 explained, in the assessment of breach of positive obligations in domestic settings, the Court bundles the factors of causation, reasonableness, knowledge, and legality. As a consequence, even though causality might be empirically diluted, this is not necessarily a problem, and it might not prevent the finding of a failure in domestic settings due to the operation of certain normative considerations related to communitarian interests. For example, although it might be difficult to establish the factual causation between a state omission and a harm (due to absence of scientific knowledge or relevant evidence), responsibility under the ECHR might not be precluded, since it might be reasonable to expect that the State should, in any case, have taken preventive measures, or because the State failed effectively to enforce the preventive measures envisioned as appropriate by the national regulatory framework.

Such normative considerations that operate within the bounded political community do not exist in extraterritorial circumstances, where the individuals who might claim any positive protective measures are not normatively related to the State that arguably should offer these measures. There is no communality between the State and these individuals that could be the basis for the identification of common interests that could guide the assessment as to how intrusive or restrained the State should be, which in turn might guide the approach to causation.

### 8.4.3.2 Involvement of various actors as a challenge to causation

The issue of causation in its factual and normative aspect is confronted with additional difficulties in extraterritorial settings. In particular, the individuals affected by the alleged omissions by a State are very likely to remain within the jurisdiction of the State on whose territory they are physically located; the latter State thus continues to owe them human rights obligations. The issue of how obligations of different States might be apportioned and shared is not addressed here,[419] but it needs to be taken into regard that the involvement of various States can affect causality in factual and normative terms. In particular, the territorial state can also contribute to harm through its own omissions, which can disrupt the lines of factual causation between the omissions of the extraterritorial state and the harm sustained by the individuals. It might be difficult to see where the contribution to harm through omissions of one State ends and that of another State begins.

Besides factual causality, normative concerns related to democratic legitimacy also arise. It is the territorial State that has the primary responsibility to ensure the human

---

[419] See W Vandenhole, 'Obligations and Responsibility in a Plural and Diverse Duty-bearer Human Rights Regime' in W Vandenhole (ed), *Challenging Territoriality in Human Rights Law* (Routledge 2015) 115; N Nedeski, *Shared Obligations in International Law* (Cambridge University Press, 2022); A Nollkaemper and I Plakokefalos (eds), Principles of Shared Responsibility in International Law (Cambridge University Press, 2016).

rights of the individuals on its territory. A different starting point would imply a fundamental erosion of the international legal system. This assumption must affect the assessment as to whose omissions should be considered normatively and legally relevant in the first place, or more important. Given the intertwined world that we live in, various omissions can be attributed to various States. When States cooperate, multiple States might be involved and there might be thus multiple omissions that might be factually possible to link to harm. Non-state actors might be also involved with their own omissions.[420] Besides abilities and practical restraints,[421] it is normative considerations based on democratic legitimacy that guide and limit causation and, consequently, the assignment of obligations for committing omissions. Jurisdiction in human rights law, understood as a normative threshold, ensures such guidance and limitation.

### 8.4.3.3 Weaknesses in the framing of the concrete obligations

Let us move one step further in the analysis by putting aside the factual and normative challenges referred to above, and instead reflect upon the content of any possible positive obligations. So far, I have explained that it might be difficult to disentangle the contributory omissions of different States, including the territorial and the extraterritorial, and that there might be many simultaneous causes (some of which might not be even related to the extraterritorial State). All of these might make factual causation weak. Still, for the sake of the argument, let us ignore this weakness and assume that the extraterritorial State should be assigned obligations, since it has in some way negatively affected individuals located beyond its borders through its conduct in the form of omissions. Under this assumption, the analysis can move to the merits, and the issue to be confronted then is whether it might be possible to frame a positive obligation with some content. In other words, how to frame the content and the scope of any substantive extraterritorial positive obligation? Could this content be so diluted to the point of being ultimately meaningless given the weak factual causation (under the assumption that any normative considerations are ignored)?

The content and the scope of the obligation has to be framed in a way that implies the undertaking of measures that can be expected somehow to remedy the alleged contributory omission. If the actual contribution is weak or indeterminate, it can be expected that the content and the scope of any positive obligations will be also weak or hard to determine.[422] For example, the State might be under the obligation to demand companies to conduct a human rights impact assessment, a measure with

---

[420] This has been framed as 'transnational composite acts'. See Altwicker 'Transnationlizing Rights' (n 6) 594.

[421] *Ilse Hess v United Kingdom* no 6231/73, 28 May 1975 (inadmissible) revealed such practical restraints. The applicants complained about the prison regime in the British sector of West Berlin. However, the Commission held that the United Kingdom could not be responsible for his situation since the United Kingdom could not alone, without the consent of the other three allied powers, modify the regime.

[422] An additional source of weakness might originate from the limited competence of the extraterritorial State in the light of the permissible basis of jurisdiction under international law and the principle of non-intervention. See Section 8.4.1.

questionable actual effect. Not to mention that conducting such impact assessments is not generally perceived as a matter of obligations corresponding to individual entitlements. Impact assessments rather only reflect practices and procedures that have human rights considerations as their background.[423]

Another measure that the extraterritorial State might be required to take is to ensure the availability of procedural mechanisms for redress. For example, the State might have to ensure that despite their location in another country, affected individuals have access to procedures that can scrutinize the liability of companies for their activities abroad.[424] This is a relatively weak procedural obligation, and in any case, as shown in Section 8.4.1.2, it is difficult to argue that the availability of procedural mechanisms for affected individuals irrespective of their location can be in principle framed as a matter of human rights obligations.

The ultimate point here is that given the weak factual causation and the limitation imposed by the principle of non-intervention, there might be very little benefit in the eventual assignment of obligations. Such obligations might be very feeble in terms of content or scope, and prone to an assessment that easily finds that they are fulfilled.[425] In addition, even if it might be possible to frame the content and the scope of any positive obligations that imply protective measures, States might have already shown a clear resistance to undertake such measures as a matter of legal obligations.

## Conclusion

This chapter has offered the first examination of the conceptual hurdles if positive obligations under the ECHR were to be applied extraterritorially. This examination confirms that human rights law is compartmentalized within sovereign state entities. Many of the problems that could arguably be addressed through the imposition of positive obligations might be global and indeed require cooperation at international level, yet our political communities are not global.[426] Human rights law is rather tied to the national community. As Besson has noted, '[t]he democratic subject remains the individual and her political community the domestic one'.[427] The analysis and the

---

[423] See Peters, 'Global Constitutionalism' (n 344) 319.
[424] Ollino, 'Justifications and Limits of Extraterritorial Obligations of States' (n 45). See also Peters, 'Global Constitutionalism' (n 344) 305: If a link between one State's policies and violations of social rights is established 'this would only mean that some remedial measures might be required as a matter of human rights law, while further, interventionist measures might on the contrary be prohibited by the victim State's sovereignty protected by the principle of non-intervention'.
[425] See also Park, *The Right to Life in Armed Conflict* (n 154) 9 and 101: 'the effect of recognizing right to life obligations, when interpreted through the principles of international humanitarian law in armed conflict, does not impose a significant burden upon States and military commanders beyond that which already governs the use of lethal force'.
[426] Besson, 'Why and What (State) Jurisdiction. Legal Plurality, Individual Equality and Territorial Legitimacy' (n 19) 132.
[427] S Besson, 'International Human Rights and Political Equality—Some Implications for Global Democracy' in E Erman and S Näsström (eds), *Equality in Transnational and Global Democracy* (Palgrave MacMillan 2014) 89, 113.

standards under human rights law are thus politically and socially contingent on the specific community.

As a consequence, once state conduct or the effects of such conduct transcend national borders, the working of human rights law seems to be disrupted. I have demonstrated that this disruption transpires not only in the communitarian underpinnings of human rights law but also in the technical conceptual aspects. These aspects concern the questions when positive obligations are triggered, what factors determine their scope and content, and how causation, knowledge, reasonableness, and balancing are assessed. In fact, one of the main findings is that these technical conceptual aspects are intimately related to communitarian nature of human rights law. In particular, the answers to all of these questions are contingent on perceptions about the role of the State in the specific political community (how intrusive or restrained should this role be), and how the various interconnected interests within this community should be protected and balanced.

The claim about the universality of human rights has not been matched with a global political community akin to that of the State, a community that could render any positive, extraterritorial, and unbounded obligations legitimate in the light of some global public interests and global public good. As a consequence, there might be no referents and thus no conceptual tools to engage properly with the technical conceptual questions about scope and content of positive obligations in extraterritorial settings.

If the specifics of human rights law as an independent body of law meant to regulate the relationship between individuals and their political communitarian organizational form, that is, the State, are seriously taken into account, then the role of the jurisdictional threshold in Article 1 ECHR can be understood in a better way and explained. Its role is to preserve the unity and the independence of human rights law as a very specific body of law that has communitarian underpinnings.

Pinning down how this role might manifest itself in different scenarios is far from easy. Fixing, shaping, and making explicit the different criteria (factual control, legal entitlement, etc) that might determine how restrictive this role should be, both at a general level and at the level of concrete cases, as well as their significance, is not easy either. This explains the uncertainties and the oscillations in the ECtHR case law. The Court has made some allusions to the communitarian nature of human rights law when offering the justifications behind the threshold; however, communitarianism as a justification has rather worked implicitly in the background.

This chapter has shown the accuracy and importance of this justification. This was achieved in two main steps. First, drawing on previous chapters, Section 8.1 demonstrated that the conceptual analysis of positive obligations is contingent on certain preconditions (ie bounded political and legal order, interdependent stakes of the individuals belonging to this order and balancing of interests that are institutionally channelled through a democratically constituted sovereign). These are important so that the analysis on the merits in terms of triggering, scope, and content of positive obligations is equipped with the necessary conceptual tools. These preconditions are not necessarily present in extraterritorial settings. Section 8.2, though, confirmed the sensitivity of the case law under Article 1 ECHR to these preconditions as modified and adjusted to the particular extraterritorial situations emerging in the different cases; yet any sensitivity has not been explicit and consistent.

The second step, discussed in Sections 8.3 and 8.4, sought to reveal and analyse the conceptual difficulties that might transpire in the assessment of breach of positive obligations if they were to be applied extraterritorially. The major finding is that due to the absence of the above-mentioned preconditions, the conceptual tools for performing the analysis on the merits might be missing. I also showed that if this absence is ignored at the threshold stage where the existence of jurisdiction is reviewed, the ultimate result might often be an automatic finding of a breach. From the perspective of States, such a result might be unjust and hard to accept.

My analysis, however, also engaged the question whether and how it might be possible to modify and adjust these tools so that they could become operational in extraterritorial settings. In some respects this might be possible. For example, not national legislation, but rather relevant legal frameworks from international law might be used as referents in the assessment of omissions. Interestingly, however, the relevance and the application of such frameworks might already be taken into account in considering whether the State has jurisdiction, and a positive finding at this threshold stage might have been precisely the one that allowed the analysis on the merits. In other respects, however, such an adjustment does not seem to be possible. This impossibility particularly came to light when I discussed the difficulties arising when an attempt is made to perform 'extraterritorial balancing'. Reconstruction of causality in extraterritorial settings also faces challenges since causality in the context of positive obligations is not limited to factual causality but also includes normative considerations related to the role of the State in the particular society.

As a warning note, it was also observed that de-territorialization and the ensuing depoliticization of human rights might come with a price. The content and scope of any positive obligations might be so weak that it might be meaningless to have them. Much more importantly, the easy finding of compliance holds its own dangers, at least two of which can be identified here. First, we need to remind ourselves that besides an independent body of law meant to confer individual legal entitlements and subjected to certain legal technicalities, human rights also serve as interpretative guidance in various areas of human activity. This guiding role might be sapped of its rigour in seeking to prevent cross-border harm, if no violation has been found on the technical side. Second, the easy finding of compliance might dissuade States from searching for solutions in other areas of international law or, more generally through other channels of cooperation. We might be thus left with two extremes: easy finding of a breach or easy finding of no breach. The challenge is how to navigate between these two. The uncertainty in the Court's case law mirrors this challenge.

Finally, it can be objected that the findings in this chapter do not advance the objectives of human rights law, which can be framed as protection of individuals irrespective of formal membership in a political community. By explaining and justifying the jurisdiction threshold with reference to communitarian considerations, States that in fact affect individuals might not be constituted as holders of human rights obligations, and questions of material justice are avoided. Gaps might be therefore created where no legal responsibility can be determined in a meaningful way. This is indeed a stark conclusion. It does not, however, negate the above-mentioned general role of human rights as offering interpretative guidance. Nor does it prevent the operation of other branches of international law whose protection possibilities might be relevant.

# Conclusion

This book engaged with the analytical difficulties in how the human rights enshrined in Articles 2, 3, and 8 of the European Convention on Human Rights (ECHR) generate positive obligations and how to find the boundaries of these obligations. It has hopefully helped in alleviating these difficulties by identifying and explaining the key analytical standards of knowledge, causation, and reasonableness that need to be considered in the determination of these boundaries and thus in the finding of breach of these obligations. The book explained the different types of positive obligations, their distinctions, and the structure of review, that is, the analytical steps followed, to ascertain state responsibility for breach of each one of them. In this way, the book situated the Court's review and reasoning regarding knowledge, causation, and reasonableness, within an intelligible framework of analysis. The book also explained the distinction between the existence of a positive obligation and the breach of this obligation, a distinction that might be blurred in the Court's reasoning. The analytical distinction between scope and content of positive obligations was also clarified.

The book described the tensions and complexities in delineating the scope and the content of each of the three types of positive obligations (ie the procedural obligation to investigate, the obligation to develop effective regulatory frameworks and the obligation to take protective operational measures). An important complexity concerning the first one is limiting the circumstances where criminal proceedings (as opposed to civil or administrative proceedings) are required as a matter of ECHR obligation. As to the second one, the oscillation between abstract and concrete review of the national regulatory frameworks for assessing their deficiencies is a notable source of complexity. As to the third, the specifications as to the types of risks, the objects of harm, and actors of harm, so that targeted operational measures are required, causes difficulties.

Irrespective of the type of positive obligation invoked, the questions about, first, the specification of the obligation and, second, the alternative formulations of such specifications, are key. The Court has developed at a very abstract level the positive obligations upon States to investigate harm, to have effective regulatory frameworks with procedural guarantees, and to take protective operational measures. This development serves the Court's constitutional role. The analytical operation of specifying the obligations, which necessary demands formulation of alternatives, is indispensable for answering whether they have been breached. Specification is therefore essential for making the analytical transition from abstract rights and abstract obligations to concrete obligations, in this way enabling the Court to deliver individual justice.

As I showed, however, the specification can only go so far since the Court is not in a position to tell States what concrete measures to take to fulfil their positive obligations. States have discretion in this area. This explains the usefulness of the reasonableness standard as invoked in the Court's reasoning when the obligations need to be specified. This invocation of the flexible standard of reasonableness enables the Court to motivate and reach a binary judgment with breach or no breach as a conclusion, when in fact different alternative measures are possible in the course of conduct that could (or should) have been adopted by the State.

The standards of knowledge (ie whether the State knew or should have known about harm or risk of harm) and of causation (ie whether the invoked alternative had a 'real prospect' of actually preventing the harm or the risk) can limit the scope of relevant alternative measures that could be considered in answering the question of breach of the obligation. At the same time, as I demonstrated, these two standards are applied in flexible ways. This flexibility can be understood in light of the objective of the human rights law review, namely reviewing the responsibility of a collective, in other words, the State. This is the entity tasked with the distribution of costs and protection within the particular society. Within this distributive framework, the identification of which and whose conduct or decisions are definitively causative to harm is difficult. Within the distributive framework, there are rather multiple and wide structures of decisions, actions, omissions, and practices. This does not only explain and justify the flexibility of the standards of knowledge, causation, and reasonableness. It is also revealing as to the type of justice that underpins human rights law. In particular, it is suggestive of distributive rather than individual corrective justice.

Even if a violation of a positive obligation is found, this does not necessary lead to an individual right to some concrete measures, which also pushes human rights law away from the notion of individual corrective justice. It also raises questions about the correlation between rights and obligations. This book was an effort to explain how rights generate obligations. The reverse question, that is, whether and how the generated obligations correlate back to rights, is a worthy candidate for another exploration and possibly another book.

In addition to these technical analytical questions mentioned above (ie breach, scope and content of obligations, types of obligations, standards for determining breach of the obligations), the book also reflected upon what is at stake for the political community when the triggering, the content, and the scope of positive human rights obligations are determined. The central challenge is how the search for a balance between intrusion and restraint by the State, between protection and freedom from invasion, defines this community and pulls the analysis of state responsibility for breach of positive obligations in different directions. How could one respond to this challenge?

The question about the role of the State in the society is much wider. Given its specific focus and methodology, the book cannot purport to have offered a comprehensive answer. However, the analysis in the book still allows me to offer the following response to the above-mentioned challenge.

First, positive obligations ultimately imply expansion of the role of the State. This needs to be openly acknowledged. It puts human rights law in tension with its historical origins and justifications, which in itself can be a warning sign.[1] A sign that can be useful when faced with 'crisis' and 'emergencies', such as the one during the COVID-19 pandemic, when the tendency has been to easily sacrifice freedoms for the arguable sake of more protection from known, unknown and/or unknowable risks.

Second, the analytical distinction between the standards of reasonableness, state knowledge, and causation is also important to face the challenge of how to resist intrusive positive obligations seen as warranted by the need to avert risks. This challenge can therefore be confronted by better awareness as to *how* intrusive measures are justified. Are they justified based on the knowledge about harm or the risk of harm? How conclusive or inconclusive is this knowledge? To what extent is the harm knowable? How immediate is the harm? Is it acceptable to take protective actions against potential risks regardless of their immediacy? Are intrusive/protective measures justified since they are expected to cause reduction in the risk of harm? How stable is this causality? Even if stable, is it still reasonable to undertake these measures since, for example, they themselves might create other forms of risks for other individuals or groups in the society? Are these other risks and individuals more certain and definitive in comparison with the certainty of averting any potential dangers through intrusive/protection measures? On which side of the scales is the harm more certain and less speculative?

Third, the identification and the assessment of alternatives is also important for averting the danger of overreach of positive obligations. The existence of alternatives presupposes that there might be measures that sufficiently serve the purpose of fulfilling positive obligations, and at the same time serve other interests, including leaving intact or causing less damage to other human rights and public policy concerns.

Fourth, despite its ambiguities, the distinction between actions and omissions as a basis for state responsibility needs to be maintained. States need to justify their actions and these justifications to be valid under human rights law, need to comply with certain strict standards so that negative obligations are not breached. In contrast, the justification of omissions is an object of more flexible standards. Human rights law does not allow States to act, arguably in fulfilment of positive obligations, by violating negative obligations. Positive obligations, whose content and scope include measures amounting to disproportionate infringement of rights, and thus in breach of negative obligations, are precluded.

Fifth, similarly to the distinction between acts and omissions, another distinction seems to be also useful. This distinction underpins the whole idea of human

---

[1] See also D McGrogan, *Critical Theory and Human Rights. From Compassion to Coercion* (Manchester University Press 2021).

rights—the distinction between general interests and interests of specific concrete individuals. It is the latter that underpin human rights law and make it distinctive. As opposed to general interests that can be considered within the reasonableness standard, the interests protected by human rights law have special normative force. What does this mean more concretely? Taking actions to limit the private and family life of specific concrete individuals for the arguable sake of protecting the lives of the unidentifiable many, is suspect. As much importantly, an argument that given the importance of the interests that the right to life protects, this right necessary generates positive obligations that have priority over those generated by, for example, the right to private and family life, is flawed.

The distinction between general interests and the interests of specific concrete individuals and the position that it is the latter interests that base human rights law, bring me back to the question of justice. It was already suggested that the review of state responsibility for breach of positive obligations pulls human rights law towards distributive rather than individual corrective justice paradigm. The specificity of human rights law as a body of law that distinguishes the interests of specific concrete individuals, pulls it back to individual justice paradigm. In any case, distributive and individual justice paradigms seem to be in a conversation within the specific political community.

This conversation was made even more evident in Chapter 8 that engaged with the question how to review breach of positive obligations when the affected individuals are not part of the conversation and the normal communitarian structures of human rights law (within which distribution happens) are disrupted. In this way, the book engaged not only with the boundaries of positive obligation in terms of their trigger and scope of measures required but also with their communitarian boundaries.

# Select Bibliography

## A

Addo M, *The Legal Nature of International Human Rights* (Martinus Nijhoff Publishers 2010)

Abresch W, 'A Human Rights Law of Internal Armed Conflict: The European Court of Human Rights in Chechnya' (2005) 16(4) European Journal of International Law 741

Afonso da Silva V, 'Comparing the Incommensurable: Constitutional Principles, Balancing and Rational Decision' (2011) 31(2) Oxford Journal of Legal Studies 273

Akandji-Kombe J, *Positive Obligations under the European Convention on Human Rights* (Council of Europe Publishing 2007)

Alexy R, 'Individual Rights and Collective Goods' in C Nino (ed), *Rights* (Dartmouth 1992) 169

Alexy R, 'On Constitutional Rights to Protection' (2009) 3 Legisprudence 1

Alexy R, *A Theory of Constitutional Rights* (Oxford University Press 2010)

Alexy R, 'The Construction of Constitutional Rights' (2010) 4(1) Law and Ethics of Human Rights 20

Altwicker T, 'Transnationlizing Rights: International Human Rights Law in Cross-Border Contexts' (2018) 29(2) European Journal of International Law 581

Ambrus M, 'The European Court of Human Rights and Standards of Proof' in L Gruszczynski and W Werner (eds), *Deference in International Courts and Tribunals: Standard of Review and Margin of Appreciation* (Oxford University Press 2014) 235

Ambrus M, 'The European Court of Human Rights as Governor or Risk' in M Ambrus and others (eds), *Risk and Regulation of Uncertainty in International Law* (Oxford University Press 2017) 99

Arai-Takahashi Y, *The Margin of Appreciation Doctrine and the Principle of Proportionality in the ECHR* (Intersentia 2002)

Arendt H, 'The Decline of the Nation State and the End of the Rights of Man' in *The Origins of Totalitarianism* (Meridian Books 1958)

Arnardóttir O, 'The "Procedural Turn" under the European Convention on Human Rights and Presumptions of Convention Compliance' (2017) 15(1) International Journal of Constitutional Law 9

Augestein D, 'The Crisis of International Human Rights Law in the Global Market Economy' (2013) 44 Netherlands Yearbook of International Law 41

Augunstein D and Kinley D, 'When Human Rights 'Responsibilities' Become Duties': the Extra-territorial Obligations of States that Bind Corporations' in D Bilchiz and S Deva (eds), *Human Rights Obligations of Business: Beyond the Corporate Responsibility to Respect* (Cambridge University Press 2013) 271

Augenstein D, 'Paradise Lost: Sovereign State Interest, Global Resource Exploitation and the Politics of Human Rights' (2016) 27(3) European Journal of International Law 669

Augenstein D, 'Torture or Tort? Transnational Tort Litigation for Corporate-Related Human Rights Violations and the Human Right to a Remedy' (2018) 18 Human Rights Law Review 593

## B

Barros A, *Governance as Responsibility: Member States as Human Rights Protectors in International Financial Institutions* (Cambridge University Press 2019)

Bates E, *The Evolution of the European Convention on Human Rights—From its Inception to the Creation of a Permanent Court of Human Rights* (Oxford University Press 2010)

Barak A, 'Proportionality and Principled Balancing' (2010) 4 Law and Ethics of Human Rights 1

Barak A, *Proportionality. Constitutional Rights and their Limitations* (Cambridge University Press 2012)

Bartels L, 'The EU's Human Rights Obligations in Relation to Policies with Extraterritorial Effect' (2014) 25(4) European Journal of International Law 1071

Bederman D, 'Contributory Fault and State Responsibility' (1990) 30 Virginia Journal of International Law 335

Bellamy R, 'The Democratic Legitimacy of International Human Rights Convention: Political Constitutionalism and the European Convention on Human Rights' (2015) 25(4) European Journal of International Law 1019

Benvenisti E, 'Sovereigns as Trustees of Humanity: On the Accountability of States to Foreign Stakeholders' (2013) 107 American Journal of International Law 295

Besson S, *The Morality of Conflict: Reasonable Disagreement and the Law* (Hart Publishing 2005)

Besson S, 'Sovereignty' in R Wolfrum (ed), *Max Planck Encyclopedia of International Law* (Oxford University Press 2011)

Besson S, 'Human Rights and Democracy in a Global Context: Decoupling and Recoupling' (2011) 4(1) Ethics and Global Politics 19

Besson S, 'Sovereignty, International Law and Democracy' (2011) 22(2) European Journal of International Law 373

Besson S, 'The Extraterritoriality of the European Convention on Human Rights: Why Human Rights Depend on Jurisdiction and What Jurisdiction Amounts to' (2012) 25 Leiden Journal of International Law 857

Besson S, 'The Law in Human Rights Theory' (2013) 7(1) Journal of Human Rights 120

Besson S, 'The Legitimate Authority of International Human Rights—On the Reciprocal Legitimation of Domestic and International Human Rights' in A Føllesdal (ed), *The Legitimacy of Human Rights* (Cambridge University Press 2013) 32

Besson S, 'The Egalitarian Dimension of Human Rights' (2013) 136 Archiv für Rechts- und Sozialphilosophie 19

Besson S, 'The Allocation of Anti-poverty Duties. Our Rights, but Whose Duties?' in K Shefer (ed), *Poverty and the International Economic Legal System. Duties to the World's Poor* (Cambridge University Press 2013) 408

Besson S, 'The Bearers of Human Rights' Duties and Responsibilities for Human Rights: A Quiet (R)evolution' (2015) 32(1) Social Philosophy and Policy 244

Besson S, 'Human Rights and Constitutional Law' in R Cruft and others (eds), *Philosophical Foundations of Human Rights* (Oxford University Press 2015) 280

Besson S, 'Science without Borders and the Boundaries of Human Rights' (2015) 4 European Journal of Human Rights 462

Besson S, 'Subsidiarity in International Human Rights Law—What is Subsidiary about Human Rights' (2016) 61(1) The American Journal of Jurisprudence 69

Besson S, 'Human Rights in Relation: A Critical Reading of the ECtHR's Approach to Conflicts of Rights' in S Smet and E Brems (eds), *When Human Rights Clash at the European Court of Human Rights* (Oxford University Press 2017) 23

Besson S, 'Concurrent Responsibilities under the European Convention on Human Rights: The Concurrence of Human Rights Jurisdictions, Duties and Responsibilities' in A van Aaken and I Motoc (eds), *The European Convention on Human Rights and General International Law* (Oxford University Press 2018) 155

Besson S, 'International Courts and the Jurisprudence of Statehood' (2019) 10(1) International Legal Theory 30

Besson S, 'Why and What (State) Jurisdiction. Legal Plurality, Individual Equality and Territorial Legitimacy' in J Klabbers and G Palombella (eds), *The Challenge of Inter-Legality* (Cambridge University Press 2019) 91

Bhuta N, 'The Frontiers of Extraterritoriality—Human Rights Law as Global Law' N Bhuta (eds), *The Frontiers of Human Rights. Extraterritoriality and Its Challenges* (Oxford University Press 2016) 1

Bomholl J and Zucca L, 'The Tragedy of Ms Evans: Conflicts and Incommensurability of Rights' (2006) 2 European Constitutional Law Review 424

Booth C and Squires D, *The Negligence Liability of Public Authorities* (Oxford University Press 2006)

Brems, E (ed), *Conflicts between Fundamental Rights* (Intersentia 2008)

Brems E, 'Human Rights: Minimum and Maximum Perspectives' (2009) 9(3) Human Rights Law Review 349

Brems E and Lavrysen L, 'Procedural Justice in Human Rights Adjudication: the European Court of Human Rights' (2013) 35 Human Rights Quarterly 182

Brems E, 'Procedural Protection. An Examination of Procedural Safeguards Read into Substantive Convention Rights' in E Brems and J Gerards (eds), *Shaping Rights in the ECHR. The Role of the European Court of Human Rights in Determining the Scope of Human Rights* (Cambridge University Press 2014) 137

Brems E and Lavrysen L, '"Don't Use a Sledgehammer to Crack a Nut": Less Restrictive Means in the Case Law of the European Court of Human Rights' (2015) 15 Human Rights Law Review 139

Brodie D, 'Compulsory Altruism and Public Authorities' in D Fairgrieve and others (eds), *Tort Liability of Public Authorities in Comparative Perspective* (British Institute of International and Comparative Law 2002) 541

Brown C, 'Universal Human Rights: A Critique' (1997) 1 The International Journal of Human Rights 41

Bydlinksi F, 'Methodological Approaches to the Tort Law of the ECHR' in A Fenyves and others (eds), *Tort Law in the Jurisprudence of the European Court of Human Rights* (De Gruyter 2011) 29

# C

Çali B, 'Balancing Human Rights? Methodological Problems with Weights, Scales and Proportions' (2007) 29(1) Human Rights Quarterly 251

Chevalier-Watts J, 'Effective Investigation under Article 2 of the European Convention on Human Rights: Security the Right to Life or an Onerous Burden on a State?' (2010) 21(3) European Journal of International Law 701

Christoffersen J, 'Individual and Constitutional Justice: Can the Power Balance of Adjudication be Reversed?' in J Christoffersen and M Madsen (eds), *The European Court of Human Rights between Law and Politics* (Oxford University Press 2011) 181

Corten O, 'The Notion of "Reasonable" in International Law: Legal Discourse, Reason and Contradictions' (1999) 48(3) International and Comparative Law Quarterly 613

Corten O and Kolb R, 'Reasonableness in International Law' Max Planck Encyclopedia of International Law (Oxford University Press 2021)

Costa J, 'The European Court of Human Rights: Consistency of its Case-Law and Positive Obligations' (2008) 26 Netherlands Quarterly of Human Rights 449

Crawford J, 'Revisiting the Draft Articles on State Responsibility' (1999) 10 European Journal of International Law 435

Crawford J, *State Responsibility. The General Part* (Cambridge University Press 2013)
Crawford J and Keene, 'The Structure of State Responsibility under the European Convention on Human Rights' in van Aaken and Motoc (eds), *The European Convention on Human Rights and General International Law* (Oxford University Press 2018) 178

## D

Decoulombier P, 'Conflicts between Fundamental Rights and the European Court of Human Rights: An Overview' in E Brems (ed), *Conflicts between Fundamental Rights* (Intersentia 2008) 223
de Schutter O, 'Globalization and Jurisdiction' (2006) 6 Baltic Yearbook of International Law 185
de Schutter O and Tulkens F, 'Rights in Conflict: the European Court of Human Rights as a Pragmatic Institution' in E Brems (ed), *Conflicts between Fundamental Rights* (Intersentia 2008) 188
den Heijer M and Lawson R, 'Extraterritorial Human Rights and the Concept of "Jurisdiction"' in L Malcom (ed), *Global Justice, State Duties* (Cambridge University Press 2013) 153
den Heijer M, 'Shared Responsibility before the ECtHR' (2013) 60(3) Netherlands International Law Review 411
Dijk P, '"Positive Obligations" Implied in the European Convention on Human Rights: Are the States Still the 'Masters' of the Convention?' in M Castermans-Holleman and others (eds), *The Role of the Nation-State in the 21st Century* (Kluwer 1998) 17
Donnelly J, 'The Virtues of Legalization' in S Meckled-García and B Çalı (eds), *The Legalization of Human Rights. Multidisciplinary Perspectives on Human Rights and Human Rights Law* (Routledge 2006) 67
Dröge C, *Positive Verpflichtungen der Staaten in der Europäischen Menschenrechtskonvention* (Springer 2003)
Duvic-Paoli L, 'Prevention in International Environmental Law and the Anticipation of Risk(s): A Multifaceted Norm' in M Ambrus and others (eds), *Risk and Regulation of Uncertainty in International Law* (Oxford University Press 2017) 141
Duttwilder M, 'Authority, Control and Jurisdiction in the Extraterritorial Application of the European Convention on Human Rights' (2012) 30(2) Netherlands Quarterly of Human Rights 137
Dworkin R, *Taking Rights Seriously* (Duckworth 1977)
Dworkin R, 'Rights as Trumps' in J Waldron (ed), *Theories of Rights* (Oxford University Press 1984) 153
Dworkin R, *A Matter of Principle* (Harvard University Press 1985) 73

## E

Ebert F and Sijniensky R, 'Preventing Violation of the Right to Life in the European and the Inter-American Human Rights Systems: From *Osman* Test to a Coherent Doctrine on Risk Prevention?' (2015) 15 Human Rights Law Review 343
Engle L, 'Anti-Impunity and the Turn to Criminal Law in Human Rights' (2015)100 Cornell Law Review 1069
Evans M, 'State Responsibility and the European Convention on Human Rights: Role and Realm' in M Fitzmaurice and D Sarooshi (eds), Issues of State Responsibility before International Judicial Institutions (Hart Publishing 2004) 139

## F

Fairgrieve D, 'Pushing the Boundaries of Public Authority Liability' in D Fairgrieve and others (eds), *Tort Liability of Public Authorities in Comparative Perspective* (British Institute of International and Comparative Law 2002) 475
Favre A, 'Fault as an Element of the Illicit Act' (1964) 52 Georgetown Law Journal 555
Fletcher G, 'The Theory of Criminal Negligence: A Comparative Analysis' (1971) 119(3) University of Pennsylvania Law Review 401
Fredman S, *Human Rights Transformed: Positive Rights and Positive Duties* (Oxford University Press 2008)
Fumerton R and Kress K, 'Causation and the Law: Preemption, Lawful Sufficiency, and Causal Sufficiency' (2001) 64 Law and Contemporary Problems 83

## G

Gattini A, 'Smoking/No Smoking: Some Remarks on the Current Place of Fault in the ILC Draft Articles on State Responsibility' (1999) 10 European Journal of International Law 397
Gerards J, 'Fundamental Rights and Other Interests. Should it Really Make a Difference?' in E Brems (ed), *Conflicts between Fundamental Rights* (Intersentia 2008) 655
Gerards J, 'The Prism of Fundamental Rights' (2008) 8 European Constitutional Law Review 173
Gerards J, 'Pluralism, Deference and the Margin of Appreciation Doctrine' (2011) 17(1) European Law Journal 80
Gerards J, 'How to Improve the Necessity Test of the European Court of Human Rights' (2013) 11(2) International Journal of Constitutional Law 466
Gerards J, 'The ECtHR's Response to Fundamental Rights Issues related to Financial and Economic Difficulties—the Problem of Compartmentalization' (2015) 13 Netherlands Quarterly of Human Rights 274
Gerards J, 'Procedural Review by the ECtHR: A Typology' in J Gerards and E Brems (eds), *Procedural Review in European Fundamental Rights Cases* (Cambridge University Press 2017) 127
Gerards J, *General Principles of the European Convention on Human Rights* (Cambridge University Press 2019)
Gerards J, 'Abstract and Concrete Reasonableness Review by the European Court of Human Rights' (2020) 1 European Convention on Human Rights Law Review 218
Gerards J, and Brems, E, 'Introduction' in E Brems and J Gerards (eds), *Shaping Rights in the ECHR. The Role of the European Court of Human Rights in Determining the Scope of Human Rights* (Cambridge University Press 2014) 1
Gerards J and Senden H, 'The Structure of Fundamental Rights and the European Court of Human Rights' (2009) 7(4) International Journal of Constitutional Law 619
Gerry A, 'Obligation to Prevent Crime and to Protect and Provide Redress to Victims of Crime' in M Colvin and J Cooper (eds), *Human Rights in the Investigation and Prosecution of Crime* (Oxford University Press 2009) 423
Giddens A, 'Risk and Responsibility' (1999) 62(1) Modern Law Review 1
Green S, *Causation in Negligence* (Hart Publishing 2015)
Greer S, 'Constitutionalizing Adjudication under the European Convention on Human Rights' (2003) 23 Oxford Journal of Legal Studies 405
Greer S, 'What's Wrong with the European Convention on Human Rights?' (2008) 30(3) Human Rights Quarterly 680
Greer S, *The European Convention on Human Rights. Achievements, Problems and Prospects* (Cambridge University Press 2006)
Griffin J, *On Human Rights* (Oxford University Press 2008)

## H

Hakimi M, 'State Bystander Responsibility' (2012) 21 European Journal of International Law 341

Hakimi M, 'Human Rights Obligations to the Poor' in K Shefer (ed), *Poverty and the International Economic Legal System. Duties to the World's Poor* (Cambridge University Press 2013) 395

Hannum H, 'Reinvigorating Human Rights for the Twenty-First Century' in D Akande and others (eds), *Human Rights and 21st Century Challenges* (Oxford University Press 2020) 13

Hertogen A, 'Letting Lotus Bloom' (2015) 26(4) European Journal of International Law 901

Hickman T, 'Tort Law, Public Authorities, and the Human Rights Act 1998' in D Fairgrieve and others (eds), *Tort Liability of Public Authorities in Comparative Perspective* (British Institute of International and Comparative Law 2002) 17

Hickman T, 'The Reasonableness Principle: Reassessing its Place in the Public Sphere' (2004) 63 Cambridge Law Journal 166

Hohfeld W, 'Fundamental Legal Conceptions as Applied in Judicial Reasoning' (1917) 8 Yale Law Journal 710

Honore T, 'Are Omissions Less Culpable' in P. Cane and J. Stapleton (eds), *Essays for Patrick Atiyah* (Oxford University Press 1991) 31

Hoyano L and Keenan C, *Child Abuse: Law and Policy Across Boundaries* (Oxford University Press 2010)

Huijbers L, *Process-based Fundamental Rights Review* (Intersentia 2019)

Husak D, 'Omissions, Causation and Liability' (1980) 30 Philosophical Quarterly 318

Hutchinson M, 'The Margin of Appreciation Doctrine in the European Court of Human Rights' (1999) 48(3) International and Comparative Law Quarterly 638

## J

Jackson M, 'Freeing *Soering*: The ECHR, State Complicity in Torture and Jurisdiction' (2016) 27(3) European Journal of International Law 817

Joseph S, 'Sovereign Debt and Civil/Political Rights' in I Bantekas and C Lumina (eds), *Sovereign Debt and Human Rights* (Oxford University Press 2018) 303

Jurkevics A, 'Democracy in Contested Territory: On the Legitimacy of Global Legal Pluralism' (2022) 25(2) Critical Review of International Social and Political Philosophy 187

## K

Kamber K, *Prosecuting Human Rights Offences* (Martinus Nijhoff Publishers 2017)

Kamber K, 'Substantive and Procedural Criminal Law Protection of Human Rights in the Law of the European Convention on Human Rights' (2020) 20(1) Human Rights Law Review 75

Kapelańska-Pręgowska J, 'Extraterritorial Jurisdiction of National Courts and Human Rights Enforcement: Qua vadis justitia?' (2015) 17 International Community Law Review 413

Kellner M and Durant I, 'Causation' in A Fenyves and others (eds), *Tort Law in the Jurisprudence of the European Court of Human Rights* (De Gruyter 2011) 449

King H, 'The Extraterritorial Human Rights Obligations of States' (2009) 9(4) Human Rights Law Review 521

Klatt M, 'Positive Obligations under the European Convention on Human Rights' (2011) Heidelberg Journal of International Law 691

Klatt M and Meister M, *The Constitutional Structure of Proportionality* (Oxford University Press 2012)

Klatt M, 'Positive Rights: Who Decides? Judicial Review in Balance' (2015) 13(2) International Journal of Constitutional Law 354

Kokott J, *The Burden and Standard of Proof in Comparative and International Human Rights Law* (Kluwer Law International 1998)

Koskenniemi M, 'Human Rights, Politics and Love' (2001) 4 Mennesker og Rettigheter 33

Kratochvil J, 'The Inflation of the Margin of Appreciation by the European Court of Human Rights' (2011) 29(3) Netherlands Quarterly of Human Rights 324

Kumm M, 'The Idea of Socratic Contestation and the Right to Justification: The Point of Rights-Based Proportionality Review' (2010) 4 Law and Ethics of Human Rights 140

Kuper A, 'The Responsibilities Approach to Human Rights' in A Kuper (ed), *Global Responsibilities. Who Must Deliver on Human Rights?* (Routledge 2005) ix

# L

Lanovoy V, 'Causation in the Law of State Responsibility' (2022) British Yearbook of International Law 1

Larsen K, *The Human Rights Treaty Obligations of Peacekeepers* (Cambridge University Press 2012)

Latty F, 'Actions and Omissions' in J Crawford and others (eds), *The Law of International Responsibility* (Oxford University Press 2015) 362

Lavrysen R, 'The Scope of Rights and the Scope of Obligations: Positive Obligations' in E Brems and J Gerards (eds), *Shaping Rights in the ECHR—The Role of the European Court of Human Rights in Determining the Scope of Human Rights* (Cambridge University Press 2014) 162

Lavrysen L, 'Protection by the Law: The Positive Obligation to Develop a Legal Framework to Adequately Protect the ECHR Rights' in E Brems and Y Haeck (eds), *Human Rights and Civil Rights in the 21st Century* (Springer 2014) 69

Lavrysen L, *Human Rights in a Positive State* (Intersentia 2016)

Lavrysen L, 'Causation and Positive Obligations under the European Convention on Human Rights: A Reply to Vladislava Stoyanova' (2018) 18 Human Rights Law Review 705

Lawson R, 'Out of Control. State Responsibility and Human Rights: Will the ILC's Definition of the "Act of State" Meet the Challenges of the 21st Century' in M Castermans-Holleman and others (eds), *The Role of the Nation-State in the 21st Century. Human Rights, International Organisations and Foreign Policy* (Kluwer 1998) 91

Lawson R, 'Life After Bankovic: On the Extraterritorial Application of the European Convention on Human Rights' in F Coomans and M Kamminga (eds), *Extraterritorial Application of Human Rights Treaties* (Intersentia 2004) 83

Lawson R, 'Really Out of Sight?' in A Buyse (ed), *Margins of Conflict: The ECHR and Transitions to and from Armed Conflict* (Intersentia 2010) 57

Lazarus L, 'Positive Obligations and Criminal Justice: Duties to Protect or Coerce' in L Zadner and J Roberts (eds), *Principles and Values in Criminal Law and Criminal Justice: Essays in Honour of Andrew Ashworth* (Oxford University Press 2012) 135

Lazarus L, 'Preventive Obligations, Risk and Coercive Overreach' in L Lavrysen and N Mavronicola (eds), *Coercive Human Rights* (Hart Publishing 2020) 249

Legg A, *The Margin of Appreciation in International Human Rights Law: Deference and Proportionality* (Oxford University Press 2012)

Leijten I, *Core Socio-Economic Rights and the European Court of Human Rights* (Cambridge University Press 2018)

Lemmens P and Courtoy M, 'Deterrence as a Key Factor in the European Court of Human Rights Case Law' in L Lavrysen and N Mavronicola (eds), *Coercive Human Rights* (Hart Publishing 2020) 55

Letsas G, 'Two Concept of the Margin of Appreciation' (2006) 26(4) Oxford Journal of Legal Studies 705

Letsas G, *A Theory of Interpretation of the European Convention on Human Rights* (Oxford University Press 2007)

Letsas G, 'The Margin of Appreciation Revisited' in A Etinson (ed), *Human Rights: Moral or Political?* (Oxford University Press 2018) 296

Loven C, '"Verticalised" Cases before the European Court of Human Rights Unravelled: An Analysis of their Characteristic and the Court's Approach to Them' (2020) 38(4) Netherlands Quarterly of Human Rights 246

Lubell N, *Extraterritorial Use of Force against Non-State Actors* (Oxford University Press 2011)

# M

MacCormick N, 'Rights in Legislation' in P Hacker and J Raz (eds), *Law, Morality and Society: Essays in Honour of H.L.A. Hart* (Clarendon Press 1977) 199

Mallory C, *Human Rights Imperialists. The Extraterritorial Application of the European Convention on Human Rights* (Hart Publishing 2020)

Mavronicola N, 'What is an "Absolute Right"? Deciphering Absoluteness in the Context of Article 3 of the European Convention on Human Rights' (2012) 12 Human Rights Law Review 723

Mavronicola N, 'Coercive Overreach, Dilution and Diversion: Potential Dangers of Aligning Human Rights Protection with Criminal Law (Enforcement)' in L Lavrysen and N Mavronicola (eds), *Coercive Human Rights* (Hart Publishing 2020) 184

Mavronicola N, *Torture, Inhumanity and Degradation under Article 3 of the ECHR. Absolute Rights and Absolute Wrongs* (Hart Publishing 2021)

Mavronicola N and Lavrysen, L, 'Introducing the Sharp Edge of the European Convention on Human Rights' in L Lavrysen and N Mavronicola (eds), *Coercive Human Rights* (Hart Publishing 2020) 1

McBride J, 'Protecting Life: Positive Obligation to Help' (1999) 24 European Law Review 43

McGrath S, 'Causation by Omissions: A Dilemma' (2005) 123 Philosophical Studies 125

McGrogan D, 'The Problem of Causality in International Human Rights Law' (2016) 65 International and Comparative Law Quarterly 615

McGrogan D, *Critical Theory and Human Rights. From Compassion to Coercion* (Manchester University Press 2021)

McHarg A, 'Reconciling Human Rights and the Public Interest: Conceptual problems and Doctrinal Uncertainty in the Jurisprudence of the European Court of Human Rights' (1999) 62 Modern Law Review 671

McMahan J, 'Killing, Letting Die, and Withdrawal of Aid' (1993) 103 Ethics 250

Meckled-Garcia S, 'On the Very Idea of Cosmopolitan Justice: Constructivism and International Agency' (2008) 16(3) Journal of Political Philosophy 245

Meckled-Garcia S, 'Do Transnational Economic Effects Violate Human Rights?' (2009) 2(3) Ethics and Global Politics 259

Meckled-Garcia S, 'Giving Up the Goods: Rethinking the Human Right to Subsistence, Institutional Justice, and Imperfect Duties' (2013) 30(1) Journal of Applied Philosophy 73

Milanovic M, 'From Compromise to Principle: Clarifying the Concept of State "Jurisdiction" in Human Rights Treaties' (2008) 8 Human Rights Law Review 411

Milanovic M, 'A Norm Conflict Perspective on the Relationship between International Humanitarian law and Human Rights Law' (2010) 14(3) Journal of Conflict and Security Law 458

Milanovic M, *Extraterritorial Application of Human Rights Treaties* (Oxford University Press 2011)
Milanovic M, '*Al-Skeini* and *Al-Jedda* in Strasbourg' (2012) 23(1) European Journal of International Law 121
Milanovic M, 'Jurisdiction and Responsibility. Trends in the Jurisprudence of the Strasbourg Court' in A van Aaken and I Motoc (eds), *The European Convention on Human Rights and General International Law* (Oxford University Press 2018) 97
Milanovic M and Papic T, 'The Applicability of the ECHR in Contested Territories' (2018) 67 International and Comparative Law Quarterly 779
Miller S, 'Revisiting Extraterritorial Jurisdiction: A Territorial Justification for Extraterritorial Jurisdiction under the European Convention' (2010) 20 European Journal of International Law 1223
Mills A, 'Rethinking Jurisdiction in International Law' (2014) 84(1) The British Yearbook of International Law 187
Möller K, 'Two Conceptions of Positive Liberty: Towards an Autonomy-based Theory of Constitutional Rights' (2009) 29(4) Oxford Journal of Legal Studies 757
Möller K, 'Proportionality: Challenging the Critics' (2012) 10(3) International Journal of Constitutional Law 709
Möller K, *The Global Model of Constitutional Law* (Oxford University Press 2012)
Möller K, 'The Right to Life between Absolute and Proportionate Protection' in S Bronitt and others (eds), *Shooting to Kill: Socio-Legal Perspectives on the Use of Lethal Force* (Hart Publishing 2012) 47
Möller K, 'Dworkin's Theory of Rights in the Age of Proportionality' (2018) 12(2) Law and Ethics of Human Rights 281
Moonen T and Lavrysen L, 'Abstract but Concrete, or Concrete but Abstract? A Guide to the Nature of Advisory Opinions under Protocol No 16 to the ECHR' (2021) 21(3) Human Rights Law Review 752
Moreno-Lax V, 'The Architecture of Functional Jurisdiction: Unpacking Contactless Control—On Public Powers, S.S. and Others v Italy and the "Operational Model"' (2020) 21 German Law Journal 385
Mowbray A, *The Development of Positive Obligations under the European Convention on Human Rights by the European Court of Human Rights* (Hart Publishing 2004)
Mowbray A, 'The Creativity of the European Court of Human Rights' (2005) 5(1) Human Rights Law Review 57
Mowbray A, 'A Study of the Principle of Fair Balance in the Jurisprudence of the European Court of Human Rights' (2010) 10(2) Human Rights Law Review 289
Mowbray J, 'The Right to Food and the International Economic System: An Assessment of the Rights-Based Approach to the Problem of World Hunger' (2007) 20(3) Leiden Journal of International Law 545

# N

Nedeski N, *Shared Obligations in International Law* (Cambridge University Press 2022)
Nickel J, 'How Human Rights Generate Duties to Protect and Provide' (1993) 15(1) Human Rights Quarterly 77
Nickel J, *Making Sense of Human Rights* (Blackwell 2007)
Nolan D, 'Negligence and Human Rights Law: The Case for Separate Development' (2013) 76(2) Modern Law Review 286

Noll G, 'The Exclusionary Construction of Human Rights in International Law and Political Theory' IIIS Discussion Paper (2003)
Noll G, 'Analogy at War: Proportionality, Equality and the Law of Targeting' (2013) 43 Netherlands Yearbook of International Law 205
Noll G, 'Theorizing Jurisdiction' in A Orford and F Hoffmann (eds), *The Oxford Handbook of the Theory of International Law* (Oxford University Press 2016) 600
Nozick R, *Anarchy, State and Utopia* (Basil Blackwell 1974)

## O

O'Cinneide C, 'A Modest Proposal: Destitution, State Responsibility and the European Convention on Human Rights' (2008) 5 European Human Rights Law Review 583
Oette L, 'Austerity and the Limits of Policy-Induced Suffering: What Role for the Prohibition of Torture and Other Ill-Treatment?' (2015) 15 Human Rights Law Review 669
Ollino A, 'The 'Capacity-impact' Model of Jurisdiction and its Implications for States' Positive Human Rights Obligations' (2021) 82 Questions of International law 81
Ollino A, *Due Diligence Obligations in International Law* (Cambridge University Press 2022)

## P

Palmisano G, 'Fault' in *Max Planck Encyclopedia of Public International Law* (Oxford University Press 2007)
Papanicolopulu I, *International Law and the Protection of People at Sea* (Oxford University Press 2018)
Park I, *The Right to Life in Armed Conflict* (Oxford University Press 2018)
Peroni L and Timmer A, 'Vulnerable Groups: The Promise of an Emerging Concept in European Human Rights Convention Law' (2013) 11 International Journal of Constitutional Law 1056
Peters A, 'Global Constitutionalism. The Social Dimension' in R Suami and others (eds), *Global Constitutionalism from European and East Asian Perspectives* (Cambridge University Press 2018) 277
Pinto de Albuquerque P, 'The Overuse of Criminal Justice in the Case Law of the European Court of Human Rights' in C van Kempen and M Jendly (eds), *Overuse of the Criminal Justice System* (Intersentia 2019) 67
Plakokefalos I, 'Causation in the Law of State Responsibility and the Problem of Overdetermination: In Search of Clarity' (2015) 26(2) European Journal of International Law 471
Pogge T, 'Recognized and Violated by International Law: The Human Rights of the Global Poor' (2005) 18(4) Leiden Journal of International Law 717
Poole T, 'Legitimacy, Rights and Judicial Review' (2005) 25(4) Oxford Journal of Legal Studies 697

## Q

Quénivet N, 'The Obligation to Investigate after a Potential Breach of Article 2 ECHR in an Extra-territorial Context: Mission Impossible for the Armed Forced' (2019) 37(2) Netherlands Quarterly of Human Rights 119
Quinn W, 'Actions, Intentions, and Consequences: The Doctrine of Doing and Allowing' (1989) 98 The Philosophical Review 287

## R

Raible L, 'Title to Territory and Jurisdiction in International Human Rights Law: Three Models for a Fraught Relationship' (2018) 31 Leiden Journal of International Law 315

Raible l, *Human Rights Unbound. A Theory of Extraterritoriality* (Oxford University Press 2020)

Ratner S, *The Thin Justice of International Law* (Oxford University Press 2015)

Raz J, *The Morality of Freedom* (Clarendon Press 1986)

Raz J, 'On the Nature of Rights' (1984) XCIII Mind 194

Reiertsen M, *Effective Domestic Remedies and the European Court of Human Rights* (Cambridge University Press 2022)

Reus-Smit C, 'On Rights and Institutions' in C Beits and R Goodin (eds), *Global Basic Rights* (Oxford University Press 2011) 26

Rigaux F, 'International Responsibility and the Principle of Causality' in M Ragazzi (ed), *International Responsibility Today. Essays in Memory of Oscar Schachter* (Martinus Nijhoff Publishers 2005) 81

Ryngaert C, 'Jurisdiction. Towards a Reasonableness Test' in M Langford and others (eds), *Global Justice, State Duties: The Extraterritorial Scope of Economic, Social and Cultural Rights in International Law* (Cambridge University Press 2013) 192

Ryngaert C, 'Extraterritorial Obligations under Human Rights Law' in M Lattimer and P Sands (eds), *The Grey Zone: Civilian Protection Between Human Rights and the Laws of War* (Hart Publishing 2018) 273

Ryngaert C, 'EU Trade Agreements and Human Rights: From Extraterritorial to Territorial Obligations' (2018) 20 International Community Law Review 374

Ryngaert C, *Selfless Intervention. Exercising Jurisdiction in the Common Interest* (Oxford University Press 2020)

## S

Salomon M, 'State of Play and the Road Ahead. A World of Poverty and Human Rights' in D Akande and others (eds), *Human Rights and 21st Challenges* (Oxford University Press 2020) 214

Saul M, 'The European Court of Human Rights' Margin of Appreciation and the Process of National Parliaments' (2015) 15 Human Rights Law Review 745

Schabas W, '*Lex Specialis*? Belt and Suspenders? The Parallel Operation of Human Rights Law and the Law of Armed Conflict, and the Conundrum of *Jus Ad Bellum*' (2007) 40(2) Israeli Law Review 592

Scheinin M, 'Just Another Word? Jurisdiction in the Roadmaps of State Responsibility and Human Rights' in M Langford and others (eds), *Global Justice, State Duties: The Extraterritorial Scope of Economic, Social and Cultural Rights in International Law* (Cambridge University Press 2013) 212

Seavey W, 'Negligence: Subjective of Objective' (1927) 41(1) Harvard Law Review 1

Shany Y, 'Toward a General Margin of Appreciation Doctrine in International Law?' (2006)16(5) European Journal of International Law 907

Shue H, 'The Interdependence of Duties' in P Alston and K Komasevski (eds), *The Right to Food* (Martinus Nijhoff Publishers 1984) 83

Shue H, *Basic Rights. Subsistence, Affluence, and U.S. Foreign Policy* (Princeton University Press 1996)

Skinner S, *Lethal Force, the Right to Life and the ECHR. Narratives of Death and Democracy* (Hart Publishing 2019)

Skogly S and Osim P, 'Jurisdiction—A Barrier to Compliance with Extraterritorial Obligations to Protect against Human Rights Abuses by Non-State Actors' (2019) 13(2) Human Rights and International Legal Discourse 99

Smet S, 'Conflict between Absolute Rights: A Reply to Steven Greer' (2013) *13* Human Rights Law Review 469

Smet S, 'The "Absolute" Prohibition of Torture and Inhuman or Degrading Treatment in Article 3 ECHR' in E Brems and J Gerards (eds), *Shaping Rights in the ECHR. The Role of the European Court of Human Rights in Determining the Scope of Human Rights* (Cambridge University Press 2014) 273

Smet S, 'When Human Rights Clash in "the Age of Subsidiarity"' in P Agha (ed), *Human Rights between Law and Politics: The Margin of Appreciation in Post-National Contexts* (Hart Publishing 2017) 55

Smet S, 'Conflicts of Rights in Theoretical and Comparative Perspective' in S Smet and E Brems (eds), *When Human Rights Clash at the European Court of Human Rights* (Oxford University Press 2017) 1

Smet S, 'Conflicts between Human Rights and the ECtHR' in S Smet and E Brems (eds), *When Human Rights Clash at the European Court of Human Rights. Conflict or Harmony?* (Oxford University Press 2017) 38

Smet S, *Resolving Conflicts between Human Rights. The Judge's Dilemma* (Routledge 2017)

Smet S, 'On the Existence and Nature of Conflicts between Human Rights at the European Court of Human Rights' (2017) 17 Human Rights Law Review 499

Somers S, *The European Convention on Human Rights as an Instrument of Tort Law* (Intersentia 2018)

Starmer K, 'Positive Obligations under the Convention' in J Jowell and J Cooper (eds), *Understanding Human Rights Principles* (Hart Publishing 2001) 139

Steel S, 'Causation in Tort Law and Criminal Law: Unity and Divergence?' in M Dyson (ed), *Unravelling Tort and Crime* (Cambridge University Press 2014) 239

Steinder H, 'Working Rights' in M Kramer (ed), *A Debate Over Rights: Philosophical Enquiries* (Clarendon Press 1998) 233

Steiner H, *An Essay on Rights* (Blackwell 1994)

Stoyanova V, 'Dancing on the Borders of Article 4: Human Trafficking and the European Court of Human Rights in the *Rantsev* Case' (2012) 30(2) Netherlands Quarterly of Human Rights 163

Stoyanova V, 'Article 4 of the ECHR and the Obligation of Criminalising Slavery, Servitude, Forced Labour and Human Trafficking' (2014) 3 Cambridge Journal of International and Comparative Law 407

Stoyanova V, *Human Trafficking and Slavery Reconsidered. Conceptual Limits and States' Positive Obligations in European Law* (Cambridge University Press 2017)

Stoyanova V, 'The Disjunctive Structure of Positive Rights under the European Convention on Human Rights' (2018) 87 Nordic Journal of International Law (2018) 344

Stoyanova V, 'Causation between State Omission and Harm within the Framework of Positive Obligations under' (2018) 18 Human Rights Law Review 309

Stoyanova V, 'Common Law Tort of Negligence as a Tool for Deconstructing Positive Obligations under the European Convention on Human Rights' (2020) 24(5) The International Journal of Human Rights 632

Stoyanova V, 'Due Diligence versus Positive Obligations: Critical Reflections on the Council of Europe Convention on Violence against Women' in J Niemi and others (eds), *International Law and Violence against Women: Europe and the Istanbul Convention* (Routledge 2020) 95

Stoyanova V, 'The Right to Leave Any Country and the Interplay between Jurisdiction and Proportionality in Human Rights Law' (2020) 32(3) International Journal of Refugee Law 403

Stoyanova V, 'The Right to Life under the EU Charter and Cooperation with Third States to Combat Human Smuggling' (2020) 21(3) German Law Journal 436

Stoyanova V, 'Fault, Knowledge and Risk within the Framework of Positive Obligations under the European Convention on Human Rights' (2020) 33(3) Leiden Journal of International Law 601

Stoyanova V, 'Framing Positive Obligations under the European Convention on Human Rights: Mediating between the Abtract and the Concrete' (2023) 23(3) Human Rights Law Review 1

Stoyanova V, 'Specification of Positive Obligations by the European Court of Human Rights and the Roles of Reasonablness, Prevention and Precaution' in A Ollino and others (eds), *The Concept of Obligation in International Law* (Oxford University Press forthcoming)

Summers A, 'Common-Sense Causation in the Law' (2018) 38 Oxford Journal of Legal Studies 793

# T

Teubner G, 'Transnational Fundamental Rights: Horizontal Effect' (2011) 40 Rechtsfilosofie and Rechtstheorie 191

Thielbörger P, 'Positive Obligations in the ECHR after the Stoicescu Case: A Concept in Search of Content?' (2012) European Yearbook on Human Rights 259

Thienel T, 'The Burden and Standard of Proof in the European Court of Human Rights' (2007) 50 German Yearbook of International Law 543

Thomas J, *Public Rights, Private Relations* (Oxford University Press 2015)

Trouwborst A, 'Prevention, Precaution, Logic and Law: The Relationship between the Precautionary Principle and the Preventive Principle in International Law and Associated Questions' (2009) 2(2) Erasmus Law Review 105

Tulkens F, 'The Paradoxical Relationship between Criminal Law and Human Rights' (2011) 9 Journal of International Criminal Justice 577

Tzevelekos V, 'Reconstructing the Effective Control Criterion in Extraterritorial Human Rights Breaches: Direct Attribution of Wrongfulness, Due Diligence, and Concurrent Responsibility' (2014) 36 Michigan Journal of International Law 129

# U

Ugrekhelidze M, 'Causation: Reflection in the Mirror of the European Convention on Human Rights (A Sketch)' in L Calflisch and others (eds), Liber Amicorum Luzius Wildhaber Human Rights—Strasbourg Views (Engel Publishers 2007) 469

# V

Valentini L, 'In What Sense are Human Rights Political?' (2012) 60 Political Studies 180

Vandenbogaerde A, 'Attributing Extraterritorial Obligations under the International Covenant on Economic, Social and Cultural Rights' (2015) 9 Human Rights and International Legal Discourse 6

Vandenbogaerde A, *Towards Shared Accountability in International Human Rights Law* (Intersentia 2016)

Vandenhole W, 'Obligations and Responsibility in a Plural and Diverse Duty-bearer Human Rights Regime' in W Vandenhole (ed), *Challenging Territoriality in Human Rights Law* (Routledge 2015) 115

Varuhus J, *Damages and Human Rights* (Hart Publishing 2016)

## W

Waldron J, 'Can Communal Goods be Human Rights?' (1987) 28(2) European Journal of Sociology 296

Waldron J, 'Rights in Conflict' (1989) 99 Ethics 503

Waldron J, *Liberal Rights: Collected Papers 1981–1991* (Cambridge University Press 1993)

Waldron J, 'Security and Liberty: The Image of Balance' (2003) 11(2) Journal of Political Philosophy 191

Wallace S, *The Application of the European Convention on Human Rights to Military Operations* (Cambridge University Press 2019)

Weigend T, 'Subjective Elements of Criminal Liability' in M Dubber and T Hőrnle (eds), *The Oxford Handbook of Criminal Law* (Oxford University Press 2014) 490

Wicks E, *The Right to Life and Conflicting Interests* (Oxford University Press 2010)

Wibye J, 'Reviving the Distinction between Positive and Negative Human Rights' (2022) 35(4) Ratio Juris 363

Wibey J, 'Beyond Act and Omissions—Distinguishing Positive and Negative Duties at the European Court of Human Rights' (2022) 23(4) Human Rights Review 1

Wheatley S, *The Democratic Legitimacy of International Law* (Hart Publishing 2010)

## X

Xenos D, *The Positive Obligations of the State under the European Convention of Human Rights* (Routledge 2011)

## Z

Zucca L, *Constitutional Dilemmas* (Oxford University Press 2007)

# Index

*For the benefit of digital users, indexed terms that span two pages (e.g., 52–53) may, on occasion, appear on only one of those pages*

'Absolutely necessary' 110
Absolute rights 104, 107–8
Abstract review 181–82, 183, 188, 190, 191–97, 199–200
Administrative/administrative proceedings/ administrative liability/administrative control 18–19, 25–26, 48–49, 69, 79–80, 123–24, 141–42, 143, 146–47, 154, 173, 175, 198, 239–40, 260, 311
Adversarial procedure 278–79
Afghanistan 262, 263
Allocation (e.g. of resources or burdens) 8, 69–70, 224
Amnesty 157–58
Arendt (Hanna Arendt) 225–27
'arguable claim' 125, 127–28, 130, 131, 132–33
Armed conflict 231, 281, 299–300
Armed groups /armed individual 10, 110–11, 149–50
Arrest 48–49, 153, 163–64, 208–9, 230–31, 232, 259, 280–81
Arrest warrant 163–65, 272n.262
Articles on the Responsibility of States for Internationally Wrongful Acts 21–22, 249n.159
Asylum/asylum- seeker 61–63, 127n.17, 201–2n.153, 239, 240n.113, 241
Attribution in international law (attributed) 10, 20, 21–22, 41, 46–47, 48–53, 54, 71, 101n.30, 129, 140n.93, 141n.105, 142, 205–6, 233–34, 239n.102, 246–47, 248–50, 251n.166, 256, 267n.241, 268–69, 270, 304–5

Baseline ('baseline comparisons') 13–14, 64, 180–81, 224
Building regulations 1–2
Burden (including, burden sharing) 8, 17n.71, 28–29, 40–41, 42–43, 53–54, 59, 70–71, 73–74, 78, 88–89, 92, 102–3, 115–16, 148–49, 167, 168, 224, 295, 301–2
'But for' test 47, 112

Carelessness 128n.22, 142, 144–45
*Case Concerning the Application of the Convention on the Prevention and Punishment of the Crime of Genocide* 22n.14, 50n.39, 288n.332
Child/children/child-parent relationship 1–2, 24n.23, 29–30, 29–30n.52, 31n.66, 34n.77, 38n.105, 38n.108, 40n.116, 56–57, 61n.102, 62–63, 74n.11, 84n.45, 85n.51, 87–88, 98, 108, 111, 114–15, 115n.97, 119–20, 127n.17, 129n.30, 132, 144n.122, 155, 166, 172n.5, 174–75, 180–81, 180n.61, 183–84, 190, 191, 200n.144, 201–2n.153, 209, 210, 210n.191, 211n.198, 212–13, 214, 238, 239, 241–42, 243, 271, 301
Civil liability 57
Civil proceedings 123–24, 128n.21, 139–42, 146–48, 150, 158
Civil remedies 69, 69n.141, 144, 147–48
Civilian (civilian target) 208, 280–81, 297
Concrete review 150–51, 174, 181–82, 185, 188–89, 190, 191–92, 193, 194–95, 196, 311
Constitutional justice 182, 183
Combatant 280–81, 297
Communitarian 4–5, 218, 219–21, 226–27, 229–30, 250, 262, 263, 273, 274, 277, 283, 304, 307, 308–9, 314
Community (including political community) 4–5, 7, 8–9, 33, 99–100, 220, 221, 222, 224–28, 229–30, 257, 273–74, 283, 292–96, 301–2, 304, 306–7, 312
Community (international) 261, 302n.410
Complicity (complicit) 254, 256
Cold War 10
Consulate 238, 240–41, 246–47
*Corfu Channel* case 22, 32n.72
Corporation 10, 58–59, 250–52, 256n.198, 285n.321, 291n.347
Corrective justice 303, 312, 314
Correlation (between rights and obligations) 12–13, 81–82, 312
Cost/cost-effectiveness 8, 28, 70–71, 73–74, 93, 102, 224, 312

'credible assertion' 130
Criminal responsibility 59n.88, 137, 140n.93, 154
Deference 82–83, 89, 90–91, 168n.275, 201n.149, 274–75
*de facto* organ 49–50
Defamation 198
Democracy/democratic (see also community and communitarian) 8–9, 106–7, 117, 131, 222–23, 224–26, 228–30, 234, 250, 263–64, 273–74, 283, 289, 290–93, 295–96, 297–98, 299, 302, 303, 304–5, 306–8

Deportation 75n.16
Detention/detention 18n.73, 60–61, 62–63, 84n.46, 111–13, 120–21n.121, 164–65, 230–31, 232, 233n.70, 280–81
Dignity 104n.44, 224n.14
Disability 62–63, 98n.15, 190, 228n.33
Disaster 1–2, 10, 39, 59, 134
Disciplinary proceedings 123–24, 139–40, 141–42, 155
Discrimination 155, 175
Distribution 3, 8n.11, 9, 13–14, 70–71, 74, 224, 229, 312, 314
Distributive justice 8n.11, 292–93, 302, 302n.412
'dynamic and evolutive' interpretation 11
'dynamic aspect' of human rights 16–17, 97–98, 186
Domestic violence 1–2, 3, 30–31, 34–35n.84, 36–37, 62–63, 65, 98, 118n.112, 155, 174, 175, 182n.66, 183–84, 187, 188–89, 192, 209–10, 211–12, 216
Due diligence 22–23, 23n.20, 256
Duty-based reasoning 17n.67
Duty bearers 9

Economic and social rights 251–52, 306n.424
Economic well-being 100, 100n.24
Education 10–11, 56, 62–63, 298–99
Effectiveness 11, 48, 69–70, 71, 85–86, 88, 130–31, 133, 135, 137, 138, 139n.88, 147–49, 150–52, 155, 160–61, 162
Embassy (see consulate)
Employee 174, 200n.144
Employer 42
Employment 62n.104, 110, 115n.96, 155, 198, 199, 202
Environment 3, 58n.79, 63, 65n.121, 66
Epistemology/epistemological 46, 63, 66, 71, 190–91, 196
Equality 8, 101, 103–4, 116–17, 222, 225–26, 245, 273–74, 294–95, 299, 302n.409
EU/EU law 277n.282
European public order 229n.38

Evidence 27, 32, 33, 45, 125–26, 132–33, 139–40, 141–46, 152–53, 160, 162, 165–66, 168, 169, 190–91, 194, 237, 298–99
*Ex ante* 11, 17, 197
*Ex post* 11, 27, 31, 91–92
Expulsion (see also deportation) 240–41
Extradition 163n.247, 165–66

Fair trial 239n.104, 299
Freedom of assembly 98
Freedom of expression 96n.7, 102, 116–17, 200, 201n.148
Food security 250–51

Health/health care 1–2, 33, 36, 46–47, 55–56, 57, 60–61, 64, 67, 68, 69–70, 76–78, 100, 104–6, 134, 136, 144n.123, 154, 174, 193, 205–6
Human trafficking 159n.233, 175n.34
Humanitarian law (international humanitarian law) 280–84, 296–98

Individual justice 311–12, 314
Industrial activities 1–2, 58n.79, 63
International Law Commission (ILC) 21–22, 49

*Jus ad bellum* 282–83
*Jus in bello* 282

Liberty/the right to liberty 111, 280, 283–84, 298–99

Medical negligence 3, 36, 37, 39, 68, 127n.18, 135, 144–45nn.123–24, 146, 148n.139, 158, 174, 192–93, 194–95

'necessary in a democratic society' 110n.72, 117, 131

Occupation 230–31, 234n.76, 246n.142, 288n.334, 291, 297n.384

*post factum* 17, 27, 117n.107, 122, 127–28, 197
Precaution 27n.40, 41, 57n.74, 65n.123, 88n.67, 187
Prison 59–60, 61, 62–63, 69, 78, 79, 99n.19, 136, 145n.124, 206–7, 208, 280–81
Proportionality 6, 8n.11, 12n.40, 13–14, 90, 110–11, 114–15, 115n.96, 116–17, 197, 282, 284–85, 294n.361, 295n.370, 296–98
*Proprio moto/Proprio moto* proceedings 148–50
Protection order (see also domestic violence) 179, 188–89, 192, 212–13, 216n.223
Public safety 100, 100n.24, 196n.121

Qualified rights 6, 91, 92–93, 96–97, 113–14, 115–16, 121–22, 293, 298–99

Remedies 17n.71, 49n.28, 57, 69n.141, 87, 123n.5, 133, 139–40, 139n.88, 142, 144, 147–48, 155n.200, 176n.36, 188–89, 198, 285–86, 306n.424
Reputation 96n.7
Restraining order 192
Rights-based reasoning 16–17
Risk aversion 4–5, 15–16, 80
Road safety 1–2
Roma 19n.81, 62–63, 85n.54, 146, 188
Rule of law 133, 237n.94

Safety at public places 1–2
Second World War 10
Science/scientific 26–28, 29–30, 32n.69, 42, 65, 67, 190–91, 304
'Significant flaw' 68, 69–70, 169
Shared obligations 304
Shared public space 225–26
Shared responsibility 250
Shared state institutions 295
Shared territory 225–26
Shared values 292n.349
Solidarity 302, 302n.412
Statism 4–5, 172, 207n.179
Subjects of international law 8–9
Subsidiarity 82–83, 89, 120–21, 179, 201n.149
Suicide 35–36, 48–49, 60–61, 98n.15, 178, 194–95, 210n.191, 216n.218

Totalitarianism 10
Trade 250–51, 287n.329

*ultra vires* 49–50, 51
Universality of human rights 9, 226–27, 229–30, 292n.355, 293–94, 301–2, 302n.409, 307
Utilitarian 99–100, 101, 121

Visa 239–41, 243n.128, 246–47, 259
Vulnerability 56, 61, 62–63, 118n.109, 188, 243

Weapon 46–47, 65n.123, 105, 110–11, 187, 250–51, 253, 254